Rock and Roll in the Rocket City

Rock and Roll in the Rocket City

The West, Identity, and Ideology in Soviet Dniepropetrovsk, 1960–1985

Sergei I. Zhuk

Woodrow Wilson Center Press
Washington, D.C.

The Johns Hopkins University Press
Baltimore

EDITORIAL OFFICES

Woodrow Wilson Center Press
One Woodrow Wilson Plaza
1300 Pennsylvania Avenue, N.W.
Washington, D.C. 20004-3027
Telephone: 202-691-4029
www.wilsoncenter.org

ORDER FROM

The Johns Hopkins University Press
Hampden Station
P.O. Box 50370
Baltimore, Maryland 21211
Telephone: 1-800-537-5487
www.press.jhu.edu/books/

2 4 6 8 9 7 5 3

Library of Congress Cataloging-in-Publication Data

Zhuk, S. I. (Sergei Ivanovich)
   Rock and roll in the Rocket City : the West, identity, and ideology in Soviet Dniepropetrovsk,
1960–1985 / Sergei I. Zhuk.
      p.   cm.
   Includes bibliographical references and index.
   ISBN 978-0-8018-9550-0
   1. Popular music—Political aspects—Ukraine—Dnipropetrovsk—History—20th century.
2. Popular music—Political aspects—Soviet Union. 3. Popular culture—Soviet Union—Western
influences. 4. Music and youth—Soviet Union. 5. Music and state—Soviet Union. I. Title.
   ML3917.R8Z58   2010
   947.7'4—dc22

                                                                                          2009047217

Woodrow Wilson International Center for Scholars

The Woodrow Wilson International Center for Scholars is the national, living U.S. memorial honoring President Woodrow Wilson. In providing an essential link between the worlds of ideas and public policy, the Center addresses current and emerging challenges confronting the United States and the world. The Center promotes policy-relevant research and dialogue to increase understanding and enhance the capabilities and knowledge of leaders, citizens, and institutions worldwide. Created by an Act of Congress in 1968, the Center is a non-partisan institution headquartered in Washington, D.C. and supported by both public and private funds.

Conclusions or opinions expressed in Center publications and programs are those of the authors and speakers and do not necessarily reflect the views of the Center's staff, fellows, trustees, or advisory groups, or any individuals or organizations that provide financial support to the Center.

The Center is the publisher of *The Wilson Quarterly* and home of Woodrow Wilson Center Press and *dialogue* television and radio. For more information about the Center's activities and publications, including the monthly newsletter *Centerpoint,* please visit us on the web at www.wilsoncenter.org.

Lee H. Hamilton, President and Director

To dear Irinushka, the love of my life, in memory of the songs
by John, Paul, George, and Ringo, which we still cherish

Contents

Figures

ream

Acknowledgments

This book is my tribute to the Soviet people in the USSR's provincial cities and towns who were ignored and forgotten by post-Soviet and Western scholars in their studies of post-Stalin socialism, which were (and still are) based mainly on material from Moscow and Leningrad / Saint Petersburg. This project started as a result of my long conversations in Moscow during 1988 and 1989 with Evgenii Kozhokin and Sergei Stankevich, the leaders of the so-called Soviet Association of Young Historians, the nongovernmental organization sponsored by Komsomol as a symbol of democratization in the difficult years of perestroika. After defending my dissertation on social conflicts in colonial New York at the Moscow Institute of World History (the USSR Academy of Sciences), and inspired by my conversations with Kozhokin and Stankevich, I brought the noble idea of the democratic historians' organization to Dnieropetrovsk, a big industrial, but still provincial, city in Soviet Ukraine.

My Dnieropetrovsk colleagues—historians such as Oleksandr Mykhailiuk, Yurii Mytsyk, Vitalii Pidgaetskii, and Serhii Plokhy—supported this idea with great enthusiasm. In 1989, we discussed and planned different projects for writing a "real" history, free of traditional Marxist-Leninist stereotypes. I proposed writing a social history of rock-and-roll music in Europe. One of my colleagues, Evgenii Chernov, asked me instead to write "a history of the perception of Western rock music among the youth of the closed Soviet society." Another friend, Igor Okhin'ko, who knew about my interest in American oral history, gave me the provocative idea to interview the "rock music fans" who lived in the "special closed Soviet rocket city, Dnieropetrovsk." In response to Igor's idea, I began interviewing various friends who knew something about "rock music consumption" in the "rocket city"—Vitalii Pidgaetskii told me the story of Arnold Gurevich, the "black music market's king" in the 1960s; and a former disc jockey, Mikhail Suvorov, revealed to me the secrets of the local "discotheque mafia." Former rock musicians from my home town—Vatutino, in the Cherkassy Region of Ukraine—such as Eduard Svichar, explained to me the details of rock music consumption in other regions of Soviet Ukraine. Some of my close friends even gave me their diaries from their high school years, which contained fascinating information about their "rock-and-roll madness."

By 1991, I already had unique material with which to begin. Therefore, my thanks go to my old friends and colleagues from Moscow, Dniepropetrovsk, and Vatutino, who provided me with the inspiration and information for this project. Unfortunately, some of them, like Igor Okhin'ko and Vitalii Pidgaetskii, did not survive the difficult period of the transition from mature socialism to bandit capitalism and died without knowing that I had fulfilled my promises.

This book is also my tribute to the Anglo-American rock musicians who inspired generations of Soviet people during the 1960s, 1970s, and 1980s. All my Vatutino classmates began listening to the music of the Beatles and Rolling Stones as early as 1965 and 1966, and they grew up listening to various styles of rock music, ranging from Eric Clapton and Jimi Hendrix to Led Zeppelin and Deep Purple. Later, when we entered our colleges, we began listening to the more serious music of the 1970s, including Pink Floyd, Yes, Genesis, and Jethro Tull. Paradoxically, we discovered the American roots of our music through our consumption of British rock. And we began to study these roots, listening to Chuck Berry, Little Richard, Bo Diddley, and our idol, Muddy Waters. Many of my friends played in amateur "beat bands," and some of them (including myself) had part-time jobs in various disco clubs during the late 1970s and 1980s. Anglo-American rock music affected our personal life as well. I still remember that my first dance with the love of my life, my future wife, took place when a local band in Kyiv suddenly began playing the Beatles songs "In My Life" and "Hey Jude." Even now, we still listen to this music of our childhood as a kind of a special nostalgic ritual. So my special thanks go to all our favorite rock musicians, who brought us the direct and most attractive ideas of the West.

Another inspiration for writing this book came from my American colleagues. I met my first American friend, Marcus Rediker, in 1983, at Nikolai Bolkhovitinov's house in Moscow. Bolkhovitinov, my dissertation adviser, had planned this meeting especially so I could discuss my dissertation chapter about the pirates of colonial New York with Rediker, who was writing a book about the Atlantic maritime world of the eighteenth century. Surprisingly to Bolkhovitinov, I discussed with my American colleague not the problems of pirate history but the problems of punk rock. So Marcus was the first American who learned about the Ukrainian "fascist punks" from me.

Then, in 1994 and 1995, as a Fulbright scholar, I went to Philadelphia and wrote my Russian book about the social history of the middle colonies of British America at the Philadelphia (now McNeil) Center for Early American Studies. During the breaks in my research work in Philadelphia, I shared my childhood experiences of Western rock musical influences in Soviet Ukraine with my American friends, including Wayne Bodle, Richard Dunn, Jack Greene, William Pencak, and Michael Zuckerman. Later, they invited me to deliver a lecture about my rock-and-roll roots during a special meeting at the Philadelphia center. A year later, my lecture was published by *Pennsylvania History* magazine. So I owe my gratitude to these, my first American friends, who were fascinated by my stories about rock music consumption in Soviet Ukraine and who urged me to write about them in English for American readers. My thanks also go to the Rockefeller Foundation, which awarded me a grant that allowed me to write my first sketches for my future project at the Bellagio Center in Italy, in November and December 1996.

In 1997, I moved with my family to the United States, and I became very busy with other scholarly projects that were important for my survival in my new academic environment, which was very different from my former Soviet experience. In 2003–4, when I was finishing the research for my first American book, *Russia's Lost Reformation,* I used my Library of Congress Fellowship in International Studies and again checked various materials at the library. Surprisingly, in the Rubinov Collection at the Library of Congress, I found a unique collection of letters from the 1970s and 1980s written by the readers of the Soviet newspaper *Literaturnaia gazeta.*

After reading these letters, I realized that my own collection of documents, which I had already accumulated in Dniepropetrovsk during perestroika, was more interesting. That is why, in the spring of 2004, I decided to finish my project about Soviet youth and cultural consumption during the Brezhnev era, using my own collection. Meanwhile, Blair Ruble and Joe Brinley of the Woodrow Wilson Center, with whom I had already discussed ideas for this project in 2003, supported me from the very beginning in pursuing the project that became this book. Eventually, Joe would also become my editor for this book. Therefore, I am very grateful to the American Council of Learned Societies, which awarded me a Library of Congress Fellowship in International Studies that allowed me to formulate the major ideas for this project in the English language, and to Blair and especially Joe, who worked with me over five years, helping me to transform my ambitious project into this book.

It would have been impossible for me to finish this book without support from various people and organizations. First of all, Ball State University awarded me a Faculty Research Grant during my first stage of research in 2005, and my colleagues in the Department of History were very supportive and helpful during this difficult period for me. I am also grateful to the Center for Russian and East European Studies at the University of Michigan, which awarded me a Teaching Development Grant, which gave me an opportunity to use particular printed materials for my research during the summer of 2007. The International Research and Exchange Board provided support for my research during the summer months in Moscow, Saint Petersburg, Kyiv, and Dniepropetrovsk. I am much indebted to the staff of the State Archive of the Russian Federation in Moscow, the Dniepropetrovsk State Regional Archive, and the Central State Archive of Non-Governmental Organizations of Ukraine in Kyiv for directing me to particularly useful material and for their tireless and good-natured assistance.

The suggestions and critical comments made by Oleksandr Beznosov, Jeffrey Brooks, Kate Brown, Eugene Clay, Karen Dawisha, Mikhail Dmitriev, Sheila Fitzpatrick, Venelin Ganev, David Goldfrank, Tomasz Kamusella, Neringa Klumbyte, Hiroaki Kuromiya, Eve Levin, Oleksandr Mykhailiuk, Dietmar Neutatz, Stephan Norris, Julia Obertreis, Serhii Plokhy, William Risch, Roman Senkus, Dmitry Shlapentokh, Lewis Siegelbaum, Kelly Smith, Mark Steinberg, Richard Stites, Gleb Tsipursky, Catherine Wanner, and Denise Youngblood improved my manuscript. Breanne Swim (Gladis), my graduate assistant in the Department of History at Ball State University, not only proofread and polished my text but also contributed fresh ideas for the book.

A deep debt of gratitude also goes out to the friends and relatives who provided fellowship, intellectual nourishment, and good cheer, and who made life quite enjoyable in Russia and Ukraine: the late Nikolai Nikolaevich Bolkhovitinov and Liudmila Antonovna Bolkhovitinova, Mikhail and Tatiana Dmitriev, Tamara Antonovna Kozintseva, Oleksandr Mykhailiuk, Eduard Svichar, and many others. Also, I want to express my great gratitude to Joe Brinley and Yamile Kahn of the Woodrow Wilson Center Press for supporting my book and polishing its text to perfection. Without their editing efforts, the book would not exist.

I thank the *Russian Review* and the Center for Russian and East European Studies at the University of Pittsburgh for permission to reprint portions of earlier versions of chapters 2, 3, 5, 10, and 11, which appeared as "Religion, 'Westernization,' and Youth in the 'Closed City' of Soviet Ukraine, 1964–84," *Russian Review* 67, no. 4 (October 2008): 661–79; and "Popular Culture, Identity, and Soviet Youth in Dniepropetrovsk, 1959–84," in *The Carl Beck Papers in Russian and East European Studies, No. 1906* (University of Pittsburgh Press, 2008).

Finally, I wish to acknowledge the most helpful and supportive person, the love and inspiration of my entire life, without whom this book would not have been possible: my wife Irina, to whom this book is dedicated.

Rock and Roll in the Rocket City

Introduction: Back in the USSR— The "Glory Days" of Late Socialism, Fascination with the West, Identities, and Scholars

Question: "Who was Brezhnev?"
Response: "The insignificant Soviet political leader during the era of the Beatles and of Alla Pugacheva."
—Old Soviet joke from the 1970s

In May 1974, Andrei Vadimov, a fifteen-year-old high school student from Dniepropetrovsk,[1] a big industrial city in Eastern Ukraine, wrote in his diary about a trip his class had taken to the Western Ukrainian city of L'viv:

We enjoyed our trip to this city very much! For us, it was like traveling to the real West. In contrast to our hometown, L'viv is open to visits from foreigners. So on L'viv's streets we even met American and Canadian tourists who spoke their native language. For me, it was the first time in my life when I saw foreigners and heard them speaking real English, my favorite language, the tongue of the Beatles, the Rolling Stones, and Deep Purple. The best result of our trip was the visit our entire class made (secretly) to L'viv's black market, where seven members of our tourist group, myself included, and our Komsomol ideologist Natasha, bought new British records of the rock opera *Jesus Christ Superstar* from Polish tourists. It was great because Ian Gillan, our favorite vocalist from the hard-rock band Deep Purple, sings in this rock opera. The Polish tourists also recommended that we buy crosses because we were Gillan's fans and Gillan sang the part of Christ in the opera.[2]

A month later, after he had returned to Dniepropetrovsk, Vadimov noted in his diary that he and his friends could not understand the opera's portrayal

1

of events. They translated its lyrics into Russian and tried to find any information about Jesus Christ in Soviet atheistic literature. In July 1974, Vadimov noted triumphantly that "today was a great day for us! My neighbor, Vasia, brought an old Russian Bible he found in his grandmother's room, and we read the Gospels and compared them to the opera lyrics." Vadimov and his five friends spent all of August 1974 reading the religious text and listening to their favorite rock opera. Driven by curiosity and inspired by their favorite music, they decided to attend a worship meeting of a local Baptist group where Vasia's grandmother was a member, and for the next year they attended these meetings on a regular basis. In December 1975, however, the police arrested them for participating in "unsanctioned" religious meetings. It turned out that the Baptists who organized these meetings were not officially registered. Only intervention by Vadimov's parents saved him and his friends from scandal.

Other contemporaries also noted the rise in the early 1970s of a similar interest in religion among many young fans of *Jesus Christ Superstar.*[3] Cases of "Jesusmania" among rock music enthusiasts coincided and overlapped with the activities of new evangelical and Orthodox leaders, who tried to attract more young people to their churches in Dniepropetrovsk. The police noted that both "the cult of *Jesus Christ Superstar*" and the "rise in religiosity" among local Komsomol members were connected to Western cultural products, which had reached Dniepropetrovsk through L'viv's black market. For the KGB officers, "the *Jesus Christ Superstar* mania" was one case among the many instances of the "dangerous consumption of Western mass culture" by Dniepropetrovsk's youth. According to the KGB's monthly reports from the 1960s through the early 1980s, Western cultural influences reached Soviet consumers directly through music records, youth periodicals, radio, and movies, and indirectly through local tourists traveling abroad and to the Western Ukrainian city L'viv.[4] The KGB officers complained that these influences produced Ukrainian nationalism, popular religiosity, and a "blind" imitation of Western youth fashions in Eastern Ukraine.

In 1991, Igor T., a retired KGB officer who monitored the students' activities in Dniepropetrovsk, recalled how the Dniepropetrovsk KGB tried to control or halt consumption of Western cultural products. These attempts triggered special ideological campaigns against the "ideologically suspicious" consumption of cultural products, which included not only Western popular music but also Ukrainian national poetry. These campaigns were related to the major ideological and political crises in the neighboring socialist countries. The first, most significant campaign started in 1968, and it was related to the role of Czech youth in the events of the Prague Spring. Both Soviet ideologists and KGB operatives were afraid that Soviet youth could imitate Czech cultural developments. The last ideological campaign began in 1981 as a direct reaction to the events in Poland and the involvement of Polish youth in the Solidarity movement.[5]

According to the KGB officers, "the literature, music and films from the West produced four subsequent waves of Western cultural influence" among Soviet youth. The first wave began in the early 1960s with the spread of Ukrainian nationalist literature through Czechoslovakia, Poland, and L'viv. As the KGB officials discovered, "this rise of Ukrainian nationalism coincided with Beatlemania, which had already affected the Czechs, and also with the spread of beat music and hippie fashions among high school and college students."[6] The KGB reacted immediately to these cultural developments by trying to prevent the imitation or repetition of the Czech events in Ukraine. The second wave of Western cultural influence, in about 1975, was "a Deep Purple mania and a cult of the rock opera *Jesus Christ Superstar*, which led to the mass popularity of hard rock and triggered an interest in religion among not only students but also young industrial workers." Another important feature of this wave was "hysteria about the Western movies which created a scandal all over the region."[7]

After this "hard-rock mania," an overwhelming majority of the youth of Dniepropetrovsk became obsessed with Western mass culture and "accepted disco dances and Western films as their way of life." This obsession was stimulated by tourism and the entertainment business, which involved both Communist and Komsomol apparatchiks who made money from the consumption of Western products by Soviet consumers. This period, from 1976 to 1980—the third wave of Western mass culture hysteria—was called "disco madness." According to Igor T., it was a direct result of the politics of détente and the relaxation of the international tensions between the Soviet bloc and the West. The fourth and the final wave of Western cultural influence was "fascist punk and heavy metal hysteria," which affected young Communists and Komsomol activists during the years 1981–84. Fearing the imitation of Polish anti-Soviet cultural developments among local heavy metal fans, the KGB and Soviet administration tried to suppress this hysteria. As Igor T. noted, all these efforts to protect the young people from "Westernization" eventually failed:

We lost the entire young generation. Instead of loyal Soviet Ukrainian patriots we now had Westernized imbeciles who had forgotten their national roots and who were ready to exchange their Soviet motherland for Western cultural products. Even more dangerous, this Westernization happened in the most strategically important Soviet city, which became a symbol for the entire Brezhnev rule in the USSR. Dniepropetrovsk, which was closed to foreigners, became ideologically polluted by anti-Soviet bourgeois influences as early as the 1970s. If this, the most secret and closed center of Soviet military industry and politics, experienced such an ideological anti-Soviet pollution so early, it was a bad omen for the entire Soviet system.[8]

This KGB officer thus emphasized that the consumption of Western cultural products had influenced Soviet youth culture and that the Soviet ideologists had failed to protect Soviet cultural identity from the polluting influences of Western mass culture.

Why did the Soviet ideologists lose their ideological war against the West in Dniepropetrovsk, the Soviet city that was closed to foreigners? How was the consumption of cultural products related to the construction of national and religious identity in this closed city? How did cultural consumption affect the political ideologies of late socialism? Why did the youth of the closed Soviet city become so Westernized by 1985 that even the KGB had to admit failure in the struggle against anti-Soviet ideas and practices?

This book seeks to answer these questions and explore the reasons for these failed ideological attempts to stop Westernization in Dniepropetrovsk, the "most strategically important" region of Soviet Ukraine, during the peak of consumption of Western cultural products before perestroika. Concentrating on three major objects of cultural consumption—literature, popular music, and films—the book considers their effects on Cold War politics and ideology, the revival of the Ukrainian national culture, identity formation, international tourism, and religion from 1960 to 1985. The consumption of Western cultural products contributed to identity formation for men and women who later became members of the post-Soviet elite. Their identities were partially constructed by what they consumed as young people during the late period of Soviet socialism—what they listened to, what they watched, what they read, and what they wore. In this way, their identities were partly the result of what they had consumed. This book explores this phenomenon in one large industrial city, where the political leaders would later shape Soviet and post-Soviet politics in Ukraine.

The "Closed City" of Dniepropetrovsk in the USSR

The consumption of Western cultural products by Dniepropetrovsk's youth was particularly worrisome for Soviet ideologists and the KGB because the city was strategically important to the entire Soviet regime—it was the site of the Soviet Union's biggest missile factory. Having been built in 1951 to produce the Soviet military-industrial complex's most powerful rocket engines, the factory had such a sensitive role that the KGB decided to close the city to foreigners in 1959. From that time, Dniepropetrovsk became one among many so-called closed cities, where the major industrial factories of the Soviet military complex were located.[9]

In addition to its strategic significance, Dniepropetrovsk also played an important role in the Soviet politics of the time. It became the launching ground for the political careers of many Soviet politicians in Moscow because of its close association with the clan of Leonid Brezhnev. And it also played an important role in the political life of Ukraine: Before perestroika, more than 53 percent of all the political leaders in Kyiv had come from Dniepropetrovsk; by 1996, some 80 percent of post-Soviet Ukrainian politicians had begun their careers in this city. The overwhelming majority of these representatives of the "Dniepropetrovsk Family" (including Leonid Kuchma, a former president of post-Soviet Ukraine, and Yulia Tymoshenko, a heroine of the "Orange Revolution" of 2004) started their careers during the late socialist period in the factories of the closed city's military-industrial complex. All these post-Soviet politicians were active consumers of Western cultural products during the Brezhnev era.[10]

This book is an attempt to explore the connections between cultural consumption, ideology, and identity formation in Dniepropetrovsk mainly during the Brezhnev era (1964–84) before the reforms of Mikhail Gorbachev. Given its closed, sheltered existence, Dniepropetrovsk became a unique Soviet social and cultural laboratory where the various patterns of late socialism collided with the new Western cultural influences. Using archival documents, periodicals, personal diaries, and interviews as historical sources, this book focuses on how different developments in cultural consumption among the youth of the "closed city" contributed to various forms of cultural identification, which eventually became elements of the post-Soviet Ukrainian national identity.

For many years, Dniepropetrovsk has provided the cadres for both the Soviet and post-Soviet political leadership, beginning with Brezhnev in

Figure 1. Shaping the Ukrainian national identity in Dniepropetrovsk, the closed city of Eastern Ukraine. Shown here is an ensemble of bandura (a Ukrainian musical instrument) players from the Babushkin House of Culture in an industrial neighborhood of the city in 1983. Photograph by the author.

Moscow and ending with President Kuchma and Prime Minister Tymoshenko in Kyiv. Modern post-Soviet Ukrainian politics now depends on the politicians and businesspeople who came from this "closed" city. To understand the current post-Soviet political situation, it is necessary to know more about the cultural influences that shaped their identities.

This book also explores how the Soviet consumption of Western popular cultural products, along with the ideology and practices of late socialism, contributed to the unmaking of Soviet civilization before perestroika. Recent studies of post-Stalin socialism in the Soviet Union explore various forms of cultural production and consumption, along with their interaction with ideology and politics. Yet the overwhelming majority of these studies —by scholars like Svetlana Boym, Hilary Pilkington, Thomas Cushman, Alexei Yurchak, and William J. Risch—are based on material from the Westernized, "open" cities of the USSR (Moscow, Leningrad, and L'viv), which were exposed to direct Western influences through foreign tourists and journalists.[11] As a result, the history of cultural consumption, including popular music, in "closed" Soviet provincial cities and villages is missing from their analyses. It is difficult to generalize about the social and cultural history of the Soviet Union when the focus is only on Moscow and Leningrad.[12] Therefore, by bringing forgotten "provincial" cities like

Dniepropetrovsk into the historical debate, this book provides new material and new directions for the study of Soviet politics and cultural consumption. The closed city of Dniepropetrovsk is a microhistorical model for analysis of the closed Soviet society and nascent post-Soviet society.

During perestroika and since the collapse of the Soviet Union, Ukrainian history and the evolution of Ukrainian politics have also been studied by various Ukrainian and Western historians, anthropologists, and political scientists.[13] Missing from this literature is a concrete, detailed historical analysis of cultural consumption and identity formation in Dniepropetrovsk, one of the most influential regions in Soviet and post-Soviet Ukraine.[14]

Cultural Consumption

This book draws on various British cultural studies of cultural consumption and identity. According to John Storey, "It is important to include cultural consumption in a discussion of identities because human identities are formed out of people's everyday actions and interaction in different forms of consumption."[15] New cultural studies concentrate on the effects of globalization—particularly on the consumption of Western cultural products such as popular music and films on the local identities of those on the margins of the Western world and in non-Western countries.[16] Cultural products from the West have been an important factor in the formation of local identities. As sociologists of music have noted, "in appropriating forms of popular music, individuals are simultaneously constructing ways of being in the context of their local everyday environments."[17] The consumption of foreign cultural products was (and still is) a process of selective borrowing and appropriation, translation, and incorporation into the indigenous cultural context.[18]

These ideas have influenced the new school of Russian cultural studies, whose exponents, such as Hilary Pilkington, continue to study the effects of globalization, cultural consumption, and local youth cultures in Soviet and post-Soviet Russia.[19] From this school, the most important idea for this book is *the role of the local cultural context,* in which the consumption of foreign cultural products is "embedded" and takes very different forms. The best studies of popular music consumption in the Soviet Union mainly explore "indigenous" popular music *production* by the famous Soviet and post-Soviet bands in the major capital cities; this book turns more toward the details of everyday music *consumption* by nonmusicians in a provincial city.[20]

Another concept that is useful for this book's analysis of the consumption of Western cultural products in the closed Soviet society is the idea of *cultural fixation.* According to the sociologist Thomas Cushman, the limited sources of foreign cultural practices always produce "an intense idealization" of the early available forms of such practices in societies with strong ideological control and limitations. In the closed Soviet society, the literature, music, and films of "an important, but limited range," Cushman explained, "[were] seized upon early on and became the central objects" upon which subsequent cultural practice was based.[21] Western cultural products became a point of *cultural fixation* for Soviet youth, who exaggerated the cultural significance of these products.

Cultural consumption is always related to ideology. After World War II, the consumption of cultural products in both capitalist and socialist countries became influenced by the ideology and politics of the Cold War. Using new approaches to cultural consumption and identity, Uta Poiger analyzes "how and why, in the postwar period, East (socialist) and West (capitalist) German encounters with American cultural products such as movies, jazz, and rock and roll were crucial to (re)constructions of German identities in the two states."[22] She reveals the direct connections between cultural consumption and Cold War politics. In her pioneering study, Poiger investigates the debates in the two German states about American cultural influences. She demonstrates how these debates revealed "the complicated intersections of gender, sexuality, class, and race in East and West German constructions of national identities."

According to Poiger, it is important to include the political aspects of the Cold War for our understanding of cultural consumption and youth culture during the postwar period. "In spite of many ideological differences," she writes, "authorities in both German states made their citizens' *cultural* consumption central to their *political* reconstruction efforts."[23] Her study demonstrates that an analysis of the consumption of foreign cultural products can be important for our understanding of postwar German politics and ideology.

This book follows Poiger's approach and concentrates on three major spheres of cultural consumption in the closed Soviet city of Dniepropetrovsk—books, popular music, and movies. Sports, classical music, and fine arts are not considered because they had no direct connections to the consumption of Western cultural products. With the *cultural fixation* of the youth in the closed socialist society on the limited sources of information about the forbidden capitalist West, the available books, periodicals, music, and films, which came directly from the West, influenced all other objects and forms of cultural consumption, including fashions, sports, and tourism. Contemporaries noted that Western mass culture, especially pop music, created a favorable impression image of the West among Soviet youth. As David Gurevich states, "Rock & roll was the battering ram that the West drove into our collective psyche. Then everything else rushed in: art, fashion, books, and, sometimes, politics."[24]

The main goal of this book is to show how an obsession with cultural products from the West revealed the most important trend in closed Soviet society—the Westernization of Soviet popular culture and Soviet ideological discourse not only in the capital cities but also in the provinces. The best way to show this trend is to concentrate on the most important spheres of cultural consumption—Western pop music, including jazz, rock, and disco; books, including those related directly or indirectly to the idea of the West, such as Ukrainian nationalism from Western Ukraine, and popular religion from the West; and movies from the West. This book also demonstrates how these spheres of cultural consumption are interconnected.

The Brezhnev Era and Socialist Consumption

Nikita Khrushchev's reforms and his attempts to develop a higher standard of living and everyday consumption for Soviet citizens started a new period of Soviet socialism. According to William Taubman, Khrushchev's dreams about the future Communist society affected the entire ideological discourse of post-Stalin socialism. During the Twenty-first Congress of the Communist Party of the Soviet Union (CPSU) in 1959, a Soviet leader pronounced that the USSR had completed the "full and final construction of socialism."[25] Soviet people needed to demonstrate a higher level of production because they would have a higher level of consumption than any country in the world within two decades. Khrushchev's emphasis on higher standards for production and consumption as the main objective of mature socialism opened the door for various interpretations of socialist consumption.

Leonid Brezhnev replaced Khrushchev as the general secretary of the CPSU's Central Committee in October 1964. His rule (1964–82) began a new chapter in "socialist consumption" in the Soviet Union. The Communists' goal was to build a better, more productive, and more humane society than capitalism. Therefore, Soviet leaders cared about forms of consumption in the USSR and about the efficient production of various consumer goods for the Soviet people, "to satisfy the needs of the builders of Communism."[26] All Soviet leaders, beginning with Vladimir Lenin and Joseph Stalin, understood that Communist society needed to prove its superiority over capitalism. However, before Brezhnev, no one publicly announced and included the idea of "socialist consumption" in the official social policy of the CPSU and Soviet state. Brezhnev pointed out that the production of consumer goods had to be the main goal of the entire socialist economy. In contrast, both Stalin and Khrushchev emphasized investment in heavy industries as the priority for both the Soviet state and people. After the decisions of the Fifteenth Congress of the CPSU in December 1927, the party directives for each five-year plan began by emphasizing this priority, trying to justify the intensive development of heavy industry with the necessity "to strengthen the military state defense system."

During the Twenty-fourth CPSU Congress, in March and April 1971, Brezhnev changed the emphasis of the directives in the USSR's Ninth Five-Year Plan. Instead of heavy industry as the top priority, the Soviet leadership turned their attention to goods for mass consumption. Brezhnev introduced "Soviet consumerism" into the official Soviet discourse as a legitimate precondition for what Communist ideologists had called "developed socialism" since 1967. The Soviet leadership planned to increase investment in the agriculture, food, and textile sectors to satisfy the growing demand by Soviet consumers during the period of "developed socialism," which was, according to Brezhnev's new theory, the "last stage before the final phase of Communist social and economic formation." In February 1976, during the Twenty-fifth CPSU Congress, Soviet leaders still prioritized the growth of the consumer sector.[27] In reality, the official emphasis on providing socialist consumers with necessary goods worked poorly, and a black market with a system of personal favors known as *blat* compensated for the lack of products and services.[28]

During the 1960s and 1970s, Soviet ideologists paid more attention to the organization of leisure time and cultural consumption among the Soviet population. Soviet consumers had to be provided not only with consumer goods but also with new services and new healthy goals for consumption. According to the ideological requirements of developed socialism, socialist consumption differed from "capitalist consumerism" and excluded notions of individual profitability and the accumulation of wealth. Soviet ideologists tried to combine the traditional Stalinist goals of "rational consumption" and the "rational use of leisure" with the new requirements of the "developed socialism" theory.[29] As Hilary Pilkington argues, this theory "attempted to show the difference between cultural relations in socialist and capitalist versions of modernity. Whilst in both societies emphasis was placed on high standards of living and development of consumer industries, Soviet society, it was claimed, was characterized by rational consumption and not cheap consumerism."[30]

In spite of the fact that Western Sovietologists have published extensively about Soviet politics, economy, society, and culture during the Cold War, the Brezhnev era is still mostly ignored by historians. The current historiography includes Svetlana Boym's and Nina Tumarkin's general surveys of the "mythologies" of everyday life in Soviet Russia from Lenin to Gorbachev, where "the Brezhnev period" is mentioned as a period of "stagnation and reaction."[31] Frederick Starr, Timothy Ryback, and Richard Stites have also written chapters on the "era of stagnation" in their historical analyses of entertainment and music in Russia and Eastern Europe.[32] Some scholars—including Ellen Propper Mickiewicz, Anne White, Dmitry Shlapentokh, Vladimir Shlapentokh, and Denise J. Youngblood—have devoted a few chapters of their books to the problems of film consumption during the Brezhnev era.[33] Historians of book consumption have analyzed the paradoxes of "the reading revolution" in the post-Stalin era.[34] After the collapse of the Soviet Union, more scholars devoted their studies to "the national question in the USSR" during the late socialist period.[35] A few historians explored problems of tourism in the Brezhnev era.[36] Many Western scholars have noted Soviet intellectuals' fascination and idealization of an "imaginary West," especially during the late socialist period.[37] However, the overwhelming majority of social historians have ignored the history of Brezhnev era, preferring to study the "Stalinist terror" or "Khrushchev thaw," instead of a boring "period of stagnation."

The scholarly neglect of this period is indicative of a stereotypical view of Brezhnev's rule as an unimportant time for Soviet history.[38] British scholars, such as Edwin Bacon, have recently noted that one of the primary reasons why the Brezhnev era has attracted so little "posthumous" analysis is the result of "the reforming discourse of the political project known as perestroika and overseen by the last Soviet leader, Mikhail Gorbachev," which declared the Brezhnev years to be "an era of stagnation." Unfortunately, this discourse became the "overwhelmingly dominant conceptualization of the almost two decades during which Brezhnev oversaw the Soviet state." Bacon and his colleagues consider this to be an inaccurate approach, because Brezhnev "brought an unprecedented stability to Soviet system, oversaw a continuing rise in living standards for his people, consolidated the USSR's position as a global superpower, and played a part in the prevention of the global nuclear conflict which many observers considered likely during those years. He stands as the most popular leader of the USSR/Russia in the twentieth century."[39] It is time for a serious historical analysis of the Brezhnev period in Soviet history, and the present volume is an attempt to do this through the lenses of the social and cultural history of everyday life in one region of the Soviet Union.

The first important studies of the Brezhnev era and cultural consumption were written by cultural anthropologists. Katherine Verdery devoted her book to the problems of national identity and cultural politics in Ceauşescu's Romania during a period that chronologically corresponds to the Brezhnev era in the USSR.[40] Another very important study for understanding cultural consumption during the Brezhnev era is that of the Hungarian scholar Anna Szemere. In her fascinating study of the underground rock music scene in Hungary, she revealed the complicated, paradoxical relationship between the socialist state and the production and consumption of rock music. She noted that "a distinction should be made between the mere adoption (co-option) of a musical idiom and that of a culture surrounding, nourishing, and making sense of that music."[41] Verdery's and Szemere's work on cultural politics during the late socialist period has influenced new anthropological studies of the Soviet Union in the West.[42]

The first serious attempt to explore the ideological aspects of everyday life during the late socialist period (especially the Brezhnev era) in the USSR was a study by the anthropologist Alexei Yurchak. He investigated the "internal shifts that were emerging within the Soviet system during the late socialist period at the level of discourse, ideology, and knowledge but that became apparent for what they were only much later, when the system collapsed."[43] He primarily used material from his hometown, Leningrad, to show how different forms of cultural production and consumption during the late socialist period, especially rock music and Western fashions, influenced Soviet youth, including Komsomol activists and officials. According to Yurchak, "rock-and-roll culture" became a part of "nonofficial discourses and practices in late socialism." In contrast to scholars such as Thomas Cushman, who insisted on the countercultural character of rock music the Soviet Union, Yurchak argued that nonofficial practices (e.g., listening and playing rock and roll) "involved not so much countering, resisting, or opposing state power as simply *avoiding* it and carving out symbolically meaningful spaces and identities away from it. This avoidance included passive conformity to state power, pretense of supporting it, obliviousness to its ideological messages, and simultaneous involvement in completely incongruent practices and meanings behind its back." He explained the reasons for the existence of unofficial practices like rock music. From the Brezhnev era until the collapse of Communism, "state power depended less and less on Soviet citizens' belief in the communist ideology, and more and more on their simulation of that belief."[44]

The Imaginary West

As Verdery and Yurchak argued, the obsession with Western cultural products became the most important feature of cultural consumption in the closed socialist society during the post-Stalin era. Yurchak especially focused on the cultural and discursive phenomenon known among social scientists as the "Imaginary West,"[45] which is "a local cultural construct and imaginary that was based on the forms of knowledge and aesthetics associated with the 'West,' but does not necessarily refer to any 'real' West, and that also contributed to 'deterritorializing' the world of everyday socialism from within."[46]

Yurchak rejected the confrontational/countercultural character of the "imaginary West" in Soviet cultural consumption. He offered a consensual/conformist interpretation of this metaphor. Using the ideas of the Russian cultural critic Tatyana Cherednichenko, he tried to show how Western music (as a part of "the Imaginary West") contributed to "the production of a whole generational identity" for the last Soviet generation. At the same time, he ignored the problems of regional, national, and religious identities that were shaped by the consumption of Western cultural products in various parts of the Soviet Union. He discarded the connections between Soviet dissidents and the idea of the West, which were very important for the practice of political dissent in the USSR. His interpretation exaggerated the role of discursive practices—thus, the visual elements, especially Western films, lost their role in influencing both ideological discourse and the local identity of Soviet consumers. In contrast to Yurchak's consensual/conformist definition of the "Imaginary West," this book offers an alternate, more countercultural interpretation of this metaphor, showing in detail the concrete connections between the identity formations in one region of the Soviet Ukraine with the "images, sounds and ideas of the West."

The major problem with Yurchak's study is its concentration only on Leningrad. Most of his material and interviews are from the Leningrad area.

Moreover, the majority of his material and information came from that city's educated elite, the loyal representatives of the Soviet middle and upper classes, and conformist Soviet intellectuals. He entirely ignored working-class youth, the major consumers of heavy metal music and adventure films in Soviet society. Another problem with his study was his uncritical attitude toward interviews. He interviewed people during the very difficult period 1994–98, which saw the transition of Russian society to post-Soviet "capitalism." Many of his interviewees tended to idealize or exaggerate their "socialist experience" as without conflicts—in contrast to the brutal reality of the "bandit capitalism" during the Boris Yeltsin era. In many cases, with his "speech acts" approach, Yurchak took his interviewees' information at face value, uncritically, without checking archival sources.[47] Therefore, he interpreted Soviet society during the late socialist period as void of any serious social problems or conflicts. He thus ignored the prevalent problems of the period—such as the involvement of Soviet officials in the activities of black market, Russification, the street gang culture, popular religiosity, nationalism, and anti-Semitism. He also underestimated the importance of the KGB and police interference in the cultural consumption of late socialism, which especially affected the provincial cities, where the majority of Soviet youth lived.[48]

This book is a serious contribution to the historiography of the Brezhnev era and seeks to add greatly to Yurchak's study of socialist cultural consumption by giving the official version (from the KGB and Communist Party archival documents) of the events alongside narratives from diaries and oral history. The archival material from my research and interviews with people from various social backgrounds in the provincial closed Soviet city of Dniepropetrovsk also bring a different perspective to the cultural history of the Brezhnev era. And I also consider common problems related to cultural consumption, such as Russification, nationalism, anti-Semitism, and popular religiosity, which were overlooked by Yurchak.

The Sources for and Organization of This Book

During perestroika, five old friends (two workers, two teachers, and one businessman) gave the copies of their diaries they had written during the 1970s to me. Reading these diaries inspired me to begin studying the consumption of Western cultural products in Soviet Ukraine. After being trained as a social historian of early America at Moscow's Institute of World

History, I came to work at the Department of History of Dniepropetrovsk University and decided to use new American methods of historical research to study the local history of cultural consumption in Soviet Ukraine. At its very beginning, this project was influenced by American oral history and the pioneering studies of Allan Nevins, popularized in Soviet books on the history of the United States. According to the methods of oral history, personal interviews can be combined with personal journals and diaries to explore the recent past.[49] As an implementation of such an approach, a close reading of five personal diaries led me to the next step in my research—personal interviews with participants in the consumption of Western cultural products.

From 1992 to 1994, I worked part time as a journalist for Serhyi Tihipko's periodicals in Dniepropetrovsk. In those days, Tihipko, the former first secretary of the regional Komsomol organization, was a rising star of Ukrainian capitalism and a founding father of Privatbank, the most successful financial organization in post-Soviet Ukraine. I interviewed him and other former Communist Party and Komsomol officials about the influence of Western cultural products on Komsomol apparatchiks. During the 1990s, I interviewed more than one hundred people of various social backgrounds, and collected personal diaries and memoirs about popular music consumption. As it turned out, this collected material covered not only topics of music but also themes of literature, nationalism, popular religiosity, and film consumption in the region of Dniepropetrovsk.

Eventually, I composed a new questionnaire and continued to interview people who lived in Dniepropetrovsk during the Khrushchev and Brezhnev eras.[50] A majority of the interviewees belonged to the generation of the people who were born between the late 1940s and early 1970s and came of age between 1964 and 1984. Half of them had college degrees, and the other half had been members of the Soviet working-class or collective farmers (i.e., people without a college education). The most interesting and informative interview was with Igor T., a retired KGB police officer who supervised "college life" in Dniepropetrovsk during the 1970s and early 1980s. Despite his obvious bias against "Westernized young imbeciles," he related precious information about the interaction between ideology and cultural consumption in the closed city. Another important interview was with Andrei Z., who in the 1970s took courses at Dniepropetrovsk City School No. 75, from which Yulia Grigian (Telegina) graduated in 1978. She eventually would become the famous oligarch and politician of independent Ukraine known as Yulia Tymoshenko. The interview with Andrei Z. provided this study with important information about Tymoshenko's childhood. In addition, some of my close friends—such as a former rock musician, Eduard Svichar; a chemistry teacher, Aleksandr Gusar; and a businessman, Vladimir Solodovnik—not only answered all the questions during their interviews but also gave me their summer diaries from their schooldays in the 1960s and 1970s.[51] These personal diaries and interviews became the major sources of information for this study.

Another group of sources for this book were archival documents from the Soviet state, Communist Party, Komsomol, and trade unions.[52] The most important materials were the "secret" KGB reports. Every month, the head of the Dniepropetrovsk Department of the KGB submitted a special report to the regional committee of the Communist Party "about the ideological crimes and political situation" in the region. These monthly reports are unique documents that demonstrate the official attitudes toward cultural consumption among the local youth. Reflecting the "closed" nature of Dniepropetrovsk, these KGB reports give an opportunity to explore in detail different stages of cultural consumption, including jazz and rock music, "banned" books, and films. In a closed city, the strict police control and detailed records of this consumption simplify the task of tracing the circulation of Western cultural products. In the 1990s, Dniepropetrovsk's historians began a unique project: a multivolume publication of the archival documents about police persecutions of "political dissidents" in the region after Stalin. This and similar published documents from the "era of developed socialism" became an important source for this book as well.[53]

The final source of information for this study was local periodicals. They included Communist Party newspapers, such as *Zoria* in Ukrainian and *Dneprovskaia Pravda* in Russian; the city administration's newspaper *Dnepr vechernii* in Russian; and the regional Komsomol's newspaper *Prapor iunosti* in Ukrainian. Various central and regional Komsomol periodicals, such as the Moscow-based magazine *Rovesnik* in Russian and the Kievan journal *Ranok* in Ukrainian, also provided important information for this study.

This book begins with an introductory chapter on the military-industrial complex and ruling elite of Dniepropetrovsk. Then each major sphere of cultural consumption is represented in each of the book's subsequent three parts, which are organized chronologically. The book's main themes—the construction of the local ideal of the West through the consumption of Western cultural products, and the inclusion of this ideal in the identity formation of Dniepropetrovsk's youth—permeate all three parts.

Part I of the book is about the 1960s, a transitional period from Khrushchev's "thaw" to Brezhnev's rule, when the major problems for the local police were the consumption of Ukrainian literature and Ukrainian nationalism, the consumption of Western "beat" music, and "Beatlemania." This consumption was mainly elitist and involved primarily the local intellectual elite of the closed city. At the same time, by the end of the 1960s, this fascination with beat music and western (cowboy) films also affected millions of working-class youth.

Part II of the book is about the 1970s and the consumption of Western adventure books and of movies made in Western capitalist countries, many of which became blockbuster hits in Soviet Ukraine during the Brezhnev era, as well as "hard-rock mania" and popular religiosity. Cultural fixation on the British hard-rock band Deep Purple began a period of the so-called democratization of Western pop music consumption, which especially influenced young workers, former peasant youth, and female audiences. This mass Westernization of local youth contributed to the Russification of the Soviet Ukrainian youth culture. At the same time, new limitations on cultural consumption imposed by Moscow in the closed city led to a growing disappointment by local elites and ordinary consumers with both the privileged position of Muscovites in socialist cultural consumption and the cultural and ideological politics of Moscow. Eventually, this opposition to Moscow contributed to the formation of local identity in Dniepropetrovsk.

Part III of the book focuses on the disco movement of the 1970s and 1980s, on tourism, and on Komsomol business. This part also deals with the reaction of Brezhnev's successor, Yuri Andropov, to the commercialization of the disco movement and the so-called fascist punk threat during the years 1982–84. Soviet ideologists considered this threat the logical result of corruption among disco activists. Therefore, the disco and punk stages of music consumption are covered here together. This final part also explores the major results of the Soviet administration's failure to stop the mass consumption of Western cultural products in Dniepropetrovsk and the Komsomol roots of post-Soviet "capitalist" business.

Overall, the primary emphasis of this book is first on the evolution and transformation of various ideas of the West, both imaginary and real—including ideas of economic prosperity, scientific progress, the market, democracy, and the like—during cultural consumption, and the influence of these ideas on identity formation in the "closed" Soviet society of late socialism.

Chapter 1

The Closed Rocket City
of Dniepropetrovsk

The city of Dniepropetrovsk (known before 1926 as Ekaterinoslav) always had an important role as the main industrial urban center of the southern Russian Empire and of Soviet Ukraine.[1] Many of the famous metallurgical and machine-building factories of prerevolutionary Russia and the Soviet Union were located in Dniepropetrovsk.[2] In 1980, the industrial enterprises of Dniepropetrovsk manufactured a significant proportion of the Ukrainian Republic's industrial products and consumer goods.[3]

The Secret Center of the Military-Industrial Complex

After 1945, however, the main economic and financial activities of the region and the city of Dniepropetrovsk became neither metallurgy nor the mining industry. The new center of the city's life was a secret military factory. The entire ideological and cultural situation in the region and the city now depended on this one factory, which became the most important part of the Soviet military-industrial complex. As early as July 1944, the State Committee of Defense in Moscow decided to build a large military machine-building factory in Dniepropetrovsk on the site of a prewar aircraft plant. In December 1945, thousands of German prisoners of war began construction and built the first sections and shops of the new factory.[4] This was the foundation of the Dniepropetrovsk Automobile Factory. In 1947 and 1948, this factory produced its first cars and special military automobiles. However, on May 9, 1951, the USSR Council of Ministers decided to transform the main shops and sectors of this factory into a secret enterprise, which would produce not only special military vehicles but also powerful rocket engines and various modern military aircraft. The former Dniepropetrovsk Automobile Factory was transferred to the Ministry of Armament of the USSR, and it received a new name: State Union Plant 586.[5]

Joseph Stalin himself suggested special, secret training for highly qualified engineers and scientists to enable them to become rocket construction specialists. He recommended introducing a new college degree at Dniepropetrovsk State University: a master of sciences in rocket construction. In 1952, the university administration formed the new Physical-Technical Department, which became the largest department at the university, admitting an average of four hundred students a year. These students received better accommodations and a higher stipend than students in other departments and colleges. The lowest stipend for this department was 450 rubles per student, whereas the highest stipend at another prestigious school, the Dniepropetrovsk Medical Institute, was 180 rubles. A special commission from Moscow selected talented undergraduate students studying physics at engineering schools all over the USSR and sent them to Dniepropetrovsk State University's Physical-Technical Department, where they resumed their studies as rocket engineers. Simultaneously, the university administration announced the admission of new freshmen students to this department. The promise of a good stipend and a glamorous career as a rocket engineer attracted thousands of talented young people to this "secret" department, which provided training specialists for only one industrial enterprise, the Dniepropetrovsk Automobile Factory.[6]

In 1954, the administration of this automobile factory opened a secret design office with the name "Southern" (Konstruktorskoe biuro Yuzhnoe in Russian, abbreviated KBYu) to construct missiles and rocket engines. Hundreds of talented physicists, engineers, and machine designers moved from Moscow and other large cities in the Soviet Union to Dniepropetrovsk to join KBYu. In 1965, the secret State Union Plant 586 was transferred to the Ministry of General Machine Building of the USSR. The next year, this plant officially changed its name to the Southern Machine-Building Factory (Yuzhnyi mashino-stroitel'nyi zavod—or, in the Russian acronym, simply Yuzhmash). The first "general constructor" and director of KBYu was Mikhail Yangel', a prominent scientist and outstanding designer of space rockets, who managed not only the design office but also the entire factory from 1954 to 1971. Yangel' designed the first powerful rockets and military space equipment for the Soviet Ministry of Defense. Moscow sent specialists and invested money in the projects of Yangel' and his colleagues. He collaborated with talented engineers, who later became the leaders of mili-

Figure 1.1. The Secret Production Building of the Yuzhmash rocket factory complex. Photograph by the author.

tary production in Dniepropetrovsk and the official directors of Yuzhmash. Two close collaborators of Yangel and of his successor, V. Utkin (who served as KBYu director during the years 1971–90), were the Yuzhmash directors Leonid Smirnov (1952–61) and Aleksandr Makarov (1961–86).[7]

In 1951, the Southern Machine-Building Factory began manufacturing and testing new rockets for the battlefield. The range of these first missiles was only 270 kilometers. By 1959, Soviet scientists and engineers had developed new technology, and as a result, KBYu started a new machine-building project making ballistic missiles. Under the leadership of Yangel', KBYu produced such powerful rocket engines that the range of these ballistic missiles was practically without limits. During the 1960s, these powerful engines were used as launch vehicles for the first Soviet spaceships.

During Makarov's directorship of Yuzhmash, KBYu designed and manufactured four generations of missile complexes of different types. These included the space launch vehicles Kosmos, Interkosmos, Tsyklon -2, Tsyklon-3, and Zenith. Under the leadership of Utkin, Yangel's successor, KBYu created a unique space rocket system called Energia-Buran. Yuzhmash's engineers had also manufactured 400 technical devices, which had been launched as artificial satellites known as Sputniks. For the first time in the world space industry, the Dniepropetrovsk missile plant organized the serial production of these Sputniks. By the 1980s, the plant had also manufactured sixty-seven different types of spaceships, twelve space research complexes, and four defensive space rocket systems. These systems were used not only for purely military purposes by the Ministry of Defense but also for astronomic research, for global radio and television networks, and for ecological monitoring. Yuzhmash initiated and sponsored the international space program of the socialist countries, called Interkosmos. Twenty-two of the twenty-five automatic Sputniks for this program were designed, manufactured, and launched by engineers and workers from Dniepropetrovsk. The Yuzhmash-KBYu facility had thus become an important center for the Soviet space industry and the Soviet military-industrial complex, as well as the main rocket producer for the entire Soviet bloc.[8]

On the eve of the collapse of the Soviet Union, KBYu had 9 regular and corresponding members of the Soviet Academy of Sciences, 33 full professors, and 290 scientists holding a PhD. These scientists and scholars awarded degrees and presided over a prestigious graduate school at KBYu, which attracted talented students of physics from all over the USSR. More than 50,000 people worked at Yuzhmash. By the end of the 1950s, Yuzhmash had become the main Soviet design and manufacturing center for various types of missile complexes. The Soviet Ministry of Defense included Yuzhmash in its strategic plans. Thus, the military rocket systems manufactured in Dniepropetrovsk became the major component of the newly born Soviet Missile Forces of Strategic Purpose.[9]

According to contemporaries, Yuzhmash was a separate entity inside the Soviet state. After a long period of competition with the Moscow center of rocket construction of V. Chelomei (a successor of Sergei Koroliov), the Yuzhmash rocket designs won in 1969. After that time, the leaders of the Soviet military-industrial complex preferred Yuzhmash's rocket models. By the end of the 1970s, Yuzhmash had become the USSR's major center for designing, constructing, manufacturing, testing, and deploying strategic and space missile complexes. The general designer and director of Yuzhmash also supervised the work of numerous research institutes, design centers, and factories all over the Soviet Union, from Moscow, Leningrad, and Kyiv to Voronezh and Erevan. And the Soviet state provided billions of rubles to finance Yuzhmash's projects.[10]

Officially, the Yuzhmash plant manufactured agricultural tractors and special kitchen equipment for everyday needs, such as mincing machines and juicers for peaceful Soviet households. In official reports for the general public, there was no mention of the plant's production of rockets or spaceships. However, hundreds of thousands of workers and engineers in the city of Dniepropetrovsk worked at this plant, and the members of their families (who constituted up to 60 percent of the city's population) knew about its "real production." This missile plant became a significant factor in the arms race of the Cold War,[11] which is why the Soviet government approved of the KGB's secrecy about Yuzhmash and its products. According to the Soviet government's decision, the city of Dniepropetrovsk was officially closed to foreign visitors in 1959. No citizen of a foreign country (even of the socialist ones) was allowed to visit the city or district of Dniepropetrovsk. After the late 1950s, ordinary Soviet people called Dniepropetrovsk "the closed rocket city."[12]

During the 1950s, the primary sponsor of improvement and renovations within the city of Dniepropetrovsk was the metallurgical industry. Then, during the 1960s and 1970s, the space industry and its biggest factory, Yuzhmash, sponsored new city programs, renovations, and new architectural projects—including the Meteor sports palace with its large indoor pool; the soccer team Dnieper; the city airport; the city's theater of opera and ballet; the Yavornitskii historical museum; the Children's World department store; the construction of thousands of modern apartment houses, libraries, and movie theaters; and the city's two-hundredth-anniversary celebration in 1976. All these and many other events and projects were initiated and financed by Yuzhmash and its talented director, A. Makarov.[13] Even the expansion and renovation of the Central Farmers' Market was related to the new role of Yuzhmash's leadership in the improvement of the city's life. The Central Farmers' Market was a reflection of the growth and strategic importance of the city. From 1958 to 1965, the city administration invested money in building a new covered hall for the market. By 1970, it had rebuilt and reconstructed the entire neighborhood surrounding the market, transforming it into a modern and convenient place for the "socialist consumption of goods and services."[14]

As a result, the Yuzhmash missile factory contributed to a new, improved level of cultural consumption for the city's residents. Yuzhmash made this new level of consumption possible because its leaders, who were the rocket city's intellectual elite, had already become the most Westernized group of Dniepropetrovsk intellectuals. All Yuzhmash engineers had unlimited access to Western scientific literature on physics and the rocket building. They also read American, British, French, and West German popular periodicals—such as *Science, Scientific American,* and *Nature*—in the special "secret" collections of Yuzhmash and local university libraries. Although these Yuzhmash engineers were not allowed to travel abroad, they all had obligatory "business trips" (*komandirovka*) to other Soviet regions and cities, including Moscow. They were the most mobile and open-minded part of the rocket city's elite. Consequently, the pioneering efforts in the popularization of Western films and new, modern forms of Western music such as jazz, rock and roll, and disco also started among the engineers and workers of the Yuzhmash factory complex, who contributed to the spread of new cultural forms and activities among those who lived in the city and region of Dniepropetrovsk.

The Brezhnev Clan and the Dniepropetrovsk Family

Dniepropetrovsk's transformation into an important center of the Soviet military-industrial complex was also related to the sudden rise of Leonid Brezhnev to power in October 1964. Brezhnev had been born in 1906 in the town of Kamenskoe (now Dnieprodzerzhinsk), near Dniepropetrovsk. He joined the Communist Party in 1931 and was elected a member of the Dniepropetrovsk City Council after graduating from the local metallurgical institute. The Stalinist purges of the 1930s removed many old Soviet and Communist officials from government positions, and these members of the Soviet elite perished in prisons and labor camps. Young people like Brezhnev filled the void created by the Stalinist repressions among leaders of the region. In 1938, young Brezhnev was elected a member of the regional committee of the Communist Party. He became the head of this committee's Department of Agitation and Propaganda the same year. By the age of thirty-two, he had became the secretary of the Communist Party committee for the Dniepropetrovsk Region—the most important industrial region of Soviet Ukraine. (As suggested above, before Yuzhmash, the region's industrial prominence had been gained through its metallurgical factories. The Dniepropetrovsk Region was a center of Soviet metal production before the 1960s.)

Brezhnev's career as the party secretary was interrupted by the Great Patriotic War, and in July 1941 he joined the army as an officer in the ideological division. After the war, the Central Committee of the Communist Party of the Soviet Union (CPSU) sent him to Dniepropetrovsk in November 1947, where he revealed himself to be a talented and ambitious organizer of the city's and region's industrial rebirth. He was elected first secretary of the Dniepropetrovsk regional committee of the CPSU the same year, and he ruled the entire region until June 1950 as party boss. His successor, who ruled from 1950 to 1955, was Andrii Kirilenko, a close friend of Brezhnev from the prewar years. Another young friend of Brezhnev, Volodymyr Shcherbytsky, who had graduated from Dniepropetrovsk Chemical Technological Institute before the war, took over the region during the periods 1955–57 and 1963–65. Two other young comrades of Brezhnev during his leadership in Dniepropetrovsk, Oleksii Vatchenko and Evgenii Kachalovskii, each assumed leadership of the region, respectively, during the periods 1965–76 and 1976–83.[15]

Thus Brezhnev began building his important connections in the region, which became his clan, which in turn would prove very useful in his struggle for power by supporting his rule during the 1960s and 1970s. Later, when he became the CPSU's first secretary and then the Soviet Union's president, he always supported all industrial projects in the Dniepropetrovsk Region and increased state investment in "the rocket factory." And he also promoted the political careers of his old friends from Dniepropetrovsk. Under his rule, many of them became prominent political figures in Kyiv and Moscow. Both contemporaries and scholars who study the "Brezhnev period" of Soviet history call this phenomenon of the rise of a group of politicians from Dniepropetrovsk the "Dniepropetrovsk mafia," or the rule of the "Dniepropetrovsk Family."[16] After Brezhnev's rise to power, Dniepropetrovsk's ruling elite influenced not only regional but also Ukrainian republican and All-Union politics.

During the 1960s and 1970s, Brezhnev's friends and close colleagues from his postwar years of rule in the region of Dniepropetrovsk went to Moscow and became prominent political figures in the Soviet "nomenclature" hierarchy. As described above, two main industries of the Soviet military-industrial complex—the metallurgical and missile-building industries—had important factories in the region of Dniepropetrovsk. Therefore, the industry of Dniepropetrovsk provided the Brezhnev ruling team with new members from 1964 to 1982. The city of Dniepropetrovsk became the location of the USSR's Ministry of Black Metallurgy and, as described above, the location of Yuzhmash, the largest Soviet missile-building factory, whose offices were staffed with Brezhnev's friends. Even after the downfall of the "Brezhnev clan" in Moscow in 1983, when Yuri Andropov began his struggle "with corruption and nepotism" among the Soviet nomenclature, the members of this clan still played a prominent role in the political life of Soviet Ukraine.

In 1990, Soviet president Mikhail Gorbachev sent a special committee to check the political situation in Ukraine. This committee represented the department in charge of the party organizations in Ukraine for the organizational sector of the CPSU's Central Committee. The report of the committee proved that 53 percent of Ukrainian executive officials came from Dniepropetrovsk.[17] Brezhnev's close friend, the first secretary of the Communist Party of Ukraine, Volodymyr Shcherbytsky, promoted the careers of other people from the region of Dniepropetrovsk. With his support, Oleksii Vatchenko became the head of the Presidium of the Ukrainian Supreme Soviet in 1976. Vatchenko ruled the Presidium until 1984 with the assistance of another politician from the region, Valentyna Shevchenko, who replaced Vatchenko in 1985. Many other members of the "Kyiv ruling class" under Shcherbytsky were also related to the metallurgical and military lobby from Dniepropetrovsk.[18]

The combination of important connections and support from Moscow and Kyiv contributed to rapid career promotion for many Dniepropetrovsk representatives in Soviet and post-Soviet politics. Another important moment in Dniepropetrovsk's political history, which affected various spheres of life in this "closed city," was the relative independence of the city's local administration from the central Ukrainian administration in Kyiv. Because of the status of Dniepropetrovsk as a "strategically important center for the military industry," different branches of the local administration were under the direct supervision of Moscow rather than Kyiv.[19]

The powerful presence of Brezhnev's clan in the Moscow central offices of the KGB and Ministry of the Interior also contributed to centralized ideological control in Dniepropetrovsk. This especially affected the KGB and police operations in the closed city. The local KGB office was always more Moscow oriented, ignoring the interests of the Ukrainian republican administration in Kyiv. At the same time, for those Moscow officials who had begun their careers in Dniepropetrovsk, this city became the testing ground for many of the All-Union KGB campaigns that they tried to initiate. As a result, Dniepropetrovsk's population experienced more ideological limitations and more brutal anti-Western campaigns by the police than people in other Soviet cities. Facing direct supervision from the Kremlin, local KGB officers and Communist ideologists tried to prove their ideological reliability and sometimes exaggerated the real "threat from the capitalist West."

Given their support from Moscow during the Brezhnev era, Dniepropet-rovsk's KGB officers were "pioneers" in organizing ideological campaigns that became models for the police in other "closed" Soviet industrial cities.[20] At the same time, the direct connections of these ideological campaigns to Moscow's leadership discredited the image of Moscow as the political center in the eyes of Dniepropetrovsk's residents. Eventually, both local elites and ordinary people complained about "Moscow's interference."

The KGB officers transformed one building in Dniepropetrovsk's Special Psychiatric Hospital, which was located in the town of Igren (now a suburban district of Dniepropetrovsk), into a special police facility for "political dissidents." All over the Soviet Union, the Igren hospital's *psikhushka* (mental asylum), especially its Section 9, became notoriously known as the worst place for political prisoners. Section 9 of the hospital was transformed into another KGB model for the treatment of various anti-Soviet criminals such as "Ukrainian nationalists, Zionists, and religious activists." The local KGB did various drug and medical experiments on its prisoners, treating the most "opinionated" political dissidents as mentally ill patients. Many religious and civil rights activists and various "bourgeois nationalists," such as the Ukrainian patriot Leonid Plyushch, called this hospital a "mental hell" because of its police system of harsh treatment and everyday humiliation organized by KGB supervisors, who protected the ideological security of the closed city.[21] Meanwhile, the local KGB officers justified the harsh treatment of political dissidents like Pliushch as necessary to ideologically protect Dniepropetrovsk, the strategically important center of the Soviet military-industrial complex.[22]

The Growth of the Region's Population and Consumption

The new status of the closed city of Dniepropetrovsk brought more state investment and contributed to the overall improvement of its inhabitants' standard of living. As a result, the region's population increased from 2.34 million in 1951 (56 percent urban) to 2.85 million in 1961 (72 percent urban). Larger salaries and a better distribution of resources also attracted mainly young people from other regions of the Soviet Union to Dniepropetrovsk. From the 1950s onward, the majority of its population was younger than thirty years of age and belonged to the USSR's major ethnic groups. In 1970, there were 3.34 million people in the region (76 percent urban); by 1984, its population had increased to 3.77 million (83 percent urban). The population of the region's main city, Dniepropetrovsk, grew from 660,800 in 1959 to 862,100 in 1970. And by 1979, the city of Dniepropetrovsk had become the "Soviet city–millionaire," with a population of 1.06 million. By the beginning of 1985, the city had more than 1.15 million people.[23]

The Dniepropetrovsk Region had a young, multinational, predominantly Russian-speaking population. Three major ethnic groups shaped its cultural development: Ukrainians, Russians, and Jews. During the peak of the period of the "international harmony and prosperity of developed socialism" in 1979, Ukrainians made up the overwhelming majority of the region's population (72.8 percent) and urban population (68.5 percent). Yet the numbers of Ukrainians decreased slightly, from 77.8 percent in 1959 to 74.5 percent in 1970 and to 71.6 percent in 1989. Due to the massive emigration of Jews from the Soviet Union, the Jewish population also decreased, from 2.7 percent in 1959 to 1.7 percent in 1979 and to 1.3 percent in 1989. The proportion of Russians in the region's population grew rapidly, from 17.2 percent in 1959 to 20.9 percent in 1970, and then to almost 23 percent in 1979 and to 24.2 percent in 1989.[24] By 1985, more than a third of the population of the city of Dniepropetrovsk was ethnic Russians. If we add to this the 3.2 percent of Russian-speaking Jews and more than 33 percent of Ukrainians who considered Russian their native language, more than 65 percent of the city's people associated themselves with Russian rather than Ukrainian culture.[25]

Overall, the standard of living in Soviet Ukraine improved after Stalin. The region of Dniepropetrovsk demonstrated rapid growth in its inhabitants' standard of living and level of consumption. According to official statistics, the most growth in the standard of living took place between 1940 and 1984.[26] The main participants in socialist consumption, who experienced an improvement in living standards, were young people. The region's youth population (people between sixteen and twenty-nine years of age) increased from 720,600 in 1959 (26.6 percent of the region's population) to 839,100 in 1983 (22.2 percent). During the same period, the number of the youth residing in the cities grew from 536,400 in 1959 (28.2 percent of the urban population) to 727, 300 in 1983 (23.7 percent).[27] For 1983, however, if we add the 234,480 local middle school students (between ten and fifteen years) in the region, this increases this most active youth population to 1.07 million—more than a third of the regional population and more than 40 percent of the urban population.[28] The majority of this youth population was influenced by Western youth fashions, music, and films, all traditionally associated with capitalist propaganda by Communist ideologists. But despite efforts by these ideologists to close the city and region of Dniepropetrovsk to foreign influences, its young people discovered their own peculiar forms of Westernization and enthusiastically consumed the cultural products of the capitalist West from the 1960s to the early 1980s.

Part I

The "Beating" 1960s: From the Khrushchev Thaw to the Brezhnev Doctrine

According to contemporaries, the first stage in the mass consumption of "the forbidden cultural products from the capitalist West" began (and it was recorded in detail by the KGB) after the official "closing" of Dniepropetrovsk in 1959, and this stage lasted until the end of the 1960s. During this 1960–70 period, Ukrainian, Jewish, and Russian "nationalist" literature and American jazz and "beat" (rock) music became the major objects of consumption among the region's growing population. According to local ideologists and KGB officers, during the 1960s, the cultural influences from these forbidden books and music contributed to the construction of what the Soviet officials termed "bourgeois nationalism" and "anti-Soviet behavior among Dniepropetrovsk's youth." (See the author's interviews with Igor T., KGB officer, Dniepropetrovsk, May 15, 1991; and with Vitalii Pidgaetskii, Department of History, Dniepropetrovsk University, February 10, 1996.) As a result, Dniepropetrovsk's KGB and Communist Party officials triggered the special ideological and police campaigns against the growing consumption of "dangerous books and music" by the young inhabitants of Dniepropetrovsk, the closed city. As it turned out, these campaigns revealed the growing importance of "the capitalist West" in the mass cultural consumption of post-Stalin socialist society.

Chapter 2

Anti-Soviet Crimes, Poetry, and Problematic Nationalism, 1960–1968

The most serious problem for KGB officers and Communist ideologists in the Dniepropetrovsk Region was the rise of Ukrainian "bourgeois nationalism" among local intellectuals, which had two primary sources: the radio, and the Westernized, "open" city of L'viv. The radio became the first source of anti-Soviet information because, during Nikita Khrushchev's de-Stalinization campaign, some restrictions on Soviet radio broadcasting were lifted and more Soviet people could listen to Western radio shows. The other source was the constant contacts between Dniepropetrovsk's intellectuals and their colleagues in the Western Ukrainian city of L'viv. Thus, "anti-Soviet information from the radio" and "Western influences from L'viv" contributed to what KGB officers called Ukrainian "bourgeois nationalism." Paradoxically, this movement became connected to popular forms of socialist cultural consumption such as reading books, listening to the radio, and recording music.

The Unexpected Results of Khrushchev's Thaw, Taras Shevchenko, and the KGB Response

The main ideological crimes of "Ukrainian nationalists" noted by KGB officers in the early 1960s were related to the new level of cultural consumption by the region's population, whose standards of living had improved since the beginning of Khrushchev's policy of de-Stalinization and the liberalization of Soviet society. One major result of this 1956–61 policy was the publication of the explicitly anti-Stalin letters and essays written by Vladimir Lenin during the last years of his life. For the first time, Soviet readers had an opportunity to learn about the conflict between Lenin and Stalin over nationality policy. In a 1922 debate about the future organization of the new federal socialist state, the Soviet Union, Lenin had categorically rejected Stalin's plan of "autonomization" (i.e., the inclusion of non-Russian Soviet republics in the Russian Federation, and the domination of Russian language and culture). Instead, Lenin had insisted on the equal representation of all republics in the federated Soviet Union out of respect for the national culture, language, history, and traditions of each Soviet republic. He asked his Russian comrades to support the national culture of each non-Russian nation and ethnic group in the Soviet Union. And he "declared war to the death on Great Russian chauvinism" to protect the national interests of each and every non-Russian ethnic group.[1] These forgotten ideas of Lenin about Soviet nationality policy became a real inspiration for Ukrainian intellectuals during the 1960s. And these ideas also triggered an interest in Ukrainian national history and culture among many Dniepropetrovsk college students.

An emphasis on technical progress and technical-scientific education was a main theme of Communist Party propaganda from the first days of Soviet history. All the Soviet leaders, from Lenin and Stalin to Khrushchev and Brezhnev, mentioned this in their reports, and all the congresses of the Communist Party of the Soviet Union included this theme in their documents. This interest in new technology brought unforeseen results among Soviet youth. In Dniepropetrovsk during the late 1950s and early 1960s, thousands of high school and college students enthusiastically designed amateur radio sets and other radio devices. Some of them even broadcast their own improvised radio shows without any state sanction. The KGB tried to prevent these activities, which they called "radio hooliganism." The Soviet police worried about the "radio hooligans'" interference with officially controlled radio waves, and also about students who listened to "bourgeois radio stations" and spread "dangerous bourgeois propaganda" among the Soviet population.

The first recorded criminal case in the KGB files was reported to the Dniepropetrovsk regional Communist Party organization on July 30, 1962. It analyzed the "anti-Soviet" behavior of A. Duplishchev, P. Belonozhko, and E. Boiko, three students at Dniepropetrovsk State University (Dniepropetrovskii gosudarstvennyi universitet, DGU). In 1960, these students designed special radio devices that permitted them to listen to foreign music and "anti-Soviet radio shows" and then to broadcast their own improvised shows. As it turned out, all the arrested radio hooligans recorded the chart-topping popular music of capitalist countries and eventually broadcast this music for local radio audiences.[2] According to the KGB report, these students not only listened to the Western radio stations but also spread "anti-Soviet information" among their classmates. The university's administration did not stop their activities. However, under police pressure the university party organization insisted on expelling these students from Komsomol and from the university. In 1961 and 1962, the KGB investigated more criminal cases about the "dissemination of anti-Soviet propaganda" among students of other colleges in the region. Some of these students not only criticized Stalin's terror but also mentioned his "mistakes in Lenin's nationality policy."[3]

For the Dniepropetrovsk party and KGB officials, a new problem related to the "Khrushchev thaw" was the growing interest in national history and national traditions among loyal intellectuals, members of the Communist Party and Komsomol.[4] Party ideologists tried to prevent the "spread of ideologically unreliable rumors." Moreover, they were afraid of an unprecedented level of "criminal activities" among young intellectuals, especially among college students. Some of these students composed anti-Soviet leaflets and attached them to city buildings. During the night of October 19–20, 1961, two students at the Dniepropetrovsk Metallurgical Institute (Dnipropetrovskii metallurgicheskii institut, DMETI), M. Lopatnichenko and P. Prodan, manufactured and placed "anti-Soviet leaflets" on the public buildings in downtown Dnepropetrovsk. These leaflets criticized the low levels of production and the standard of living in the USSR, which lagged behind Western countries. They also contained demands for the "Ukrainian Republic's independence from the USSR." The KGB recorded six other similar cases between 1961 and 1962. All these crimes were committed by students from the local colleges, such as the Engineering and Construction Institute of Dnipropetrovsk (Dnipropetrovskii inzhenerno-stroitel'nyi institut, DISI), DMETI, and DGU. This was a dangerous trend for the local administration. Party apparatchiks demanded that the KGB stop these activities among local students and investigate the reasons for this unprecedented rise in "anti-Soviet crimes."[5]

The KGB organized a special investigation and discovered that college seminars on the Communist Party's history had become forums that officially permitted criticism of Stalin. The DMETI student Prodan, who was arrested for pasting anti-Soviet leaflets on buildings, actively participated in all discussions during the seminars on the history of the party and demonstrated erudition and good knowledge of Lenin's works and party documents. He was one of the best and most talented students in his seminar's group. According to the KGB reports, "criticism of Stalin," led him to "very dangerous generalizations" about the lack of democracy in the Soviet political system. The instructor for the seminar, M. Zvenkovskaya, did not censor Prodan's criticism and even supported his generalizations about negative elements in the Soviet political system. KGB officials reporting this case to the regional party organization acknowledged that Khrushchev's campaign of de-Stalinization had confused and disoriented city intellectuals and created problems for ideologically controlling the strategically important city of Soviet Ukraine.

The KGB operatives interpreted rising interest in Ukrainian national history and national traditions among loyal Soviet intellectuals as Ukrainian nationalism. For the KGB, the main center of Ukrainian nationalism in Dniepropetrovsk was the university, and especially its Historical-Philological Department.[6] The first KGB "nationalist" case directly related to cultural consumption involved A. Ovcharenko, a student in this department.[7] In 1960, he wrote his master's thesis (*diplomnaia rabota*) about a controversial poem by Taras Shevchenko, a nineteenth-century Ukrainian poet and the founding father of the Ukrainian literary tradition. Shevchenko wrote "A Poem-Fantasy" (Mysteria) titled "A Great Cellar" (Velykyi Liokh) in 1845. This poem is about the tragedy of Ukrainian history portrayed through the laments of "three souls, three crows, and three *kobza* players."[8]

According to Shevchenko, these images symbolized Ukrainians who died after the annexation of Ukraine by the Russian Empire. The main idea of the poem is that Bohdan Khmel'nytsky, a Ukrainian Cossack leader (*hetman*), made a dangerous mistake when, in Pereyaslav in 1654, he signed an agreement that approved the joining of Ukraine to Russia.[9] After this alliance, Ukrainians became slaves of the Russian tsars; Peter I and Catherine II, "the worst enemies of Ukraine," annihilated the freedoms and privileges of Ukrainian Cossacks and destroyed Zaporizhian Sich, Baturin, and other centers of Cossack power in Ukraine. After this, Russian rulers ("*moskali*" and "*katsapy*" in the poem) exploited and humiliated Ukrainians. Thousands of Ukrainian peasants and Cossacks died while building the city of Saint Petersburg, railroads, and other construction projects for the Russian crown. Due to these tragic events, the souls of dead Ukrainians still meet in Subbotiv, the hometown of Khmel'nytsky near Chyhyryn, to lament and denounce his decision to betray the independence of Ukraine and join Russia. Shevchenko used the metaphor of "the Great Cellar" or "the Great

Coffin" to portray a Ukraine enslaved: After 1654, the Russians dug a "huge cellar [*liokh*] of slavery" for Ukrainians. The Russian Empire became a "cold and oppressive underground prison." And Khmel'nytsky's church in Subotiv, in the poetic imagination of Shevchenko, was transformed into a symbol of slavery and death ("a burial place") for all of Ukraine. According to Shevchenko, Khmel'nytsky, a "friend" of Tsar Alexis, betrayed and humiliated Ukraine: "All nations of the world now are laughing at Ukraine and making fun of Ukrainians who, by their own will, have traded their freedoms for slavery in Russia." The ending of the poem is very optimistic and prophetic, however: "Do not laugh, strangers, at poor orphan Ukraine, because this Church-Coffin will fall apart and from its ruins the free Ukraine will arise! And this Ukraine will remove a darkness of slavery, and then turn the light of Truth on, and Ukraine's oppressed children will pray in freedom at last!"[10]

Shevchenko's poem offered a historical concept that differed from the traditional interpretations of Soviet historiography. In contrast to a positive portrayal of the Pereyaslav agreement as a symbol of friendship of two brotherly Slavic nations,[11] Shevchenko described it as a tragic act of betrayal and humiliation for Ukraine. He presented the great modernizers of Imperial Russia, Peter I and Catherine II, as the most brutal executioners and torturers of the Ukrainians, and as ending all hopes for an independent Ukraine. Of course, the very fact that Ovcharenko chose this poem for his research raised suspicions among his classmates, who denounced him to KGB officers. As a result, the KGB considered Ovcharenko's thesis "a nationalistic deviation" and complained about it to his professors. Despite the KGB's pressure, his professors not only tried to avoid any ideological criticism of Ovcharenko's work but also fully supported his thesis. Moreover, Ovcharenko's mentor K. Dmukhovsky, an associate professor in the Department of Philology, suggested that he just remove some sentences "that looked too nationalistic" and eventually awarded the thesis a B grade ("good"—*dobre*).[12]

The KGB officials, who were outraged by the indifference shown by university professors to such nationalistic transgressions, organized a special investigation. They discovered that in 1960, Ovcharenko, with his classmates O. Zavgorodnii and O. Trush, from the Department of Philology, and M. Leliukh, a student at the Dniepropetrovsk Medical Institute, were part of Dnipro, a student group at the university. They read books on Ukrainian history and culture, recited Ukrainian poetry, and studied Shevchenko's works. As it turned out, Leliukh had organized this group and composed its program and rules. According to KGB records, he was notorious among his classmates for his anti-Soviet remarks and nationalistic ideas. In 1959, during a seminar on political economy at the Medical Institute, Leliukh used his own interpretation of Marxist theory to prove the necessity of economic autonomy for Ukraine within the USSR. In 1960, he used these same ideas in his program for Dnipro. As the KGB described it, Leliukh "included an idea of a separation of Ukraine from the Soviet Union." It was fortunate for other participants of this group that they had no time to discuss this document; in 1962, after graduation from the university, they left Dniepropetrovsk for their new job assignments. This departure spared them from arrest. As the main organizer of the group, Leliukh was eventually arrested and sent to jail in November 1962 for "nationalistic propaganda."[13]

It is noteworthy that Leliukh's group attracted loyal Komsomol members, whose interest in Ukrainian history and traditions was stimulated by two developments in cultural production and consumption in Soviet Ukraine during 1959 and 1961, which were connected to the official discourse of post-Stalin socialism. First, the assigned readings for students in the Department of Philology now included more books in Ukrainian written by classical Ukrainian writers like Shevchenko. Second, the Communist Party's cultural program under Khrushchev stressed the creation of a new Soviet humanistic culture, "socialist in essence" and "national in form." This led to state sponsorship of ideological campaigns to celebrate national poets, such as Shevchenko, who were "opponents of the oppressive tsarist regime" and "predecessors of socialist national cultural revival."[14] The 140th anniversary of Shevchenko's birth and the centennial of his death (respectively, in 1954 and 1961) were marked by the publication of multivolume collections of his works in Ukrainian. The reading of his controversial poetry (both anti-Russian and pro-Ukrainian) in Ukrainian schools by millions of students led to an interest in Ukrainian history in forms that differed from the ideology of Soviet internationalism. Some of these forms were labeled nationalistic deviations by the KGB.[15]

"The West Will Help Us": Young Poets and the Revival of Ukrainian Culture

At the beginning of 1960, another group of young, patriotically inclined poets attracted the KGB's attention. Most were DGU students who joined the literary workshop at the Palace of Students in Dniepropetrovsk. Natalia

Televnaya, a young Soviet official, organized this workshop as a base for a future club of "the creative youth," following the example of the Kyiv Komsomol organization, which combined elements of the jazz club with serious intellectual discussions.[16] According to KGB reports, the young, talented poets, members of the literary workshop, denied the "traditions of socialist realism," insisted on new "revolutionary approaches to a changing reality," and called themselves "the generation of the '60s" (*shestydesiatnyky*). During their meetings at the Palace of Students, KGB officers discovered, they not only listened to American jazz but also experimented with nationalist ideas, reading and disseminating texts written by famous figures in the Ukrainian national movement of the nineteenth and twentieth centuries. These young poets also discussed problems of the medieval and modern history of Ukraine, "idealizing the role of *hetmans* and Ukrainian Cossacks."[17] Although their ideas of national history were expressed in the traditionally accepted Marxist forms—none of these "experimental poets" denied the theory of "class struggle" or the progressive character of socialism —they were interpreted by the police as "nationalist propaganda."

By 1965, this group of poets expanded to include more college students who wrote their own poetry in Ukrainian. The KGB officers focused their activities on this group of young poets, such as Oleksandr Vodolazhchenko, Ivan Sokul'sky, Oleksandr Zavgorodnii, V. Semenenko, P. Vakarenko, and Grigorii Malovik.[18] One member of this group, Vodolazhchenko, was responsible for the spread of Ukrainian books printed in West Germany, and he was interrogated by KGB officers in 1965. As a result, he repented and promised to avoid any "nationalistic activities." However, after a conversation with KGB representatives, on the same day, he said in public:

> We must fight not only for the preservation of the Ukrainian language because this is not a very important question for this given period, but we must struggle for the preservation of the nation, the national cadres. It is necessary that Ukrainians have to stay to work in Ukraine, that we have fewer ethnically mixed marriages. We must work hard in this direction [*sic*].[19]

According to KGB reports, similar ideas were shared by many people in the Philology and Physical-Technical departments of DGU, at DISI, and among young artists and men and women of letters. Despite numerous interviews and warnings at the KGB offices, these poets still met with each other. Moreover, they boasted to each other of their courage during the KGB interrogations and they tried to expose those who had denounced them to the police.[20]

On the eve of the new year, 1966, DGU students, including Vodolazhchenko and Ivan Sokul'sky, organized a group of sixteen young people to meet in the classrooms of the Agricultural Institute (Dniepropetrovskii sel'sko-khoziaistvennyi institut, DSKHI) and DGU for recitals of national Ukrainian Christmas and New Year's songs (called *koliadky* and *shchedrivky* in Ukrainian). They had official permission from the DGU Communist Party committee and the Komsomol regional committee to meet and recite the *koliadky,*[21] and they borrowed Ukrainian national costumes from the Palace of Students. Late in the evening of December 31, 1965, they donned their costumes and visited the apartments of their professors from DGU, DISI, and DSKHI, where they staged the national rituals of Ukrainian New Year celebrations. But when they tried to visit officials of the regional party committee in a special residence building in downtown Dniepropetrovsk, they were stopped by the police. It is noteworthy that the KGB report emphasized that the "lyrics of the *koliadky* had no bad or harmful content."[22] The report also noted that Vodolazhchenko and Sokul'sky—both quite intoxicated—called each other "*pan*" ("my lord" in Ukrainian). The KGB officer wrote:

> They began to express their admiration and joy at what they had done. They declared that their activities would be recorded in the history books because they were the first people who got a permission to perform Ukrainian *koliadky* in public. They regarded this as a big victory for Ukrainian culture. Vodolazhchenko even suggested writing about this to the Polish periodical *Our Word,* which could inform the Ukrainians abroad, in Canada, and other countries.[23]

These young Soviet Ukrainian patriots expected that all progressively minded people in the West would support their actions and approve them. The young patriots obviously idealized the level of support for Ukrainian nationalism in the "progressive West." According to their contemporaries, the idealized image of "the intellectual free West" inspired Dniepropetrovsk's poets to seek support for their actions among Western intellectuals as well. They thought that the official Soviet international policy of peaceful coexistence of socialist and capitalist countries would help "to improve the national situation among socialist nations such as Ukraine and Russia."[24]

The groups of Ukrainian culture enthusiasts mainly consisted of college students and young female workers from local factories. On January 7, 1966, many students joined a group of *koliadky* singers to celebrate Orthodox Christmas, using old national Ukrainian rituals and folk songs. The local Komsomol periodical published an article that same day praising "an important cultural initiative of young people who tried to restore the local customs of ordinary people who settled in the Dnipro Region many years ago and who laid a foundation for a modern Ukrainian socialist civilization."[25]

DGU, pressured by the KGB, then tried to accuse one of the main organizers of this group, Ivan Sokul'sky, a fourth-year student (a junior) in the Department of Philology, of what they called "Ukrainian nationalism." Sokul'sky, who felt offended by these accusations, prepared a special article for a local periodical with the title "Am I Nationalist?" in which he denied all the accusations. He even planned to sue I. Iarmash, deputy secretary of the DGU Communist Party committee, for calling him "a Ukrainian bourgeois nationalist." When the local Dniepropetrovsk television station prepared a special show devoted to the poets, like Sokul'sky, who belonged to a university literary association called Gart ("Tempering" in Ukrainian), KGB officials insisted on the removal of Sokul'sky's name from the script. Moreover, they used Sokul'sky's classmates to denounce him and other participants in the performance of *koliadky* rituals. As these officers had suspected, the Gart newspaper *Gart* resisted their pressure and kept publishing poetry by Sokul'sky and his friends.

Eventually, under pressure from the KGB, on May 5, 1966, Sokul'sky was expelled from the section of Ukrainian language and literature in the Department of Philology for the "nationalistic ideas he put in his poems."[26] According to KGB reports, Sokul'sky and his friends had disseminated "ideologically dangerous literature" and advocated releasing all people arrested for "nationalistic activities" from jail. After a long interrogation, the KGB "persuaded" Sokul'sky to stop his patriotic activities. After 1966, he worked in different places in various positions, including as proofreader at the local energy plant's newspaper. Another friend of Sokul'sky, O. Zavgorodnii, who worked as a journalist at the district newspaper, was also persecuted by the KGB. In conversations with KGB officers, Zavgorodnii again and again tried to defend his poetry as "an expression of normal Soviet patriotism."[27] According to the KGB reports for 1966, the young poets were interrogated daily for their alleged "nationalistic activities" during October and November 1966 by the KGB officers.[28]

On October 10, 1967, another young poet from Dniepropetrovsk, My-khailo Chkhan, who worked as an engineer-researcher at dmeti before he gained membership in the Union of Writers of Ukraine, complained about the bad cultural situation in his city to his colleagues, the poets of L'viv:

> The local administration carries out subtle and consistent politics of Rus-sification in Dniepropetrovsk. Nowadays it is not necessary to take a Ukrainian language exam to be admitted to a college here. The language of instruction is Russian in all colleges and the university now. They do not use Ukrainian in factories or offices anymore. That is why ordinary people are convinced that the Ukrainian language has no practical use. Therefore they turned to Russian and replaced their Ukrainian with the Russian language now.[29]

The KGB feared active contact between Dniepropetrovsk's intellectuals and their colleagues in L'viv and Kyiv because their discussions contributed to the spread of anti-Soviet and nationalistic ideas. The city of L'viv was the major source of trouble for KGB operatives because all the ideologi-cally dangerous literature came to Dniepropetrovsk from this city.[30]

KGB Reports about Ukrainian, Russian, and Jewish Nationalism

During the period 1960–67, KGB reports to the regional Communist Party committee had only a few details about "anti-Soviet ideological crimes" in the Dniepropetrovsk Region. The year 1968, when Soviet troops crushed an attempt to reform socialism in Czechoslovakia, became the busiest time for KGB officials since "closing" the city of Dniepropetrovsk in 1959. Since 1968, KGB officials had offered more details about "anti-Soviet activities" in the region. On July 4, 1968, the head of the Dniepropetrovsk Department of the KGB, N. Mazhara, sent secret information about the ideological sit-uation in the region to the first secretary of the Dniepropetrovsk Regional Committee of the Communist Party of the Soviet Union.[31] This KGB offi-cial noted that during a six-month period, the police had discovered 184 printed documents with "anti-Soviet content," widely circulated among the regional population; 95 of these documents derived from the Ukrainian na-tionalist organization Ukrains'ka golovna vyzvol'na rada, 14 from the Russian anticommunist organization Narodno-Trudovoi Soiuz, 61 from various religious organizations, and 14 from "socialist revisionist international organizations" (mainly from Albania). Mazhara noted that some of the religious and "revisionist" literature came from socialist countries, such as Poland and Romania, and some of the "nationalistic" literature came from Czechoslovakia. Many of these documents reached Dniepropetrovsk through L'viv. The KGB detected an increase in anti-Soviet and "politically harmful" activity in the region; there were 60 cases of such activities during the whole year of 1967, but for only five months in 1968 there were 194 such cases.[32]

Mazhara's report testifies to the growth of a new kind of cultural consumption among the region's population during the years 1967–68. The most popular type of banned literature were the pamphlets of Ukrainian nationalists (95 cases) and religious publications (61 cases). Of the 194 detected cases of anti-Soviet activity during the five-month period in 1968, the most typical were the "dissemination of foreign anti-Soviet literature" (183 cases); the "spread of ideologically and politically harmful notions, slander about Soviet reality" (62); "manifestations of nationalist character" (47); "antisocietal acts of religious tendency" (20); and the "circulation and keeping at home of handwritten and printed material of anti-Soviet and politically harmful content" (12). Almost 56 percent, a majority of the "anti-Soviet criminals" (109 of 194), were intellectuals (31 students, 27 college teachers, 30 representatives of the "creative intelligentsia," and 21 members of the "technical intelligentsia").[33] Those most active in the processes of cultural production and consumption in the region became the main violators of the Soviet rules for cultural consumption in Dniepropetrovsk. Given this city's strategic importance, the increase of anti-Soviet cultural production and consumption required special attention from all branches of the local administration—not only the political police but also the region's ideological and educational organizations.

According to Mazhara's KGB report, in February 1968 a teacher from Dniepropetrovsk Construction Technical School (Tekhnikum), M. Kukushkin (b. 1915), told his colleagues: "Given the automation of production in the capitalist world, an industrial worker is transformed into an engineer, and therefore in a future the working class they will disappear. That is why the teaching of Karl Marx is outdated and many people in the West now accept the new contemporary theories, replacing Marxism with the new ideas." During one meeting with his colleagues, Kukushkin said that "honesty is a relative notion. . . . A Soviet spy, carrying out a special intelligence assignment, acts dishonestly toward the foreign country where he is living.

At the same time an American soldier, by participating in a war in Vietnam, performs his duties for his motherland and acts honestly." Similar ideas were shared in public by professors from dmeti and DGU.[34] Dniepropetrovsk's professional writers added nationalist elements to these kinds of critical discourse, which became very popular among local intellectuals. Six out of 28 (i.e., 21 percent) members of the Dniepropetrovsk Branch of the Union of Writers of Ukraine "demonstrated their nationalist sympathies in public."[35]

To prevent the spread of "anti-Soviet, revisionist ideas from Prague," the KGB initiated a special ideological campaign in 1968 to "suppress any demonstration of pro-Western or nationalist sentiment."[36] This campaign used traditional Stalinist ideological discourse, which emphasized the necessity of vigilance and Communist ideological "purity," especially in ideologically important sources of propaganda such as newspapers, radio, and television. The KGB complained to local Communist Party officials that on February 3, 1968, the Komsomol regional newspaper *Prapor iunosti* ("A Banner of the Youth" in Ukrainian) devoted its entire issue to the anniversary of the birth of Grigorii Petrovskii, a Bolshevik, after whom the city of Ekaterinoslav had been renamed Dniepropetrovsk in 1926. This issue focused on Petrovskii's friends, the prominent figures in the party and the Soviet state, like Iona Yakir, who perished during the "Stalinist purges." The KGB officers explained that this focus was a very dangerous ideological trend. They wrote, "You are not supposed to mention purges, if the content and tone of the material would not demand this."

The KGB feared that material about the cult of personality would provoke anti-Soviet ideas among readers.[37] It analyzed the ideological contents of all the articles in local periodicals and of local radio and TV shows. Between 1966 and 1968, it found that the most popular articles and shows included material about people who were persecuted by the Soviet police either in Stalin's times or in more recent years. Therefore, the KGB officials recommended that party and Komsomol ideologists strengthen control over the means of disseminating mass information in the city of Dniepropetrovsk. They explained how dangerous it was to publish or demonstrate open criticism of the Soviet system of power in a strategically important region with an ethnically diverse population. For example, they showed how rumors about social unrest among the workers of Krivoi Rog in 1968 had spread throughout the region. Many workers who were dissatisfied with their low standard of living and low wages used local publications that criticized the Soviet system to justify their actions, and in June 1968 they took to the streets to demonstrate, with anticommunist slogans. It was a peaceful demonstration and the police arrested, but later released, all the ringleaders of this "anti-Soviet" event.[38]

Yet an overwhelming majority of the criminal cases (more than 70 percent) reported by the KGB from 1960 to 1968 concerned displays of nationalism. Almost 60 percent of these were related to Ukrainian nationalism, and 10 percent were about Russian and Jewish nationalism.[39] It is noteworthy that the cases of so-called anti-Soviet nationalist behavior in the KGB's files were about the idealistic attempts of young people to cleanse socialist reality from "distortions" and "deviations" of Communist ideals and to make a life under socialism better and closer to the Leninist ideal of mature socialism. This kind of discourse existed in Soviet society all the time, but Khrushchev's de-Stalinization campaign and his romantic attempt to build Communism in the near future energized and justified this discourse, especially between 1961 and 1968.

In October 1967, Mikhail Mikhailov, a DGU student, had an intensive correspondence with his close friend Nikolai Polesia, a former DGU student who had moved to Kyiv State University. In their letters, they criticized the corrupt system and the immoral behavior of the Soviet officials who accepted bribes, cheated on their colleagues, and so on. They had encountered this kind of corruption when they worked as students at a brick factory and on collective farms. In their idealistic vision of Communism, this behavior contradicted its major ideals; therefore, all honest Soviet citizens should struggle with such distortions of socialism. Polesia suggested that Mikhailov organize a special "ideological" group for "the struggle with the everyday, all-suppressing, dull reality" in the name of "a better Communist future."

Polesia, Mikhailov, and other college students, who were later interrogated by the KGB, wanted to "make Soviet reality fit the classical Leninist model of socialism." They tried to defend "the Leninist theory of equality for all nations and national languages under socialism." Therefore, they accused the Communist leadership in Dniepropetrovsk of "ignoring Leninism, of organizing an anti-Marxist campaign of Russification, and of persecution of the socialist Ukrainian national culture."[40] These young Ukrainian idealists were simply following the main ideas of official Soviet discourse about nationalities under socialism.[41] Dniepropetrovsk's students just took for granted the major elements of this policy and tried to criticize distortions of it in the closed city.

All the cases of so-called Ukrainian bourgeois nationalism stemmed from the same discourse of improving the "Soviet socialist model" and implementing the Communist Party program's objective "to create Soviet culture, socialist in its content and national in its forms."[42] In October 1967, Vasyl Suiarko, a twenty-one-year-old freshman at the Dniepropetrovsk Mining Institute, planned to form a nationalist organization and to put the Ukrainian national flag (yellow and blue) on the main building of the institute on November 7, the fiftieth anniversary of the October Revolution. As the police later discovered, in the summer of 1966, Suiarko had come to Dniepropetrovsk to take the institute's admission examinations. There, he met Oleksandr Golovchun, and they spent time together talking about creating an underground student organization of Ukrainian nationalists. Suiarko boasted that he had read books about the history of Ukraine that were forbidden by the KGB, and that he had personal contacts with "the writer-nationalist Korzh" in the city of Dniepropetrovsk. As it turned out, Suiarko had invented the entire story for his friend Golovchun to demonstrate how brave he was; his information about Korzh was borrowed from a BBC radio show. He failed his exams in 1966 and was admitted to the institute only the next year. When he returned to Dniepropetrovsk in 1967, he again met Golovchun and continued to play the role of the "active Ukrainian nationalist" for him.[43] This childish game led to the fantastic project to put the Ukrainian flag on the main building of the institute. This plan was denounced by another student to the KGB.[44]

Suiarko and Golovchun were arrested by the police and later released and expelled from Komsomol and the institute. As Suiarko admitted in a conversation with a KGB officer, he thought that as an ethnic Ukrainian he fit the role of organizer of a Ukrainian nationalistic group. He believed that such an organization would be important in awakening national feelings among local Ukrainians and improving socialist society. In the Ukrainian city of Dniepropetrovsk, he noted, local department stores did not sell Ukrainian national clothing or Ukrainian national literature. According to many local Ukrainians, this was a "distortion" of "Leninist national policy" and created "a Russified version" of "socialist cultural consumption" that contradicted the main principles of "mature socialism," as declared by Leonid Brezhnev himself.[45] Suiarko also acknowledged that he had borrowed some arguments for his plan from foreign radio broadcasts such as the BBC, the Voice of America, and the Voice of Canada for Ukrainians. Cultural consumption—listening to the radio—thus led to an activity that was interpreted by the KGB as "nationalistic" and therefore as a dangerous, "anti-Soviet" crime.[46]

Another criminal case was related to the unique manifestation of "Russian anticommunist nationalism." A group of high school students from the city of Krivoi Rog tried to disseminate leaflets with Russian nationalistic and anti-Soviet propaganda, using information from the radio stations Liberty and the Voice of America. The leader of this group, a high school senior, Nikolai Kondratenko, also invited young workers from the local mine in Krivoi Rog to join his anticommunist underground movement. According to the KGB's information, this group was organized on May 28, 1968. As Kondratenko confessed during the police investigation, the main goal of his organization was to struggle with the Soviet regime and "provide conditions for the flourishing of the Russian nation." According to him, Soviet Communists had destroyed the Russian nation by dissolving it into an artificial international supernational formation called the "Soviet people." All ethnic groups had disappeared into this new entity. He referred to the new party program of 1961, which connected the approaching of mature Communism in the Soviet Union with the merger of all nations. He expressed his fear that Russian ethnic identity would be replaced with Soviet national identity as a result of the formation of the Soviet nation-state and the supraethnic "Soviet people."[47] As was noted by Yitzhak Brudny, a scholar who studied Russian nationalism during the late socialist period, the new party program promoted this new idea of a Soviet national identity.[48]

In planning his new organization, Kondratenko followed the ideas of Narodno-Trudovoi Soyuz (NTS), an anticommunist Russian organization. He had learned about NTS from the radio shows of the BBC and Voice of America. According to his plan, his new organization would include various sections such as a political one for anticommunist propaganda; a foreign section, for establishing connections with the leadership of NTS abroad; and a propagandist section, for a disseminating leaflets with information from the BBC, Voice of America, and Liberty radio stations. All participants in this group were arrested and later released. Some were expelled from Komsomol, but the majority received only minor administrative punishments.

According to KGB officers, the high school students confessed that they just wanted to "correct the Soviet reality and improve the economic situation" in the region. Some students dreamed about "a new ideal of life with more and better goods for consumption." They told the police that they knew about such an ideal of life from foreign radio broadcasts. All of them, except Kondratenko, were driven not by anti-Soviet motivation but by a desire to improve the Soviet reality. Kondratenko still insisted on his critical position about Communism and the "antihuman national policy" in the Dniepropetrovsk Region. Eventually, Kondratenko was sent to a mental asylum because he was the only member of the group who persisted in his anticommunist ideas.[49] The Kondratenko case was the only criminal case about Russian nationalism in the relatively Russified region of Dniepropetrovsk.

During the 1960s and 1970s, according to KGB reports, cases of Jewish nationalism were more numerous than the criminal activities of "young Russian nationalists" in the region. These cases of Jewish nationalism were usually called "Zionism" in the KGB documents. At the end of May 1968, eight students from two Dniepropetrovsk high schools who "studied the Jewish religion formed the Israel National-Democratic Party." These students planned to disseminate leaflets that would justify the "aggression and expansion of Israel in the Middle East." In addition, they obtained radio equipment, which they planned to use to illegally broadcast "the true news about Israel" to the region's people, who they thought were being "deceived by the official Soviet propaganda" about the Jewish religion and the state of Israel. According to the police investigation, these students threatened to break windows in official buildings and set fires in downtown Dniepropetrovsk. Their main goal was "to attract attention to the problems of the Jewish state, which was betrayed by Soviet politicians." With terrorist acts against official Soviet buildings in Dniepropetrovsk, these Jewish students wanted to demonstrate their solidarity "with the sufferings of their brothers and sisters in Israel."[50]

In 1967 and 1968, both high school students and older people of Jewish origin sought to publicly vindicate the politics of Israel and to support the decisions of the Israeli government. In May 1968, a vendor with a newspaper kiosk in downtown Dniepropetrovsk, Eva Budovskaia, illegally distributed Jewish religious periodicals among her young customers. According to KGB reports, some local Jews who visited the Dniepropetrovsk synagogue publicly demonstrated their pro-Israel sympathies and intentions to immigrate to Israel. The KGB linked pro-Israel ideas to the rise of anti-Soviet activities among Jewish youth in Dniepropetrovsk. According to KGB informers, "the young Jews were especially insolent because they knew about their protection by the state of Israel and their possible migration to the West." As one agent noted, "These young Zionists expected that the entire capitalist West would protect them against the anti-Semitism of the Soviet officials."

These young Jews organized groups to study Jewish religion and culture. All of them supported "ideas of Zionism to restore the historical Jewish state in Palestine." They regularly listened to Western radio shows and had lively correspondence with their relatives and friends in the United States and Israel. Overall, in Dniepropetrovsk the police recorded at least twenty cases of such "Zionism" among young Jewish intellectuals from 1968 to 1972.[51] After a mass Jewish migration from Dniepropetrovsk during this period and the beginning of a new wave of the anti-Soviet dissident movement, local KGB officers concentrated more on the spread of Ukrainian nationalism in the region rather than on "the diminishing influence of Zionism."[52]

As KGB reports noted, the rise of Ukrainian nationalism in Dniepropetrovsk was the result of demographic and political developments after 1956. According to a KGB decision, former political prisoners who had been indicted for "Ukrainian bourgeois nationalism" and had served their prison terms in the Gulag were released after the Twentieth Party Congress but were not allowed to return to their homes in Western Ukraine. These prisoners, called Banderovtsy in official documents, were either members or supporters of the Ukrainian Insurgent Army (known as the UPA), the Organization of Ukrainian Nationalists, and/or members of the Ukrainian Greek Catholic Church (a Uniate Ukrainian Greek-rite Catholic Church) from the Trans-Carpathian and Galician regions of Western Ukraine.[53]

When the Soviet army suppressed these patriotic and anti-Soviet movements after 1945, thousands of adherents were sent into exile far from Ukraine—in Siberia and Kazakhstan. KGB officials tried to prevent any contacts between these former political prisoners and their homeland in Western Ukraine. By the mid-1960s, many of theses ex-prisoners had settled in eastern, more Russified, regions of Ukraine. KGB officials tried to control the movement of these "Ukrainian nationalists" there and isolate them among the more diverse, and less Ukrainian, population of the Dniepropetrovsk and Donetsk regions. By 1967, 1,041 former political prisoners who were labeled "Ukrainian nationalists" from Western Ukraine had settled in the region of Dniepropetrovsk alone,[54] posing a danger to the ideological and political control of the region because they lived not only in the countryside but also in strategically important cities such as Dniepropetrovsk.

On December 18, 1967, KGB officers discovered that ex-prisoners had established a very busy correspondence with the members of their families who had migrated abroad after 1945. One emigrant wrote to his relatives in Soviet Ukraine from Canada:

I suggest that you join the Communist Party, Komsomol, and please, get more and better education whenever it's possible. But do not forget in your soul and your heart that you are Ukrainians. When you get higher offices of government and get higher education, then Ukraine will be free. . . . The more Ukrainians join the Communist Party, the more influence these Ukrainians will get among the ruling elites. Only Ukrainians who will be members of the ruling elite could save our Ukrainian collective farmers [*rabiv-kolgospnykiv*] from the Moscow yoke.[55]

Likewise, the KGB established special surveillance over Oleksandr Kuz'menko, a bus driver from Dniepropetrovsk. During the Nazi occupation, he was elected team leader of a "Ukrainian youth" nationalist organization in the Dniepropetrovsk district called Lotskamenka. In 1944, when the Soviet troops liberated the city, Kuz'menko was sent for eight years to labor camps for "the crime of collaboration with Nazi occupants." In 1956, he came back to Dniepropetrovsk and became a target of a new KGB investigation. Now he was suspected of spreading "anti-Soviet rumors" and criticizing "Soviet reality." As the KGB discovered, by the beginning of 1968, Kuz'menko had already established close relations with different "nationalistically disposed" people in Kyiv, including Ukrainian writers such as Ivan Dziuba and Oles' Honchar and the descendants of Taras Shevchenko. It is noteworthy that the links to Shevchenko's relatives were considered in official correspondence as "ideologically dangerous."

Among Kuz'menko's "connections," the KGB discovered the people who played an important role in the economic life of the region. One was Ivan Rybalka, a Communist and one of the executives of the important research center of the USSR Ministry of Metallurgy. Rybalka used his office typewriter for disseminating "nationalistic" literature, which he acquired in Kyiv and L'viv. In many cases, as it turned out, the patriotic Ukrainian poetry (even by Shevchenko) that was used by Rybalka aroused suspicions. The KGB officers worried that local intellectuals like Rybalka had become intermediaries between the ex-prisoners and their nationalist relatives in Western Ukraine.[56]

"The Western Connection": Ivan Sokul'sky
and His Creative Youth Club

The Western Ukrainian city of L'viv was always the major source of trouble for the KGB's operatives in Dniepropetrovsk. During the 1960s, forbidden nationalist literature, the most popular Western records of "degenerate rock and roll," and all other "bad" cultural influences came from L'viv. The leaders of the young poets' group that attracted the attention of the Dniepropetrovsk KGB either had direct contact with L'viv intellectuals or had graduated from L'viv State University. Ivan Sokul'sky, who we met earlier in the chapter, took classes there for one year before entering DGU. His close friend and supporter Volodymyr Zaremba, who covered Sokul'sky's career in his articles in local periodicals, also came to Dniepropetrovsk from L'viv.

In 1964, after graduating from L'viv University, Zaremba got a job as a full-time journalist for the Komsomol newspaper *Prapor iunosti.* From the first days of his Dniepropetrovsk career, he attracted KGB attention because of his "aggressive pro-Ukrainian and anti-Russian position." In one conversation after his arrival in Dniepropetrovsk, Zaremba complained about Russification and how Russians and Jews ousted Ukrainians from leading positions of power in the city.[57] As one KGB informer noted, he always demonstrated his contempt to colleagues who spoke Russian instead of Ukrainian and called them traitors. Zaremba distributed copies of Ivan Dziuba's pamphlet *Internationalism or Russification* among his friends and maintained close connections with famous nationalists in L'viv like Mikhailo Kosiv and Bohdan Goriv. "I worry about our Ukrainian nation now," he used to say, "but I believe that our Soviet system of power will fall apart soon and then the Ukrainian language will become popular again among all the people in Ukraine."

In November 1965, the KGB called Zaremba to visit its office for "a prophylactic interview" about his "nationalistic declarations." After this meeting, he still maintained his old contacts in L'viv and established new ones in Dniepropetrovsk—with Ivan Sokul'sky and his group. In 1966, after two years of struggle against Russification in *Prapor iunosti,* Zaremba accepted a new job in the youth department of the Dniepropetrovsk regional radio station. In 1968, Zaremba again attracted the KGB's attention: He proposed a public celebration (including sending information using all means of mass distribution) of the anniversary of Shevchenko's reburial, which took place on May 22, 1968, in Kaniv, and had an important symbolic meaning for all Ukrainian patriots.[58] Under pressure from the KGB, Zaremba was expelled from Komsomol in June 1968. A month later, he was also fired from the radio station. After that, he worked as a freelance journalist and a poet, but his actions were always under KGB surveillance.[59]

In 1968, KGB investigators again concentrated their attention on a group of young poets connected to Sokul'sky.[60] "The most active members of this group were Bohdan Uniat and Mikhailo and [his wife] Tatiana Skorik, former undergraduate students, who had been expelled from Kyiv State University for 'displays of nationalistic character.'"[61] The main reason for punishing the Skoriks and Uniat was their support of Matvii Shestopal, their professor in the department of journalism at Kyiv State University, which fired Shestopal for his "nationalism." On March 12, 1965, sixty-seven students in the department, including Skorik and his wife, signed a letter to the university's administration requesting that Shestopal be reinstated. They vowed to quit their study at the university if it insisted on firing Shestopal. The university retaliated by expelling all sixty-seven students, who were future journalists. Since the beginning of 1968, Mikhailo Skorik had worked as a journalist in the department of culture, science, and schools of the editorial board of the daily Communist Party newspaper *Zoria,* and his wife had worked as a proofreader (corrector) at the Komsomol newspaper *Prapor iunosti.* After their arrival in Dniepropetrovsk in 1968, the Skoriks joined Sokul'sky and Zavgorodnii's group.[62]

In 1966, workers at the Pridneprovsk Energy Plant created their own literary club at the Palace of Culture in Pridneprovsk, a suburban district of Dniepropetrovsk. By April 1968, this club had disbanded and the plant's administration asked Komsomol members to revive it. Komsomol commissioned Viktor Sysoev, a young Communist and engineer, who had recently published some of his poems, to do this. Sysoev asked his colleagues from the energy plant's newspaper for help. Sokul'sky, who worked for this newspaper part time, supported this idea with a great passion.[63]

As a further development, Sokul'sky proposed to invite all young poets in Dniepropetrovsk to "an evening of poetry" at the Pridneprovsk Palace of Culture. This would be the beginning of a new literary organization. Sokul'sky told his friends that he had official approval for this idea. According to him, the new group, which he called "the Club of Creative Youth," would include sections for poetry and literature, architecture, music, and tourism. He prepared the text of the official invitation for the first meeting on April 13, 1968. Mikhailo and Tatiana Skorik, and others from the group at Dniepropetrovsk University, took an active part in this "evening of poetry," reading their poems and discussing various cultural problems.

The next day, April 14, all the participants in this event went to the village of Nikol'ske (in the district of Solene) and visited the spot where the legendary Kievan prince Sviatoslav had been killed by Turkic nomads on his way back from Byzantium to Kyiv in 972. Sokul'sky and others recited their poetry and discussed problems of cultural development in Dniepropetrovsk. According to KGB informers, they also criticized the official cultural policy in the city as an expression of "Russian chauvinism." They complained about the low prestige accorded the Ukrainian language and the Russification of all spheres of life in Ukraine. According to another KGB informer, "during these poetic discussions on the spot of Sviatoslav's death, Sokul'sky proposed to meet more often and use 'the Club of Creative Youth' at Pridneprovsk Energy Plant for promoting national ideas." As it turned out, the young poets decided to combine poetic discussions with entertainment, including American jazz.[64]

Many young intellectuals liked the idea of the new literary club. On April 24, 1968, Dniepropetrovsk regional radio included information from "M. Skorik" about "the Club of Creative Youth" in "the latest radio news." This information presented the "evening of poetry" in Pridneprovsk as a special session of the literary club. Skorik appealed to people who considered themselves "creative youth" to visit this club in Pridneprovsk on a regular basis.[65] Uniat was in charge of a special exhibition "The Books of Young Poets," and Mikhailo Skorik contacted the local periodicals. But the major organizer of all the events, who sent letters of invitation and communicated with the Komsomol and Communist Party apparatchiks, was Sokul'sky. The KGB tried to stop his activities and prevent the meetings of this club under the leadership of "the famous young nationalist."

When Sokul'sky announced the next meeting of the club on May 14, 1968, the DGU administration (under pressure from the KGB) organized special "countermeasures" to keep university students busy on campus; they had to stay in their classrooms to clean, repair desks, and so on. Only four students were able to attend the May 14 meeting. Sokul'sky understood the situation and decided again asking the energy plant's administration for help. Komsomol and party leaders responded to an invitation and agreed to participate in a meeting of "the Club of Creative Youth." The KGB ruined Sokul'sky's plans, however. On May 16, a KGB officer visited a party committee at the energy plant and urged the local administration to stop the activities of the new club, which according to the KGB combined "propaganda of Ukrainian nationalism with American jazz." Its recommendation was very clear: "Because of Sokul'sky's nationalistic ideas, it is impossible to allow him a leadership role in the literary organization of Dniepropetrovsk youth."[66]

During the KGB's investigation of the club, the police discovered that Uniat had read "anti-Soviet and nationalistic poems and other anti-Soviet literature" at the meetings of young poets. In May 1968, under pressure from the KGB, Mikhailo Skorik was expelled from the Communist Party. Fearing KGB persecution, Uniat quit his job and left Dniepropetrovsk, hoping to avoid arrest and interrogation. Sokul'sky also quit his job at the newspaper and tried to avoid any contacts with his friends.[67] Thus, the noble patriotic ideas of these idealistic young Ukrainian poets were destroyed by police interference.

Paradoxically, all the enthusiasm of Dniepropetrovsk's youth for national ideas, poetry, and history was inspired by Khrushchev's "thaw" and the public exposures of Stalin's "deviations" from and "distortions" of Lenin's nationality policy. During the 1960s, many young patriots in the Dniepropetrovsk Region sincerely believed that their poetic and other activities in support of national cultures would lead to a restoration of the "real, internationalist, and human, Leninist model of socialism." But the KGB ruined these young enthusiasts' hopes and dreams about the flourishing of national cultures in the region. In destroying Sokul'sky's group in 1968, the KGB ignored the growing enthusiasm of young Ukrainian patriots for national issues, which stemmed from their discovery of Lenin's nationality policy. Following the directives of the KGB's head, Yuri Andropov, the Dniepropetrovsk police tried to suppress any demonstration of "pro-Western nationalism" and any attempt to create "nationalistic" organizations that were reminiscent of "the revisionist socialism" in Czechoslovakia. For them, the most dangerous similarity of the events in Dniepropetrovsk to the events in Prague in 1968 was the combination of "nationalistic poetry with American jazz" among Dniepropetrovsk's youth.[68]

Chapter 3

The Campaign against the Novel *Sobor* and the End of the National Literary Revival

In 1968, a new ideological campaign pursued by the KGB began as a reaction to another case of cultural consumption—the publication, reading, and discussion of one particular novel, *Sobor* (*The Cathedral* in Ukrainian), by Oles' Honchar, which became the catalyst for a new wave of repressions and KGB persecutions that involved all those in Dniepropetrovsk who already had problems with the KGB because of "Ukrainian nationalistic activities."[1] *Sobor* was first published in January 1968, in the first issue of the literary magazine *Vitchyzna* (*Motherland* in Ukrainian); a paperback edition appeared in a special series, "Novels and Tales," in March of that same year.

In *Sobor,* Honchar told the story of a small town, Zachiplianka, on the banks of the Dnieper River, where workers at the local metallurgical plants were trying to preserve an old Cossack cathedral from attempts by local Communist Party officials to destroy it. Using the cathedral as a symbol of Ukrainian national and cultural awakening, Honchar addressed a number of important problems for the development of the Dnieper region: the threat of industrial pollution and the betrayal of national values and ideals; the role of old Cossack traditions; and the preservation of the Ukrainian language, culture, and natural environment.[2] He based his novel on a real event and a real historical monument: the Cathedral of the Holy Trinity in Novomoskovsk, near Dniepropetrovsk. This cathedral is a unique historical monument. It was built by a self-taught Ukrainian Cossack architect, Iakym Pogrebniak, in the 1770s with funds from the Zaporizhian Cossacks. In its construction, the workers did not use any iron nails; everything was made of wood.[3] After the Soviet government closed the cathedral, Dniepropetrovsk's party leaders planned to demolish it. Honchar was among those patriots concerned about national history who fought to preserve the cathedral. Many of the characters and locations in his novel therefore have counterparts in the real world. Eventually, under pressure from local intellectuals (including some Communist ideologists), the Dniepropetrovsk regional administration "left the cathedral in peace," and it was saved.[4]

The first secretary of the Dniepropetrovsk regional Communist Party committee, Oleksii Vatchenko, recognized himself in the character in *Sobor* named Volodymyr Loboda, a career-minded apparatchik who betrays his father and plans to destroy the cathedral. Vatchenko was enraged, and in March 1968 he began a personal vendetta against Honchar, who was then the head of the Ukrainian Writers' Union. During the first three months of 1968, the novel received only positive official reviews in Ukrainian periodicals; but by the end of March, it had become the target of negative and nasty criticism. Moreover, Vatchenko organized an attack on Honchar during the Plenum of the Communist Party of Ukraine (CPU) in Kyiv on March 29, 1968. Vatchenko accused Honchar of distorting socialist reality and idealizing the Cossack past and of nationalism. Petro Shelest, the CPU's first secretary, tried to tone down criticism because Nikolai Podgorny, head of the USSR Supreme Council, supported Honchar. Later on, the state publishing house stopped issuing *Sobor,* and Honchar himself was replaced as head of the Writers' Union in May 1970. Yet he was never expelled from the Communist Party or arrested, despite Vatchenko's efforts to punish him.[5] In the Dniepropetrovsk Region, however, Vatchenko started a mass ideological campaign against the novel that affected local intellectuals and the city's cultural life, creating an atmosphere reminiscent of Stalinism.[6]

In a special report on May 15, 1968, KGB officials noted that despite the official criticism of the novel by party ideologists, a majority of ordinary readers in Dniepropetrovsk condemned the "ideological hunting of a great Ukrainian writer and his masterpiece." According to KGB informers, during the years 1968–69, a majority of Dniepropetrovsk intellectuals expressed admiration for Honchar's novel as a patriotic anthem "written in the best traditions of Soviet socialist realism."[7] One admirer, M. Vorokhatskii, wrote to the regional party committee: "Your ideological campaigns against *Sobor* look ridiculous and shameful. They are testimony of your helplessness. Ordinary Soviet people think differently. They respect this honest piece of writing." Addressing part of his letter to I. Moroz—a professor of philosophy at Dniepropetrovsk State University (Dniepropetrovskii gosudarstvennyi universitet, DGU) who had published official criticism of *So-*

bor in the local party daily newspaper—Vorokhatskii noted that party critics "tried to judge the novel by standards of the 'cult of personality' and carried out a black and dirty mission of denunciation, which does not suit educated people." And he suggested to local ideologists that they "implement a real Leninist national policy in Dniepropetrovsk and publish a serious article about Leninist national policy in Ukraine and how local leaders ignore this policy nowadays."[8]

During the spring of 1968, *Sobor* became the most popular book among young intellectuals in the Dniepropetrovsk Region, especially university students. According to the KGB, the region's students called Honchar's novel "an epoch-making book" that was "widely read, even during classes, by everyone."[9] Then, suddenly, a local newspaper published an "Open Letter of the University Freshmen in the Department of History," expressing very negative criticism of the novel. For the many students in that same department of DGU who loved the novel, this article was a shock. They decided to discuss the book and this negative letter together and to send their response to the newspaper with their rejection of "the freshmen's letter," which they considered a fake.

On May 20, two sophomore students in the DGU History Department, Yurii Mytsyk and Viktor Lavrishchev, without any consultation with the department's administration, announced a debate about *Sobor* to be held on May 22.[10] After reading this announcement, F. Pavlov, the department's chair, visited the classroom where the classmates of Mytsyk and Lavrishchev were loudly discussing the situation. They were indignant because the local periodicals had published only negative reviews of *Sobor.* Most frustrating for the student historians was the fact that the "Open Letter" had come from their department. They told Pavlov that "the whole letter was falsified; it was a fraud, prepared under pressure from the university administration because some freshmen, whose names were included in this letter, confessed they had never read this novel."

Pavlov, wishing to calm these students down, gave them his personal permission to hold a debate. Another professor, V. Biletsky, a secretary of the departmental Communist Party committee, met Mytsyk and Lavrishchev on May 21 and supported their idea as well. Under pressure from the KGB, however, the DGU administration and the party committee interfered and canceled the event. Meanwhile, the KGB established secret surveillance over Mytsyk, Lavrishchev, and the other students who were Honchar's most active fans. Lavrishchev and Mytsyk had long, unpleasant conversations with the chair of their department. Eventually, on May 22, the university threatened to expel them, and both men ceased any discussion of Honchar's novel with their classmates. These threats and subsequent pressure from the KGB traumatized the students. Mytsyk, who in the 1970s entered graduate school in the same department and later became a teacher of Slavic history there, never mentioned this story to his colleagues or students. Moreover, he became carefully guarded and avoided any conversation about politics or Ukrainian patriotism in his department.[11]

Meanwhile, Vatchenko asked the KGB for help in his ideological witch hunt. He was enraged when several Dniepropetrovsk writers (including S. Zavgorodnii, V. Korzh, and V. Chemeris) prepared a very friendly letter congratulating Honchar on his fiftieth birthday and praising *Sobor* as "a cleanser of our souls." Vatchenko insisted on the removal of this phrase from the official letter. V. Vlasenko, the chair of Ukrainian literature at DGU, prepared a "warm and emotional" letter from his department with congratulations for Honchar, who was the university's most famous alumnus. However, under pressure from the DGU Communist Party committee, which was following Vatchenko's orders, Vlasenko canceled his trip to Kyiv for Honchar's anniversary celebration and destroyed the department's letter.

As the KGB officers complained in their report, many writers turned down a request from the party daily newspapers *Dneprovskaia pravda* and *Zoria* to join the "anti-Honchar" campaign.[12] KGB informers noted that some students at DGU thought that "keeping silent" about Honchar's birthday at the university was an official party reaction to the rumors that Pope Paul VI had nominated Honchar for the Nobel Prize in Literature in 1968. Many local young intellectuals, who had been inspired by *Sobor,* complained about the constant interference of Moscow ("the center") in the cultural life of "the Dnieper region," which had led to Russification and "a loss of the national character." During 1968 and 1970, fearing "*Sobor*'s bad influence," the KGB even collected information about Honchar's personal life, hoping to find scandalous and discrediting facts, and it sent this information to Vatchenko for his ideological campaign.[13]

In May and June 1968, Vatchenko invited I. Grushetsky, head of the Party Commission of the CPU's Central Committee, to Dniepropetrovsk and arranged special meetings with representatives of various party organizations. Vatchenko and other officials of the regional administration orchestrated public meetings at which local leaders presented vituperative criticism of Honchar. They submitted various reports and complaints about the "nationalistic" and "anti-Soviet deviations" of the author and his novel. Grushetsky collected all these documents and took them to Kyiv to make a case against Honchar. Vatchenko thus tried to justify his ideological policy and demonstrate the people's support for the anti-*Sobor* campaign as a struggle against "Ukrainian bourgeois nationalism" in the strategically important closed city of Dniepropetrovsk.[14]

"A Letter from the Creative Youth of Dniepropetrovsk" and the Anti-Ukrainian Campaign

The KGB and Communist Party ideologists used the campaign against the novel *Sobor* as a pretext for suppressing any sign of a Ukrainian nationalist movement and for punishing those who had displayed enthusiasm and persistence in defending Ukrainian language and culture. In June 1968, Ivan Sokul'sky, Mykhailo Skorik, and Volodymyr Zaremba wrote "A Letter from the Creative Youth of Dniepropetrovsk," in which they documented the KGB's suppression of Ukrainian patriots. From September to December 1968, this letter was sent to the various offices of party, Komsomol, and Soviet organizations and to the colleges in Kyiv and Dniepropetrovsk. With the assistance of several Dniepropetrovsk intellectuals—including Mykola Kul'chytsky; Viktor Savchenko, a graduate student at the Dniepropetrovsk Metallurgical Institute; and Oleksandr Kuz'menko, a bus driver—the letter reached not only the political leaders of Ukraine but also Ukrainian émigré centers abroad. The following spring, foreign radio stations like Liberty included the text of the letter in their broadcasts.[15] In June 1969, the KGB arrested Sokul'sky, Kul'chytsky, and Savchenko for writing and disseminating the letter. In February 1970, the Dniepropetrovsk court, using KGB information about the letter writers' anti-Soviet actions, indicted them as political criminals.[16]

The text of "A Letter from the Creative Youth of Dniepropetrovsk" is a good demonstration of the loyal, pro-Soviet intentions of its authors—who called themselves "young progressive Ukrainians, who were brought up in Soviet schools and colleges, educated with works by Marx and Lenin, Shevchenko, and Dobroliubov." In the letter, they criticized the "anti-Ukrainian" campaign in Dniepropetrovsk that had been started by the local administration in reaction to the publication of *Sobor.* They called this campaign "a wild and stupid persecution of honest Ukrainian citizens, who are the devoted builders of Communism," a persecution that could be compared only with the actions of Maoists in China.[17] The letter opened with a list of Communists and Komsomol members who had been punished for supporting Honchar's novel and for their "concern over the fate of the Ukrainian language and Ukrainian culture in a Russified city of Dniepropetrovsk." It named Sokul'sky and other talented young Ukrainians who had been accused by the KGB of a "fantastic conspiracy of 'Ukrainian bourgeois nationalism,' invented at the KGB headquarters on Korolenko Street."[18]

At the same time, in the letter, its authors sought to demonstrate that the police had not punished those apparatchiks who had committed real crimes of murder or rape—because of their ideological loyalty. They appealed to Marxism-Leninism and accused their opponents of betraying Vladimir Lenin's ideas. They invoked Karl Marx's positive characterization of the Cossack Zaporizhian Sich as "a democratic republic." They reminded readers of the Marxist approach to history and the need to appreciate everything progressive in the past—including the famous Cossack cathedral in Novomoskovsk featured in *Sobor.* They noted that "for a contemporary Ukrainian, Soviet patriotism includes respect for the national dignity and national pride of the great and talented Ukrainian people." "If we are Marxists," they wrote, "we need to change this [Dniepropetrovsk] reality to make it fit Leninist norms and Soviet laws rather than to persecute all progressive-thinking Ukrainian citizens who are loyal to Marxism-Leninism."[19] They finished their letter with an appeal to the leaders of the Ukrainian government to protect Ukrainian culture from Russification. They also requested punishment for those who had started the anti-Ukrainian ideological campaign in Dniepropetrovsk. "Such campaigns," they reminded Ukrainian leaders, "sow the seeds of animosity and hatred in the relationship of two brotherly, socialist nations, Russians and Ukrainians."[20]

The authors of "A Letter from the Creative Youth," Sokul'sky and his group, shared with their opponents certain basic ideas that belonged to the dominant Soviet ideological discourse. The case of this letter was related to the debate over national cultural consumption in Ukraine during Nikita Khrushchev's de-Stalinization campaign. The official interpretation of this case dismissed the pro-Soviet and anti-Stalinist spirit of the letter. Dniepropetrovsk's Communist Party newspapers tried to present the letter as "an expression of militant nationalism, which is the most dangerous form of ideological struggle, which the intelligence and propagandist centers of international imperialism used in their confrontation with socialism." Yet Dniepropetrovsk's journalists had problems with this description of the letter and could not find among Sokul'sky's arguments a serious foundation for the legal interpretation of his actions as "criminal activities." According to the Dniepropetrovsk periodicals, Sokul'sky's main crime was his concern for Ukrainian language and culture in the "Russified city of Dnie-propetrovsk." KGB officials and Communist ideologists also had problems with the claim that Sokul'sky had committed an "anti-Soviet crime," because they shared with Sokul'sky and his friends the same ideological language of Marxism-Leninism—the same arguments of the "progressive development of mature socialism." Yet both sides of the conflict had to portray their opponents' behavior as a "deviation" from Soviet cultural production and consumption (i.e., reading and writing in Ukrainian). Each side had to blame the other of "a betrayal of Leninist nationality polity" or "anti-Soviet provocations."[21]

Even the Soviet police and court found it hard to justify their decisions and accusations related to the actions against "A Letter from the Creative Youth" by Sokul'sky and his group. As it turned out, one of the men arrested, Victor Savchenko, had not participated at all in circulating the letter but had been accused because of circumstantial "evidence." Two people (one of them a KGB informer) had seen the letter among other "anti-Soviet documents" in Savchenko's apartment. As a result, on November 17, 1969, he was arrested and included in the "anti-Soviet nationalist group of Sokul'sky." According to the KGB, reading and keeping "suspicious literature" at home was a crime. Savchenko, who was very interested in Ukrainian history, had borrowed photocopies of two books about Ukrainian history, by M. Braichevs'ky and Mykhailo Hrushevsky, from Sokul'sky; and, again, reading these "nationalist" books was considered a crime by KGB officials. The police also discovered tapes of "forbidden American jazz and beat music" among Savchenko's possessions. Despite KGB pressure, the court did not send Savchenko to prison; but after his trial, he was fired from the Metallurgical Institute and had to abandon his career in Soviet academia.[22]

On August 26, 1971, the Dniepropetrovsk regional committee of the Communist Party of the Soviet Union passed a special resolution about preventing the spread of anti-Soviet and politically harmful documents. This special resolution from Moscow—a response to a similar Central Committee resolution issued on June 28, 1971—was a "secret document" sent to all regional party committees. Local leaders used this resolution to suppress any "ideological deviation" in the region. They noted that the police had discovered fifty titles of anti-Soviet "samizdat materials" in the region of Dniepropetrovsk. According to this party document, the most "dangerous" among these was "A Letter from the Creative Youth," because it had been sent abroad and published in the centers of anti-Soviet propaganda. Using phraseology supplied by Moscow, local leaders justified their persecution of young Ukrainian patriots as a struggle with the "anti-Soviet nationalistic conspiracy of Sokul'sky's group."[23]

The Suppression of the Ukrainian Patriotic Movement among Dniepropetrovsk's Youth

The ideological campaign of the years 1968–69 in Dniepropetrovsk created a model for the suppression of any "ideological deviation" in the region. Using the 1971 resolution by the Communist Party of the Soviet Union and resolutions issued in 1973 "about the prevention of the spread of anti-Soviet materials," KGB officials and party ideologists punished any expression of Ukrainian patriotism.[24] Thus, Ivan Sokul'sky, who was released from prison in December 1973, was arrested again in April 1980 for writing Ukrainian nationalistic poetry—that is, for his "cultural production." In January 1981, the Dniepropetrovsk court sentenced him to ten years in prison for "Ukrainian nationalism." His interest in cultural production and consumption of Ukrainian poetry thus cost him almost thirteen years of life spent in prison and labor camps.

Sokul'sky was released from prison in August 1988. Having been weakened by his many years of suffering and humiliation, he died in June 1992.[25] Thus the post-Stalinist cultural revival in Ukraine confused and disoriented young Ukrainian intellectuals. And as with Sokul'sky, some of them even paid with their own lives for what the Communist ideology considered Leninist nationality policy—"a creation of culture, socialist in its essence, but national in its form." Soviet Ukrainian writers always supported this policy. Even ten years later, in 1980, they still "emphasized 'the national spirit and national character' of the writer's craft, and warned against 'the violation of the balance, in one direction or the other, of the national in form and socialist in content formula that governs Soviet cultural policies.'"[26]

After 1970, and until perestroika, any Ukrainian "deviation" in "cultural production and consumption" was destroyed immediately by the KGB. In the years 1973–74, it suppressed even the slightest signs of "Ukrainian nationalism" among local intellectuals. For instance, Mykola M. Tretiakov, a thirty-three-year-old engineer at the Dniepropetrovsk agricultural machine-building corporation, was arrested for "the dissemination of anti-Soviet rumors." As it turned out, Tretiakov had sent more than forty-five letters to

Figure 3.1. The funeral on June 22, 1992, of Ivan Sokul'sky, a pioneer of the Ukrainian literary revival during the Brezhnev era, who became a legendary dissident in the closed city of Dniepropetrovsk. Photograph by the author.

various newspapers and local Soviet administrators in the region with complaints about the "Russification of the Ukrainian national culture" and "the need to develop the national culture of socialist Ukraine." In the spring of 1974, he was indicted under Article 187 of the Ukrainian Soviet Socialist Republic's Criminal Code "for spreading false ideas that discredited the Soviet state and social order."[27]

KGB officers discovered that the most popular books in Tretiakov's personal collection included historical novels by Soviet Ukrainian writers—novels by Semen Skliarenko, for example, about the princes of Kievan Rus' such as Sviatoslav and Volodymyr. All the arrested members of Sokul'sky's literary group also owned these books. They had also tapes of forbidden Western jazz and rock ("beat") music in their music collections. Among Tretiakov's possessions, the police discovered "an amateur audiotape" with a recording of the song "Ukrainian Cossacks," a Ukrainian cover of "Venus," the song by the Dutch rock band Shocking Blue. It is noteworthy that only this song and two other songs by the Ukrainian rock band Smerichka represented "modern beat music" in Tretiakov's audio collection. His music collection mostly included traditional Ukrainian folk songs. There were no songs in any language other than Ukrainian on his tapes. He was not a rock music fan at all.[28] But his choice of the Shocking Blue and Smerichka songs is a remarkable example of his appropriation of Western musical forms to express his Ukrainian identity.

One volume in Tretiakov's book collection attracted special attention from the KGB. This was a historical novel by Ivan Bilyk, a famous Soviet Ukrainian writer, about Attila, leader of the legendary Huns, who defeated the Roman Empire in the fourth century AD. According to Bilyk's interpretation, Attila was the first successful Ukrainian leader, and his real name was Hatylo, a purely Ukrainian name. This novel was criticized for its "distortion of historical truth" and for Ukrainian nationalism as well. After 1974, the KGB ordered that all copies of this novel be withdrawn from the public libraries as "anti-Soviet material." Within two years, Bilyk's book was removed from circulation all over Ukraine.[29] During the period 1975–78, the police found that some college students had an "unhealthy interest" in Ukrainian historical novels. A few "forbidden" books, including Bilyk's, were confiscated from Dniepropetrovsk students by 1980. But these transgressions were considered minor, and nobody was arrested.[30]

No significant case of "nationalist dissent" was recorded by the KGB after 1974. The participation of a few Dniepropetrovsk intellectuals, including Sokul'sky, in the Ukrainian Helsinki Group after 1975 was an exception to the rule.[31] Sokul'sky joined this group in October 1979, was arrested by the KGB on April 11, 1980, and sent to prison next year again. Overall, after the "anti-Ukrainian" campaign of the years 1968–69, the region of Dniepropetrovsk no longer had scandalous cases of Ukrainian nationalism.[32] Many Ukrainian patriots, such as the young writer Victor Savchenko and the young historian Yurii Mytsyk, had to keep silent and hide their interest in the revival of Ukrainian culture until the era of perestroika.

Some Ukrainian intellectuals, such as the artists Volodymyr Makarenko and Feodosii Humeniuk, chose to leave the closed city of Dniepropetrovsk and move to the safer Russian ground of Leningrad, where they could enjoy freer expression for their Ukrainian patriotic ideas. Both Makarenko and Humeniuk, who were painters, represented the Ukrainian artistic avant-garde and elaborated national, especially Cossack, themes in their paintings. Both had started their artistic careers at the Dniepropetrovsk School of Fine Art. Makarenko left Dniepropetrovsk for Leningrad in 1963. Later,

Humeniuk followed Makarenko and also moved to Leningrad. Both of them participated in two exhibitions of Ukrainian avant-garde art in Moscow (November 22–December 7, 1975; and March 12–22, 1976). These shows attracted the attention not only of foreign guests, who were ready to buy Ukrainian paintings, but also of the KGB. When Western journalists wrote articles presenting these exhibitions as revealing a new, innovative development in Ukrainian national art, the KGB officers interpreted the shows as "nationalistic demonstrations seeking financial support from the West." Makarenko grew tired of KGB control and emigrated from the USSR to France in 1980.

In 1977, after the second Moscow exhibition of Ukrainian avant-garde art, Humeniuk "was deprived of his residence permit in Leningrad" by the KGB and moved back to Dniepropetrovsk. However, he could not stand the oppressive ideological atmosphere of the closed city. Under pressure from the KGB, the local press began a campaign against him and his artistic experiments. As a result, this last representative of the Ukrainian artistic revival in the closed city left Dniepropetrovsk for Leningrad in 1983 and never came back. Likewise, many talented Ukrainian artists who began their careers in Dniepropetrovsk could not stand the KGB's severe pressure and moved after 1969 to the open cities of Russia with less ideological control, like Moscow and Leningrad. These Ukrainian artistic emigrants included M. Malyshko, Nina Denisova, V. Loboda, Liudmyla Loboda, V. Iegorov, O. Borodai, and V. Soloviov.[33]

Starting in 1968, local KGB and Communist Party officials began complaining about the interference of the Moscow authorities in their struggle against "bourgeois nationalism" and "Western cultural influences" in the closed city. Both Oleksii Vatchenko, the Dniepropetrovsk party leader, and N. Mazhara, the head of the local KGB office, failed to punish Oles' Honchar, whose novel *Sobor* had first provoked the "nationalistic" movement in Dniepropetrovsk. They thought that "Moscow's protection" saved Honchar's career in 1969. Dniepropetrovsk's Soviet and party administrators were confused by the controversial decisions of the "political center" in Moscow, which demanded "persecution of the nationalists" and, at the same time, "protected them from punishment." Many contemporaries noted that after 1969, despite their dependence on Moscow, both Dniepropetrovsk KGB and party ideologists complained about the "deficiencies of Moscow's planning" of the region's ideological and cultural supervision. One KGB officer commented on this situation: "It is very easy to sit comfortably in

Moscow and send us controversial orders about our ideological enemies. The very difficult thing is to carry out these orders and find these enemies among the loyal Soviet citizens."[34]

Conclusion

Both those Ukrainian patriots like Oles' Honchar who participated in the literary and artistic revival of the years 1968–69 and their persecutors, the KGB and Communist Party officials, were not always happy with Moscow's supervision of the ideological and cultural developments in the region of Dniepropetrovsk. This gradual opposition to Moscow among the region's intellectual and political elite became part of the ideological situation and cultural practices, especially after Khrushchev's controversial de-Stalinization, that confused and disoriented both leaders and their subjects—and that became especially obvious during the anti-*Sobor* campaign.

It is noteworthy that the Ukrainian literary and artistic revival in the closed city of Dniepropetrovsk in the years 1968–69 revealed the connections between local patriotic intellectuals and their idealized image of a "Western world" that could protect them from persecutions by Soviet officials. These Ukrainian intellectuals appealed to Soviet ideologists and referred to Marxism and old Leninist concepts about nationalities in the USSR. They also turned to their audience in the West for support by sending letters complaining about Russification in Ukraine to Western radio shows.

The KGB also discovered another "Western" connection among the young poets in Dniepropetrovsk. In the 1960s, the police realized that Western popular culture in the form of jazz and so-called beat (rock) music affected not only a few "dissident nationalistic" poets but also thousands of young people in the closed city. This is the subject of the next chapter.

Chapter 4

The First Wave of Music from the West: The Consumption of Jazz

Although books about Ukrainian nationalism were popular among young intellectuals in Dniepropetrovsk, Western popular music—both jazz and rock—was the most desirable object of cultural consumption during the late socialist period. In Dniepropetrovsk, which was closed to direct foreign influences in 1959, the main sources of pop music consumption were foreign radio stations and two black markets for foreign music downtown. An unprecedented rise in foreign music consumption during the 1960s attracted the attention of both KGB officers and Communist Party ideologists.

The KGB Reports about Western Popular Music Consumption

Using information from their agents among the student population, KGB officials in Dniepropetrovsk reported to the regional secretary of the Communist Party of the Soviet Union on how the "bourgeois radio stations" were shaping the behavior of Soviet youth in the region. KGB informers shared Soviet propagandist clichés when they pointed out that everything bad in "Soviet real life" came only from the capitalist West and not from Soviet life itself. Thus the KGB report of December 1962 noted that "some students in the student hostels listened to the anti-Soviet broadcasting, blindly imitated melodies of American jazz and rock and roll, played cards for money, drank alcohol, met women of easy virtue, some of them even blamed the Soviet power for all their financial problems."[1]

In reports to their KGB supervisors, Komsomol leaders also deplored the Western anti-Soviet influences that came through foreign music and radio.

According to them, "an excessive consumption of foreign music" led to a rise in alcohol drinking among adolescents (a 35 percent increase for 1964) and college students. The major complaint of the Komsomol ideologists was about intoxicated Westernized students who attacked and physically abused the representatives of college authorities. After their raids of the student dormitories in 1965, the Komsomol officials noted that "students demonstrated their apathy toward public life, and understood incorrectly the questions of the contemporary international and domestic situation(s)." The most dangerous fact, however, for these apparatchiks was that all student rooms had obvious signs of capitalist cultural influence, such as audiotapes of "beat music" and pictures of the Beatles and Rolling Stones. In some rooms, students listened regularly to foreign radio stations and recorded foreign music on their tape recorders.[2]

In January 1968, KGB officials analyzed data about how the inhabitants of Dniepropetrovsk consumed information from foreign radio stations. The police checked more than 1,000 letters sent to different radio stations throughout the world by listeners from the region of Dniepropetrovsk during 1967. According to their analysis, 36 percent of all letters were sent to radio stations in Canada, 31 percent to stations in the United States, and 29 percent to stations in England. The overwhelming majority of correspondents were young people; 38.8 percent of listeners were younger than eighteen years, 28 percent were between eighteen and twenty-eight, and 32.2 percent were older than twenty-eight.[3] The KGB analysts noted that 37 percent of these listeners to and consumers of Western radio information asked in their letters for the radio stations to send them records, albums, manuals for fashionable dances, or radio guides with a timetable for different Western radio stations. Nearly 25.5 percent of the listeners asked the stations to "fulfill their musical request" to play their favorite song, 13.7 percent asked for help establishing "friendship with citizens of other countries," and 23.5 percent gave answers to various questions to contests and quizzes organized by the stations.[4]

This analysis of these letters is indicative of the main content of cultural consumption among the listeners to Western radio in the Dniepropetrovsk Region. The overwhelming majority of the letter writers were mainly interested in new music, popular culture, and fashion—not in politics. It is noteworthy that the KGB censors could not find any critical anti-Soviet comments or expressions of ironical or skeptical attitudes toward Soviet values in the letters. Nevertheless, the police noted the negative influence of Western radio information on some of its consumers. A student at the Engineering Construction Institute, Stanislav Banduristyi, told his classmates during discussion about the Vietnam War that he regularly listened to the Voice of America and disagreed with the interpretation offered by the Soviet media. Still, a majority of Soviet listeners were interested only in Western music. Evgenii Chaika, a sixteen-year-old student at Dniepropetrovsk High School No. 42, wrote numerous letters to the BBC radio station about his love of rock-and-roll music. "It is impossible not to love the Beatles [Bitlov]," he wrote in one letter. "I have listened to their music since 1963. I want to listen to their song "19th Nervous Breakdown" again. [Apparently, he confused the Beatles with the Rolling Stones.] And I have something else in mind. Please send me chewing gum as well." Another listener, nineteen-year-old Vladimir Dmitriev, who worked as a technician at the Dniepropetrovsk House of Technique, asked radio stations in the United States and England to help him organize correspondence with the citizens of these countries. His main requests were about jazz and rock music records.[5]

In 1969, the KGB organized a special public campaign in the local periodicals to stop "the radio hooligans" who literally "polluted the city radio waves with the musical cacophony" of "heinous" rock and roll.[6] According to the Dniepropetrovsk police, the local radio hooligans still recorded and then broadcast foreign music on a regular basis for local audiences during the 1970s and 1980s. The number of radio hooligans increased in only one year from 475 in 1970 to 685 in 1971. These numbers continued to rise. The KGB annually recorded 3,000 cases of illegal radio broadcasting from almost 700 local amateur radio stations. During 1971 in Dnieprodzerzhinsk, the second industrial city of the region, the local police organized more than 150 raids, arrested 120 radio hooligans, and confiscated their radio and sound-recording equipment, which cost on average more than 3,500 rubles. More than 90 percent of these "radio music criminals" were younger than twenty-five years old.[7]

The spreading popularity of Western popular music became a major problem for both the local police and Communist ideologists. Over a six-month period in 1972, Komsomol activists and the police organized more than 100 raids against hippies and people who traded foreign music records in downtown Dniepropetrovsk. More than 200 music *fartsovshchiks* (black marketers) were arrested during those raids. The police confiscated hundreds of foreign music records, thousands of audiotapes with Western popular music, and "264 copies of illegal printed material, called samizdat." KGB officers noted the important role of L'viv, a Western Ukrainian city, as a major distributing source of Western music records and illegal printed material of "undisguised anti-Soviet nature" for Dniepropetrovsk's black market. After 1972, Dniepropetrovsk leaders still complained about a rapid increase of rock music consumption. At the beginning of the 1980s, KGB reports had to admit the failure of all ideological efforts to halt the spread of Western pop music in the region and city of Dniepropetrovsk.[8]

The KGB reports emphasized the dangerous influence of Western pop music on Soviet youth. Annual reports of KGB officials to the regional committee of the Communist Party of the Soviet Union made a clear connection between anti-Soviet behavior and an unhealthy enthusiasm about Western mass culture.[9] It is noteworthy that KGB officers and Communist ideologists emphasized the negative "Westernized" role of the L'viv on local youth. This negative image of L'viv would affect all ideological campaigns against Western "bourgeois" cultural consumption in Dniepropetrovsk.[10] Western popular music affected not only young enthusiasts of Western mass culture but also KGB officials and party apparatchiks. During the 1960s, both the elitist families of the Soviet "nomenclature" and the ordinary families of local workers and intellectuals became involved in new forms of cultural consumption that had nothing to do with what the party ideologists called "the Soviet style of life."

American Jazz, Leonid Kuchma, and Stylish Youth

The first and the most lasting Western musical influence in the city of Dniepropetrovsk came from American jazz. Because of the "closed conditions" of this city, information about the spread and popularity of new Western musical influences throughout the city was practically nonexistent for Western visitors and foreign guests who wrote about American jazz in the USSR.[11] Like the youth of many other Soviet urban centers, such as Moscow and Kazan, the youth of Dniepropetrovsk had become affected by the fashion for jazz music by 1955. In the 1950s, the only source of information about jazz was the radio. Many young city dwellers listened to foreign radio music shows. The most popular radio show was Leonard Feather's *Jazz Club USA* on the Voice of America. Since 1955, Dniepropetrovsk jazz fans had tuned their radio sets to a new show on the Voice of America, *Music USA,* with Willis Conover at the microphone.[12] Thousands of young people fell in love with jazz after listening to Conover's shows. Both KGB reports and memoirs of contemporaries noted the tremendous popularity of these shows, even among engineers from the secret departments of the Yuzhmash rocket factory complex.[13]

Jazz became very popular among students of the city and region in the middle of the 1950s. As contemporaries noted, students of the Physical-Technical Department at Dniepropetrovsk State University (Dniepropetrovskii gosudarstvennyi universitet, DGU) organized their own jazz-band as early as 1960. They called this band an *estradnyi* orchestra because the word "jazz" was not popular among the university's leaders in those days. Igor Kos'ko, the new chair of the department, loved jazz and played different musical instruments himself. He supported his students, visited their jazz sessions, and protected them from Communist Party ideologists who opposed jazz music.

All major musicians of DGU jazz band came from the jazz band of the Physical-Technical Department in the early 1960s. The department's band used to play at a special student club on Shevchenko Street in downtown Dniepropetrovsk. Long lines of people waited outside in hopes of getting extra tickets for these concerts. Many talented professional jazz and rock musicians started their musical careers playing long jazz sessions at the club on Shevchenko Street. One of these musicians was a son of Igor Kos'ko, Oleg, who after graduating from the Physical-Technical Department played with different jazz bands all over Ukraine and eventually became a legendary Ukrainian jazz pianist in the 1970s. Many young students—freshmen and sophomores—visited these jazz concerts and danced at the club on Shevchenko Street. Among them was Leonid Kuchma, a future president of independent Ukraine, who in those days was a freshman in the Physical-Technical Department.

Kuchma was born in August 1938 in the small village of Chaikino in the northern Ukrainian province of Chernigov, located on the border of Russia and Byelorussia. His parents were poor Ukrainian peasants who worked on a small collective farm. Because the village was located on the border of Russia, the majority of the local population spoke Russian rather than Ukrainian. Moreover, the official politics of Russification discouraged knowledge of Ukrainian in the province. As a result, Chaikino had only one middle school, with Russian as the language of instruction. Kuchma's father was killed in World War II in 1944, leaving his mother to raise three children by herself. It was a very difficult time for millions of peasants, who struggled to survive the famine of 1946 and the problems of the postwar economic crisis in the Ukrainian countryside.

Like many other village children, Kuchma had to work hard in school and on the collective farm, assisting his parents and performing special field assignments for his school. He joined the group Oktiabriata at the age of eight years, and the All-Union Soviet Pioneer organization at the age of eleven. Similar to other Soviet children of this age, he experienced the special program of ideological indoctrination and upbringing through mass youth organizations and the entire system of Soviet education. As a typical Soviet school student, he blindly believed in Communism and internationalism. He spoke only Russian, he rejected the idea of God, and he was ready to die for his "great socialist motherland." He became an active Komsomol member in high school.[14]

Postwar Soviet schools stressed, foremost, the importance of new technical skills and scientific expertise for the "future builders of Communism."[15] Many contemporaries noted that before the end of the 1960s, there was a cult of knowledge and respect for the professions of teachers, engineers, and doctors among the Soviet people, especially in rural areas.[16] Kuchma's mother supported her son's goal to continue his studies after finishing seven years of primary and middle school in Chaikino. She understood clearly that a professional career for her son in a city would bring him a better life and save him from hard work on a collective farm. There was no high school in Chaikino, so when Kuchma entered a high school in the nearby village of Kostobobrov in 1952, his mother paid his rent and supported him until his last day in school.

Throughout his high school years, Kuchma dreamed of becoming a teacher, but he later changed his mind and chose a career as an engineer. As he recalled, rumors about the high stipend made him change his mind and enter the DGU Physical-Technical Department instead of teaching. He had only a poor peasant mother to support him, so he had to rely only on his own finances. Stipends for pedagogical students were much lower than what the "secret" department offered. After graduating from Kostobobrov High School and successfully passing the admission exams, he was admitted as a student to the DGU Physical-Technical Department in 1955.[17]

From 1955 to 1960, Kuchma was a typical Soviet undergraduate student who spent his time not only in classrooms, laboratories, and libraries but also attending numerous parties and concerts, playing the guitar, dancing, playing sports games, and dating girls. It was a very important time for establishing the necessary personal connections for his future career. He realized at an early age how important political activity was, especially for a peasant boy such as himself without any connections in a big city. With this in mind, he chose to play a more important role in the Komsomol organization in his DGU department. In 1958, he organized a special student group in the department that went to the Siberian region to help harvest the "newly colonized virgin lands" (*tselina* in Russian). His Komsomol activity and his ability to communicate with older colleagues helped him get a good job as a "rocket engineer" at the Yuzhmash factory's secret design office in 1960 after his graduation from the university.[18]

After a year in his new career as an engineer, Kuchma was elected one of the secretaries of the Yuzhmash Komsomol committee. In their memoirs, contemporaries tried to stress Kuchma's engineering talents as a young constructor. However, it appears that he was more talented as an organizer of public activities among the young workers and engineers of the plant than a genius at rocket building. After 1966, he was officially assigned as a main engineer-constructor of rocket engines and worked as the first secretary of the Yuzhmash Komsomol committee. He was a talented executor of the interesting, innovative ideas of two of his bosses—the main constructor, Mikhail Yangel, and the director of Yuzhmash, Aleksandr Makarov. With their support, he made a career as a political leader, and in 1980 he was elected the first secretary of the plant's Communist Party committee.

Thus, in 1980, Kuchma became an official member of the ruling Communist nomenclature and enjoyed the privileges of the party bureaucracy. In 1982, he took a position as the deputy head of the Yuzhmash factory's secret design office, and in 1986 during perestroika, he became the successor of Makarov as the new director of Yuzhmash.[19] Throughout his entire career, he orchestrated a very important network of business and party connections, which created an important political order of influence in his struggle for power in post-Soviet Ukraine.

The basis for this network was created through Kuchma's close friends, who at the end of the 1950s and beginning of the 1960s became the enthusiastic consumers of new music and new fashions. These young consumers not only listened to jazz and danced to the new melodies but also tried to imitate the new songs on their musical instruments. Young Kuchma played the guitar, and in his DGU days during student parties in the dormitories often played the new "hits" from the repertoire of the student jazz band. Some of the future Soviet and post-Soviet politicians also began their student careers as a part of this jazz band. One of them, Vitalii Doguzhiev, in the 1980s became a minister of general machine building (i.e., rocket building) industry of the USSR. On the eve of perestroika, he was the first deputy of the Soviet prime minister. Another enthusiast of American jazz from DGU, a future member of the "Kuchma presidential team" in the 1990s, Vladimir Gorbulin, became the first director of the National Space Agency of Ukraine and was a head of the Council of National Security and Defense of Ukraine.[20]

This early 1960s generation was a good example of the new "stylish" cultural consumption, which became a part of the jazz culture in the Soviet Union. Kuchma and his friends tried to imitate the fashions and hairstyles of *stilyagi* ("stylish men" in Russian), a trend among Soviet youth that became popular during the late 1940s and 1950s and was influenced by mass enthusiasm about jazz in 1955.[21] A majority of *stilyagi* came from the Soviet middle class, privileged families with relatively good financial situations that permitted their children to use expensive tape recorders and wear fashionable dress.[22] According to one of the most prominent representatives of the *stilyagi* generation, the Soviet jazz musician Alexei Kozlov, a typical Moscow "stylish man," had "narrow short pants, big shoes, long chequered jacket with bright and long ties . . . with Tarzan-like long hair combed straight back and smeared generously with briolin."[23]

The stylish Dniepropetrovsk youth tried to imitate this Moscow "style." After frequent visits to Moscow, engineers and university students who worked for Yuzhmash brought the latest Moscow fashions back to Dniepropetrovsk. The relatively high stipends of the students in the DGU Physical-Technical Department allowed them to spend some money not only on liquor but also on new "stylish" clothing. As a result, the new American fashions and style of the English "Teddy Boys" affected the students of the "most secret university department," which had been under direct KGB surveillance since 1959.[24]

The "stylish" cultural consumption worked through a system of socialist market and Soviet *blat*—a system of informal personal connections, which Alena Ledeneva defined as "the use of personal networks and informal contacts to obtain goods and services in short supply and to find a way around formal procedures."[25] As an example of such *blat* relations, in the period 1959–61, Kuchma's classmates regularly visited the student dormitory tailor shop and asked Abram Solomonovich, a local tailor, to narrow their trousers hem from 33 centimeters (the Soviet standard at the time) to a "stylish" width of 18 centimeters. Despite the official prohibitions, Solomonovich agreed to do this for an additional fee. The students and the tailor became part of an informal network, which survived all the official limitations and changes in Soviet cultural policy.

During the early 1960s, future rocket engineers such as Kuchma and his comrades used their high student stipends and bought Bulgarian shirts with square collars and white or light-colored jackets in the central department store, TsUM, in downtown Dniepropetrovsk. They brought these Bulgarian shirts to Solomonovich and asked him to make them look "stylish," similar to their photo cards with portraits of Elvis Presley and Western movie stars. Even in the 1970s, until his emigration to Israel, Solomonovich took care of fitting all shirts at the waist and tailoring the so-called hippy jeans, American T-shirts, and leather jackets that the new student generation asked him to alter and make stylish according to the hard-rock or glam-rock dress codes.[26] Another *blat* network that students used to create a stylish look was located in one downtown hair salon (behind the central department store for children, the Children's World), where a famous barber, Ziama, created the most fashionable stylish hairstyles for student Teddy Boys. In spite of all the official prohibitions, the hairdresser Ziama helped students in their "stylish jazz" cultural consumption for an extra fee.[27]

The first jazz club in Dniepropetrovsk that hired musicians to play American jazz in a special small "combo" band was opened near a big chemical factory that manufactured automobile tires. This youth jazz club became the most popular place for "stylish entertainment" among Kuchma's class-mates. In 1961, Komsomol enthusiasts of jazz named this club Chipollino, which derived from the funny name of a popular character in a children's book by the Italian Communist writer Gianni Rodari. Many jazz musicians from the university jazz band visited Club Chipollino. Some of them joined the local "combo" because the club administration paid money for each gig. Against university rules, the club managers permitted musical improvisations and innovations, which attracted crowds of young people who not only drank alcohol and danced but also enjoyed serious American jazz.[28] During 1964 and 1965, Club Chipollino was still a favorite place for the city's most popular jazz sessions. These music sessions became an improvised job competition for many young jazz musicians. The local officials responsible for culture and entertainment and the directors of the palaces of culture visited these jazz sessions and hired the most talented musicians to play in the orchestras that were under their supervision. Thus, the consumption of jazz became linked to the financial aspects of cultural production in the city of Dniepropetrovsk. Through Club Chipollino, many amateur musicians got their first professional jobs.[29]

Local ideologists tried to stop the "stylish" consumption of jazz music and fashions. Ivan Nasekan, a director of the Dniepropetrovsk Palace of Students, asked the police and Komsomol activists to interfere and stop the dangerous capitalist influences among the student youth. When the local students, who were jazz fans, approached him about organizing a jazz club at the Palace of Students, he rejected and forbade playing jazz or any modern music on the premises of his palace. From 1964 to 1967, Nasekan and other Komsomol ideologists used old publications from the Soviet central periodicals about the bad influence of capitalist jazz for their ideological campaign against this "new" music.[30] Eventually, even the most conservative critics of jazz had to accept this new music. Due to practical issues of youth entertainment and the organization of leisure time, Komsomol activists learned how to deal with jazz clubs.

From the beginning, jazz clubs attracted not only talented musicians but also talented managers and organizers of restaurants, who realized that they could make money from local youth by using the new music and a growing enthusiasm for jazz. By 1966, three of the first jazz clubs in Dniepropetrovsk were transformed into popular restaurants with crowded dance floors where local musicians played not only jazz but also the new popular "beat" music.[31] Club Chipollino became a restaurant called Yunost' (the Youth) in 1966; the second jazz club in the city, Dnipropvs'ki zori (the Dnieper Dawn), became another regular café with live music. The only jazz club that continued to function until 1968 as mainly a music club was a small café, Mriia (a Dream). It was built and supervised by Yuzhmash in downtown Dniepropetrovsk on Kirov Avenue in the spring of 1967. The administration of the missile-building factory allowed its Komsomol organization to transform this place into a youth club. This club immediately became a center of the jazz movement for the entire region. Club Mriia organized special jazz concerts, lectures, and musical competitions on regular basis. As a result of Mriia's activity, Dniepropetrovsk became the location of prestigious jazz festivals called Yunost'. These festivals attracted young and talented jazz musicians from other cities of the Soviet Union. The most popular of these festivals took place during 1968, 1969, and 1970.[32]

In 1968, KGB officials complained about the anti-Soviet "style of life" of Mriia's patrons. According to KGB reports, the Yuzhmash Komsomol committee promised the police to "introduce the youth of the city to modern jazz music and help them understand such music correctly." The KGB discovered, however, that the club was not a center for the musical education of the young generation. Club leaders such as Yurii Boisagolov had no musical education and were engaged exclusively in the propaganda of American jazz music, considering it the best in the world. A majority of club members shared the notion that only the United States provided professional jazz musicians with proper training in music conservatories. Meanwhile in the Soviet Union, there were neither professional training classes for jazzmen nor special jazz departments in musical schools or conservatories. The KGB officers also criticized the "loud ear-rending melodies" of the musical tapes, which were used for dance parties at the club. According to their comments, "Such music had nothing to do with the socialist style of life." The founders of the club, Boisagolov, Gennadii Smirnov, and Aleksandr Leifman, were young, highly educated engineers from local factories. They provided the club with audiotapes and music information. As the KGB officers reported, many inexperienced young people, including "frivolous girls of easy virtue," visited the club. Some of them, especially girls, "blindly imitated fashions and habits of capitalist world," and some of them "used to dress like vulgar people, drank alcohol, and smoked inside the club."[33]

Sometimes the club's leaders organized special musical parties or "jazz sessions" after the official concerts, behind closed doors. According to one KGB source, a typical after-concert party was a session organized to honor the saxophonist Pishchikov and his quartet, who were the famous participants in a jazz competition in Tallinn. On this night, admission for this concert was relatively expensive—1 ruble (the average price for a club admission was 30 kopecks).[34] There were refreshments for musicians—brandy, wine, snacks. After the end of his performance, Pishchikov stayed in the club for the special concert for a "selected audience" after 1 am, a very late time according to Soviet standards. A majority of the audience had left; only those who knew about the private jazz sessions stayed in the club all night long. As the KGB source noted, "An atmosphere in the club was reminiscent of the witches' Black Sabbath. A jazz session concert lasted till 3 am in the morning. There were hysterical shouts, whistles, moans."

The KGB officials tried to make their own analysis and interpret their information. A lack of musical education, a complete ignorance of Western popular culture, and traditional ideological clichés led them to very conflicting conclusions, which did not help Soviet understanding of the new phenomenon in the youth culture. Sometimes, the KGB documents gave incorrect definitions and explanations that were far from reality. They criticized the activities of jazz Club Mriia for "propaganda of abstractionism in music, which was developed by the American and British jazz musicians."[35] According to this report and the memoirs of participants in the jazz sessions, Club Mriia played not only "quiet" jazz but also "loud" rhythm and blues and rock and roll.[36] The main venue for popularizing new music was the official Club Mriia, which was organized under the auspices of Komsomol.

Despite the constant criticism by KGB, Dniepropetrovsk's Komsomol leaders actively participated in the All-Union jazz club movement, which was initiated by the central Komsomol authorities after the Moscow International Youth Festival in 1957. According to Alexei Kozlov, a Moscow musician, who played jazz in the clubs organized by Komsomol, the International Youth Festival in Moscow triggered a mass interest in Western popular culture, which eventually affected all of Soviet entertainment. After this festival, Communist ideologists allowed some elements of Western mass culture into the Soviet system of cultural consumption. These elements had nothing to do with the traditional Soviet ideological discourse and cultural forms of "the mature socialism." Kozlov wrote:

> On the one hand, this event gave birth to the entire generation of dissidents of various levels of courage and openness, from Vadim Delone and Piotr Yakir to "the inner migrant intellectuals who silently defied the system." On the other hand, a new generation of party and Komsomol functionaries appeared. They were the conformists with double layers, who understood everything inside their soul, but ostensibly demonstrated their loyalty to the system. After the Youth Festival of 1957, jazz got a special protection and guidance from Komsomol. In two years, all district Komsomol organizations began to open jazz clubs, then jazz cafés, and later started the annual jazz festivals first in Tartu and Tallinn (in Estonia), then later in Moscow and in other cities—Leningrad, Gorkii, Voronezh, etc.[37]

That is why Dniepropetrovsk Komsomol ideologists supported the initiative of the Yuzhmash enthusiasts of jazz. For the entire decade, they sponsored the spread of jazz as an alternative to the new forms of cultural consumption among the young population of the region. They tried to protect the established canons of jazz culture, which the Komsomol elite had already accepted as "ideologically permissible" from the new music of rock and roll after 1957.[38] Even in 1973, the Dniepropetrovsk Komsomol leaders still supported jazz festivals and ignored the growing interest in rock and roll among the local youth. They considered rock the negative commercial by-product of "the progressive jazz music culture."[39]

Despite its popularity among the Soviet intellectual elite and Komsomol ideologists, jazz did not represent a product for mass cultural consumption among the young people of the city and region of Dniepropetrovsk. Only a tiny minority of local youth were real enthusiasts of jazz. In contrast to

Moscow and Leningrad, Dniepropetrovsk's consumers of American jazz rarely used the jazz records self-made from X-ray plates. The black market in downtown Dniepropetrovsk never had many of these recordings, which were called by contemporaries "the records on ribs," or "jazz on bones" (recordings of jazz music), or "rock on bones" (recordings of rock music).[40] By the middle of the 1960s, the major form of recordings for all Western music (including jazz) was audiotapes.

Meanwhile, the real mass cultural consumer revolution took place in the region of Dniepropetrovsk after 1965. According to contemporary participants in the region's popular music consumption, during the period 1961–64 the city of Dniepropetrovsk's music black market usually consisted of approximately 10 constant sellers and no more than 40 buyers of music products on market day—usually Sunday. After 1965, with the arrival of new products—records and tapes of rock music—the average number of black market sellers increased to 50 (and up to 200 *fartsovshchiks* in 1972). During the same period, the number of regular customers at the city music market grew to more than 600 on market days.[41]

These changes were the result of three important developments in the history of local cultural consumption. The first development was the growth of production and the availability of relatively cheap tape-recorders for young consumers. The second was the growing variety of foreign radio shows devoted to rock-and-roll music. The third was the beginning of Beatlemania in the city of Dniepropetrovsk in the fall of 1964. The combination of these developments contributed to the mass growth of cultural consumption, which involved thousands of young residents of the region of Dniepropetrovsk, beginning with students at middle schools and high schools and influencing people of middle age.

Conclusion

Even during the first stage of the consumption of Western music—jazz—in the closed city of Dniepropetrovsk, contemporaries noticed major developments that would influence the important cultural and ideological practices of both the ruling elite and common consumers of Western cultural products. First of all, jazz affected the fashions and lifestyles of local youth, who incorporated more Western cultural elements into their everyday life. At the same time, to control this consumption, local ideologists had to accommodate new Westernized cultural forms of the "stylish" youth culture and in-

clude them in their ideological practices. As a result, jazz led to a controversial ideological situation between the city's youth and local ideologists.

By the mid-1960s, after Soviet officials incorporated American jazz as
"progressive" and as "good, cultured" consumption in their official ideological practices, they tended to "use" jazz against any new cultural influences from the West, including so-called beat music. Provincial ideologists
from the closed city lagged behind the new ideological and cultural fashions that came from Moscow. This led to new tensions between "the ideological practitioners" in Dniepropetrovsk and their ideological supervisors
in Moscow, who justified the consumption of Western products that were
unacceptable in the orthodox Marxist worldview of the local KGB and Soviet officials. However, the practical needs for career making and adjusting
to the central directives from Moscow modified their anti-Western tastes
and forced them to not only accept but also use the new forms of cultural
consumption for their political and financial survival. Thus the first wave of
cultural consumption in the 1960s, that involving jazz, demonstrated the
ability of both Soviet officials and common consumers to make money on
new music and build new entrepreneurial connections, which would become the foundation for a lucrative music business in the closed city of the
1970s.

Chapter 5

Beatlemania, Shocking Blue, and the Ukrainian Cossacks

In the mid-1960s, rock-and-roll music became the most important component of Westernization for an entire way of life, especially for urban youth.[1] According to contemporaries, rock music shaped the behavior, tastes, and ideas of Soviet youth during the 1960s:

> The authorities automatically banned any Western music, from Canned Heat to James Brown. To Soviet ideological pundits, the Beatles were every bit as subversive as a miniskirt or Nabokov. You needed to be somewhat politically inclined (and nothing breeds political apathy the way Communism does), as well as have some command of English and the proper connections, to get hold of and read *1984*. You needed friends in high places to see *Midnight Cowboy*. But rock was readily available from the numerous radio stations like Radio Luxembourg or the BBC (the unjammed, English-language edition), and we lapped it up with a gusto unimaginable in the West. For Westerners, it was a music to dance or drop acid to; for us, when you multiplied the Beatles' youthful vitality by the forbidden-fruit factor, it was more than a breath of fresh air—it was a hurricane, a release, the true voice of freedom. We paraphrased Mayakovsky's line "I'd learn Russian just because it was spoken by Lenin" to read: "I'd learn English just because it was spoken by Lennon."[2]

The entire generation of Soviet intellectuals that grew up in the 1960s was influenced by the Beatles' music and Anglo-American rock and roll. As a former interpreter for Mikhail Gorbachev wrote in his memoirs:

I am sure that the impact of the Beatles on the generation of young Soviets in the 1960s will one day be the object of studies. We knew their
songs by heart. A typical group of young people would have someone
playing the guitar surrounded by a group listening or singing along with
varying proficiency. To the Beatles, even more than to my teacher of pho-
netics, I owe my accent. But I and my friends and contemporaries owe
them something else too. In the dusky years of the Brezhnev regime they
were not only a source of musical relief. They helped us create a world
of our own, a world different from the dull and senseless ideological
liturgy that increasingly reminded one of Stalinism. Our generation
chose their melodies—and also their freedom, their mistakes, their
crises. I believe that only some of us in those years drew inspiration from
Andrey Sakharov, for we had not yet matured enough to understand his
vision. But the Beatles were our quiet way of rejecting "the system"
while conforming to most of its demands.[3]

Those who grew up in Soviet Ukraine confirmed the important influence
that rock music became during the 1960s and 1970s. Vitalii Pidgaetskii,
who graduated from Dniepropetrovsk University in the 1970s and became
a professor of history there ten years later, recalled: "Oh, rock music, great
music of the Beatles and Rolling Stones was everywhere, in every room
where students had their drinking party. You could not imagine dancing,
dating, making love without Beatles music in our student life in the late
1960s."[4]

Yulia Tymoshenko, a heroine of the 2004 Orange Revolution, also
stressed the strong influences of Western pop music in her youth. In 1975,
while in high school, she wrote in an autobiographical essay: "I liked music by Bach, Mozart, and Strauss. I liked also the modern rock bands such
as the Beatles, Manfred Mann, Led Zeppelin, and others." She confessed in
this essay that she was not able to imagine everyday life without modern
rock music.[5]

Serhii Tihipko, a leader of the Komsomol organization in the Dniepropetrovsk Region during the 1980s, and now a prominent political figure in
independent Ukraine, characterized the situation in Dniepropetrovsk during the 1970s in the same way: "When I came to Dniepropetrovsk after my
high school years in Kishinev, I found the same popular music there. The
majority of young people spent more time listening to the music of Deep
Purple and Pink Floyd than reading books."[6] According to a Ukrainian amateur rock musician, Eduard Svichar, who was a college student in Kyiv at

the end of the 1970s, "Rock hysteria influenced all thinking parts of Ukrainian youth, especially in the 1970s and 1980s; so it was impossible even to imagine any conversation of young people without mentioning such names as Led Zeppelin, King Crimson, Yes, Genesis, Peter Gabriel, Phil Collins, or Dire Straits."[7]

The Popularity of Beat Music

At the end of the 1950s, American rock and roll reached Dniepropetrovsk's youth audience along with jazz music. College jazz bands sometimes included the new "beat" hits of American rock and roll groups in their concerts. In 1960, young music enthusiasts played and even sang popular songs by Elvis Presley and Bill Hailey during drinking parties in the dormitories of Dniepropetrovsk State University (Dniepropetrovskii gosudarstvennyi universitet, DGU), sometimes with their own Russian lyrics. Boris Severniuk, one of the classmates of Leonid Kuchma, used to imitate Elvis Presley and attracted crowds of students who liked the new music and fashions.[8]

American rock musicians were not always popular among young audiences in Dniepropetrovsk during the early 1960s. American rock and roll was introduced as a by-product of American jazz. The first jazz music consumers were predominantly local intellectuals—college students, physicians, teachers, professional engineers, and scientists from Yuzhmash, the city's rocket factory complex, and its other industrial plants and technical institutions. Therefore, the first rock music fans also represented the intellectual elite of the region and the city. The market for foreign records and audiotapes was the same. People who collected tapes and records of music by Duke Ellington or Miles Davis sometimes also bought recordings of music by Elvis Presley or Little Richard.

Everything changed after 1964, when the first original (*firmennyi*) Beatles album *A Hard Day's Night* appeared in the music market on Lenin Street near the Railroad Palace of Culture in downtown Dniepropetrovsk. During November of that year, the city's usual consumers of Western music were divided about this new record on the market and the rumors about this new band with a strange name. One group of these local consumers rejected the Beatles record as a "product of dance pop music that had nothing to do with serious jazz." The overwhelming majority of these consumers, however, liked this record. As it turned out, the Beatles' music attracted a younger and jazz-illiterate audience to Dniepropetrovsk's music market.

These young people still represented the city's upper middle class—with money, social status, and reputation—but their age and musical tastes had changed. They were much younger (mainly high school students and freshmen and sophomores at the local university and colleges), they included more female fans, and instead of jazz or American rock and roll they loved the "noisy" British rock music that they called "beat music."[9]

In small towns near Dniepropetrovsk, such as Sinel'nikovo and Pavlograd, the first recordings of Beatles albums appeared during 1965 and 1966. According to the personal diaries of two young enthusiasts of this music, Vladimir Solodovnik and Aleksandr Gusar, their relatives, who were undergraduate students at Moscow colleges, brought tapes with recordings of two Beatles albums, *A Hard Day's Night* and *Rubber Soul,* to their hometowns of Sinel'nikovo and Pavlograd during their college winter break in February 1966. Local high school students fell in love with the strange sounds and catchy melodies of the Beatles. They could not understand the lyrics, but they loved this music and made their own tape-recordings of Beatles songs. By the end of 1966, in the small towns of the Dniepropetrovsk Region, all households with tape recorders had at least one Beatles song in their music collection on audiotapes.[10]

The central Ukrainian Komsomol newspaper from Kyiv, *Molod' Ukrainy,* first published information about the Beatles in May 1964. In a brief passage under a blurred photograph of the Beatles, there were only three sentences. A Kyiv journalist wrote that the Beatles, "an English vocal quartet, was famous for their silly hairstyle and shouting that replaced normal singing."[11] Dniepropetrovsk's newspapers ignored the new cultural phenomenon in Western music related to the strange name Bitly (the first and most popular Russian/Ukrainian translation/nickname for "the Beatles"). In December 1964, the Dniepropetrovsk mass media was preoccupied with the visit of an Azerbaijani singer, Muslim Magomaev, to the city. Magomaev was a rising Soviet popular music star, and his visit attracted more official attention than the emerging popularity of the Beatles, which the Komsomol newspaper *Prapor iunosti* called "A Fashionable Illness." For the young journalists who worked for this newspaper, Magomaev and the Italian singer Robertino Loretti were more important cultural figures than "four Liverpool lads who forget to do their haircut [*sic*]."[12]

In the late 1950s, the Soviet government had created a network of "music studios," which were audio recording stores (*musykal'nyi salon,* or *muzykal'naia studia* in Russian) where people, for the relatively high price of 2 rubles, could record holiday greetings with popular songs on a small flexible vinyl disc. These music studios also allowed people to record their favorite melodies for money. In 1965, Dniepropetrovsk's music studios sold not only audiotapes and holiday greetings with songs by popular Soviet *estrada* (pop music) stars such as Edita Piekha and Eduard Khil', and by popular guitar poets such as Aleksandr Galich, Bulat Okudzhava and Vladimir Vysotsky, but also recordings of "foreign beat music." Many contemporaries considered the act of recording audiotapes and their subsequent distribution as the first stage of a new Soviet mass culture phenomenon, which was called tape-recording publishing (*magnitizdat* in Russian). The historian Richard Stites noted that "by the mid-1960s guitar poetry was in its heyday." He wrote:

> The three major figures, Okudzhava, Galich, and Vysotsky were joined by dozens of lesser-known figures in a kind of alternative culture. Galich and Vysotsky went beyond Okudzhava into the lore of the underworld, the street, and the camps, drawing on materials that were already widely sung in private circles.[13]

These audiotapes (*magnitofonnye zapisi* in Russian) and holiday greetings with Vysotsky's songs became the most popular product in Dniepropetrovsk's music studios after 1965. This practice of official music recording prepared a foundation for a relatively lucrative business. The people who were in charge of recording these holiday musical greetings tried to satisfy the growing demand for new music. As a result, when young people asked for recordings of "beat" music instead of Vysotsky's songs, the music stores had to include Beatles songs on the list of the available music. In 1965, the most popular hits for these recordings were "Can't Buy Me Love" and "And I Love Her." The music from the album *A Hard Day's Night* triggered an interest in other Beatles songs, which were recorded on thousands of "musical greeting cards" in Dniepropetrovsk.[14]

By the beginning of the academic year 1965–66, high school students and undergraduate students at DGU became regular customers of the city's largest audio recording store, on Karl Marx Avenue in downtown Dniepropetrovsk. As it turned out, one individual who was responsible for recording musical greeting cards was also an active participant in the music black market on Lenin Street, a few blocks away. He made a lot of money by trading new foreign records and audiotapes. In August 1965, he became the first Dniepropetrovsk resident to buy, in L'viv, an East German record (on the Amiga label) with a compilation of Beatles songs. He bought the new Beatles album *A Hard Day's Night* for 40 rubles at Dniepropetrovsk's music black market and sold more than a hundred tapes with music from this album for 10 rubles each. Also in 1965, the songs from two old Beatles albums, *Please Please Me* and *With the Beatles,* became the primary material for the musical greeting card collection of the entire city of Dniepropetrovsk.[15]

In the mid-1960s, the number of musical greetings cards with "beat music" increased dramatically in the city of Dniepropetrovsk. According to Mikhail Suvorov, whose friend worked at the central audio recording store on Karl Marx Avenue, three songs out of the top ten hits of 1965 belonged to the Beatles, three others were bard songs, two were foreign popular songs by the French singer Edith Piaf or the Italian singer Robertino Loretti, and two were Soviet *estrada* songs by Eduard Hil' and Edita Piekha. By the end of 1968, the most popular hits were rock songs—six out of ten were rock songs, with the Beatles and the Rolling Stones leading this hit parade.[16] According to official statistics, in 1965, 90 percent of all the musical greeting cards made in Dniepropetrovsk included popular songs by Soviet composers, while fewer than 10 percent had recordings of Western songs. In 1970, however, more than 90 percent of these cards had "Western beat music," mainly songs by the Beatles and the Rolling Stones. In April of that year, Zinaida Soumina, an official in the city of Dniepropetrovsk's administrative apparatus, complained about this phenomenon. "We are not against consumption," she claimed. She continued:

> But this should be a *cultured* consumption. Take a look at our city offices of music recording and what our youth is consuming there as "music." They are recording the tapes with songs of Vysotsky [10 percent], music by the Beatles [Bitlov] [90 percent]. Where is the real cultural consumption here? You can't see that our young people are recording classical music by Tchaikovsky or Glinka. They still prefer the dances with their boogie-woogie to the concerts of classical music. They still wait when the fresh music records from the West will appear on the city black market. In search for the recordings of their Western idols, young people forget their national roots, their own national culture.[17]

In 1971, nine of the ten most popular songs in Dniepropetrovsk belonged to the "beat music" category, and only one of them was a Vysotsky song.[18] These figures also reflected the situation in the music markets of other Ukrainian cities, especially in the Odessa, Kyiv, and Cherkassy regions. By the middle of the 1970s, rock music had become the most popular form of cultural consumption in the "closed city" of Dniepropetrovsk.[19]

The Beatles' "invasion" of Dniepropetrovsk led to the transformation of former jazz bands into rock bands. Officially, they continued to be called *estrada* ensembles. Yet they imitated the Beatles not only in their music but also in the style and structure of their ensembles. The most popular bands were groups of four or five musicians. The DGU jazz band split into a large *estrada* ensemble and a smaller one, which was called the "beat group." In 1966, everybody had called this smaller group a vocal instrumental ensemble.[20] This name change reflected developments in official cultural policy. Soviet ideologists accepted the existence of Komsomol bands that played popular music. However, they rejected the foreign idea of a rock-and-roll band and replaced it with a Soviet substitute. In 1966, the Soviet Ministry of Culture sponsored so-called vocal instrumental ensembles (*vokal'no-instrumental'nyi ansambl'* in Russian, or VIA). The paradox was that all the early Soviet VIAs still imitated the melodious Beatles, only in the "Soviet style," and singing in the Russian language.[21] Dniepropetrovsk's colleges followed this pattern and supported new "beat groups," which were now officially called VIAs. During the 1970s and 1980s, DGU produced various VIA bands. Seven rock bands were officially registered by the university administration in 1979. The most famous was the band Dniepriane (which had been established in 1968), which fused various "beat" influences with Ukrainian folk music.[22]

The Engineering and Construction Institute of Dniepropetrovsk (Dniepropetrovskii inzhenerno-stroitel'nyi institut, DISI) also became fertile ground for various styles of the new "beat music," which included not only the Beatles and the Rolling Stones but also Cliff Richard, the Doors, and Creedence Clearwater Revival. By the beginning of the 1970s, only the Beatles' music style survived among DISI bands. The best Beatles-style band was Maki (Red Poppies), which was officially accepted by the DISI administration as its vocal instrumental ensemble. This was also a typical development for other regions of Ukraine. The melodious, harmonious style of Soviet VIAs, based on the accepted musical forms of Western rock music, became an acceptable official norm for Soviet *estrada* in the 1970s. And some of these norms were incorporated into traditional Soviet mass songs.[23]

By 1972, the Soviet form of a rock band—the VIA—had become the most popular in Dniepropetrovsk. All fifty palaces (houses) of culture in the city had their own rock band by 1972.[24] In 1978, all fourteen outdoor dance floors in the city had a professional VIA that played at least twice a week.

In the region of Dniepropetrovsk, Soviet rock bands were the leading form of popular music production and consumption. Despite all the efforts by Communist ideologists to promote classical and folk music, Soviet youth preferred music performed by VIAs. According to the official statistics for 1979, 240 palaces of culture in the region had 48 folk music bands, 148 brass bands, and 353 vocal instrumental (rock) bands. The most lucrative part of the entire entertainment business for these "socialist clubs" was a dance floor with a live local rock band playing. By 1979, 71 palaces of culture had their own dance floor with an officially assigned VIA. All these bands had a set of music instruments typical for a "beat" band of the 1960s, which included three electric guitars (lead, rhythm, and bass) and drums. Later, some bands also got keyboards, percussions, and a brass section. Still, the Beatles' style and structure prevailed in Soviet VIAs, even during the 1970s.[25]

The first consumers of the Beatles' music in 1964 and 1965 were children from the wealthy families of the city and region of Dniepropetrovsk. Sometimes, their parents—scientists, engineers, Communist apparatchiks, and KGB officers—would bring Beatles albums back from their visits abroad. The first known place where Beatlemania struck the region was School No. 9 in Dniepropetrovsk, a "special-language" school for privileged children that used English as its language of instruction. As early as December 1964, students brought in audiotapes with two Beatles albums, *A Hard Day's Night* and *The Beatles for Sale,* and organized a tape exchange. All these students came from very respectable families of Communist apparatchiks and KGB officers.[26]

Young Yuzhmash scientists and engineers, who visited Moscow and other Soviet centers of spaceship construction, brought back tape-recordings of Beatles songs, together with audiotapes of songs by Galich, Vizbor, and Vysotsky—the famous Soviet bards of the 1960s. Some of these young engineers included in their audiotape collections recordings of entire Beatles albums. Sometimes, they did not know the name of the band whose music they had recorded. They just liked the sound and the melodies. As a result, through the families of these Yuzhmash scientists and engineers, the Beatles' music spread among high school and college students in Dniepropetrovsk, and then to the region's other cities and towns, such as Dnieprodzerzhinsk, Novomoskovsk, Sinel'nikovo, and Pavlograd.[27] Before 1964, the original Beatles albums had reached only one city in the region, Krivoi Rog, which was open to foreigners. Some of these foreigners, who came from the developing countries of Asia, Africa, and Latin America, were students at local colleges, and they brought in original rock records as early as 1963.[28] Besides the Yuzhmash scientists and engineers, these foreign students at Krivoi Rog's colleges became the main suppliers of Western "beat music" recordings to local music markets during the 1960s.

Because of Beatlemania, Communist ideologists worried about the growing Westernization of Dniepropetrovsk's students. The Beatles' "mod" style of fashion and "mop-top" hairstyles spread among many high school students and undergraduate students in local colleges during 1965 and 1966. Dniepropetrovsk's newspapers called these "Beatles' men" "traitors" and portrayed, ironically, how they blindly imitated their foreign idols, substituting their "good Slavic names with unpronounceable foreign names" such as Alfred, Max, and Rex, and replacing their "normal dress with foreign fashions."[29] For the Dniepropetrovsk police, this growing consumption of rock-and-roll by the local population was an alarming sign of "creeping dangerous bourgeois influences" among the city's youth. According to Evgenii Chaika (in a letter to the BBC radio station), this rock consumption had started at least in 1963 and was connected to the strange name "Bitly" (again, a translation/nickname of "the Beatles"). As KGB documents attested, by 1967 the Beatles' music has become the most popular object of consumption among students and their young teachers. A KGB officer reported in 1968 that Elena Suratova, a forty-three-year-old English-language teacher at the Chemical Mechanical Technical School (Technikum), "brought the records with music of foreign songs, performed by Bitly, which she had received from the foreigners, to her school and organized a regular collective listening to the Beatles music by her students [*sic*]."[30]

The Beatles' music opened a road to other Western rock musicians in the regional music market. The music of the Rolling Stones became especially popular among young consumers of new "beat music" recordings after 1965. For many high school and college students who bought tape-recordings of this music, it was difficult to tell the difference between the names of the bands or titles of their songs. Sometimes, students attributed Rolling Stones songs to the Beatles. But as the KGB case of Chaika demonstrated, young enthusiasts of the new music did not care about correct titles or names.[31]

An entire new subculture of rock music fans appeared in the Dniepropetrovsk Region at the end of 1967. After 1967, the consumers of "beat music" paid more attention to the origin of the music, the names of the musicians, and the titles of the songs. More local rock fans began to study the English language in order to understand their favorite songs. And many of these fans later became undergraduate students in the Department of English Language, part of the DGU Faculty of Philology. The most remarkable rock influence, which triggered their interest in the English language, came from the 1967 Beatles album *Sgt. Pepper's Lonely Hearts Club Band.* This record reached Krivoi Rog's market as early as August 1967. By the end of that month, this album was available in Dniepropetrovsk in its original vinyl form for a price of 60 to 100 rubles. (The average monthly salary for a young secondary school teacher or engineer was 90 to 100 rubles in the late 1960s.) Young students could buy a tape-recording of the entire album for 25 rubles on the music market or its separate songs for 5 to 10 rubles in the city's official music studios. Young "Beatles' men" looked for the sleeve of this album because the original Beatles lyrics were printed on it. They copied these lyrics and disseminated them among their friends. Young enthusiasts also collected records, tapes, poetry, photos, posters, and various paraphernalia for the British bands. And they began translating rock lyrics from English into Russian or Ukrainian. Some of them tried to imitate this music and joined local bands, which covered the most popular songs of their favorite "beat groups."[32] By 1967, the most popular recordings among young consumers were those of the Beatles and the Rolling Stones. After 1967, a real "cult" of the Beatles among the Soviet youth sparked an interest in any musician who had a certain relation to this legendary group. Thus, rumors about Jimi Hendrix covering *Sgt. Pepper's Lonely Hearts Club Band*'s "title" song immediately after the release of this album made Hendrix a new cult figure among young Soviet "Beatles men." Information about Eric Clapton playing guitar with George Harrison in his song "While My Guitar Gently Weeps" on the Beatles' *White Album* triggered a mass interest in Clapton's music and especially in the bands, like Cream, in which he participated. Rumors about John Lennon's friendship with Keith Moon, a drummer for the band the Who, and with Harry Nilsson, Elton John, and David Bowie, made their music attractive to millions of Soviet Beatles fans in the early 1970s. "Without You"—a hit song by Badfinger, a British band sponsored by the Beatles—was covered by Nilsson, Lennon's friend, and became the most popular "slow" song on Soviet dance floors.[33]

After 1967, more European and American rock music became available on the Dniepropetrovsk market. The Dutch band Shocking Blue, with their hits "Venus" and "Shocking You," became as popular as the Rolling Stones and the Who. According to popular demand in the city's music studios during the period 1968–70, the uncontested leaders were mainly European rock musicians—the Beatles, the Rolling Stones, Shocking Blue, Cream with Eric Clapton, Procol Harum, Jimi Hendrix (considered British by the local fans), the Yardbirds with Jeff Beck, Elton John, and the Who. The Australian band the Bee Gees, with hits such as "Holiday" and "I Can't See Nobody," followed suit. Only four American rock bands had reached the Dniepropetrovsk music market by the end of the 1960s: the Doors, Creedence Clearwater Revival, Simon and Garfunkel, and Santana.[34] By the end of 1970, according to the number of tape-recordings and albums sold in Dniepropetrovsk, the most popular American rock band was Creedence. During that year, five of the ten most popular vinyl records on the black market on Lenin Street in downtown Dniepropetrovsk were recordings by Creedence.[35] As early as 1970, the local Ukrainian rock bands that played for various dance floors and dance halls—in places ranging from small towns to the big industrial cities such as Dniepropetrovsk—covered the hits of Creedence, such as "Suzie Q," "I Put a Spell on You," and "Down on the Corner."[36]

Some Moscow authors considered Elvis Presley and Bob Dylan to be the most popular American rock musicians among Soviet youth during the 1960s.[37] However, according to a multitude of sources, the overwhelming majority of rock music fans in provincial cities like Dniepropetrovsk ignored the music of Presley and Dylan. The tapes with their music reached a mass, local audience only after Beatlemania, and they were few and of bad quality. Many young consumers of popular music could not appreciate Dylan's songs because they did not understand his lyrics in English and they preferred the more "rhythmic" and melodious music of the Beatles and Creedence Clearwater Revival. As one young rock fan wrote in his summer school diary in August 1966, after reading a Soviet magazine with a positive review about Dylan, "What did they find progressive and good in this slow and boring muttering to a guitar (by Dylan)? I would rather prefer the catchy melodies of the Beatles or Rolling Stones than this boring Dylan stuff! It's hard to believe that such bad music as songs by Bob Dylan came from America, the motherland of rock and Creedence." Local rock bands in Dniepropetrovsk never performed Dylan's songs in the 1960s, because even the most enthusiastic rock fans ignored his "boring and slow music." They preferred American music that was "more energetic and more like rock and roll" by the Doors and Creedence.[38]

Ukraine's Shocking Blue Story

In 1970, Ukrainian rock bands incorporated five major international rock hits into their repertoire for dance parties: "Girl," by the Beatles; "As Tears Go By," by the Rolling Stones; "The House of the Rising Sun," by the An-

imals; "Suzie Q," by Creedence Clearwater Revival; and "Venus," by
Shocking Blue. Musicians covered these songs with their own lyrics in
Ukrainian. Though the Ukrainian versions of "Girl," "As Tears Go By," and
"Suzie Q" represented romantic poetry about love, a traditional topic for
Soviet bands, their cover of "Venus" in Ukrainian was very different.[39]

Originally, the Dutch band Shocking Blue had released the song "Venus"
in 1969 as a single. In 1970, the band included this song on their album *At
Home,* which became very popular not only in Great Britain but also in other
European countries. As a Dutch sociologist wrote, "Shocking Blue played
brilliant, concise, almost classical American rock and roll, and its song
'Venus' with the alien, mechanical vocal sound of Mariska Veres became a
major hit in Holland and the rest of Europe in the second part of 1969 and
number 1 in America in early 1970."[40] The Shocking Blue hit "Venus" was
aired on BBC radio shows throughout 1970. Even Viktor Tatarskii, a Soviet
radio journalist, included "Venus" in his popular radio show on the Moscow
radio station Maiak (the Beacon) in December 1970. At the beginning of
the 1970s, this song became a symbol of beat music all over the Soviet
Union.[41]

The local music studios all over Ukraine put Shocking Blue's hit "Venus"
in their musical material for greeting card recordings, together with popular Soviet songs by Muslim Magomaev, Eduard Khil, and Edita Piekha. The
average Dniepropetrovsk consumer of popular music ordered more greeting cards with recordings of "Venus" than with recordings of popular Gypsy
songs or folk songs by Zykina or Vysotsky. Before 1970, only young customers had asked for musical greeting cards with foreign music, predominantly by the Beatles and Rolling Stones. But after 1970, even middle-aged
people of thirty and forty years now ordered the Shocking Blue song.[42]

To some extent, the immense popularity of "Venus" was connected to the
new Ukrainian version of its lyrics. Many local Ukrainian rock bands covered "Venus" with their own unusual lyrics in Ukrainian, unlike the traditional poetry of Soviet pop songs. The Ukrainian version of "Venus" became a song about the Ukrainian Zaporizhian Cossacks who fought with
the foreign enemies of the Ukrainian people, trying to defend their native
land and religion. The new Ukrainian lyrics were simple but catchy:
"Dnipro flows into the Black Sea, and there will be a disaster for the Turks,
when the Cossacks will arrive and kill all the Turks. Hey Cossacks, Zaporizhian Cossacks. . . ."[43]

This song about the Zaporizhian Cossacks set to the melody of "Venus"
had five or six versions in different parts of Ukraine. It became very popu-

lar not only among young fans of rock music but also among those who visited dance parties and loved to dance. Even the Russian-speaking audience in Dniepropetrovsk danced when "The Cossacks" version of "Venus" came on. This was the beginning of a new phenomenon: the "Ukrainization" of English rock songs. A similar indigenization of English rock music took place among Russian rock musicians as well.[44] The Russian band Poiushchie gitary (Singing guitars) from Leningrad covered "Yellow River," a popular song by the American band the New Christie Minstrels, with Russian lyrics about Karlsson, a funny character from a fairy tale by the Swedish writer Astrid Lindgren. The Moscow rock band Vesiolye rebiata (Funny guys) covered the Beatles song "Drive My Car" from the *Rubber Soul* album with Russian lyrics about a "small old car" and released this song on the Melodia label.[45]

The tremendous popularity of the Ukrainian version of "Venus" was an interesting example of new types of cultural consumption among young Ukrainian rock music fans. Even Russian-speaking dance hall visitors in Dniepropetrovsk did not feel offended by this song that idealized the Ukrainian Cossacks; they preferred the Ukrainian version to the English original. To some extent, the popularity of this patriotic theme about the Ukrainian Cossacks paralleled the growing interest in the Soviet Ukrainian historical novels in Dniepropetrovsk during the 1960s and early 1970s. According to librarians' statistics, along with traditionally popular adventure stories by Alexander Dumas and Arthur Conan Doyle, the most popular books among the city's young readers were historical novels about ancient Ukrainian heroes written by Semen Skliarenko, Ivan Bilyk, and Pavlo Zagrebel'nyi.[46]

Significantly, neither Communist ideologists nor KGB operatives objected to this Ukrainian version of "Venus" on Dniepropetrovsk's dance floors. In the 1970s, the DGU rock band from the Physical-Technical Department still sang "The Cossacks" to the melody "Venus." As one police officer noted, "It is better to have Soviet young people dance to their national song 'Cossacks' than to American rock and roll."[47] The ideological priorities to limit "dangerous" Western influences on Soviet youth thus led the authorities to approve an idealization of the Ukrainian national past as an alternative to an idealization of the capitalist present. Such permission to consume pop music is remarkable because it followed so closely the 1968 KGB campaign of persecution against young local poets like Ivan Sokul'sky for the very same activity: the idealization of Ukrainian national history.

The popularity of "The Cossacks" contrasted with the story of Smerichka, the Ukrainian rock band (a vocal instrumental ensemble) from the region of Chernivtsi in Western Ukraine.[48] This band's first original songs, written by the talented medical student Volodymyr Ivasiuk, reached the local audience in Eastern Ukraine by 1970. At this time, the majority of Dniepropetrovsk's consumers of pop music fell in love with Smerichka's music, which was broadcast on the radio and TV almost every night. Ukrainian Komsomol leaders supported this band, and the Ukrainian Republic's festival of popular music awarded it a gold medal. In 1971, the Ukrainian Ministry of Culture praised the band as "the best Komsomol music ensemble in the country" and called it "the best model for contemporary Soviet *estrada* [popular music] that responded to the requirements of the life today."[49]

Moreover, Komsomol ideologists used the band Smerichka's music as an antidote against Western rock music. In Dniepropetrovsk, Komsomol leaders recommended that local rock bands play the music of Smerichka instead of Western rock and roll. This produced an unexpected result. Many musicians who had played the Smerichka's songs in the years 1970–71 now avoided the group because its songs had become "the official Soviet" music. To follow the official recommendations to include Ukrainian Soviet songs in their repertoire, they continued to perform their favorite, "The Cossacks."[50] Likewise, when Smerichka's songs became part of the official Soviet *estrada,* local rock fans lost interest in the Ukrainian band. According to the sale of "greeting card recordings," "Chervona Ruta" and other songs by Smerichka were the top hits in 1970–71 among Dniepropetrovsk's pop music consumers, mostly middle-aged people and recent migrants from the countryside. But after 1971, the young generation of rock music fans ignored Smerichka. Even Ukrainian-speaking fans of rock preferred the "real rock" that they associated with Western musicians like Shocking Blue.[51] The melodious and catchy Ukrainian pop songs had lost the competition with American and European rock hits. Ukrainian rock enthusiasts wanted to identify themselves with the "authentic" West to look "cool" and "trendy."[52] And once Smerichka became integrated into Soviet music propaganda, it lost its rock music status and "stylish rock appeal." As one fourteen-year-old Ukrainian rock music fan wrote in his diary during August 1972,

> When I heard those songs "Chervona Ruta" and "Vodograi" [songs by Ivasiuk for Smerichka] the first time in my life, I loved them. I thought these guys would be our Ukrainian Creedence [Clearwater Revival] or the Beatles. Now it sounds like old folk music or Soviet *estrada.* I hate

these peasants' songs. The only real "cool" song in Ukrainian that I am aware of is still "The Cossacks" [a cover of the Shocking Blue song "Venus"].[53]

The choice of the Ukrainian language for a cover of the popular Shocking Blue song "Venus" by Ukrainian musicians signified a very important cultural construction of meaning through association in expressing the local Ukrainian identity in the Russian-speaking city of Dniepropetrovsk. According to Harris M. Berger, a sociologist of music, much of human "identity in everyday life is achieved through linguistic behavior, and, capitalizing on this fact, singers and songwriters use forms of talk from the social world around them to publicly think about, enact, or perform their identities. Construed broadly to include the use of multiple dialects and registers, the issue of language choice in music is central to these processes."[54] As Maria Paula Survilla has noted, language choice can play the role of "an aural trigger that connects the idea of cultural rebellion with music rebellion" via rock.[55] But the Dniepropetrovsk case demonstrates that this language choice depended on the origin of the music. The local Ukrainian rock music enthusiasts in the closed city still preferred "the original Western" music rather than an officially imposed Soviet Ukrainian version of it.

Conclusion

Overall, during the 1960s and early 1970s, young local consumers preferred the cultural products that they associated with the emotional world they imagined. They identified with the world of "Western rock music." This music framed their sense of identity through the direct experiences it offered, enabling them to place themselves in imaginative cultural narratives. According to Simon Frith, "The experience of pop music is an experience of identity: In responding to a song, people are drawn, haphazardly, into emotional alliances with performers and with the performers' other fans.... [Therefore] music symbolizes and offers the immediate experience of collective identity."[56] The "imaginary West" played a central part in this cultural narrative. To some extent, listening to rock music became a way to cultivate "hopes and ideals of the imaginary West." Dniepropetrovsk's rock music consumers sought to recover cultural meaning, which had deliberately been removed from their daily life in the closed city and relocated in a distant cultural domain they called "Western rock."[57]

The basis for this imaginary musical world was connected to the beat music of the 1960s. From 1964 to 1970, the Beatles' music paved the way for other types of Western popular music to enter Dniepropetrovsk by creating a new group of cultural consumers that was constantly expanding through sales of rock tapes and records by legal and illegal distribution outlets. The members of this growing group of cultural consumers constantly aligned themselves with Westernized music, which they frequently altered and indigenized rather than simply imitated. And at the same time as they made Western music their own through their changes, they rejected attempts by Soviet ideologists to force cultural feelings for officially sanctioned music that was similar to Western versions. These new consumers wanted to make their own choices about music—choices that would affect their identity formation.

Chapter 6

Sources of Rock Music Consumption

The consumption of rock-and-roll music in Soviet Ukraine depended on changes in supply and demand and reflected the general trends of cultural consumption in the Soviet Union in the late 1960s and early 1970s. For the new generation of rock music consumers, the first and most popular source of rock was not foreign radio stations such as the Voice of America or the BBC. Instead, most developed their first taste and enthusiasm for this new music on the dance floors in their schools, in offices, or at private parties, when they were first exposed to the new rhythms and melodies. Through their friends in school, they began to listen seriously to rock music recordings. They began creating their own audiotapes, which they then exchanged with their friends. Some of them went to a black market, such as the "music market" in downtown Dniepropetrovsk, while others went to the city music studios to ask about new tape-recordings.

In contrast to other big Soviet cities that were open to foreigners, Dniepropetrovsk lacked the foreign tourists who usually brought "fresh music information from the West." During the 1970s in Kyiv's black market, 25 to 50 percent of all new Western music records came directly from foreign visitors. In port cities like Odessa, almost 50 percent of all new popular music records came from foreigners, and the other 50 percent was brought by Soviet sailors and fishermen who visited foreign countries on a regular basis.[1] But the closed city of Dniepropetrovsk had no such sources. Dniepropetrovsk's music enthusiasts who were interested in fresh Western recordings had to go to the black markets of the open cities—Moscow, Odessa, Zaporizhie, and L'viv. By 1970, the black market in downtown L'viv had become the major source of new Western music for Dniepropetrovsk's residents. So the closed city's KGB officers worried about the "growing new Western influences and boogie-woogie" from L'viv.[2]

The Roles of the Record Label Melodia
and of Soviet Radio Stations

For many rock music consumers who wanted to avoid the black market, the state-owned record label Melodia (Melody) became another, albeit incomplete and belated, source of music by 1975. Melodia responded to the growing demand among young music consumers. Its first attempt to satisfy this demand was the release of two songs, three years after their original release in England—"Girl," by the Beatles; and "(I Can't Get No) Satisfaction," by the Rolling Stones—in a Soviet compilation of pop music in 1968. But Melodia did not reveal the true names of these two famous rock bands. On the compilation sleeve, it only put the words "English people's [*narodnaia*] song: vocal and instrumental ensemble (England)."[3] From 1971 to 1975, without any official permission from the Western record companies, Melodia released six small records (*minions* in Russian, the Soviet version of single-song records) with the most popular Beatles hits. It also released at least two *minions* with songs by the Rolling Stones, including "As Tears Go By," "Paint It Black," "Ruby Tuesday," and some others. The Moscow rock band Vesiolye rebiata covered the Beatles songs "Ob-La-Di, Ob-La-Da" in English and "Drive My Car" in Russian and released its own *minion* on Melodia. In 1975, a new compilation, *Vocal Instrumental Ensembles from England,* featured the Beatles song "Birthday," from the *White Album* of 1968.[4] From 1974 to 1984, Melodia released two *minion* compilations with John Lennon's songs from the *Imagine* album, and two *minions* with a few songs from the albums *Ram* and *Band on the Run* by Paul McCartney and Wings.[5] By 1976, in many cases without revealing the name of the performers or songwriters, Melodia's compilations included music by the Animals, Bob Dylan, Simon and Garfunkel, Elton John, Creedence Clearwater Revival, the Bee Gees, Deep Purple, Slade, Sweet, and T. Rex. All these Melodia recordings, released without any official permission from the Western record companies, became the first available source of this music for the youngest Soviet rock music fans, mainly middle school and high school students, who had just begun their search for recordings of their favorite music.

As a reaction to the rising interest in jazz and rock music, the USSR Radio Committee created a special music journal to promote new forms of art and music: *Krugozor* (Wide Vision). Melodia was involved in the release of this journal, which included small records with popular songs by foreign musicians and sometimes even rock music from Europe and the United States. Melodia provided *Krugozor* with the necessary music information. Other journals, such as *Klub i khudozhestvennaia samodeiatel'nost'* (*Club and*

Amateur Art Activities), followed *Krugozor*'s example and released small records with songs by popular Western musicians in special "music appendixes."[6] By 1968, popular youth magazines like *Rovesnik* (in English, *Contemporary*, or *A Person of the Same Age*), *Smena* (*Successors*), and *Yunost'* (*Youth*) began publishing material about Western rock music. Many of Dniepropetrovsk's rock-and-roll fans turned to these publications for more information about their favorite musicians.[7]

In 1967, radio journalist Viktor Tatarskii created the most popular music show in the history of Soviet radio for the station Maiak ("beacon"). In the same year, he created the show *Vstrechi s pesnei* ("Meetings with a song"), which popularized Soviet popular songs (*estrada*). From 1968 to 1975, Tatarskii and journalist Grigorii Libergal hosted a show on Maiak called *Zapishite na vashi magnitofony* (Please make your own tape recording), broadcasting the latest music hits along with Tatarskii's commentary. Maiak's administration tried to stop him from playing "loud music" and several times stopped the show. After 1976, Tatarskii devoted new shows at other Moscow stations to jazz and *estrada*. For the central radio station Yunost ("youth"), Viktor Tatarskii and other young radio journalists, such as Ekaterina Tarkhanova, Vladimir Pozner, and Igor Fesunenko, organized *Na vsekh shirotakh* (On all latitudes) and *Muzykal'nyi globus* (Musical globe), covering popular music including jazz and rock and roll.[9]

However, for many Ukrainian rock music fans, the most popular source of music was a "socialist Romanian" radio station broadcasting from Bucharest. From 1965 to 1973, thousands of Ukrainian enthusiasts tape-recorded the long hours of this Romanian station's pop music shows. According to many contemporaries, including KGB operatives, the Romanian station's signal was stronger than that of the Voice of America or the BBC. For this reason more young people from Dniepropetrovsk listened to Romanian radio than to capitalist stations. But unfortunately for Ukrainian rock music fans, when the Romanian Communist leaders took more conservative and nationalist directions in their cultural policy, they changed the content of their radio shows and completely purged "capitalist rock music" from Romanian radio in the middle of the 1970s.[10]

The Black Market and Arnold Gurevich

For serious music lovers, the best source of recordings and information was the black market, or the music market, in downtown Dniepropetrovsk. During Beatlemania, from 1964 to 1970, the city's "beat music" fans had their music market on what they called the Broadway—the central stretch of Karl Marx Avenue, the main street in downtown Dniepropetrovsk, between Serov Street and Moskovskaya Street, which sometimes was called simply the Broad. To some extent, local rock music enthusiasts followed the example of the jazz fans and *stilyagi* ("stylish men") in Moscow, Leningrad, Kazan, Kyiv, and Odessa, who had their own favorite places for gathering during the 1950s.[11] In Dniepropetrovsk, the Broad became a place for the music market selling popular British and American vinyl records. Most of the foreign records at this market came from large Soviet cities that were open to foreigners. In the years 1964–65, the Inturist hotels for foreign tourists in these cities established special bars and cafés that attracted their foreign guests by allowing them to use their own currency. The Inturist bars in Kyiv, Odessa, L'viv, and Zaporizhie became favorite haunts for Dniepropetrovsk's music black marketers, who traded Soviet souvenirs for Western records.[12]

Eventually, all these records appeared on the Broad. During the period 1964–70, the majority of those who traded records and tape-recordings on the Broad were college students. Many of these students came from the English-language section of the Philological Department of Dniepropetrovsk State University. Knowledge of English was useful during their business operations, which required them to read the labels and printed lyrics of the songs. During the 1965–66 academic year, the most famous music businessman from the Broad for both the "beat music" consumers and the police was Aron (Arnold) Gurevich, a university student whose major was English language and literature.[13]

Arnold, as he preferred to call himself, had listened to the BBC, the Voice of America, and other Western radio stations as early as 1961, when he was a senior at Dniepropetrovsk High School. He liked American jazz, rhythm and blues, and American literature. He practiced his English by listening to radio shows in English. And beginning in 1963, when the Dniepropetrovsk KGB tried to jam Western broadcasts in Russian, he started listening to radio shows in English only.

At about this same time, Arnold's parents' friends, who worked as engineers for Yuzhmash, Dniepropetrovsk's rocket factory complex, and visited Moscow and other Soviet centers of the spaceship industry, introduced him to new rock-and-roll music. They brought the first original British records of "beat music," including the Beatles' 1964 album *A Hard Day's Night,* into the Gureviches' apartment. Moreover, they showed Arnold their audiotapes with recordings of other British musicians, and they explained how

Figure 6.1. Downtown Dniepropetrovsk. This is a part of Karl Marx Avenue known in the 1960s and 1970s as the Broad, a meeting place for rock music fans and hippies. The building on the right was the location of the offices of the Komsomol city committee and Sputnik, the Komsomol travel agency. Photograph by the author.

they had bought all these records and tapes from the *fartsovshchiks* (black marketers), paying 10 rubles for a tape and 50 rubles for an original record. Because they were good friends with Arnold, they suggested that the young student copy their tapes for free. They explained that he could sell copies of these tapes to his classmates at the university, and then, using this money, he would be able to buy an original (*firmennyi* in Russian) Beatles album in Moscow.

In December 1964, Arnold made twenty tapes with a recording of *A Hard Day's Night* and tracks by Little Richard and Chuck Berry, and he wrote all the tracks' names in English, with a correct translation in Russian, on the tapes' boxes. By the end of December, he had sold all his tapes at 10 rubles each. His fellow students, who loved this new music, were ready to pay for his good recordings with professionally prepared labels including Russian translations. He sold twenty more audiotapes during an examination session at the university in the middle of January 1965.

Now Arnold, who before had only his monthly stipend of 30 rubles as pocket money, had suddenly earned 400 rubles in one month and could buy railway tickets to Moscow to buy original Western records of his favorite music. During the winter break of early February 1965, he arrived in Moscow and went directly to Smolenskaya Square near a Metro station downtown, which in the 1960s was famous for its black market for Western music. He bought his favorite Beatles album for 40 rubles there and established important connections with Moscow's *fartsovshchiks.* The black marketers explained that he could have original Western records for a reduced price if he would buy more than five. So he bought ten more records at a reduced price of 25 rubles each, and he promised the *fartsovshchiks* to return during the spring break.

As a result of Arnold's Moscow deal, he not only brought to Dniepropetrovsk all the Beatles albums—*Please Please Me, With the Beatles, A Hard Day's Night, Beatles for Sale*—but also the records of bands that were completely new for him, such as the Rolling Stones and Manfred Mann.[14] Then, during 1965, he discovered a new source of Western music records: the L'viv black market, where he established friendly relationships with Polish tourists who sold various Western goods, including music records. For many years, these tourists from Poland provided him with the most popular Western music records. According to KGB data, by 1970 his Polish connections in L'viv had resulted in a mass influx of "bourgeois" music records into the closed city of Dniepropetrovsk.[15]

Expanding his business, Arnold made new audiotapes and sold them not only to college students but also to people who manufactured recordings of musical greetings for money in the city's music studios. Thus songs by the Beatles, Rolling Stones, and Manfred Mann reached a wide audience in Dniepropetrovsk. As a result of Arnold's activities, which to some extent shaped the new cultural consumption of youth in Dniepropetrovsk, the most popular hits for tape-recording in May 1965 included not only the Beatles songs "Can't Buy Me Love" and "And I Love Her" but also Manfred Mann's "Do Wah Diddy Diddy."

Arnold also made more money than he had expected. After two more trips to Moscow, he had built his own collection of beat music. By the beginning of September 1965, he had enough money to hire other local college students, such as Boris (Bob) Poplavskii, to trade records and audiotapes for him. These "Arnold's agents" visited Moscow's black market, bought new foreign records for Arnold, copied them, and sold the tapes not only in Dniepropetrovsk but also in other cities in the region, such as Novomoskovsk, Sinel'nikovo, and Pavlograd. Moreover, Arnold had established favorable connections with the members of important families in Dniepropetrovsk, including Communist Party apparatchiks, KGB officers, and other representatives of the city's elite. By the end of 1965, Arnold had made a fortune using his new connections and trading audiotapes to young members of elite families. The police and Communist ideologists knew that people like him had accumulated "a large amount of money in their bank accounts [*vklady v sberegatel'nykh kassakh* in Russian]," but no one arrested him. Eventually, he was expelled from the university in December 1966 because its administration had decided to get rid of this student who was involved in "black market activities."[16]

Because Dniepropetrovsk was a closed city, people like Arnold became its most important sources of information about new trends in Western popular culture. They shaped the musical tastes and major forms of cultural consumption in the city's market for pop music. By the end of the 1960s, Arnold (Aron Gurevich), "Man" Kabatskii, Yurii Bonar, Vladimir Oskevich-Rudnitskii, and a few others controlled the entire market for rock music in the city. And this music market sold not only vinyl records and audiotapes but also posters, music journals, badges, and other rock music paraphernalia. During the 1970s, musical instruments, including homemade and imported electric guitars, drums, and keyboards, became available at the market. The people who controlled the market became very wealthy. Sometimes they bribed local officials and the police. Their customers were mainly the children of Communist Party apparatchiks, KGB officials, and police (*militsia*) officers, along with the managers and directors of the local factories. Rock music dealers like Arnold had the financial resources to lend money to other people and invest capital in other adventurous schemes.[17]

Worried Apparatchiks and Officials

With the success of the black market, the city administration, KGB officials, and Communist Party apparatchiks worried about the growing popularity of Western rock music and the influence of the black marketers on local youth. That is why, during the period 1968–74, the Dniepropetrovsk City Committee of the Communist Party (CCCP) discussed the problems of the illegal music market every month. On November 17, 1970, one of the CCCP's secretaries prepared a special report (*spravka*), "On the measures in the

struggle with enthusiasm about 'popular music' and manifestations of unhealthy interest to the decadent culture of the West."[18]

Moreover, after the KGB complained about the ideological problems in
the city, the local police established strict control and surveillance over the
meeting places of stamp collectors (*philatelists*), numismatists, and other
people who distributed foreign records and audiotapes among youth—
especially in the parks near the Railroads' Palace of Culture and the Volo-
darsky textile factory in downtown Dniepropetrovsk. Between January
1969 and November 1970, the police observed three meetings of forty
young people who called themselves "hippies." Some of them had foreign
music records. The city police dispersed their meetings, and after November 1970 there were no public demonstrations of "hippie" behavior among
local youth.[19]

Although the police stopped the "hippie" movement in Dniepropetrovsk
in 1970, they failed to prevent the spread, and growing popularity, of Western rock music. They periodically organized raids in localities where music
fans sold and bought records. After many arrests, the police confiscated a
huge collection of records (mainly albums) by British and American rock
bands. The largest collections on this rock-and-roll market (more than 100
records) belonged to G. L. Roshal and K. A. Tsukur, students at the medical
and chemical-technological institutes, who sold each music album for 50 or
100 rubles.[20]

The limits of the socialist economy prevented some rock music dealers
from expanding their financial activities. Many dealers emigrated to Israel
or the United States in the middle of the 1970s. Those who stayed in
Dniepropetrovsk laid a foundation for a new stage of rock music consumption. They built important business connections, not only with the rock music markets in Moscow but also with the neighboring "open" cities of Krivoi
Rog and Zaporizhie and the famous Ukrainian centers of *fartsovshchiks,*
such as L'viv and Odessa. *Fartsovshchiks'* families, like the Fedins in downtown Dniepropetrovsk, expanded their activities and combined trade in
music records with trade in clothing, especially American jeans, which became the most popular object of trade on the Soviet black market during the
1970s.[21]

The spread of rock music records and tapes became the main concern for
Communist Party ideologists and the local police in Dniepropetrovsk. An
obsession with the new music replaced their old fears of "hippie" meetings,
which had dominated KGB and party documents between 1967 and early
1970. After 1970, the major target for police raids in downtown Dniepro-

petrovsk was not groups of hippies but meetings of young fans of the Beatles, the Rolling Stones, the Doors, and Creedence Clearwater Revival, who bought, sold, and exchanged the records and tapes of their favorite bands. As it turned out, music recording studios (*punkty zapisi musyki*) became another important venue for spreading this new music.[22] Party and Komsomol ideologists tried to establish tight control over all the "offices of music recordings" and substitute tapes of rock music with recordings of Soviet musicians and mainstream popular music from the Soviet bloc. As an alternative to the spread of rock music, local ideologists intensified different forms of "ideological" work in schools, parks, clubs, and dance halls, including special lectures and concerts of classical and Soviet popular music. Finally, the CCCP decided to ask specialists, musicologists, and English-language teachers to evaluate the music on confiscated records.

Both KGB officers and party apparatchiks wanted to figure out how to treat this new music, which sounded very different from the old music of American jazz musicians. These officials were familiar with old traditional jazz, because some of them even had their own private jazz collections. Meanwhile, directives from the central authorities in Moscow and Kyiv lagged behind the new trends in the local youth culture. Dniepropetrovsk officials needed the opinions of local composers and musicians who were professionally trained and ideologically reliable. One of these local experts, a member of the USSR Union of Composers, V. Sapelkin, submitted a special report to the CCCP in late November 1970.[23]

After listening to almost a hundred music albums of American and British origin, Sapelkin acknowledged that all the music tracks had been composed, arranged, performed, and recorded "professionally with very good quality." At the same time, he emphasized that he had received a very bad impression of this music because of its monotonous rhythms, the limited character of its melodious tools, and its gloomy and oppressive themes. He opposed the use of this music for education because "the means of dramatic influence of this music included *khripenie gortaniu* [a guttural wheezing], hysterical shouts, wild laughter of madmen, barking of the dog, cries of a goat, and other projections of erotic character." He presented this rock music as a manufactured product not intended for normal human psychology or psychological health, and he warned against publicly listening to it, especially by young audiences. Such expert opinions became a justification for outlawing and prohibiting new Western music in Dniepropetrovsk in 1970.

Sapelkin's recommendations were prevalent until the end of the 1970s, not only in KGB and Communist Party records but also in the recommendations for the lecturers for Znanie (Society of Knowledge). Znanie was an organization advocating the popularization of ideologically reliable scholarly information among Soviet citizens. It had been officially created and sponsored by the Communist Party of the Soviet Union for the purpose of educating people in different spheres of knowledge, from history and foreign politics to physics and astronomy. As late as 1979, the lecturers for Znanie (the majority of whom came from local colleges) avoided presenting rock music, which they criticized as "capitalist propaganda."[24] The "closed" existence of the local apparatchiks in Dniepropetrovsk created local principles and rules of ideological games that were very different from the situation in the capital cities of the Soviet Union, such as Moscow and Leningrad, where rock music culture literally flourished in the 1970s.[25]

Therefore, Dniepropetrovsk's ideologists were unprepared to comply with the new requirements about youth entertainment that came in 1975 from Moscow. The central Communist Party and Komsomol authorities sponsored a new ideological campaign promoting "ideologically reliable forms of Komsomol entertainment," which had the foreign name of "discotheques." Suddenly, the local authorities had to organize special youth clubs with the same Western music these ideologists had tried to prohibit in 1970. At the same time, the local administration had to deal with mass cultural consumption among Soviet youth. During the 1970s, a new period of democratization of pop music consumption was triggered by two very different forms of Western music: hard rock and disco music.

Conclusion

The 1960s were the first stage of growth in Dniepropetrovsk's consumption of Western cultural products, which connected both music and literature in the cultural practices of Soviet youth with the ideological practices of the KGB and Communist officials in the closed city. Moreover, this consumption led to the rapid distribution of Western music and also revealed the direct and growing connections between black market dealers like Arnold Gurevich and the majority of young rock music consumers.

These black market sources of rock music consumption contributed to the commercialization of Soviet youth culture during the 1960s, even in closed cities like Dniepropetrovsk. The new beat music culture brought to the market those elements in the local youth culture that emphasized the businesslike, profit-oriented, and enterprising aspects of young rock fans' behavior. The KGB became aware of these new developments in rock music consumption. However, the police and Soviet ideologists could not stop this consumption, which now affected various social groups among Soviet youth. By the end of the 1960s, the consumption of Western music in the closed city was loosing its elitist and mostly male character. With the introduction and consequent popularity of the new beat music, the consumer base expanded to include more young people, women, and the working class.

Part II

The Hard-Rocking 1970s: The Beginning of Mass Westernization

The early 1970s in Dniepropetrovsk were a period of "mass Westernization" of the local youth. This mass Westernization included the consumption of books written by Western writers, movies from the West, and especially music from the West—hard rock—which influenced not only youth fashions but also popular religiosity in the region.

By 1976, this mass consumption of Western cultural products contributed to the homogenization of the local youth culture and to Russification. This process began with the mass popularity of Western adventure classics among local middle school and high school students. In contrast to the traditionally didactic and boring stories in the Soviet books that were obligatory for children's reading, Soviet students found Western adventure, detective, and science fiction stories more exciting and interesting. Ironically, the old Western adventure classics of the nineteenth century, which represented all these genres, were recommended by the Soviet middle school and high school curricula for "extracurricular reading" during school breaks. In this way, Western adventure books became available to, and tremendously popular among, the youth of the closed city of Dniepropetrovsk.

Chapter 7

Western Adventure Stories and Ukrainian Historical Novels: Problems of the Homogenization of Soviet Culture

In June 1964, a twelve-year-old middle school student from the town of Sinel'nikovo, near Dniepropetrovsk, wrote in his summer school diary:

> Now we have summer break till the end of August. The first thing I did today was to visit the City Children's Library and borrow the first volume of Mayne Reid's works with my favorite novels, *The White Chief* and *The Quadroon*. I will start my holidays with these Mayne Reid masterpieces. Then I will continue with *The Leatherstocking Saga,* James Fenimore Cooper's novels about Indians and Nathaniel Bumpo. And I will finish with my favorite fantasy and mystery stories by Edgar Allan Poe.[1]

Seven years later, another middle school student from the city of Dniepropetrovsk made his reading plans for the summer break of 1971:

> All spring I dreamed about those six rose volumes of my Mayne Reid which wait for me on our living room's bookshelves. Of course I will start again with *The White Chief* and *The Quadroon* in the first volume. My plan is to finish all Mayne Reid's volumes, especially one with *The Headless Horseman,* during June. I had already read these novels during my winter break. Now I need to read all volumes one by one. Then in July and August I plan to read three books that my parents presented me as my birthday gifts, *The Three Musketeers* by Alexander Dumas, *The Last of the Mohicans* by James Fenimore Cooper, and *The Adventures of Sherlock Holmes* by Arthur Conan Doyle. If I have time, I will also finish ten volumes by Jules Verne that my mother strongly recommended

me to read. But, of course, I must read Dumas and Conan Doyle first. Mom told that it was very difficult to get [*dostat'*] these books. She bought them in the "downtown book market," and she paid the local black marketers fantastic prices for these books to make me happy.[2]

Similar themes appeared in the summer school diary of another middle school student from a neighboring industrial town. At the end of May 1973, he celebrated the beginning of his summer break by reading *The Headless Horseman* by Mayne Reid. This fourteen-year-old student noted:

> I am glad to finish all these boring studies and readings for my class. Now I can read what I like. I will go to our town's library and will borrow the volumes of Mayne Reid. Then I will read *The Hound of the Baskervilles* by Conan Doyle, a collection of Edgar Allan Poe's stories, Louis Bousse- nard's *Captain Daredevil* [*Le Capitaine Casse-Cou*], and *The Count of Monte Cristo* by Dumas, which my father bought from the black mar- keters in Dniepropetrovsk last month. I also plan to read a collection of Jack London's stories, all six volumes of James Fenimore Cooper, and my favorite novels of Walter Scott, *Ivanhoe* and *Quentin Durvard.*[3]

These summer school diaries demonstrate several similarities in book consumption among the schoolchildren of the Dniepropetrovsk Region dur- ing the summer breaks of 1964, 1971, and 1973. The most desirable books for reading by middle school students were the adventure stories of old Western authors.[4] In their diaries, these children never mentioned books by Soviet authors or Ukrainian literature as an object of their book consump- tion. Often, parents also grew up reading the same "Western adventure clas- sics" that they suggested to their children. More than one hundred people who were interviewed from 1989 to 2007 confirmed that Western adven- ture literature was immensely popular in the Brezhnev era. People from dif- ferent backgrounds, such as the librarian Evgen Prudchenko and the histo- rian Yurii Mytsyk, who were adolescents during the 1960s and 1970s, fell in love with adventure books by Mayne Reid, Louis Boussenard, James Fenimore Cooper, Edgar Alan Poe, Robert Stevenson, Arthur Conan Doyle, Jules Verne, and Alexander Dumas. Foreign literature dominated their lists of favorite books. In interviews, they could only recall a few Ukrainian or Russian adventure and detective stories that captivated their imagination. As Prudchenko recalled, "Nine of ten books which I had read in my child- hood belonged to the Western adventure classics."

It is noteworthy that both Mytsyk and Prudchenko recalled that a majority of Western adventure classics were published in the Ukrainian language. In the 1960s and early 1970s, the most popular adventure books were available for Dniepropetrovsk's children in a Ukrainian rather than a Russian translation. Prudchenko read his first Reid book in Ukrainian, when he was ten years old in 1970. Mytsyk recalled that the first adventure book in his life was *Treasure Island* by Stevenson in Ukrainian translation.[5] However, because of the immense popularity of Western adventure classics among Dniepropetrovsk's book consumers, even Ukrainian translations disappeared from the city's bookstores by the end of the 1970s. According to diary accounts, the Dniepropetrovsk black market then accommodated growing reader demand.[6]

Because traditional Soviet locations for the consumption of children's books, like libraries and bookstores, were not able to satisfy this growing demand, the black market gradually became the most important location for book consumption under late socialism. According to school diaries, the majority of the books in students' households came from the black market in downtown Dniepropetrovsk during their final school years, 1975 and 1976.[7] Other contemporaries confirmed the growth of the black market trade in books in the region beginning in the late 1960s.[8] In Dniepropetrovsk, the book market and music market merged by the mid-1970s. The same *fartsovshchiks* (black marketers) offered their clients *The Three Musketeers* by Dumas, or the record *Abbey Road* by the Beatles, or a pair of Levi's jeans. Entire dynasties of black marketers, such as Sergei Fedin's family, combined a lucrative trade in books, records, and other goods that were popular among local consumers. The Soviet administration, police, and Communist ideologists tried to stop this growing illegal trade in books and records. But they failed.[9]

According to Stephen Lovell, a British historian of book consumption in the Soviet Union during late socialism, "Until the mid-1950s, mass reading was library-based, and the masses could thus be directed towards the appropriate books. By the end of the 1950s, however, private collections started to catch up with libraries; the demands of readers became more varied, and the unwieldy publishing system was unable and unwilling to respond."[10] As many Soviet and Western scholars argued, during the urbanizing "revolution" in the Soviet Union in the 1960s, people "became better educated, migrated to the cities, moved out of communal flats, and gained slightly more disposable income." Soviet researchers also called this period "the book boom."[11] During the 1960s and 1970s, "recent migrants to the

— Чим же ти займаєшся?
— Літературою. Беру книжку в бібліотеці, сплачую вартість у десятикратному розмірі, а продаю — у двадцятикратному.

Figure 7.1. Drawing captioned "What do you do for you living? I do literature. I borrow a book at the public library, then pay ten times as much for this book as a lost book, and afterward I sell it for twenty times as much on the black market." From *Perets,* 1982, no. 19, 7.

city were inclined to regard books as a means of symbolic adaptation to the 'higher' urban culture." As a result, "the size of workers' private collections had doubled over 10–15 years," and "there were in 1985 ten times more books in homes than in libraries."[12]

The development of book consumption in Dniepropetrovsk followed the All-Union patterns. It was prestigious among Soviet industrial workers to

Figure 7.2. Cartoons, with captions reading, on the left: "Edik changed completely. Recently he traded only foreign dress, but now he loves books"; and on the right: "Do you need Pushkin, Stendhal, or Hugo? . . ." From *Perets,* 1976, no. 2, 3.

have an extensive book collection at home. In some regions, the number of industrial workers who had more than 100 volumes at home increased from 16 percent in 1966 to more than 45 percent in 1978.[13] This "book boom" stimulated black market connections all over the Soviet Union.[14] Lovell gives an excellent explanation of mass book consumption in Soviet society:

> Books were so sought-after in the late Soviet period not just because of an atavistic Russian hunger for the Word; a more crucial factor was the lack of alternative sources of entertainment and social or material status symbols. It is surely the case that any commodity beyond the basic material necessities acquires symbolic value under the conditions of the *kul'tura defitsita.* In the absence of a market, the fetishization of culture replaces that of money and exchange value.[15]

Despite being a closed city, Dniepropetrovsk's problems with book consumption were also typical throughout the Soviet Union. But at the same time, Dniepropetrovsk demonstrated local peculiarities. A comparison of the city's and region's library records with private school diaries provides us with important information about the evolution of book reading and consumption, especially among young readers.

School Book Diaries, Yulia Grigian (Telegina), and Book Choice

During the 1960s and 1970s, Russian- and Ukrainian-language teachers encouraged their students to write personal diaries, especially during summer school breaks. Sometimes they suggested that the students write a "diary of books." Teachers expected students to write down brief summaries of each book they read. In some schools in the Dniepropetrovsk Region, students began these diaries in the fifth grade. Most students hated keeping reading lists. However, a few of these students kept writing their "book journals" for many years. These book records are a unique source of information about book consumption among the youth of Dniepropetrovsk. Two of the most detailed book diaries were used in this study. They cover books read by the authors from February 1970 until June 1975. The authors of these documents—Aleksandr Gusar, whose native language was Ukrainian, and Andrei Vadimov, an ethnic Russian—recorded all the books they read from their fourth year until their ninth year in school. For a five-year period, they commented on a description of the plot, the language of the book, the number of pages, and their evaluations of each book.

During the first year of their book diaries, in 1970, Gusar read eighty books and Vadimov read seventy-eight books. Each student followed the recommended reading list from his teacher. Due to the centralized system of Soviet education and the universal curriculum for all Soviet schools, the two teachers of Russian literature used the same lists of recommended reading for summer breaks. This is why Gusar and Vadimov often described the same volumes in their book diaries. They read books by Russian classic writers, such as V. Korolenko's novel *The Blind Musician,* and Soviet writers, such as Yu. Olesha's novel *Three Fat Men* and V. Kataev's series of novels, *The Waves of Black Sea,* about revolutionary events in the southern Ukrainian city of Odessa. All these books were recommended by the Soviet curriculum for fifth-grade students. Both students also read a series of fairy

tales written by A. Volkov, who adapted *The Wizard of Oz* by L. Frank
Baum. Using an original American idea and plot for his first novel, *The Wizard of Emerald City,* Volkov composed new stories that fit the official requirements for Soviet children's books and wrote three new novels about
the adventures of an American girl, Elly, from Kansas.[16]

Adventure literature and science fiction by Western writers take a promi-
nent place in these book diaries. As recounted in the quotations above, each
student read adventure novels by Mayne Reid, James Fenimore Cooper, and
Robert Louis Stevenson, as well as science fiction stories by H. G. Wells.
There were only a few books by classical Ukrainian writers recorded in the
book diaries for 1970. Both students read collections of the stories by Marko
Vovchok, a prominent female Ukrainian writer of the nineteenth century.
Each student read at least one book every two months in Ukrainian. Usually these Ukrainian books were adventure novels by Soviet Ukrainian writers like N. Trublaini, Yu. Bedzyk, and Yu. Dol'd-Mykhailyk; Ukrainian
translations of Russian historical novels by Z. Shishova; or translations of
Romanian detective novels by the Romanian writer T. Konstantin. On average, twelve-year-old readers read 20 percent of their books in Ukrainian
(mostly Western adventure stories) and 80 percent in Russian. Approximately 80 percent of the books they read represented Soviet literature, and
fewer than 20 percent were foreign literature.[17]

In 1971, Gusar read sixty and Vadimov read fifty-six books. Besides the
obligatory Russian classical books—such as *Dubrovsky* by Aleksandr
Pushkin and *Taras Bulba* by Nikolai Gogol—foreign historical and adventure novels and science fiction obviously prevailed in their records (60 percent in Gusar's diary and 53 percent in Vadimov's diary). Both of them fell
in love with "European medieval history," reading about the adventures of
Ivanhoe and Quentin Durvard, the heroes of Walter Scott, and the heroes of
The Black Arrow by Stevenson, of *Notre-Dame of Paris* by Victor Hugo,
and *Three Musketeers* by Alexander Dumas. Gusar and Vadimov reread
Mayne Reid's novels and began reading Jules Verne's science fiction. Both
of them reread a collection of stories about the detective Sherlock Holmes
by Conan Doyle. Gusar left a note about Conan Doyle's book on December 31, 1971: "I read this book the fourth time [*sic*]."

During the sixth grade, Gusar and Vadimov preferred only foreign or
Soviet adventure and detective literature (either in Russian or Ukrainian).
Overall, the number of Ukrainian books they read decreased. Only 15 percent of their books were in Ukrainian.[18] In 1972, Gusar read fifty and Vadimov read forty-six books. More than 60 percent of all the books they read

were foreign science fiction by Verne and Arthur C. Clarke, detective stories by Conan Doyle, and stories about the pirate Captain Blood by Raphael Sabatini, as well as novels by James Fenimore Cooper, Mark Twain, and Alexander Dumas. Almost 20 percent of all the books they read represented Russian and Ukrainian classical literature (Pushkin, Gogol, Tolstoy, and Nechui-Levytskyi). Fewer then 20 percent represented Soviet historical and detective stories. Only three books in both the students' records (fewer than 6 percent) were in Ukrainian.[19]

In 1973, their last year in middle school (the eighth grade), the two fifteen-year-old students read more classical Russian and Ukrainian literature, as was required by the Soviet curriculum. Gusar read seventy books and Vadimov read sixty-six. More than 23 percent of the books now included classical works by writers such as Denis Fonvizin, Aleksandr Griboedov, Aleksandr Pushkin, Mikhail Lermontov, Nikolai Gogol, and Taras Shevchenko. Despite this increasing reading load, both students still read foreign books for leisure. More than 40 percent of the books in their records represented adventure novels by Alexander Dumas; science fiction by Verne, Conan Doyle, and Wells; horror and mystery stories by Edgar Allan Poe; adventure stories by Bret Harte; and detective stories by Agatha Christie and Georges Simenon. Almost 26 percent of all the books represented Soviet science fiction (mainly A. Beliaev's novels) and Soviet historical and detective stories. Both students read more than 15 percent of all the books mentioned in their diaries, including detective stories by Christie, in the Ukrainian language.[20] A similar proportion of books—40 percent of foreign literature (mainly adventure tales and science fiction), 30 percent of obligatory Russian and Ukrainian literature (Tolstoy, Anton Chekhov, Maxim Gorky, Panas Myrnyi, Lesia Ukrainka, and Oles Honchar), and 30 percent of Soviet contemporary literature for entertainment—was recorded during the years 1974–76 in the book diaries. Almost 20 percent of all books, including foreign detective stories and obligatory (*programnaia literature*) books from Ukrainian classical literature, were in Ukrainian.[21]

During their last grades in high school, both readers, the Ukrainian speaker Gusar and the Russian speaker Vadimov, began reading Ukrainian historical novels in Ukrainian written by Soviet writers such as Semen Skliarenko and Ivan Bilyk. Gusar, a sixteen-year-old, who was always more interested in science (especially chemistry) than in the humanities, was thrilled by Bilyk's novel *Mech Areia* and decided to read more books about Ukrainian history, including those about the Kievan princes Sviatoslav and

Volodymyr and about the legendary Zaporizhian Cossacks. In his summer diary, in June 1975, Gusar wrote:

> My father criticizes me for reading in Ukrainian and reminds me that for my career and studies at Dniepropetrovsk University I will need a good knowledge of Russian. But I can't stop reading Bilyk's novel. My friend whose mother is a librarian gave me this copy in the Ukrainian language. He told me that this book was forbidden to read and removed by the authorities from circulation. However, I am so impressed by what I have read in Bilyk's novel. It turned out that the Hun leader from the fourth century AD, great Attila who controlled all of Eurasia, was our Ukrainian ancestor, Prince Hatyla. It is unbelievable! We were a great and ancient nation even before Kievan Rus'! And now we, Ukrainians, are transformed into a nation of stupid and timid peasants.[22]

This entry from Gusar's school diary is a good illustration of the role of Ukrainian historical novels in identity formation in the Dniepropetrovsk Region. Gusar, who idealized Western rock music and whose native language was Ukrainian, under the influence of his parents switched to writing in Russian from Ukrainian in his diary in 1975. The same year, he still continued reading his favorite Ukrainian books, and in his dairy he expressed an obvious pride in the past achievements of the Ukrainian nation.

On the one hand, Gusar followed a typical road toward Russification. He entered Dniepropetrovsk University, where the language of instruction was Russian, and he switched to Russian to communicate with his classmates. As Kenneth Farmer noted, "Official Soviet policies in the Ukraine have tended to reinforce the prestige of Russian over Ukrainian, and to encourage the adoption of Russian by Ukrainians seeking upward mobility."[23] Eventually, Gusar adopted the Russian language. He also publicly criticized the stupidity and incompetence of Ukrainian intellectuals and the Soviet conservatism of the local Ukrainian apparatchiks, whom he felt personified all the reactionary developments of the Soviet reality. On the other hand, he wanted to know more about the history of his nation. He read Ukrainian historical novels and idealized the glorious past of Ukraine, which he contrasted with the backward, anti-Western elements in contemporary Soviet Ukrainian culture.[24]

According to contemporaries, more high school students (both Ukrainian and Russian speaking) read Bilyk's and Skliarenko's novels.[25] Vladimir

Solodovnik, a Russian-speaking high school student who entered Dniepro-petrovsk University in 1976 was also enthusiastic about Ukrainian histori-cal novels by Skliarenko during the late 1960s and early 1970s.[26] This in-formation corresponds to the records of Dniepropetrovsk's public libraries. According to these records, Ukrainian historical novels became the most popular books among young readers from fifteen to seventeen years of age during the period 1970–75. Besides traditionally popular adventure and de-tective stories and science fiction by foreign authors, novels about Ukrain-ian history were in great demand in all the city's central libraries. Some con-temporaries witnessed a growing demand for Ukrainian historical books, even on the black market, where the most popular book in the years 1975–76 was Bilyk's novel *Mech Areia.*[27]

Another Dniepropetrovsk high school student, Yulia Grigian (Telegina), was also a participant in book consumption in the closed city during the 1970s. Yulia, who in 1978 changed her last name into Tymoshenko after her marriage, became widely known in the 1990s as the "gas princess" of the Ukraine and in 2004 as the "Joan of Arc" of the Orange Revolution. Born in 1960, she was the daughter of an Armenian taxi driver, Grigian, and a Russian technical worker, Telegina. As Yulia's classmates recalled, she lived in a typical working-class neighborhood, in a typical Krushchevka apart-ment building on Kirov Avenue, not far from the jazz club sponsored by the Yuzhmash rocket factory.[28] She grew up in this apartment house, which was known to the neighbors as the "taxi driver's house" because all the inhabi-tants of the gray five-story building were employees of the Dniepropet-rovsk city taxi depot. Yulia's parents, as a taxi driver and the controller of the taxi depot, had received their small apartment from their employer. Af-ter her parents' divorce, as Yulia recalled later, her mother worked hard to support the entire family:

> To earn more money, my mother worked extra hours and was in constant attendance at the taxi depot. She also had to support my grandmother and her sister's family. I grew up under the conditions when I knew that it was very difficult to save an extra penny. We had to count only upon ourselves.[29]

According to her classmates, Yulia was a relatively good, but not an ex-cellent, student. Instead of studying hard at home preparing for classes, she preferred to spend her free time outside, watching movies and playing games with her friends. Yet, because of her good memory and quick-wittedness, she always got good grades in school. She recalled, "During my childhood, I did not play the girl games, did not have dolls and avoided friendship with other girls. I preferred friendship with boys, who were more active and inventive than our girls. I was not an aggressive child but I liked the boys' games, especially soccer."[30] Later, in her high school composition, she added: "I am fond of sports, especially of ping pong, skating, and also of sport games such as volleyball, basketball." During this period of time, she entered a special city sports club and joined "a section of sports gymnastics" there. She became a professional female athlete and won the special high rank of "a candidate for a master of Soviet sports" in gymnastics. But during one of her training drills, she fell from the parallel bars and broke her collarbone.[31]

After this accident, she quit sports and spent more time at home. While recuperating, she began reading books. Her reading preferences were shaped by her friends and neighbors, predominantly local boys. Like many of her classmates, she preferred foreign literature with a Russian translation. During the 1970s, until her admission in 1978 as an undergraduate student to the Department of Economics at Dniepropetrovsk State University, she read mostly Western adventure and science fiction stories. The most popular writer for her and her classmates was Alexander Dumas.[32] After 1976, her tastes were also influenced by "girls' literature." The female reading audience in Dniepropetrovsk voraciously read sentimental "love stories" by the nineteenth-century French author Georges Sand. Russian prerevolutionary classic writers with romantically themed stories, such as the "officially permitted" Ivan Turgenev and the "officially forbidden" Ivan Bunin, also influenced female audiences. At the end of the 1970s, even the romantic poetry of the forbidden Russian poet Marina Tsvetaeva circulated among the students at Dniepropetrovsk High School No.75, from which Yulia graduated in 1978. There was no Ukrainian book or poetry among the popular literature, which was read by the students of this school with Russian as the official language of instruction. Even in the Special City School No. 9, where the official languages of instruction were Ukrainian and English, an overwhelming majority of students preferred reading books in Russian.[33] Yulia became a typical representative of this Russian-speaking young generation of Eastern Ukrainians in the 1970s. In post-Soviet times, this generation of Soviet youth would take part in building a new Ukrainian identity among those who never spoke the Ukrainian language during the 1970s.

The Sociology of Book Consumption in Dniepropetrovsk

In 1975, a large proportion of the books in demand at the city libraries of Dniepropetrovsk corresponded to trends that Gusar and Vadimov had noted. Almost 40 percent of the books checked out that year from the main Dniepropetrovsk library were books written by foreign authors, 25 percent were books by prerevolutionary Russian and Ukrainian authors, and 35 percent were books by Soviet Russian and Ukrainian writers. Almost 70 percent of all these books were in Russian and 30 percent were in Ukrainian.[34] To some extent, these numbers correspond to the library statistics in other regions of the Soviet Union during the 1970s.[35] In 1977, in the city libraries of Dniepropetrovsk, more than 98 percent of all readers checked out works of fiction (*khudozhestvennaia literatura*), 65 percent borrowed foreign fiction in Russian, 25 percent borrowed Russian classic literature, 20 percent borrowed books in Ukrainian, and 80 percent borrowed Soviet Russian literature on regular basis.[36]

After 1975, the situation in the book market and in the libraries' records changed. During the late 1970s, new book consumers asked for more foreign literature in Russian translation and for fewer books in Ukrainian. By 1984, the leaders in Dniepropetrovsk book consumption (both on the black market and in public libraries) were books written by Western authors who were traditionally popular among the Soviet reading audience throughout the 1960s and 1970s. Alexander Dumas, Mayne Reid, Arthur Conan Doyle, and Jules Verne, with the addition of Georges Sand, Guy de Maupassant, Jack London, and Somerset Maugham, became the most-read foreign authors among Dniepropetrovsk readers. The proportion of foreign books among all books checked out of the central city library increased from 42 percent in 1979 to almost 60 percent in 1984. At the same time, the number of books in Ukrainian that were checked out plummeted from 30 percent to less than 8 percent.[37]

During the period 1980–84, popular books in Ukrainian (including the books by the forbidden Mykhailo Hrushevsky, Bilyk, and other Ukrainian writers) disappeared from the Dniepropetrovsk black market after they became less profitable for local book dealers. More than 60 percent of all books read in 1980 in Dniepropetrovsk came from private collections and the black market. The majority of private book collectors ignored literature in Ukrainian. They preferred to buy only books in Russian.[38] According to many contemporaries, the books in Ukrainian that people still read and checked out were mainly representatives of *programnaia* literature—books required in the schools for obligatory reading according to the existing Soviet curriculum. These books included works by classical Ukrainian writers such as Taras Shevchenko and Panas Myrnyi, or Soviet Ukrainian writers such as Mykola Bazhan and Pavlo Tychyna. In many cases, local high school students did not read the original works of these writers. They visited the city libraries and took notes from and summarized literary criticism about the Ukrainian literature they were supposed to study. These students used these notes and their summaries for their school papers and tests in Ukrainian literature.[39]

One Dniepropetrovsk librarian, Evgen D. Prudchenko, emphasized that in contrast to the 1960s and 1970s, when young readers loved to read books in Ukrainian, in the 1980s the overwhelming majority of Dniepropetrovsk's youth had stopped reading books in Ukrainian.[40] As Vitalii Pidgaetskii, a former professor of history at Dniepropetrovsk University noted, by the end of the Brezhnev era in Dniepropetrovsk, the overwhelming majority of local readers had lost interest in Ukrainian history and books. According to Pidgaetskii, among the local intellectuals in the 1980s, it became unfashionable to read Ukrainian literature:

Everybody boasted what book of the new Western author he or she read. People were reading a Soviet magazine, *Inostrannaia literatura* [Foreign literature in Russian], and books by fashionable writers from the West. They forgot Ukrainian literature. The Western authors—American, French, German, and Italian—ousted all the Ukrainian writers from local book consumption. Of course, all the new Western books were published in Russian translations. I think that the mass popularity of foreign literature contributed to a gradual replacement of the Ukrainian language with Russian in Dniepropetrovsk's book market. To some extent this popularity of Western literature became a factor in the growing Russification of the local reading audience in Dniepropetrovsk.[41]

Pidgaetskii's observations about the role of book consumption in the Russification of Dniepropetrovsk demonstrate the ties between cultural consumption and social and ethnodemographic developments in Eastern Ukraine. Even the official Soviet scholars of reading and book consumption noted that the popularity of foreign books in Russian translation and Soviet Russian literature among non-Russian readers in national republics such as Ukraine led to a replacement of national languages with Russian in everyday book consumption.[42]

Conclusion

As the summer school and book diaries of those who grew up during the 1970s demonstrate, Soviet youth often read the same books and reacted in similar ways in their book consumption because of the universal standard-ized curriculum of Soviet schools. According to this curriculum, their re-quired reading lists contained books by Western authors that were more popular than books by Soviet and Ukrainian authors. Western adventure novels became tremendously popular among the young and adult audi-ences. In many cases, Dniepropetrovsk's readers preferred Western novels because of the growing fashion to show their connection to the literary prod-ucts of the West. To read (or in many cases, to have in their private collec-tion) prestigious editions of works by fashionable Western authors like Alexander Dumas and Agatha Christie became a sign of a "cultured, civi-lized" person. To have Ukrainian books in private collections was "unfash-ionable" and "out of time."[43] Local readers mainly requested Western books in Russian at the local libraries. By the beginning of the 1980s, books by Western authors (in Russian translation) became the most desirable object of cultural consumption in the closed city.

These trends in cultural consumption also affected the local black mar-ket. In the 1960s and early 1970s, besides foreign music records and Amer-ican jeans, Ukrainian books (especially historical novels and forbidden "na-tionalist literature") were the most popular objects among Dniepropetrovsk's black market customers. After 1975, these customers lost interest in books in Ukrainian. Even good Ukrainian translations of the most fashionable Western authors disappeared from the Dniepropetrovsk book market.

By the mid-1970s, "the reading boom" in the closed city of Dniepro-petrovsk had influenced the black market tremendously and contributed to new skills and building new social and economic connections among the black marketers. The "music mafia," a group of the most notorious *fartsov-shchiks,* who usually sold records and audiotapes, grew throughout the 1970s and gradually established complete control over the book market in Dniepropetrovsk.

The members of this "music mafia" began trading books—particularly foreign books in Russian translations—during the 1970s. By uniting trade in Western books and music, they built connections between book and mu-sic consumption in the closed city. These "music mafia" members, who also included thousands of rock music enthusiasts, became known as the "dis-cotheque mafia" by the end of the 1970s. The members of this "mafia" dominated and influenced all major forms of cultural consumption—especially trade in books and records—in the closed city. Through their connections with Komsomol officials, they built their first "legal businesses" after 1985 and influenced both the economic practices and business ethics of the new post-Soviet Ukrainian elite.

Chapter 8

Crimes from the West: Westerns, the Mafia, and Crime Films

During the 1970s, the mass popularity of foreign films, especially those from the West, became a major concern of both the KGB and Soviet ideologists. Dniepropetrovsk's youth ignored the ideological message of Soviet films and preferred only Western films, which provided local audiences with images and ideas that influenced youth fashions and behavior, and also contributed to identity formation in the closed city. As a result of the practical commercial needs of Soviet officials responsible for releasing movies, these Western films "coexisted" with Soviet films on Soviet screens. Local movie consumers were confused by mixed messages from critics, the KGB, and ideologists about which films were good and which were bad. Moreover, the mass consumption of foreign films with soundtracks dubbed in Russian also contributed to the mass Russification of the young generation of Eastern Ukraine during the 1970s.

Film Consumption Problems in Dniepropetrovsk

Movie theaters were an important socializing location for youth in the city and region of Dniepropetrovsk during the late 1960s and 1970s. The most popular place for the socialization of Soviet youth during the Brezhnev era was the dance floor (*tantsploshchadka*). During the late 1970s, a new form of entertainment, the disco club, enhanced possibilities for the socialization and communication of young people. At the same time, traditional forms of Soviet entertainment, such as movie theaters, attracted both young and middle-aged people.[1] According to some contemporaries, young people sometimes preferred movie theaters to a dance floor. As Evgen D. Prudchenko, a librarian at the Central Library of Dniepropetrovsk Region, noted, "Normally, you can visit a disco club twice or three times a week, when it has a dance party, usually on Wednesdays, Saturdays, and Sundays. The city movie theaters were open seven days a week."[2]

In the Dniepropetrovsk Region, the number of movie theaters increased from 867 in 1960 to 1,214 in 1984, with the number of moviegoers also growing from 51.5 million in 1960 to 54.3 million in 1984.[3] In the city of Dniepropetrovsk alone, the number of modern movie theaters grew from three in 1950 to sixteen in 1980. On average, each city dweller attended from fourteen to seventeen movie performances a year. According to the All-Union film magazine *Sovetskii ekran,* these numbers were close to the general Soviet statistics. In the USSR, the average Soviet citizen visited movie theaters eighteen times during 1966 and nineteen times during 1970.[4] According to the All-Union survey of *Sovetskii ekran*'s readers younger than fourteen years old, Soviet middle and high school students were the most active consumers of movies. In the year 1972–73, almost half these readers watched from ten to thirty films monthly. Almost 30 percent of the young filmgoers watched two films per day on television, and a half of these visited a movie theater once or twice a week.[5] According to the personal diaries of Dniepropetrovsk middle school students, during the normal school week in the 1970s, each of them watched two or three movies a week. During the school breaks, they usually watched six to seven films a week.[6]

Another favorite place for city filmgoers was a palace (or house) of culture. Each palace of culture in Dniepropetrovsk had also a film projector and movie auditorium. All Soviet palaces of culture usually showed movies during weekends. Palaces of culture in the larger cities showed films every night. The number of palaces of culture in Dniepropetrovsk with movie auditoriums grew from 16 in 1950 to 56 in 1980. In the entire region, the number of palaces of culture with movie auditoriums increased from 560 in 1970 to 652 in 1984.[7]

According to official statistics, Soviet films were the most popular. Some films—especially Soviet comedy, adventure, and detective films—achieved sensational popularity among filmgoers. During the period 1968–70, four films had phenomenal box office success all over the USSR. In 1969, a comedy film directed by Leonid Gaidai, *Brilliantovaia ruka (Diamond Arm),* attracted 76.7 million moviegoers. Another comedy by the same director, *Kavkazskaia plennitsa (Caucasian Captive),* attracted 76.5 million people annually. A comedy film about the Soviet Civil War, *Svad'ba v Malinovke*

(*A Marriage in Malinovka*), was a success with 74.6 million viewers. The first part of the adventure movie about the Soviet spy who penetrated Nazi intelligence during World War II, *Shchit i mech* (*Shield and Sword*), boasted 68.3 million moviegoers annually. The sequel to *Neulovimye mstiteli* (*The Elusive Avengers*), the film about young heroes of the Civil War, *Novye prikliuchenia neulovimykh* (*New Adventures of the Elusive Avengers*), attracted 66.2 million younger filmgoers.[8]

Dniepropetrovsk's audiences also loved these films. Soviet films were very popular in the city and the region during the 1970s, and even in the early 1980s. Besides these traditional blockbusters, new foreign films from the West attracted young moviegoers as early as the 1960s. Film consumption in Dniepropetrovsk became more and more "Westernized." The local ideologists and KGB operatives constantly complained about the negative role of "films from the West" that "transformed a spiritual world" of the Soviet youth and "polluted the pure soul of the Soviet child with alien ideas and dangerous expectations."[9]

According to the former Soviet and now American sociologist Vladimir Shlapentokh, movies from Western countries were especially popular among Soviet intellectuals and Soviet youth. As he noted, "of 250 to 300 films shown each year" in the Soviet Union, "the number of foreign origin does not exceed 25 to 30, a ratio of 10 to 1. . . . Although there is no direct data on the attendance at foreign movies, there is much indirect evidence that shows they are quite popular, often more so than Soviet ones. According to official data, among the ten most attended movies, two were foreign, which means that the average popularity of a western movie is at least two times higher than a Soviet film."[10] Just in 1973 alone, the main Soviet authority for the acquisition and distribution of foreign films, Soveksportfilm, bought more than 150 feature films from seventy countries. During the period of détente, this number grew. More Western films reached Soviet moviegoers by the end of the 1970s than in the previous decade. During the entire Brezhnev era, the few Western movies released in the Soviet Union played a more significant role in the "Westernization" of Soviet youth than Western popular music or books.[11]

Authentic American Westerns and Their Substitutes

The first American movie that influenced millions of Soviet children at the end of the Khrushchev era was the American western *The Magnificent Seven.*

This remake of the Japanese classic *Seven Samurai,* directed by John Sturges and featuring the Russian-born movie star Yul Brynner, was originally released in the United States in 1960.[12] During the summer of 1962 and the fall of 1963, it appeared in movie theaters all over the Soviet Union and became an immediate sensation among young moviegoers. It was the first original American western film that had ever reached the Soviet audience since the 1940s. (Stalin only permitted one original American western, John Ford's *Stagecoach,* renamed *The Trip Will Be Dangerous,* to be shown in Moscow after the war.)[13] During the first years of the Brezhnev era, this film was widely shown in the region of Dniepropetrovsk. In the summer of 1966, *The Magnificent Seven* was still the most popular movie in the city. During the summer, most local schools were on summer break. Thousands of students visited Dniepropetrovsk's movie theaters, which showed this American western as early as June 20 and kept it on screens until the end of August.[14]

The immense popularity of western films such as *The Magnificent Seven* among local youth worried Dniepropetrovsk's ideologists. Young Pioneers and Komsomol members only wanted to watch the action and adventure stories portrayed in western films. They ignored boring Soviet movies. Local journalists singled out the most popular films among Dniepropetrovsk's moviegoers during the summer of 1966. Their list included films such as *The Magnificent Seven, Thief of Baghdad, Lemonade Joe, The Iron Mask,* and *Scaramouche.* There was no Soviet film on this list.[15] On July 19, 1966, a fourteen-year-old high school student wrote in his summer diary:

> Today I watched *Velikolepnaia semiorka* [*The Magnificent Seven*] for the fifth time during this year. It is a great film full of action and humor. I want more "cowboy films." Unfortunately, we have none of them in our movie theaters except the Czech comedy *Lemonade Joe.* Tomorrow I will go to watch another "cool" [*klassnyi*] film, *The Three Musketeers.* Day after tomorrow, I and my friends will go to see *The Iron Mask,* a French sequel to *The Three Musketeers.* Jean Marais played a role of old D'Artagnan, who is in charge of the man in the iron mask. If I will find some extra money, I plan to watch another French film with Jean Marais, *The Mysteries of Paris.*

And he added later, "People praised a new American comedy *V dzhaze tol'ko devushki* [*Some Like It Hot*] as a funny film. I need to watch it as well."[16] It is noteworthy that this Soviet high school student did not mention a single Soviet movie in his diary. During the entire summer of 1966, he only watched Western adventure and comedy films. According to his diary, his favorite films included two American movies (one a western and the other a comedy) and three French historical adventure films based on Alexander Dumas's and Eugène Sue's novels.[17]

In the 1970s, Dniepropetrovsk's youth still preferred Western action films. They still loved to watch either French "historical" films about adventurous musketeers and beautiful Angelique or "cowboy" films.[18] The summer diaries of local students were preoccupied with such adventure films. The Communist Party and Komsomol leaders noted the same preferences not only among high school and vocational school students but also among local young workers and intellectuals. According to Serhiy Tihipko, "cowboy" movies and western films led to mass hysteria (*massovaia isteria*) and "a weird imitation of cowboy style of behavior" among the local youth.[19]

During the Brezhnev era, the Soviet administration released only two original American western movies on screen, *My Darling Clementine* and *Mackenna's Gold*. The first film, directed by John Ford, was a black-and-white western classic of 1946. This western featured famous American movie stars such as Henry Fonda. Fonda played the role of Wyatt Earp, who became the marshal of the Arizona town Tombstone to avenge the death of his brother.[20] The central Soviet film magazine, *Sovetskii ekran,* immediately praised this film after its release in the Soviet Union in 1975.[21] A Soviet journalist wrote a very positive review, describing it as "a real masterpiece even after 30 years of its original release in the USA, which still looks fresh as a great and talented jewel of the western genre." As this journalist noted, "In his movie, Ford contrasted a character with a revolver, a central figure of the traditional western with the everyday human truths, a purity of the simple life, eternal earth; the earth that absorbs everything, from the most bitter to the highest elements, and that always remains the everlasting earth which is necessary for the human survival."[22]

It is noteworthy that the most respectable Soviet film magazines praised and idealized the western genre, which, according to Dniepropetrovsk's ideologists, was an expression of American imperialism and aggression.[23] Soviet film critics usually rejected the movies of American film directors and actors who criticized the Soviet Union or made anti-Soviet films. The American actor John Wayne was officially considered a symbol of American imperialism and militarism by the Soviet press. Therefore all his films, including classic Hollywood westerns, were banned in the Soviet Union.[24]

In the 1970s, Dniepropetrovsk's KGB officers used reviews by Soviet film critics of "the reactionary cowboy John Wayne" to justify their official prohibition of American westerns in the closed city. As a result, *My Darling Clementine* did not last long in Dniepropetrovsk's movie theaters. This Hollywood western was shown in the city for less than a month in February 1975.[25] Unfortunately for Soviet youth, this interesting western was released too late. Moreover, it was a black-and-white film and too slow and boring for young Soviet moviegoers.[26]

As recently as 1974, these young moviegoers enjoyed another American production, *Mackenna's Gold,* which became a cult western movie for millions of young filmgoers all over the Soviet Union. This American western in color was directed by J. Lee Thompson, and it had been released in the United States in 1969. When it reached Soviet audiences in 1974, it produced a real sensation, especially among young moviegoers. Even Soviet film critics praised it as a "real authentic American western." Though they criticized the film for not being a masterpiece, they contrasted it positively with "the bad substitutes" of western films that flourished on Soviet film screen for decades.[27] The overcrowded movie theaters all over the Soviet Union during showings of *Mackenna's Gold* testified that the Soviet audience's hunger for American adventure films grew during the 1970s.[28]

Between 1966, the last year of the showing of *The Magnificent Seven* in Soviet movie theaters, and 1977, the year of the immense popularity of *Mackenna's Gold* among Soviet filmgoers, the most popular form of adventure film on the Soviet screen was what one Soviet film critic called "the substitutes of the American westerns."[29] These substitutes primarily consisted of cowboy films from the socialist European countries. One of these films was *Lemonade Joe, or a Horse Opera,* a musical parody of Hollywood westerns from the Czech director Oldrich Lipsky that was released by the Barrandov Films studio in Prague in 1964. In the film, the main character, Lemonade Joe, dresses in white from head to toe and rides into a town called Stetson City, bringing law and order and lemonade (called Kolaloka) to the frontier, while rescuing a beautiful girl from the clutches of a bad guy who drinks only hard alcohol. The beverage Joe promotes, Kolaloka, ensures that all the film's characters who were killed in the shooting are all brought back to life, and the ending is presided over by Joe's father, president of the Kolaloka Company. In this scene, Joe and his girlfriend "go off on the next stagecoach and, in true capitalist fashion, a new company and a new drink are created: Whiskykola, which can be drunk by both teetotallers and alcoholics."[30] American film critics also praised this Czech satire of American westerns as "a delightful, thoroughly enjoyable and hilarious from the start to finish."[31] From 1965 to 1970, *Lemonade Joe* was shown all over the Soviet Union and was also praised by more Soviet film critics.[32]

According to contemporaries, various jokes from this Czech film became part of the street jargon in Dniepropetrovsk and other Soviet cities. After *The Magnificent Seven,* the Czech parody became the most popular western film among Dniepropetrovsk youth at the end of the 1960s.[33] If American westerns were most popular among young audiences, especially among middle and high school students, *Lemonade Joe* became a favorite of young intellectuals, especially college students. As Vitalii Pidgaetskii, a former professor of history from Dniepropetrovsk University, recalled, knowledge of the jokes from the Czech film became a marker of intellectual ability and a good sense of humor:

> Everybody had to demonstrate his level of intelligence and mention some jokes from this film in a conversation with his intellectual friends. Jokes about "Kolaloka" beverage or "mixture number one," meaning a heavy fuel of alcohol, sulphuric acid, and pepper, survived the film and existed in the student society till the beginning of the 1970s. For many young intellectuals, a Czech film parody about cowboys became a connecting point between our boring life in the closed Soviet city and an opened society of free and humorous spirit which we associated with the West and Czechoslovakia as a legitimate socialist substitute [*zamenitel*] of the capitalist West.[34]

In 1967, a new "socialist substitute" for American westerns reached Dniepropetrovsk's movie theaters. This was *The Sons of Great Mother Bear,* an East German film released by the DEFA film studio in 1965–66.[35] From this time on (until the beginning of the 1980s), what were called East German "Indian films" dominated the Soviet screen. And because of Gojko Mitic, a Yugoslavian student of physical education turned actor who played major parts in the DEFA Indian films, these films became the most important type of western movie for many children. These films about the resistance movement of indigenous American people during the expansion of white settlers in the eighteenth and nineteenth centuries were the most important and influential substitutes for Hollywood westerns in Soviet popular culture. One eleven-year-old boy wrote in his summer diary on June 22, 1970, "In the evening I saw a bright advertisement that on June 24–25, our local theater will show the films about the Indians. I will go to watch these movies without fail (if my mom will give me money for the tickets)." Two days later, on June 24, he added a new entry in his diary:

> Tonight I watched *The Sons of Great Mother Bear* and *Chingachgook, the Great Snake,* about the American Indians. I had read such books before. [He obviously referred to the novels by the East German author Liselotte Welskopf-Henrich and American writer James Fenimore Cooper.] The first film is about the Dakota tribe and their brave chief Tokei-ito, and how they struggled with white greedy settlers who were looking for gold on the Indian tribal land. Eventually the Dakota Indians escaped from the reservation and settled on the free land. The second film is based on Cooper's novel *Zveroboi* [*The Deerslayer*] and tells a story of the friendship of a white trapper and a Delaware Indian Chingachgook. Hurons stole a Chingachgook's bride. A Delaware Indian with his white friend saved her. I liked these films very much, and I watched them a fifth time.[36]

The Sons of Great Mother Bear and *Chingachgook, the Great Snake* were two of twelve East German films produced by the DEFA studios between 1965 and 1983. These DEFA Indian films were shot on location in Yugoslavia, Czechoslovakia, Romania, Bulgaria, and the Soviet Union, and were produced by East German film directors such as Josef Mach, Richard Groschopp, Gottfried Kolditz, and Konrad Petzold. They articulated "an outspoken critique of the colonialism and racism that fueled the westward expansion of the United States."[37] According to scholars who study East German films,

> [The DEFA Indian movies] contain many of the ingredients that make for a good Hollywood western: the ambush of the stage coach, the attack on the railroad, fist fights and shoot-outs, swinging bar doors, Indians on the war path attacking an army fort, etc. And like most Hollywood westerns, these films have a clear division of good guys and bad guys— except that in the DEFA films sympathy lies exclusively with the tribe and their heroic chief [always played by Mitic] in their struggle against greedy white settlers, treaty-breaking army colonels, corrupt sheriffs, imperialist oil magnates, and plantation owners.[38]

At the same time, the DEFA Indian films played a very important ideological role. For the people in socialist countries, they provided their own, socialist, alternative to capitalist forms of entertainment like Hollywood westerns.[39] Initially, socialist ideologists used Mitic's films as a "socialist response" to capitalist westerns and promoted Mitic as a positive role model in contrast to the superheroes of Hollywood.[40]

Although the Soviet officials responsible for releasing the DEFA Indian films in the USSR supported Mitic's anticapitalist message, Soviet film experts ignored this message and apparently preferred traditional Hollywood westerns. From the beginning of the DEFA Indian films' popularity in 1967, official Soviet film critics were unenthusiastic about the German "substitutes" for Hollywood westerns. *The Sons of Great Mother Bear* was severely criticized in *Sovetskii ekran* as "a bad and stupid imitation of the old Hollywood western films," which, according to a Soviet journalist, were "the best representatives of the cowboy-Indian movie genre." Soviet film critics even called the DEFA Indian films as "the funeral repast [*pominki*] for the classic westerns." Despite their critical Marxist analysis of "the Hollywood capitalist movie industry," they acknowledged the authenticity and inventiveness of the American westerns such as *The Magnificent Seven,* which just recently had captivated Soviet moviegoers in 1963–66.[41]

When, in 1968, a new DEFA film with Mitic, *Chingachgook, the Great Snake,* was released in the Soviet Union together with the West German productions of *Shatterhand Is a Friend of the Indians* (*Vernaia ruka—drug indeitsev*) and *Winnetou—a Chief of Apaches,* Soviet journalists also brutally criticized these imitations of American westerns. The West German director Harald Reinl made a film trilogy based on the novels of the German writer Karl May about the friendship of a white trapper, Old Shatterhand, and an Indian chief, Winnetou.[42] Although this trilogy had originally been released before the DEFA films, Soviet movie theaters showed both the West German and DEFA westerns ("the films about cowboys and Indians," according to the Soviet terminology) during the same period, 1968–72. Soviet journalists ridiculed the numerous mistakes and inconsistencies in the DEFA and West German film adaptations of classic novels by Cooper and May. They recommended that Soviet filmgoers (especially the young ones) reread the literary originals rather than watch these "bad and awkward interpretations of the old good American classical westerns."[43] Despite all this criticism, an overwhelming majority of the readers of the most popular Soviet film magazine, *Soviet ekran,* praised the West German film *Winnetou—a Chief of Apaches* as one of the best foreign films of 1969. According to the All-Union statistics about the phenomenal box office success of this film and a survey of the magazine's readers, *Winnetou—a Chief of Apaches* became even more popular than all the DEFA Indian films among Soviet film-goers by the end of 1969.[44]

By the late 1960s, even childhood identity in Dniepropetrovsk was affected by the German westerns. Local children now preferred to play cowboys and American Indians, and they imitated the behavior of their favorite heroes played by Mitic and West German actors. All personal diaries of local middle school students at the end of the 1960s and beginning of the 1970s included entries about playing games of American Indians during their summer school breaks. Usually the images from Indian films inspired various games imitating events in the films.[45]

Both Communist ideologists and KGB operatives worried about this new cowboy fashion on the streets of Dniepropetrovsk. As one KGB officer complained,

> You will hardly see the Soviet patriotic games among our kids nowadays. They forgot their old games in the Reds and the Whites, in the Russians and the Germans [Nazis]. All they know is the games in American cowboys and Indians. Where are the games about Ukrainian Cossacks and Turks, about our own Ukrainian history?[46]

He praised the cartoon films of the Ukrainian director V. Dakhno about the adventures of the Ukrainian Cossacks and the film *Chiortova diuzhina* (*The Hell's Dozen*) as good examples of Ukrainian patriotic adventure movies. *The Hell's Dozen* was a new historical feature film made in an Odessa studio by the Ukrainian director V. Savchenko about a group of Zaporizhian Cossacks who escaped into the Caspian Sea from the oppression of the Russian Empire under the rule of Catherine the Great.[47]

During the late 1960s and the 1970s, even conservative Ukrainian film critics who had at first rejected any cowboy movie as "ideological pollution," finally acknowledged the favorable role of the DEFA Indian films because of their "positive anticapitalist message." They especially praised two actors who represented the anti-imperialist and anti-American spirit of East German films. On of these was Mitic; and the other was the American protest singer Dean Reed, who lived in East Germany and publicly criticized the imperialistic politics of the United States. A Ukrainian film magazine published a series of articles written by East German journalists about the positive role of the DEFA Indian films and their stars such as Mitic and Reed. Many young filmgoers in Dniepropetrovsk interpreted the publication of these articles as giving official approval of their favorite genre.[48]

During the same period, Soviet ideologists supported the idea of showing Soviet adventure films about the Civil War, such as the series *Elusive Avengers* and *Beloe solntse pustyni* (*The White Sun of the Desert*). In these films, the Reds played the role of the good Indians and the Whites substituted for the bad cowboys.[49] Soviet ideologists considered these films to be an antidote against "the cowboy film mania" among Soviet youth. Although they acknowledged the American western clichés of these films, they tried to use such patriotic Soviet films to combat the growing interest in Western action films. In practice, this led to a strange situation: The young audience could watch DEFA Indian films, Western adventure films, and Soviet adventure films such as *Beloe solntse pustyni* during the same week, on the same day, sometimes in the same theaters.[50]

In Dniepropetrovsk, a series of Indian film showings began on January 17, 1967, with *The Sons of Great Mother Bear* playing in all central city movie theaters. In July 1968, *Shatterhand Is a Friend of the Indians* began playing; and in August, *Chingachgook, the Great Snake* followed. In December 1969, the West German Indian film *Winnetou—a Chief of Apaches,* a sequel to *Shatterhand Is a Friend of the Indians,* captivated the imagination of Dniepropetrovsk's moviegoers.[51] During the period 1970–73, the DEFA Indian films with Mitic—such as *Sled Sokola* (*A Track of Falcon*), *Belye volki* (*The White Wolfs*), *Otseola: The Seminoles' Chief,* and *Tekumse* —became the most popular among the non-Soviet adventure films on Dniepropetrovsk's screens.[52]

The famous Western European substitutes for Hollywood westerns, the Italian cowboy films known as spaghetti westerns, did not affect Dniepropetrovsk's moviegoers. To some extent, this lack of effect was related to the ideological disapproval of this genre by Soviet film critics. These critics accepted the authenticity of the old Hollywood westerns as the classics of the genre. For them, the Italian cowboy films were "the worst commercial and purely capitalist imitations" of the old classics. Traditionally, Soviet film critics highly praised the Italian Neorealist film directors like Vittorio De Sica, Luchino Visconti, and Federico Fellini.[53] The Italian cowboy films did not fit the traditional Soviet description of progressive Italian moviemaking. They looked like bad "inhuman imitations" of the American movies. Soviet film magazines criticized Italian cowboy film directors as "repetitious and greedy people of poor taste and imagination." Some critics even accused the Italian master of spaghetti westerns, Sergio Leone, of an "Americanization of the Italian cinema."[54] After such criticism, the Soviet administration preferred to buy films from progressive Italian directors rather than Italian spaghetti westerns from the "commercial imitators of Hollywood" such as Leone.

Occasionally, the Soviet audience could watch Leone's spaghetti westerns in Moscow during the special film programs of the International Film Festivals or the Weeks of Friendship with Italy.[55] In June 1971, Aleksandr Gusar, a middle school student from the Dniepropetrovsk Region, came with his mother to visit his older brother, an undergraduate student of physics at Moscow Physical Technical Institute. His brother brought Gusar and his mother to a Moscow movie theater where they watched Leone's spaghetti western *For a Few Dollars More*.[56] This film had already been shown in 1969 in Moscow as "a nonparticipant of the Moscow International Film Festival" and had attracted crowds of Soviet moviegoers. During the summer of 1971, some old westerns such as *The Magnificent Seven* and *For a Few Dollars More* were included in a "cowboy" film program of the special retrospective movie theater (*kinoteatr povtornogo fil'ma*) in downtown Moscow. Aleksandr's brother, who knew that such film programs did not exist in provincial Soviet cities, decided to bring his family to a showing of the foreign westerns that were impossible to find in Dniepropetrovsk. As Gusar noted the words of his brother,

> You can't watch the real westerns from the West in your closed city. Only one Soviet city, Moscow, permits to do this. Enjoy the freedom of the open city![57]

In contrast to Moscow, Dniepropetrovsk had more limits on Western cultural products, including Italian spaghetti westerns.

Only one Italian spaghetti western, *Zolotaia pulia* (*A Golden Bullet*), reached moviegoers in the Soviet provincial cities such as Dniepropetrovsk in 1968. This film with the original Italian title was *Quien Sabe?* was made in 1966 by the Italian director Damiano Damiani.[58] Because of Damiani's pro-Soviet and leftist sympathies, the Soviet authorities released all his major films in the Soviet Union in the 1960s and 1970s. *Zolotaia pulia* was the first of Damiani's film to reach the Soviet audience. Franco Solinas, a Marxist writer who adored Sergei Eisenstein's films, wrote the script for *Zolotaia pulia*. Moreover, *Zolotaia pulia* was considered by Soviet film critics as an anti-American film and therefore ideologically reliable, with its obvious allusions to the recent assassinations of American political leaders and violence.[59] *Zolotaia pulia*, which is set at the height of the Mexican Revolution (1910–17), tells the story of a Mexican gunrunner, El Chuncho; his half-brother, Santo, a fervent revolutionary and priest; and a gringo outlaw, Bill Tate. Bill was an American assassin who killed a revolutionary Mexican general for money. El Chuncho, who had liked the young gringo from the beginning, was so enraged by Bill's crime that he rejected the money Bill offered and shot the American as a traitor of the revolution.[60]

From the end of 1968 to the beginning of the 1970s, *Zolotaia pulia* competed with the DEFA Indian films on the screens of Soviet Ukraine. It is noteworthy that the young female filmgoers, who were predominantly middle and high school students, preferred Mitic's films. The older (and mainly male) audience, college students and young professionals, praised Damiani's western. As the seventeen-year-old Vladimir Solodovnik noted in his diary in 1968, "only excited kids without brains could enjoy stupid Gojko Mitic films, everybody who thinks a little bit will watch *Zolotaia pulia.*"[61] The former singer for the band Dniepriane, Tatiana Yeriomenko, thought that the young female audience preferred the DEFA Indian films because they had less violence and "more humanity" then the "bloody" Western adventure films, including Damiani's western. The female audience found the romantic image of handsome Mitic more attractive than the realistic and brutal male characters in Damiani's film.[62] The future female politicians of post-Soviet Ukraine, such as Yulia Tymoshenko, grew up in the 1970s watching DEFA westerns and dreaming about having boyfriends who looked like Mitic. For them, Mitic was not only their first action movie hero but also an idealized image of "the man from the West."[63]

The only original western film that attracted both male and female audiences was *Zoloto Makenny* (*Mackenna's Gold*), a real Hollywood western in color. This 1969 American movie, directed by J. Lee Thompson, became a blockbuster film in the city and region of Dniepropetrovsk immediately after its release in the Soviet Union, during the entire time of the school summer break, from June to August 1974.[64] *Mackenna's Gold* told a romantic story of adventure, love, greed, and a search for lost treasure that was typical for all kinds of westerns on the Soviet screen. However, for the Soviet audience of the Brezhnev era, *Mackenna's Gold* was the first authentic Hollywood western. Many young viewers of this film had never seen a real Hollywood western. Only the older viewers remembered *The Magnificent Seven,* which was released during the Khrushchev era. For the young generation of filmgoers, *Mackenna's Gold* was a real cultural product from the real, authentic West: the United States of America. It was not an East German or Winnetou substitute for a western film; it was the real thing.[65]

The main character in *Mackenna's Gold,* Marshal Sam Mackenna (played by Gregory Peck), learns during his travels in the Arizona Territory in the 1870s that the secret lost treasure of the fabulous Golden Canyon is protected by the local Indians as a sacred place. He is captured by the Mexican bandit Colorado (Omar Sharif), who has long sought to kill Mackenna. But Colorado must keep Mackenna alive because the marshal is the only living person who knows the route to the Indian treasure in the Golden Canyon. Eventually, Mackenna not only escapes alive but also gains a beautiful girl and the Indian gold as his prize, while Colorado fails and loses his gang and his spoils. Some American film critics considered *Mackenna's Gold* to be a mediocre western film, without "a single redeeming quality."[66]

For Soviet filmgoers, however, *Mackenna's Gold* was the best western film they had ever seen. Its setting contributed to its immense popularity. The beautiful landscapes of Arizona and the naked body of the beautiful Indian girl shown in the film became part of authentic American exotica. As Vitalii Pidgaetskii noted, Soviet moviegoers finally saw the real American West on a big screen in color with familiar actors who became legitimate representatives of progressive American cinema in the Soviet Union. Pidgaetskii particularly referred to Peck, the favorite American movie star among Soviet film critics.[67] The film's music also attracted the young Soviet audience. Its original musical score was written by the legendary Quincy Jones. José Feliciano sang the theme song "Old Turkey Buzzard." In the Soviet release of the film, a popular Soviet singer, Valerii Obodzinskii, covered the theme song with a new one in Russian about how gold led humans to destruction. Still, even with this change, the song sounded like a new non-Soviet, Western popular song that was similar to the Western "beat music" of the 1960s. As a result of all these elements, *Mackenna's Gold* became a box office success and Obodzinskii's song about gold was a hit in 1974.[68]

According to the summer diaries of high school students, *Mackenna's Gold* was shocking to many Soviet people who were used to the traditional clichés of the DEFA Indian films. Andrei Vadimov watched this film each weekend during late August 1974 and considered it to be the best representative of the "cowboy films." He noted in his diary, "I can't stand these faked Indians in the DEFA films anymore [*sic*]."[69] As a fifteen-year-old student, Gusar wrote on August 12, 1974, after watching this film,

I fell in love with this movie from the beginning. I had never seen such films before. I am unable to compare this film to any adventure movie about cowboys and Indians. *Zoloto Makenny* is a unique movie. I would never watch Gojko Mitic films after this masterpiece of adventure films.

Gusar watched this film more than twenty times during the year 1974–75.[70] Twelve-year-old Mikhail Suvorov watched it more than fifty times.[71] Even fifteen-year-old Natalia Vasilenko and Tatiana Yeriomenko, who hated the violence and shootings in western films, watched this movie no fewer than ten times.[72] All Soviet youth loved *Mackenna's Gold.* Fascination with this American film was noted everywhere in the Soviet Union.[73] Sometimes this fascination affected school discipline, especially during June 1974, when this film premiered in Dniepropetrovsk. Instead of participating in school Komsomol meetings, the classmates of Mikhail Suvorov, a future disco movement activist, and of Yulia Grigian (Tymoshenko), a future Ukrainian prime minister, left school for a neighboring movie theater and took their place in the long lines of people at the theater box office waiting for a ticket for *Mackenna's Gold.* As Suvorov explained, many of his classmates who ignored the Komsomol meeting were very good students and loyal Komsomol members. All of them were punished by a school principal, who, a week later, organized a special meeting of his school Komsomol members and criticized "the ideological danger of such imperialist movies" as *Mackenna's Gold.*[74]

Because of the immense popularity of *Mackenna's Gold,* the traditional box office hits, both the DEFA Indian films and West German Winnetou series, became less appealing to audiences by the end of 1974. Even the best of the West German films about Winnetou, *The Treasure of Silver Lake,* which had been widely shown in all Dniepropetrovsk's movie theaters just a week before the release of *Mackenna's Gold,* failed to attract the young filmgoers. According to movie statistics and the personal diaries of contemporaries, only two western films continued to attract an audience during the period 1974–79. One was the western substitute, the old Czech western parody of 1964, *Lemonade Joe.* The other popular western was an authentic American western movie, *Mackenna's Gold.*[75]

The Sandpit Generals, Martial Arts, and Gangs in Film

For the Communist Party and KGB apparatchiks, the mass popularity of American films such as *Mackenna's Gold* raised questions about the "dangerous imitation" of Western capitalist cultural forms by local youth. A

KGB officer who had supervised the activities of Dniepropetrovsk's youth in the 1970s and 1980s noted, "Three feature films from the West produced real hysterias of imitation among Dniepropetrovsk secondary school and college students. These movies were two American films, *Mackenna's Gold* and *The Sandpit Generals,* and one British film, *O Lucky Man!*" The British film, directed by Lindsey Anderson, was connected to the old "rock music obsession," which revealed itself again in August 1975 when rock-and-roll fans waited in long lines for a movie ticket to watch the legendary Alan Price from the British band the Animals perform his songs for this film.[76]

However, two American films created more serious problems than "the rock music obsession." According to police records, the first two films were connected to an increase in crime among Dniepropetrovsk's youth. Soviet officials complained that the imitation of American films had led to numerous criminal acts on the city's streets. "We knew that these American films [*Mackenna's Gold* and *The Sandpit Generals*] were made by the leftist sympathizers of our country," a KGB officer told, "but the forms of behavior portrayed in these films were inappropriate for our Komsomol young people. Our youth blindly imitated the antisocial criminal behavior of their film heroes, American cowboys and juvenile delinquents from *Generaly peschanykh karierov.*"[77]

This KGB officer referred to the American film, *Generaly peschanykh karierov* (*The Sandpit Generals*), which became a real cult film for millions of young filmgoers all over the Soviet Union. Originally released in 1970 in the United States under the title *The Defiant* (or *The Wild Pack*), this movie was produced and directed by Hall Bartlett. The film never became popular in the United States like it did in the Soviet Union. Based on a novel by the Brazilian writer Jorge Amado, *Captains of the Sand* (*Capitães da areia*), this movie tells the story of a gang of homeless children led by Pedro Bala ("a bullet" in English). Set in Bahia, Brazil, the film follows the adventures of Bala's gang of underage outlaws as they steal, rape, find love, practice *capoeira* (a Brazilian form of martial arts), and follow their African-Brazilian religion. During the summer of 1971, under the title *The Sandpit Generals,* this film was shown at the Seventh Moscow International Film Festival.[78] In 1973, *The Sandpit Generals* was released in the Soviet Union to the general public.[79]

Millions of Soviet young people fell in love with this American film in 1973 and 1974. Its soundtrack, by Darival Caymmi, became a point of cultural fixation for Soviet rock music fans, who had previously listened to the Beatles and Deep Purple and rejected Soviet *estrada* songs (pop music). On this soundtrack, they discovered musical themes that they connected to their perception of authentic Western music.[80] Meanwhile, Soviet film critics praised both the film's realistic anticapitalist story and music. They noted that the film's criminal storyline ended in a mass demonstration against the capitalist establishment, and its theme song by Caymmi became the musical symbol of youthful social protest against the capitalist system of social injustice and exploitation. Strangely enough, the official appraisal of the film as a decent and honest critique of capitalist society coincided with the popular fascination with the film among its young Soviet audience.[81] This fascination, mixed with nostalgia, is still evident in the numerous Web site reviews of this film written by former Soviet citizens.[82] Like many cultural products of the West, *The Sandpit Generals* became a typical cultural fixation for Soviet youth.

In November 1973, *The Sandpit Generals* reached Dniepropetrovsk's movie theaters. During the entire month of November, the American film became a box office hit in all the city's major theaters. By December, youth throughout the region preferred only this film over the other blockbusters on Soviet screens.[83] The local administration responsible for the film's distribution in the Dniepropetrovsk Region decided to show *The Sandpit Generals* again during the summer of 1974. In July and August of that year, the film successfully competed with another American sensation of the season, *Mackenna's Gold*.[84] Both Andrei Vadimov and Aleksandr Gusar, fourteen- and fifteen-year-old high school students, expressed their fascination with Bartlett's film in their diaries. On June 28, Gusar wrote: "I remember each scene from *Generaly* [*The Sandpit Generals*]. But still I am going to watch this film the third time tomorrow and memorize a melody of this song by heart."[85] When the Soviet youth magazine *Rovesnik* published the lyrics and sheet music of the song, many young enthusiasts of the story about Brazilian criminal gangs copied the Russian translation of the song's lyrics from the magazine into their notebooks. As Vadimov noted on August 16, "We have a long line of my friends waiting for an issue of *Rovesnik* with this famous song and its Russian text by a Soviet poet B. Sen'kin. Everybody wants to write down the lyrics in their albums and notebooks. I copied this text by myself into my diary together with lyrics from *Jesus Christ Superstar*. The song from *Generaly* sounds like a real American song, only in Portuguese!"[86] Thus, this high school student treated the lyrics from his favorite American film as a cultural object worthy of keeping, along with another symbol of authentic Western cultural products, the lyrics from his favorite rock opera.

Dniepropetrovsk's Communist Party and Komsomol leaders worried about growing crime rates among local youth in the 1970s. According to the official data, more than 28,000 young people committed various crimes annually in the city. Almost 72 percent of all crimes in the city were committed by young people. During a discussion of the criminal situation and leisure time of local youth in 1975, both the police and Komsomol ideologists noted the negative role of the "films from the West" in "producing the negative role models for personal behavior." Many arrested young "hooligans" associated themselves either with Colorado, the gang leader in *Mackenna's Gold,* or with the young criminals in *The Sandpit Generals.*[87] Some police officers emphasized emotional factors such as Western popular songs, including the soundtrack from *The Sandpit Generals,* which led to the imitation of "the alien forms of martial arts, fistfights and karate." The police complained about widespread criminal acts of violence and "hooliganism," which involved "a use of forbidden forms of foreign wrestling." Some of the young criminals cited the film *The Sandpit Generals* as their information source about these forms of wrestling.[88] As a KGB officer explained, "These acts if imitation were reminiscent of the two criminal film manias in the late 1960s; one was related to three French comedy films about Fantomas and another was a reaction to a Japanese film *A Judo Genius [Judo Saga].*"[89]

The Cult of *Fantomas* and Film Noir in the Closed City

The French remake of the legendary "film noir" series of 1913–14 by the French director Louis Feuillade about a mysterious criminal, Fantomas, was produced and directed as a *Fantomas* trilogy by Andre Hunebelle in 1964–66. It was released in the Soviet Union during the summer of 1967 and was immediately well received by Soviet film critics.[90] The trilogy's first film, titled *Fantomas,* reached Dniepropetrovsk's movie theaters in July 1967. The second film, *Fantomas Enraged,* was released in Dniepropetrovsk a few months later.[91] The third film, *Fantomas against Scotland Yard,* was shown in Dniepropetrovsk's movie theaters six years later, in 1973. As had happened before, this French film, originally released in color, was shown in black and white in Soviet movie theaters.[92]

In the first film, the criminal mastermind Fantomas, a man of a thousand artificial faces, becomes unhappy with Fandor, a journalist who has written a fictive interview with him. He kidnaps Fandor and threatens to kill him, but first goes about ruining the journalist's reputation by committing a sensational crime in Fandor's guise. As a good boxer, Fandor performs spectacular fistfights, sometimes even beating the best of Fantomas's bodyguards. On the trail is a police *commissaire*, Juve, so Fantomas commits a crime looking like him. Soon Fandor and Juve, with the help of Fandor's girlfriend Hélène, are on the mastermind's trail, but Fantomas escapes with the help of various technical devices, from fantastic remote control to a minisubmarine. In the second film, Fantomas plans to create a superweapon that would allow him to dominate human wills and establish global domination. Because he needs assistance from serious researchers, he kidnaps talented scientists for his fantastic project. And again his nemeses, Juve, Fandor, and Hélène, pursue him, and finally Fantomas flees from them by transforming his automobile into an airplane. In the third and last film of the series, Fantomas wants to extort money from rich Scottish landlord in exchange for his life. Juve, Fandor, and Hélène arrive at a Scottish castle to protect the owner and to catch Fantomas. Eventually they almost catch the criminal, but he escapes using both an intercontinental ballistic missile and a bicycle.[93]

In these French films, the mysterious criminal Fantomas, disguised in special masks and attire to imitate the images of other people, commits various crimes using the identities of these people. As a result, the police always suspect somebody who is innocent but whose identity has been used by Fantomas. This leads to funny situations involving police chases, fistfights, and other elements of eccentric comedy, which attracted Soviet youth tired of boring didactic stories about the young heroes of the Civil War, or Great Patriotic War. The young filmgoers interpreted the word "Fantomas" as "the fantastic masks," which referred to the fantastic ability of the mysterious criminal to change his image and use other people's identities. The focus on the various technological innovations in the *Fantomas* trilogy, which many critics considered an imitation of the James Bond movies forbidden in the Soviet Union, also attracted Soviet youth.[94]

Traditionally in Soviet popular culture, modern technological elements, innovative gadgets, machines, and robots became elements of future society, which was always associated with communism in the Soviet imagination. Therefore, Soviet young people loved science fiction and films that involved the elements of such technological fantasies.[95] Both Vitalii Pidgaetskii and Vladimir Solodovnik acknowledged that the *Fantomas* films attracted their classmates at the end of the 1960s not only with very funny and humorous stories but also with their portrayal of unusual details that looked like elements of science fiction. As Solodovnik mentioned in his summer diary in August 1968, "I again went to watch *Fantomas razbushevalsia* [*Fantomas Enraged*] tonight because I like to see various technical devises which Fantomas used in this film and especially how Fantomas' car could be transformed into airplane [Solodovnik referred to a final scene from the movie when Fantomas, imitating Bond's films, escaped a police chase by transforming his automobile into an aircraft]."[96] In the second film of the trilogy, police *commissaire* Juve also tried to emulate Fantomas with his own technical inventions. Juve used a fake hand, cigars, and crutches to disguise the guns he planted for shooting criminals. Soviet fans imitated some of Juve's devices and manufactured them at home. The police complained about "hooligan acts of disrupting public order" in the region of Dniepropetrovsk that involved Fantomas and Juve gadgets.[97]

Another secret of the *Fantomas* films' box office success in the Soviet Union was related to the three French actors who played the major characters: Jean Marais, as the journalist Fandor and as Fantomas; Mylene Demongeot, as Fandor's fiancée; and Louis de Funès, as the police *commissaire* Juve. These actors became familiar faces to millions of Soviet filmgoers. Because of the limited number of film images associated with the West, these three actors, who appeared in other French films on Soviet screens in the 1960s and 1970s, became the symbols of the real West in the movies. As Pidgaetskii noted, at the end of the 1960s "the Soviet kids knew if Jean Marais, Louis de Funès, or Mylene Demongeot would be in a film it guaranteed that the film was funny and worth seeing." As he joked, these actors were "the guarantors of the real (not faked) West" in the film. For many young people from Dniepropetrovsk, a good and funny film was only associated with "a movie from the real West."[98]

Unfortunately for Soviet ideologists and the police, the "funny films from the real West," like the *Fantomas* trilogy, created problems among local youth. The images and ideas in these French comedies became related to a rise in crime in the city and region of Dniepropetrovsk. Many violent crimes and "acts of hooliganism" committed by young people at the end of the 1960s and beginning of the 1970s had direct connections to the *Fantomas* movies. Sometimes young thieves, after committing an act of robbery, left a written note: "Fantomas did it." To intimidate their neighbors, young hooligan jokers who smashed a window could put a handwritten note *"Do skoroi vstrechi, Fantomas"* (See you soon, Fantomas). This phrase from the French film became the most popular joke among the young hooligans of Dniepropetrovsk after 1967. Many brutal hooligan acts were committed by the young imitators of the French Fantomas. The police complained about a gang of Fantomas who used various disguises and terrorized the working-class neighborhoods in the city of Dniepropetrovsk in 1968 and 1969.[99]

According to the police, one movie contributed to the region's criminal situation more than other crime films. This was the Japanese film *Genii dziu-do* [*A Judo Genius,* known in America as *Judo Saga*]. Originally released in 1965 as a remake of an old Akira Kurosawa movie, this film was directed by Seichiro Uchikawa, and it featured the Japanese star Tosiro Mifune. At the beginning of the Brezhnev era, this Japanese movie was shown throughout the Soviet Union.[100] In January 1967, it reached Dniepropetrovsk and immediately became a cult film, especially for young male moviegoers. As one young twelve-year-old enthusiast of the DEFA Indian films wrote in June 1970:

> I loved only Gojko Mitic's films about American Indians. Tonight (June 28, 1970) I saw a very different film which changed my perception of wrestling and self-defense. This was the Japanese film *Genii dziu-do*. The story takes place in Tokio in 1883. The school of Japanese wrestling Judo won over one of jujitsu. The main character is a real genius of judo wrestling who prevailed over everyone. He was challenged by a representative of the new-for-him school of wrestling, karate. The genius of judo reads and studies patiently the rules of the new-for-him wrestling techniques. His intelligence and patience help him to win in a deadly fight with a karate man.

A few days later, he added: "Under the influence of *Genii dziu-do* our friends decided to organize a circle of karate and school of Japanese wrestling, and I will join this circle immediately."[101] Eventually the author of this diary, Aleksandr Gusar, like many other fans of the Japanese movie, would become an enthusiast of the new Asian school of martial arts, karate. As one KGB officer explained, after 1967, "a Fantomas mania" coincided with a "karate mania" in the region of Dniepropetrovsk. By 1970, hundreds of karate groups had appeared in many cities and towns of the region. The police complained about brutal, violent crimes committed by the enthusiasts of *Genii dziu-do*.[102] During the 1970s, the local police banned all karate groups. Eventually, when the central Ukrainian authorities in Kyiv permitted karate training in 1981, Dniepropetrovsk's administration continued the ban on karate and similar types of Asian martial arts.[103]

This Japanese film influenced millions of Soviet youth, who wrote letters to the Soviet film magazines asking for material about their favorite movie, actors, and Japanese martial arts. The most popular Soviet film magazines, such as *Sovietskii ekran* and *Iskusstvo kino,* which were the most readable periodicals among the young filmgoers in the city and region of Dniepropetrovsk, had to respond to this mass popularity of the Japanese film about martial arts.[104] The popularity of Asian martial arts, especially karate, at the end of the 1960s in industrial cities such as Dniepropetrovsk had thus been triggered by the remake of Akira Kurosawa's film about a judo genius. Many Soviet young people, who were curious enough to learn from the Soviet publications about the origins of their favorite film, discovered for themselves that Kurosawa's films were remade even into their favorite American western films such as *The Magnificent Seven.* As Andrei Vadimov noted in his diary in January 1973, "I read today in the film magazine [he referred to an article about *Genii dziu-do* in *Iskusstvo kino*] about my favorite film about Japanese schools of wrestling. I was surprised that a Japanese film by the director Kurosawa created a story for my favorite American cowboy movie, *The Magnificent Seven.* It is strange to know how Japan contributed to our images of the real American West which we had taken for granted."[105]

Films about the Italian Mafia

Other Western depictions of violence, like movies about the Italian Mafia, also influenced Dniepropetrovsk's filmgoers during the Brezhnev era. According to both Western and Soviet film critics, the best political films about the Italian Mafia were made by the Italian film director Damiano Damiani.[106] Two of his best films about organized crime were popularized in the Soviet Union in the early 1970s. Soviet ideologists and KGB officers considered them as a serious alternative to other "Western films about crime." The first Damiano film about the Italian Mafia was an adaptation of Leonardo Sciascia's novel *Day of the Owl.* In this film, released in 1968, the young police inspector Bellodi (played by Franco Nero) begins his investigation of Mafia crimes in Sicily but encounters a wall of silence and isolation. As a result, all his efforts to discover the truth about these crimes fail. This film was released in the Soviet Union in 1969 under the title *Sova poiavliaetsia dniom (The Owl Appears during the Daylight).* From the first days of its release, Soviet ideologists used it as counterpropaganda for the

Western style of life.[107] On July 19, 1970, a twelve-year-old Gusar noted in his diary: "Tonight I and my Mom watched an Italian color film *Sova poiavliaetsia dniom* in the summer movie theater. This is a detective story about the killings committed by an organization Mafia. How fortunate we are that we live here in the Soviet country! It looks like Mafia is ruling the West!"[108] This was the exact reaction that Soviet ideologists hoped to get from the Soviet audience after watching Damiani's film. These films offered a criticism of the Western capitalist system, a vituperative critique that had already been part of everyday Soviet propaganda.[109]

The most successful and impressive political film about the Mafia was Damiani's 1971 movie *Priznanie komissara politsii prokuroru respubliki* (*Confessions of a Police Captain*). According to Howard Hughes, this movie "remains Damiani's best and most controversial film." In this film, the Italian movie star Franco Nero plays Traini, "a young district attorney assigned to investigate an assassination attempt with police captain Bonavia (Martin Balsam)."[110] Eventually, Traini discovers that his supervisors, representatives of elite of Italian jurisprudence, are connected to the Mafia. All the new facts about the Mafia's criminal activities, which Captain Bonavia had submitted to the young district attorney's office, have become known to the Mafia leaders. Bonavia realizes that he is powerless in the struggle with the Mafia, because even his bosses are part of the same system of organized crime. In an act of despair, he shoots and kills a leader of the Mafia group by himself. He is then indicted for premeditated manslaughter and sent to prison. The final scene is the most tragic and heartrending in the film: A bleeding Bonavia is dying in the prison movie theater after being stabbed in the prison dining room by the criminals who had worked for the Mafia. Everybody is laughing at the jokes of the comedy film being shown in the theater. Nobody pays attention to the former police captain who is silently dying in his theater seat, covering his wound.

Confessions of a Police Captain was shown for the first time in the Soviet Union as part of the program of the Seventh Moscow International Film Festival during the summer of 1971. Even traditionally conservative Soviet film critics who covered the festival praised Damiani's film as "an important contribution to the progressive humanistic tradition of Western filmmakers."[111] Soviet ideologists in Ukraine immediately followed this positive evaluation of Damiani's film. They promoted the release of this film all over Ukraine during the fall of 1972. *Confessions of a Police Captain* reached the city of Dniepropetrovsk at the end of September 1972 and immediately became a blockbuster in local theaters.[112] Moreover, this film became a real box office success all over the Soviet Union. According to the All-Union readers' survey of *Sovetskii ekran, Confessions of a Police Captain* was the most popular foreign film of 1972 in the USSR after the British movie *Romeo and Juliet,* which beat all the records for foreign film released in the country.[113] Even two years after its release in the Soviet Union, Damiani's film remained competitive with new Western adventure films, such as *Mackenna's Gold* and *The Sandpit Generals.* As both Gusar and Vadimov noted in their summer diaries in June 1974, *Confessions of a Police Captain* was still the best film about the Italian Mafia on the Soviet screen.[114] During the summer of 1974, according to movie theater statistics for the region of Dniepropetrovsk, besides *Mackenna's Gold* and *The Sandpit Generals,* the most popular foreign film was *Confessions of a Police Captain.*[115]

Soviet ideologists in Ukraine were always more cautious and conservative than their colleagues in Moscow. Conservative attitudes influenced the Ukrainian Soviet apparatchiks who were responsible for releasing foreign films in the republic. Many contemporaries, including famous Soviet filmmakers such as Eldar Ryazanov, complained about this "notorious" conservative attitude of the Ukrainian ideologists toward film releases in Soviet Ukraine.[116] In Dniepropetrovsk, local ideologists were even more conservative and reactionary than their supervisors in Moscow and Kyiv. They blindly followed the recommendations from the center. Moreover, Dniepropetrovsk's leaders added new local restrictions for the strategically important secret city, which had to be "closed" to all the dangerous ideological influences of Western capitalist propaganda. For these local leaders, publications of the major Soviet expert in the Italian cinema like Georgii Bogemskii became the most important directives in their ideological work in the closed city.[117] Bogemskii recommended Damiani's films for the Soviet audience as the best political Italian movies about "the bad negative essence of the Western capitalist reality." Even the Ukrainian film magazine *Novyny kinoekranu* published a positive article by Bogemskii about Damiani's film in May 1972 and reprinted some of Bogemskii's old material about Italian filmmakers.[118] During the 1970s and early 1980s, a series of Italian films about the Mafia were released in Ukraine. At least half these films were directed by Damiani.[119] In the Soviet imagination, the major actor in Damiani's films, Franco Nero, became the most popular image of the Western man besides the familiar faces of the American protest singer Dean Reed and the French actors Jean Marais and Alain Delon. The Soviet film magazine *Sovetskii ekran* promoted the image of Franco Nero as a hero of the "progressive Western cinema" and as an attractive and progressive critic of the capitalist way of life.[120]

During the 1970s, Italian films about the Mafia became the most important ideological tool for diverting young Soviet filmgoers from their favorite westerns and foreign adventure films. On the one hand, Dniepropetrovsk's ideologists tried to discredit the popularity of the West in the popular imagination of local filmgoers by using Damiani's films. On the other hand, they tried to stop a rise in crime among local youth. Instead of films about the criminal Fantomas, Japanese martial arts, or Hollywood western themes, which triggered various forms of criminal activity, Soviet ideologists and KGB operatives promoted anti-Mafia films.[121] But eventually they failed. Despite the popularity of Damiani's films, local young filmgoers preferred their favorite Western adventure films about crimes, including westerns and gangster films. Moreover, the official promotion of Damiani's films did not stop the rise of crime among local youth. Instead, more and more filmgoers began using the term "Mafia" in their description of the local everyday realities of corruption in those Soviet organs of power that had failed to prevent the catastrophic growth of crime in the city and region of Dniepropetrovsk.[122]

Chapter 9

Idiocy and Historical Romance from the West: Comedy and Historical Films

According to contemporaries of the events, the most popular movie genre among ordinary Soviet filmgoers was comedy. Of course the main block-busters were the Soviet comedies, especially the eccentric comedies of Leonid Gaidai.[1] Among foreign films, the most popular were American and French comedies. The first American comedy to open in the Brezhnev era in Dniepropetrovsk was Stanley Kramer's 1963 *It's a Mad, Mad, Mad World*, which would became the new movie sensation. It was first released in the Soviet Union in late 1965, and it was shown in Dniepropetrovsk for the first time in full theaters with all the tickets sold out during January and February 1966.[2] According to Soviet film magazine statistics, this became one of the most popular foreign films shown in the Soviet Union in 1966.[3]

Kramer's hilarious comedy tells the story of a search for buried treasure by at least a dozen people, all played by then-well-known entertainers. After a car accident, a group of complete strangers (including Milton Berle, Jonathan Winters, Sid Caesar, Phil Silvers, and others) witness how a dying driver (Jimmy Durante) identifies the location of some hidden money. This story of buried treasure triggers a conflict-ridden hunt, watched over carefully by a suspicious cop (Spencer Tracy). This treasure hunt involves more and more people and creates various humorous situations. As an eleven-year-old, Aleksandr Gusar summarized the film in his summer diary on May 31, 1970: "My Mom and I watched a very funny, two-part [*dvukhseriinyi*] American film in color about a search for money which was buried under the trees, a combination of which looked like the English letter 'W.' The main characters were chasing each other for more than two hours; then they found money and lost everything at the end."[4]

Another young moviegoer, fourteen-year-old Vladimir Solodovnik, during the first show of the American comedy in March 1966, also noted that this film was funny and dynamic. However, at the same time he felt very uncomfortable about the main story, a search for money. "It looks like everybody [in the film] was driven crazy by this search," he wrote. "The capitalist West is mad about money." He concluded this entry with a remarkable passage: "So our propaganda was correct; in America a human greed and lust for money is the most important driving force. Even the American filmmakers such as Stanley Kramer demonstrated this in their movies."[5]

Such ambiguous feelings about the themes in Kramer's film were also present in the writing of another boy, twelve-year-old Andrei Vadimov, who noted that "it is funny to watch this hunt for money, but it's good to know that we live in a normal country, safe and comfortable, without this American madness about money."[6] Many Soviet filmgoers were shocked by the realistic portrayal of human greed in Kramer's film. One viewer thought that it made America look "like an abnormal dysfunctional country" compared with the normality and stability of the Soviet Union.[7] This American comedy about "a mad hunt for money" played the role of the "negative other" from the West in the imagining of "normal" Soviet identity by young filmgoers at the start of the Brezhnev era.

Strike First, Freddy! and Dreams of the West

Despite the portrayals of the "abnormalities of the capitalist society," Western comedy films, especially American and French ones, attracted millions of young Soviet moviegoers. "The idiocy from the West," as Soviet ideologists characterized Western comedy films, created a sensation among young audiences. On the eve of the Brezhnev era, British films about the adventures of a funny character, Mister Pitkin, produced the first wave of "hysteria" about Western comedies among Soviet filmgoers. Even in 1966 these comedies, which had been originally released in Britain in 1958, triggered in Dniepropetrovsk an "unhealthy enthusiasm among the young moviegoers, who created long lines of people waiting for an extra ticket."[8] The second wave of "hysteria" in Dniepropetrovsk was related to the release of French comedy films about Fantomas in 1967.[9]

This mass "unhealthy enthusiasm" about Western comedies peaked in 1969. That year, the release of the Danish comedy film *Strike First, Freddy!* (*Bei pervym Freddi!*) created a scandalous sensation all over the Soviet

Union, especially in Dniepropetrovsk. As Soviet journalists explained in their critical articles, this Danish comedy film was about the "stupid but funny adventures of Freddy, a small traveling salesman, who got involved in the gangster and spy games." This Danish parody of gangster films, which "ridiculed anti-Soviet hysteria in the West," had many funny episodes set in very clean, attractive Western urban neighborhoods.[10] Moreover, this comedy included a few explicit erotic moments, which were not cut by the Soviet censors. As a result, this film attracted numerous young Soviet moviegoers eager to see the real West with real supermarkets full of various fantastic products, with naked girls, and with trendy clothes, all of which were shown uncut and in color.

In the spring of 1969, the young fans of the Danish film literally stormed a Moscow movie theater Mir (the World) and fought with the police to get to the box office.[11] This *"Freddy* hysteria" reached Dniepropetrovsk in July 1969 with events similar to those in Moscow.[12] As Andrei Vadimov, a thirteen-year-old enthusiast of the Danish comedy noted,

> I saw *Bei pervym Freddy* the second time. It is amazing how funny this film is! I laughed all the time. How wonderful are the shops, cars, dress, and everything looks fantastic in this film! It is like another planet, not just Denmark! I want to travel there and see it with my own eyes! How pretty is Freddy's girlfriend! They showed her naked body. Of course she had a light transparent dress on her. But you can see everything on the screen! I will never tell this to my Mom, but I'd love to live in Freddy's country, to drive his fantastic cars, to have his fashionable clothes and his beautiful girls![13]

Soviet children discovered their own images of the West in this Danish parody film, which they associated with the Western standard of life. They began constructing their own "positive imagery" of the West based on elements from Western films, which were available to them in their everyday cultural consumption. The major elements of this construction were cars, supermarkets, and beautiful women or handsome men.

Comedies from the United States

In the same entry quoted above, Andrei Vadimov wrote, "Two weeks ago, I saw another funny film which could be compared to this Danish parody

[*Bei pervym Freddy*]. This was an American comedy titled *Vozdushnye prik-liuchenia* [*The Air Adventures*]. I saw that film ten times. And I remember the first time I saw this film with my Mom in 1968, and we had to stay in the long, long line of the people for many hours to get our tickets. The American comedy was even more popular than *Bei pervym Freddy* in Dnie-propetrovsk those days."[14]

Here, Vadimov referred to another wave of the Western comedy "mad-ness" triggered by a comedy that was originally released in the United States in 1965 under the title *Those Magnificent Men in Their Flying Ma-chines.* The director Ken Annakin made this marvelous comedy about the historic 1910 London-to-Paris air race, which involved the greatest aviators from around the world. These aviators came together when a stuffy, but very rich, newspaper publisher decided to sponsor an airplane race across the English Channel, offering £10,000 to the winner. The funny escapades be-tween the American, British, French, German, Italian, and Japanese teams resulted in the most daring and hilarious in-flight acrobatic stunts ever caught on film. American reviewers highly praised this comedy, which fea-tured "thrilling aerial photography and some stupefying stunt flying."[15]

In the Soviet Union, *Those Magnificent Men in Their Flying Machines* was released in 1968 under the title *Vozdushnye prikliuchenia* (*The Air Ad-ventures*). In November 1968, it reached Dniepropetrovsk and became a box office hit in all the major movie theaters of the city and the region. The popularity of this American comedy reached its peak during May and June 1969.[16] In the 1970s, a similar American comedy film, *Bol'shie gonki* (*The Great Race*), also became the favorite movie for the local youth of the en-tire region. It was released in the Soviet Union relatively late in 1976, ten years after its original release in the United States. In June and July 1976, during the school summer break, *Bol'shie gonki* was the major attraction for millions of secondary school and college students in the region. Many young filmgoers fell in love with the film, which had a plot similar to that of the previous American blockbuster, *Vozdushnye prikliuchenia.*[17]

According to All-Union statistics, American comedy films such as *The Great Race* produced large profits. As Val Golovskoy noted, "76 million seats were sold for *The Great Race;* that is, the USSR made about 23 mil-lion rubles if the average admission charge for the period is taken to be 30 kopeks."[18] Teachers and Communist and Komsomol ideologists com-plained about the tremendous popularity of these "eccentric idiotic come-dies from America," which attracted Dniepropetrovsk children "like a mag-net."[19] Nevertheless, *The Great Race* never became as popular as *The Air*

Adventures had been. During the 1970s, the local movie theaters still showed the American comedy about the air race of 1910.[20]

According to contemporaries, *Those Magnificent Men in Their Flying Machines* was the last American comedy film that became an object of cultural fixation for millions of young Soviet moviegoers. Aleksandr Gusar watched this "hilarious American comedy in color" during his summer school breaks in 1970 and 1971, and he always noted "a very long line of people waiting to watch this American movie about funny adventures of international aviators."[21] For a ten-year-old Yulia Grigian (the future Yulia Tymoshenko) and her classmates, this film was the first American film they saw in their life. Many years later, they would recall how this film provided their imagination with the first very attractive and funny images of life in the West.[22] Many of the film's funny episodes about technology looked very innovative to many young enthusiasts of science and technology. Moreover, some of them discovered episodes unusual for the Soviet screen, especially erotic elements, which included the shots of a nude girl. As one filmgoer described his emotions about these episodes, "I was shocked that they did not cut a scene with a naked female body and episodes when a main female character was losing her skirt, showing her underwear." Yet he wrote in his diary that the portrayal of the old airplanes in the American film, rather than its erotic scenes, was the major attraction for him and other filmgoers such as his friends and classmates.[23]

At the same time, during the 1970s the young filmgoers in Dniepropetrovsk were losing interest in the American comedy films of the 1960s, which still were being widely shown all over the region. The Soviet Union did not release any new American comedies in the 1970s. Filmgoers were forced to watch the same old foreign films again.[24] As a result, new French comedy films replaced old American favorites. As the young authors of the summer diaries noted in 1971–72, "Everybody loved only the French films with Louis de Funès and Bourvil." Gusar explained that "we were tired of the artificial tricks and unnatural situations of the American comedies." And he continued, "After all these funny escapades in American comedies with various technical devices, I feel very uncomfortable, very unreal. What is the point? The French films are more humane and real, despite all those grimaces and tricks of Louis de Funès. Funès' comedies are silly and naïve, but they are more humane than American films."[25] It is noteworthy that this juxtaposition of American films as artificial and French comedies as humane and natural was present in many diaries and testimonies of contemporaries who lived in the region through the 1970s. During the 1970s,

French comedies became the most popular foreign comedy films in the city and region of Dniepropetrovsk.

Louis de Funès, Bourvil, and the
Cult of French Comedy Films

As early as 1967, the *Fantomas* trilogy introduced a very talented French actor, Louis de Funès, to Soviet audiences.[26] From 1967 until the early 1980s, this French comedian captivated the imagination of millions of Soviet moviegoers. De Funès (Louis Germain de Funès de Galarza, 1914–83) was the biggest French box office star of all time in both France and the Soviet Union.[27] And the partner of de Funès in all the most popular French comedy films was Bourvil (André Raimbourg, 1917–70). Bourvil started as an accordionist in Normandy dance halls and later sang in Parisian cabarets and on the radio, where he was discovered by filmmakers. His previous experience contributed to his on-screen images, "a simple and quiet peasant type," who fit very well with "the effusive and arrogant type" of de Funès' characters.[28] Both de Funès and Bourvil became most successful when they played partners in films directed by Gérard Oury (1919–2006). Their most popular comedy films, which brought them glory not only in France but also in the Soviet Union, were *Le Corniaud / The Sucker* (1965) and *La Grand vadrouille / Don't Look Now, We're Being Shot At* (1966), in which both of them starred.[29]

At the end of 1967, the French comedy *Le Corniaud,* under the Russian title *Razinia (A Scatterbrain),* was released in the Soviet Union. In December 1967, this film appeared in Dniepropetrovsk's movie theaters.[30] For the first time, local fans of de Funès, who played Commissaire Juve, their favorite character from the *Fantomas* series, could see him on a screen together with Bourvil. The film had a typical plot for Western comedies released in the Soviet Union. An overwhelming majority of these films were gangster or spy parodies. *Le Corniaud* tells the story of Antoine Maréchal (played by Bourvil), a shopkeeper from Paris. While leaving his apartment in Paris for a vacation in Italy, he suffers an accident that completely destroys his car. Léopold Saroyan (played by de Funès), the director of an import-export company, is the owner of the fashionable automobile that ruins Maréchal's car. Saroyan can only compensate the shopkeeper for his ruined trip by offering to drive his American friend's Cadillac from Naples to Bordeaux, all expenses paid. However, unknown to Maréchal, Saroyan is the leader of a criminal organization, and the Cadillac is filled with drugs, gold, and diamonds. Maréchal departs for his destination, oblivious of both his cargo and Saroyan, who discreetly follows him to watch over the delivery. Unfortunately, a gang of Italian criminals discovers Saroyan's plan and attempts to steal the car. When Maréchal becomes aware of the plan while crossing the border, he turns the tables on both Saroyan and the Italian gangsters.

During the 1970s, this film triggered the mass popularity in the Dniepropetrovsk Region of the new movie attraction from the West known as the Funès-Bourvil comedies. As the high school student Vladimir Solodovnik noted in 1969, "now every kid in the region memorized jokes from *Razinia* and tried to imitate tricks of Funès and Bourvil whenever they can."[31] The popularity of these French comedies reached its peak in June 1971, when a new film was released in the Soviet Union.[32] It was another French comedy, *Bol'shaia progulka* (*The Big Stroll*). Originally released in 1966 in France as *La grande vadrouille,*[33] this film also starred de Funès and Bourvil. It is set in 1943 during the Nazi occupation of Paris. An Allied British bomber plane is shot down over Paris by the Germans. Its crew (with Terry Thomas as the flight captain) lands there by parachute. The British pilots decide to meet at the Turkish Bathhouse after landing in Paris. Then, with the help of some French civilians (de Funès as the conductor Stanislas and Bourvil as the housepainter Augustin), they try to escape over the demarcation line into the southern part of France, which was not occupied by the Germans. After many humorous and sometimes dangerous adventures, the French patriots and British pilots not only successfully flee from their enemies but also fool both the German police and Nazi troops who desperately want to capture these fugitives.[34]

According to many Western film critics, *La grande vadrouille* was one of the highlights in the careers of de Funès and Bourvil and one of the biggest office successes in French film history. In France, this film attracted 17.7 million viewers, "while the 777,000 tickets that the film sold in Sweden provided an indication of its international success."[35]

Immediately after its release in France, Soviet film critics declared *La grande vadrouille* to be the best antifascist comedy produced in the West. They called French comedians "the true representatives of the French working people." For Soviet journalists, Bourvil became a favorite representative of poor peasants and craftsmen of France, "a peasant Piero from the village of Bourvil."[36] Many Soviet ideologists praised not only the themes of the antifascist resistance movement in the French comedy but also "the apparent sympathy of the creators of the film towards the democratic elements of French population" that struggled with the Nazi occupation. Given the fact that Bourvil died in 1970, before the Soviet release of *La grande vadrouille,* some Soviet reviewers considered the film "the Swan song of Bourvil, as his last stroll in filmmaking."[37]

The local ideologists in Dniepropetrovsk read positive reviews of *La grande vadrouille* and followed the official Soviet critics' positive evaluation of the Funès-Bourvil partnership in French comedy films. After the success of *La grande vadrouille* among Dniepropetrovsk's moviegoers and its official approval by Moscow's film experts in 1971, all new Funès-Bourvil comedies were released in the region. According to contemporaries, the French comedies of de Funès dominated Dniepropetrovsk's film market during the first half of the 1970s. By 1976, all the comedies with de Funès—beginning with the famous series about the funny adventures of the gendarme Cruchot from Saint Tropez and ending with the less-known films about Oscar, or the "one-man orchestra"—were being shown throughout the region.[38]

As entries in personal diaries testify, these films attracted young filmgoers not only because French comedies were fun to watch but also because they demonstrated elements of modern Western technology and machinery that were lacking in everyday life in the Soviet "rocket city." Aleksandr Gusar mentioned his joy after seeing *Bol'shaia progulka* in late May of 1973. But he especially noted his reaction after June 27 and 29, 1973, when he saw *Razinia* and *Malen'kii kupal'shchik* (*Le petit baigneur* in French; *The Little Bather* in English). Gusar was shocked by the modern technical details of Western life that he noted in both films. "It is fantastic how they use machines in France!" he wrote after watching *Malen'kii kupal'shchik.* "Everybody drives cars and can operate different machines. And what the machines! If in the films about Fantomas, everything looks like science fiction, in the new film everything, including yachts, is real. How I dream just to live in such a society! It is easy living in the West! And we are missing all this technology in our everyday life here in the Soviet industrial city!"[39] By showing the details of the everyday Western life, French comedies such as *Malen'kii kupal'shchik* triggered comparisons between the realities of Western and Soviet lifestyles among the young filmgoers in Dniepropetrovsk.[40]

After they watched Western comedy films, the image of the West was associated by these young filmgoers with an idealized notion of easy living. In this idealized world, there were no social problems in the West, which was very different from the traditional image of the capitalist "oppressive" West in Soviet propaganda. Another contemporary of these events emphasized that the funny plot and attractive details of everyday life in the Western comedies "strengthened this feeling of the easy careless living in the West." As a result, the Soviet viewer had negative impressions of the difficult realities of everyday life in the Soviet Union, "when people worked hard, earned a little, and lived without convenient modern Western machines."[41]

During the late 1970s, new French comedy films with the young comedian Pierre Richard replaced the eccentric comedies with de Funès in Soviet movie theaters. These new films incorporated elements of social criticism about the "capitalist reality, exploitation, and humiliation of the human being in the West," which were considered by Soviet ideologists as the positive ideological concepts for cultural consumption by Soviet filmgoers.[42] Yet a majority of Soviet filmgoers ignored these aspects of social criticism and enjoyed the humorous plots and portrayal of "modern Western life."[43]

French Historical Films versus Soviet Ukrainian Movies

Vitalii Pidgaetskii, who became a professor of history at Dniepropetrovsk University during the late 1970s, recalled that Western movies triggered his interest in reading historical novels and encouraged his ambition to become a professional historian.[44] Pidgaetskii's colleagues in the Department of History, including Yurii Mytsyk and myself, who grew up during the 1960s and 1970s in cities like Dniepropetrovsk, were also influenced by Western historical epic films, which were released for the first time in the Soviet Union in the late 1950s and 1960s.[45]

The first historical movies that immediately became box office hits in Soviet movie theaters were French adventure films about the history of France in the seventeenth and eighteenth centuries. As Pidgaetskii noted,

It was a paradox, that in Soviet Ukraine the French tradition of historical films such as *Fanfan the Tulip, The Mysteries of Paris, The Three Musketeers, The Iron Mask, The Adventures of Angélique,* and *The Black Tulip,* rather than Ukrainian films, captivated the imagination of millions of Soviet young people. They had no films about the Kievan princes or the Ukrainian Cossacks in the 1960s. These Soviet youth discovered history through the "epic costume films" [*kostiumirovannye istoricheskie fil'my*] from the West. During the Khrushchev thaw, these films were mainly French historical movies. At the beginning of the Brezhnev era, American historical films added a Hollywood flavor to the images of ancient Greece and Rome, and conquered the hearts of Soviet kids all over the Soviet Ukraine.[46]

Western "epic costume films" contributed to the construction of positive, optimistic images of the West among young Soviet filmgoers. The French comedy *Fanfan the Tulip* became the most popular historical adventure movie for the entire generation of people who grew up during the Brezhnev era. Originally released in France in 1952 as *Fanfan la Tulipe,* this film was directed by Christian-Jaque and featured Gérard Philippe and Gina Lollabrigida. It reached Dniepropetrovsk during the last years of Khrushchev's rule.[47] It tells the story of Fanfan, a handsome young peasant, who joins the army to escape marriage and because a gipsy girl predicted he would get glory and the king's daughter as a wife. The gypsy girl was in fact Adeline, the daughter of the recruiting officer. Once he has discovered this stratagem, Fanfan refuses to forget this dream and decides to fulfill the destiny of the fake prediction. Set during the reign of King Louis XV, the film is full of funny adventures and well-made fighting and fencing scenes. Young filmgoers especially loved its fight sequences and love story intrigues. As a result, this film became the most popular Western adventure film up until the 1970s.[48] Even in March 1970, this old French movie was still considered to be a box office success and was included in the film program for the spring school break at Dniepropetrovsk's palaces of culture and movie theaters.[49] During the summer school breaks in 1970 and 1972, all "summer movie theaters" that showed old films also included *Fanfan the Tulip* in their program. As the summer school diaries of students from various Dniepropetrovsk schools testify, old French historical films with fencing scenes and fights such as *Fanfan the Tulip* became the cult films and a new cultural fixation for numerous young filmgoers during the 1970s.[50]

A comparison of the entries in summer school diaries with published lists of the movies shown in the city of Dniepropetrovsk during the 1960s and the 1970s demonstrates the continued popularity of French "historical costume films." These movies—*The Mysteries of Paris, The Three Musketeers, The Iron Mask, The Adventures of Angélique,* and *The Black Tulip*—were released in the Soviet Union after *Fanfan the Tulip,* and had the similar love intrigues and fencing/fighting scenes. Instead of Philippe, all these films featured new French stars, who performed all the fencing and fistfight scenes. These actors were Jean Marais and Alain Delon who played a bandit and his twin brother in *Black Tulip*.[51]

Marais was in two French historical romantic movies that reached the Soviet audience at the beginning of the 1960s after *Fanfan the Tulip*. The first film was *The Mysteries of Paris* (*Les Mystères de Paris;* 1963), a film adaptation by the director André Hunebelle of the sentimental novel by the French author Eugène Sue (1804–57).[52] The second film, *The Iron Mask* (*Le Masque de fer;* 1963), directed by Henri Decoin, tells the story of the Three Musketeers, D'Artagnan, and the imprisonment in an iron mask of the identical twin of King Louis XIV.[53] Soviet moviegoers watched these films simultaneously with two other French films about the adventures of the Three Musketeers and D'Artagnan, which were released in the Soviet Union as one film in two parts under the title *The Three Musketeers* during the early 1960s. These French films—*Les Trois mousquetaires: Les ferrets de la reine* (known in the United States as *The Fighting Musketeers*) and *Les Trois mousquetaires: La vengeance de Milady* (known in the United States as *Vengeance of the Three Musketeers*)—were made in 1961 by the French director Bernard Borderie. All these films maintained the status of box office hits throughout the Brezhnev era all over the Soviet Union.[54]

These films became a target for criticism by the Dniepropetrovsk administration, especially during the peak of their popularity in the region between 1965 and 1975.[55] On the one hand, all these French historical films brought stable and guaranteed ticket sales and, therefore, fulfilled the film show plans in the region. On the other hand, these films created problems for both the Soviet apparatchiks and the police. The local police complained that imitation of the fist fights and fencing scenes from the "Jean Marais and Alain Delon movies" among young filmgoers had led to real street fights in the city of Dniepropetrovsk. A group of arrested adolescent hooligans in June 1966 confessed that they practiced in their street fights the tactics and boxing techniques of Rodolphe de Sombreuil, the main character from the film *The Mysteries of Paris* played by Marais.

The administration of Dniepropetrovsk's hospitals also complained about treating numerous wounds on local adolescents who became fascinated with D'Artagnan's and Black Tulip's techniques of fencing. Thousands of the young fans of French historical films manufactured their own "musketeer's swords" from wood and organized mass fencing matches in the yards of the region's towns and cities.[56] As Vladimir Solodovnik noted in his diary, the release of these French films contributed to the growing popularity of Dumas's novels among Dniepropetrovsk's youth. He wrote in June 1966, "Everybody was impressed with the films about musketeers, and now more and more people ask about Alexander Dumas's books. Meanwhile, I see how local kids are fighting in the streets using their homemade swords and wounding each other."[57]

The most serious problem for Dniepropetrovsk's ideologists was the ideological unreliability of French historical films. According to these local ideologists, some of them contained explicit erotic scenes and propagated immorality and "Western degeneration." Dniepropetrovsk's leaders especially worried about the immense popularity of the French "historical epic costume films" on the adventures of Angélique. The first film in this series, *Angélique, marquise des anges,* was originally released by the director Borderie in France in 1964. The third film in the series, *Angélique et le roy* (released in the United States under the title *Angélique and the King*), came out in 1966. These films, based on the novels by Anne and Serge Golon, tell about the erotic adventures of beautiful Angélique in the royal court of the Sun King, Louis XIV. In the Soviet Union, *Angélique and the King* was released in the fall of 1968, while *Angélique, marquise des anges* reached Dniepropetrovsk a year later in November 1969. Both films produced a sensation all over the Soviet Union.[58]

In Dniepropetrovsk, for the entire month of October 1968 and November 1969, traffic downtown was paralyzed by the long lines of people waiting for an extra ticket to the two central movie theaters that were showing films about Angélique.[59] Contemporaries testified to a fascination among young filmgoers about the portrayal of the intimate details of the Angélique's love affairs onscreen. Neither criticism by the local ideologists or protests by prudish teachers could stop the showings of these films. Even in the early 1970s, these films were listed among the most popular movies in Dniepropetrovsk.[60] At the beginning of the 1970s, the young female audience, including twelve-year-old Yulia Grigian (later Tymoshenko) and fourteen-year-old Natalia Vasilenko, still enjoyed the adventures of beautiful Angélique and the handsome musketeers. As they confessed later, these French adventure films helped them to construct their own images of ideal sexually attractive men and women. Visual images of the French actresses such as Mylene Demongeot (who played Milady in a film about the Three Musketeers) and actors such as Alain Delon influenced perceptions of sexuality among girls and boys in Dniepropetrovsk and awoke their own sexuality and sexual fantasies.[61]

The Soviet ideologists also worried about a lack of patriotism and the "ideological blindness" of filmgoers who watched French historical films. They preferred Western epic costume films and adventure films to boring

Soviet movies "about the ideologically correct historical past." Local youth ignored Soviet Ukrainian films about the Ukrainian past because all these movies were slow, boring, and too didactic. These films—based on Ukrainian classics, such as Ivan Franko's *Zakhar Berkut* about the Mongolian invasion and *Yaroslav Mudryi* about the great princes of Kievan Rus—were shown in almost empty movie theaters.[62] Only a few filmgoers visited the showing of *Chertova diuzhina,* a Ukrainian adventure film about the Zaporizhian Cossacks.[63]

Dniepropetrovsk's ideologists had to order the administration of secondary schools and local colleges to send their students to watch the ideologically correct films about the Ukrainian past, Russian Imperial history, and Soviet revolutionary events. From the late 1960s through the 1970s, thousands of the secondary school and college students had to waste their time after classes watching Soviet historical films in the city's theaters. According to the reports of the administration of the local movie theaters, only the "enforced attendance" of high school and college students under the guidance of their teachers saved Soviet historical films from box office failure, including *War and Peace, Zakhar Berkut, Yaroslav Mudryi,* the film-ballet *Spartacus* with A. Khachaturian's music, and numerous films about Lenin.[64]

Spartacus and *The 300 Spartans:* Ancient History in American Films

At a meeting of local ideologists and KGB personnel in December 1968, Oleksii Vatchenko, the first secretary of the Dniepropetrovsk regional Communist Party committee, recommended using not only Soviet historical films but also the new Western historical movies based on the Marxist theory of class struggle as an antidote to the current local fascination with French epic costume films such as *The Three Musketeers* and *The Adventures of Angélique.* As one participant in this meeting recalled, Vatchenko criticized the Dniepropetrovsk theater administration for "indulging the low taste of the young fans of fights and eroticism." Instead of *The Three Musketeers, The Iron Mask,* and *The Adventures of Angélique,* he recommended showing *Spartacus.* To the surprise of the audience, the regional party leader referred in his speech to the American movie *Spartacus,* which had recently been released in Dniepropetrovsk.[65]

During two months of 1967, in February and March, this film, *Spartacus,* had become a box office hit in the entire region of Dniepropetrovsk.

The film had an important combination of historical romance, adventures, and romantic and fighting scenes, which attracted a mass audience and satisfied the ideological requirements of the political leadership in the "closed" city.[66] *Spartacus,* produced by Kirk Douglas, who also played the lead character, and directed by the thirty-year-old director Stanley Kubrick, had its world premier on October 7, 1960, in New York City, seven years before it reached the Soviet audience.

The film tells the story of the most famous slave rebellion in ancient Roman history during the period 73–71 BC. This rebellion was led by the Thracian slave Spartacus (Kirk Douglas), who was trained as a gladiator by Lentulus Batiatus (Peter Ustinov) in his school for gladiators at Capua, near Rome. During the rebellion, Spartacus organizes a disciplined army of former slaves and gladiators. After numerous glorious victories of the slave army over the Roman legions, Spartacus is betrayed by Sicilian pirates and defeated by the troops of the Roman general Marcus Crassus (Laurence Olivier).[67] Some scholars consider this film a "leftist" response to Cold War developments by liberal American filmmakers.[68] The film's reception in the United States was problematic from the early beginning, and it attracted the attention of Soviet ideologists. As an American film historian recalled,

> On the left, the *Communist Worker* (a newspaper of the American Communists) criticized apostate [Howard] Fast [author of the book on which the film was based; he quit the Communist Party] as heavy-handed, albeit praising [Dalton] Trumbo [author of the film's screenplay] for putting the Roman Legions in what the reviewer took to be Nazi regalia. Others found the production itself an instance of working-class heroics. . . . On the right, *Spartacus* was attacked by the American Legion and by syndicated gossip columnist Hedda Hopper: "That story was sold to Universal from a book written by a Commie and the script was written by a Commie, so don't go to see it."[69]

In the Soviet Union, official film critics praised the film from its release in early 1967. They discovered "a serious class analysis" of historical facts in the film, which was "different from the merely entertaining quality of the French historical films about musketeers." Yurii Khaniutin, a Soviet film critic, following the Western Leftist evaluation of the film, emphasized "an obvious historical philosophical warning" against the "totalitarian regime" that he found in the film. Of course, the Soviet journalist referred to only one form of totalitarianism accepted by the Soviet ideologists, Western fascism. According to Khaniutin, the rise of General Crassus to power demonstrated "the elementary logic of the beginning of a totalitarian regime." Soviet journalists always portrayed Kirk Douglas favorably as "an opponent of the capitalist system and as a fighter with social injustice and inequality in imperialistic America."[70] This is why the local ideologists supported the release of this American film in Dniepropetrovsk as an ideologically approved "counterbalance" to French adventure films. In the 1970s, this film was still on the screen in numerous palaces of culture in the Dniepropetrovsk Region. All available summer school diaries had entries for July 1970 about the immense popularity of *Spartacus* among young filmgoers in the city and region of Dniepropetrovsk.[71]

In September 1970, another American historical film, *The 300 Spartans,* captivated the imagination of *Spartacus* fans. This movie became a box office success for two months of September and October 1970 in the city of Dniepropetrovsk. Together with the French films about musketeers, this American movie guaranteed a planned ticket sale in the regional movie theaters until 1975.[72] *The 300 Spartans* had been directed by Rudy Mate and produced by the American company Twentieth Century Fox in 1961. Based on the events described in Herodotus' *History,* the film tells the story of the battle of Thermopylae in 480 BC between 300 Spartan soldiers led by King Leonidas and the Persian Army led by King Xerxes.[73]

Both American films, *Spartacus* and *The 300 Spartans,* started a mania of imitation among local youth. Thousands of children in the region organized new games in the yards. They now pretended to be either Romans and gladiators, or Spartans and Persians. Moreover, during the early 1970s, the administrations of the local libraries discovered a growing interest among young readers in relatively esoteric literature about ancient Greece and Rome. Adolescents who previously had only been interested in adventure or detective stories now asked librarians for popular editions of ancient Greek authors such as Plutarch and Herodotus. As one contemporary recalled, his mother, who was in charge of the trade union libraries in the region during the 1970s, complained about three waves of "young readers' excitement [*azhiotazh*]." The first wave was connected to the growing interest in literature about Western popular music, especially the articles about rock music in the youth magazine *Rovesnik.* The second wave was triggered by a mass hysteria about the rock opera *Jesus Christ Superstar,* which led to an interest in literature about the Gospels and Jesus Christ. The third and last wave was related to American films about the great heroes of ancient history. Middle and high school students asked for books about Spartacus and the events of the Greek-Persian wars.[74] After reading these books, some local fans of the American movies discovered numerous mistakes and anachronisms in both films. Despite these annoying discoveries, they still preferred the Western epic costume films to the boring productions of patriotic stories about the Soviet past. After watching *The 300 Spartans* in September 1970 and being forced to watch the new Soviet film about the Great Patriotic War together with his school in the city movie theater, one twelve-year-old middle school student wrote in his diary, "Our school principal [*director*] should send us to watch the interesting historical films such as *Spartacus* and *The 300 Spartans,* rather than waste our time on these long and boring films about the war."[75]

Franco Zeffirelli's *Romeo and Juliet* and the Failed Popularity of Soviet Cinema in the Closed City

In 1972, a new Western historical romantic movie created problems for both the local ideologists and schoolteachers in Dniepropetrovsk. This was the British-Italian movie *Romeo and Juliet.* This film, directed by the great Italian director Franco Zeffirelli and originally released in England in 1968, reached Dniepropetrovsk's theaters in May 1972. For more than two months, it became a film sensation and a box office hit in the entire region.[76] Even before the film's official release in the USSR, Soviet critics had already praised it "as a bright and remarkable event in the world's cinema and international Shakespeariade."[77]

After the first months of enthusiasm about *Romeo and Juliet* in 1972, Soviet journalists noted its incredible popularity, especially among young audiences. Ukrainian youth fell in love with this film as well.[78] As one thirteen-year-old fan wrote in his diary on July 21, 1972: "Today together with my mother and brother, we watched an Anglo-Italian film in color and on the wide screen, *Romeo and Juliet.* I liked this film very, very, very much. This is the best film about love that I had ever seen in my life."[79] Yulia Grigian (Tymoshenko) and her twelve-year-old classmates watched Zeffirelli's film many times in 1972, and they memorized entire dialogues and scenes from it.[80]

When the Soviet film magazine *Sovetskii ekran* organized its regular readers' survey of the feature films' popularity in 1972, it turned out that the most popular foreign film in the Soviet Union was *Romeo and Juliet.* According to readers' letters, this film was more popular among young filmgoers than any Soviet film that was released that year. An analysis of the letters demonstrated that Soviet middle and high school students were the most active consumers of Western romantic historical movies such as *Romeo and Juliet.* The editors of *Sovetskii ekran* received thousands of letters from children younger than fourteen years who confessed that *Romeo and Juliet* was more important to them than any Soviet film.[81] Young Soviet filmgoers loved every moment of this, their favorite movie. A song from the film composed by the Italian composer Nino Rotta became a popular hit even among rock music fans. Millions sent letters to youth periodicals and asked for the lyrics of Rotta's song. Under immense pressure from these enthusiasts, in 1974 *Rovesnik* published brief information about the film, including the sheet music and lyrics in English of this song.[82]

The young audience ignored the new Soviet movies and preferred to wait for hours in the long lines of people at the theater box offices for an extra ticket to watch this old Western blockbuster, which had been originally released many years ago. As one Komsomol leader in Dniepropetrovsk complained, the immense popularity of Western romantic movies such as *Romeo and Juliet* undermined all efforts by the local Komsomol activists to carry out the important ideological campaigns devoted to patriotic education among the local youth.[83] As a result, all the ideological actions of Komsomol in Dniepropetrovsk's movie theaters failed after May 28, 1972, the date of the official release of Zeffirelli's film in the region. Aleksandr Gusar, who was a new Komsomol member, noted that all his friends ignored their school administration's recommendation to watch patriotic Soviet historical films and celebrate the upcoming fiftieth anniversary of the Soviet Union's formation by seeing ideologically reliable Soviet movies. "Even our Komsomol activists," he wrote, "went to watch *Romeo and Juliet* instead of the film *Ukroshchenie ognia,* which we had to watch after our classes today."[84]

KGB officials worried about the lack of good patriotic Soviet films in Dniepropetrovsk. During the 1970s, they discovered that all the most popular historical films shown in the region were foreign ones, including the new box office hits of the early 1970s such as the West German, Italian, and Romanian movies about ancient Roman history and the struggle of the Dacians, the indigenous Romanian tribes, with the expansion of the Roman Empire into the Balkans.[85] Conversely, they were afraid of the immoral patterns of behavior portrayed in Western romantic historical movies. Thus they expressed their concern about the portrayal of nudity in *Romeo and Juliet* and the vulgar scenes of eroticism in another short-lived Western movie sensation of 1969, the American film *One Million Years B.C.*, with "Raquel Welch in a two-piece fur bikini."[86]

Despite numerous complaints about the domination of foreign films on the movie screens of Dniepropetrovsk by the KGB and Communist Party apparatchiks, Western movies were still prominent in the repertoire of local theaters throughout the entire Brezhnev era. Overall, the overwhelming majority of the films released in the region were Soviet. However, if we add the titles of old movies played at local palaces of culture and the summer movie theaters to the titles of new films, we see a growing proportion of foreign films in the 1960s and 1970s. In 1966, almost 60 percent of all the movies shown in the city of Dniepropetrovsk were of foreign origin, and 50 percent were from the West. Nine years later, in 1975, almost 90 percent of the films were foreign, and almost 80 percent were Western.[87]

"The Fewer Western Films, the Better for Soviet Youth!" Television, Ideology, and an Invasion of Films from the West

During the Brezhnev era, technological innovations affected film consumption in the region of Dniepropetrovsk. More movie theaters accepted the new type of screens and the new film projecting technology with a special wide-format screen. A special movie theater, Panorama, with the new wide-format screen was built in downtown Dniepropetrovsk. This screen was especially good for the "epic costume films," a majority of which were of foreign origin. As a result, new technology emphasized the better quality of Western films.

Meanwhile, during the 1970s, television became a more popular form of entertainment than movies in the Soviet Union.[88] In 1972 and 1973, the two most popular Soviet TV film series—about Soviet spies in the years of the Civil War and World War II—dealt a devastating blow to the profits of movie theaters in Dniepropetrovsk. During the evening, when these favorite spy films were being broadcast on Soviet television, even traditionally popular Western box office hits were shown in almost empty theaters.[89]

The administration of Dniepropetrovsk's movie theaters and palaces of culture tried to attract a new audience to compete with television. Despite all official criticism, Western (even ideologically unreliable) movies were a better means of income than the patriotic Soviet films. According to the administration, the best way to compete with television was to show foreign feature films that were not allowed to broadcast on Soviet TV. As traditionally, only TV film series for children made in socialist countries and rare TV films based on classical foreign literature from capitalist countries appeared on Soviet TV during the Brezhnev era.[90]

As this situation unfolded, the local theater administration encountered a serious problem. On the one hand, it tried to promote only progressive Western films that criticized the capitalist way of life. On the other hand, it needed to produce profits in the movie theaters. The most popular films were foreign ones that had no elements of obvious criticism of capitalist society. Illusions of the West came with Western films to the closed city. Local filmgoers associated Western life with the onscreen images. Despite all anti-Western propaganda, filmgoers saw a good, interesting life with a lot of exciting moments. The lifestyles portrayed in Western movies, especially in comedy films, looked much better than the realities of Soviet life. The movie screen images of a careless and colorful life full of adventures became an important source for the idealization of Western lifestyles and contributed to a long tradition of illusions about the West. To some extent, in the Soviet imagination, life in the West was always associated with idealized images from these foreign films.[91]

At the same time, the Soviet Ukrainian films (as with Soviet movies in general) were losing popularity in comparison with foreign films. Moreover, the local administration in Dniepropetrovsk tried to avoid showing those Ukrainian films that had no official approval from Moscow. As a result, Ukrainian films in the Ukrainian language completely disappeared from Dniepropetrovsk's movie theaters. During the 1970s, the city's young audience was gradually losing interest in Ukrainian cinema. In 1969 and 1972, only two Ukrainian feature films attracted the attention of these local filmgoers: *Annychka* and *Bilyi ptakh z chornoiu vidznakoiu* (*The White Bird with the Black Mark*). Both were controversial movies about developments in Western Ukraine during World War II. They had been highly praised by the Moscow critics.[92] However, both films had disappeared from the city's theaters by the end of the 1970s. Moviegoers obviously preferred Russian-language Soviet films or foreign films that were dubbed in Russian.

The ideological limitation of cultural consumption in the closed city led to the parochialism and provincialism of its cultural life. Local leaders like Oleksii Vatchenko limited the number of Soviet Ukrainian films in the

Ukrainian language released in the region. At the same time, they tried to limit the dangerous influences of Western movies in the secret city. As Vatchenko used to say, "the fewer Western films, the better for Soviet youth."[93] As a result, Dniepropetrovsk's filmgoers could choose from fewer newly released Western films than in the "open" Soviet cities. Many excellent Western films, which had been highly praised by the Moscow critics, were not shown in the region. Some movies only had a very limited release and were restricted to selected theaters. So families from Dniepropetrovsk had to visit the other open cities to see Western films that would never be shown in the closed city. Andrei Vadimov noted in the summer of 1970 that his parents had to visit their relatives in Moscow to see *The Apartment,* the American comedy directed by Billy Wilder. After reading a positive review of this film in *Sovetskii ekran,* Vadimov's parents decided to visit their Moscow relatives during their vacation in August 1970 and see this good American comedy with famous stars such as Jack Lemmon and Shirley MacLaine. They knew that the conservative leaders of Dniepropetrovsk could not allow the release of this film in the closed city.[94]

Many representatives of Dniepropetrovsk's political and intellectual elite complained about the ideological limits imposed by both the political center (in Moscow) and the KGB on the distribution of popular Western films in the region. It became especially obvious during the mid-1970s, at the peak of détente, when new foreign movies were released in Moscow but were not shown or delayed for release in Dniepropetrovsk. In 1975, Sydney Pollack's anti–Central Intelligence Agency film *Three Days of the Condor* was released in the United States. In a few years, it reached Moscow, and it was praised by the Soviet film critics as "a progressive and honest exposure of the brutal capitalist realities of contemporary American life."[95] Dniepropetrovsk's filmgoers, including the families of the local elite, expected to watch this American movie soon. But they were disappointed, because this movie was only shown in the closed city many years after its official release in Moscow. As some contemporaries of the events noted,

By the end of the 1970s, a majority of Dniepropetrovsk intellectuals openly criticized the cultural politics of Moscow, which not only limited the access of local consumers to Western cultural products but also stifled the local cultural life and contributed to its closed provincial character. Everybody, including the local leaders, blamed Moscow for the limits in consumption of those cultural products which Muscovites enjoyed themselves. Everybody was envious of Moscow![96]

Conclusion

As the stories of these films have shown, the majority of Dniepropetrovsk's people were able to consume only a limited number of those Western cultural products that were winnowed by local ideologists from the already limited choices offered by Moscow. In many cases, these products reached local consumers too late and thus had lost their contemporary appeal and connections with reality. With a strong fixation on Western cultural products such as movies, local consumers (especially the young ones) tended to idealize the separate elements of Western reality that were missing in their own everyday lives. Through such consumption, they reinvented their own "West," which still matched the dimensions of their own Soviet realities. Images from the movie screen were taken out of their cultural context and incorporated into the everyday lives of local youth. As we have seen, a majority of the Western films that reached an audience in Dniepropetrovsk were already outdated and did not correspond to the contemporary cultural developments in the West during the time of their release in the closed city. Moreover, the local consumers in this city closed to foreigners had no opportunity to compare the realities of Western life with the movie images of these lifestyles. As a result, local filmgoers had a distorted and inadequate understanding of the West. All these limitations on cultural consumption eventually contributed to the conservative, parochial, and very provincial perception of the outside world among the young people who grew up in Dniepropetrovsk during the Brezhnev era.[97]

At the same time, the consumption of Western films in the closed city revealed important social and psychological tensions among the local population. The consumers of this closed Ukrainian city criticized the cultural limitations from the center—from Moscow. Even the Russian-speaking consumers of cultural products were frustrated with the ideological interferences from Moscow and from local leaders who followed Moscow's orders. This was the beginning of regional opposition by local consumers in Dniepropetrovsk to the cultural politics of Moscow, which affected their everyday cultural consumption. This regional "envy" of Moscow became a very important element in shaping the local identity of the closed city.

Chapter 10

The Democratization of Rock Music Consumption

The period of popularity of Anglo-American rock music (or beat music) from 1964 to 1969 in the big cities of Soviet Ukraine, such as Dniepropetrovsk, was a time of elitist cultural consumption. It was the Soviet elite—Communist Party and police officials, engineers, lawyers, and college professors, the members of the "upper middle class"—who could afford foreign recordings of rock music.[1] The fans of Jimi Hendrix and a few hippies, who appeared on Dniepropetrovsk's main thoroughfare in 1968 and 1969 and flaunted their long hair and new American jeans, and who demonstratively rejected cultural consumption on the black market and any relations with the material world, represented the wealthy families of Dniepropetrovsk's ruling elite. The local police arrested at least forty people who called themselves "hippies" and who tried to imitate that American lifestyle. According to contemporaries and participants, they were inspired by Western rock music and information about the American and European hippie movement that was published in the Soviet Komsomol magazine *Rovesnik* in December 1967.[2]

Some of these local hippies were the children of KGB officers, one was the son of a secretary of the regional committee of the Communist Party of the Soviet Union, two were the children of a famous lawyer, and some were the children of respectable physicians and professors at the local university. In the spring of 1972, after long conversations between their parents and KGB operatives, Karl Marx Avenue—the main thoroughfare of Dniepropetrovsk, whose central stretch was called the Broadway, or just the Broad —was cleared of both hippies and black marketers.[3] Yet hippie fashions survived all persecutions. During the 1970s, most young rock music fans tried to imitate the "hippie style," which included obligatory long hair, a pair of bell-bottom American jeans, a Western T-shirt, a leather jacket, and plat-form shoes. At the beginning of the 1970s, this look was so closely associ-ated with the hippie image that the combination of American jeans and long hair was called "hippism" (*hipiza* in Russian). But by the end of the 1970s, after this fashion had spread among millions of Soviet consumers, people gradually forgot about its hippie origins. Jeans became a part of everyday life not only for young enthusiasts of rock music but also for the middle aged, including members of the ruling Communist elite.[4]

Deep Purple Mania and Hard Rock during the 1970s

Communist ideologists tried to stop any new forms of rock music con-sumption among the young residents of the city and region of Dniepropet-rovsk. Yet the black market in music survived and was revived again in late 1972, this time not on the Broad but in different locations throughout the city. In the period 1971–74, musical tastes changed and consumers changed as well, now representing not only the upper middle class but also the lower-middle and lower classes. Representatives of working-class families, stu-dents at vocational schools (*professional'no-tekhnicheskoe uchilishche,* in Russian, or PTUs),[5] joined college students in favoring the new, loud, and aggressive music, which was called hard rock in the 1970s and heavy metal in the 1980s.

Thousands of boys and girls from vocational schools bought audiotapes of hard-rock music because they loved to dance to it in the city dance halls where they socialized. They found the dance floor to be the most conven-ient place for communication with other people of the same age, and music provided the necessary emotional background. This dance music (mainly British hard rock) initiated a period of democratization of rock consump-tion in Soviet cities. The first phase of this democratization was related to the popularization of old "beat music" songs with a heavy "bluesy" sound. These songs, which became a link between the elitist music consumption of the 1960s and the democratic music consumption of the 1970s, came from the Beatles' last albums—such as the *White Album, Abbey Road,* and *Let It Be*—that had already included elements of hard rock. Along with Beatles melodies, this new generation of consumers also discovered the heavier and more aggressive music of Led Zeppelin and Deep Purple, as well as the less heavy music by Paul McCartney and Wings that was good for dancing.[6]

By the middle 1970s, the center of rock music consumption had moved from traditionally elitist and selective forms of trade in the downtown black markets to the locations where the overwhelming majority of the new music consumers lived—the hostels and dormitories of college students, of students at *tekhnikums* (technical schools that gave a basic education in engineering, etc.), and of PTU students. These consumers wanted the new, loud, and aggressive hard rock of the 1970s and the heavy metal of the 1980s, and this trend in consumption spread much more rapidly than Beatlemania had done among the earlier generation of individual consumers living in city apartments. Many contemporaries considered these developments as the "democratization of rock music consumption."[7] Two factors shaped the music markets in student dormitories. The first factor was a growing supply of original Western music records and audiotapes. These audiotapes spread among dormitory inhabitants faster than among individual consumers of the new music in their apartments. The second factor was a rising demand for the new forms of entertainment like Western-style discotheques, which would match the new style of life associated with Western popular music.[8]

The "democratization" of rock music consumption started with "hard-rock mania." Sometimes, contemporaries called this "Deep Purple mania," because the British rock band Deep Purple had become the most desirable object of cultural consumption on Soviet dance floors. By 1973, Deep Purple mania had affected high school and vocational school students, including a thirteen-year-old girl at City School No. 75, Yulia Grigian (Telegina), who eventually would become the famous oligarch and politician of independent Ukraine known as Yulia Tymoshenko.[9] To some extent, this Deep Purple mania in Dniepropetrovsk was a delayed reaction to the All-Union cultural phenomenon that influenced the musical preferences and tastes of millions of Soviet young people, especially in Leningrad and Moscow. This Soviet "Deep Purple generation" of the 1970s included not only Yulia Tymoshenko, a future Ukrainian prime minister, but also Dmitry Medvedev, a future Russian president and successor of Vladimir Putin.[10] By 1975, Deep Purple mania had spread among the young population of all Soviet industrial cities. As a Soviet jazz musician, Aleksei Kozlov, recalled,

After 1972, all over the Soviet Union the overwhelming majority of the local bands imitated the British hard rock of Deep Purple or Black Sabbath. Young enthusiasts of rock and roll now preferred only hard-rock music. Especially popular was the album *Deep Purple in Rock,* especially the song "Smoke on the Water." [This is an obvious mistake. This song came from the album *Machine Head.*] It is noteworthy that such music was popular among all the dance floor guests in Moscow. Deep Purple's music united both the intellectual students and the uneducated working-class youth from the Moscow region, who were called "bumpkins" ["*urla*" in Russian].[11]

Anything related to the British band Deep Purple immediately attracted the attention of thousands of Dniepropetrovsk's rock music consumers. When Viktor Tatarskii of the Moscow radio station Maiak (the Beacon) devoted a few of his twenty-five-minute Sunday broadcasts to Deep Purple in 1973, Dniepropetrovsk's playgrounds, soccer pitches, and volleyball fields stood empty because boys were instead recording their favorite songs from the radio.[12]

The popularity of Deep Purple sparked interest in other hard-rock bands from Great Britain. The second-most-popular band in Dniepropetrovsk in the period 1971–76 was Uriah Heep. A majority of high school, vocational school, and college students all over the region (and all over Soviet Ukraine) fell in love with the loud and aggressive sound of this British hard-rock band.[13] As was recently recalled by Eduard Svichar, an amateur rock musician from the Cherkassy Region who also lived in Kyiv during the same time, "We, the generation of the seventies, preferred the sound and rhythm of Uriah Heep and Deep Purple to the slow and boring sound of the beat music of the sixties. After the growing popularity of Uriah Heep by 1975, Black Sabbath and Led Zeppelin replaced the Beatles and Rolling Stones in our music collections."[14] Natalia Vasilenko, who visited parties at Dniepropetrovsk's dance floors (*tantsploshchadka* in Russian) during her high school and college years from 1974 to 1979, noted, "Even in 1977, at the peak of a disco madness, during the mass popularity of ABBA, Boney M, and Donna Summer, we still loved to dance to 'July Morning' by Uriah Heep, 'Soldier of Fortune' by Deep Purple, and 'Stairway to Heaven' by Led Zeppelin."[15]

During the period 1972–76, two other "manias" influenced rock music consumption in the city and region of Dniepropetrovsk. The first spread when the British rock band Slade triggered an interest in glam-rock music. The second was related to a star of British glam rock, Marc Bolan, and his band T. Rex. The unusual sounds and strange voices of the bands Slade, T. Rex, and another glam-rock sensation, the group Sweet, made them symbols of real rock music for millions of young Soviet fans from Leningrad to Odessa, from L'viv to Dniepropetrovsk.[16] As Vladimir Solodovnik, a young enthusiast of hard-rock music in 1975, noted:

> In the early 1970s, we began listening to Deep Purple, Uriah Heep, Black Sabbath, Ten Years After, Manfred Mann's Earth Band, and Led Zeppelin. We loved this music because it was heavier and more aggressive than the "beat music" of the 1960s. Then, after 1972, Slade, Sweet, and T. Rex became even more popular among Dniepropetrovsk's kids. These mainly working-class children had no idea of the Beatles or Animals. They did not like the sophisticated music of Pink Floyd. They needed the rhythm and aggression in the new hard-rock music. They preferred the simplicity and rudeness of Slade to the complex musical ideas of Deep Purple and Led Zeppelin. Slade and T. Rex opened a door to new bands with a heavy sound and simple music that was easy to understand and dance to. Sweet, Geordie, Gary Glitter, Suzi Quatro, Nazareth, Grand Funk Railroad, Alice Cooper, and ZZ Top followed Slade and T. Rex in popularity. High school students and students at vocational schools [PTUs] were the main consumers of this simple and aggressive music, which became a typical emotional background for collective fistfights on the dance floors in the 1970s. Young men of low education found in this music an expression of their "manliness," their masculinity.[17]

Other contemporaries observed similar developments in other Ukrainian cities. Dniepropetrovsk State University students—such as Aleksandr Gusar, who came from Pavlograd, and Vladimir Sadovoi, from Novomoskovsk—noted that local bands in these small towns usually performed the songs of Slade, Sweet, or T. Rex during dance parties in the middle of the 1970s. Svichar explained that the audience at the city's dance halls had changed by 1976:

> Few college students visited the city dance floors. PTU students and people without any education identified themselves with the more masculine music of heavy metal for dancing. PTU boys used to come to a dance floor after heavy drinking. They did not bother with sophisticated music. They just needed a heavy rhythm, catchy melodies, and loud sound. They usually had collective fights on the dance floor. We played the music they required. Nine of ten songs that we performed in 1976 were covers of Deep Purple, Grand Funk Railroad, Uriah Heep, Nazareth, Manfred

Mann, Slade, Sweet, Geordie, or T. Rex songs. . . . Deep Purple started a hard-rock music sensation on Soviet dance floors in 1972. Then the music of Slade and T. Rex laid a foundation for mass music consumption among both male and female audiences of Soviet dance floors. Boys loved fast numbers not only for dancing but also for fights. Girls preferred slow numbers for slow dances with their boyfriends. Eventually, Deep Purple mania and Slade mania in the Soviet cities prepared the young audience for the reception of the commercial heavy metal of the AC/DC style in the late 1970s.[18]

As we can see, the spread of this new music, which became known as heavy metal, contributed to the democratization of Western pop music consumption among Soviet youth. Even those who knew nothing about rock and roll now loved to dance to the music of Deep Purple, Slade, or T. Rex. In contrast to the consumption of jazz and beat music, which was still the elitist hard rock of the early 1970s led to mass pop music consumption, which had affected millions of Soviet young people by the end of the Brezhnev era.

The popularity of hard rock (and glam rock) among the new generation of young music consumers in the Soviet Union during the 1970s intrigued many scholars who write about popular music in the USSR. These writers noted how quickly after Beatlemania Soviet pop music consumers diverted their interest toward the British pioneers of heavy metal like Led Zeppelin, Deep Purple, Black Sabbath, and Uriah Heep. The most plausible explanation for this phenomenon came from an interpretation of similar developments during the same period among Anglo-American fans of hard rock. According to Will Straw, a music sociologist, the major characteristic of hard-rock and heavy-metal music was "its consistent non-invocation of rock history or mythology in any self-conscious or genealogical sense." He discovered that people with a limited educational background in America used this music as an expression of their aggressive masculinity. The heavy-metal look (long hair, denim jackets, and jeans) "came to acquire connotations of low socioeconomic position." As a result of their low social status and educational background, consumers of heavy rock music were not interested "in tracing the roots of any musical traits back to periods preceding the emergence of heavy metal."[19]

We can see certain parallels with the situations of Soviet hard-rock and heavy-metal consumption. Up until 1975, Soviet rock music consumers were predominantly from the middle and upper-middle classes—college students, the children of the college professors, teachers at secondary schools, physicians, and Communist Party and state functionaries (including police officers), whose musical preferences included different styles of popular music—from Jim Hendrix to the Beatles, from Cream to Deep Purple. After 1975, a new generation of pop music consumers emerged; the males among these consumers (predominantly representatives of lower-working-class families), in many cases students at vocational schools or young industrial workers, preferred only hard-rock music, from Led Zeppelin to AC/DC, while the females preferred the "light" dance tunes of Soviet *estrada* (pop music) or disco music.

Many contemporaries of these events noted a significant social factor that contributed to this development: the influx of young migrants from rural villages to the city. The majority of all PTU students and college students came from Ukrainian peasant families. During their years of study, they were adjusting to the new urban conditions of life, and they began consuming the popular music of the city en masse.[20] As Yurii Mytsyk, a historian who lived in Dniepropetrovsk at that time, explained, these young Ukrainian peasants experienced the shock of encountering a new lifestyle. They were losing their old peasant identity, cultural preferences, and stereotypes. In a Russified Ukrainian city like Dniepropetrovsk, many of these migrants adopted the new style of behavior that they had experienced in vocational school and college dormitories.[21] To some extent, they replaced elements of their Ukrainian peasant identities with new elements of urban popular youth culture, including not only the "obligatory" American jeans and long hair but also dancing to new music, especially hard rock and disco. Many police officers and Communist ideologists expressed their concerns about this transformation.[22] During police interrogations, PTU students who were arrested for different crimes during the late 1960s and 1970s blatantly denied their Ukrainian identity. In conversations with the police officers, these students, former Ukrainian peasant children, stressed that they "were not bumpkins [*byki,* or *baklany*] from the village." They explained to the police that they wore Western dress and listened to Western rock music because they wanted to look "cool" (*firmenno*) and "stylish" (*modno*).[23]

As Mytsyk noted, "PTU and college students, former Ukrainian peasant children, became the victims of Soviet cultural unification during mature socialism." This cultural unification or homogenization, according to some scholars, affected Ukrainian children in big industrial cities like Dniepropetrovsk. When these children left their villages for Dniepropetrovsk and tried to adjust to an urban lifestyle, they became completely im-

Figure 10.1. The beginning of the official, "theoretical" part of a disco program in one of the student dormitories of Dniepropetrovsk, November 1981. Photograph by the author.

Figure 10.2. The dance part of a disco program in one of the student dormitories of Dniepropetrovsk, November 1981. Photograph by the author.

Figure 10.3. A typical vocal instrumental ensemble, September 1980. Photograph by the author.

mersed in the cultural homogenization of this big industrial Soviet city.[24] Many of them lost the major features of their Ukrainian identity. They tried to speak Russian instead of Ukrainian; they wore new, fashionable Western dress; they listened and danced to the new, fashionable music; and they stopped reading Ukrainian literature. Urban Soviet mass culture—influenced by Western pop culture—filled a vacuum in the development of the Ukrainian peasants who moved to the cities. Soviet cultural homogenization, which involved millions of young people migrating from villages to the cities, laid the foundation for the consumption of Western mass culture during the late socialist period. Paradoxically, this process included the mass consumption of cultural products that had previously been rejected as dangerous tools of imperialist propaganda, such as American rock and roll and disco clubs.[25]

The democratization of rock music consumption during the mid-1970s led to the mass spreading of rock music products among the young people of the region of Dniepropetrovsk. A variety of this music became an integral part of the youth fashion, first in big cities such as Dniepropetrovsk, Krivoi Rog, and Dnieprodzerzhinsk, and then in smaller towns such as

Sinelnikovo, Novomoskovsk, and Pavlograd. By 1975, a majority of rock fans had recordings of the most popular hard-rock bands in their audio collections. Besides the obligatory Deep Purple, Led Zeppelin, Uriah Heep, and Black Sabbath, these consumers of the new rock music also obtained tapes of T. Rex, Queen, Slade, and Sweet at the Dniepropetrovsk music market. Although new styles of rock music were represented on the black market during the 1970s, from David Bowie to Pink Floyd, King Crimson, Yes, and Genesis, typical local consumers preferred music that could be easily performed and could be played at dances rather than for serious listening.[26]

As a result, the dance floor shaped the musical tastes of the overwhelming majority of those who consumed the new popular music during the 1970s. First, catchy and energetic melodies of glitter and glamour versions of British hard rock by such bands as Queen, Slade, Garry Glitter, and Sweet, which were available by 1976 on Dniepropetrovsk's music market, completely replaced the more sophisticated and longer compositions of intellectual rock bands like King Crimson, Emerson Lake & Palmer, Yes, early Pink Floyd, early Genesis, and Jethro Tull at dance parties. What remained for consumption by dance audiences included various slow ballads that could be played as "slow dance music."[27]

The Dance Floor as Center of
Pop Music Consumption

The dance floor (*tantsploshchadka*) in Soviet palaces of culture and various dormitories was the real arena of popular music consumption among Soviet youth. From the Stalinist era onward, the Soviet government and Communist ideologists paid attention to the organization of leisure time and entertainment for the Soviet people. Through ideologically reliable forms of artistic entertainment, Soviet leaders tried to shape the aesthetic tastes and worldview of Soviet cultural consumers.[28] For them, the main place for the collective organization of leisure time and entertainment was a Soviet palace (or house) of culture, which usually had libraries, special concert halls, movie theaters, and rooms for various cultural activities of numerous associations of singers, musicians, dancers, artists, and the like. According to the educational objectives of the Soviet government, these associations existed for amateurs who worked in collectives. Those who wanted to express themselves in any artistic or musical sphere had the opportunity to visit a palace of culture and participate. The Soviet state offered free education for amateur artists and musicians, providing them with the necessary music instruments and artistic tools at the palaces of culture.[29]

The dance floor was an important part of these palaces of culture and usually occupied the central place in the building. In the cities, palaces of culture were surrounded by parks of culture and relaxation, with outdoor dance floors. Millions of Soviet people spent their leisure time on these dance floors, dancing to the music of local bands whose members either worked at the local palace of culture or were hired to play for dance parties. To Soviet ideologists in the city of Dniepropetrovsk, a dance floor became not only a place for entertainment but also an arena of ideological confrontation between "bourgeois mass culture" and socialist forms of leisure.[30] In Dniepropetrovsk, an overwhelming majority of dance hall participants consisted of high school students, vocational school students (PTUs), technical school (*tekhnikum*) students, and college students.[31]

The regional administration maintained the palaces of culture by investing money in new buildings and equipment. Their number in the region increased from 997 in 1975 to 1,021 in 1985. In the city of Dniepropetrovsk alone, the number of houses of culture with dance floors grew from 52 in 1973 to 65 in 1985.[32] By the end of the 1970s, the best 240 palaces of culture among the 1,020 in the region belonged to the industrial trade unions. In 1983, these trade union palaces had 82 officially registered dance floors. During 1981–83, they organized more than 12,000 dance parties that had more than 2.8 million regular participants. Approximately 376 rock bands —called vocal instrumental ensembles—and orchestras played for these dance parties. In 1983, more than 5,000 musicians were hired to play by the trade union palaces of culture. According to Komsomol statistics, in 1978 in the city of Dniepropetrovsk 14 of the most popular dance floors had regular bands. All these dance floors had existed since the beginning of the 1960s, and all of them were funded by the industrial trade unions.[33]

Dniepropetrovsk's Communist ideologists tried to establish tight ideological control over the dance floors. Youth dormitories with indoor dance floors (for students and young workers) became an object of attention for the Komsomol apparatchiks. In the city of Dniepropetrovsk alone, at least a third of its young population (more than 70,000 people) lived in 235 city dormitories during the years 1978–79. All of them visited local dance floors on a regular basis.[34] Communist ideologists worried about Western influences that affected students in their dorms, including dorm dance floors. According to official statistics, the number of college students who lived in dormitories increased from 20,300 in the years 1975–76 to 27,800 in

1984–85. At the same time, the number of technical school students living in dorms grew from 18,800 to 21,700. All these students became active consumers of Western cultural products and participants in various dance parties at their dorms.[35]

On March 4, 1972, Oleksii F. Vatchenko, the first secretary of the Dniepropetrovsk regional committee of the Communist Party of the Soviet Union, delivered a speech at the annual conference of the regional Komsomol organization. He spoke about the dangerous Westernization of the local students and about Komsomol's failure to fight the capitalist cultural influences in the dormitories and on the dance floors of the city. He reminded Komsomol activists that

> it is impossible to stay indifferent to various perversions in the student society about fashion, music, and arts. What we see [on the dance floor] —untidy appearance, extremely long hair among certain boys, beards that look like they were borrowed from the pages of foreign magazines— all this does not fit an image of the Soviet young man. This influence of alien morals is a result of a blind imitation of bourgeois fashions that Komsomol organizations do not repulse. As a matter of fact, our dance floors at both palaces of culture and student dorms now popularize the morality and manners which are alien to Soviet culture. They engage in propaganda of trashy foreign music. Dances are now transformed into vulgar body movements that are reminiscent of savage orgies rather than cultural entertainment. Remember that this kind of entertainment could lead young men to other, more dangerous, displays of [anti-Soviet] behavior, such as political indifference, skepticism, neglect of the Soviet citizen's duties. . . . We need to find new forms of work with our youth. We must cultivate a love of real art and good music. If we bring this good music to the dance floor as well, we will eventually decrease the influence and number of spreaders of music records and tapes with trashy and degenerate Western music among the young audience.[36]

Responding to the orders of the party leaders, Komsomol activists organized annual raids of the local dance floors during the period 1972–75. These activists constantly complained about the Westernization of young audiences on the dance floor. But the Communist ideologists failed to outlaw dancing to Western music.

Beginning in the early 1960s, many Soviet organizations in the region had started making money from young people's music consumption on dance floors. The administrations of the local palaces of culture, restaurants (or canteens), and even food stores near popular dance floors had a vested interest in the rising attendance at neighboring dancing parties. The young guests of the local dance floors were ready to pay not only for admission but also for alcoholic and nonalcoholic beverages and food provided by local stores and restaurants/canteens offering catering services. This kind of consumption led to increased profits for not only those who organized dance parties but also for those who catered to the young participants in these parties. That is why the Soviet apparatchiks who were in charge of the palaces of culture and nearby local restaurants/canteens and food stores resisted any attempt to interfere with their profits. As a result, the Communist ideologists responsible for the ideological reliability of youth entertainment were unable to shut down the popular dance floors, despite constant complaints about the consumption of Western music. The officials involved in the beverage and food catering businesses simply ignored ideological pressure and used various forms of resistance to preserve their profits.

The most scandalous case of such resistance involved the trust of canteens in the downtown Kirov District of Dniepropetrovsk. From 1972 to 1983, the Kirov trust provided alcoholic beverages and snacks to the young guests of popular youth clubs and dance floors in the city. Whenever Komsomol apparatchiks filed an official complaint about certain ideological transgressions related to the dance floor or youth club located near the Kirov trust of canteens, the administration always rejected their complaints. The trust administration and local entertainers united their efforts in a struggle against overzealous Komsomol activists. As a result, the material interests of the catering service prevailed over the ideological concerns of the Komsomol apparatchiks. A secretary of the Komsomol organization at Yuzhmash, the rocket-building plant, complained in 1972 that the Kirov trust did not permit any dance party at the youth club Mriia without special conditions in their agreement about providing catering services for the dance party. This condition included the obligatory sale of a minimum alcohol consumption per person: 350 to 400 grams of vodka for each participant in the dance party. Any attempt to break this agreement led to the automatic cancellation of the Komsomol dance parties.

Eventually, the sale of alcohol became part of catering services for all youth clubs and parks of culture and relaxation in downtown Dniepropetrovsk. As late as 1983, despite numerous efforts by Komsomol activists to cancel the services of the Kirov trust of canteens for youth entertainment, the regular visitors to dance floors kept drinking the beer and vodka provided by the trust. During the 1980s, the trust established special relations with the city Komsomol and trade union leaders and became the main provider of catering services for popular and profitable disco clubs downtown.[37]

Communist ideologists also failed to control the ideological level of music played on the dance floor. During 1975, the Komsomol city committee organized special raids of the local restaurants, cafés, and various dance floors at the palaces of culture and the city parks. The officials making these raids discovered that all the bands playing included Western rock music in their repertoire. These bands had a special official approval for their music program. However, they followed this program only when the official representatives were present. Usually the bands alternated between fast (Western) and slow (Soviet) dances. At the end of the party, they played only Western music.[38]

A typical dance party was described by the participants in the Komsomol raid on January 25, 1975, when officials visited the local trade union palace of culture in downtown Dniepropetrovsk. According to the official report of the Komsomol activists who took part in this raid, the dance floor was open at 8 pm. The admission fee was 50 kopecks for every guest of the dance party. More than 200 young people, ages sixteen to nineteen years, arrived at the beginning of a dance. Some of them were already drunk. The palace of culture offered a buffet, which was officially open until 8 pm. In fact, they served beer and snacks for all participants until 10 pm. The dance floor stayed open until midnight, with attendance increasing to up to 500 people.

As the administration of this raided downtown trade union palace admitted, dance parties brought usually profits of 300 to 500 rubles per night, or 6,000 rubles per month. Using this money, they were able to buy musical instruments and pay a relatively good salary to their musicians. Each member of the local vocal instrumental ensemble that played on a dance floor officially earned no more than 100 rubles per month. In reality, these musicians could make much more money at the palace of culture. They earned an additional "nonregistered" 100 to 300 rubles for each dance over playing the same instruments at private events, such as weddings and birthday parties. For these rock musicians, the local palace of culture was a good official cover, and dance parties were a good testing ground for new popular music, including Western rock and roll. According to the official Komsomol report on the January 1975 raid, the band "played waltz, tango, shake, *kazachok* [a popular Soviet dance of the 1960s], and contemporary Soviet *estrada* songs."

Figure 10.4. A student wedding party on the embankment of the Dnieper River, August 1979. Photograph by the author.

The report on this January 1975 raid also contained complaints about the immense popularity of "the pieces of perverted Western music which attracted all young people to this dance floor." "When the young guests recognized familiar Western melodies," the Komsomol observers wrote, "they ran to this dance floor like mad men and asked the musicians to repeat these songs again and again." All these participants immediately stopped dancing and left the dance floor when the band began to play Soviet songs. Usually ten to fifteen couples danced to the waltz, while the overwhelming majority of dancers went out to smoke in a palace foyer and waited for their "ace great" (*baldiozhnaia*) music. When the band resumed playing this "cool" (Western rock) music, the dancers returned to the dance floor, formed circles of five to ten people each, and danced "their perverted shakes."[39]

Other local rock musicians who were active at this time described similar situations for the city's other dance floors. For instance, the musicians who used to play in the band at the Chkalov Park of Culture and Relaxation in downtown Dniepropetrovsk admitted that they "usually played obligatory Soviet hits, especially at the beginning of a dance." As one former musician explained,

There were the songs from repertoire of Alla Pugacheva and various Soviet VIAs [vocal instrumental ensembles, *vokal'no-instrumental'nyi ansambl'* in Russian]. But when we saw that the representatives of the ideological committees who checked our repertoire left the dance floor, we stopped playing Soviet *estrada*. Then we played what our audience loved the most—the Western hot stuff. For more than an hour we performed the hits of Deep Purple, such as "Smoke on the Water," "Sail Away," and "Highway Star," and Uriah Heep's favorites, such as "July Morning." For our tough male audience, we played the fast numbers of Slade or T. Rex; for our girls, we performed the obligatory slow songs such as Led Zeppelin's "Stairway to Heaven." Usually one of our friends informed us about a visit of suspicious-looking middle-aged people, who might be the KGB or Communist apparatchiks. In this case we again switched to the boring Soviet *estrada* numbers. The administration of Chkalov Park clearly understood that our Western music attracted more people to their dance parties. That is why they did not care about our musical tastes. What they did care about was their profits. The more people visited our dance floor, the better their financial situation became. Therefore our local supervisors told us to "play what you like but avoid scandals." Moreover, our administration often asked us to play for other extra gigs—for official ceremonies, weddings, private parties at their houses. They were interested in keeping us as an active music band because we attracted people and created immense popularity for the Chkalov Park dance floor with our British hard-rock sound.[40]

As we can see, during the democratization of rock music consumption, Dniepropetrovsk's dance floors became not only sources of emotional satisfaction and socialization for local young consumers but also very important sources of profit for both Soviet officials and musicians. Therefore, by 1975, dance music was contributing to building new business enterprises, which united the efforts of both ideological supervisors and music providers as advocates for dance parties in the closed city.

Conclusion

From 1971 to 1975, the new, loud, heavy, and aggressive music of the British hard-rock bands like Deep Purple replaced traditionally popular

Anglo-American beat music on the Dniepropetrovsk music market. In contrast to the consumption of jazz and beat music, which was still elitist, the hard rock of the early 1970s led to mass pop music consumption, which affected millions of Soviet young people by the end of the Brezhnev era. This new heavy hard rock also triggered the so-called democratization of Western pop music consumption in major industrial Soviet cities like Dniepropetrovsk. And the British hard-rock bands paved a road for various versions of glam rock, glitter rock, and eventually even disco music on the Dniepropetrovsk music market. This music attracted new young consumers—mostly high school, vocational school, and technical school students and young industrial workers—who enjoyed this music collectively on dance floors or in their dormitories.

Gradually, by the mid-1970s, a new commercial element appeared as an important aspect of rock music consumption. The dance floor (*tantssploshchadka*) became a significant part of Soviet entertainment. This entertainment business was a place of interaction between musicians and official organizers of entertainment at the local palaces of culture, also Communist (in many cases, Komsomol) ideologists, on the one hand, and the enthusiasts of rock music with their own extensive collections of this music who provided the dance floors with important music information, on the other. The overwhelming majority of these enthusiasts were also active participants in the black market who made money by trading precious music information, original music records, and tapes. Some of these *fartsovshchiks* (black marketers) became integrated into the system of Soviet entertainment.[41] Dance floors thus united the official representatives of Soviet entertainment and Communist ideology with the representatives of the technically illegal black market of popular music in a very special form of cultural production and consumption.

At the same time, the young Ukrainian consumers were losing their Ukrainian identity on the dance floor by identifying themselves with Western hard-rock musical culture rather than Soviet Ukrainian musical culture. During the 1970s, a majority of young male Ukrainians constructed their own identity by rejecting elements of Ukrainian popular culture. They tried to look and behave "coolly," like their Western idols of hard rock and glam rock.

Chapter 11

Popular Religiosity in the Dniepropetrovsk Region: Cultural Consumption and Religion

In 1968, in his report to the regional Communist Party committee, Nikolai Mazhara, head of the Dniepropetrovsk KGB Department, complained that the "rise in religiosity" among local Komsomol members was connected to Western cultural products. The KGB detected increased anti-Soviet and "politically harmful" religious activity in the region. The KGB officer especially noted that antireligious campaign of 1960–61 did not stop "the anti-Soviet crimes of religious activists in the region." Mazhara also expressed his concern about "the growing popular religiosity among the local youth, who read more religious books, including the Bible, listened to more religious radio shows, recorded more religious sermons and music, and collected more religious objects of art than they had done before 1967."[1]

The KGB official called all this "the anti-Soviet consumption of the products of religious culture [*potreblenie produktov religioznoi kul'tury*]." According to him, this "dangerous cultural consumption," which came from the capitalist West, threatened to destroy the Soviet identity of local youth "with anti-Soviet religious elements." The police even arrested young people for trading crosses and icons at the local farmers' markets.[2] KGB reports from the 1970s mention high school and college students in the region reading the Gospels. Even local tourists became involved in a very unusual form of cultural consumption: On their trips abroad, they bought Bibles, Orthodox crosses, and icons and brought them back to Dniepropetrovsk. According to KGB reports, 90 percent of all transgressions occurring on tourist trips were related to "popular religiosity."[3]

187

During the 1970s and 1980s, Mazhara and his successors in the Dnie-propetrovsk KGB constantly reminded local ideologists about the need to protect Soviet cultural identity from the polluting influences of religion and Western mass culture.[4] Popular religiosity also became part of cultural consumption in the region of Dniepropetrovsk. Religious cultural consumption was a serious problem for both Communist ideologists and KGB officials.[5]

Khrushchev's Antireligious Campaigns and the Spread of Popular Religiosity

Nikita Khrushchev started his de-Stalinization campaign in 1956 in an attempt to cleanse Soviet society from any deviation of socialism, preparing the road for building a new Communist society in the USSR. According to Khrushchev's plans, this society had no space for religion. Therefore, his ideas for the liberalization of the Soviet society and culture coexisted with an offensive against religion and popular religiosity; which at times was even worse than Stalin's antireligious campaigns.[6] In the USSR during the years 1960–61, the number of Orthodox congregations decreased from 14,000 to fewer than 8,000. In Ukraine, only 49 Orthodox parishes survived these campaigns.[7]

Khrushchev's antireligious emphasis contributed to the KGB's operations against organized religion in the region of Dniepropetrovsk. In addition to the traditional ideological justification for these "operations," KGB officials now used another very important argument for their antireligious activities: an ideological vigilance in the strategically important region of the Soviet military complex aimed at the prevention of any connection of local religious organizations to foreign religious centers. The KGB considered these centers to be part of an anti-Soviet imperialist strategy. The KGB had to protect the Dniepropetrovsk military-industrial complex from any "ideological provocation of anti-Soviet imperialist propagandist centers," including religious ones from the West.[8] Besides the spread of "dangerous" Western mass culture and Ukrainian nationalism in the region, the growth and spread of popular religiosity, especially among young people, became a major concern for both KGB officers and Communist ideologists in the region from the 1960s through the 1980s. According to KGB statistics, by 1964 more than 3 percent of the Dniepropetrovsk Region's inhabitants were members of various religious congregations.[9] KGB officers thought that this growth of popular religiosity was due in part to overzealous Dnie-propetrovsk ideologists and Soviet officials, who by 1967 had closed 203 of the region's religious congregations.[10] KGB statistics confirmed these concerns about the "growth of religion in the region"; from a third to a half of the region's entire newborn infant population was baptized in a church during the 1960s.[11]

On December 12, 1963, a KGB official complained to Volodymyr Shcherbytsky, the first secretary of the regional Communist Party committee, that the forced closing of the meeting houses and churches provoked the "anti-Soviet actions of sectarian preachers and priests of the Orthodox Church." The KGB operative feared that local religious activists would ask the political leaders of the "Western capitalist countries" to interfere in "Soviet atheistic politics." After the closing of his church in the village near Dniepropetrovsk, the Orthodox priest Vasilii Kremena tried to calm his parishioners and promised them that "people from the West will take care of our religious situation, they will help us, and we will resume our religious service at the same church." Another priest, Vlas Tereshchenko, told his followers after the official closing of their church in the village of Bogdanovka, "These house-dogs [*Barbosy*] closed our churches and took our liberties. But we must stand firmly and fight for Jesus Christ. Only our God's laws are the real laws for us."[12] The Orthodox priest Nikolai Petrov, from a nearby district, delivered a long sermon in May 1963 with vituperative criticism of the Soviet administration. He began his sermon with a reference to the recent disturbances in the mining town of Krivoi Rog, where thousands of workers organized demonstrations against inadequate supplies of food:

> The events in Krivoi Rog were organized not only by ordinary workers. Organizers of the events included no less than 30 percent of Communists, who shouted, "It is enough to feed us only with macaroni!" It is not surprising that these events happened. Look at our collective farmers; they are paid only 40 kopeks a day. Their living conditions are appalling. But do not worry; the time is coming when the Germans and Americans will come again and liberate us.[13]

Orthodox believers did not forget closed or sometimes destroyed churches. As KGB operatives reported, the former parishioners of Vlas Tereshchenko continued unsanctioned religious meetings at their old church locations five years after their church had been demolished. According to the KGB report, on June 18, 1967, during the holiday of the Holy Trinity, two hundred of Tereshchenko's parishioners met at the location of their demolished church, held religious ceremonies, and celebrated a holiday dinner together. For many years afterward, Orthodox believers from

Bogdanovka's congregation remained loyal to their old priest Tereshchenko and organized religious meetings in open fields on a regular basis. The persistence of Bogdanovka Christians was a reaction to the rash decision of the local administration to close and demolish the old and very popular church.[14]

One KGB report concluded that the "illegal" closing of religious buildings by Dniepropetrovsk officials had prompted local Orthodox (mainly young) followers to join nearby Christian sects, especially Pentecostal groups, and in some places had even led to an unprecedented increase of new, and sometimes illegal, religious groups.[15] The growth of various Protestant sects in the region became a major concern of the KGB. A powerful stimulus behind this increase in popular religiosity was the creation of the "Initiative Group" among the Soviet Baptists in August 1961. Growing dissatisfaction with the conformism and formalism of the official leadership of the All-Soviet Union of Evangelical Christian Baptists led to divisions within and between congregations and resulted ultimately in the creation of a new organization in 1965—the Council of Churches of Evangelical Christian Baptists—uniting those who disagreed with the policies of the official Union. Though the officially recognized Baptist communities followed Soviet laws and demonstrated their loyalty to the Soviet administration, the dissenting Baptists, who were called *initsiativniki,* caused real problems for the police and administrative officials; though they tended to sever relations with the Soviet state, when they did deal with officials they were usually confrontational, and they quickly became famous for using music and technology to provoke conflict and debates among the evangelicals of the Dniepropetrovsk Region.[16]

The main problem for the local police in Dniepropetrovsk was the proselytizing efforts of different churches among the local youth through what the KGB called the "modernization of religion."[17] KGB operatives were surprised by Christian groups' effective use of radio, musical instruments, record players, and tape recorders in their missionary efforts. Pentecostals and Baptists were the most active and successful in their missionary activities among Dniepropetrovsk's youth.[18]

Tape Recorders and Other Objects of Socialist Consumption among Dniepropetrovsk's Evangelicals

"Leaders of the Pentecostal sect," wrote a KGB officer in a 1963 report, urge their followers to "buy tape recorders, record . . . their religious ceremonies, and then during an absence of their leaders to organize [prayer

meetings] using the tapes of previous worship meetings. After these recommendations, all Dniepropetrovsk sectarians immediately bought tape
recorders."[19] Tape-recording equipment was still considered expensive for
local consumers, but Pentecostals became the most prominent participants
in this facet of Soviet cultural consumption, buying more tape recorders in
the region than nonreligious dwellers during the period 1962–65. As some
contemporary observers noted, the sectarians became real pioneers in tape-
recording technology, inviting young specialist engineers to help and using
various advanced techniques (including Western ones) in their recording
and performance of religious services and ceremonies.[20]

Television sets were another popular item of cultural consumption
among sectarians. As a KGB officer reported, "To conceal their meetings
for worship from persecution (especially in the evenings), leaders of the illegal sectarian groups advised their coreligionists to buy television sets and
perform religious ceremonies on the pretext of collective watching of TV
shows."[21] It is noteworthy that during the 1960s and 1970s, Soviet evangelicals were always associated in the Communist ideologists' imagination
with antimodern behavior. According to official Soviet propaganda, Christian believers were outdated, backward people who rejected cultural and
technological progress. Suddenly, KGB operatives had to admit that evangelicals had become the most active participants in the socialist cultural
consumption.[22]

The Baptist dissenters' uncompromising attitude toward the Soviet administration, support of young members and their organization of music
bands and children's choirs attracted hundreds of former members of conformist Baptist churches to the new groups of *initsiativniki*. In May 1965, a
bus with thirty such Baptist dissenters from Krivoi Rog arrived in a village
near Dniepropetrovsk where local Baptists held their meeting for worship.
These *initsiativniki* asked for permission to preach. When the local "official"
minister denied their request, the dissenters began an improvised meeting for
worship with preaching, praying, and singing. They told the local Baptists
that the dissenters' preaching "was closer to God because they rejected any
collaboration with Soviet state." Therefore, they preached that conformist
Christians must remove themselves from "communities of traitors whose
meetings were sanctioned by the state and as a result, were transformed into
loyal elements of the state machine." The dissenters brought violins, guitars,
mandolins, and some electrical equipment, including amplifiers.

These guests, school students among them, transformed their improvised
meeting into an interesting religious concert with songs, the recitation of religious poems, and collective praying. Not only the local Baptists but also

Figure 11.1. A regional meeting for worship of Baptist dissenters in the forest near Dniepropetrovsk, November 8, 1968. Photograph by the author.

Figure 11.2. The Orthodox Cathedral of the Transfiguration, which housed the Museum of the History of Religion and Atheism during the Brezhnev era. Photograph by the author.

Figure 11.3. The old Lutheran church, which was used as the Library of Foreign Literature during the Brezhnev era. Photograph by the author.

their nonreligious neighbors were attracted by the music and joined the growing crowd of people around the bus of these "musical guests." An "official" minister of the local Baptist congregation sent for the police to arrest the "uninvited guests" and stop their propaganda among his coreligionists. But it was too late. The damage had been already done to his congregation. Before the police came, the dissenters left the place, but some local Baptists joined the *initsiativniki* and quit their old community. As they later explained to their minister, the dissenters were "closer to them and corresponded better to their ideal of Christianity than their own community's cautious traditional style of worship."[23]

Pentecostal leaders also changed their methods for missionary activities. They now targeted not only the young people but also older people who had personal problems, such as death in their family or divorce. As one of the sectarians told a KGB informer, "We need to study all neighborhoods to figure out real problems of the nonbelievers and collect information about families with scandals, drinking problems, divorce, analyze the reasons of all these family problems, and then to direct all our attention and influence on members of such 'problematic' families." It is noteworthy that local sectarians sometimes provided "the old and lonely members of their sect with tape recorders and radio sets to be sure that their members would listen and record the religious radio shows."[24] By using new forms of cultural consumption, sectarians offered emotional help to people with personal problems. When the Soviet administration and party organizations ignored these problems and paid no attention to ordinary people who needed care and help, then local sects appeared and provided care and assistance. According to KGB complaints, this lack of attention from Soviet and Communist Party officials to the personal problems of people who suffered was a major reason for the missionary success of sectarians. KGB reports from 1963 to 1973 noted this fact and criticized the local administration, party, and Komsomol officials for their loss of interest in the real human problems of the region's ordinary residents.[25]

Both the KGB operatives and Soviet officials noted how a new level of cultural consumption among sectarians affected youth who were attracted to the dissenters' meetings of worship by music and new cultural forms of religious rituals. In their report of December 28, 1965, these officials complained of the growth of illegal youth organizations among both the Baptists and Pentecostals under the influence of the Baptist dissenters. The *initsiativniks* used new methods and music, which attracted more young people to the radical evangelical movements in the city of Dniepropetrovsk. Three young preachers among these dissenters—Ivan Garkusha, Anna Chaban, and Pavel Malyi—formed new evangelical groups of former Baptists and Pentecostals in the city. These groups denied any state control and, as a result, grew faster than old evangelical congregations. They used religious concerts to attract the local youth to their meetings for worship.[26] The growing popularity of new technical and musical forms in the propagandist efforts of the dissenters affected all old evangelical congregations. Young members now desired more music and more singing during their meetings for worship. They referred to the success of dissenters to justify their efforts to bring new musical forms into the religious life of their traditional communities.

In December 1965, young activists from registered Baptist congregations in Dniepropetrovsk approached their presbyter, Shchukin, and asked him to allow them to organize special musical training and rehearsals each Saturday when they could sing new hymns, play new musical instruments, and use new musical equipment and recording technology. To justify their request, they mentioned how the *initsiativniki* attracted youth to their meetings for worship by playing modern musical instruments, using modern melodies and arrangements for psalms and theatrical declamations of religious poetry, which transformed traditional religious ceremonies into an emotional and attractive performance for young people. Young activists argued that the incorporation of modern musical forms into traditional religious meetings would both retain all those young people who loved singing and who enjoyed modern music and bring back those young Baptists who had begun visiting the dissenters' meetings looking for modern musical forms. The administration of registered Baptist congregations finally permitted musical rehearsals for their young activists. However, under pressure from Soviet officials who interpreted this as a transgression against Soviet religious laws, the ministers had to cancel these rehearsals. As a result, many young Baptists continued to prefer the dissenters' meetings. Old Baptist congregations were losing the struggle for popularity to the *initsiativniki.*[27]

The Baptist dissenters tried to attract young people to their meetings and make them active participants, equal to the old members of traditional congregations. As one leader of the Krivoi Rog *initsiativniki,* F. Petrakov, emphasized during a congress of the Baptist presbyters in February of 1966, the main reason for the split of local Baptists was the prohibition of children from participation in the meetings for worship. As he said, "They [the conformists] ousted our youth from the choirs and forbade baptism of the young people till the age of eighteen years, and limited baptism of those below thirty years." As a result, conformist leaders banned any creative activity of the youth and stopped their missionary work. Petrakov urged the conformist Baptists to separate from the Soviet atheist state and intensify missionary work among the youth of the region.[28]

Even during the 1970s, the radical evangelicals were still more efficient in their usage of new technologies than were the traditional Baptists preachers. In 1972, one Baptist dissenter, Nikolai Iarko, used his tape recorder to play religious sermons in the passenger trains running between Dniepropetrovsk and its neighboring towns. According to the police, Iarko had recorded foreign religious radio shows and then included some fragments of popular music by the Beatles to make his Baptist "message" more attractive, especially to younger passengers.[29]

The influence of young evangelicals in the 1970s forced the leadership of the region's moderate Baptists to adjust their strategy to the new realities. They even borrowed some new ideas and technology from their rivals, the *initsiativniki.* The new head of the region's Baptists, Venedikt Galenko, used "modern" music, guitar bands, and youth choirs to attract more visitors to worship meetings. With the same goal in mind, he organized a dinner on New Year's Eve 1972, which featured a special religious concert with live music and the airing of a variety of tape-recorded sermons, including recordings of some foreign radio shows. Galenko also invited some of the city's other evangelicals, especially *initsiativniki,* to attend the dinner meeting. The event was a great success. Loud music and free food—which included sausages, cheese, buns, lemonade, tea, sweets, and so on—attracted many young people to this meeting. But Soviet officials were not at all pleased. "These new methods" of religious propaganda, they complained to Galenko, "were not desirable because they included elements of Western modernization."[30]

Galenko must not have heeded these concerns because, some six months later, on June 22, 1973, he received a special order from the city administration directing him to "stop this transformation of worship meetinghouses into cafés and forbid the organization there of special music parties with dinners and concerts." The order further required the city's Baptist leaders to remove all radio, music, and tape-recording equipment from their meeting-houses, and to remove amplifiers, musical instruments, benches, and other concert equipment from the yards of these meetinghouses. All religious concerts were banned in Dniepropetrovsk, and children were prohibited from attending religious meetings.[31] Thus, Soviet officials tried to stop the "Western modernization" of the Dniepropetrovsk Region's evangelical movement, but it failed to do so; and in fact, despite police persecution, the movement not only became more modernized but also more radical, especially among those under twenty-five years of age, who during the 1970s comprised 25 percent of the membership.[32]

Tape-recordings of foreign broadcasts were not the only problem for Soviet officials worried about the increasing influence of popular religiosity at this time. In 1968, the KGB reported that Christians from a variety of denominations also were listening directly to foreign radio stations. More than 500 Christians (mainly Baptists) from the Dniepropetrovsk Region had organized meetings where participants could listen to foreign radio shows about religion, as a result of which more than 300 individuals had tried to "establish written correspondence with leaders of foreign religious centers and their radio stations." What bothered the KGB officials in particular were letters that Dniepropetrovsk Baptists tried to send to the World Council of Churches and to the United Nations complaining of religious persecution in the region. According to the KGB, in 1968 alone the police had detected illegal activities on the part of nine groups of *initsiativniki* (500 members), eight groups of Pentecostals (600 members), and five small groups of Jehovah's Witnesses (30 members).[33]

In the years 1967–68, the police also reported the growth of the Jewish religion in the region. In one synagogue in the city of Dniepropetrovsk, there was an increase of visitors from 35 to 50 people on workdays and 250 on the Sabbath to 3,000 during the big Jewish holidays. At least half of these were "Jews younger than forty years of age."[34] According to the KGB reports, some local Jews who visited the Dniepropetrovsk synagogue demonstrated in public their "Jewish religiosity," pro-Israel sympathies, and intentions to immigrate to Israel. The KGB linked pro-Israel ideas to the rise of the anti-Soviet activities among Jewish youth in Dniepropetrovsk. According to the KGB informers, "the young Jews were especially insolent because they knew about their protection by the state of Israel and their possible migration to the West." As one agent noted, "these young Zionists expected that the entire capitalist West would protect them against the anti-Semitism of the Soviet officials." These young Jews organized groups to study Jewish religion and culture. All of them supported "ideas of Zionism to restore the historical Jewish state in Palestine." They regularly listened to Western radio shows and corresponded with their relatives and friends in the United States and Israel. Overall, in Dniepropetrovsk the police recorded at least ten cases of such "Zionism" among young Jewish intellectuals from 1968 to 1972.[35]

"Modernization" among Orthodox and Evangelical Believers

At the same time, the KGB was sounding the alarm about the growth and modernization of evangelical and Jewish groups, it also was tracking the growing influence of the Orthodox Church. An alarming number of young married couples, mostly Komsomol members, still observed the rite of Baptism for their newborns. In 1970, 34 percent of all newborns in the region were baptized in the Orthodox Church, while 42 percent of all funerals in the region were performed according to Orthodox rituals. Some local college students even entered Orthodox seminaries. The police calculated that by the end of 1976 there were roughly seventy-three thousand activists of the Orthodox Church in the region. The KGB connected the Church's growing popularity with the new leaders of the Dniepropetrovsk Diocese, including the new and very ambitious bishop Antonii (whose civil name was Onufrii I. Vikarik).[36]

During the 1970s, the Soviet government initiated a special voluntary money collection project known as the Soviet Fund of Peace among Soviet people. All Soviet organizations and religious congregations were supposed to collect money from their members for this fund. In reality, the Soviet government also used this fund for military needs. Bishop Antonii understood this and tried to resist collecting money in his parish for this fund. His main reason for resistance was the desire to stir up religious activities among clergy of the region. He publicly announced that the local Orthodox Church must decrease contributions to the Soviet Fund of Peace and, instead, Christians should create additional funds for the improvement of missionary activities among the local youth. Antonii told his audience:

> This is not a fund of peace, but a fund of preparation for a war. We have to think how to spread Christ's teaching among people. For this objective, we need to increase missionary activities and invest money in these activities. Therefore, it would be better to spend our funds on these activities than to waste them in the Fund of Peace, which has nothing to do with peace at all.[37]

In 1971, Bishop Antonii tried to replace Orthodox officials who were secret KGB informers with new, honest religious activists in his diocese. He declined candidates for different offices in a diocese if he knew about their collaboration with the KGB, or if they were recommended by Soviet officials for this job. He also tried to restore the leading position of the Orthodox Church among Christian believers of the region. He organized a special missionary campaign against Protestant sects and invited young members of these sects to join Orthodoxy. Antonii even promoted the church careers for those young talented sectarians who renounced their old sect and converted to Orthodoxy. As a result of his efforts, he raised the prestige and position of the Orthodox Church in the region by 1970. Moreover, he organized the purchase of new music and technical equipment for the needs of the local Orthodox Church. KGB officers called this the "Westernization of the Church." As a result, the KGB organized a special campaign to discredit the bishop and remove him from office.[38] Eventually, under pressure from the KGB, Bishop Antonii was removed from the region, and KGB representatives reestablished their control in the diocese. In their April 13, 1973, letter to the USSR Council of Ministers, the local Soviet officials supported KGB recommendations to remove Antonii from his office because of "his refusal to collaborate with Soviet administration in the region of Dniepropetrovsk and his modernization of the church."[39]

During the 1970s and the 1980s, the KGB officials also worried about the new, modernized propagandist efforts of non-Orthodox Christian denominations. They noted how modern forms of cultural consumption—such as music recording technology, theatrical performances, guitar bands, and orchestras—attracted more young people to these religious groups. According to their records, the most successful in the "modernization of cultural consumption" were Baptist groups. When the police reminded Baptist ministers that the involvement of children in religious rituals was a crime, the Baptist leadership just ignored the police interference. Even in a small Baptist congregation of seventy-eight members near the city of Dniepropetrovsk, the police recorded seven transgressions of Soviet laws, including children's involvement in the choral and musical activities of the congregation from September 1976 to March 1977.[40]

KGB and Soviet officials noted the "radicalization of evangelical movement in the region" during approximately the same time. A. Kirichenko, a presbyter of Dniepropetrovsk city congregation of Evangelical Christian Baptists, publicly ignored the local Soviet administration. As Soviet officials complained in December 1975, without official permission, Kirichenko and his followers tried to organize a religious meeting of city Evangelical Christian Baptists, which was dedicated to the one-hundredth anniversary of the founding of the Baptist city congregation. Moreover, a radical Baptist presbyter invited the *initsiativniki* to collaborate together against state atheism. Kirichenko removed all those who were loyal to the Soviet administration from their offices in the city congregation. He did not allow official representatives of the Soviet administration to visit Baptist meetings for worship. In his sermons, he always criticized the Soviet administration. "This administration," he preached in February 1976, "always oppressed us and they still oppress us now. We can't expect any leniency from Satan anymore."[41]

In June 1976, Kirichenko organized the "Brotherly Council," with twenty-nine representatives from different districts of the city. His goal was to restore the democratic spirit of the early church and avoid state control over religious activities. Eventually, under pressure from the KGB, radical evangelical preachers like Kirichenko were removed from their offices in Baptist congregations. As a result, some young members of the officially registered Baptist congregations left their communities and joined radical nonconformist groups of the *initsiativniki*.

It is noteworthy that the main concern of both KGB and Soviet local officials was the modernization of cultural consumption among Dniepropetrovsk evangelicals. KGB operatives and Communist apparatchiks worried about new forms of cultural consumption, such as the spread of tape-recordings of foreign radio shows, the popularity of religious tapes and books, and the combination of "modern guitar music" with elaborate theatrical performances. During the early 1980s, new cultural forms attracted young people, including Komsomol members, who initially visited these religious meetings purely out of curiosity, not because of religious propaganda.[42] In January 1980, the KGB discovered an underground Christian printing-press in the suburban zone of Dniepropetrovsk with thousands of audiotapes of religious preaching and piles of religious literature. As it turned out, all these books and tapes were objects of very intense cultural consumption by thousands of the local evangelicals. The most radical of them used both tapes and books in their underground biblical school, which became popular among curious young consumers of this religious information.[43]

Popular Religiosity and Western Rock Music

A peculiar case of cultural consumption connected the world of Western rock music with religion in the region of Dniepropetrovsk. According to contemporaries, it was the music of the Beatles, and especially George Harrison's songs, which toward the end of the 1960s provided the first link between the world of Western popular music, on the one hand, and religion in the region of Dniepropetrovsk, on the other. All Beatles fans knew about Harrison's interest in Indian culture and religion. "When we listened to Harrison's experiments with the sitar and other Indian musical instruments in the such Beatles songs as 'Norwegian Wood' and 'Within You Without You,'" one former beat music enthusiast noted, "we decided to collect all information about the Indian cultural roots of the Beatles' music, and we discovered, surprisingly for us, all sorts of Eastern religions, including Hinduism, Krishnaism, and Buddhism, that had inspired our idol, George Harrison."[44]

In the late 1960s, teachers from Dniepropetrovsk's high schools routinely complained that students were spending their class breaks reading popular books on the history of Indian religion and drawing symbols of "Eastern mystic religions" in their notebooks. According to teachers' reports, all these enthusiasts of Indian religion were *bitlomany* (Beatles fans).[45] Both teachers and librarians noted that young beat music enthusiasts cut out any pages from the Komsomol magazine *Rovesnik* containing information about the Beatles, and also pages from books about Indian history and religion.[46]

The police connected the rising interest in Eastern religions among Komsomol *bitlomany* to the Soviet hippie movement. In May 1970, ten young hippies (all high school students) were arrested in downtown Dniepropetrovsk for shouting "Hare Krishna" slogans and "exposing symbols of the Buddhist religion." The police thought the arrests would put an end to public demonstrations by "Soviet Hinduists and Buddhists."[47] But they did nothing to prevent some *bitlomany* from pursuing their exploration of Indian philosophy and religion. "I tried to figure out the meaning of the strange phrase 'Gura Deva Om' from the Beatles song 'Across the Universe,' which was on their *Let It Be* album," fifteen-year-old Vladimir Solodovnik wrote in his diary in June 1971. "I read everything in our school library about Indian religion, and I discovered more than I expected."[48] This eventually led Solodovnik and his friends to begin reading literature about Krishnaism on a regular basis in the 1970s. Two of his classmates became serious followers of Krishna in the 1980s. During the period 1972–82, they and other "Krishnaists" from the closed city went to neighboring cities that were open to foreigners. There they met tourists and students from India and established the contacts with Indian guests who brought new information about Indian religions. During perestroika, some old Beatles fans from Dniepropetrovsk joined new religious groups of Buddhists and Krishnaists. Even now, they still recall how it was music by the Beatles that inspired their interest in what, for Ukraine, was such an exotic religion.[49]

The American rock band Creedence Clearwater Revival also played a strange role in connecting the world of Western pop music and popular religion in the Dniepropetrovsk Region. As contemporaries recall, Creedence Clearwater Revival triggered interest in folk-rock music among local amateur musicians. Local Soviet ideologists were only too happy to support the notion of using Soviet Ukrainian folk bands as an alternative to "Western mass culture," and as a result the region saw the formation of several local folk-rock bands that incorporated Ukrainian folk elements into their music.[50] To the KGB's horror, however, some of these bands used old Ukrainian folk songs with religious content, "popularizing Christian images and symbols." As former folk-rock musicians recalled, their experiments with Ukrainian religious songs led them to "rediscover the Ukrainian religious past." Despite KGB efforts to ban Christian Ukrainian folk songs from public performance, officers complained that Dniepropetrovsk rock musicians always played "Ukrainian nationalist songs of Christian character." And

Figure 11.4. Dniepriane, a Ukrainian folk-rock band, giving a concert at the main building of Dniepropetrovsk State University on Gagarin Avenue, August 31, 1980. Tatiana Yeriomenko, the band's singer, is at the far right. Major representatives of the university's administration, including its president, V. I. Mosakovskii, are standing on the platform to the left. Photograph by the author.

Dniepriane, the local university folk-rock band, actually performed these songs during a trip to England in October 1981.[51]

The most striking link between Anglo-American rock music and popular religiosity among Dniepropetrovsk rock fans was provided by music of the British hard-rock band Deep Purple. Deep Purple's immense popularity shaped the music preferences of Soviet youth in the early 1970s. Dniepropetrovsk's rock music enthusiasts idealized and venerated everything related to this band. Therefore, when rumors surfaced in Moscow and Leningrad about members of Deep Purple performing in a rock opera about the last days of Jesus Christ, it set off a scramble among fans to get tapes of the opera. The album of Andrew Lloyd Webber's rock opera *Jesus Christ Superstar* had been released in 1970 (before it became a Broadway sensation in 1971), and by 1973 the original vinyl recordings, as well as taped recordings, could be found on the music black markets of all major Soviet industrial cities, Dniepropetrovsk included. It became the most popular object of cultural consumption among Soviet hard-rock fans because Ian

Gillan, the lead singer of Deep Purple, sang the part of Jesus Christ. Thus, in the imagination of young rock music consumers, Webber's opera was connected directly to the legendary British band.[52] Soviet intellectual consumers justified their interest in this product of Western mass culture by its very genre. According to Soviet cultural standards, the opera always represented a more sophisticated musical form than just a popular song. Many young classical and jazz musicians were attracted to Webber's opera as an example of elitist culture. As a result, after 1972 *Jesus Christ Superstar* became a new phenomenon of Soviet cultural consumption, which involved not only college students and ignorant working-class enthusiasts of rock music but also young intellectuals all over the Soviet Union.[53]

The biblical story behind the opera triggered an interest in the history of Christianity on the part of thousands of Soviet rock fans. They scoured local libraries for any information about the Gospels and Jesus Christ. Though the Bible was officially banned from Soviet libraries, young fans of Webber's opera could use any number of the multitude of atheistic books about the Gospels. Boring tomes of atheistic propaganda that had long been gathering dust suddenly became best sellers in local bookstores and were put on waiting lists in libraries. Dniepropetrovsk's librarians complained during 1972 and 1973 about this sudden interest in atheistic literature, especially books about Jesus Christ and origins of Christianity.[54] Even such notorious classics of antireligious propaganda as Zenon Kosidovskii's *Stories about the Gospels* and Leo Taksille's *Funny Gospels* became objects of cultural consumption among local rock fans.[55] *Nauka i religiia,* a Soviet atheistic periodical, gained instant popularity among young readers, who spent hours in the reading rooms of local libraries looking for information about the Gospels, Jesus, the crucifixion, Judas, and Mary Magdalene.[56] This Jesus mania also resulted in new fashions; besides long hair, jeans, and T-shirts, a big cross worn around the neck became an important accessory for completing the new image of the young rocker in Dniepropetrovsk.[57]

To some extent, the new religious interest of rock fans resulted in greater attendance at Orthodox churches and sectarian worship meetings, especially on important Christian holidays such as Easter. Young people liked to watch the Easter religious services "just for fun," but for others there was also the added sense of adventure surrounding attendance at such forbidden events as Easter mass at the central Cathedral of the Holy Trinity in downtown Dniepropetrovsk, a "rush" that was amplified by the feeling of danger they experienced as they ran from the police who were chasing them.[58] As one rock music fan recalled, on April 28, 1973, he and some of his friends who had just taped *Jesus Christ Superstar* and were fascinated with this music went to the Cathedral of the Holy Trinity to watch the Easter Eve ceremony. There they found hundreds of other kids—rock fans with long hair, jeans, and metal crosses. They whistled tunes from Webber's opera, showed each other their crosses, and eventually tried to push their way through a thick crowd of police and *druzhinniki* (members of the people's patrol) to enter the cathedral. They were prevented from doing so by the police, who instead arrested some of these drunken "Jesus Christ fans." According to one officer, "This crowd of young men shouted disapprovingly," but in due course they left the premises. Soviet officials promptly restricted access to the cathedral and stopped young people from entering. As these officials later reported, their efforts led to a decrease in the number of Komsomol members who visited the cathedral during the Easter holidays.[59]

Many young people whose interest in the Gospels had been ignited by Webber's rock opera later became Christian believers. Some of them joined local Orthodox communities, while others began visiting local Baptist or Pentecostal worship meetings. As contemporaries noted, those who were involved in the "Jesus" hysteria eventually discovered the real text of Holy Scripture through either their Christian relatives or friends. Young rock fans tried to compare the real description of the events with a portrayal of the "Jesus story" in the rock opera. They made handwritten copies of the opera lyrics, read the Gospel of Saint John word by word, and compared the Russian text with the English lyrics. Many students of English from Dniepropetrovsk University spent hours of their free time translating the opera's lyrics and cross-checking their translation with the biblical text in Russian.[60]

Some of these students later entered religious schools and became either Orthodox priests or Baptist ministers. One of them, Valerii Likhachev, who graduated with honors from the Department of History of Dniepropetrovsk University in 1978 and worked on the university's archeological expedition, applied and was admitted to an Orthodox seminary in Leningrad in 1983.[61] Aleksandr Gusar remembers how his high school classmates gathered at his house to compare the text of the Gospels, which belonged to Gusar's grandmother, with their two Russian translations of the lyrics from the original album sleeve of *Jesus Christ Superstar*. Throughout 1974, they would listen to these records almost every evening. It is noteworthy that it was their interest in the biblical stories that led some of Gusar's friends to breach the Soviet bounds of permissibility. Two of them joined the local Baptist community, two others became active participants of the local Pentecostal church, and one later became a prominent preacher among the local Adventists.[62]

Figure 11.5. The Orthodox Cathedral of the Holy Trinity, the location of the first demonstration of the *Jesus Christ Superstar* fans. Photograph by the author.

Something similar occurred in another town near Dniepropetrovsk, when some close friends of Vladimir Solodovnik began their biblical studies by listening to Webber's opera and checking the Russian translation of its lyrics. Five of these friends converted to the Baptist faith by the end of the 1970s. Each one of them started out as an ordinary participant in the "Jesus" hysteria of the early 1970s, adopting all the usual elements of the fashionable youth culture of the time—long hair, crosses, jeans, and an idealization of hippies. But after they joined their local Christian communities, these symbols of the rock music culture were replaced by purely Christian symbols, and elements of religious piety and Christian ethos, rather than rock-and-roll music, became the most important factors shaping their identity.[63]

As we see, despite official criticism and prohibitions, the Dniepropetrovsk Region's young people linked prohibited music and religion together in their own version of cultural consumption, which contributed to a new style of life and cultural identification. Paradoxically, by the end of the

1970s, songs from Lloyd Webber's opera were included in Soviet main-stream popular culture. Even Soviet television broadcast musical shows (such as the "Benefit Performance" of the actress Larisa Golubkina), during which Soviet musicians covered some songs from Webber's opera in Russian.[64] However, it needs to be noted that the initial enthusiasm of 1972 and 1973, which led to the "Jesus hysteria," emphasized the non-Soviet and nonatheist elements in the local popular culture. Despite a partial incorporation of these elements into the Soviet establishment of entertainment, they continued to contribute to an interest in popular Christianity and Western religions among Dniepropetrovsk's youth.

The music and lyrics of the British band Black Sabbath also contributed to the growing interest in religion among Ukrainian rock fans. Two of these fans, Eduard Svichar and Mikhail Suvorov—whose curiosity had been piqued by the pictures they had seen of band members with crosses on their chests, and who in general were fascinated by the band's heavy rock music and mystical lyrics—combed through Soviet atheist magazines in an effort to find answers to their questions about Black Sabbath's religious symbols, and about religion in general. Both Svichar and Suvorov eventually discovered a rare prerevolutionary edition of the Russian Orthodox Bible. It became their first religious text. Inspired by the British band's religious symbolism, Svichar even decided to visit Orthodox churches and monasteries in an effort to speak with priests about religion. According to Svichar, after his spiritual search for religious truth and his visits to various churches in Kyiv, he became so disappointed with the Soviet system of higher education and Komsomol indoctrination that he dropped out of college and returned to his hometown in the Cherkassy Region, where he continued to play rock music.[65]

Although Soviet officials did their best to discourage or prevent unauthorized public displays of religiosity, they were realistic enough to try to co-opt or divert the movement by adopting some of its features. As early as 1976, for example, Communist and Komsomol ideologists in Dniepropetrovsk tried to use Western music, including fragments of *Jesus Christ Superstar,* in an antireligious campaign that locals tellingly termed "Keep the youth busy during the big religious holidays." Communist ideologists continued to rely on the old standby of *subbotniks,* which kept many high school and university students busy with various labor activities during the most popular religious holidays, particularly Easter.[66] But Dniepropetrovsk's ideologists also tried their hand at new tactics. The Dniepropetrovsk Komsomol, for example, organized unusually long dance parties (sometimes until 2 am) at the downtown discotheque Melodia during the Easter holidays of 1977, 1978, and 1979.[67] According to some of the organizers of these parties in 1977, the most popular melodies, which were requested five or six times in a row, were arias from *Jesus Christ Superstar.* The disk jockeys obliged, although some would accompany musical fragments from the opera with their own atheistic commentary.[68]

None of these measures, however, stopped people from attending religious ceremonies during the Easter holidays. According to police data, during the Easter holiday of April 9–10, 1977, 63,000 people visited Orthodox churches in the city of Dniepropetrovsk, 6,300 young people watched religious ceremonies inside these churches, and 2,300 young people participated in the consecration of the paschal bread. These people were not, the police noted, religious activists; rather, they were ordinary Soviet citizens who were "just curious about what was going on." These groups of young people included some whose curiosity had been triggered by the very rock opera the authorities had tried to use in their antireligious, anti-Easter dances.[69] During the period 1981–83, the Soviet administration approved special plans for using Komsomol discotheques and mass dance parties "with a goal to distract the youth from participation in religious rituals of Christian holiday Easter." During those anti-Easter discotheques, local disc jockeys would sometimes play music, including some old songs from *Jesus Christ Superstar,* which qualified as "ideologically dangerous for the Soviet youth." Komsomol ideologists ignored this during the holidays because they felt that popular music should keep youth away from churches. Therefore, they permitted the "lesser evil" of Western rock music in their struggle with the "larger evil" of religion. As a result, the cultural consumption of "bourgeois" music became a peculiar ideological tool in the Communist ideological struggle against what was considered more dangerous for the Soviet way of life: religion and cultural consumption related to this peculiar form of "anticommunist ideology."[70]

Documents generated by Dniepropetrovsk's trade unions and Komsomol tourist agencies also demonstrate the ongoing influence of Webber's opera on popular religiosity among locals who traveled abroad. This is an important point because the overwhelming majority of these tourists were the most loyal and ideologically reliable Soviet citizens. In 1983 an electrician from the Dneprovskaia mine, Viktor Rybakov, bought a Russian-language Bible in Hungary and tried to bring it back with him to Dniepropetrovsk. When a leader of the tourist group asked him to hand it over to the KGB operative accompanying them, Rybakov replied that he would keep it, "because I need this book in my life." Eventually the KGB officer confiscated Rybakov's Bible at the Soviet border.[71] Throughout the 1970s and early 1980s, tour group leaders regularly complained about how tourists from Dniepropetrovsk attempted to smuggle in silver crosses, Bibles, and Orthodox icons from their trips to socialist countries, particularly Bulgaria and Yugoslavia. More than 60 percent of the tourists involved in these crimes mentioned Webber's opera as an inspiration for their curiosity in religion.[72]

Popular Religiosity Statistics

Despite every official effort, organized religion and popular religiosity remained vibrant phenomena in both the rural and industrial districts of the Dniepropetrovsk Region. From 1980 to 1984, according to KGB estimates, some 50,000 to 60,000 of the region's inhabitants visited Orthodox churches on a regular basis, whereas from 1978 to 1984 some 4,000 to 6,000 people (including 100 people who were under thirty years of age) routinely visited Dniepropetrovsk's Cathedral of the Holy Trinity. During these same years, anywhere from 250 to 400 people participated on a regular basis in Passover celebrations in the city's central synagogue.[73] According to official statistics, 9 percent of all newborns in the region were baptized in the Orthodox Church, 24.5 percent in one city district alone. Among the 158 parents who baptized their children in the city of Dniepropetrovsk, 104 (65.8 percent) were Komsomol members, 7 were engineers, 11 were elementary and secondary school teachers, and 5 were college students.[74]

Neither Communist ideologists nor KGB operatives were able to annihilate religion in the region. Even on the eve of perestroika, Komsomol and Communist members still baptized their children according to religious rituals and followed some religious rules in their private life. Sometimes, when these regional residents faced serious personal problems and when they lost hope in finding support from the state, they preferred to send their financial donations to the local Orthodox monastery rather than to the Soviet Peace Fund.[75] On the eve of perestroika in 1984, organized religion held the same position and infrastructure as it had twenty years ago in the region. According to official data, "the registered religious people" made up only 3 percent of the entire population, and at least 2 percent of these religious people lived in Dniepropetrovsk itself.[76] More young people had now joined this category of "religious people." In 1982, among 146 new converts to the Baptist faith in the region, 44 were young people between eighteen and thirty years of age. By 1984, among 165 new converts, 53 were young people.[77] Despite various restrictions and prohibitions, more than a third of all new converts in the communities of evangelicals in the region were young people. As the KGB officers noted, this increase of young evangelicals in the region was partially result of the new forms of cultural consumption that made the meetings for worship more attractive than the boring Komsomol meetings.[78] As we can see, neither official ideological indoctrination nor police persecutions were able to destroy popular religiosity and organized religion in the region of Dniepropetrovsk. The existence of religious people, even though only 3 percent of the population, was proof that officially sanctioned cultural consumption in the region took different directions and forms. By the 1980s, popular cultural consumption (including its religious expressions) became more distanced from Communist ideological discourse than its ideologists could have anticipated in the 1960s. Paradoxically, popular music from the West, which was used by Soviet ideologists as atheistic propaganda, also contributed to the spread of the popular religiosity among local youth.

Conclusion

During the second phase of cultural consumption (1971–75) in the closed city of Dniepropetrovsk, the themes of Ukrainian culture and history were gradually replaced with the "ideas, images and sounds from the West" in local Ukrainian popular culture.[79] Now Dniepropetrovsk's youth read more books in Russian and watched their favorite Western films dubbed in Russian. They consumed more information about their favorite rock music from Soviet youth periodicals and radio in Russian language as well. The "book boom" of the 1970s, the tremendous popularity of Western films, and the democratization of rock music consumption, which involved millions of the young industrial workers and peasant migrants to industrial cities—all this led to a gradual Russification of popular culture in Dniepropetrovsk.

This Russified version of the regional Ukrainian identity coexisted with the elements of religious identity among the generation of the 1970s. Growing interest in popular religion, especially Christianity, was not only a reaction to the mistakes in the ideological efforts of Soviet officials but also a direct result of the consumption of Western rock music. During the Brezhnev era, Western cultural products such as rock music were not simply an important component of everyday cultural consumption—they were a significant contributing factor in the spread of popular religiosity among the youth of the strategically important region of Dniepropetrovsk. Music from the West became an important factor in the formation of a local identity in the closed city. As sociologists of music have noted, "in appropriating forms of popular music, individuals are simultaneously constructing ways of being in the context of their local everyday environments."[80]

The consumption of Western popular music in Dniepropetrovsk was a process of selective borrowing and appropriation, translation, and incorporation into the indigenous cultural context. Music by the Beatles, Creedence Clearwater Revival, Black Sabbath, Deep Purple, and Andrew Lloyd Webber was a point of *cultural fixation* for thousands of young people in Dniepropetrovsk. Everyday living conditions in Ukraine's closed city led to the extreme idealization of any popular cultural product from the West. Through their cultural fixation on authentic Western or imitative music forms, Dniepropetrovsk's rock music consumers built their own religious identities using the elements of Christianity, Ukrainian folk culture, and Hinduism present in their favorite songs.

During this second phase of cultural consumption, it also became obvious that the major cultural and ideological influences that shaped the identities of local ruling elites and ordinary consumers in Dniepropetrovsk came through two different, but Westernized and "open," Soviet cities. One was the Western Ukrainian city of L'viv. The second city was Moscow, the capital of the Soviet Union. By 1976, besides their traditional opposition to L'viv's "dangerous" Western and nationalistic influences, the representatives of Dniepropetrovsk's ruling elite also became frustrated with the cultural politics from Moscow. Local Soviet officials (including the KGB operatives) were confused and embarrassed by this politics. They did not understand this politics and feared the negative reaction from Dniepropetrovsk's consumers. Various restrictions from Moscow in book, film, and music consumption provoked anti-Moscow feelings not only among local intellectuals but also among a majority of industrial workers. Of course, serious economic problems (a lack of food supply, manufactured goods, etc.) were the major reasons behind this growing discontent. Dniepropetrovsk residents who visited Moscow's food stores and shops in the 1970s knew that "Muscovites had no problems with distribution of major goods." As many contemporaries noted,

> After visits to Moscow we felt very bad about Muscovites—they had everything for consumption on the shelves in their stores, but we had

nothing to buy in Dniepropetrovsk shops, in the city which was a major center of the entire Soviet military industrial complex! Muscovites not only bought the best manufactured products from all over the world, they also watched the best foreign films and listened to the best Western music which was banned in our closed city. Some of Western movies, books, and music records, which Muscovites freely enjoyed, never reached the closed city, or came to us with a great delay. It was unfair! We were outraged by the Muscovites' privileges in consumption and envied them very much.[81]

This perception of "envy of the Muscovites' privileges in Soviet consumption" became a very important development in regional identity formation in Dniepropetrovsk. Even the Russian-speaking population of the closed city identified itself with local (Ukrainian) economic and cultural interests rather than with Moscow's (Russian) economic and cultural practices. Despite the growing Russification of Dniepropetrovsk during the 1970s, the local population (including the young, enthusiastic consumers of Western cultural products) gradually distanced itself from Moscow, which was associated with "unjust privileges for Muscovites" and various restrictions and limitations on regional consumption in "the provinces." During perestroika, these feelings of "provincial envy of Moscow" in Dniepropetrovsk would be used by Ukrainian nationalist politicians to enroll and mobilize local young activists in their anti-Russian (and anti-Moscow) independence movement.

Part III

The "Disco Era," Antipunk Campaigns, and Komsomol Business

From 1976 to 1985, the Dniepropetrovsk Region lived through the peak of official "Westernization," which was connected to the Komsomol "disco movement"; through the various profitable (and sometimes illegal) business activities of the Komsomol and trade union tourist agencies, including the commercial success of the new disco entertainment industry; and through the anti–rock music ideological campaigns that targeted "fascist punks" and "corrupt Komsomol activists." During this period, Westernization, Russification, and commercialization influenced not only students and workers, who were the ordinary consumers of Western cultural products, but also the young generation of Dniepropetrovsk's Komsomol activists. The new Komsomol enterprises like tourism and music entertainment helped to promote these Komsomol ideologists' careers and brought them profits.

Their life experiences during this "disco era" shaped the identities of these Komsomol members—such as Yulia Grigian (later Tymoshenko), Victor Pinchuk, Serhiy Tihipko, and many others—who would become the typical representatives of "the Dniepropetrovsk political clan" in post-Soviet Ukraine. As a result of their life in the closed city of Dniepropetrovsk during this era, they developed a very cynical and practical approach to the ruling ideology, which had replaced highly moral Communist ideals with pragmatic, profit-oriented goals based on their ideals of Westernization. Dniepropetrovsk's provincial character, along with the confusing impact of developments in Western mass culture, which reached the closed city indirectly and too late, contributed to their moral cynicism, and to the very provincial and parochial worldview of the future Ukrainian politicians who grew up during the disco era in the closed city of Soviet Ukraine.

Chapter 12

Taming Pop Music Consumption: From *"Tantsploshchadka"* to Discotheque

Dance floors (*tantsploshchadka*) in Soviet parks and palaces of culture became the primary location for new forms of Soviet entertainment in the mid-1970s. These forms, known as discotheques, were promoted by the All-Union Komsomol in Moscow as the most progressive and ideologically safe venues for Communist entertainment for Soviet youth. The Komsomol discotheque movement reached Ukraine in 1976 and affected cultural consumption not only in Kyiv and its other Westernized cities but also in the "closed rocket city" of Dniepropetrovsk.

The Beginning of the Disco Movement in the Rocket City

According to Artemy Troitsky, the first "typical" Soviet discotheque was organized in Moscow in 1972. Troitsky and his friend, Aleksandr Kostenko, rented special musical equipment from their musician friends and operated this "dancing enterprise" inside a café at Moscow University. As Troitsky noted, they developed a special program organization for this discotheque event, which became a model for other Soviet discotheques. "The first hour was dedicated to listening; that is, I played music by 'serious' groups like Jethro Tull, Pink Floyd, King Crimson, and talked about their histories. . . . After the 'listening' hour, people spent the next three expressing themselves on the dance floor."[1]

Komsomol ideologists had already tried to use similar forms of musical lectures as early as 1966 at different youth clubs in many Soviet cities, from Moscow and Kyiv to Kazan and Dniepropetrovsk. Even local branches of Znanie (Society of Knowledge) organization, which usually worked under control of the ideological departments of regional Communist Party committees, provided this kind of musical lectures with subsequent dance parties to popular music.[2] To some extent, Troitsky and his friends used traditional Soviet musical propaganda and transformed it into a new form of musical entertainment, which imitated Western forms and fashions.

If dance parties in Moscow mostly followed Troisky's model, the new discotheques of Riga and other cities in the Baltic republics during the years 1973–74 developed more flexible forms and styles of presentation, sometimes without the "obligatory thematic" part of musical lectures. They drew on the Eastern European model of the "socialist discotheque," which had existed from the late 1960s in many European socialist countries. In the years 1971–72, the Yugoslavian model became the most popular form of disco club in the countries of the Soviet bloc.[3]

By 1975 discotheques, as a new form of youth entertainment, became part of the official ideological campaign among Komsomol ideologists. Timothy Ryback, the first Western scholar to write about Soviet discothe-

— Папашо, чи вам не соромно: всі звуть мене Геральдом, лише ви — Грицьком!

Figure 12.1. Drawing captioned "Dad, shame on you, everybody calls me Gerald, only you call me Grytsko!" From *Perets,* 1975, no. 1, 14.

Figure 12.2. Drawing captioned "They call us lazy people. Let them dance like we do every day in the restaurant!" From *Perets*, 1977, no. 11, 9.

— А ще кажуть, що ми ледарі. Нехай хто спробує ось так витан- цьовувати кожного дня в ресторані.

Figure 12.3. Drawing captioned "Hey son, I can't recognize you. You look like a foreigner." From *Perets*, 1976, no. 15, 8.

— Ой, синочку, ти якийсь геть не наш став!

Figure 12.4. Drawing captioned "Please ask them not to play so loudly." "I would, but they will not listen." From *Perets,* 1977, no. 16, 7.

Figure 12.5. Drawing captioned "Without words." Notice the name of the band Nightingale on the drum. From *Perets,* 1976, no. 8, 11.

ques, noted that "discomania" in the Soviet Union and official fascination with Western disco music began in Riga, the capital of Latvia. The Latvian Republic Cultural Workers Trade Union and Latvian Komsomol organized the first Soviet (*mezhrespublikanskii*) Discotheque Festival and Competition in Riga as "the first national effort to assess the effectiveness of the dis-

— Хелло! Ви з Техасу?
— Ні, ми з Борщагівки.

Figure 12.6. Drawing captioned "Hello, are you from Texas?" "No, we are from Borshchagovka." From *Perets,* 1979, no. 17, 11.

cotheque as a means of ideological indoctrination." The oldest and most famous disco clubs from five cities—Riga, Ventspils, Kaunas, Tartu, and Tashkent—competed in this festival. Hundreds of Komsomol ideologists from all over the Soviet Union took part as observers and judges in the Riga competition. From October 23 to 30, 1976, the first Soviet disco clubs presented, as Timothy Ryback wrote, a "discotheque format, combining music, light shows, and Communist propaganda in an attempt to appease ideological watchdogs without alienating youthful audiences."[4] By the end of 1978, Moscow had registered 187 Komsomol-sponsored discotheques. Latvia had more than 300 disco clubs of different kinds. In 1978, Ukraine had 16 disco clubs in Kyiv, 16 in L'viv, and 10 in Odessa. The majority of these clubs followed the same pattern, which Ryback called "the prototypical Soviet disco of the late 1970s: flashing lights, mirrored walls, and Western disco tunes."[5]

According to the Ukrainian participants in the discotheque movement, as early as 1974 former youth clubs in the Ukrainian cities already used forms of the dance parties and musical lectures, which were similar to what in 1976 was called "the discotheque for young people" (*molodiozhnaia*

Мал. О. МОНАСТИРСЬКОГО

— Рятуйте наші уші!

Figure 12.7. Drawing captioned "Save our ears from this music!" From *Perets,* 1980, no. 2, p. 13, by O. Monastyrskyi.

diskoteka in Russian). In the years 1974–75, all major Ukrainian cities, including Kyiv, Odessa, and L'viv, already had the dance parties that imitated Western disco clubs.[6] Under the influence of the Baltic "discotheque initiative," the Komsomol organization of Ukraine tried to emulate and imitate the new form of youth entertainment. The All-Union Komsomol leadership supported this initiative as a new venue for Communist education and for organizing ideologically reliable leisure for Soviet youth. The Komsomol city committee of Dniepropetrovsk became involved in this new ideological campaign as early as 1976. Different spontaneous forms of the discotheque movement already existed in many locations in the city, especially in vocational school and college dormitories, where local Komsomol activists organized dance parties on a regular basis and used recordings from the popular music enthusiasts who provided these parties with not only music but also information about the music. These dances without live music became known as "the dances to the tape recorder's music" (*tantsy pod magnitofon*). It was of course cheaper for the organizers of leisure-time activities to use a tape recorder than to invite a band to play.

The Komsomol city committee decided to transform the old youth clubs that already existed in Dniepropetrovsk into new disco clubs, which were promoted by the Komsomol leadership from Moscow. Mriia, the old youth club, a pioneer of jazz music in the city, was under the jurisdiction of the administration of the Yuzhmash rocket factory complex. By 1976, this club—legendary for its Ukrainian jazz—had been turned into an ordinary café. Sometimes local rock bands played live in this café, but most of the time Mriia functioned like a restaurant.[7] The intellectual aura had disappeared from Mriia. Komsomol activists and enthusiasts of rock music from Yuzhmash decided to transform this place into the new Komsomol music club.

As the wealthiest and the most influential industrial enterprise in the region, Yuzhmash sponsored the first professional disco club in Dniepropetrovsk. Both the trade union and Komsomol organizations of this factory used special "recreational" funds assigned to them by its administration to buy music and audio equipment for their dance parties, for the factory's jazz and rock bands, and to organize leisure-time activities in the numerous dormitories that belonged to Yuzhmash. The major part of this equipment and the financing for these activities was concentrated in the Palace of Culture of the Machine Builders, a magnificent building of the Stalinist Empire style, which was located on Rabochaia (the Workers') Street, not far from the central entrance checkpoint for entering the Yuzhmash complex. In December 1976, using this equipment and music audiotapes from local enthusiasts of Western pop music, Stanislav Petrov and Valerii Miakotenko, who worked at the Palace of Culture of the Machine Builders, organized a New Year's Eve dance party structured like a Baltic discotheque. This party included a disc jockey's special announcements and intellectual commentary about the music, and new technology, including home-made equipment for various special video and audio effects, such as "color music" (*son et lumière; tsvetomuzyka*) lights. Miakotenko, who was the manager of the local rock band Vodograi, also organized a special concert of amateur musicians and included this in the dance program. And he asked musicologists and teachers of music from the local music schools to provide professional commentary about modern music.[8]

Figure 12.8. The central entrance checkpoint of the Yuzhmash rocket factory complex on Rabochaia Street. Photograph by the author.

After this successful dance party, Petrov and Miakotenko decided to use the old club Mriia for their discotheque. The Komsomol district committee supported this decision, and in February 1977 Mriia became the location of the first discotheque officially registered by the city Komsomol organization. The first director and manager of this disco club (or "club of music lovers") was Petrov. At the beginning, this club had two official leaders and disc jockeys—the musician-manager Miakotenko and the musicologist Natalia Fesik. During February 1977, the disco club at Mriia had three meetings, with an average number of forty participants, mainly young workers and engineers from Yuzhmash, but also high school and undergraduate college students. Local enthusiasts of popular music, architects, designers, artists, and engineers helped to decorate and prepare the club's building and interior, and they also made and assembled the sophisticated equipment used for visual and audio effects.[9]

As Petrov explained to the discotheque's guests, the club's main goal was to spur "a campaign against musical illiteracy." "Although we all love music," he noted, "we do not know everything about it. We need a consistent system of music education. We can't understand music without the assistance of specialists-musicologists." The same evening, a local musicologist, who became one of the first commentators ("disc jockeys") at this disco club, organized a special lecture about the songs of the Soviet composer David Tukhmanov. This lecture responded to the increasing interest in Tukhmanov's new album, *On the Wave of My Memory,* among the club's young guests. Both Communist and Komsomol ideologists praised this kind of presentation in youth clubs as "a new positive form of popular music consumption" in the city.[10]

The city Komsomol committee invited the pioneers of the Soviet discotheque movement from Riga, the capital city of Latvia, to show the main forms and methods for organizing Komsomol music entertainment for the local enthusiasts and activists of this movement. These Latvian pioneers of the disco club movement were Normund Erts and Karlis Upenieks, members of the special council of youth entertainment at the Riga city Komsomol committee, and the organizers of discotheques at the Riga Club of the Printers and at the radio factory VEF, which also belonged to the Soviet military-industrial complex. It is noteworthy that the Riga guests from the VEF factory and the Dniepropetrovsk hosts from the Yuzhmash factory were part of the same financial and economic machine, which provided the Soviet military with sophisticated equipment and ammunition. Both the VEF and Yuzhmash factories had better funding and equipment for organizing the disco clubs than other Soviet industrial plants. Moreover, any ideological and entertainment initiatives (including the disco club idea) from these secret factories were supported by the KGB as ideologically reliable, in contrast to initiatives from "immature college students."[11]

These guests from Riga summarized the major results of their various experiments in the organization of discotheques. And Dniepropetrovsk's Komsomol leaders followed the suggestions of their guests. After this visit, they promoted two types of disco club programs recommended by the Latvians. One was the "program for enlightening and education," called the "discotheque club." The other was the "program for dance and entertainment," called the "discotheque dancing hall."[12] The Latvian guests demonstrated their own discotheque programs in three locations in the city of Dniepropetrovsk—at the Palace of Students in Taras Shevchenko Park, at the Yuzhmash club Mriia, and in the park pavilion Dnieper Dawn in the Chkalov Park of Culture and Relaxation downtown. They explained to their hosts that the first "socialist" discotheque was organized in the German Democratic Republic in 1962 and that they had followed this East German model. The most impressive disco programs of the Latvian guests, which

Figure 12.9. The legendary Palace of Students in Taras Shevchenko Park. This was the location of the most significant student cultural activities, including jazz and rock music concerts, and the beginning of the discotheque movement. Photograph by the author.

Figure 12.10. A picturesque panorama of the Dnieper River near Taras Shevchenko Park. Photograph by the author.

were praised by the local Komsomol newspaper, covered the music of the "socialist rock musician Cheslav Nieman from Poland and the anti-imperialist American singer Bob Dylan."[13]

The practical advice of the guests from Riga was very important for the Dniepropetrovsk enthusiasts of discotheques. According to the hierarchy of the typical Soviet cultural consumer in the 1970s, the Baltic region represented the "authentic" West in its Soviet socialist form. If a Western cultural form such as the disco club was presented by "Westernized" Soviet people such as Latvians, it immediately gained authenticity and proof of ideological reliability in the minds of Dniepropetrovsk's Komsomol ideologists. The visit from the Latvian guests thus not only symbolically approved the beginning of the discotheque movement in the region of Dniepropetrovsk but also started a process of imitating Baltic cultural forms. These forms were considered ideologically reliable because they came from the Westernized Soviet region, not from the capitalist West.

In the years 1977–78, then, the local administration of Dniepropetrovsk opened new bars and cafeterias with elements of Baltic variety shows, including "erotic dances" and other "exotic" cultural forms, which looked like Western ones. Using the ideas of Baltic entertainers, the local administration opened a popular music bar, the Red Coral, on the embankment of the Dnieper River. This club had a Latvian variety show and live music from a rock band, which featured the famous guitarist Vladimir Kuz'min, who became a living legend of Soviet rock music in the 1970s. Each evening, more than five hundred young rockers waited in line to get into their favorite music show at the Red Coral. Despite the relatively high price of admission—5 to 10 rubles, compared with an average price of 50 kopecks to 1 ruble for a ticket to a regular dance floor—the Red Coral became the most popular venue for rock music fans in the city.[14] In 1977, the seventeen-year-old Yulia Grigian (later Tymoshenko) and her classmates joined these crowds of rock fans.[15] From 1977 to 1981, places such as the Red Coral and Maiak (the Lighthouse) restaurant in Taras Shevchenko Park became symbols of collaboration between the local Ukrainian and Baltic organizers of leisure time and entertainment for youth. The beginning of this collaboration was initiated during the Komsomol discotheque campaign of 1976.[16]

Responding to pressure from above, from the Central Committee of Komsomol in Moscow, which urged the local Komsomol organizations to participate in a new All-Union initiative for youth entertainment, the Dnieprope-

Figure 12.11. The building housing the restaurant and bar Maiak (the Light-house), a famous location of rock and disco music activities in Taras Shevchenko Park. Photograph by the author.

trovsk Komsomol city committee decided to officially support the Yuzhmash disco club. Moreover, the local Komsomol functionaries understood that they were losing contact with even ordinary Komsomol members, who were bored with the traditional, ideological Komsomol events, such as regular meetings with official reports and elections of new officials, *subbotniks,* lectures, and so on. They tried to reestablish ideological control over the new forms of cultural consumption and the new, growing disco movement, which involved thousands of the young enthusiasts of Western pop music throughout the entire region of Dniepropetrovsk.[17]

The city Komsomol leaders invited young disc jockeys from the Yuzhmash discotheque to be leaders of the central city disco club, which was created with the support of the Komsomol city committee. Valerii Miakotenko, who, as described above, had worked with Stanislav Petrov at the Yuzhmash cultural centers during the period 1973–76 organizing various dance parties, became the first official disc jockey of this Komsomol enterprise. On May 15, 1977, the Komsomol apparatchiks officially announced the opening of the first city discotheque at the building of the Palace of Students in Taras Shevchenko Park in the city's so-called student district. All the city's major colleges and the State University were located near this park. Thus, from the 1960s to the 1980s, the park, including its famous (and only one for all Ukraine) Palace of Students, became a favorite place for rest and leisure activities among the city's thousands of college students.[18]

To control and direct the central discotheque and the city's other disco clubs, the Komsomol functionaries recommended the creation of a new bureaucratic organization, a special Council of the City Discotheque. Under the guidance of the Komsomol city committee, the organizers of this Komsomol "enterprise" elected a disc jockey, Miakotenko, as chairperson of this council and formed three special council sections. The first was the scenario-producing section, and it addressed the major problems of selecting material, writing a script, producing the show, and staging a dance. The second was the section of presenters. Its main goal was to prepare the disc jockeys and anchors responsible for presenting information and organizing the elements of the variety show, and inviting clowns, mimes, and jugglers. The third was the technical section, and it addressed technical issues related to audio and video equipment, music recording and producing devices, light effects technology, and so on.[19]

Natalia Fesik and Miakotenko, the two disc jockeys who had been officially approved by D. Fedorenko, the secretary of the city Komsomol committee, opened the first meeting (*zasedanie*) of the city discotheque on the evening of May 15, 1977. They introduced the first music program from a series they called "Vocal Instrumental Ensembles from the Brotherly Soviet Republics." This first evening was devoted to "Pesniary: Music of the Byelorussian Folk in Modern Rhythms," the most popular theme from this series. Fesik and Miakotenko covered the biographies and musical achievements of the Byelorussian rock band Pesniary (whose name in English translation means "Singers"), which was famous for popularizing Byelorussian folklore and its rock-and-roll arrangements. For more than an hour, the disc jockeys played music and showed photo slides to illustrate the main ideas of their presentation. The second and the longest part of the event was devoted to dances. Fesik and Miakotenko made comments for each melody they played (half these melodies were foreign and half were Soviet). During a break, local mimes and jugglers performed various tricks and entertained the audience. At the end, both Komsomol and Communist ideologists praised the high "ideological and educational level" of the central city discotheque and characterized it as an example of "really good cultured" consumption "under the reasonable ideological supervision" of the city Komsomol leadership.[20]

During its first year, the city central discotheque sponsored the organization of branch discotheques at different places, such as the Mining Institute, the Mechanic-Mathematical Department of Dniepropetrovsk University, Yuzhmash, and the Radio Factory. By July 1978, there were eleven officially registered discotheques in the city of Dniepropetrovsk. The majority of these disco clubs had the official support of the central city discotheque. Yet the organizers of the discotheque movement were still complaining about a lack of funding, music, and visual information. Miakotenko had his own ambitious plans for his discotheque. He shared these plans with the local journalists:

> Our main goal is to transform the central city discotheque into a special cultural center, which would provide all important information, materials, and recommendations for all enthusiasts of popular music. First, we need to organize our own photo laboratory to supplement music information with visual information. It is easy for an audience to understand the story we are telling, when we show photos or video clips about a particular musician or a band. We need to organize our own disco ballet and school of modern dance. This school will educate our audience and help to develop the elements of good dancing culture. Our disco club has to bring the new forms of cultural consumption for our young guests.[21]

According to Miakotenko, the central city disco club should help to develop "positive" forms of the "really good cultured" consumption, which would be ideologically reliable and "positive and elevated" from an aesthetic point of view.[22] Later, Miakotenko told journalists that "the discotheque had to teach and educate young people, not just entertain."[23] At the same time, the local journalist who interviewed Miakotenko reminded readers that the disco club needed funding to function. This same journalist then suggested that the club should introduce an entrance fee and use the money for financial needs. The local ideologists from Komsomol and the Communist Party supported this idea of financial independence for the disco club and approved this idea officially in 1978.[24]

Disco Club as Komsomol Business

Eventually, the city administration permitted the opening of a central city disco club in the big park pavilion Dnieper Dawn in Chkalov Park downtown in October 1978. The city administration also allowed the disco club to function as a "financially independent enterprise under auspices of the city Komsomol organization." The organizers of this disco club were allowed to introduce entrance fees and use the money for their financial needs, which included buying and fixing music equipment.[25]

By January 1979, the central city disco club had the name Melodia ("Melody" in Russian) and had moved to a new, more spacious location—the large park pavilion Dnieper Dawn. In two years, 1978–79, Club Melodia became a successful business enterprise, which brought profits to its organizers and made them famous among Ukrainian Komsomol ideologists. The city Komsomol organization used the talents of the young architects, designers, and artists who were students of the Dniepropetrovsk Engineering-Building Institute to decorate and prepare the rooms of the pavilion in Chkalov Park for a new disco club. Even though much money was invested in this building, the results exceeded all expectations. On average, the disco club met six times a week.[26] Each meeting attracted 300 to 500 visitors. By charging 1 ruble as an admission fee from each guest, the organizers of this disco club made almost 500 rubles profit for every evening.

During the period 1979–83, admission payments alone created a profit of approximately 3,000 rubles a week. The disco club also had a bar that served alcohol and a hall with vending machines and various game machines. In 1983, alcoholic beverages and games brought in an additional 5,000 rubles every week. The new equipment and catering service required participation from other departments of the local Soviet administration responsible for the provision of food and beverages. Very soon, both Komsomol and Soviet apparatchiks recognized the profitability of the new disco club. By 1983, Melodia had become a kind of joint venture that combined the efforts of people from the different offices of the city administration. Still, the Komsomol ideologists tried to play the main role in controlling this new "ideological enterprise." The enterprise became the first stable source of profit for the local administration, including the Komsomol apparatchiks. According to official records, Club Melodia brought in a monthly profit of more than 60,000 rubles in the period 1981–83. In fact, the organizers of this business earned an additional "nonregistered" (by the accountant's books) 20,000 rubles each month.[27] The leaders of Melodia tried to invent something new to attract more people to the club's meetings. Eventually, they cut back on the theoretical "music lecture" part of the meetings. As Miakotenko commented, "We try to make our presentations and commentaries in a laconic and emotional way." "We had no right to forget," he

Figure 12.12. The legendary discotheque Club Melodia, in Chkalov Park in downtown Dniepropetrovsk. Photograph by the author.

continued, "that our guests came to us after a long working day and they just wanted to relax, dance, and communicate with their friends."[28]

According to a local journalist, in January 1978 Miakotenko limited the entire "theoretical part" to only brief comments. They were devoted to a new sensation of Soviet *estrada* (pop music), the record *The Mirror of My Soul* by the Soviet superstar Alla Pugacheva. This record had just been released in 1978 on the Soviet Melodia label and was very popular among the club's female audience. Miakotenko finished his thematic part in less than an hour. Then a dance followed. To demonstrate his ideological reliability and the program's political correctness, he included some material from official Soviet radio and TV shows about the contemporary political situation in the world, especially in the United States, because a majority of his musical material came from that part of the globe. Other than these political comments, which came from the official Soviet sources of mass information, the entire program of the disco club offered more contemporary dance music than ideological indoctrination. Miakotenko mostly played hits by Donna Summer, ABBA, Boney M, and the Bee Gees.[29]

Miakotenko's decision to join the Komsomol city discotheque led to a division inside the Yuzhmash disco club in 1977. One of its founders,

Stanislav Petrov, had to use different locations for this club because the administration of the rocket factory, including its Komsomol apparatchiks, did not want to be involved in the "leftover" of what was considered the city Komsomol's object, Miakotenko's disco Club Melodia. As a result of this attitude, Petrov, who still worked at the Palace of the Machine Builders and had access to expensive music equipment and funding from Yuzhmash, was left alone with a few rock music enthusiasts from the factory to continue the activities of the Yuzhmash club. With all Komsomol apparatchiks' attention directed to the central city discotheque, Petrov used his temporary independence from Komsomol supervision during 1977–78 to develop new forms of entertainment and business advertisements.

Using his connections among the city's industrial, Communist, and trade union leaders, Petrov attracted not only many young and middle-aged guests to his dance parties but also various sponsors (besides the Yuzhmash administration), who could advertise their products and services during the disco club's activities. These products and services included everything from a new toothpaste, which was available at the central department store, to special sports events in the city's stadiums and gymnasiums and new movies and plays at the local theaters. Under Petrov's leadership, the Yuzhmash disco club, now called Courier, became the most popular youth club among those who loved serious rock music because its ideological control was minimal.

Moreover, after 1978, the city disco Club Melodia looked more like a commercial place for dancing and drinking rather than a music club for serious intellectual discussions. Petrov used advertisements of different public and state organizations (sports stadiums; the philharmonic music center; *kinoprokat,* a regional committee responsible for delivering new movies; etc.) to establish important relations with the leaders of these organizations. In response to "good favors" from Petrov (reminiscent of what A. Ledeneva called *blat),* the leaders of these sports stadiums, movie theaters, concert halls, and the like provided Courier with a location, audience, and sometimes even substantial financing.[30]

The ideological and financial success of Melodia and Courier during the years 1977–78 inspired other enthusiasts of popular music to organize their own independent local discotheques. Thus, at the beginning of 1978, the disco club Your World was organized at the Pridneprovsk Chemical Factory in the industrial city of Dnieprodzerzhinsk, not far from the region's capital city. By the end of that year, there were eight registered disco clubs in this city.[31] Also, all the colleges (university and institutes) in the region of Dniepropetrovsk organized their own disco clubs.

In contrast to the factory-based discotheques, the college disco clubs were more oriented toward the intellectual student audience, who preferred serious rock music to official Soviet *estrada*. The thematic programs of student disco clubs always covered classic rock bands such as the Beatles, Rolling Stones, Doors, Creedence Clearwater Revival, Led Zeppelin, Deep Purple, King Crimson, Jethro Tull, Yes, Genesis, and Pink Floyd. Of course, the student disc jockeys always included some anti-imperialist criticism in their political comments. Thus, in a program devoted to the Beatles in November 1979, they often covered Paul McCartney's 1972 song "Give Ireland Back to the Irish" as an example of the anticapitalist spirit of rock and roll and pointed out that this song was banned in the West.[32] In 1979, the city of Dniepropetrovsk alone had more than twenty discotheques. Each college (including the university) had organized one "main college discotheque" and allowed each student dormitory to open its own "dorm disco club" as well.[33]

The rapid spread of the discotheque movement made the Dniepropetrovsk Region exemplary for many Soviet ideologists, who, in their propaganda for new forms of socialist leisure for Soviet youth, used the success of the Dniepropetrovsk central discotheque as a proof of ideological efficiency. The region was praised by Komsomol ideologists in Kyiv for "the efficient organization of the disco club movement." In 1979, the city of Dniepropetrovsk became the location for the "first All-Ukrainian final festival contest of discotheque programs."[34] The city Komsomol organization of Dniepropetrovsk had also prepared a special report about the achievements of the city disco Club Melodia, which summarized the major forms and methods of "music entertainment" in the city.

In October 1979, this published report was widely circulated among the participants of the All-Ukrainian festival competition. Many guests of the city used this publication as a guide for their disco club activities.[35] During the first year of its existence, Melodia had organized 175 thematic dance parties with special music lectures attended by more than 60,000 young people.[36] In 1979, the many apparatchiks involved in this movement were promoted and rewarded for "excellent ideological and educational activities among the regional youth." By the beginning of 1982, more than 560 youth clubs with 83 officially registered discotheques existed in the region of Dniepropetrovsk. In the region's capital city, there were 31 officially registered disco clubs in 1983.[37] Despite the Communist ideologists' criticism that discotheques spread bourgeois mass culture among the local youth, the Komsomol leaders maintained their collaboration with the activists of the discotheque movement.

"Bad" Music Consumption and the
Ideological Threat of L'viv

In 1980, new attempts by Soviet ideologists and Komsomol apparatchiks in Moscow to stop the "bad" cultural consumption and capitalist ideological influence on the dance floor led to new legislation regulating Soviet discotheques. From July to August 1980, the Soviet discos were regulated, first by a joint Ministry of Culture and the Komsomol resolution "On Measures for Improving the Activity of Amateur Associations, Hobby Clubs, and Discotheques," and then by a "Model Statute for the Amateur Discotheque."[38] "Amateur discotheques" were defined as "one form of organization of the population's leisure time, the development of amateur arts, the satisfaction of spiritual needs and interest in music on the basis of a comprehensive utilization of artistic and audiovisual technological aids."

According to these All-Union regulations of 1980, the Soviet disco club "had to create interesting, emotionally filled patriotic and informational programs, which have a perceptible effect on the socialization and formation of the aesthetic tastes of young people."[39] In theory, the difference between a discotheque and a regular dance party was that a Soviet disco club had some educational content. As was noted by Anne White—a scholar who studied the Soviet system of entertainment and houses of culture—this situation was "connected with the fact that discos were officially viewed as originally having been channels for Western propaganda, and the solution found has been to fill them with counterpropaganda."[40]

The All-Union resolution of 1980 about discotheques criticized the lack of control exercised by cultural and Komsomol organizations and complained about "the small use made of classical and folk music in disco programs." Soviet ideologists noted that Western and samizdat materials were used in their preparation, with "the commentary element retransmitting bourgeois culture, and quite frequently exerting a negative influence on the socialization of Soviet young people."[41] A few years later, in 1982, a new resolution—published by the Ministry of Culture, Komsomol, and the Soviet trade unions—reiterated their criticism of "bad" cultural consumption in many Soviet disco clubs: "Many disco programs which are prepared for public participation are not registered with the cultural organs. They rarely take patriotic themes or use Russian classical or contemporary Soviet music. Responsible organizations were ordered to exert more control and to make available more methodological guidance to disco planners."[42]

In trying to adhere to these regulations and recommendations from the center, the local ideologists and Komsomol apparatchiks worked to prevent

Western mass culture consumption in Dniepropetrovsk. Even before the central regulations about disco clubs reached the city, the local Communist ideologists had recommended that all Komsomol organizations "improve ideological and political focus of discotheques, youth clubs and cafés, and to strengthen an ideological control over entertainment of the local youth."[43] On November 11, 1980, the city Komsomol committee had a special meeting to address the problems of "bad cultural consumption" in local discotheques. Following recommendations from Moscow, the local Komsomol leaders organized a special "city inspection-competition of the disco programs" on November 29–30, 1980, in the Shinnik Palace of Culture, which belonged to the Automobile Tire Factory. Each disco club in the city had to present one disco program for this inspection-competition. As result of this inspection-competition, the Komsomol organizers decided that the best programs belonged to Melodia, the Yuzhmash discotheques, and the Shinnik Palace of Culture. The major concern of Komsomol organizers was the lack of educational development in all programs and "an obvious domination by Western musical forms."[44] After 1980, articles in local publications about the disco clubs changed their tone and became more critical of fascination with discotheques. They began criticizing disco clubs for their commercialization and promotion of low vulgar tastes and "bad" musical culture.[45]

Meanwhile, in 1980 Valerii Miakotenko, the old disc jockey, left Melodia for a new commercial organization created by the Dniepropetrovsk Komsomol for the supervision and centralization of funding of all forms of youth entertainment—music, theater, and discotheques. This organization, which supervised not only ideology but also the profits of musicians and disco clubs, was a part of an institutionalization of the region's discotheque movement. It was called DOOMAD (the abbreviation for the Dniepropetrovskoe oblastnoe ob'edinenie muzykal'nykh ansamblei i diskotek, the Dniepropetrovsk Regional Union of Music Ensembles and Discotheques). DOOMAD, which had been created as result of the USSR Komsomol leaders' initiative, connected Komsomol apparatchiks with the trade union officials who were responsible for leisure-time activities and entertainment. After 1980, the discotheque movement was connected to both apparatchiks and "the activists of the Dniepropetrovsk black market," who provided fresh musical information and material for the disco clubs' dance programs. The new leaders of the central city disco Club Melodia represented a new generation of discotheque leadership, which depended on both "black market" and Komsomol ideological support. These young activists of Melodia—the club's head, Oleg Litvinov; the disc jockey, Sergei Novikov; and the sound engineer, Mikhail Suvorov—made their disco club "events" more commercial, combining the alcohol bar, videogames, and dancing, and brought more profits to doomad. As a result, despite the constant criticism of their activities in the local press, they still had the support and protection of their Komsomol supervisors.[46]

At the beginning of the discotheque movement in Dniepropetrovsk, besides the obligatory hits of Soviet *estrada,* the classic rock ballads such as "House of the Rising Sun" by the Animals, "July Morning" by Uriah Heep, or Badfinger's hit "Without You" in an interpretation by Harry Nilsson still dominated the music programs of the main disco clubs. However, after 1976, disco music from the West (mostly Euro-disco) had begun replacing traditional rhythm and blues, heavy blues, and hard rock on Dniepropetrovsk's dance floors. During that year, the Swedish band ABBA's hits— such as "S.O.S." and "Money, Money, Money"—became the most popular melodies for "cultural consumption" by young customers of Dniepropetrovsk's disco clubs. During the years 1976–77, the new disco stars added to ABBA. In 1977, the most popular dance melodies were Donna Summer's hit "Love to Love You Baby" and songs by the West German disco band Boney M, such as "Baby, Do You Wanna Bump," "Sunny," "Daddy Cool," and "Ma Baker." Donna Summer and Boney M (and later Eruption, another West German sensation) became the dominant names on Dniepropetrovsk's music market until the end of the 1970s. Even disco songs by Bee Gees from the film *Saturday Night Fever,* which reached Dniepropetrovsk disco clubs in 1978, could not compete with the West German "kings" of disco. During the official celebrations of the two-hundredth anniversary of the founding of the city of Dniepropetrovsk in 1976, disco music was endorsed by the city's leaders as an officially approved form of music for mass entertainment. Since 1976, this kind of music had not only dominated local dance parties and discotheques but also become part of the musical programs of numerous "Western-style" bars and restaurants, which had been opened all over the city because of the city's anniversary.[47]

The city's Komsomol ideologists and their KGB supervisors now faced a very serious problem. Young pop music consumers apparently preferred Western musical hits to Soviet ones. A majority of rock music enthusiasts completely rejected what they called Soviet *estrada.* Therefore, Komsomol ideologists began to encourage discos that played mainly Soviet music, including songs from the national republics. The apparatchiks responsible for the discotheque movement supported the Ukrainian band Vodograi or the

Byelorussian band Pesniary because they represented Soviet tradition, in contrast to the alien forms of Western pop culture. To show their ideological loyalty and local patriotism, many disc jockeys in Dniepropetrovsk included comments about "glorious Ukrainian history" and criticized "capitalist exploitation in the Western countries."[48] Even in their comments about Ukrainian history, they (as loyal Soviet citizens) always emphasized the class struggle. Still, their stories were about the Ukrainian Cossacks or melodious Ukrainian poetry, which were not very popular subjects among the local KGB operatives.

Eventually, the KGB supervisors had to accept these stories and national Ukrainian music on the local dance floors. For them, it was less evil than capitalist music from the West.[49] It is noteworthy that both the KGB and Komsomol apparatchiks praised the patriotic approach of Dniepropetrovsk's discotheques, in contrast to the famous L'viv disco clubs in Western Ukraine. One KGB officer who visited both L'viv and Dniepropetrovsk during April and May 1979 criticized "a lack of patriotic themes in L'viv disco programs and bad pop music on L'viv dance floors":

Only Western rock and disco music dominated in L'viv. L'viv disco clubs did not include Ukrainian popular songs in their programs. L'viv disc jockeys did not cover problems of Soviet or Ukrainian history and culture. Their comments were only about the Western style of life. It is a paradox, but our Dniepropetrovsk discos [in a mainly Russian-speaking city!] had more Ukrainian music and presented more information about our Soviet Ukrainian culture in one week than all L'viv discos did in the entire month. I was pleasantly surprised when I heard at the Dniepropetrovsk disco club a good story about our Ukrainian Cossacks' struggle with Turkish invaders for the freedom of our Ukrainian nation. You would never hear such stories in L'viv disco clubs. Their disc jockeys talk only about the most fashionable trends in American pop culture. L'viv disc jockeys ignored completely the Western Ukrainian popular music of the band Smerichka. We should praise our Dniepropetrovsk entertainers for promoting the good Soviet Ukrainian music of Smerichka and other Ukrainian Soviet musicians. We need to support our Dniepropetrovsk initiatives in the disco movement in contrast to the Americanized disco clubs in L'viv. Patriotic material about our Ukrainian history and culture on the Dniepropetrovsk dance floor will educate young people, while an idealization of American pop culture and ignoring Ukrainian history and culture in L'viv disco clubs will confuse and disorient our Soviet citizens and transform them into apolitical cosmopolitans.[50]

During the period 1978–82, according to Mikhail Suvorov, the Dniepropetrovsk city Komsomol committee discussed the city disco club repertoire almost every month. The main focus of these discussions was the patriotic theme of music education on the dance floor. As Suvorov recalled, in October 1979, a KGB supervisor who visited the Komsomol city committee during a discussion of the disco club repertoire, requested the "old Cossacks' song" instead of "stupid" Western disco. This KGB officer recommended playing "a patriotic song about Ukrainian Cossacks instead of the Western crap that dominated the local disco clubs." When the surprised Komsomol ideologists tried to figure out what kind of song it was, they realized that the KGB officer was referring to the Ukrainian cover of the old Shocking Blue song of 1969.[51] The Komsomol leaders and KGB officers complained about the bad Western influences from the discotheques in L'viv; local ideologists tried to protect the patriotic character of youth entertainment from the Westernized trends emanating from L'viv. The major concern of the Komsomol apparatchiks was "the total domination of American music hits" in L'viv disco programs. The main advice for disc jockeys in Dniepropetrovsk was to avoid this "bad and ideologically harmful L'viv disco experience."[52]

Conclusion

As we have seen again, the themes of good and bad cultural consumption became involved in the evaluation of the disco club movement in Soviet Ukraine. But this time, it also included the problems of national history and culture. The paradox was that to prove their ideological reliability, the Dniepropetrovsk ideologists invoked elements of Ukrainian culture in opposition to the dangerous Westernization of the city's and region's youth culture.

This time, Westernization was associated not only with the "capitalist West" but also with L'viv, the most Westernized city of Western Ukraine. This was an aspect of the ambiguity in the Soviet ideology of mature socialism in addressing the problems of leisure and entertainment among the youth of national republics such as Ukraine. On the one hand, Communist ideologists had to resist Western cultural influences on the dance floor, using any available Soviet music genres, including Ukrainian ones. On the other, they confused the young consumers of mass culture by officially supporting and elevating cultural forms that were usually associated in Soviet ideological discourse with so-called bourgeois Ukrainian nationalism.

However, by the beginning of the 1980s, to the Komsomol ideologists responsible for the discotheque movement in the region of Dniepropetrovsk, problems of profitability had become more important than the promotion of Soviet pop songs sung in Ukrainian on the dance floor. The Komsomol disco clubs combined forms of ideological indoctrination, like musical lectures, with forms of Soviet youth entertainment, like the dance party. This combination now involved more Western cultural products and, at the same time, brought more material profits to the Soviet officials in charge of the discotheques. The Komsomol initiatives of 1975–76 had attempted to control and regulate the consumption of Western music by incorporating elements of Communist indoctrination. But these efforts had led to unexpected results. The Komsomol ideologists who had first gotten involved in the discotheque movement primarily to guarantee its socialist character had ended up becoming part of the profit-making disco club business, which had nothing to do with the Marxist-Leninist theory of cultural enlightenment and Communist indoctrination.

Chapter 13

The Komsomol Magazine *Rovesnik* and the Ideology of Pop Music Consumption

The development of the discotheque movement in the Dniepropetrovsk Region reflected general trends in the new cultural policy of late socialism and socialist consumerism. Communist ideologists and Komsomol leaders officially supported the discotheque movement. The Soviet music recording company Melodia released the first licensed Western music records to satisfy the growing demand among young Soviet consumers for Western music and, at the same time, to respond to the new ideological requirements for Soviet entertainment.

Between 1970 and 1975, without any official permission from Western recording companies, Melodia had already released musical compilations that included popular Western rock songs. In 1976, Melodia signed its first official contract with the Dutch recording company Old Ark to facilitate the release of the album of the Dutch rock band Teach In.[1] It was the first original Western musical record that Melodia released with an official license. After this, many Western records reached Soviet consumers through official channels. These records represented different styles of Western music —from Billie Holiday's *Greatest Hits in Jazz* to the ex-Beatle John Lennon's *Imagine* and Paul McCartney and Wings' rock album *Band on the Run,* which appeared on the Melodia label in 1977, four years after its original release in England.[2] Popular journals such as *Krugozor* and *Klub i khudozhestvennaia samodeiatel'nost* released various compilations of Western music on "flex discs," which were included as the music appendixes to these journals.[3] In general, Melodia was too slow and inefficient to satisfy the growing Soviet demand for the consumption of Western culture in the 1970s and 1980s. In contrast to the slow reaction of the official recording com-

239

pany, the Soviet black market provided young consumers with all fashionable Western music products without any delays.

The beginning of détente in U.S.-Soviet relations and the relaxation of international tensions also resulted in some changes in youth cultural consumption.[4] Young Western popular music enthusiasts could not only listen to Soviet music records with pop Western music hits but could also watch their musical idols on Soviet television. The Central Soviet TV program always prepared a special music variety show, which was shown on New Year's Night. During the late 1960s and early 1970s, this show usually included a long concert with famous Soviet and foreign musicians and actors that were predominantly from socialist countries. This show was called *Novogodnii Ogoniok* (The New Year Merry Twinkle). Various Soviet celebrities, politicians, journalists, artists, musicians, and singers were invited to *Ogoniok* as guests. Some sat at tables with wine, champagne, and snacks, while others played music, danced, or sang.

Classical music, traditional folk music, and Soviet popular songs dominated *Novogodnii Ogoniok*. Sometimes popular singers from socialist countries, such as Karel Gott from Czechoslovakia or even Dean Reed from the United States, appeared as guests. Millions of Soviet fans of Western pop music were pleasantly surprised that after a traditional long and boring show on the early morning of January 1, 1975, the central Soviet TV station broadcast an unusually long concert of Western pop music stars. These stars included the most popular names played in the Soviet discotheques, such as ABBA, Boney M, the Dowley Family, Donny Osmond, Silver Convention, Joe Dassin, Amanda Lear, Smokey, and Baccarat.

After 1975, Soviet TV aired similar shows at least once a year, usually very late at night. Beginning on January 11, 1977, Soviet TV broadcast an annual special, *Melodies and Rhythms of Foreign Estrada,* that showed the most popular Western rock and disco stars—the only opportunity Soviet fans had to see their idols on TV. Soviet TV also broadcast variety shows with Russian covers of western hits by Soviet bands. The "TV Benefit Performances"of Soviet film stars such as Larisa Golubkina (1975) and Liudmila Gurchenko (1978) and Evgenii Ginzburg's show "Magic Lantern" (1976) offered very good covers of songs from *Jesus Christ Superstar* and Beatles and Paul McCartney albums by Soviet bands such as Moscow's Vesiolye rebiata and Leningrad's Poiushchie gitary.[5]

Dniepropetrovsk's young consumers of Western popular music also relied on printed information. Besides a few editions of Polish, Czech, East German, Hungarian, and Bulgarian youth magazines, which came through official channels of distribution for Soviet mass media, and rare issues of British, French, and West German music magazines, which came through the black market, young Dniepropetrovsk residents relied mainly on Soviet youth newspapers and magazines to get information about their favorite musicians. These publications included both All-Union titles, such as *Komsomol'skaia Pravda, Yunost'*, and *Smena*, and Ukrainian republican periodicals, such as *Molod' Ukrainy* and *Ranok*. Traditionally, the Ukrainian periodicals were more cautious and conservative than the Moscow-based ones. Therefore, young readers in Dniepropetrovsk preferred the periodicals from Moscow. According to contemporaries' and librarians' statistics, the most popular publication among Dniepropetrovsk's consumers of popular music was the Soviet youth journal *Rovesnik* (in English, *Contemporary*, or *A Person of the Same Age*), which was established in 1962 by the All-Union Komsomol to cover the major problems of international youth culture and politics. *Rovesnik* published important information about Western popular culture in the Russian language. By 1982, in 211 trade union libraries the absolute favorite magazine among young readers was *Rovesnik*. During the 1970s and 1980s, young readers between the ages of fifteen and twenty-one years preferred this journal to any other Komsomol publication. The beginning of the mass popularity of *Rovesnik* coincided with the peak of the discotheque movement in the region.[6]

The Youth Magazine *Rovesnik* (1964–84) and the Realities of Local Music Consumption

Young readers were not only looking for more information about music but also for public approval from official sources. *Rovesnik* became the most reliable official source for this information because it used foreign publications as sources and covered popular topics of youth culture abroad.[7] Even the local Komsomol ideologists who were in charge of the region's disco club movement acknowledged this fact. Mikhail Suvorov noted that Komsomol supervisors always checked the content of disc jockeys' comments about Western music with information from *Rovesnik*.[8] This journal became an important and officially sanctioned source of information for both young pop music consumers and their local Komsomol ideologists. *Rovesnik* also reflected the central Komsomol officials' reactions to new music and youth fashions from the West. Thus, without studying the contents of this magazine, it is difficult to understand the peculiarities of local cultural consumption in closed provincial Soviet cities such as Dniepropetrovsk. There-fore, an analysis of *Rovesnik* issues can add important ideological dimen-sions to our understanding of the popular cultural consumption of Soviet youth.

The first article about rock-and-roll music appeared in *Rovesnik* in Feb-ruary 1964. It was a small critical essay about "Beatlemania" in England, whose author explained the popularity of the Beatles' music as due to two factors: the simplicity of their melodies and their loud sound.[9] At the very beginning, this Soviet magazine presented rock musicians as representa-tives of the decadent bourgeois culture of the West. However, in its July 1964 issue, a Soviet correspondent who visited the working-class clubs in England acknowledged the popularity of the Beatles' music among "the young British proletarians whose rock bands tried to imitate the Beatles' music and sound."[10] After 1964, *Rovesnik* shared such an ambiguous ap-proach to this new music, which reflected the confusion of Soviet ideolo-gists with regard to the new cultural phenomenon. On the one hand, they considered rock music to be a product of capitalist culture and therefore ide-ologically harmful. On the other hand, they acknowledged that it was a part of the social protest of Western working-class youth against the capitalist establishment. In contrast to their traditional criticism of purely "capitalist movements" among British youth, such as "rockers" and "mods," Soviet journalists praised working-class singers such as Pete Seeger and Woody Guthrie, "who were worthy of the song."[11] In July 1965, *Rovesnik* pub-lished the sheet music and lyrics of Mark Traverse's song "Sixteen Tons." From this time on, almost every issue of the journal included the sheet mu-sic and lyrics of the most popular songs among young Western workers.[12]

In response to growing interest from readers in Western popular music, *Rovesnik* began publishing more about this music on a regular basis. Dur-ing the year 1965–66, the magazine followed the prevailing ideological hierarchy of Western music, as approved by the Soviet ideologists. The first and most positive category, from the Communist ideological point of view, was the group of Western songs called "*narodnye pesni rabochikh,*" or working-class songs, traditionally associated with the music of Woody Guthrie and Pete Seeger. The second place in this hierarchy belonged to the "popular ordinary people's chant" ("*populiarnoe-narodnoe penie*") of American folk bands such as the Kingston Trio and Peter, Paul, and Mary. Jazz, still considered the music of "the oppressed and exploited Afro-Americans," was also well respected, along with the folk songs of working people. Soviet journalists criticized the type of music that they called "pop music of capitalist entertainment." The leaders of this pop music category were the Beatles. The journalists of *Rovesnik* described the Beatles' music as "a pretentious cacophony instead of music."[13] In 1966, these journalists added a new category to their hierarchy of music from the West: "big beat" music. *Rovesnik*'s music correspondents divided this beat music into two subdivisions. One was the positive, progressive beat of Bob Dylan, Joan Baez, and Barry McGuire, who represented "a good folk tradition of the American working class." The other subdivision was negative beat music, which they characterized as "for entertainment only"; this included "loud beat bands," particularly the loud rhythmic dance music of the Beatles. In July 1966, *Rovesnik* even published the sheet music and lyrics of Bob Dylan's song "Blowing in the Wind" to illustrate the "progressive anticapitalist spirit of American working-class songs."[14] Almost every year, *Rovesnik* praised Dylan's music work as the most important contribution to modern popular culture in the West.[15]

The first positive mention of the Beatles' music appeared in the February 1967 issue of *Rovesnik*. They were mentioned in an article about an American singer, Dean Reed, who had popularized some of the Beatles' songs and included them in his repertoire during his concert in Moscow in 1966.[16] This positive public appraisal of the Beatles' music only added to the Beatles' popularity among Soviet rock music fans. Reed was an American-born radical singer who had criticized American imperialism and racial discrimination. Later, he immigrated to the Soviet bloc, where he became a citizen of East Germany. He was accepted by the Soviet ideologists as a positive representative of Western rock music. After 1967, he became the most popular figure of Western popular culture for young Soviet consumers of rock music.[17] All Komsomol publications, including *Rovesnik,* devoted more attention to Reed than to any other pop star from the West.

In the September 1967 issue of *Rovesnik,* A. Volyntsev, who usually covered jazz topics for the journal, published a long article about new developments in Western rock music.[18] In this article, Volyntsev praised the music of Ray Charles and the Beatles as the most positive and progressive phenomena of contemporary Western popular culture. He emphasized the long-lasting humanistic effects of the Beatles' music, in contrast to the decadence of popular bourgeois music by groups like Sonny and Cher, the Monkees, and the Troggs. He demonstrated extensive knowledge of musical material and gave a relatively objective portrayal of the situation in Western pop music:

> By the 1960s, rock-and-roll fashion in the USA had been over, and big beat moved to Europe. The English quartet, the Beatles, contributed to the immense popularity of this music. The participants in this quartet cre-

ated a music which reflected correctly the emotions of the modern English teenagers. . . . The Beatles are the musicians of great talent, but their talent is exploited impetuously and mercilessly by [a capitalist industry of entertainment]. As a result, the best products of their musical talent are dissolving in a sea of mediocre musical recordings.[19]

Volyntsev's article sparked a series of articles in the Komsomol media that reevaluated the representation of the Beatles' songs as the most progressive Western popular music. Other Soviet newspapers and magazines followed *Rovesnik*'s example—1968 and 1969 witnessed more positive articles about the Beatles in the Soviet press.[20] In 1969, this idealization of the Beatles' music on the pages of *Rovesnik* reached its peak. The Beatles' cartoon film *Yellow Submarine* was glorified as a cultural "protest against imperialistic war and sufferings of the people and a hymn to a beauty of this world, pleasures of simple life and love."[21]

With its publication of many positive and professionally written articles about Western rock music, *Rovesnik* (together with Tatarskii's music shows on the Maiak radio station) became the most popular and reliable source of information for millions of Soviet rock music fans.[22] According to a librarians' analysis of readers' records (*chitatel'skie formuliary* in Russian) at the reading rooms of the main libraries in the regions of Dniepropetrovsk and Cherkassy in Ukraine, *Rovesnik* was the most widely read Komsomol magazine during the period 1967–84. Besides *Rovesnik,* young Dniepropetrovsk residents also liked to read *Sovetskii ekran* (Soviet screen), *Zhurnal mod* (Fashion magazine), *Tekhnika molodiozhi* (Technique to the youth), *Radio, Za rubezhom* (Abroad), *Vokrug sveta* (Around the world), and *Novoe vremia* (New times).

The system of Soviet public libraries required those librarians who were in charge of reading rooms to make a monthly analysis of the periodicals chosen by readers. By the end of each year, the librarians submitted their calculations to the director of the library. According to calculations from the State Public Library of the Dniepropetrovsk Region, during the period 1965–70, 55 percent of readers read *Rovesnik* at least once a month. In 1971–75, this number increased to 82 percent; and by 1976–80, it had risen to 95 percent. During the period 1981–85, the number of regular readers of *Rovesnik* reached a peak, almost 100 percent of library users read this magazine.[23] Contemporaries noted that during the 1970s, young enthusiasts of rock music signed the list of readers to get a fresh issue of this popular magazine in the public library's reading room.[24]

Some librarians complained that the young zealots of rock music vandalized the issues of *Rovesnik* by cutting off the pages with the sheet music and lyrics of their favorite songs. This happened for the first time in the spring of 1968, when *Rovesnik* reprinted the Animals' song "House of the Rising Sun" as "the old American folk song."[25] In its December 1968 issue, *Rovesnik* reprinted the Beatles song "A Hard Day's Night." During the January 1969 school break, young beat music enthusiasts cut out pages of the magazine with the sheet music and lyrics of this song in the reading rooms of the two central libraries in Dniepropetrovsk, the main city library and the main regional library downtown.[26] The same thing happened in 1969 and 1970, when *Rovesnik* reprinted the sheet music and lyrics (sometimes in Russian) of hits such as "Lady Madonna," "Yesterday," "Girl," and "Back in the USSR," and John Lennon's "Give Peace a Chance."[27] Some of these issues of *Rovesnik* just disappeared from the libraries; they were stolen by Beatles fans. Even the central Lenin Library of the Soviet Union in Moscow suffered from the depredations of numerous Beatles fans who cut the pictures of their idols from the issues of *Rovesnik* in the 1970s.[28]

The next British band, after the Beatles, that was reevaluated by *Rovesnik* as a progressive and antibourgeois beat group was the Rolling Stones. In the spring of 1969, A. Valentinov, another Komsomol expert on Western rock music, presented the Rolling Stones as an antiestablishment rock band and praised their songs as "a sincere protest against capitalist exploitation." According to his description, their song "(I Can't Get No) Satisfaction" was "an emotionally strong expression of anxiety and frustration with a contemporary bourgeois Western world."[29] Despite such positive characteristics of the Rolling Stones, *Rovesnik*'s articles were very ambiguous about the commercialization of rock music. In 1973, the magazine continued to praise the early songs of the Rolling Stones that were "based on the old rhythm and blues traditions." At the same time, it rejected the band's "cynicism and capitalist commercialization of its music in the 1970s." Nevertheless, the editorial board of *Rovesnik* tried to satisfy the interests of a new generation of readers. Young rock music fans asked the journal to clarify "the rumors that the Rolling Stones were forbidden in the USSR." In its response to satisfy readers, *Rovesnik* devoted a long article to an analysis of the new developments in the Rolling Stones' music. Thus, in 1973, *Rovesnik* initiated a new series of articles under the title "Examining Our Mail (Answering the Letters of Our Readers)."[30] During the 1970s and 1980s, this series in *Rovesnik* predominantly covered themes of popular culture, especially topics of popular music.

Overall, *Rovesnik* commented on all the most important contemporary developments in Western popular culture. In its December 1967 issue, the journal published the first article in the Soviet press about the hippie movement in London.[31] This pioneering essay triggered interest in this new phenomenon among Soviet youth. A year later, another Soviet popular magazine, *Vokrug sveta* (Around the World), also published a long article about Western hippies.[32] Many young Dniepropetrovsk residents learned about this "hippie movement" from the 1967 *Rovesnik* article and the Soviet TV show *Mezhdunarodnaia panorama* (International Panorama) on New Year's Eve 1968.[33]

During the summer of 1972, *Rovesnik* again reacted quickly to the new *Jesus Christ Superstar* fashion, which started in the West with the rock opera by Andrew Lloyd Webber. This "Jesus" fashion became very popular among Soviet youth in the big cities as early as the end of 1971.[34] Young consumers of rock music in Dniepropetrovsk compared information from *Rovesnik* with facts from Tatarskii's Soviet radio shows about *Jesus Christ Superstar.* Despite the ideologically correct criticism of the "idealization of the Jesus revolution among the Western youth," young Dniepropetrovsk consumers of rock music were happy to read about the most popular music product they were buying on the city's music black market from June to September of 1972. According to Vladimir Solodovnik, the *Rovesnik* articles helped to explain the background of the music of Webber's opera and the origins of the new "Jesus" fashion in Western pop culture to Soviet youth.[35]

Despite the obvious intention of *Rovesnik*'s journalistic attempts to cover new cultural developments in the West in a timely fashion, on average, *Rovesnik*'s information was usually one year late. In the summer of 1972, *Rovesnik* wrote about the rock opera *Tommy* by the Who, which had been released in 1969; in November 1973, the magazine published a short article about the success of the jazz-rock band Blood, Sweat, and Tears during its 1970 concert tour of Yugoslavia, Romania, and Poland; in 1974, the magazine covered the U.S. Osmond Brothers band two years after it reached the highest point of its popularity in England.[36] Many enthusiasts of rock music in the region of Dniepropetrovsk were disappointed that *Rovesnik*'s coverage of Creedence Clearwater Revival and Shocking Blue, the most popular American and Dutch rock bands on the region's music market, came too late, after both groups had already disbanded.[37] Even the positive and professionally written article about Deep Purple, the most popular British hard-rock band among Soviet youth, appeared in *Rovesnik* in 1975, when this pioneering heavy metal rock group was already falling apart.[38]

From the beginning of *Rovesnik*'s coverage, Komsomol journalists considered the propaganda of American anti-imperialist and antiwar songs as the most important aspect of its articles from an ideological point of view. This antiestablishment, antibourgeois appeal of the new music was a constant topic in these *Rovesnik* articles. Any kind of public criticism of the capitalist establishment by rock musicians or related public scandals attracted the attention of *Rovesnik*. Those musicians who participated in the working-class movement, communist parties' activities, or antiwar, anti-imperialist actions in Western countries became the heroes of *Rovesnik* articles. These musical heroes of *Rovesnik* were Woody Guthrie, Pete Seeger, Bob Dylan, Phil Ochs, and Joan Baez.[39] Another group of American pop musicians that symbolized class struggle against the "oppression of American capitalists" were the African American founders of jazz and rhythm and blues. For *Rovesnik,* all black musicians, from the jazz "kings" such as Louis Armstrong to the "queens" of soul music such as Aretha Franklin, were the indisputable representatives of "the cultural opposition to international imperialism."[40] From the middle of the 1970s onward, Komsomol ideologists emphasized the idea that American rock music was a result of the class struggle of exploited black musicians who invented jazz, rhythm and blues, and reggae as the music of their cultural protest against capitalist exploitation and racial discrimination in the United States.[41]

Starting in the mid-1970s, the Beatles' music, including the solo careers of John Lennon, Paul McCartney, George Harrison, and Ringo Starr, became the standard for progressive anti-imperialist Western rock music to *Rovesnik* journalists. They presented Beatles songs (especially those from the 1972 John Lennon and Yoko Ono album *Sometime in New York City*) as the "best and the most talented music created in all of Western rock and roll." One *Rovesnik* journalist praised Lennon's songs as "a continuation of the traditions of Bob Dylan, Pete Seeger, and Phil Ochs."[42] In the July 1973 issue, *Rovesnik* reprinted several chapters from *The Authorized Biography of the Beatles* by Hunter Davis.[43] This glorification and idealization of the Beatles as musicians continued and survived all new trends and music fashions at the end of the 1970s and beginning of the 1980s. Even in 1983, *Rovesnik* was still fascinated with the Beatles. During August of that year, the journal resumed publication of chapters from the newly revised edition of Davis's *Authorized Biography.* The Beatles' music, according to the famous Soviet composer Andrei Petrov, was "the most talented fruit of the entire Western rock-and-roll culture."[44]

Throughout the 1970s and 1980s, *Rovesnik* covered the entire history of rock music. All the major figures of this music, the representatives of all the major currents of Western popular music, which were popular on the Soviet music markets, including Dniepropetrovsk's, appeared in the pages of this magazine. The music of the late 1960s was represented by material about the Doors and Jim Morrison, in addition to numerous articles about the Beatles, the Rolling Stones, and the Who. Other artists—like Elton John; David Bowie; Led Zeppelin; Queen; Slade; Rainbow; Uriah Heep; Emerson, Lake, and Palmer; Pink Floyd; the Sex Pistols; and the Clash—were also popular subjects for the articles about music history in the 1970s, covering the different styles of heavy metal, psychedelic, progressive, punk rock, and "new wave."[45]

In 1977, *Rovesnik* began a series of articles about music for discotheques with a small piece about a Swedish band, ABBA. In 1979, the Bee Gees and their disco music became a new popular subject in the pages of the magazine. In its April 1979 issue, *Rovesnik* published a very long essay about the organization of disco clubs in the socialist countries of Eastern Europe. During 1977 and 1978, readers of the magazine had already recommended starting a special column devoted to discotheques, "In Assistance to Disc Jockeys" (*V pomoshch vedushchemu diskokluba* in Russian). In response to this request, in November 1979 Leonid Pereverzev, the most popular and qualified music critic writing in this journal, presented the first essay in a series about the new dance music, titled "The Phenomenon of Disco Music," for the new column requested by readers.[46]

Marxist class analysis and official ideological approaches to music shaped the presentation of musical information in *Rovesnik*. Thus, according to ideological requirements, journalists concentrated their attention on cultural developments in neighboring socialist countries. Young rock music enthusiasts hated this approach.[47] By giving the socialist countries' priority in coverage, journalists put information about the readers' favorite Western rock musicians only after an obligatory article about rock bands from the socialist camp. That is why in 1977 a regular reader of *Rovesnik* could find a good article about Slade, the most popular British band on the Soviet music market during those years, only after reading material about Puhdys, an East German band completely unknown in Dniepropetrovsk.[48] In the September 1979 issue, information about the former Deep Purple guitarist Ritchie Blackmore's band Rainbow from England and the band the Eagles from California appeared in tandem with articles about East German and Czech rock bands, such as Regen Macher and M. Effekt.[49]

Prices on the Dniepropetrovsk and Kyiv music markets reflected more closely the demands of local rock music consumers than information in *Rovesnik*. Nobody was interested in East German, Polish, or other socialist rock bands in the city's music market. By the end of 1979, the most popular and expensive music products in these two Ukrainian cities had nothing to do with the socialist countries at all. Two record albums, *Bee Gees Greatest* and Pink Floyd's *The Wall,* cost approximately 100 to 125 rubles each.[50] The British band Supertramp's album *Breakfast in America* and Rainbow's LP *Long Live Rock 'n' Roll* were sold for 60 rubles each. At the same time, the Polish rock band Czerwone Gitary's (Red Guitars) record *Czongla Pada* (Rain Is Falling) and the Hungarian band Omega's album could be sold for only 25 rubles each.[51]

The only socialist musical product that became surprisingly popular on the music market in Dniepropetrovsk in 1976–77 without any coverage by *Rovesnik* was the Soviet record *On the Wave of My Memory* (*Po volne moei pamiati*) by the young Soviet composer David Tukhmanov. Tukhmanov composed songs using various styles of Western rock music, from heavy blues to progressive rock, and he used exotic lyrics derived from classical international poetry, from the ancient Greek poet Sappho and the English poet Percy Bysshe Shelley to such Russian poets as Anna Akhmatova and Maksimilian Voloshin. Tukhmanov invited talented musicians from various well-established Soviet rock bands, such as Aleksandr Barykin, Mekhrdad Baadi, and Sergei Belikov, and together they made a good conceptual album of Soviet rock music.[52] This record was released in late 1975 on the Melodia label, and it officially cost 2 rubles and 50 kopeks in record stores. Because of the growing demand and limited supply of Tukhmanov's album in official department stores, its price reached 10 to 30 rubles on the black market by the middle of 1976.[53] But this album was an exception to the rule. The overwhelming majority of records on the market represented Western popular music, and consumers wanted to know more about this music rather than read about vocal and instrumental groups from socialist countries.

Rovesnik Recommendations, *O Lucky Man!* and Serious Rock Music

The main problem for Komsomol ideologists, including authors of *Rovesnik,* was how to tell good (and progressive, from an ideological point of view) Western music from bad (and dangerous, from an ideological point of view) Western music. Both Western originals and socialist versions of rock and disco music were officially used for entertainment, for dance parties everywhere in the Soviet Union.[54] With the beginning of the officially approved discotheque movement in the USSR in the middle of the 1970s, Komsomol ideologists struggled with traditional Communist criteria for Western popular music. According to these criteria, only working-class songs of class struggle and social protest were worthy for consumption by Soviet youth. Products of Western mass culture such as dance music had to be censored by Marxist ideological experts before they were allowed for cultural consumption in the USSR.[55]

However, the overwhelming majority of songs popularized on the Soviet dance floor had nothing to do with class struggle, capitalist exploitation, or imperialistic wars. Fashionable Western music for dances not only attracted millions of Soviet members of Komsomol but also began to bring profits to those who distributed these records. Soviet consumers preferred to buy light music for dances rather than serious music for listening. They were ready to pay astronomical prices for foreign records, for admission to fashionable disco clubs, and for concerts of light music. Even the official Soviet label Melodia released Western records, which in general usually consisted of light dance music. According to *Rovesnik*'s readers, the overwhelming majority of Western records released by Melodia from 1976 to 1983 did not include classical rock albums. All these records were "music for legs, not for the head." As one reader, an engineer, I. Sharapov, the organizer of a nonprofessional disco club, wrote:

Look at what was shown on the Soviet TV, who was invited to visit our country with concerts, or whose music records were released on Melodia label. They were—ABBA, Boney M, the Dowley Family, Donny Osmond, Silver Convention, Joe Dassin, Amanda Lear, Smokey, Baccarat, Genghis Khan, New Seekers, the Mamas and Papas, Teach In, Lipps Inc., Demise Russos, Cliff Richard, Robert Young, Paul Anka, Diana Ross, Pussycat, Gibson Brothers. It looks like monotonous picture, doesn't it? It is either sweet pop or light and sometimes very silly disco. Where is real rock music in this list? Where is music that is very true, sincere and innovative, progressive, and with an element of protest? It appears in very rare cases: the movie *O Lucky Man!* with Alan Price's songs, concert tours of Elton John and B. B. King, and one album by John Lennon (*Imagine*) and by Paul McCartney (*Band on the Run*). That is it. As we see, the lion's share of Western products, which were released in our country, belonged to the very "specimens of mass culture" that B. N. Pastukhov, the first secretary of the Central Committee of the All-Union Soviet Komsomol, recently criticized in his report to the Fifth Plenum of the Komsomol Central Committee. . . . It looks for me that now there is one of the most radical solutions [in transforming our discotheque movement as a means of education of good musical taste among mass audience]. We need to use the best specimens of the "rock music classics," which were tested by time, in a contrast to an invasion of a disco style and commercial rock that had pushed our youth in a direction of the careless, thoughtless entertainment and wastes their time. The characteristic feature of progressive Western rock music (in a hidden or explicit form, gradually or straightforward, with sarcastic remarks, chaotic or consistently) is that this music condemns the capitalist reality and bourgeois morals. We need to use this feature of Western rock music in the Soviet discotheque movement.[56]

At the end, he offered the main criteria for differentiating between good music and bad music:

From the start, we must reject any disco products which contain elements of anarchism, pornography, Neofascism, and violence. The main criteria for our selection [of good music for discotheques] include: humanity, pacifism, social criticism, lyricism, sincerity in music and poetry, innovations, good melody, good taste in music, progressive political convictions of a performer. There are many examples of such rock music in the West that correspond to these criteria. And we need to use them.[57]

Sharapov shared a typical approach of Soviet consumers of Western rock music. To some extent, they "imagined" this music. Because Western music often came from audiotapes, the Soviet consumers of these tapes did not even have accurate images of the original Western records or their favorite musicians. A majority of Soviet rock music consumers simply invented ideas and images of Western pop music for themselves. For instance, Aleksandr Gusar, who began to collect audiotapes with rock music recordings as early as 1972 while he was in high school, drew pictures of his favorite musicians in pencil as he imagined them with long hair, in American Levi's jeans, playing electric guitars. He could not understand the English lyrics of rock songs, so he invented his own Russian translations of these songs. Thus, he interpreted the Rolling Stones' song "Paint It Black" as a protest song against racial discrimination in capitalist society. Gusar honestly believed that the Marc Bolan–T. Rex songs "Children of Revolution" and "20th Century Boy" were political action songs calling for a socialist revolution among Western youth.[58] Another rock music fan, Mikhail Suvorov, recalled how he and his classmates from the Dniepropetrovsk high school invented not only lyrics but also stories about their favorite musicians. They tried to collect any information they could about rock music, not only songs but also visual images of rock bands. "We wanted to see our 'rock idols' alive," noted Suvorov, "not just listen to their music! We were envious of Polish kids who had an opportunity to watch the Beatles movies in Warsaw, when we read about this in Soviet newspapers. We wanted to see the real Western rock band alive on the movie screen in our hometown, Dniepropetrovsk!"[59] To feed their rock music imagination, Soviet rock music fans needed images of their idols.

That is why, in 1975, the British film *O Lucky Man!*—which Sharapov mentioned in his letter—created a sensation among Soviet enthusiasts of serious rock music. This film, from the "ideologically progressive" British director Lindsay Anderson, gave a very critical portrayal of the modern British capitalist society. Showing the adventures of a coffee sales agent, Mick Travis (played by Malcolm McDowell), Anderson analyzed the major problems of British imperialism—the exploitation of developing countries by the advanced Western nations, greed, the military industrial complex, dangerous antihuman scientific experiments for profit's sake—all of which fit very well into Soviet anticapitalist propaganda. The most important fact for Soviet rock music consumers was that Alan Price, a British rock musician from the legendary band the Animals, took part in this film, playing live with his new band. Soviet rock music fans knew Price as a founder of the Animals and were familiar with his keyboard arrangements in the song "House of the Rising Sun," an international hit in the mid-1960s. Hundreds of rock bands in the region of Dniepropetrovsk used to play this song for slow dances, covering the original with either Russian or Ukrainian lyrics. For rock music fans, Price was a living legend of real British rock music.

The film *O Lucky Man!* was released in Great Britain in 1973, but it was shown widely in the Soviet Union two years later.[60] When the film reached Dniepropetrovsk in the late summer of 1975, thousands of young enthusiasts of rock music went to the main movie theaters downtown that were showing the film. Rumors spread all over the region of Dniepropetrovsk that Price and his band had recorded and performed live the entire new album of his songs for the film. Soviet rock music fans were able not only to see how a professional British rock star played the instruments but also to read his sheet music and lyrics, which appeared on the screen. Long lines of young people waited for movie tickets at the box offices. As KGB officers recalled, the police were sent to control a situation near the movie theaters Rodina (Motherland) and Panorama in downtown Dniepropetrovsk, where young rock music consumers stormed the box offices and doors. The police had to stop riots and fights near the main entrance to the theaters.[61]

Many high school children skipped their classes and stood in the lines of people waiting for tickets to the film. Vladimir Solodovnik, who lived in the town Sinel'nikovo, near Dniepropetrovsk, went to Dniepropetrovsk together with his classmates to get tickets for a show at the Rodina Theater. Tickets for a movie of standard length (a one-part film, of an hour and a half, known as *odnoseriinyi film* in Russian) usually cost 35 kopeks; tickets for a two-part movie (*dvukh-seriinyi film* in Russian) like *O Lucky Man!* cost 70 kopeks. Yet it was impossible to get these tickets through legitimate means. The black marketers bought the majority of these tickets and made a lot of money selling them to visitors to Dniepropetrovsk who were anxious to watch *O Lucky Man!* In late August 1975, black market ticket prices reached 2 to 5 rubles. Solodovnik and his friends paid a very high price (for a Soviet high school student) to get tickets for the popular British film.[62]

As police officers complained, this hysteria surrounding *O Lucky Man!* in 1975 was the second mass campaign of Westernization that affected the youth of Dniepropetrovsk after the "Jesus Christ" movement, connected to the popularity of music and themes from the rock opera *Jesus Christ Superstar* in 1972–74.[63] Similarly, the "Alan Price hysteria" also took place in Kyiv, Cherkassy, Odessa, and other cities of Soviet Ukraine in 1975–76.[64] For the young Soviet consumers of rock music in closed cities such as Dniepropetrovsk, the British film with Price, a real rock-and-roll legend, was a unique opportunity to see a performance of a real rock star on the movie screen. Rock music fans from the "open" Soviet capital cities were more fortunate. They at least had a chance to see live performances of rock musicians from the West or their substitutes from socialist countries, who occasionally gave concerts during the 1970s. Rock music enthusiasts in Dniepropetrovsk had no such opportunity. As one high school student noted in his diary in September 1975,

My cousins in Kyiv and Moscow saw every month live performances of the very good rock bands from Hungary and Poland who covered the hits from repertoire of Deep Purple, King Crimson, and Uriah Heep. We, who reside in Dniepropetrovsk, are cut off from all these Western influences. We are satisfied if we have a concert or two of a very bad Russian band from Moscow or Leningrad. Finally, this August, we had real rock music of the real British band on the movie screen. This was a film *O Lucky Man!* All my classmates watched this film at least twice. I read in *Rovesnik* that our socialist brothers in Poland saw the Beatles movies in the 1960s. How lucky they were! They watched the gods of beat music on the screen. They had an authentic, real rock! Meanwhile, we are satisfied with our own, socialist, "substitutes" for this music. We are happy if we watch Czech or Polish music parodies with elements of beat music, or stupid Romanian comedy about modern pop music, or boring Soviet film with good beat music of the wonderful Soviet rock musician Aleksandr Gradskii from Moscow. Now, for the first time in their lives, all lovers of serious music watch not the Soviet substitute for beat music but the authentic rock in the authentic British setting in *O Lucky Man!* on the screen here, in Dniepropetrovsk.[65]

It is noteworthy that in his diary the author mentioned the most popular musical films of socialist countries that contained the elements of rock music and popularized a socialist version of Western beat music. In his opinion, all these films were just substitutes for the original Western rock music. He referred to films such as a Czech music parody, *Esli by tysiacha klarnetov* (*If I Would Have a Thousand of Clarinets*), released in the Soviet Union in 1967; a Polish music comedy, *Samozvanets s gitaroi* (*A Pretender with a Guitar*), released in Dniepropetrovsk in December 1971; a Soviet-Romanian musical, *Pesni moria* (*The Songs of the Sea*); and a Soviet musical film by Andrei Mikhalkov-Konchalovskii, *Romans o vliublionnykh* (*A Romance about the Lovers*), which reached Dniepropetrovsk's audiences in December 1974.[66]

The reception of the film with Alan Price's music in the Soviet Union in 1975 was similar to the reception of Beatles films in the West in 1964 and 1966.[67] The main difference was that Soviet rock music fans had very limited information about their musicians. They wrote to various Komsomol periodicals and Soviet radio stations and asked questions about rock music. Local Komsomol ideologists asked similar questions as well. They tried to differentiate between bad and good music. Suvorov remembered how— after long discussions about the film *O Lucky Man!*—the Komsomol activists from his school wrote a letter to *Rovesnik* with a question about the music of Price for this film. In 1976, the journalists of *Rovesnik* responded to thousands of letters with similar requests and questions about the British film. *Rovesnik* even published a small article about Price and reprinted the sheet music and lyrics of the song "O Lucky Man!"[68]

Sharapov's letter to *Rovesnik* about criteria for serious progressive rock music, and similar articles from other issues of *Rovesnik,* were recommended by Dniepropetrovsk's Komsomol leaders for a discussion in local disco clubs. During the spring of 1981, many discotheque organizers in the region used these articles to justify their musical programs and the scripts for their dance parties.[69] Moreover, the local Komsomol apparatchiks literally followed the music recommendations from the *Rovesnik* articles. When they organized special events of ideological indoctrination, which required "ideologically correct Western music," they requested assistance from their discotheque activists. Serhiy Tihipko, a former first secretary of the Komsomol regional committee in Dniepropetrovsk, recalled that during the 1980s, Komsomol ideologists always asked the discotheque activists to help them find musical material that was praised on the pages of *Rovesnik* as progressive Western pop music.[70]

Suvorov, who worked in various capacities at the disco called Club Melodia from 1977 to 1985, noted how important the *Rovesnik* recommendations for the Dniepropetrovsk Komsomol officials were:

After 1980, when John Lennon was assassinated, the central Komsomol administration asked the local Komsomol ideologists to prepare music events about Lennon's songs as an example of progressive anticapitalist music of the West in the struggle against war and imperialism. But by this time, the Soviet official label Melodia had released only one John Lennon album, *Imagine,* and a few songs like "Give Peace a Chance" in the music magazine *Krugozor.* Therefore, when one Komsomol apparatchik approached us and requested anticapitalist songs by Lennon, such as "Power to the People," "Sunday Bloody Sunday," or "Woman Is the Nigger of the World," I had to ask "my connections" from the "music market" to bring me the tapes with Lennon's songs. Another time, the same apparatchik had to deliver a lecture on the old (of the early 1970s) Soviet ideological campaign in support of an American Communist, Angela Davis, who was arrested then by the U.S. government. And he needed again a "rare" Lennon song, "Angela," from the album of 1972, *Sometime in New York City.* He read about this in *Rovesnik.* A similar situation was repeated when the Komsomol ideologists requested from "the discotheque people" tapes with recording of Pete Seeger's, Bob Dylan's, and Joan Baez's songs, which became very important items in official Communist music ceremonies devoted to the international solidarity of workers. And again, the main source of information about these songs was *Rovesnik*. When at the end of 1984 *Rovesnik* published information about the anti-imperialist and anti-American ideas of the Bruce Springsteen's album *Born in the U.S.A.*, Dniepropetrovsk's Komsomol ideologists asked the organizers of our Komsomol discotheque to include Springsteen's songs in a dance program. And again we had to go to the music market and pay for the tapes of Springsteen's album. And I explained this to our ideological supervisors. But they did not care about our sources. What they needed was an ideological efficiency and immediate response to the ideological suggestions of their bosses from Moscow.[71]

To pay tribute to the goals of Communist education, Komsomol ideologists had to be critical about "bourgeois music for entertainment." At the same time, they were responsible for mass entertainment as a means of education for Soviet youth. Therefore, Komsomol ideologists and discotheque activists needed to find a compromise for how to deal with the new popularity of dance music among young people. Eventually, they agreed to permit a certain amount of Western music in dance programs. At the same time, they popularized any "progressive anti-imperialist act" of Western musicians; they supported an official dissemination of information about such anti-imperialist musicians and urged the organizers of dance parties to play the music of such musicians. The local Komsomol officials tried to adjust the recommendations from *Rovesnik* to "the requirements of ideological education" in the closed city of Dniepropetrovsk and to the suggestions of the old Communist and KGB apparatchiks who had more experience with ideological work in this strategically important region.[72] Sometimes this led to a controversial situation when the local disco club organizers were inspired by *Rovesnik* articles and then encountered resistance from Dniepropetrovsk's ideologists, who tended to be more cautious than the journalists from Moscow.

In 1980, Dniepropetrovsk's Komsomol ideologists criticized certain local disco activists for playing songs by the British musician Manfred Mann in their dance program. For some reason, these ideologists had received confusing information about the anti-Soviet actions of this musician, who supposedly had criticized the Soviet invasion of Afghanistan. Dniepropetrovsk's discotheque enthusiasts, including local college students, wrote letters to *Rovesnik* and asked for correct information about Manfred Mann. In response to these letters, *Rovesnik* journalists published an essay about the "progressive character of the Manfred Mann's Earth Band music." They explained to Dniepropetrovsk's incompetent ideologists that Manfred Mann always supported "the left, socialist ideas and criticized imperialism." Moreover, this musician joined the British Communist Party in 1983 and expressed "pro-Soviet sympathies in public." After this article, Dniepropetrovsk's ideologists changed their attitude and supported the popularization of Manfred Mann's music in disco clubs of the region.[73]

Many Komsomol disco club organizers sincerely believed in the progressive character of the Communist culture. They treated experimental music of the West as part of an international phenomenon of revolution and cultural experimentation, which would transform the entire world in the direction of social justice, equality, and a higher level of cultural development. These Komsomol enthusiasts of rock music also shared what Alexei Yurchak, who lived in Leningrad during the same period of time, called the idealization of the "future-oriented aesthetics of rock music." As Yurchak correctly noted, this "futuristic, avant-garde, experimental aesthetics remained an important part of the ethos of socialism even during the late Soviet period, despite strict party control."[74] To some extent, this experimental aesthetics shaped the tastes of many disco club activists, who were traditionally fans of "progressive rock music" from the West.[75]

The Domination of *Popsa* over Serious Music on the Dance Floor

With the democratization of rock music consumption during the end of the 1970s, these criteria for "progressive" rock bands, which were shared by people such as Sharapov and Yurchak, were replaced by different requirements and demands. Only the most serious rock music consumers, who mainly represented the intellectual minority of Soviet urban youth, followed the criteria and aesthetic of Sharapov and Yurchak. The overwhelming majority of popular music consumers preferred the "light and primitive" rhythms of disco or the aggressive and simple tempo of heavy metal bands, such as Ritchie Blackmore's Rainbow, Iron Maiden, the Scorpions, AC/DC, and Kiss.[76]

On the basis of the recommendations of the youth periodicals like *Rovesnik,* the disc jockeys and engineers of the central city discotheque in Dniepropetrovsk organized a sociological survey among its regular visitors in November 1979 (when they interviewed 200 people), September 1980 (350 people), and December 1981 (400 people). Almost 95 percent of those who answered the questions visited the discotheque at least once a week. A total of 80 percent of them were Komsomol members, 40 percent were female visitors, and 60 percent were male visitors. And 10 percent were high school students fifteen to seventeen years old (from eighth to tenth grades); 20 percent were from vocational schools (*proftekhuchilishche*), sixteen to seventeen years old; 30 percent were young workers, seventeen to twenty-two years old; 10 percent were students of technical schools (*tekhnikums*); and 30 percent were college students or "young specialists" with a college degree, eighteen to twenty-five years old. As we can see, only one-third of regular participants in dance parties organized by the central discotheque were local intellectuals with college degrees. As a result, the young democratic majority of these participants had very different musical tastes and preferences from those of Soviet intellectual youth like Sharapov and Yurchak. Only 5 percent of the regular (both male and female) visitors preferred serious music by King Crimson, Yes, Genesis, and Pink Floyd, and they requested that each evening a disc jockey play at least one song from Pink Floyd's albums *Dark Side of the Moon, Wish You Were Here, Animals,* and *The Wall.* Almost 10 percent of visitors (all of them male guests) loved to dance to heavy music by old hard-rock bands such as Deep Purple, Led Zeppelin, Nazareth, Queen, Slade, Sweet, Suzi Quatro, Uriah Heep, and Black Sabbath. Hard-rock music fans also included in their list old songs by the Beatles from their last albums. By the end of the dance program, they always requested the songs "Birthday" and "Helter Skelter" from the Beatles' *White Album* of 1968. Approximately 30 percent of all visitors, an overwhelming majority of whom were female, also preferred Soviet *estrada* (pop music), especially songs by Alla Pugacheva and Yurii Antonov, while 10 percent of visitors liked unofficial Soviet rock bands such as Mashina vremeni (Time Machine). Almost 80 percent of both female and male visitors preferred Western disco music, especially ABBA, Boney M, Eruption (its most popular song was "One Way Ticket"), the Italian composer Toto Cutugno, the Bee Gees' songs from *Saturday Night Fever,* and songs by the American band Blondie (with the most popular hit of 1979 and 1980, "Heart of Glass"). Most shocking for the Komsomol ideologists was the fact that 70 percent of all male visitors and 60 percent of female guests preferred music by AC/DC and Kiss. Though male visitors requested songs from the AC/DC albums *Highway to Hell* (1979) and *Back to Black* (1980) and Kiss's song "Rock and Roll All Nite," female audiences always asked for three Kiss hits "for slow dances when ladies would invite gentlemen to dance"—"Hard Luck Woman," "I Was Made For Lovin' You," and "Beth." Ukrainian popular music (including Ukrainian folk rock) disappeared from the repertoire of the Dniepropetrovsk disco club. Nobody requested Ukrainian songs.[77]

As early as the 1970s, Dniepropetrovsk consumers began to categorize two different groups of music products. One was called "a proper rock music" and the other was dismissed as "mere popular music" ("*popsa*" or "*estrada*," in Russian). This differentiation came from the old Soviet ideological tradition to consider the serious, sophisticated, and experimental cultural product as a priority for Soviet cultural consumption as a means of ideological education. Many Soviet disc jockeys used this differentiation to justify their music preferences when they played "serious rock" rather than "light disco," which was "*popsa*" for them. That is why Dniepropetrovsk's disc jockeys were reluctant to include punk music or "new wave" in their repertoire because that music was not serious enough for them and was different from the traditional standards of hard rock of Deep Purple, Led Zeppelin, Uriah Heep, and Queen or from the intellectual rock of King Crimson, Yes, Genesis, and Pink Floyd. Even before the official prohibitions of punk rock, local Komsomol discotheque activists disliked this kind of music because it sounded "primitive" and not sophisticated enough. According to Mikhail Suvorov, he and his friends from the central Dniepropetrovsk city discotheque tried to avoid playing Western *popsa* even if an audience demanded this music during dances. Nevertheless, because of popular demand and pressure from their Komsomol supervisors, who were interested in the real profits of the region's disco clubs at the end of the 1970s and during the 1980s, they played more and more "light dance music."[78]

By the beginning of the 1980s, further divisions appeared in the disc jockeys' discourse: Western music and Sovdep music. In his organization for upcoming dances, Suvorov always used Sovdep, an abbreviation of Sovet Narodnykh Deputatov (Soviets of People's Deputies), to mark the names of songs of Soviet pop music on a paper with the discotheque program. This abbreviation had negative connotations about the Soviet system of power, but many rock music enthusiasts still used it.[79] Sovdep included not only official Soviet *estrada* (*popsa*) but also the majority of the Soviet vocal instrumental ensembles, which were obligatory items for any dance program in the Soviet discotheques. When Suvorov was invited to a special closed dance party of the Dniepropetrovsk regional Komsomol apparatchiks in December 1983, he brought a copy of his program of dances and showed this program to the person responsible for this special dance party. This apparatchik, who knew the tastes of his colleagues, crossed out all the Soviet songs marked as "Sovdep" and left only the most popular hits of Western pop music. Doing this he noted, "We do not need Sovdep *popsa,* we want to have fun. Bring us more hot hits for this evening."[80] "O man, what a night it was," Suvorov recalled:

> All these Komsomol activists drank too much. They were openly dating each other. There were a lot of young beautiful girls among guests from district Komsomol organizations. They attracted the attention of male apparatchiks. Even young KGB officers came to this closed dance party. They invited young female Komsomol activists to dance. At the beginning of the evening, I tried to play mainly Soviet *estrada*—Alla Pugacheva, Yurii Antonov, Sophia Rotaru—and included also some officially approved Western hits—"Hey Jude" and "Birthday" by the Beatles, "Angie" and "Start Me Up" by the Rolling Stones, "Child in Time" and "Soldier of Fortune" by Deep Purple, and various disco trash by Boney M and Eruption. By the end of this long evening, I was very tired and I played music for this drunken Komsomol audience without announcing the names of the bands. And suddenly I realized that the most popular music in this room that night were the forbidden songs by Kiss. I had an old tape of "slow" and "fast" dance numbers of this band. The KGB guys who wanted to dance with our beautiful Komsomol activists asked me to play the same songs again and again because their partners loved this music. All these songs were the Kiss's hits—"Hard Luck Woman," "Sure Know Something," "I Was Made for Lovin' You," and "Beth." Between midnight and two in the morning, I played only these songs. And after this party, one drunken KGB officer came to me and thanked me for playing Kiss music, which his new young date knew and liked. I was shocked that he recognized the music. As I realized that many of the Komsomol guests recognized this music as well. But they did not care. And this was a time of the official Komsomol banning of fascist punk music of Kiss and AC/DC.[81]

Other disco activists witnessed the same hypocrisy in organizing the elite dance parties for the Westernized young apparatchiks who represented both Komsomol and KGB personnel in the Cherkassy Region of Ukraine.[82] The author of this study had the same experience in December 1983 at another closed Komsomol discotheque on the island of Khortytsia in the city of

Zaporizhie in the building of the Regional Komsomol School (Zonal'naia Komsomol'skaia shkola), where all Komsomol activists throughout southern Ukraine, including Dniepropetrovsk, had special classes on Communist indoctrination, the organization of atheist propaganda and entertainment, and the like. After the classes, the local disc jockeys from Zaporizhie played dance party music for students of this Komsomol School. They included forbidden Western music (e.g., Kiss songs) in their program and did not announce the title or name of the performer. According to other witnesses, this kind of practice was common for Komsomol discotheques not only in Dniepropetrovsk and Zaporizhie but also in all the industrial cities of Soviet Ukraine, such as Kyiv, L'viv, Donetsk, and Odessa.[83]

At the same time, the people responsible for the organization of discotheques noticed another very important trend in the repertoire of disco programs in Soviet Ukraine at the end of the 1970s and beginning of the 1980s. Previously, all Ukrainian disc jockeys included Ukrainian hit songs in the Ukrainian language as at least a part of their obligatory "patriotic" program. However, during the period 1980–84, popular songs in Ukrainian disappeared from disco programs. This change was especially remarkable in the closed city of Dniepropetrovsk, whose central disco clubs were famous for their reliable patriotic programs with the inclusion of the obligatory Ukrainian songs in Ukrainian.[84] As Suvorov noted, a central city disco club stopped playing songs in Ukrainian as early as 1982. Dniepropetrovsk disc jockeys replaced "official Ukrainian *estrada*" songs with pop hits in foreign languages, mainly in English, Italian, and Russian. Even Komsomol ideologists and young KGB officers, who had their own disco dance party in December 1983, preferred only Western or Russian Soviet songs. The main organizer of this dance party, Suvorov, recalled that he had brought a special audiotape with a recording of pop music in Ukrainian, expecting that apparatchiks would pay a special tribute to the officially accepted pop songs in Ukrainian. Eventually, he realized that nobody cared about Ukrainian music. The young ideologists in the closed cities of Soviet Ukraine demonstrated their own preferences in pop music consumption, which completely excluded Ukrainian popular culture.[85]

By the end of the Brezhnev era, both ordinary Komsomol members and their leaders shared the same tastes and music preferences, which corresponded to the ideological patterns approved by the official articles in *Rovesnik,* the most popular youth magazine among the young consumers of pop music in Dniepropetrovsk. The major emphasis on Western pop music typical for *Rovesnik* eventually justified the exclusion of not only official

Soviet *estrada* but also Ukrainian pop music from the everyday cultural consumption in Russified cities like Dniepropetrovsk.

Western Music, Identity Formation, and Russification

The main result of the mass consumption of Western musical products in Dniepropetrovsk was the Russification of its Ukrainian youth culture. To some extent, this was related to the origins and sources of information about new music that the local youth consumed. During the 1970s, all the official Soviet recordings of Western music were released on the state-owned label Melodia, with comments in Russian only. All the best radio shows about rock music were of foreign or Russian origin.[86] Young consumers of Western popular music in Dniepropetrovsk also relied on Russian periodicals because the Ukrainian editions were more cautious and conservative than the Moscow-based ones. The Ukrainian Komsomol magazine *Ranok* always published awkwardly written articles with incompetent criticism of the developments in the Western youth culture. Sometimes local readers were appalled by the ignorance and incompetence of Kyiv journalists. "I am tired of reading this mixture of lies and fantasy in *Ranok*," wrote one young enthusiast of rock music, "these guys from Kyiv invented that American hippies was a satanic sect with a mixture of palmistry, astrology, and black magic, and that hippies were looking for a virgin girl for their devilish black mass ritual and couldn't find such girls among themselves. I would rather read a boring Feofanov book about rock music than Kyiv magazines." Because of this disappointment, he stopped reading Ukrainian youth periodicals as early as 1974 and read only *Rovesnik*.[87] Many Ukrainian rock fans preferred *Rovesnik* as well. As a result, the most popular youth magazine among the local rock music fans was the Russian-language journal *Rovesnik*.

The Russian language became the major language of local rock bands. Starting in the mid-1970s, the repertoire of student concerts changed dramatically. In fact, the Russian language ousted the Ukrainian one in the major concerts organized in Dniepropetrovsk during the 1970s. In June 1982, during the traditional music festival "The Student Spring" in Dniepropetrovsk, all college rock bands performed songs in Russian. Even the Ukrainian folk-rock band Dniepriane performed fewer songs in Ukrainian than usual. One journalist complained about the lack of national Ukrainian songs in the repertoire of the student bands in comparison with previous music festivals during the 1970s.[88] During the 1980s, more local college rock bands switched from the Ukrainian language to Russian.[89] Local Komsomol periodicals also emphasized that in the early 1980s disco clubs stopped playing Ukrainian music.[90] Some Ukrainian-speaking enthusiasts of rock music by the end of the 1970s began speaking Russian and replaced their native language with Russian. In writing his diary, Aleksandr Gusar, who was a native Ukrainian speaker, switched from Ukrainian to Russian during the summer of 1976. During the period 1971–75, he wrote his diary exclusively in Ukrainian. As he explained in his diary in August 1976, the language of the young rocker should be English or Russian rather than Ukrainian. That is why he switched to Russian.[91]

We can argue that (besides the official policy) rock music consumption during the 1970s led to Russification as the main trend in the cultural development of the Dniepropetrovsk Region and especially of the city of Dniepropetrovsk.[92] The search for the authentic West deeply affected the process of identity formation for the millions of young Soviet consumers of Western cultural products. In the closed city of Dniepropetrovsk, these consumers tried to identify themselves only with the West or its legitimate substitutes, which by the end of the 1970s had lost any connections with Soviet Ukrainian culture. In the imagination of these consumers, the official Soviet Ukrainian culture represented all the most conservative, backward, and anti-Western elements in their life. "Only idiots and peasants listen to Ukrainian *estrada,* the normal *razvitye* [smart, intelligent] people listen to real rock music from the real West," wrote Andrei Vadimov, a future activist of the discotheque movement in the city of Dniepropetrovsk, in September 1976. The same year Gusar, a future organizer of a dorm disco club at Dniepropetrovsk University, noted in his high school diary: "You must be stupid enough to claim that Ukrainian *estrada* songs are better than Western rock music. Ukrainian music exists only for bumpkins. All intelligent youth listen now to classic rock from the West [*sic*]."[93]

By accepting the real West as a part of their identity, these young rock music fans and discotheque activists rejected the official Soviet version of their own ethnic identity. As we have seen, this process of identification with the West also affected the Komsomol ideologists who eagerly participated in the consumption of Western cultural products during the Brezhnev era. In contrast to their official denial of the corrupting influences of the capitalist West, these apparatchiks preferred Western cultural products to Soviet ones. Their musical preferences, fashions, and dance parties demonstrated the surprising Westernization of these young ideologists in the closed city of Soviet Ukraine. They consumed more Western cultural products than products of Soviet Ukrainian culture. This preference was especially obvious at the beginning of the 1980s.

Eventually, this process of identification with the real West leveled national cultural differences among the active consumers of Western mass culture and contributed to what some scholars called a homogenization of Soviet culture that meant a mass Russification of the youth culture in Eastern Ukraine during the 1970s.[94] For many rock music enthusiasts in the closed city of Dniepropetrovsk, only the Russian mass media offered interesting and relatively reliable information about the main trends and developments in Western popular culture. The youth magazine *Rovesnik,* published in Russian, became the most popular source for this kind of information. By the middle of the 1980s, the young Ukrainian consumers of Western cultural products mainly preferred their sources of information to be in the Russian language rather than Ukrainian.

Chapter 14

Antipunk Campaigns, Antifascist Hysteria, and Human Rights Problems, 1982–1984

Discotheques became a main responsibility for Komsomol officials when, after the death of Brezhnev, Yuri Andropov, the new Soviet leader, began his campaign against corruption in the Communist Party and Komsomol. During the period 1982–84, according to Soviet and Western scholars, the Soviet leadership was concerned "with the social control of young people, mentally through improved ideological training and physically, through the greater regulation of their leisure time and activity."[1]

Andropov emphasized the need for discipline and ideological purity. In his speech at the July 1983 Plenum of the Central Committee of the Communist Party of the Soviet Union, he declared war on Western pop music: "It is intolerable to see the occasional emergence on a wave of popularity of musical bands with repertoires of a dubious nature."[2] He pointed out the dangerous ideological confusion created by Western popular music, which had become the main object of consumption for millions of Soviet young people, and he reminded Komsomol that leisure-time activities were "the battleground for fierce ideological conflict between Communist and bourgeois ideologies." He suggested special counterpropagandist efforts that would protect the mentality of the "young builders of the initial stage of developed socialism" from the "distortions, confusion, and antisocial patterns of behavior" associated with Western degenerate music.[3]

In response to these suggestions, Komsomol introduced special counterpropagandist measures that affected the discotheque movement in 1983–84. In the Dniepropetrovsk Region, the local ideologists used a special Komsomol seminar for disco activists, established between October 1982 and May 1983 on the premises of the prestigious Illich Palace of Culture in downtown Dniepropetrovsk, to control music programs and purge those

265

leaders of disco clubs who resisted collaboration. By 1984, more than half the 100 discotheques in the region had been closed by Dniepropetrovsk ideologists for "ideological unreliability."[4] In December 1983, all the college rock bands and disco clubs in the city participated in a special antiwar and anti-American concert organized by the regional Komsomol organization in the Dniepropetrovsk city circus building. In this way, they demonstrated their loyalty and ideological reliability. Dniepropetrovsk's Komsomol leaders presented this event both as a propagandistic action in support of the official policy of the Soviet state and as proof of their efficient ideological work in the discotheque movement.[5]

After Andropov's death in 1984, the new Soviet leader, Konstantin Chernenko, began a fresh round of criticism of Komsomol's ideological work among Soviet youth. According to Communist ideologists, Komsomol had failed to combat new temptations, the blind imitation of Western fashions, and the lack of interest in politics. The leadership accepted this criticism and called "for a mobilization of Komsomol forces to patrol the performances" of local rock bands and check "the repertoires of Soviet discotheques."[6] During the same year, the USSR Ministry of Culture, and, later, the USSR Ministry of Higher and Specialized Education, issued special orders about "the regulation of activities of vocal-instrumental groups and improvement of the ideological-artistic standard of their repertoires." These orders were used to strengthen ideological control of local rock bands and discotheques all over the Soviet Union.[7] New Soviet legislation now threatened to punish people who provided the thriving Komsomol discotheque movement with musical material. The activities of sound engineers and discotheque activists involved in the mass production of recordings came under the articles in the Soviet Criminal Code regarding entrepreneurial activities (Article 153) or the practicing of an illegal trade (Article 162).[8]

On October 1, 1984, the USSR Ministry of Culture issued a list of sixty-eight Western rock bands and thirty-eight Soviet "unofficial" rock bands whose music was not recommended for playing in public places within the city limits of Moscow. The list of "forbidden Western bands" included the favorites of Soviet youth, such as Kiss, AC/DC, Black Sabbath, Alice Cooper, and Pink Floyd. The list of ideologically unreliable Soviet bands included those especially popular among high school and college students, such as Aquarium, Kino, and Nautilus Pompilius. All these bands were officially prohibited for cultural consumption by all Soviet youth. By the end of 1984, many regional Komsomol committees in Ukraine, including the one in Dniepropetrovsk, were using these lists in their campaign to purify the pop music consumption of Komsomol members. They wanted to replace "bad, uncultured" bourgeois music with "good, cultured," and ideologically reliable, socialist music.[9]

The Soviet Version of Punk

In Ukraine, Andropov's campaign against rock music converged with another old ideological campaign, which targeted so-called fascist punks. It began in the years 1980–81, as a result of confusing information in the central Soviet periodicals, where British punks were presented as neofascists and as skinheads. Therefore, all the Western music that was associated with the punk movement and used fascist symbols had to be prohibited for mass consumption in the Soviet Union. As Artemy Troitsky explained, the periodicals' description of punks as fascists confused and disoriented thousands of Communist ideologists in provincial cities such as Dniepropetrovsk. He noted:

> The only thing anyone knew about punks was that they were "fascists" because that's how our British-based correspondents had described them for us. Several angry feature articles appeared in the summer and fall of 1977 with lurid descriptions of their unsavoury appearance and disgraceful manners, including one that quoted sympathetically a diatribe from the *Daily Telegraph.* To illustrate all this, a few photos of "monster" with swastikas were printed. . . . The image of punks as Nazis was established very effectively, and in our country, as you should understand, the swastika will never receive a positive reaction, even purely for shock value.[10]

For many discotheque activists, the new antipunk campaign was a shock. In Dniepropetrovsk, the local disc jockeys played the music of British punk rock bands like the Sex Pistols and the Clash as an obligatory, ideological part of their dance programs during 1979 and 1980. This was in accord with the critique of the "political agenda" of progressive rock and punk musicians offered by *Rovesnik,* the central Komsomol magazine. It praised the anticapitalist spirit of "young English rock musicians" who followed the traditions of legendary, intellectual rock bands like Pink Floyd. Komsomol journalists from Moscow wrote about the collaboration between the Clash and British Communists in their struggle against racism and neofascism, and about the criticism of capitalist reality in Pink Floyd's album *The Wall.*[11] KGB officials and Communist ideologists in Dniepropetrovsk followed conflicting ideological recommendations from their Kyiv supervisors: They interfered in local youth clubs and banned the music of any musician who was associated with the word "punk." According to the KGB's taxonomy from Kyiv, the "punk movement" was considered a part of international neofascism. Therefore, music by the Clash or the Sex Pistols was forbidden in the region of Dniepropetrovsk as early as 1980.

The first public scandal of the new antipunk campaign took place at Club Melodia at a dance party on the eve of 1981. As one organizer of this party recalled, the program was officially approved by the city Komsomol committee. The ideological part of the program was devoted to the theme "the World Celebrates New Year." The disc jockey began with a summary of the major political and musical events of the last year. He told the audience that three of the most popular musicians among Soviet youth had died in 1980: the Russian bard and guitar poet Vladimir Vysotsky; a popular French singer, Joe Dassin; and the ex-Beatle John Lennon. After playing their songs, the disc jockey mentioned a *Rovesnik* article about the Clash, and then noted the strange behavior of Komsomol apparatchik who was in charge of the party. In the middle of "London Calling" by the Clash, this apparatchik and two KGB officers approached the disc jockeys and ordered them to stop playing "the fascist music." Then one of the Melodia leaders tried to explain that *Rovesnik* had praised the Clash as an anticapitalist, "leftist" British band. As one disc jockey, Mikhail Suvorov, recalled:

> The KGB people did not listen to us. They interrupted our party for one hour. They checked all our tapes of the dance program. Eventually they confiscated all our music records and tapes with recordings of the Sex Pistols, the Clash, AC/DC, Kiss, and 10cc. The KGB officers punished our Komsomol supervisors for giving us permission to play the music of "fascist punks." One of these Komsomol supervisors tried again to refer to the *Rovesnik* articles in his defense. A KGB officer dismissed this as misinformation. "We know better," he told us. "All this music crap you are playing is a part of the fascist anti-Soviet conspiracy. You call this music punk rock, we call this stuff neofascism. When one of our discotheque enthusiasts interfered and told the KGB people that AC/DC and Kiss were not punk rock bands, he was arrested by the police and removed from the

dance floor. Two organizers of this dance party argued that it was a violation of human rights, and they were also arrested by the KGB.[12]

This was the beginning of a long ideological campaign waged by both Communist Party ideologists and KGB officers. After 1980, nobody tried to play punk rock at dance parties anymore.

According to Vladimir Demchenko, who worked in the 1980s as a public lecturer for the regional lecture society Znanie (Society of Knowledge) in Dniepropetrovsk, local ideologists used "a description of a British punk" from the atlas of TASS (the Telegraph Agency of the Soviet Union), the secret digest of the foreign press for Communist propagandists; the main identifying sign of a fascist punk was his shaven head. Apparently, it was a misunderstanding, because the author of the original article dealt with British skinheads, and he compared punks and skinheads as the most fashionable trends in Western popular culture. In a confusing translation from English into Russian, a typical punk had shaved temples or, to put it correctly, according to this description, a punk's hair had to be removed over his ears. When this interpretation was included in an ideological portrait of "fascist punk," Komsomol ideologists were ready to identify as a punk any young man with long hair and a ponytail. As a result, many heavy metal fans from the Dniepropetrovsk Region were arrested during the years 1983–84 because the ignorant policemen were not able to tell one fashionable hairstyle from another or distinguish between "hard rock" and "punk rock."[13]

The police and Komsomol activists thought punk and fascism were the same. All Komsomol propagandists and the people in charge of discotheques in the Dniepropetrovsk Region received special notices about punk ideology with Russian translations of British punks' phrases. This information was reprinted in many articles by the Dniepropetrovsk journalists who covered this antipunk campaign. The journalists for the youth periodicals quoted the punk slogans:

> Live by today's day only! Do not think about tomorrow! Do not give a damn about all these spiritual crutches of religion, utopia, and politics! Forget about this. Enjoy your day. You are young, and do not hurry to become a new young corpse [*sic!*].

Dniepropetrovsk's journalists usually added their comments about the antihuman essence of "fascist punk music": "These were slogans of punks, preachers of bestial cynicism and meanness, who were the real spiritual mongrels of the twentieth century."[14]

Symbols of Nazi and Other Anti-Soviet Images and Ideas

Antipunk hysteria resulted in the prohibition of bands that were tremendously popular among Soviet high school and vocational school students. AC/DC and Kiss had nothing to do with the punk movement at all, yet after 1980, the local Komsomol apparatchiks officially considered them "fascist, anti-Soviet bands." Komsomol ideologists in Kyiv "discovered" elements of insignia from Nazi Germany in the names of these bands. The combination "SS" presented as a symbol of lightning in their logos was interpreted as an expression of the musicians' fascist ideology. Komsomol leaders in Dniepropetrovsk followed the recommendations of the Kyiv "experts" and tried to ban the music of "fascist rock-and-rollers."[15]

By the end of 1982, two British bands had been added to the list of "pro-fascist, anti-Soviet bands": the heavy metal group Iron Maiden and the "art pop" rock group 10cc, which was famous for its ironic, intellectual lyrics and interesting melodic arrangements. Komsomol ideologists explained to KGB officers that these bands were especially dangerous because of their "hellish, antihuman imagery, fascist symbols, and anti-Soviet lyrics." They cited the name "Iron Maiden," derived from the name of a medieval torture device; the group's artistic symbol, or mascot, a ten-foot rotting corpse named Eddie; and their 1982 album *The Number of the Beast,* which contained images of a "fascist satanic cult." The name of the second group was mistakenly reinterpreted as "Ten SS," referring to Hitler's secret police, the SS (Schutz-Staffel). Given the fact that the English letter C is the equivalent of the letter S in Russian and Ukrainian, the cc (cubic centimeters) was pronounced "ess-ess," and local Komsomol ideologists immediately characterized 10cc as a "fascist name." Moreover, in 1978 the band released its album *Bloody Tourists* with a song—a musical parody of the anti-Soviet hysteria during the Cold War—titled "Reds in My Bed." The refrain of this song shocked the Soviet censors: "I've got Reds in my bed, I'm not easily led to the slaughter, and while the Cold War exists, I'll stay warm with the Commissar's daughter. . . . Let me go home. You're a land full of misery. I don't like your philosophy. You're a cruel and a faceless race." Of course, nobody on a Soviet dance floor cared about these lyrics, and nobody understood a word of this song; they just loved the melody. The major songs from *Bloody Tourists*—including "Reds in My Bed," "Dreadlock Holiday," "For You and I," "Life Line," and "Tokyo"—became hits in discos during 1979–83. Appalled by this "music propaganda" of "anti-Soviet, fascist ideas," Komsomol ideologists asked the police and KGB to help to remove this "dangerous" music from the cultural consumption of Soviet youth. In the period 1981–84, hundreds of these forbidden records were confiscated from young rock fans in the region. The overwhelming majority of these records were albums by AC/DC, Kiss, Iron Maiden, and 10cc.[16]

This antipunk and antifascist hysteria affected even the music of Pink Floyd. This band traditionally was considered by Soviet ideologists as an anticapitalist "progressive" band, and Soviet television and radio occasionally broadcast its music. "One of These Days," from the 1971 album *Meddle,* was used by the political television show *International Panorama* as its theme song in the 1970s. Some popular songs by Pink Floyd were included in compilations by the music journal *Krugozor.* "Money" from *Dark Side of the Moon* was praised as "an anti-imperialist anthem" of Western, progressive youth culture. The idealization of Pink Floyd by the Soviet youth media reached a peak with the release of the band's album *The Wall* in 1979,[17] but the official attitude changed in 1983. Its new album, *The Final Cut,* written by Roger Waters, criticized imperialistic aggression all over the world and concentrated mainly on the Falklands War between Argentina and Great Britain. According to Waters's lyrics, three major imperialist powers threatened to destroy the world: the United States, Great Britain, and the Soviet Union. Two tracks, "Get Your Filthy Hands Off My Desert" and "The Fletcher Memorial Home," openly criticized the expansionism of "Mr. Brezhnev and the Party," including the Soviet invasion in Afghanistan. According to KGB officers, Komsomol experts recognized Brezhnev's name in *The Final Cut* lyrics, and they included Pink Floyd in the list of "forbidden musicians" for discotheques because of the group's "distortion of Soviet foreign policy." By the end of 1983, all ideological departments of the regional Komsomol organizations in Ukraine had received a complete list of "forbidden music bands" with Pink Floyd at the top.[18]

Soviet cultural consumption of Western products was always very limited and censored. On the one hand, forms of this consumption were regulated by various ideological requirements; on the other hand, they were influenced by consumers' demands. The more the ideological experts tried to ban a product, the more desirable it became. This happened with music by Kiss and AC/DC, which became the most profitable items sold on the music market in Dnipropetrovsk. Both central Komsomol and local periodicals disoriented and confused their readers when they directly connected criminal anti-Soviet and neofascist behavior with "forbidden music."

The first public scandal, which involved both "fascist music" and the display of "fascist symbols," took place in the closed city during the fall of

1982. The city police arrested two college students, Igor Keivan and Aleksandr Plastun, who had their own collections of Western records with "fascist symbols" and who demonstrated their "Neo-Nazi" behavior in downtown Dniepropetrovsk. These students were dressed in T-shirts with images of Kiss and AC/DC, which attracted the policemen, who interpreted such images as "fascist." After the arrest of Keivan and Plastun and the confiscation of their "fascist" records, the police sent information about these students' anti-Soviet behavior to their colleges.

In December 1982, the entire city and region of Dniepropetrovsk experienced the beginning of the antifascist and antipunk campaign. The Dniepropetrovsk City Committee of the Communist Party of the Soviet Union approached Nadezhda A. Sarana, an old Communist who had been a member of the antifascist resistance during World War II, to write a letter about the dangerous fashion of "fascist punks." On December 22, they staged an open public meeting with participation from all Communist and Komsomol activists in downtown Dniepropetrovsk. During this meeting, all the activists supported Sarana's letter against the punks and "declared war on punk movement" in the closed city. Later, under KGB pressure, the local ideologists organized a special public trial of Keivan, Plastun, and another young punk, Vadim Shmeliov, who were expelled from Komsomol and their colleges in January 1983. The KGB officers were especially outraged about an attempt by Keivan and Plastun to "interpret" this punishment as a violation of their human rights. From this time on, all the region's Komsomol organizations began to purge members who were suspected of unusual enthusiasm for the forbidden music.[19]

After this scandal, both Communist ideologists and KGB operatives reminded the local Komsomol activists about the ideological danger of Western capitalist culture, and they illustrated this danger with the case of a Polish youth who actively participated in the anti-Soviet movements of the early 1980s. During 1982 and 1983, Aleksandr Amel'chenko, a lecturer for the Dniepropetrovsk branch of the organization Znanie, delivered a series of special lectures about the ideological threat of Western pop music. He visited the major districts and towns of the region and discussed the problems of this threat with local activists. In October 1983, he sent some of his material to local periodicals and answered various questions from young rock music fans. In his lectures and articles, he emphasized that "the youth was the country's future." That is why "the ideological enemies of the USSR tried to confuse and pollute the Soviet youth and undermine the ideological basis of the Soviet Union. Moreover, they tried to distract Soviet audiences with so-called human rights."[20] He wrote:

> Our class enemies try to catch the politically unstable, inexperienced young people, to blunt their vigilance [*prytupyty ii pyl'nist'*], try to ignite the national hostility and to seduce with attractive sides of the bourgeois way of life. The main tools of ideological inculcation are music, movies, and fashions. Through these tools they organize various ideological provocations [*diversii*]. Our opponents try to weaken our youth spiritually; undermine its class self-awareness, its ideological convictions and beliefs, its loyalty to the Communist ideals, revolutionary fighting, and the working traditions of the older generation; distract [*vidvernuty*] Soviet youth from active social and political activities, to sow in the souls of young people seeds of consumption, greed [*korystoliubstva*], infantilism, and political nihilism; and therefore they try to transform the youth into a power that undermines foundations of the socialist order, or at least, transforms young people into a passive, inert mass.[21]

Local journalists in Dniepropetrovsk had no adequate information and relied mainly on general criticism and the recommendations of Communist and Komsomol ideologists who ordered periodic coverage of the criminal cases related to rock music consumption. During the early 1980s, every issue of the local newspapers contained material that portrayed the ideological danger of the Western music consumption.[22] Dniepropetrovsk's journalists were so intimidated by the anti–rock music campaign that they rejected any public demonstration of preferences for Western cultural products as an act of betrayal. Therefore, they took an active part in a campaign against a Leningrad rock band, Zemliane (people of the Earth, in Russian), during the spring of 1984. It was the second concert of this band in the closed city in 1984. At the time of their first concert, in January 1984, local journalists had applauded the band.[23]

But during the spring the situation changed. To advertise their concert in Dniepropetrovsk, the Leningrad rock musicians used a photograph of Igor Romanov, their lead guitarist, who was dressed in a T-shirt with the U.S. flag on it. Moreover, according to the local journalists, during their concert in the closed city, Zemliane played songs of "forbidden fascist and punk bands." As a result, the Dniepropetrovsk Komsomol newspaper organized an anti-Zemliane campaign, accusing the Leningrad musicians of "a betrayal of socialist principles of music performance." Despite readers' support of the popular Leningrad band, the journalists, together with local KGB officials, insisted on punishing these musicians for their low ideological level and for promoting "capitalist standards of antihuman mass culture." In April 1984, the administration of "Leningrad Concert," an organization responsible for Zemliane's concert tours, punished the musicians; their concerts were banned, and they had to rewrite their repertoire. After this scandal about the Zemliane's concert, Dniepropetrovsk officials stopped inviting "suspicious" rock bands from Moscow and Leningrad.[24]

Dniepropetrovsk's Heavy-Metal Fans as Fascists

This anti-rock campaign especially affected Dniepropetrovsk fans of heavy metal. When, in 1983, the Dniepropetrovsk police arrested ten students from the local vocational school for "acts of hooliganism," they discovered various symbols of Nazism and the American Ku Klux Klan being used by these students. As it turned out, Sergei Onushev, Aleksandr Rvachenko, and their friends had made special white robes, put the words "Ku Klux Klan" on them, and tried to "imitate acts of this American fascist organization."[25] The leader of this "fascist" group was Onushev, who "used to play at home the music tapes of bands which belonged to the profascist movement—Kiss, Nazareth, AC/DC, Black Sabbath." Dniepropetrovsk ideologists established a direct connection between the fascism in Onushev's group and this music. According to them, Kiss provoked the Soviet students to commit inhuman fascist acts. As a journalist commented:

> What kind of art did the musicians of Kiss represent? They tear apart live chickens and vomit in public during their performances. This band Kiss is a group of four hooligans, who selected SS Nazi symbol as the symbol of their band. Nevertheless, the show businessmen transform them into the idols of the contemporary youth and proclaim them as "trendsetters" in popular culture.[26]

Another case that attracted the attention of local journalists concerned Dmitrii Frolin, a student from the Department of Philology at Dniepropetrovsk University. As a result of the antipunk and antifascist campaign, he was arrested by the police in 1983 and expelled from both Komsomol and the university in 1985 for "propaganda of fascism." According to the local ideologists, his activities were the direct result of "intensive listening" to the music of "fascist bands" such as Kiss and AC/DC. As one local journalist wrote:

> Our Soviet books paradoxically coexisted with fascist and racist slogans on Frolin's bookshelves. These slogans were written in Gothic script in both the English and German languages with phrases such as "Only for Whites," etc. Over his bed, Frolin put a fascist cross and a poster with distorted in nonhuman grimaces and ugly decorated faces of members of the band Kiss. [Frolin paid 40 rubles for this Kiss poster on the "black market."] In addition, he had a variety of audiotapes with the music of Kiss and AC/DC. Just press a button on his tape recorder and you will hear this music.

And then the journalist made his own ideological comments:

> Let's think about all this! They, the musicians of AC/DC, call themselves the devil's children. Their song "Back in Black" became an anthem of the American Nazi Party. During a Komsomol meeting, Dmitrii justified his behavior, "I do not consider my collecting of such things a crime. This is just a mere collecting. It does not matter what is a subject of this collection. These items reflect a certain period of history of the people. As a Soviet citizen and human being, I have my human rights, which are protected by both Soviet and international law. I consider that a listening to my favorite music, collecting and listening to music records are part of my private life. And I have a right to protect my privacy according to Soviet and international laws."[27]

In December 1983, the local youth periodical published the results of a sociological analysis of Dniepropetrovsk's youth compiled by the Komsomol scholars. According to this article, in many student dorms in Dniepropetrovsk's colleges, the special Komsomol raids had discovered images of the American band Kiss, "on which any observer could easily find without any difficulties the SS symbols and Nazi signs." Moreover, a majority of the student population in Dniepropetrovsk "preferred T-shirts with the signs of the U.S. military and insignia of the capitalist countries, the political and military enemies of the Soviet Union." Dniepropetrovsk students bought these T-shirts on the black market and wore them even during their classes while in college.[28]

Komsomol journalists published their translations of the most notorious anti-Soviet songs, which became the hits in the late 1970s and early 1980s in local disco clubs. As it turned out, the most popular dance songs had obvious or hidden anti-Soviet messages. The journalists used the articles of the Soviet ideologists from Moscow or Kyiv about various anti-Soviet rock bands. The range of these bands was wide—from British musicians such as Boy George and Culture Club to West German disco bands such as Genghis Khan. The material about these bands was published under the title "Be Careful! The Western Poison!"[29] Similar themes appeared in all central and local Komsomol periodicals during the years 1983–84. In the closed city of Dniepropetrovsk, the KGB monitored this campaign and criticized local ideologists for losing control over cultural consumption among the local youth. Each week a KGB supervisor recommended that Komsomol apparatchiks read and analyze material from the local periodicals about the threat of punk fascist culture.

According to KGB officers, "a youth culture of fascist music" was also connected to the idealization of Hitler and Ukrainian nationalist leaders, such as Stepan Bandera, during World War II. Since 1938, Bandera had led the radical branch of the Organization of the Ukrainian Nationalists, which became a center of military resistance to the Soviet Army after 1944 in Western Ukraine. After the suppression of the anti-Soviet activities of Bandera's troops, he became a heroic symbol for many Ukrainian patriots. In 1983 and 1984, the police arrested members of "a fascist Banderite group" who were students at the Dniepropetrovsk agricultural college. These students—Konstantin Shipunov and his five followers—listened to "fascist rock music," organized their own "party," and popularized the ideas of Nazi leaders and Ukrainian nationalist politicians. They criticized the Russification of cultural life in Ukraine, emphasized the necessity of Ukrainian independence from the Soviet Union, and insisted on protecting the human rights of all Ukrainian patriots. In a conversation with a police officer, Shipunov referred to the Final Act of the Conference on Security and Cooperation in Europe, which had been signed in Helsinki by the Soviet leaders together with thirty-four other heads of state on August 1, 1975. According to him, the Final Act especially emphasized the protection of human rights. Meanwhile, he said, by arresting the Ukrainian patriots like him, the local police had violated their human rights and broken international laws.[30]

The criminal cases of Dniepropetrovsk "fascist" heavy metal fans revealed the surprising connections between different forms of cultural consumption in the closed city during the period 1982–84. The arrested members of Onushev's and Shipunov's groups confessed that they were inspired by the images of the "clean, intelligent, and civilized" Nazi officers portrayed in the Soviet TV series *Seventeen Moments of Spring* (1973). This TV movie about Stirlitz (Viacheslav Tikhonov), a Soviet agent posing as a Nazi officer in Hitlerite Germany in the spring of 1945, during the final months of World War II (and based on a novel by Yulian Semenov, a famous Soviet writer of mystery and spy novels), became a real blockbuster during the 1970s and early 1980s in the USSR. Many "fascist" heavy metal fans and local "punks" tried to imitate the dress and behavior of the Nazi characters in this old Soviet TV film.[31]

Another relatively new detail revealed during this antipunk campaign shocked the KGB officers. All the members of Dniepropetrovsk's "fascist punk" groups referred to their "human rights as Soviet citizens" during their arrests and interrogation. Some of them appealed by even writing letters to the central Soviet and Komsomol administration in Moscow in an attempt to find protection "against a violation of their human rights" by the Dniepropetrovsk police and the KGB. After the public trial of Keivan and Plastun in 1982, when these student "punks" had publicly accused the police of violating their human rights, the KGB recommended that local ideologists in the future avoid such public trials of "intellectual fascist punks." The KGB officers feared that the public reference to the issue of human rights would be used in anti-Soviet propaganda and "discredit the antipunk campaign."[32]

As early as December 1983, the Dniepropetrovsk regional Komsomol committee reported to the Ukrainian Komsomol Central Committee in Kyiv that in February and March 1983, local ideologists had encountered the beginning of a punk movement in the city of Dniepropetrovsk. But from the spring through the fall of that year, they mobilized all activists and "Soviet patriots," organized special counterpropaganda events all over the city and region, and finally stopped this "fascist movement." A secretary of the Dniepropetrovsk regional committee, O. Fedoseiev, finished this report with this phrase: "As a result of our antipunk campaign, there are practically no young people who would imitate 'punks' in the region."[33]

In the years 1984–85, the Dniepropetrovsk police discovered new groups of "fascist-punks" with hundreds of followers. Only a few of them had anything to do with Nazi ideology or fascism. All ten groups, after being arrested by the police, were found to have used various fascist symbols and paraphernalia, have painted their faces "in punk fashion," and have shaven temples without hair. Because Komsomol had said repeatedly that the main sign of punk behavior was "shaven temples of the head," this was enough to be arrested on the streets of Dniepropetrovsk during the period 1983–85. Hundreds of rock music fans were detained, and their records and audiotapes were confiscated in the region of Dniepropetrovsk as a result of the antipunk and antifascist campaign.[34]

According to contemporaries, anti–rock music campaigns in Dniepropetrovsk did not stop Western pop music consumption. Moreover, they contributed to the immense popularity of forbidden Western cultural products among young consumers and also among their ideological supervisors, who had already appreciated and enjoyed these products very much.[35] And as mentioned above, the KGB officers and local ideologists noticed a new, surprising result of the antipunk campaign in the closed city. During the years 1982–84, the young "fascist punks" began to refer to the Western idea of human rights. Beginning with the case of Keivan and Plastun, all local "punks" who were arrested publicly mentioned that their human rights were protected by both Soviet and international laws. Moreover, even the local Komsomol activists in the discotheque movement raised this issue of human rights during their debates with the police and KGB officials. The most unpleasant discovery for the local KGB officers who supervised student activities in the city was the involvement of the political elements in the discussion of forbidden Western cultural products, such as rock music. Dniepropetrovsk's rock music fans referred to the international documents, signed by the Soviet leaders, about the protection of human rights. After 1975, they frequently raised the issue of human rights when the police harassed them. As KGB officers argued, through the consumption of Western heavy metal and punk music, both rock music enthusiasts and the young Komsomol activists who had become involved in the disco club business tried to form their own notion of human rights, which became an important part of their self-identity.

At the same time, the antipunk, antifascist campaign in the closed city revealed growing frustration with the position of the central authorities in Moscow about the ideological situation in provincial cities like Dniepropetrovsk. Many young Komsomol enthusiasts of rock music, such as Mikhail Suvorov and Aleksandr Gusar, wrote letters complaining about the "illegal" persecutions of Dniepropetrovsk's rock music fans by the local police and KGB to central Komsomol periodicals like *Komsomol'skaya Pravda* and *Rovesnik*. The parents of persecuted students who had been expelled from colleges also complained to Moscow. But Moscow did not help and did not stop the persecutions of "fascist punks," which continued in Dniepropetrovsk—even during the first years of perestroika, in 1985–87. Many Russified rock music fans now opposed not only the local ideologists and police but also Moscow, the center of their "ideological and cultural oppression."[36] As a result, by the mid-1980s, fewer young consumers of Western cultural products in the closed city identified with Moscow as their cultural center.

Chapter 15

Tourism, Cultural Consumption, and Komsomol Business

From the very beginning of the USSR, the Soviet consumption of Western mass culture products was connected to tourism, which became another important aspect of socialist leisure. Both international and domestic tourism provided Soviet consumers with new foreign goods that were missing from Soviet stores. In the closed Soviet society, international tourism created an opportunity for real cultural dialogue with foreigners. Moreover, such tourism satisfied the growing demands for music material and information about Western popular music. It is impossible to understand the dynamics of cultural consumption in the closed Soviet society without considering tourism.[1] Soviet tourism played an important role in socialist cultural consumption. On the one hand, it had to satisfy new demands for leisure time and socialist consumer goods and services; on the other hand, it had to contribute to the intellectual wealth of cultural consumption by widening the cultural horizons of members of the developed socialist society.

Tourism, particularly international tourism, became a very important testing ground for notions of cultural consumption, especially by the end of the Brezhnev era. International tourism grew during the period of developed socialism. As early as 1929, under Stalin's rule, the Soviet government created a special tourist agency, Inturist (an acronym formed from two Russian words, "Innostrannyi turist," "Foreign tourist" or "International tourist"), to serve foreign tourists who visited the USSR. Late in 1964, with the transition to the consumerist society of developed socialism, the All-Union Administration for Foreign Tourism introduced state control over all forms of international tourism. In a few years, it changed its name to the State Committee for Foreign Tourism. This committee established control over the old agency, Inturist, and two new ones, which were created later: (1) the international youth tourist organization Sputnik, the Komsomol travel agency (since 1958); and (2) the All-Union Central Council of Trade Unions' international travel agency. According to G. Dolzhenko, the first historian of Soviet tourism, the number of foreign tourists who visited the Soviet Union increased from 486,00 to 711,000 between 1956 and 1960. Approximately 2 million tourists visited in 1970, and 6 million more visited by 1985. Almost 60 percent of all these tourists came from socialist countries. The number of Soviet tourists who traveled abroad also grew from 561,000 in 1956 to more than 1.8 million in 1970 and more than 4.5 million by 1985.[2]

At the local level in Ukraine, domestic tourism was governed by the Republican Tourism and Excursion Board. Similar to the rest of the USSR, domestic tourism was the most popular form of tourism in the Dniepropetrovsk Region of Ukraine. The local KGB office was reluctant to permit mass international tourism because of the strategic, secretive status of Dniepropetrovsk.[3] The KGB officials did not encourage international tourism in this strategically important region and tried to stop any active forms of domestic tourism, which could have led to a breach of secrecy. Despite the KGB's cautious attitude toward tourism in this region, the local administration promoted

Figure 15.1. Karl Marx Avenue in downtown Dniepropetrovsk, showing the building of the Regional Trade Union organization. The trade union travel agency was (and still is) located in this building. Photograph by the author.

forms of health-oriented tourism as an aspect of the new Communist Party's strategy. Soviet apparatchiks in Dniepropetrovsk closely followed the new party directives about cultural consumption and the creation of better living conditions for Soviet citizens. According to these party directives, tourism was part of socialist consumption.[4] In Dniepropetrovsk, a number of tourist facilities developed during the Brezhnev era.[5]

Tourism in the "Closed" City

In Soviet Ukraine, outgoing international tourism was governed by the Trade Union Republican Board Tourism Department and by the Komsomol organization Sputnik. Incoming foreign tourists were welcomed by the Ukrainian branch of Inturist and by Sputnik. Given the status of Dniepropetrovsk as "the closed city," foreign tourists were not allowed to visit the city. In fact, only one industrial city in the province of Dniepropetrovsk, Krivoi Rog, was open to foreigners, most of whom were students of the local mining college and represented the socialist and developing countries. Therefore, Dniepropetrovsk's branches of the Trade Union Tourism Department and Sputnik were more preoccupied with the local inhabitants of the region who traveled abroad than they were with incoming foreign tourists. An overwhelming majority of the local outgoing tourists participated in so-called international cultural tourism. They bought special traveling "plans," which consisted usually of a trip abroad for a week or two. They visited specially appointed places in foreign countries chosen according to officially approved travel itineraries and travel expenses, and they stayed in hotels strictly designated by the Soviet tourist authorities. The authorities took care of all travel documents for Soviet tourists, and they provided foreign passports and visas along with an allocated amount of foreign currency per tourist. Few tourists went abroad as business tourists; these were mainly visiting scholars and scientists who also had their own travel plans, called "creative business trip" (*tvorcheskaia komandirovka*).[6]

The majority of Dniepropetrovsk's tourists who participated in international travel did so in groups of thirty-four to forty people, which were closely monitored by representatives of the Soviet tourist administration. All these representatives (usually Soviet, trade union, party, and Komsomol apparatchiks) were approved by KGB offices and required to submit reports about their tourist groups to both their local tourist administration and the KGB immediately after the group's return back to Dniepropetrovsk. The first organization to introduce international group tourism in the region was the regional council of Dniepropetrovsk trade unions, which in 1961 planned to send 613 local tourists abroad. However, under pressure from the KGB, the council had to limit this number to only 551.[7] In 1966, all the region's trade unions sent 1,299 local tourists abroad.[8] Ten years later, in 1976, despite all KGB restrictions, 4,931 people traveled abroad through the trade union travel agency.[9]

Not until 1972 did the KGB permit new forms of travel abroad—the Komsomol-sponsored tourism of international groups via Sputnik.[10] The ideological basis for supporting Komsomol's international tourism in the region came from the Communist Party's directives. As early as 1973, Leonid Brezhnev pointed out that the "international connections of Komsomol, the contacts of Soviet boys and girls with the youth from foreign countries, became the crucial part of the entire Soviet foreign policy."[11] Following these directives, the tourist administration sent only groups of ideologically reliable and KGB-approved industrial workers, engineers, collective farmers, and teachers who could adequately represent the Soviet politics. Each tourist group also had one or two "nonofficial" representatives of the KGB and Komsomol apparatus. One member of this group usually directly represented the regional Komsomol committee of Dniepropetrovsk. In 1977, for example, all twenty-eight group leaders were high regional or district Komsomol apparatchiks.[12]

In 1973, Dniepropetrovsk's Sputnik organized trips to the city of Krivoi Rog for 125 foreign tourists, mainly from Poland and Czechoslovakia, and for more than 6,000 Soviet tourists from 160 cities in the Soviet Union. At the same time, Komsomol tourist organization sent more than 8,000 local tourists throughout the Soviet Union and 430 tourists from the region to 23 foreign countries; 380 of these tourists were traveling abroad the first time in their lives. According to the data of the regional Communist Party committee, during 1973, more than 4,000 tourists from the region of Dniepropetrovsk visited foreign countries through both trade union and Komsomol travel agencies. This was only a tiny fraction (0.1 percent) of the growing regional population of 3.5 million people.[13]

The number of young tourists who went abroad increased in the region. In 1976, almost 5 percent of all Ukrainian Sputnik tourists who traveled abroad represented the Dniepropetrovsk Region. Still, for a region basically closed to foreigners, this number was significant. Other "open" regions of Ukraine, such as Cherkassy or Lutsk, sent fewer local tourists abroad.[14] In 1977, altogether 815 young tourists from Dniepropetrovsk visited 18 foreign countries. The majority, 747 of these (92 percent) were in 22 tourist groups that went to the socialist counties, and only 68 (8 percent) were in 5 groups that visited capitalist countries.[15]

Overall, the overwhelming majority of Dniepropetrovsk tourists who went abroad did so through the trade unions. According to Sputnik reports, 1,000 local tourists went abroad in 1979 and 1,245 traveled in 1981. During the same years, the trade union tourist agency sent 5,242 tourists abroad and 5,400 tourists to local areas. Only 18 percent of all international tourists from the region used the Komsomol travel agency. During the 1980s, more than 1,000 young tourists from the region annually visited foreign countries. Usually 90 percent of them visited socialist countries and 10 percent went to capitalist and developing countries.[16]

From the beginning, international tourism in the closed city of Dniepropetrovsk was directly connected to cultural consumption among its population. Officially, all travelers going abroad from the region qualified as cultural tourists. The recent cultural and sociological studies of tourism portray "cultural tourists" as those who "gaze collectively upon certain objects which in some ways stand out or speak to them."[17] Yet for the Soviet tourists, their travels were a unique opportunity not just to "gaze" on certain objects of the alien world but also to memorize their own entire experience of visits to non-Soviet places. A tourist trip abroad was a rare and remarkable occasion, when even Soviet ideologists and loyal subjects of the Soviet state felt very uncertain about foreign lifestyles. On the one hand, due to indoctrination with Communist beliefs, Soviet tourists were skeptical and critical about everything non-Soviet. On the other, they were attracted to and stunned by what they experienced during their travel abroad.[18] For Soviet tourists who traveled abroad for the first time, everything looked, smelled, tasted, and sounded different. As one character in a popular Soviet comedy film of 1969 asked her husband, who had just returned from his foreign trip: "Did you taste Coca-Cola? How was it?" The wife was so anxious to know how the product that official Soviet propaganda always associated with Western consumerism and life tasted. She was obviously more interested in a physical, almost physiological, experience of travel abroad than she was in the cultural objects (museums, historical sights, etc.).[19]

Soviet people wanted not only to gaze but also to touch, smell, and taste what Western tourists took for granted and considered merely ordinary consumer goods not worthy of tourist attention (e.g., a can of Coca-Cola or a pair of Levi's jeans). The leaders of tourist groups from Dniepropetrovsk who traveled abroad from 1964 to 1984 complained about these problems in their official reports. Most tourists were more interested in visiting shopping centers and local stores than they were in seeing museums and other important objects of "cultural tourism."[20] According to former leaders of tourist groups, both the trade unions' and Komsomol tourist delegations spent more time in shops than in museums during their travels in Hungary, East Germany, Egypt, and India.[21] At the same time, the KGB officers who were members of those tourist groups, and sometimes group leaders themselves, testified that even group supervisors were more interested in the material aspects of consumption of foreign goods and services than they were in the cultural and educational aspects of their travels. Some of them made a lot of money, trading Soviet badges and coins with foreigners.[22] The traditional complaint of all KGB reports about international tourist groups from Dniepropetrovsk during the period 1972–82 contained the same phrase: "A majority of our group preferred to go shopping together rather than participate in excursions."[23]

Because of Dniepropetrovsk's status as "the USSR's strategically important military center," this region had direct supervision from Moscow. Normally, the regions of Ukraine had direct supervision from the central Ukrainian administration in Kyiv. The special status of the "rocket city" affected many spheres of life, including tourism. The Dniepropetrovsk tourist administration was more flexible and had less control from Kyiv.[24] By the end of the 1970s, the local tourist administration had developed its own travel itineraries, which were more attractive to local consumers. During 1974 to 1982, the most popular destinations for Dniepropetrovsk tourists in trips organized by Sputnik were socialist countries, such as Yugoslavia, Bulgaria, East Germany, Hungary, Czechoslovakia, and Poland. The most popular tourist travel plans through Trade Union Tourist Department included a "Mediterranean cruise trip on the steamboat from Odessa" and "cultural travels to Egypt and India."[25]

Soviet travel agencies took care of the preparation of travel documents (passports and visas) and currency. The amount of hard currency allowed to the individual tourist depended on the country of destination and duration of the trip. For two weeks of travel in capitalist or developing countries, one tourist was usually allowed to exchange no more than 150 rubles in Dniepropetrovsk (between 1972 and 1984). For a trip of the same duration to Bulgaria or East Germany, a tourist usually exchanged a maximum of 10 or 15 rubles. Even in official reports, the tourist group leaders complained about the humiliation of Soviet tourists abroad when they lacked enough hard currency to behave decently. As A. Kurochkin, the leader of a group that participated in a Danube River cruise in 1968, complained, "Our tourists felt very constrained in their financial spending when they could not visit a toilet or drink water because of lack of cash."[26] On rare occasions, like a Danube cruise in October 1978, the Soviet tourist authority permitted up to 300 rubles for individual exchange.[27] Of course, many enterprising members of the Soviet elite, who were interested in foreign consumer goods, brought items to trade during their travels. These objects—for "friendly exchange"—included everything from bottles of vodka to Soviet badges. Sometimes KGB and custom officers allowed these items to cross the Soviet border.[28] In exchange, Dniepropetrovsk tourists could bring more foreign goods home. Cultural tourists became real cultural consumers of those foreign products they had dreamed about but were unable to find in the Soviet official stores or black market. Some of these products, such as foreign music records, became the most desirable objects of consumption among many tourists, from the regular members of tourist groups to group leaders. Eventually, these "cultural tourists" from Dniepropetrovsk contributed to a growing market for Western popular music, which became an important part of cultural consumption in the region.

Local tourists who needed more foreign currency for their shopping abroad tried to illegally bring more Soviet goods, souvenirs, and extra Soviet currency abroad. Sometimes a scandalous number of tourists from Dniepropetrovsk were arrested for this crime. In 1972, during a trip to Yugoslavia, twenty-two members of a tourist group were fined for an attempt to illegally bring extra cash across the Soviet border. All these tourists were the best representatives of local Communists. Moreover, these "tourist criminals" made up the overwhelming majority of the entire tourist group (twenty-two of thirty-four). Many reliable Communist activists, journalists, and teachers were arrested for bringing jewelry, Soviet photo cameras, and cigarettes on the foreign trip. At the end of the trip, the Soviet police fined many Dniepropetrovsk tourists for bringing too many foreign products back to the Soviet Union. The Soviet customs officers calculated the price for foreign goods, such as tape recorders and records, according to the amount of Soviet currency allowed for each foreign trip. If the calculated price in rubles was higher than an officially allowed sum for tourist exchange, the police confiscated the imported goods from tourists. During the period 1972–84, each tourist group of thirty-four people returning from its trip abroad had on average three to ten cases of smuggled foreign goods or broke the rules of foreign currency exchange.[29]

The relative growth of outgoing international tourism after 1975 was, to some extent, a result of the Soviet government's propagandist efforts to demonstrate to the world that the USSR literally followed a section of the Final Act of the Conference on Security and Cooperation in Europe. This section acknowledged that less-restricted tourism was essential to the development of cooperation among nations.[30] After the United States began negotiating tourism agreements with Egypt, Hungary, Yugoslavia, and Poland in 1978, these countries became more attractive to Soviet tourists as well because of a new influx of tourists from the United States. Soviet tourists saw new opportunities for consumption in these countries.[31] An overwhelming majority of organized international tourists went not to the developing countries such as Egypt and India but to the relatively stable and loyal socialist countries such as Hungary, East Germany, and Bulgaria. Yugoslavia was also very popular among Soviet tourists. However, the local KGB officers and Communist ideologists, who loved to travel there, did not want to encourage local tourists to buy travel plans to socialist Yugoslavia, which was not an official member of the Soviet bloc. According to the unwritten hierarchy of international tourism in Dniepropetrovsk, the best place to travel was the very capitalist world—including the United States, France, England, and Italy. The second (less Westernized) place in this hierarchy belonged to the developing countries such as India and Egypt. Yugoslavia, as the most Westernized socialist country, took the third position. Other European socialist countries belonged to the fourth position. Asian socialist countries and Cuba took the last place in this hierarchy.[32]

During the 1970s and 1980s, Dniepropetrovsk's international tourists usually traveled to European socialist countries via train from Kyiv. If the tourists' destination was Poland or East Germany, they went through the railway station of Brest in Byelorussia. If they traveled to Hungary, Czechoslovakia, or Yugoslavia, they went through the railway station of Chop in Western Ukraine. Another popular travel plan included a sea trip from Odessa in Ukraine to Bulgaria and Romania. Such Mediterranean cruises, which included visits to big ports on the Mediterranean Sea, were organized by trade unions and were available only to experienced tourists whose background was double checked by the KGB. The KGB office had an unwritten rule for local international tourists. No one was allowed to visit a capitalist or developing country without previous experience traveling to socialist countries. If during travel to a socialist country, a tourist did not make ideologically harmful mistakes (buying pornography, anti-Soviet products, etc.), and demonstrated only the loyal behavior of a Soviet patriot, the KGB would permit the individual to travel to capitalist countries. Any travel abroad also required a special recommendation from certain Komsomol, Communist, and trade union organizations of which the potential tourist had to be a member. It usually took at least a couple of months for the Soviet travel agency to check all the candidate's documents for travel abroad. Even Communist Party and Komsomol apparatchiks complained of the long bureaucratic procedures of this "security" checking, which usually involved not only a special KGB officer but also representatives of the Komsomol administration, the party, and trade unions.[33]

The direct representatives of the trade union and the Komsomol administration in the international tourist groups always used their official trips abroad for their own consumption (which sometimes was not very cultural consumption at all). On many occasions, as a gesture to their supervisor, they brought a gift back from their tourist assignment as a token of their loyalty.[34] Usually these direct representatives used their special status and brought to Dniepropetrovsk some foreign goods that were impossible to obtain in the Soviet Union. The overwhelming bulk of these goods was Western fashion items such as jeans, cigarettes, records of popular music, and perfumes. Sometimes these goods included popular books in Russian, which had been printed in the Soviet Union and sent to other socialist countries as part of a cultural mission to promote Soviet culture and the Russian language among members of the Soviet bloc. These books, especially adventure novels by Alexander Dumas and Arthur Conan Doyle, were extremely popular in the 1970s among the Soviet reading audience but were unavailable in Dniepropetrovsk's bookstores. Two major publishing houses in Dniepropetrovsk reprinted boring collections of Brezhnev's works and other ideological literature of the Communist Party and ignored the growing demand for more popular and readable books.[35] Because of the ideological paradoxes of trade policy between members of the Soviet bloc, these books in the Russian language (including Russian classical literature) became available in many socialist countries that were a travel destination for many Soviet tourist groups. As a result, many tourists used their trips as an opportunity to bring these books from Bulgaria or Hungary back to Dniepropetrovsk.[36]

After the first international tourist groups returned to Dniepropetrovsk, their leaders reported to their administration the unhealthy enthusiasm of Dniepropetrovsk's tourists for Western products, especially jeans and music records. After 1974, all groups' leaders complained that a majority of tourists were preoccupied with finding cheap shops selling popular records.

Instead of participating in the intensive cultural programs in Sophia or Budapest, these tourists spent their time in the downtown parts of these cities looking for records.[37] Besides reports of frequent cases of drinking among Dniepropetrovsk's tourists, complaints about pop music consumption were a typical part of the official reports after each tourist trip abroad. In 1978, the leaders added new complaints about tourists buying various music equipment. According to group leaders' reports from 1978 to 1985, new Western reel-to-reel tape recorders and small audiocassette players became the ultimate item many tourists hoped to acquire during their entire trip.[38] As many contemporaries testified, Komsomol activists and group leaders were the most active participants in this cultural consumption during their tourist trips. The leaders of tourist groups not only participated in shopping sprees together with their fellow travelers; they also tried to use their connections with customs authorities in Chop, Brest, and Odessa to obtain permission to bring music equipment back to Dniepropetrovsk.

Overall, Komsomol activists, who made up a major part of these tourists, preferred visits to capitalist countries because they were allowed more currency and had more opportunity to buy various goods. However, by the end of the 1970s, they had brought back more rock albums and music information from socialist countries than from other parts of the world.[39] The main reason for this was that the KGB and Communist ideologists usually considered the music products and information from socialist countries as more ideologically reliable than any music information from the Western countries. As a result, they permitted Komsomol tourists to bring more cultural products like books and records from the countries of the Soviet bloc.[40]

After 1976, the most desired object of cultural consumption during the tourists' trips abroad was records of Western popular music. Many international tourists had lists of music records that had been requested by local consumers. Before 1970, only two out of ten records on Dniepropetrovsk's black market came directly from the local tourists who traveled abroad. During the period 1972–80, on average, four to five out of the ten most popular rock albums were brought to the city by local tourists from their travels to foreign countries.[41] As one sixteen-year-old high school student described the situation in the Dniepropetrovsk's black market in August 1975:

Today [August 24], I planned to buy a real Western stuff at Dniepropetrovsk music market. My friends told me that a big group of our local tourists just recently returned from Hungary and Poland and they brought new music records on the market. I had fifty rubles that I had earned this summer in kolkhoz. Today, in Dniepropetrovsk's music market, I saw all my favorite albums by Deep Purple, Uriah Heep, Geordie, Gary Glitter, Slade, and Sweet, which were brought from the socialist countries. It is amazing, what a selection of the rock records our socialist friends have! But I decided to buy only one album (for 45 rubles) of my new favorite group T. Rex. . . . Now, finally, I have a real British record from socialist Hungary (not the tapes) with my favorite songs "Children of the Revolution" and "20th-Century Boy." As a member of our school Komsomol committee, I will recommend these songs that sound like a revolution to our school's administration for the school dance instead of the boring Soviet Ukrainian songs about love. . . . Next week a new group of Dniepropetrovsk tourists will return from Yugoslavia—from the real West, not from Poland, Hungary, or Bulgaria. I call Yugoslavia the real West because this country has no limits for music information, like other socialist countries do. . . . We expect the albums of Shocking Blue and *Jesus Christ Superstar,* which we had ordered to buy through one member of this tourist group last June. Perhaps, we can ask these tourists to bring us new albums of Pink Floyd and King Crimson next time. I feel envious of these guys who can go to Yugoslavia and see how the West lives![42]

This diary entry is a testimony about the direct connections between international tourism and the growing consumption of Western cultural products, especially rock music records, among the youth of the closed city of Dniepropetrovsk during the Brezhnev era. Moreover, this document demonstrates that even young Komsomol activists like Aleksandr Gusar not only participated in the black market but also spread information about new Western music among their classmates and school administration. It is noteworthy that the main source of this information was local tourists traveling to the socialist countries, which Gusar included in his peculiar hierarchy of the West. According to him, socialist Yugoslavia was the real West, whereas other foreign socialist countries just approximated to his ideal of the West, which he associated with access to his favorite rock music.

The music records brought by local tourists after their travel abroad were a part of the very important cultural consumption that affected not only many young inhabitants of the region of Dniepropetrovsk but also their Komsomol ideologists, who were responsible for the consumption of rock and disco music among local youth. Because of the All-Union Komsomol Discotheque Campaign, which reached Dniepropetrovsk in 1976, both

Komsomol leaders and Komsomol activists became involved in the organization and supervision of various forms of popular music consumption. After 1976, the Central Committee of the All-Union Komsomol required
Dniepropetrovsk's Komsomol leaders to actively participate in the new discotheque movement, which was triggered by the Komsomol of the Baltic
republics in 1974–75.[43]

The main goal was to keep ideological control over dance floors, where
a majority of Soviet youth spent their free time. Therefore, the local Komsomol leaders who were responsible for the organization of leisure time became participants in a new network of connections and personal relations,
which by 1985 had begun being called the "discotheque mafia" in Dniepropetrovsk. Suddenly, the loyal young Komsomol functionaries found themselves in a very ambiguous situation. They had to communicate with those
who provided dance parties with the most popular music but whose ideological preferences were questionable. These people were connected to
the black market of rock music, which had flourished in downtown Dniepropetrovsk since the early 1960s. Because of the necessity of getting ideologically reliable music for disco clubs, the Komsomol ideologists now
had to depend on material unavailable through traditional sources. At the
same time, Dniepropetrovsk's enthusiasts for rock music, who were organizers of the first Komsomol discotheques as well, were able to get the necessary material through the black market. Nondirectly, the Komsomol ideologists became involved with new connections and sometimes even with
the very murky and illegal activities of rock music providers from the black
market. The primary sources for music were two black market areas that
still existed in downtown Dniepropetrovsk despite many efforts by the authorities to arrest dealers in Western music records.[44]

As Valerii Miakotenko, a leader of the discotheque movement in the city
noted, "a contemporary dance party could not exist without fresh music information from the black market." To get this information, a disco club activist had to go to a music market in downtown to buy a music record for
60 to 80 rubles each or to record a new album on his audiotape for 3 to 5
rubles, or even 15 to 16 rubles, a record. To survive in this situation and be
able to buy everything new on the black market, Miakotenko explained to
a journalist, this activist had to organize his own small business of trading
records, tapes, and other music products.[45]

Eventually, the Komsomol ideologists and discotheque activists developed mutual interests and became more and more dependent on each other.
Starting in 1978, the Komsomol disco clubs, especially Melodia, estab-

lished stable connections with the Sputnik apparatchiks, who used these clubs as their venues for various occasions, private parties, and business meetings. The discotheque activists assisted the Komsomol apparatchiks with dance parties, which were officially recorded in Komsomol reports as special events for tourist groups. In exchange, the Komsomol leaders provided ideological protection to various city disco clubs and shared profits with their organizers. Sometimes this led to financial crimes when Komsomol apparatchiks from Sputnik privatized public funds and tried to hide the unregistered profit of their tourist-disco business. At the end of 1981, a special commission discovered financial transgressions of many leaders of Sputnik and trade union tourism who were involved in murky dealings with people from various Komsomol disco clubs and cafés.[46]

This ambiguity in the attitudes of the Komsomol apparatchiks toward the music market was especially evident in the 1980s. Serhiy Tihipko, who since 1984 had worked as the Komsomol apparatchik in Dniepropetrovsk, was an eyewitness to these developments.[47] While a student at a local college during the years 1977–82, Tihipko listened to Western rock music and knew that some of his rock music tapes reached him through the black market. When in 1984 he became responsible for Communist propaganda among the youth of the Dniepropetrovsk metallurgical *tekhnikum* (technical school) and dealt with the organization of dance parties and discotheques, he faced a very serious problem. How was it possible to organize an ideologically reliable and politically loyal mass event based on music and video material that came from "ideologically unreliable and politically incorrect sources?" Music products from the capitalist countries were still only available through the illegal black market. As Tihipko recalled, some of his Komsomol colleagues, trying to avoid the Dniepropetrovsk black market, used Sputnik as a new venue for getting music information and products from the socialist countries. They considered these products to contain more reliable and correct material for proper Communist propagandist actions. Tihipko's department was responsible for organizing various leisure-time events for local youth. These events included lectures, visual agitation, special testing of the level of ideological maturity of Komsomol members, and also using discotheques as a "venue for ideological propaganda." Eventually, Tihipko became involved in various counterpropagandist activities, checking the ideological purity and political correctness of all forms of leisure in the city of Dniepropetrovsk, including dance parties and Komsomol tourism.[48]

The Adjustment of Apparatchiks to the Anti-Rock Campaign and the Roots of Perestroika

Inspired by the antipunk campaign of 1983, Komsomol ideologists like Tihipko "moved against recording studios, discotheques, and underground record networks."[49] Many disco clubs were closed in 1984–85. In the Dniepropetrovsk Region, the local ideologists organized a special survey of all disco clubs. In March 1984, they permitted only thirty-two discotheques that belonged to the trade union palaces of culture and fourteen disco clubs under the supervision of the Ukrainian Ministry of Culture to keep functioning. During 1984, the number of closed disco clubs reached a peak in the region. In the city of Dniepropetrovsk, the local administration closed seventeen discotheques "because of their low ideological level." By the beginning of perestroika, instead of a thriving discotheque movement, the closed city had only seventeen officially permitted disco clubs.[50] Many talented disc jockeys and music engineers, such as Mikhail Suvorov, left Komsomol discotheques in 1985–86 and moved to the safer ground of other ideological institutions, far away from the dangerous restrictions surrounding rock music.[51]

In 1983–84, the police organized special raids on music market locations in downtown Dniepropetrovsk. They were looking not for black marketers but for the anti-Soviet music products, including records and audiotapes of Kiss and AC/DC songs. Thousands of original Western records were confiscated, and hundreds of people were arrested during those two years. The police were shocked by what they discovered. The overwhelming majority of the arrested black marketers of Western music were very young people. They were mainly high school, vocational school, and technical school students age fourteen to eighteen years. This was a striking contrast to the demography of the black market in the 1970s. During the previous decade, a majority of music *fartsovshchiks* (black marketers) had been college students who were much older, usually eighteen to twenty-five years. Another unpleasant discovery for the police were the professionalism and organizational talents of the young music *fartsovshchiks*. These black marketers organized the trading of records according to their popularity and availability. In their peculiar hierarchy, original Western (*firmennye*) records took the highest rank; records from socialist countries, known as *demokraty,* took second place; and Soviet records, *ofitsionki,* were the least popular. The leaders of these young black marketers, who were Dniepropetrovsk high school students, established a well-organized network of business that connected the open cities of Ukraine such as Zaporizhie and Odessa with Dniepropetrovsk and many small towns in the region.

At the same time, the KGB noticed that the Western Ukrainian city of L'viv had lost its significance as a source of music information for the local black marketers during the 1980s.[52] By the beginning of 1985, the police had destroyed the city's once-thriving rock music market. But they were not able to halt its music consumption. Disco clubs, restaurants, and bars still existed in the city. Their administration still was interested in "fresh" Western popular music because it had become part of a very lucrative business. The "disco club enterprise" became the first stable source of significant material profit for the local administration, including Komsomol apparatchiks. In the years 1981–83, according to the official records, the Melodia club brought in a monthly profit of more than 60,000 rubles. In fact, the organizers of this business earned an additional "nonregistered" 20,000 rubles each month.[53]

Because of the anti–rock music campaign, the people in charge of musical entertainment had to find other sources for music information and products to satisfy the growing demands of Dniepropetrovsk's consumers. The neighboring cities Krivoi Rog and Zaporizhie, which were open for foreigners, became more important locations for obtaining fresh music products for Dniepropetrovsk's consumers. The local Komsomol leaders, who were responsible for entertainment, also had to explore nontraditional sources of music products and establish connections with providers of new music. International tourism became a major source of new material for rock music consumption during the years 1983–85. In 1972, only 30 percent of all records and audiotapes of Western popular music came directly through the channels of international tourism to Dniepropetrovsk's music market. By the end of 1984, more than 90 percent of all fresh Western music reached Dniepropetrovsk's music dealers via local tourists who traveled abroad, including those who used the services of the Komsomol travel agency.[54]

Many sources for the consumption of banned pop music came to Dniepropetrovsk through the representatives of the ruling Soviet elite, who visited foreign countries as the members of local tourist groups. According to discotheque activists, in 1979 the KGB supervisors of local tourism brought to Dniepropetrovsk the original rock music albums later banned by Communist ideologists. One KGB tourist returning from a trip to Hungary, and another from a trip to Poland, brought the albums *Highway to Hell* by AC/DC and *Dynasty* by Kiss for their own children, who were active participants in the city's music market. Through these KGB children, tapes of AC/DC and Kiss music became available to thousands of rock music consumers in the region many months before foreign students brought these albums to Krivoi Rog, a city open to foreign tourists.[55]

During the anti–rock music campaign, the Komsomol apparatchiks who had an opportunity to go abroad brought new music records, audiotapes, cassettes, and audio and video equipment. According to Mikhail Suvorov, during the crisis of 1983–84, when the music market was closed by the police, the same Komsomol apparatchik who had once asked Suvorov about rare songs by Lennon brought the new music records (of the forbidden Blondie and Iron Maiden) to the central city discotheque. All these records had been bought by the apparatchik in Hungary when he was the leader of a local tourist group. In 1984, 90 percent of all foreign music material in the central disco club of Dniepropetrovsk came directly from local Sputnik tourists who had visited European socialist countries. According to the active participants in the Dniepropetrovsk music market, approximately nine out of ten songs at the dance party in Melodia usually came from the material that belonged to such tourists. From February to December 1984, more than 1,500 young tourists from Dniepropetrovsk went abroad. Each member of this group (1,026 in the Sputnik annual report) brought to the city at least one music record of Western origin or another kind of music information.[56]

The irony of this situation was that, given the ideological requirements, these Komsomol leaders and activists had to demonstrate how effectively they performed their duties in the organization of youth entertainment. However, due to narrowing channels of music information by the anti-rock campaign, the leaders depended more and more on their old discotheque movement network, which necessarily involved the old enthusiasts for rock music who were connected to the black market. In addition, they also used domestic and especially international tourism. This involvement in the consumption of popular music produced a very important network of connections for the region's new Komsomol elite. After the beginning of the discotheque movement in 1976–77, they became active organizers, supervisors, and participants in this system of rock music consumption. By 1985, they had access to all the major forms of profit from this consumption.

Moreover, as the young ideologists of the Soviet state, they had a legitimate right to participate in all these means of profit. Through their discotheque connections, Komsomol leaders started a new type of entertainment: video salons. The first video recording equipment appeared in Dniepropetrovsk's radio shops in the fall of 1982. Any attempt to use a videocassette recorder (VCR) and to show foreign films to make money in private homes was considered a crime, and people who tried to profit by doing this were punished.[57] The first public scandal (in September 1983) involving illegal trade in VCRs and videocassettes demonstrated the links between the activists of the discotheque movement and the representatives of the "restaurant business" in the closed city.[58] During the years 1983–84, all criminal cases of illegal VCR use involved the disc jockeys and music engineers of the most respectable disco clubs in Dniepropetrovsk.[59]

According to contemporaries, the first foreign videocassettes, which reached the Dniepropetrovsk market in 1982–84, contained video clips and film concerts of the "classic" British rock musicians, such as Pink Floyd and Queen. During this time, the most popular musical video film was *Jesus Christ Superstar,* an old American movie (1973) directed by Norman Jewison and starring Ted Neeley. This video of the legendary rock opera by Andrew Lloyd Webber and Tim Rice became the most desirable object among local consumers during the entire 1980s. Sergei Pulin, young professor of English at Dniepropetrovsk University, brought his own copy of this video to the rocket city from his trip to England in 1984. During the period 1985–88, he showed this video in the Communist Party's special lecture halls in downtown Dniepropetrovsk during his public lectures about the history of the famous rock opera. The Communist Party's lecture society, Znanie, sponsored all his "atheistic" lectures and used a foreign VCR, which had been bought by local Soviet officials during their tourist travels abroad.[60] Those who visited Pulin's lectures about British rock opera later recalled:

> The first foreign videocassettes were brought to the closed city by the Soviet officials after their tourist trips abroad. All these videos had music films. The American version of *Jesus Christ Superstar* was the most popular video in 1984. I remember that we even watched this video during Pulin's public lectures, which were officially sanctioned by the local Communist ideologists. Music videos opened the road to other video products. The new videocassettes had the American action movies such as *Rambo I: First Blood,* and *Rambo II.* In 1984, the second wave of video products brought American gangster films like *The Godfather I* and *The Godfather II* and horror films like *Jaws.* But still, the music video films prevailed. It was a real obsession. Now we could see all our idols in action, playing legendary rock music hits. Even during perestroika, Dniepropetrovsk's inhabitants preferred videos with Webber's

rock opera, and with music clips by Queen, Iron Maiden, Dire Straits, Peter Gabriel, and Michael Jackson.[61]

In the period 1986–88, as some contemporaries noted, this "obsession" with rock music shaped even the consumption of video products. When Russell Mulcahy's action fantasy film *Highlander* (1986), starring Christopher Lambert and Sean Connery, reached local video consumers in Dniepropetrovsk, it immediately produced a sensation. The major reason for this was not the action scenes of fighting in the film but rock music score for this movie, which was composed and performed by the legendary British rock band Queen.[62] As the KGB officers recalled, from 1983 to 1987, almost 60 percent of all confiscated video products in Dniepropetrovsk had Western popular music, 30 percent were American action and gangster films, and less than 10 percent were horror and "erotic" films.[63] As we can see, the majority of the first videos in the local market were musical films.

These connections of music and videos in local consumption led to the first attempts to use video music clips of Western rock musicians for dance programs in the local disco clubs as early as 1984. However, Communist ideologists and KGB officers interfered and forbade the usage of VCRs during dance parties. They referred to "central orders from Moscow," which allowed the use video equipment only for the officially sanctioned "Komsomol video salons" rather than for dances.[64] By the end of 1984, responding to these KGB suggestions, Komsomol activists together with their discotheque friends started an initiative to organize an official Komsomol video business. Only in 1986, during Mikhail Gorbachev's perestroika, did the city administration permit the opening of so-called video salons in Dniepropetrovsk.[65] Like the discotheque movement, video salons became a relatively lucrative business, and young Komsomol leaders used both their legal connections in tourist organizations and regional Soviet administration and their nonformal connections with rock music enthusiasts to succeed in this business. After 1976, these new forms of cultural consumption, especially popular music and (after 1984) video, became a means for the creation of new managerial and business connections that would contribute to the post-Soviet political and business activities of former Komsomol elites.

Another paradox of the ideological campaigns of late socialism was that the lists of forbidden Western musicians and films, which were widely used by Communist ideologists and Komsomol activists in their campaign to purify the markets of pop music consumption in Dniepropetrovsk, had not reached Soviet customs officers and frontier guards before 1986. As a result, many forbidden items continued to flow into the Dniepropetrovsk music market via Soviet apparatchiks who traveled abroad. During the anti-rock campaign in the Dniepropetrovsk Region, international tourism became an important source for feeding music information to the centers of leisure, which still needed the new music for dancing and fun. Two main organizations, Komsomol and the trade unions, along with their corresponding tourist agencies, were competing for this music information—and for favors from the people who controlled the music market of Dniepropetrovsk. These people were called the "discotheque mafia" by the local police. By 1985, the practical aspects of these apparatchiks' careers tied the Dniepropetrovsk music market (including the people from the "discotheque mafia"), international tourism, and Komsomol and the trade unions' structures into one important network of business connections. Nine out of ten "Komsomol business enterprises" in Dniepropetrovsk during perestroika were created by these Komsomol activists who were directly connected to the "discotheque mafia" of the Brezhnev era, to these people who introduced new forms of cultural consumption in the closed city, such as disco clubs and video salons.[66]

The crisis of 1983–84 created a unique situation, when the Soviet apparatchiks responsible for pop music consumption by young people used all elements of the discotheque network to survive and succeed. This complicated system of interconnections and mutual obligations with elements of personal favors had begun many years ago, before 1976. Everybody depended on other participants in this system.[67] The beginning of the discotheque movement in 1976 added a new element to this system—the people from the music market, who provided the organizers of leisure time with the necessary music information and products for mass consumption.

Perestroika and Komsomol Business

In the middle of the 1980s, when perestroika created favorable conditions for the old managerial skills of Komsomol activists, this system produced new activities for cultural consumption—video salons—that became a new business that brought to its organizers more profits than traditional disco clubs. The video business used the same infrastructure and network as the discotheque movement—namely, international tourism, Komsomol activists, trade union bosses, and the "discotheque mafia." This network contributed to the business careers of two other fans of Western popular music: Yulia

Tymoshenko and her husband, Oleksandr.[68] In 1978, after her graduation from City School No. 75, Yulia Grigian (Telegina), the daughter of an Armenian taxicab driver, Grigian, and a Russian technical worker, Telegina, a talented student and fan of the British rock music, married Oleksandr Tymoshenko, a son of a member of the city Communist Party committee connected to the administration of Yuzhmash, the largest rocket factory in the Soviet Union.

Widely known in the 1990s as the "gas princess" of the Ukraine and in 2004 as the "Joan of Arc" of the Orange Revolution, Yulia Tymoshenko began her extraordinary career in 1978 as an ordinary Komsomol member of the student organization at the Department of the Economy at Dniepropetrovsk State University. This department was opened on the initiative of the Yuzhmash administration in 1977 to provide training for qualified economists in the growing military-industrial complex of Dniepropetrovsk. Yulia graduated with honors from the Department of the Economy in 1984 and began her first job as an engineer-economist through the connections of her father-in-law, Gennadii Tymoshenko. For five years, she worked at the Lenin machine building plant, another factory that belonged to the Soviet military-industrial complex. In 1979, she gave birth to a daughter, Yevgenia, and until 1988 she and her husband enjoyed the life of a typical Soviet upper-middle-class family, living in their own one-bedroom cooperative apartment. They continued to watch Western movies and listen to Western pop music, and they occasionally visited and danced in famous disco clubs in downtown Dniepropetrovsk.[69]

Perestroika changed the lifestyle of the young Tymoshenko family. Gennadii Tymoshenko recommended that his son and daughter-in-law to join the cooperative movement and promised his support through the city party and Soviet administration. In 1988, the young Tymoshenkos used their old connections in the world of Komsomol discotheques to open a public service enterprise, a video-rental shop in Dniepropetrovsk. They opened their business with 5,000 borrowed Soviet rubles. The profits made from this first venture were used to open their video rental chains. They used the experience of Komsomol apparatchiks, who brought the first VCRs in Dniepropetrovsk through Sputnik. The people from the discotheque movement helped provide these apparatchiks with Western videotapes and an audience that was ready to consume the new Western cultural products. Former discotheque enthusiasts tested the new business practices and proposed the idea of video salons, which had already become the most popular and fashionable form of entertainment in the Soviet capital cities, such as Moscow, and the Baltic republics since 1984. As a result, during perestroika both the Komsomol and the "discotheque mafia" provided infrastructure for these salons in the city.

In 1987, when the KGB again opened the city of Dniepropetrovsk to foreigners, the Yuzhmash rocket factory imported thousands of VCRs using barter agreements with South Korean businessmen. As a regional Communist Party apparatchik, who was in charge of movies distribution throughout the Dniepropetrovsk Region (*kinoprokat*), Yulia Tymoshenko's father-in-law had access not only to these Korean VCRs but also to local movie theaters, which provided the first mass audience for video shows. With these family connections, and using the traditional discotheque infrastructure, Yulia Tymoshenko organized the Komsomol cooperative Terminal, which controlled a chain of video salons with Yuzhmash VCRs in 1988. The main base of the Tymoshenko "video enterprise" was the location of the former central Komsomol disco club of the entire region of Dniepropetrovsk: the Palace of Students in the Taras Shevchenko Park of Culture and Relaxation in downtown Dniepropetrovsk.[70]

In 1989, Yulia quit her old engineer-economist job and became a leader of the Terminal cooperative. The same year, another participant of the disco movement, Serhiy Tihipko, was elected as first secretary of the Komsomol organization of the Dniepropetrovsk Region. He not only supported the Tymoshenko enterprise but also brought his additional discotheque and Sputnik connections into Terminal. In this way, both disco activists and Komsomol apparatchiks contributed to the growth and popularity of the Tymoshenko business.[71]

All the elements of the initial Tymoshenko business had already been developed during the Brezhnev era, when the cultural consumption of late socialism combined the structures of Soviet international tourism and the ideological efforts of Komsomol activists into one network of important business and managerial relations. Mass rock and disco music consumption among Soviet youth involved Komsomol and trade union apparatchiks. International tourism and discotheque enthusiasts provided these apparatchiks with important music and video material for their business of entertainment. Without these relations, it is impossible to imagine the development of post-Soviet capitalism. In 1991, after the collapse of the Soviet Union and organized Soviet state tourism, the representatives of the Brezhnev-era Komsomol elite, such as Tymoshenko, who used the same Soviet network of connections and experiences, demonstrated again that a skillful adjustment of this network to a new economic situation was an important foundation for success in the post-Soviet business activities. The initial capital of Terminal, the music and video Komsomol enterprise of Yulia Tymoshenko created during "the disco era" of late socialism, will be a foundation for her future business and political career during the new, post-Soviet capitalist era.

Conclusion

By the end of perestroika in 1991, more than a hundred Komsomol businesses had emerged in the closed city of Dniepropetrovsk. Ten of the most successful enterprises survived the brutal, post-Soviet competition during the 1990s and created "new business corporations" in Dniepropetrovsk, such as Yulia Tymoshenko's "Gas Empire," Serhiy Tihipko's Privatbank, and Aleksandr Balashov's Trade Corporation.[72] The overwhelming majority of these successful post-Soviet businesses (nine out of ten) were organized by or directly connected to the "discotheque mafia"—a network of rock music enthusiasts, black marketers, Komsomol ideologists, entertainers, and representatives of the Soviet tourist agencies. In this way, the consumption of Western cultural products, like music and videos during the late 1970s and early 1980s, contributed to capitalist entrepreneurship in post-Soviet Ukraine.

As a former disco club activist explained,

By providing local consumers with the music and videos they demanded, organizing their leisure, we, the members of the "discotheque mafia," revived the infrastructure of capitalism during the Brezhnev era. Our business activities united the efforts of small businessmen from the black market with the interests of Communist ideologists in one network. By 1985, we had similar tastes in Western products and common interests in our mutual business. Therefore, all of us involved in this business identified ourselves with local material interests rather than with the All-Union Soviet ideological goals and values. Both local Komsomol "businessmen and businesswomen" and local party ideologists discovered that they had to protect their local interests from the interference of Moscow, a political center whose behavior became unpredictable and dangerous for local interests, especially during the 1980s. It did not matter that we represented Russians, Ukrainians, Jews, and Armenians in our local music/video business. Now we had our own, regional, Dniepropetrovsk business interests and we were ready to represent them. We do not now need ideological control from Moscow. Our business activities unite us against such a control.[73]

Some contemporaries noted how the business activities of the new Komsomol "entrepreneurs" in the 1980s contributed to the regional identity of the former Soviet closed city.[74] Many of these "entrepreneurs" who were not ethnic Ukrainians became active participants in the Ukrainian independence movement in 1988–91 in an attempt to protect their regional business interests rather than their national cultural interests. In the 1990s, the former members of the Dniepropetrovsk "discotheque mafia" and their former ideological supervisors became an integral part of the business and political life of independent Ukraine.

Conclusion: "Between Moscow and L'viv"—The Closed City as an Ideological Failure of Late Socialism

Vitalii Pidgaetskii, first a student and later a professor of history at Dnie-propetrovsk University during the Brezhnev era, emphasized the impor-tance of Western cultural products in the identity formation of the youth in the closed city of Dniepropetrovsk:

> Living in the closed city under Brezhnev, we had more restrictions than Muscovites or people from other Soviet open cities had. That is why we worshipped any cultural product that came from the magic West. For us, the West was a kind of the symbolic mirror. Looking in this mirror, we tried to invent our own identity and understand what we were living for. To some extent, we constructed ourselves looking in this magic mirror of the forbidden and censored capitalist West. Sounds of Western popu-lar music or images from Western films intertwined with our Ukrainian, Russian, and Jewish cultural forms and produced a strange mental mix-ture in our heads, which was cemented by our dominant Soviet cultural stereotypes. We constructed our identity through a comparison of this mental mixture with the mirror of the West that we had already discov-ered in rock music, disco clubs, forbidden books, and Western movies. However, the construction of our identity depended on a supply of West-ern images, ideas, and sounds. Two open and Westernized Soviet cities influenced this supply immensely, and therefore contributed to identity formation in Dniepropetrovsk. L'viv brought us various forbidden cul-tural products from the West; Moscow imposed ideological control over our consumption of these products.[1]

303

The closing of the strategically important city of Dniepropetrovsk in 1959 led to tightened ideological control over its cultural consumption and revealed the role of Moscow and L'viv in the consumption of Western cultural products and shaping local identity in the closed city.[2] Four major stages of consumption of Western cultural products affected local identity formation before perestroika.

The First Stage: 1960 to 1970

From the early 1960s, as result of Khrushchev's liberalization, Western cultural products reached Soviet consumers everywhere, including provincial cities like Dniepropetrovsk. Western adventure novels, movies, and popular music became objects of cultural consumption in the closed city as well. Forbidden anti-Soviet literature from the West, including books about Ukrainian history and culture, also reached readers in the region and city of Dniepropetrovsk. Radio, tourists, and the black market provided local consumers with the major forbidden cultural products from the West, including so-called anti-Soviet nationalistic literature. For KGB officers, the major source of both "Ukrainian nationalistic books from the West" and Western "degenerate" popular music was the Western Ukrainian city of L'viv.

During the 1960s, Dniepropetrovsk's young intellectuals organized public discussions about the problems of Ukrainian national culture and history, based on ideas they had heard from their connections in L'viv. They were inspired by Khrushchev's "thaw" and public exposure of Stalin's distortions of Lenin's nationality policy. During the 1960s, many young patriots, including Ivan Sokul'sky's group, sincerely believed that their creative efforts in support of national cultures would lead to a restoration of the Leninist model of socialism. However, the KGB ruined the youth's hopes and dreams about flourishing of national cultures in the Dniepropetrovsk Region. Following directives from Moscow, the Dniepropetrovsk police tried to suppress any demonstration of pro-Western nationalism and any attempt to create nationalistic organizations, which were reminiscent of "revisionist socialism" in Czechoslovakia.

During the 1960s, American jazz and rock-and-roll (beat) music also influenced cultural consumption in the closed city. To control the consumption of Western music, which was elitist and mostly male at the beginning, local ideologists had to incorporate new Westernized cultural forms of the "stylish" jazz culture into their ideological practices. This led to a controversial relationship between the city's youth and local ideologists. By the mid-1960s—after the incorporation of American jazz as "progressive," and of "good, cultured" consumption in their official ideological practices— Soviet officials attempted to use jazz against any new cultural influences from the West, including rock-and-roll or beat music. Provincial ideologists from the closed city lagged behind the new ideological and cultural fashions, which came from Moscow. Constantly changing directives from Moscow during the 1960s led to new tensions between "the ideological practitioners" in Dniepropetrovsk and their ideological supervisors in Moscow, who ideologically justified the consumption of Western products that were unacceptable in the orthodox Marxist worldview of local KGB and Soviet officials. However, practical needs (of career making and adjusting to the central directives from Moscow) modified their anti-Western tastes and forced them not only to accept but also to use the new forms of cultural consumption for their political and financial survival.

Both young Ukrainian patriots, who participated in the poetic and artistic revival during the years 1968–69, and their adversaries, the KGB and Communist Party officials, were not always happy with Moscow's supervision of the ideological and cultural developments in the region of Dniepropetrovsk. This gradual opposition to Moscow among Dniepropetrovsk's intellectual and political elite became part of the ideological situation and cultural practices, especially after Khrushchev's controversial de-Stalinization. Both leaders and their subjects became confused and disoriented by this policy, which was revealed especially during the antireligious and the anti-*Sobor* campaigns. Soviet ideologists and KGB officers in the closed city did not understand why changes in Moscow's cultural politics and ideological practices affected traditional forms of Soviet cultural consumption. By the end of the 1960s, under pressure from Moscow, local ideologists had to accept forbidden (and traditionally considered to be anti-Soviet) Western cultural products like jazz and rock music as legitimate elements of Soviet entertainment.

The first waves of cultural consumption in the 1960s—jazz and beat music—demonstrated the ability of both Soviet officials and common consumers not only to accept the new forms of cultural consumption that were promoted by Moscow but also to make money by using these forms, especially by using jazz and rock music products. During this time, local officials began to build their entrepreneurial connections, which would become the foundation for lucrative music business in the closed city in the 1970s. Before 1964, American jazz music products prevailed on Dniepropetrovsk's music market. From 1964 to 1970, the Beatles' music replaced jazz on the local music market and paved the way for other Western music (mainly British beat music) by creating a new group of cultural consumers that was constantly expanding through legal and illegal distribution outlets.

During the 1960s, the rapid distribution of Western music revealed the direct and growing connections between the black market dealers like Arnold Gurevich and a majority of young rock music consumers. The black market as a source of rock music consumption contributed to the commercialization of Soviet youth culture during the 1960s, even in closed cities like Dniepropetrovsk. The new beat music culture brought market elements in local youth culture, which emphasized the businesslike, profit-oriented, enterprising behavior of the young rock music fans. By the end of the 1960s, the consumption of Western music in the closed city was losing its elitist and mostly male character. With the introduction and consequent popularity of the new beat music, the consumer base expanded to include more young people, women, and the working class.

The Second Stage: 1971 to 1975

During the period 1971–75, Western films and British hard-rock music became the most desirable objects of cultural consumption in the closed city of Dniepropetrovsk. A majority of the population in the closed city had to consume the limited number of Western cultural products that were permitted by local ideologists from the already limited choice offered by Moscow. In most cases, these products reached the local consumers late, causing them to lose their contemporary appeal and connections to reality. Through such consumption, they reinvented their own West, which reflected the dimensions of their own Soviet realities. Images from the movie screen were taken out of their cultural context and incorporated into the everyday lives of local youth. A majority of the Western films that reached Dniepropetrovsk were already outdated and did not correspond to contemporary cultural developments in the West during their release in the closed city. Moreover, local consumers in the city closed to foreigners had no opportunity to compare the realities of Western life with the movie images of such a life. As a result, local filmgoers had a distorted and inadequate understanding of the West. These limitations on cultural consumption eventually contributed to the conservative, parochial, and very provincial perception of the outside world among the young people who grew up in Dnie-propetrovsk during the Brezhnev era.

At the same time, the consumption of Western films in the closed city revealed important social and psychological tensions among the local population of Dniepropetrovsk. The consumers in this closed Ukrainian city criticized the cultural limitations from the center, Moscow. Even Russian-speaking consumers were frustrated with the ideological interferences from Moscow and from local leaders. It was the beginning of regional opposition by local consumers to the cultural politics of Moscow, which affected their everyday local cultural consumption. This regional "envy" of Moscow be-came a very important element in the shaping of the local identity in the closed city.

By the mid-1970s, a "reading boom" and growing interest in Western adventure novels influenced the black market tremendously and contributed to new social and economic connections among black marketers (*fartsov-shchiks*) in the closed city. The "music mafia," a group of the most notori-ous *fartsovshchiks,* who usually sold records and tapes, grew through the 1970s and gradually established complete control over the book market in Dniepropetrovsk. People in the "music mafia" began trading books—par-ticularly foreign books in Russian translations during the 1970s. By uniting trade in Western books and music, they built connections between book and music consumption in the closed city. This "music mafia" group, which also included thousands of "rock music enthusiasts" by the end of the 1970s, be-came known as the "discotheque mafia." The members of this "mafia" dom-inated and influenced all major forms of cultural consumption—especially trade in books and records—in the closed city. Through their connections with Komsomol officials, they built their first "legal businesses" after 1985 and influenced both the economic practices and business ethics of the new post-Soviet Ukrainian elite.

During the same period, *cultural fixation* on British hard-rock bands like Deep Purple led to what contemporaries called the *democratization of rock music consumption.* Millions of high school and vocational school students and young industrial workers, both men and women, joined the growing group of rock fans in the Soviet cities. In contrast to jazz and beat music consumption, which was still elitist, the hard rock of the early 1970s led to mass pop music consumption, which affected millions of Soviet young peo-ple by the end of Brezhnev era. Gradually, by the mid-1970s, a new com-mercial element appeared as an important aspect of rock music consumption. The dance floor (*tantsploshchadka* in Russian) became a significant part of the new business of Soviet entertainment and the democratization of music consumption, which affected musicians, official organizers, Communist (in many cases, Komsomol) ideologists, and the active participants in the black market who made money by trading original records and tapes. Thus, dance floors united official representatives of Soviet entertainment and Communist ideology with the representatives of the technically illegal black market for popular music in a very special form of cultural production and consumption.

During the years 1971–75, the "ideas, images and sounds from the West" replaced the themes of Ukrainian culture and history in local Ukrainian popular culture. Now Dniepropetrovsk's youth read more books in Russian and watched their favorite Western films dubbed in Russian. They consumed more information about their favorite rock music and Western films from Soviet youth periodicals (especially *Rovesnik*) and radio (especially Viktor Tatarskii's shows) in the Russian language. The "book boom" of the 1970s, the tremendous popularity of Western films, and the democratization of rock music consumption, which involved millions of young industrial workers and peasant migrants to industrial cities—all these led to the gradual Russification of popular culture in Dniepropetrovsk.

This Russified version of regional Ukrainian identity coexisted with elements of religious identity among the generation of the 1970s. A growing interest in popular religion, especially Christianity, was both a reaction to mistakes in the ideological efforts of Soviet officials and a direct result of Western rock music consumption. During the Brezhnev era, Western cultural products such as rock music were not simply an important component of everyday cultural consumption—they were a significant contributing factor in the spread of popular religiosity among the youth of the strategically important Dniepropetrovsk Region. Music from the West, especially Andrew Lloyd Webber's rock opera *Jesus Christ Superstar,* became an important factor in the formation of local identity in the closed city. As sociologists of music have noted, "in appropriating forms of popular music, individuals are simultaneously constructing ways of being in the context of their local everyday environments."[3]

The consumption of Western popular music in Dniepropetrovsk was a process of selective borrowing and appropriation, translation, and incorporation into the indigenous cultural context. Music by the Beatles, Creedence Clearwater Revival, Black Sabbath, Deep Purple, and Andrew Lloyd Webber was a point of *cultural fixation* for thousands of young people in

Dniepropetrovsk. Everyday living conditions in Ukraine's closed city led to the extreme idealization of any popular cultural product from the West. Through their cultural fixation on authentic Western or imitative music forms, Dniepropetrovsk's rock music consumers built their own religious identities using the elements of Christianity, Ukrainian folk culture, and Hinduism present in their favorite songs.

The Third Stage: 1976 to 1981

The third stage of cultural consumption in the closed city of Dniepropet-rovsk, from 1976 to 1981, was characterized by the rise of the discotheque movement, which involved both rock music fans and Komsomol ideologists. Komsomol disco clubs combined forms of ideological indoctrination such as musical lectures with forms of Soviet youth entertainment such as the dance party. This combination now involved more Western cultural products and, at the same time, brought more material profits to the Soviet officials in charge of discotheques.

The Komsomol initiatives of the years 1975–76 attempted to control and regulate Western music consumption by incorporating elements of Communist indoctrination, which led to unexpected results. The Komsomol ideologists who first became involved in the discotheque movement primarily to guarantee its socialist character ended up becoming part of a profit-making business, which had nothing to do with the Marxist-Leninist theory of cultural enlightenment and Communist indoctrination. And by accepting the real West as a part of their identity, young rock music fans and discotheque activists rejected the official Soviet version of their own ethnic identity. This process of identification with the West also affected the Komsomol ideologists who eagerly participated in the consumption of Western cultural products during the Brezhnev era. In contrast to their official denial of the corrupting influences of the capitalist West, these apparatchiks preferred Western cultural products to Soviet ones. Their musical preferences, fashions, and dance parties demonstrated the Westernization of the young ideologists in the closed city of Soviet Ukraine. They consumed more Western cultural products than products of Soviet Ukrainian culture.

Eventually, this process of identification with the real West contributed to the mass Russification of the youth culture in Eastern Ukraine during the 1970s. For many rock music enthusiasts in the closed city of Dniepropet-rovsk, only the central, mainly Russian, means of mass media offered interesting and relatively reliable information about the main trends and developments in Western popular culture. The youth magazine *Rovesnik,* published in Russian, became the most popular source of such information. By the middle of the 1980s, young Ukrainian consumers mainly preferred the sources of information in the Russian language rather than in Ukrainian.

During the 1970s, all the major cultural and ideological influences that shaped the identities of both local ruling elites and ordinary consumers in Dniepropetrovsk came through two different, but Westernized and "open," Soviet cities. One was the Western Ukrainian city of L'viv. The other was Moscow, the capital of the Soviet Union. By 1976, besides their traditional opposition to L'viv's "dangerous" Western and nationalistic influences, the representatives of Dniepropetrovsk's ruling elite had also become frustrated with the cultural politics of Moscow. The local Soviet officials (including the KGB operatives) were confused and felt embarrassed by this politics; they did not understand it, and they feared the negative reaction of Dniepropetrovsk's consumers. Various restrictions from Moscow on book, film, and music consumption provoked anti-Moscow feelings not only among the local intellectuals but also among a majority of industrial workers. Thus, the perception of "envy of Muscovites' privileges in Soviet consumption" became the most important development in the regional identity formation of Dniepropetrovsk. Even the Russian-speaking population of the closed city identified with local, Ukrainian economic and cultural interests rather than with Moscow's Russian economic and cultural practices.

Despite the growing Russification of Dniepropetrovsk during the 1970s, local residents—including the young, enthusiastic consumers of Western cultural products—gradually distanced themselves from Moscow, which was associated with "the unjust privileges for Muscovites" and various restrictions and limitations on regional consumption in "the provinces." During perestroika, these feelings of "provincial envy of Moscow" in Dniepropetrovsk would be used by Ukrainian nationalist politicians to enroll and mobilize local young activists in their anti-Russian and anti-Moscow independence movement.

The Fourth Stage: 1982 to 1985

The fourth stage of the consumption of Western cultural products in the closed city of Dniepropetrovsk, from 1982 to 1985, was a period of KGB persecutions of the local fans of the heavy-metal rock groups AC/DC and

Kiss, who were mistakenly punished as fascist punks. This antipunk campaign had begun as early as 1980, but it reached its peak in the years 1982–84, as a belated reaction by Dniepropetrovsk's KGB to Moscow's directives about the danger of the international fascist punk movement. According to the KGB, Soviet fascist punks were similar to the groups of Polish youth that were involved in the Solidarity movement. During this time, the police blamed all Soviet punks for fascist, anti-Soviet activities and banned all cultural products that had any supposed connection to fascist punks.

As this antipunk, antifascist campaign in the closed city ran its course during the years 1982–84, the KGB officers and local ideologists noticed a new, surprising result of the campaign: The young "fascist punks" referred to Western notions of human rights. Moreover, even the local Komsomol activists in the discotheque movement raised this issue of human rights during their debates with the police and KGB officials. As the KGB officers argued, through the consumption of Western heavy metal and punk music, both rock music enthusiasts and the young Komsomol activists involved in the disco club business were trying to form their own notion of human rights, which became an important part of their self-identity.

At the same time, the antipunk, antifascist campaign in the closed city revealed the growing frustration with the directives from the central authorities in Moscow about the ideological situation in provincial cities like Dniepropetrovsk. Many young Komsomol enthusiasts of rock music wrote letters complaining about the "illegal" persecutions of Dniepropetrovsk's rock music fans by the local police and KGB to central Komsomol periodicals in Moscow. The parents of persecuted students who were expelled from colleges also complained to the Moscow authorities.

But Moscow did not offer to stop persecuting the "fascist punks" in Dniepropetrovsk, even during the first years of perestroika in the period 1985–87. Many Russified rock music fans now opposed not only the local ideologists and the police but also Moscow, as the center of their "ideological and cultural oppression." As a result, by the mid-1980s, fewer young consumers of Western cultural products in the closed city identified themselves with Moscow as their cultural center. During the 1980s, this disappearance of Moscow as the cultural and ideological center contributed to an identity crisis for the youth in the closed city.

During the antipunk campaign, the KGB discovered that mass rock and disco music consumption among the Soviet youth involved Komsomol and trade union apparatchiks. International tourism and discotheque enthusiasts provided these apparatchiks with important music and video material for the entertainment businesses. Without these relations, it is impossible to imagine the development of post-Soviet capitalism. The Dniepropetrovsk "discotheque mafia"—a network of rock music enthusiasts, black marketers, Komsomol ideologists, entertainers, and representatives of the Soviet tourist agencies—contributed directly to the region's business activities both during and after perestroika.

After 1991, the people from the "discotheque mafia" organized nine out of ten capitalist corporations in Dniepropetrovsk, including Yulia Tymoshenko's business. Despite the KGB's efforts to suppress the dangerous consumption of Western capitalist cultural products, this consumption influenced all the types of capitalist entrepreneurship that were pursued in post-Soviet Ukraine. Moreover, the business activities of the new Komsomol "entrepreneurs" in the 1980s contributed to the formation of regional identity in the former Soviet closed city. Many of these "entrepreneurs" who were not ethnic Ukrainians—such as Yulia Tymoshenko, Aleksandr Balashov, and Mikhail Suvorov—became active participants in the Ukrainian independence movement in 1988–91, attempting to protect their regional business interests rather than their national cultural interests. In the 1990s, as former members of the Dniepropetrovsk "discotheque mafia," they became an integral part of the business and political life of independent Ukraine, and they openly opposed Moscow in politics.

Summing Up

The Communist ideologists and KGB officers who controlled cultural consumption in Dniepropetrovsk created a confusing and disorienting ideological situation for the local youth. They promoted Western forms of entertainment, such as the discotheque. And at the same time, they tried to limit the influence of capitalist culture by popularizing expressions of Soviet nationalism, including Ukrainian music and history. They feared the rise of Ukrainian bourgeois nationalism and tried to suppress any extreme enthusiasm for Ukrainian poetry and history—yet the entire system of Soviet education was designed to promote the progressive cultural models of socialist nations, in contrast to the "degenerate capitalist culture" of imperialist nations. As a result, the young members of the mature socialist society in Dniepropetrovsk adopted elements of Western mass culture as well as the controversial ideas of Taras Shevchenko and images of Zaporizhian Cossacks as part of their cultural identification.

Cultural consumption also depended on the changing demographic situation in the 1960s and 1970s. The constant in-migration of non-Ukrainian ethnic groups, combined with ideological pressures, led to Russification as the main trend in the region's cultural development, and especially in the city of Dniepropetrovsk. Employment at Yuzhmash, the city's rocket factory complex, a high priority for KGB officials, also contributed to the city's growing Russification.[4] Moreover, the Ukrainian language was steadily losing ground to Russian during the 1970s and 1980s. An overwhelming majority of non-Ukrainian ethnic groups preferred Russian to Ukrainian, and more Ukrainians chose Russian as their native language. In 1979, 12.6 percent of all Ukrainians in the region claimed that Russian was their native language. By 1989, this proportion had grown to 15.2 percent, and in the cities it had increased from 16.4 to 18.9 percent.[5]

Among local Soviet youth, reading books and popular magazines, watching movies (especially Western ones), and listening and dancing to popular music (including Western rock and roll and disco) became the major elements of intensive cultural consumption. However, the young people of Dniepropetrovsk not only consumed but also produced new cultural forms that challenged the traditional notions and ideological discourse of local apparatchiks. Moreover, local ideologists tried to use different forms of entertainment, such as the discotheque, for Communist (especially anticapitalist and antireligious) propaganda. The use of Western music as propaganda made it legitimate for everyday ideological activities and justified its immense popularity. KGB and Communist Party ideologists tried to neutralize this popularity by promoting Soviet and Ukrainian cultural models.

This situation left the young people who lived in Dniepropetrovsk confused and disoriented. The prevailing ideological discourse, and the changing demographic situation, emphasized the cultural role of only one language, Russian. At the same time, the young generation was urged to respect certain heroes of national Ukrainian history—such as the Cossack rebels, Bohdan Khmel'nytsky, and Taras Shevchenko—and related aspects of Ukrainian culture.[6] After many years of such indoctrination, this generation was ready, in the period of Ukrainian independence, to consume the familiar forms of Ukrainian culture as legitimate symbols that connected their former Soviet ideological discourse to the new, post-Soviet one. Because of the ideological confusion of late Soviet socialism, these symbols became intermixed with various forms of both Soviet and Western popular culture. Such a situation created very peculiar, regional types of identity formation among local youth.

The Dniepropetrovsk version of cultural identification differed significantly from the Ukrainian forms associated with less-Russified regions of

Ukraine. The people growing up in the last generation of late socialism in Dniepropetrovsk developed their national identity through a dual process: first, of seeing themselves as the cultural descendants of late Soviet civilization, with some elements of Western mass culture and Ukrainian national forms; and second, of opposing the extreme Westernization and Ukrainization associated with Western Ukrainian cities such as L'viv. During the Brezhnev era, L'viv played an ambiguous role in the identity formation of Dniepropetrovsk. L'viv provided the closed city not only with Ukrainian national ideas but also with Western cultural products, which became the city's most desirable objects of cultural consumption.

At the same time, Moscow was always identified as the political and ideological center of Soviet civilization. For the people of Dniepropetrovsk, Moscow acted as an ideological supervisor that, on the one hand, set certain cultural standards and fashionable trends for the Soviet provinces, including the Dniepropetrovsk Region, and, on the other, interfered in and limited local forms of cultural consumption. By the 1980s, Moscow had become the object of the "cultural envy" for millions of consumers in the Dniepropetrovsk Region. Traditionally, the capital city of the USSR had better access and distribution of consumer goods, including Western cultural products, than provincial cities like Dniepropetrovsk. During the Brezhnev era, local consumers (both the ruling elites and ordinary citizens) began identifying themselves with their regional interests and ideas rather than with Moscow's ones. By the beginning of perestroika, even the Russian-speaking people of Dniepropetrovsk distanced themselves from Moscow and tried to protect their own regional interests and local sources of consumption from Moscow's control.

As some contemporaries noted during the Brezhnev era, Dniepropetrovsk's youth created their own regional, Russified version of Ukrainian Soviet identity as a result of living in the closed city, "with hypertrophied emphasis on the consumption of forbidden, but desired, Western cultural products."[7] The search for the authentic West was an important part of a process of identity formation for millions of young Soviet consumers of Western cultural products. In the closed city of Dniepropetrovsk, consumers tried to identify only with the West or its legitimate substitutes—resulting, by the end of the 1970s, in their disconnection from Soviet Ukrainian culture. In the imagination of these consumers, official Soviet Ukrainian culture represented the most conservative, backward, and anti-Western elements of their life. Therefore, by accepting the real West as a part of their identity, they rejected the official Soviet version of their ethnic identity. Eventually, this process of identification with the real West leveled out and concealed national cultural differences among the active consumers of Western mass culture—contributing to what some scholars called the homogenization of Soviet culture, which meant a mass Russification of youth culture in Eastern Ukraine during the 1970s.

Cultural consumption in Dniepropetrovsk also led to what KGB and Communist Party officials considered deviational forms of youth activity. These activities were more than "arts of resistance to dominant political culture" and "strategies of the weak."[8] The new Soviet youth culture that originated during Brezhnev's rule was more a result of the transformation and consumption of dominant internal Soviet cultural practices and also new Western cultural influences.

According to Michel de Certeau, in social systems such as the city of Dniepropetrovsk, "the imposed knowledge and symbolisms [by the ideologists] become objects manipulated by practitioners [the Soviet youth] who have not produced them." Using de Certeau's ideas, we can say that the young people of Dniepropetrovsk subverted practices and representations that were imposed on them from within—not by rejecting them or by transforming them (though that occurred as well), but in many other, different ways. These young Soviet consumers of popular culture "metaphorized the dominant order: they made it function in another register. They remained within the system which they assimilated and which assimilated them externally. They diverted it without leaving it."[9] They used the sphere of leisure as the main arena of their cultural transformation. Simultaneously, books, rock and disco music, dance halls and discotheques, and films became their alternatives and spurs for transformations of the dominant cultural practices during late socialism. At the same time, the tastes and activities of the new youth culture resulted in new values and demands for cultural consumption, which gradually replaced and transformed traditional Soviet values and Communist ideological practices, even among the young Komsomol elite of the late 1970s and 1980s.

During the Brezhnev era, through cultural consumption and tourism, the people of the closed city developed their own "hierarchy of the West." In their imagination, the authentic West was associated only with Western developed industrial countries, such as the United States, Canada, the United Kingdom, France, Italy, West Germany, and the Netherlands. The developing countries of Latin America, Asia, and Africa took second place to the authentic West in their imaginary hierarchy. And Dniepropetrovsk's consumers put all the European socialist countries in the third position in their "hierarchy of the West," calling these countries "the substitute for the West."

These socialist "substitutes for the West" had their own hierarchy. Yugoslavia took the highest position among all the socialist substitutes. All Soviet consumers considered Yugoslavia the most authentic substitute for the "capitalist West." Hungary, East Germany, Poland, and Czechoslovakia took the next places after Yugoslavia in this ranking of the socialist substitutes. The last positions in this hierarchy of substitutes belonged to Bulgaria and Romania.

Finally, Dniepropetrovsk's consumers also developed an idea of the "Soviet West," which was less prestigious than the socialist substitutes for the West but was more accessible and real for the cultural imagination of Dniepropetrovsk's consumers. The Soviet West included the Baltic republics of Estonia, Latvia, and Lithuania, as well as Western Ukrainian cities such as L'viv.

"The West" became a constructive element in identity formation among the local youth during the Brezhnev era in the closed city. The association of "the West" with everything modern, progressive, and fashionable affected both Russian- and Ukrainian-speaking people. In various forms of cultural identities—Soviet, ethnic, religious, music, regional—in the region of Dniepropetrovsk, "the West" played a prominent role. And despite the region's Russification, especially through mass cultural consumption, the local version of Ukrainian national identity also became connected to the idea of the West. In the imagination of young Ukrainian patriots from Dniepropetrovsk, "the West" was always associated with the Western Ukrainian city of L'viv, where the Ukrainian language and Ukrainian culture prospered. In their imagination, "the authentic West" would be able to help and support a renaissance of Ukrainian culture in the Russified city of Dniepropetrovsk. The appeal of Dniepropetrovsk's Ukrainian poets to the West, their request for help from the West, turned them into political dissidents, and triggered police persecution in the period 1969–72.

Similar connections with the West by Dniepropetrovsk's religious population through attempts to modernize religious denominations in the region also contributed to antireligious campaigns there. Moreover, as the KGB discovered, the mass consumption of Western cultural products also influenced popular religiosity in the region. On the eve of perestroika in 1984, "registered religious people" made up 3 percent of the entire population, and at least 2 percent of these religious people lived in Dniepropetrovsk itself.

The most significant result of this "Westernization" of mass cultural consumption in the region was the involvement of young Communist apparatchiks in the process. Komsomol activists and local ideologists—who not only consumed Western cultural products, such as popular music and films, but also participated in the disco movement and tourism by the end of the Brezhnev era—promoted various forms of Western mass culture in Dniepropetrovsk. Eventually, these young Komsomol activists, such as Yulia Tymoshenko and Serhiy Tihipko, realized that their favorite idea of "the West" could bring profits. For this reason, "the West" became the central element of the first business enterprises in Dniepropetrovsk during the late socialist period. By selling Western films and music and organizing tourist trips abroad, young Communist apparatchiks, many of whom had ties to the closed city's secret rocket factory, discarded the ideological limitations of developed socialism and incorporated values that were associated with the "capitalist West."

The late Brezhnev era was the most important period for the spread of these values among Soviet youth. The story of "Western mass culture" in Dniepropetrovsk during the Brezhnev era highlights the complete failure of Soviet ideologists and the KGB to protect the youth of this strategically important center of the Soviet military-industrial complex from the "ideological pollution" of the Cold War confrontation between the "capitalist West" and the USSR's socialist ideological system. At the same time, it shows how the tastes and activities of the new "Westernized" youth culture created new values and demands for cultural consumption that gradually transformed and replaced traditional Soviet values and Communist ideological practices.

It can be said that the mass consumption of Western cultural products in the closed Soviet society contributed to the spread of cynicism among young people. The oppressive ideological atmosphere of Dniepropetrovsk as a closed city contributed not only to ideological and cultural confusion but also to the moral issue of ideological cynicism. The people of Dniepropetrovsk and other Russified regions of Eastern Ukraine dealt with this confusion and cynicism all the time.[10] As a consequence, the new, post-Soviet Ukrainian politicians, who had grown up in the region, brought their ideological and cultural confusion and resulting cynicism to the new post-Soviet politics of Ukraine.

Appendix: The Methodology
for the Interviews

This appendix explains the methodology used to conduct the interviews that are cited throughout the book. First, it gives the advertisement for local newspapers, radio, and television that was placed to find people to interview. Then it gives the questions asked in the interviews.

Advertisement for Local Newspapers, Radio, and Television

How well do we remember our lives before the collapse of the Soviet Union? Our feelings and experiences of the Soviet years are documented in personal writings, diaries, and correspondences that date to that time. These are important historical documents that should not be allowed to vanish. We are conducting a sociological and historical study of the period between the 1960s and the aftermath of the "Orange Revolution," and we are looking for personal written (or recorded) accounts of daily life at that time. We plan to interview you about everyday life during late socialism. You will be compensated (with cash) for each oral interview and/or your personal account of your daily life. We guarantee your privacy and confidentiality.

The Questions Asked in the Interviews

1. How old are you? What did you do from 1964 to 1984?
2. Can you describe a school that you had attended during this period of time?

3. Do you remember the most popular books that you and your friends read during the
   (a) 1960s?
   (b) 1970s?
   (c) 1980s?
4. Do you remember the most popular songs (and dances) that you and your friends listened to (and attended) during the
   (a) 1960s?
   (b) 1970s?
   (c) 1980s?
5. Do you remember the most popular films that you and your friends watched during the
   (a) 1960s?
   (b) 1970s?
   (c) 1980s?
6. Did you participate in any form of Soviet tourism? What were your impressions from your tourist travels, especially your trips abroad during the period from the 1960s to the 1980s?
7. Do you remember the most popular TV and radio shows that you and your friends watched and listened to during the
   (a) 1960s?
   (b) 1970s?
   (c) 1980s?
8. Did you participate in the discotheque movement in the late 1970s and early 1980s? What was the major source of music information for you during those days?
9. How often did you use the black market to get a favorite music recording or piece of clothing during the
   (a) 1960s?
   (b) 1970s?
   (c) 1980s?
10. What were your connections to the new post-Soviet leaders from the 1960s to the 1980s?
11. What were the most popular periodicals during your youth from the 1960s to the 1980s?
12. What did you think about the United States and other Western countries during the period from the 1960s to the 1980s?
13. Do you remember your favorite American songs, films, and books during the period from the 1960s to the 1980s?

14. What was the most remarkable cultural influence on you during the period from the 1960s to the 1980s?
15. What were the most important political and social skills of the Soviet era that helped you to survive and prosper after 1991?
16. Do you remember technical devices that you used for listening to and recording popular music?
17. How often did you visit church and/or religious meetings during the period from the 1960s to the 1980s? What was your attitude toward religion in those days?
18. What national language did you use at home, in school, and at work during the period from the 1960s to the 1980s?
19. Do you remember the most popular Ukrainian song during the period from the 1960s to the 1980s?
20. Do you remember any book written by a Ukrainian author that impressed you and aroused your interest in this author's work during the period from the 1960s to the 1980s?
21. How often did you buy things at the black market during the period from the 1960s to the 1980s? What did you usually buy there?
22. How often did you visit libraries during the period from the 1960s to the 1980s? Where did you get the most popular books—from the library, from personal collections, or through black marketers?
23. What did you like and dislike about the United States of America during the period from the 1960s to the 1980s?
24. Can you single out positive and negative aspects of your everyday life during the Brezhnev era?
25. What nationality do you think you belong to? When did you begin to identify yourself with this national group? Why?

Notes

Notes to the Introduction

1. The name of the city is a combination of two names—the Dniepro (Dnieper) River; and Grigorii Petrovskii, the famous Bolshevik and the first president of Soviet Ukraine. After 1991, this name had a new spelling—"Dnipropetrovs'k." Throughout the book, I use the spelling "Dniepropetrovsk," which was commonly used in the Soviet era.

2. Summer school diary of Andrei Vadimov, Dniepropetrovsk, May 20, 1974. He kept his diary in Russian from May 1970 to September 1977. This diary covers the events of his various (mainly summer) school breaks.

3. Ibid., July 15, 1974. Author interview with Vitalii Pidgaetskii at the Department of History, Dniepropetrovsk University, February 10, 1996; author's interviews with Mikhail Suvorov, Dniepropetrovsk, June 1, 1991, with Andrei Vadimov, Dnieprope-trovsk, July 20–21, 2003; and with Eduard Svichar in Vatutino, Cherkassy Region, Ukraine, June 8, 2004.

4. Derzhavnyi arkhiv Dnipropetrovs'koi oblasti (hereafter DADO), f. 19, op. 52, d. 72, ll. 1–18.

5. Author's interview with Igor T., KGB officer, Dniepropetrovsk, May 15, 1991. I should note that the perilous state of the USSR in the spring 1991 most likely contributed to the nature of this KGB officer's comments; he is a Ukrainian, and after 1991 he supported the idea of Ukrainian independence.

6. Author's interview with Igor T., May 15, 1991. Compare with the KGB reports in DADO, f. 19, op. 52, d. 72, ll. 1–18.

7. Author's interview with Igor T., May 15, 1991.

8. Ibid. Dniepropetrovsk's periodicals expressed similar concerns about the Westernization of local youth as early as the 1960s, at the beginning of the Beatlemania. These newspapers called the local enthusiasts of rock music "traitors" and portrayed, ironically, how they blindly imitated their foreign idols; substituted their "good Slavic names with foreign unpronounceable names," such as Alfred, Max, and Rex; and replaced their "normal dress with foreign fashions." See T. Savytskyi, "Perevertni," *Zoria,* June 6, 1965. See also the criticism of the "new music" in "Chaikovs'kyi i modni rytmy," *Prapor iunosti,* July 23, 1965.

9. *Dnepropetrovskii raketno-kosmicheskii tsentr: Kratkii ocherk stanovlenia i razvitia—DAZ-YuMZ-KBYu—Khronika dat i sobytii* (Dniepropetrovsk, 1994); A. G. Bolebrukh et al., eds., *Dnipropetrovs'k: vikhy istorii* (Dniepropetrovsk, 2001), 209–11, 229. See also Yurii Lukanov, *Tretii presydent: Politychnyi portret Leonida Kuchmy* (Kyiv, 1996), 13; and V. P. Gorbulin et al., eds., *Zemni shliakhy i zoriani orbity: Shtrykhy do portreta Leonida Kuchmy* (Kyiv, 1998), 6, 24–31. On the Soviet concept of "closed" cities—including Perm, Kuibyshev, and others—during the late socialist period, see Paul R. Josephson, *New Atlantis Revisited: Akademgorodok, the Siberian City of Science* (Princeton, N.J.: Princeton University Press, 1997). On the Dniepropetrovsk Region, see Vladimir A. Kozlov, *Neizvestnyi SSSR: Protivostoianie naroda i vlasti 1953–1985 gg.* (Moscow: OLMA Press, 2006), 408–16. Compare with Kate Brown, "Griddled Lives: Why Kazakhstan and Montana Are Nearly the Same Place," *American Historical Review* 106, no.1 (February 2001): 17–48.

10. Vyacheslav Pikhovshek et al., eds., *Dnipropetrovsk vs. Security Service* (Kyiv, 1996), 8; "Ukrains'kyi Nezalezhnyi Tsentr Politychnykh Doslidzhen'," in *"Dnipropetrovs'ka sim'ia": Informatsia stanom na 25 lystopada 1996 roku,* ed. V. Pikhovshek et al. (Kyiv, 1996), 15.

11. The pioneering studies in English on the Soviet cultural consumption concentrate mainly on Leningrad and Moscow. See Svetlana Boym, *Common Places: Mythologies of Everyday Life in Russia* (Cambridge, Mass.: Harvard University Press, 1994); and Hilary Pilkington, *Russia's Youth and Its Culture: A Nation's Constructors and Constructed* (London: Routledge, 1994). The sociology of rock music consumption in Leningrad is covered by Thomas Cushman, *Notes from Underground: Rock Music Counterculture in Russia* (Albany: State University of New York Press, 1995). Alexei Yurchak wrote an excellent anthropological study of late socialism that focuses mainly on Leningrad. See Alexei Yurchak, *Everything Was Forever, Until It Was No More: The Last Soviet Generation* (Princeton, N.J.: Princeton University Press, 2005). Another good study of Soviet hippies concentrates on L'viv: William Jay Risch, "Soviet 'Flower Children': Hippies and the Youth Counter-Culture in 1970s Lviv," *Journal of Contemporary History* 40, no. 3 (July 2005): 565–84. Also see another recent study focused on Moscow: Vladislav Zubok, *Zhivago's Children: The Last Russian Intelligentsia* (Cambridge, Mass.: Belknap Press of Harvard University Press, 2009). For a more balanced approach, see Catherine Wanner, *Burden of Dreams: History and Identity in Post-Soviet Ukraine* (University Park: Pennsylvania State University Press, 1998). See also a good collection of essays about the Brezhnev era: Edwin Bacon and Mark Sandle, eds., *Brezhnev Reconsidered* (New York: Palgrave Macmillan, 2002).

12. See these recent post-Soviet studies that have added two provincial Russian towns, Samara and Ulianovsk, to the traditional focus on Moscow: Hilary Pilkington, Elena Omel'chenko, et al., *Looking West? Cultural Globalization and Russian Youth Cultures* (University Park: Pennsylvania State University Press, 2002); and Elena Omel'chenko, *Molodiozh: Otkrytyi vopros* (Ulianovsk: Simbirskaia kniga, 2004).

13. See, especially, Ihor Sklovs'kyi, *Robitnycha molod' v etnosotsial'nykh zryshenniakh Ukrains'kogo suspil'stva: 70-ti—pochatok 90-kh rokiv XX stolittia* (Kirovograd, 2001); and these books in English: Serhy Yekelchyk, *Ukraine: Birth of a Modern Nation* (New York: Oxford University Press, 2007); Serhy Yekelchyk and Oliver Schmidtke, eds., *Europe's Last Frontier? Belarus, Moldova, and Ukraine between Russia and the European Union* (London: Palgrave Macmillan, 2007); Blair Ruble, *Creating Diversity Capital: Transnational Migrants in Montreal, Washington, and Kyiv* (Wash-

ington and Baltimore: Woodrow Wilson Center Press and Johns Hopkins University Press, 2005); Hiroaki Kuromiya, *Freedom and Terror in the Donbas* (New York: Cambridge University Press, 2003); Wanner, *Burden of Dreams;* Catherine Wanner, *Communities of the Converted: Ukrainians and Global Evangelism* (Ithaca, N.Y.: Cornell University Press, 2007); Kenneth C. Farmer, *Ukrainian Nationalism in the Post-Stalin Era: Myth, Symbols and Ideology in Soviet Nationalities Policy* (The Hague: Martinus Nijhoff, 1980); Andrew Wilson, *The Ukrainians: Unexpected Nation* (New Haven, Conn.: Yale University Press, 2002); Taras Kuzio, *Ukraine: State and Nation Building* (London: Routledge, 1998); Bohdan Nahaylo, *Ukrainian Resurgence* (Toronto: University of Toronto Press, 1999); and Marta Dyczok, *Ukraine: Movement without Change, Change without Movement* (London: Routledge, 2000). See also good studies of cultural production in Soviet Ukraine under Stalin: George O. Liber, *Soviet Nationality Policy, Urban Growth and Identity Change in the Ukrainian SSR 1923–1934* (New York: Cambridge University Press, 1992); idem, *Alexander Dovzhenko: A Life in Soviet Film* (London: British Film Institute, 2002); Serhy Yekelchyk, *Stalin's Empire of Memory: Russian-Ukrainian Relations in the Soviet Historical Imagination* (Toronto: University of Toronto Press, 2004).

14. For an example of the focus on L'viv and Donetsk, see Claudia Sabic and Kerstin Zimmer, "Ukraine: The Genesis of a Captured State," in *The Making of Regions in Post-Socialist Europe: The Impact of Culture, Economic Structure and Institutions— Case Studies from Poland, Hungary, Romania and Ukraine,* ed. Melanie Tatur (Wiesbaden, 2004), vol. 2, 107–354. Another good sociological survey of 1991 also completely ignored Dniepropetrovsk: N. I. Chernysh, I. V. Vasilieva, et al., eds., *Natsional'na samosvidomist' studets'koi molodi (Sotsiologichnyi analiz)* (Toronto: Canadian Institute of Ukrainian Studies Press, 1993). Even a good study on Ukrainian evangelicals concentrates mainly on the Kharkiv Region: Wanner, *Communities of the Converted.*

15. John Storey, *Cultural Consumption and Everyday Life* (London: Arnold, 1999), 135, 136. As Madan Sarup observes, "Our identities are in part a result of what we consume. Or to put it another way, what we consume and how we consume it says a great deal about who we are, who we want to be, and how others see us. Cultural consumption is perhaps one of the most significant ways we perform our sense of self. This does not mean that we are what we consume, that our cultural consumption practices determine our social being; but it does mean that what we consume provides us with a script with which we can stage and perform in a variety of ways the drama of who we are." Madan Sarup, *Identity, Culture and the Postmodern World* (Edinburgh: Edinburgh University Press, 1996), 105, 125. According to British scholars, "Human self is envisaged as neither the product of an external symbolic system, nor as a fixed entity which the individual can immediately and directly grasp; rather the self is a symbolic project that the individual actively constructs out of the symbolic materials which are available to him or her, materials which the individual weaves into a coherent account of who he or she is, a narrative of self-identity." See in detail: John B. Thompson, *The Media and Modernity: A Social Theory of the Media* (Cambridge: Polity Press, 1995), 207, 210; Storey, *Cultural Consumption,* 135, 136, 147. Simon Frith emphasized that the consumption of books, music, and films "constructs human sense of identity through the direct experiences it offers of the body, time and sociability, experiences which enable people to place themselves in imaginative cultural narratives." See Simon Frith, "Music and Identity," in *Questions of Cultural Identity,* ed. S. Hall and P. du Gay (London: Sage, 1996), 122, 124. As John Thompson noted, "These are narratives which people will change over time

as they draw on new symbolic materials, encounter new experiences and gradually re-define their identity in the course of a life trajectory." See Thompson, *Media and Modernity,* 210.

16. On globalization and the consumption of Western popular music in Eastern Europe, Asia, Latin America, and Africa, see Peter Manuel, *Popular Music of the Non-Western World: An Introductory Survey* (New York: Oxford University Press, 1988); Deanna Campbell Robinson et al., eds., *Music at the Margins: Popular Music and Global Cultural Diversity* (London: Sage, 1991); Nabeel Zuberi, *Sounds English: Transnational Popular Music* (Urbana: University of Illinois Press, 2001); and Harris M. Berger and Michael Thomas Carroll, eds., *Global Pop, Local Language* (Jackson: University Press of Mississippi, 2003). On the consumption of Western music in Communist China, see Nimrod Baranovitch, *China's New Voices: Popular Music, Ethnicity, Gender, and Politics, 1978–1997* (Berkeley: University of California Press, 2003). On cultural consumption, including American pop music, and identity formation in European countries, see Simon Frith, *Sound Effects: Youth, Leisure, and the Politics of Rock 'n' Roll* (New York: Pantheon Books, 1981); Simon Frith and Andrew Goodwin, eds., *On Record: Rock, Pop, and the Written Word* (New York: Pantheon Books, 1990); Dick Bradley, *Understanding Rock 'n' Roll: Popular Music in Britain, 1955–1964* (Philadelphia: Open University Press, 1992); Mel van Elteren, *Imagining America: Dutch Youth and Its Sense of Place* (Tilburg: Tilburg University Press, 1994); Bernard Gendon, *Between Montmartre and the Mudd Club: Popular Music and the Avant-Garde* (Chicago: University of Chicago Press, 2002); Hugh Dauncey and Steve Cannon, eds., *Popular Music in France from Chanson to Techno: Culture, Identity and Society* (Aldershot, U.K.: Ashgate, 2003); and David L. Looseley, *Popular Music in Contemporary France: Authenticity, Politics, Debate* (New York: Berg, 2003).

17. Andy Bennett, *Popular Music and Youth Culture: Music, Identity and Place* (New York: St. Martin's Press, 2000), 198.

18. The consumption of foreign goods and services "is always embedded in local circumstances." See van Elteren, *Imagining America,* 4, 18.

19. Hilary Pilkington, "'The Future Is Ours': Youth Culture in Russia, 1953 to the Present," in *Russian Cultural Studies: An Introduction,* ed. Catriona Kelly and David Shepherd (New York: Oxford University Press, 1998), 371. She noted that after 1953, the material base for growing cultural consumption among Soviet youth "was continued urbanization, the extension of the average period of education (leading young people to enter paid employment and start their own families later), an increasingly leisure-oriented society and, not least, a flourishing second economy." According to Pilkington, as a result of "a permanent deficit of consumer goods" in Soviet society, "artifacts of Western youth culture became key units of currency (home-produced recordings, blue jeans, bell-bottoms, badges, and Western rock albums) and their exchange and sale became a central part of Soviet youth cultural practice."

20. S. Frederick Starr, *Red and Hot: The Fate of Jazz in the Soviet Union 1917–1980* (New York: Limelight Editions, 1985); Artemy Troitsky, *Back in the USSR: The True Story of Rock in Russia* (London: Omnibus Press, 1987); Timothy W. Ryback, *Rock around the Bloc: A History of Rock Music in Eastern Europe and the Soviet Union* (New York: Oxford University Press, 1991); Richard Stites, *Russian Popular Culture: Entertainment and Society since 1900* (New York: Cambridge University Press, 1992); and Sabrina Petra Ramet, ed., *Rocking the State: Rock Music and Politics in Eastern Europe and Russia* (Boulder, Colo.: Westview Press, 1994). The last collection has two articles

devoted to Belarus and Ukraine: Maria Paula Survilla, "Rock Music in Belarus," in *Rocking the State,* ed. Ramet, 219–42; and Romana Bahry, "Rock Culture and Rock Music in Ukraine," in *Rocking the State,* ed. Ramet, 243–96. Unfortunately, a major part of this material covers the period after 1985. See also these studies based on Moscow and Leningrad sources: Cushman, *Notes from Underground;* Yngvar Bordewich Steinholt, *Rock in the Reservation: Songs from the Leningrad Rock Club, 1981–86* (New York: Mass Media Music Scholars' Press, 2004); Michael Urban with Andrei Evdokimov, *Russia Gets the Blues: Music, Culture, and Community in Unsettled Times* (Ithaca, N.Y.: Cornell University Press, 2004); Polly McMichael, "'After All, You're a Rock and Roll Star (At Least, That's What They Say)': *Roksi* and the Creation of the Soviet Rock Musician," *Slavonic and East European Review* 83, no. 4 (2005): 664–84; and Yurchak, *Everything Was Forever.* See also Eric Shiraev and Vladislav Zubok, *Anti-Americanism in Russia: From Stalin to Putin* (New York: Palgrave, 2000), 19–21; and Yale Richmond, *Cultural Exchange and the Cold War: Raising the Iron Curtain* (University Park: Pennsylvania State University Press, 2003), 11–13, 205–9. See also this collection of essays about Soviet youth: Jim Riordan, ed., *Soviet Youth Culture* (Bloomington: Indiana University Press, 1989); and this study of the youth entertainment in the Soviet Palaces of Culture: Anne White, *De-Stalinization and the House of Culture: Declining State Control over Leisure in the USSR, Poland and Hungary, 1953–89* (London: Routledge, 1990). Compare with David MacFadyen, *Red Stars: Personality and the Soviet Popular Song, 1955–1991* (Montreal: McGill–Queen's University Press, 2001).

21. Cushman, *Notes from Underground,* 43.

22. Uta G. Poiger, *Jazz, Rock, and Rebels: Cold War Politics and American Culture in a Divided Germany* (Berkeley: University of California Press, 2000), 1.

23. Ibid., 9, 2. Also see her articles: Uta G. Poiger, "Rock 'n' Roll, Female Sexuality, and the Gold War Battle over German Identities," *Journal of Modern History* 68 (September 1996): 577–616; and Uta G. Poiger, "A New, 'Western' Hero? Reconstructing German Masculinity in the 1950s," *Signs: Journal of Women in Culture and Society* 24, no. 1 (1998): 147–62.

24. David Gurevich, *From Lenin to Lennon: A Memoir of Russia in the Sixties* (San Diego: Harcourt Brace Jovanovich, 1991), 128. Compare with Andrei Makarevich, *"Sam ovtsa": Avtobiograficheskaia proza* (Moscow: Zakharov, 2002), 53, 90–91, 109–10, 116–18.

25. See William Taubman, *Khrushchev: The Man and His Era* (New York: W. W. Norton, 2003), 509 ff.

26. See the first scholarly biography of Brezhnev, published as a book in the Russian (formerly Soviet) series "Life of the Remarkable People": Leonid M. Mlechin, *Brezhnev* (Moscow: Molodaia gvardia, 2008). In the 1930s, during the Stalinist regime, the Communist Party and Soviet leadership always had to think about material consumption under socialism as a measure of their achievements in the historical struggle of a socialist system with a capitalist one. On "Soviet consumption" under Stalin, see Elena Osokina, *Za fasadom "stalinskogo izobilia": Raspredelenie i rynok v snabzhenii naselenia v gody industrializatsii, 1927–1941* (Moscow, 1998); Catriona Kelly and Vadim Volkov, "Directed Desires: Kulturnost' and Consumption," in *Constructing Russian Culture in the Age of Revolution: 1881–1940,* ed. C. Kelly and D. Shepherd (New York: Oxford University Press, 1998); Natalia Lebina, *Povsednevnaia zhizn' sovestskogo goroda: Normy i anomalii. 1920/1930 gody.* (Saint Petersburg, 1999); Sheila Fitzpatrick, *Everyday Stalinism: Ordinary Life in Extraordinary Times—Soviet Russia in the*

1930s (New York: Oxford University Press, 1999); and Jukka Gronow, *Caviar with Champagne: Common Luxury and the Ideals of the Good Life in Stalin's Russia* (Oxford: Berg, 2003), esp. 69–86. On tourism and consumption during late Stalinism, see also Anne E. Gorsuch, "'There's No Place Like Home': Soviet Tourism in Late Socialism," *Slavic Review* 62, no. 4 (Winter 2003): 760–85. And on "Stalinist culture as a particular Soviet incarnation of modern mass culture," see also David L. Hoffmann, *Stalinist Values: The Cultural Norms of Soviet Modernity, 1917–1941* (Ithaca, N.Y.: Cornell University Press, 2003), 10; on mass consumption under Stalin, see 118–45.

27. Leonid I. Brezhnev, *Report to the 24th Congress of the CPSU 1971* (Moscow: Progress, 1971), 12–53; Leonid I. Brezhnev, *Report to the 25th Congress of the CPSU 1976* (Moscow: Progress, 1976), 99; and Leonid I. Brezhnev, *Leninskim kursom* (Moscow: Politizdat, 1972), vol. 3, 24, 124, 235. On consumption and developed socialism, see A. Butenko, "O razvitom sotsialisticheskom obshchestve," *Kommunist,* 1972, no. 6, 48–58; and J. R. Millar, "The Little Deal: Brezhnev's Contribution to Acquisitive Socialism," *Slavic Review* 44, no. 4 (Winter 1985): 694–706. On a new "revisionist" approach to this problem, see Mark Harrison, "Economic Growth and Slowdown," in *Brezhnev Reconsidered,* ed. Bacon and Sandle, 38–67; Mark Sandle, "A Triumph of Ideological Hairdressing? Intellectual Life in the Brezhnev Era Reconsidered," in *Brezhnev Reconsidered,* ed. Bacon and Sandle, 135–64; and Mark Sandle, "Brezhnev and Developed Socialism: The Ideology of *Zastoi?*" in *Brezhnev Reconsidered,* ed. Bacon and Sandle, 165–87. Compare with the Cold War studies of the Brezhnev era: J. Seroka and S. Simon, eds., *Developed Socialism in the Soviet Bloc* (Boulder, Colo.: Westview Press, 1982); D. Kelley, *The Politics of Developed Socialism* (New York: Greenwood Press, 1986); and T. L. Thompson and R. Sheldon, eds., *Soviet Society and Culture* (Boulder, Colo.: Westview Press, 1988). Despite the negative treatment of Brezhnev's economic policy as a part of infamous "stagnation," even the typical American textbook in Soviet history for undergraduate students had to acknowledge this: "Criticizing the USSR's poor economic performance, [Brezhnev] singled out 'Group B' (consumer goods) enterprises. He castigated ministerial-level officials for treating consumer goods as 'something secondary and ancillary.'" See Woodford McClellan, *Russia: The Soviet Period and After* (Upper Saddle River, N.J.: Prentice Hill, 1998; orig. pub. 1986), 227, esp. 224–28. New textbooks in Soviet History usually ignore Brezhnev period. Compare with a sketchy overview of post-Stalin development by Nicholas V. Riasanovsky and Mark D. Steinberg, *A History of Russia, Seventh Edition* (New York: Oxford University Press, 2005), 529 ff. A much better overview is given by Ronald Grigor Suny, *The Soviet Experiment: Russia, the USSR, and the Successor States* (New York: Oxford University Press, 1998), 421–46.

28. See a pioneering study of this system in English language: Alena V. Ledeneva, *Russia's Economy of Favours: Blat, Networking and Informal Exchange* (New York: Cambridge University Press, 1998).

29. In the new interpretation of Soviet consumerism, the Stalinist "noble objectives of education and cultural growth of Soviet citizens" still dominated the ideological discourse of the Brezhnev era. On this, see Gorsuch, "'There's No Place,'" 781; and Kelly and Volkov, "Directed Desires," 293. See also Yurchak, *Everything Was Forever.*

30. She emphasized that in the Soviet Union, "consumption was not interpreted as an evil in itself. Indeed the consumption of spiritual and leisure artifacts (cinema, concerts, theater, and fashion) was considered a normal part of responsible free-time activity (and reflected the much propagandized rapid rise in the material well-being, level of

education, and culture of young people)." At the same time, she noted that "consumption, however, was sharply contrasted to consumerism, which represented the disharmony of material and spiritual demands and which turned people into the slaves of things. The development of rational needs was the way in which consumption in socialist society was differentiated from consumerist psychology alien to socialism. Rational needs did not express narcissistic pleasure principles based on the use of particular commodity forms for self-gratification but rather allowed for the all-round harmonious development of the individual without contradicting the social good." Pilkington, "'Future Is Ours,'" 373.

31. See Mlechin, *Brezhnev;* Boym, *Common Places;* Nina Tumarkin, *The Living & the Dead: The Rise and Fall of the Cult of World War II in Russia* (New York: Basic Books, 1994); and Nina Tumarkin, *Lenin Lives! The Lenin Cult in Soviet Russia* (Cambridge, Mass.: Harvard University Press, 1997).

32. See Starr, *Red and Hot,* especially his chapter "The Rock Inundation, 1968–1980," 289–315; Ryback, *Rock around the Bloc,* 50–65, 102–14, 149–66, 211–22; and Stites, *Russian Popular Culture,* especially his chapter "The Brezhnev Culture Wars 1964–1984," 148–77.

33. See Ellen Propper Mickiewicz, *Media and the Russian Public* (New York: Praeger, 1981); White, *De-Stalinization;* Dmitry Shlapentokh and Vladimir Shlapentokh, *Soviet Cinematography 1918–1991: Ideological Conflict and Social Reality* (New York: Aldine de Gruyter, 1993); and Denise J. Youngblood, *Russian War Films: On the Cinema Front, 1914–2005* (Lawrence: University of Kansas Press, 2007). On the cultural consumption of Indian films by Soviet moviegoers after Stalin, see Sudha Rajagopalan, "Emblematic of the Thaw: Hindi Films in Soviet Cinemas," *South Asian Popular Culture* 4, no. 2 (October 2006): 83–100; and Sudha Rajagopalan, *Indian Films in Soviet Cinemas: The Culture of Movie-going after Stalin* (Bloomington: Indiana University Press, 2009).

34. See, especially, Stephen Lovell, *The Russian Reading Revolution: Print Culture in the Soviet and Post-Soviet Eras* (New York: St. Martin's Press, 2000).

35. Ben Fowkes, "The National Question in the Soviet Union under Leonid Brezhnev: Policy and Response," in *Brezhnev Reconsidered,* ed. Bacon and Sandle, 68–89; Gerhard Simon, *Nationalism and Policy toward the Nationalities in the Soviet Union: From Totalitarian Dictatorship to Post-Stalinist Society,* trans. Karen Forster and Oswald Forster (Boulder, Colo.: Westview Press, 1991); Yitzhak M. Brudny, *Reinventing Russia: Russian Nationalism and the Soviet State, 1953–1991* (Cambridge, Mass.: Harvard University Press, 1998).

36. G. P. Dolzhenko, *Istoria turizma v dorevoliutsionnoi Rossii i SSSR* (Rostov, 1988), 150. See also Denis J. B. Shaw, "The Soviet Union," in *Tourism and Economic Development in Eastern Europe and the Soviet Union,* ed. Derek R. Hall (London: Belhaven Press, 1999), 137–40. On tourism and the Soviet trade unions, see Blair Ruble, *Soviet Trade Unions: Their Development in the 1970s* (Cambridge: Cambridge University Press, 1981). See also the papers in a recent collection about tourism in socialist countries, especially Karl D. Qualls, "'Where Each Stone Is History': Travel Guides in Sevastopol after World War II," in *Turizm: The Russian and East European Tourist under Capitalism and Socialism,* ed. Anne S. Gorsuch and Diane P. Koenker (Ithaca, N.Y.: Cornell University Press, 2006), 163–85; and Christian Noack, "Coping with the Tourist: Planned and 'Wild' Mass Tourism on the Soviet Black Sea Coast," in *Turizm,* ed. Gorsuch and Koenker, 281–304.

37. See, especially, Maurice Friedberg, *A Decade of Euphoria: Western Literature in Post-Stalin Russia, 1954–64* (Bloomington: Indiana University Press, 1977); Maurice Friedberg, *Russian Culture in the 1980s* (Washington, D.C.: Georgetown University Press and Center for Strategic and International Studies, 1985); Ellen Mickiewicz, *Split Signals: Television and Politics in the Soviet Union* (New York: Oxford University Press, 1988), 32–34; Vladimir Shlapentokh, *The Public and Private Life of the Soviet People: Changing Values in Post-Stalin Russia* (New York: Oxford University Press, 1989), 139–52; Vladimir Shlapentokh, *Soviet Intellectuals and Political Power: The Post-Stalin Era* (Princeton, N.J.: Princeton University Press, 1990), 120–21, 123–25, 150, 225–26; and Robert D. English, *Russia and the Idea of the West: Gorbachev, Intellectuals, and the End of the Cold Wa*r (New York: Columbia University Press, 2000).

38. For a good summary of the post-Soviet sociological studies in Russia devoted to the problems of "Homo Soveticus" in historical anthropology during late socialism, see L. D. Gudkov, "Pererozhdeniia 'Sovetskogo cheloveka' (Ob odnom issledovatel'skom proekte Levada-Tsentra)," in *Odissei: Chelovek v istorii—2007—Istoria kak igra metaphor* (Moscow: Nauka, 2007), 398–436.

39. Bacon and Sandle, *Brezhnev Reconsidered,* 1, 4, 19; compare this with the good scholarly analysis of Brezhnev's diplomacy given by Vladislav M. Zubok, *A Failed Empire: The Soviet Union in the Cold War from Stalin to Gorbachev* (Chapel Hill: University of North Carolina Press, 2007).

40. Katherine Verdery, *National Ideology under Socialism: Identity and Cultural Politics in Ceauşescu's Romania* (Berkeley: University of California Press, 1991). See also her next book: Katherine Verdery, *What Was Socialism, and What Comes Next?* (Princeton, N.J.: Princeton University Press, 1996). Following Antonio Gramsci's theory of cultural hegemony, Verdery demonstrates how both cultural production and consumption became tools of ideological control in socialist society. According to her, "culture's 'means of production'" became important to the bureaucratic drive to "accumulate allocative power." In socialist countries, means of cultural production included not only certain forms of accumulated knowledge but also language. As Verdery noted, for a Communist Party "bent on transforming consciousness, control over language is one of the most vital requirements." Verdery, *National Ideology,* 89.

41. According to Szemere: "Without an appropriate amount of space and freedom for music activities to be structured, on the grassroots level at least, by fans and musicians themselves, the music becomes vulnerable and corruptible, politically and commercially alike. The control exercised over the production, dissemination and use of pop and rock music in socialist societies, has involved the hegemony's attempts to isolate the sound or the idiom—once co-opted—from a set of extramusical and contextual elements constituting rock as a distinctive cultural practice. The underlying intention, even if not the result of such intervention is de-contextualization, through which the music, due to the indeterminacy of its meaning as a non-representational form of communication, becomes capable of functioning either as conventional entertainment (de-politicization), or, in case of more offensive state policies, of serving as a 'spoonful of sugar' to help the ideological medicine go down (re-politicization)." Szemere is cited in *Music at the Margins,* ed. Robinson et al., 77–78. See also her study: Anna Szemere, *Up from the Underground: The Culture of Rock Music in Postsocialist Hungary* (University Park: Pennsylvania State University Press, 2001).

42. The important influence came also from Verdery, *What Was Socialism.* See also Wanner, *Burden of Dreams.*

43. Yurchak, *Everything Was Forever,* 32.

44. As a result, the Soviet culture of late socialism, he notes, "included two coexisting, and often incongruent, spheres of everyday life: the official and the nonofficial spheres. Practices in the official sphere were observed and controlled by the state and involved real and simulated support of the official ideology. Virtually every Soviet citizen participated in both spheres on a daily basis." Alexei Yurchak, "Gagarin and the Rave Kids: Transforming Power, Identity, and Aesthetics in Post-Soviet Nightlife," in *Consuming Russia: Popular Culture, Sex, and Society since Gorbachev,* ed. Adele Marie Barker (Durham, N.C.: Duke University Press, 1999), 80; see also A. Yurchak "The Cynical Reason of Late Socialism: Power, Pretense and the *Anekdot,*" *Public Culture* 9, no. 2 (1997): 161–62; and Yurchak, *Everything Was Forever.*

45. For how various scholars used this metaphor before Yurchak, see English, *Russia and the Idea of the West,* 22; and Gordon K. Lewis, *The Growth of the Modern West Indies* (New York: Monthly Review Press, 1968), 57 ff.

46. Yurchak, *Everything Was Forever,* 34–35, 161–62. He begins a genealogy of this metaphor with Michel Foucault's ideas. See Michel Foucault, *Aesthetics, Method, and Epistemology,* ed. James Faubion (New York: New Press, 1998), 312.

47. On his methods, see Yurchak, *Everything Was Forever,* 29–33. The same idealization of the interviewees' information and credulity is obvious in William Jay Risch's study of L'viv. Risch took at face value all information from people who exaggerated the significance of the hippie movement for the local youth culture. See Risch, "Soviet 'Flower Children.'" Overall, Yurchak concentrates only on the intellectual elites of Leningrad and Moscow. See the similar, sometimes even more elitist, approach in the recent book about the Soviet intelligentsia: Zubok, *Zhivago's Children.* Compare these elitist studies with a fascinating illustrated book about everyday life in the USSR during the 1960s, Leonid Parfionov, *Namedni. 1961–1970. Nasha Era* (Moscow: Kolibri, 2009).

48. Even the list of forbidden rock bands, which Yurchak published in his book, came from the Ukrainian provincial town of Nikolaev. With only a few exceptions, all Yurchak's information derived from his hometown, Leningrad / Saint Petersburg. See Yurchak, *Everything Was Forever,* 214–15.

49. On Allan Nevins and oral history, see Gerald L. Fetner, *Immersed in Great Affairs: Allan Nevins and the Heroic Age of American History* (Albany: State University of New York Press, 2004), 140–42. On Soviet American studies, see Sergei I. Zhuk, "Colonial America, the Independence of the Ukraine, and Soviet Historiography: The Personal Experience of a Former Soviet Americanist," *Pennsylvania History* 62, no. 4 (1995): 468–90.

50. See the appendix for an explanation of the methodology I used in interviewing people.

51. Throughout this book, these diaries are cited as "summer school diaries," but sometimes the entries are also from other school breaks that were not during the summer months.

52. I also used readers' records (*chitatel'skie formuliary*) and librarians' monthly reports (*mesiachnye otchioty*) for the 1970s from the Dniepropetrovsk Central City Library and the Dniepropetrovsk Central Regional Library.

53. I refer to the collection under this title: *Reabilitovani istorieiu* [Those who were rehabilitated by history], ed. V. V. Ivanenko: vol. 1: *Vidrodzhena pam'iat'* (Dniepropetrovsk', 1999); vol. 2: *Svidchennia z mynuvshyny: Movoiu dokumentiv* (Dniepropetrovsk', 2001); vol. 3: *Mynule z girkym prysmakom: Represii v istorychnii retrospektyvi radians'kogo suspil'stva* (Dniepropetrovsk', 2002). I also used other collections of published documents, e.g., *Vinok pam'iati Olesia Honchara: Spogady—Khronika,* ed. V. D.

Honchar and V. Ia. P'ianov (Kyiv, 1997); and *Ternystym shliakhom do khramu: Oles' Honchar v suspil'no-politychnomu zhytti Ukrainy,* ed. P. T. Tron'ko, O. G. Bazhan, and Yu. Z. Danyliuk (Kyiv, 1999).

Notes to Chapter 1

1. The city of now called Dniepropetrovsk was founded on the location of Ukrainian Cossack settlements by the Russian Imperial administration in 1776. It was called Ekaterinoslav, or "Glory of Catherine" in Russian. In 1926, the local Soviet administration decided to change the name of the city. Ekaterinoslav sounded too "old fashioned," too "Imperial Russian," because it was connected to the "oppressive regime" of the Empress Catherine II. The Regional Congress of the Soviets voted in 1926 to rename the city. Its new name was a combination of the name of the Dnieper River with the last name of Grigorii Petrovskii, head of the All-Ukrainian Executive Committee of the Soviets, an "old Bolshevik" and a member of the "Old Leninist guard." Petrovskii was considered the most famous organizer of the working-class movement in the region of Ekaterinoslav before the Revolution of 1917. See A. G. Bolebrukh et al., eds., *Dnipropetrovs'k: Vikhy istorii* (Dniepropetrovsk: Grani, 2001), 156. The region of Dniepropetrovsk is located in the middle of the Dnieper River Valley in the southeastern part of Ukraine. Its neighbors in the North are the regions of Poltava and Kharkiv; in the South, the regions of Zaporizhie and Kherson; in the West, the regions of Nikolaev and Kirovograd; and in the East, the region of Donetsk. The region of Dniepropetrovsk occupies 31,900 square kilometers, or 5.3 percent of the entire territory of Ukraine. Historically, this region became a melting pot for the multinational Russian Empire. See I. V. Vasiliev et al., eds., *Istoria gorodov i siol Ukrainskoi SSR v 26-ti tomakh: Dnepropetrovskaia oblast'* (Kyiv: Glavnaia redaktsia Ukrainskoi Sovestskoi Entsiklopedii, 1977), 9; and Sergei I. Zhuk, *Russia's Lost Reformation: Peasants, Millennialism, and Radical Sects in Southern Russia and Ukraine, 1830–1917* (Washington and Baltimore: Woodrow Wilson Center Press and Johns Hopkins University Press, 2004), 33–59.

2. Before 1941, Dniepropetrovsk became the most urbanized region of Soviet Ukraine. Almost 53 percent the region's population lived in sixteen cities and towns. See Vasiliev et al., *Istoria gorodov i siol,* 55; and Bolebrukh et al., *Dnipropetrovs'k: Vikhy istorii,* 159–64.

3. Bolebrukh et al., *Dnipropetrovs'k: Vikhy istorii,* 219. A total of 5.4 percent of steel, 9 percent of rolled iron, 28 percent of all pipes, 62 percent of combine beet harvesters, 27.9 percent of television sets, and 8.5 percent of knitted wear in Ukraine was produced in the city of Dniepropetrovsk.

4. K. A. Markov, "Uchastie nemetskikh voennoplennykh i internirovannykh v vosstanovlenii narodnogo khoziaistva Dnepropetrovskoi oblastiv pervye polevoennye gody," in *Voprosy Germanskoi istorii: Ukrainsko-nemetskie sviazi v novoe i noveishee vremia—Mezhvuzovskii sbornik nauchnykh trudov,* ed. S. I. Bobyliova (Dniepropetrovsk, 1995), 158–72.

5. Yurii Lukanov, *Tretii president: Politychnyi portret Leonida Kuchmy* (Kyiv, 1996), 12.

6. V. P. Gorbulin et al., *Zemni shliakhy i zoriani orbity: Shtrykhy do portreta Leonida Kuchmy* (Kyiv, 1998), 9, 62–63.

7. Irina V. Strazheva, *Tiulpany s kosmodroma* (Moscow, 1978); V. P. Platonov and V. P. Gorbulin, *Mykhailo Kyz'mych Yangel'* (Kyiv, 1979); A. P. Romanov and V. S. Gubarev, *Konstruktory* (Moscow, 1989); M. I. Kuznetskii and I. V. Stazheva, eds., *Baikonur: Chudo XX veka—Vospominania vevteranov Baikonura ob akademike Mikhaile Kuz'miche Yangele* (Moscow, 1995); M. I. Kuznetskii, ed., *Baikonur, Korolev, Yangel* (Voronezh, 1997); Leonid M. Mlechin, *Brezhnev* (Moscow: Molodaia gvardia, 2008), 372–79.

8. See the descriptions of the Yuzhmash rocket production in English by Rex Hall and David J. Shayler, *The Rocket Men: Vostok and Voskhod, the First Soviet Manned Spaceflights* (Chichester: Praxis, 2001), 316 ff; Asif A. Siddiqi, *Sputnik and the Soviet Space Challenge* (Gainesville: University Press of Florida, 2003), 97, 113, 114, 164, 177, 285; and Mike Gruntman, *Blazing the Trail: The Early History of Spacecraft and Rocketry* (Reston, Va.: American Institute of Aeronautics and Astronautics, 2004), 287 ff.

9. *Dnepropetrovskii raketno-kosmicheskii tsentr: Kratkii ocherk stanovlenia i razvitia—DAZ-YuMZ-KBYu—Khronika dat i sobytii* (Dniepropetrovsk, 1994); Bolebrukh et al., *Dnipropetrovs'k: Vikhy istorii,* 209–11, 229. See also Lukanov, *Tretii president,* 13.

10. Gorbulin et al., *Zemni shliakhy i zoriani orbity,* 6, 24–31.

11. "Paritet z Amerikoiu stvoriuvavsia i v Dnipropetrovs'ku," in *Zemni shliakhy i zoriani orbity,* ed. Gorbulin et al., 20–37. Many specialists consider the unique rocket complex SS-18 (a missile system known as a "soil-soil" type) manufactured by Yuzhmash as an important material factor that pushed Soviet and American administrations in the direction of détente during the first half of the 1970s. Americans called these Soviet rockets "Satan" missiles.

12. Bolebrukh et al., *Dnipropetrovs'k: Vikhy istorii,* 211.

13. Ibid., 211–12.

14. Valentina I. Lazebnik, *Oziorka nasha: Istoricheskii ocherk o Dnepropetrovskom Tsentral'nom rynke,* ed. G. A. Efimenko (Dniepropetrovsk, 2001), 167–85. The most popular name for this market from prerevolutionary times was Oziorka.

15. Vasiliev et al., *Istoria gorodov i siol,* 72; Bolebrukh et al., *Dnipropetrovs'k: Vikhy istorii,* 233. See also recent books about Brezhnev: Aleksandr Maisurian, *Drugoi Brezhnev* (Moscow, 2004); and Mlechin, *Brezhnev.*

16. "Ukrains'kyi Nezalezhnyi Tsentr Politychnykh Doslidzhen'," in *"Dnipropetrovs'ka sim'ia": Informatsia stanom na 25 lystopada 1996 roku,* ed. V. Pikhovshek et al. (Kyiv, 1996); Bohdan Nahaylo, *The Ukrainian Resurgence* (Toronto: University of Toronto Press, 1999), 36, 69; Andrew Wilson, *The Ukrainians: Unexpected Nation* (New Haven, Conn.: Yale University Press, 2000), 162.; Mlechin, *Brezhnev,* 387 ff.

17. Vyacheslav Pikhovshek et al., eds., *Dnipropetrovsk vs. Security Service* (Kyiv, 1996), 8. Along with the Physical-Technical Department of Dnipropetrovsk State University, the Dnipropetrovsk Metallurgical Institute also opened the road to the political careers of many of Brezhnev's close friends, who in the 1970s and 1980s became important members of the Kremlin Nomenclature. Nikolai Tikhonov, a former head of the Dnipropetrovsk Sovnarkhoz during the 1930s, ruled the Soviet Union from 1980 to 1985 as the head of the USSR Council of Ministers. He was also one of the deputies of the Soviet prime minister between 1966 and 1976, and the first deputy to the prime minister from 1976 to 1980. Another deputy to the Soviet prime minister, I. Novikov, was also a graduate of the Dnipropetrovsk Metallurgical Institute. Nikolai Shcholokov, who graduated from the same institute in 1933, was the All-Union Soviet minister of public order from 1966 to 1968, and from 1968 to 1982 he was the USSR's minister of the in-

terior. Georgii Tsynev, who graduated from the same institute in 1932, worked as one of the deputies of the head of the KGB from 1970 to 1982. From 1971 to 1976, he was also a member of the Central Revision Committee of CPSU. Tsynev was the first deputy to the head of the KGB from 1982 to 1989. Victor Chebrikov, who graduated from the Dniepropetrovsk Metallurgical Institute in 1950, was one of the leaders of the city party organization in Dniepropetrovsk from 1961 to 1971. In 1971, he became the head of the personnel department of the USSR's KGB and the first deputy to the head of this organization. From 1982 to 1989 Chebrikov was the head of the KGB. See also in "Ukrains'kyi Nezalezhnyi Tsentr Politychnykh Doslidzhen'," 11–12, 272–74.

18. Kriuchkov, a Yuzhmash representative, was in charge of the Department of Defense on Shcherbytsky's team. Aleksandr Kapto, who worked as a secretary of both the Dniepropetrovsk Komsomol organization and the All-Ukrainian Komsomol in Kyiv in the 1960s, was in charge of the Department of Culture in the Central Committee of the Communist Party of Ukraine (CPU) from 1978. Shcherbytsky's assistant from 1972 to 1984 was Konstantin Prodan, who began his career in the Komsomol organization of the city of Dniepropetrovsk. As a contemporary political analysts noted, "Officially Prodan was put in charge of industrial production, though, according to insiders of the former CPU Central Committee, his principal function was 'maintaining' contact with Leonid Brezhnev's assistant Georgii Tsukanov in Moscow." See Pikhovshek et al., *Dnipropetrovsk vs. Security Service,* 33–34; and "Ukrains'kyi Nezalezhnyi Tsentr Politychnykh Doslidzhen'," 48–103.

19. Author's interview with Serhii Tihipko, a director of "Privatbank" in Dniepropetrovsk, October 12, 1993. See also the author's conversations with Karlo A. Markov, Dniepropetrovsk University, April 12, 1992; and with Natalia V. Bocharova, Dniepropetrovsk University, March 15, 1993.

20. The phrase "pioneers of ideological campaigns" belongs to a local retired KGB officer. See my interview with Igor T., KGB officer, Dniepropetrovsk, May 15, 1991. On interference of Moscow representatives of the Dniepropetrovsk clan in the local KGB business in 1968, see Derzhavnyi arkhiv Dnipropetrovs'koi oblasti, f. 19, op. 52, d. 72, ll. 1–18.

21. See, especially, the memoirs of the Ukrainian dissident Leonid Plyushch, who was transferred from a regular prison to Igren *psikhushka* for his "nationalism" and spent 1973–74 there: Leonid Plyushch, with a contribution by Tatyana Plyushch, *History's Carnival: A Dissident's Autobiography,* ed. and trans. Marco Carynnyk (New York: Harcourt Brace Jovanovich, 1979), 304–26, 340–49.

22. Author's interview with Igor T., May 15, 1991.

23. Tsentral'noe Statisticheskoe Upravlenie Dnepropetrovskoi oblasti, *Dnepropetrovshchina v tsifrakh: K 40-letiu pobedy v Velikoi Otechestvennoi voine,* ed. L. G. Glushkina (Dniepropetrovsk, 1985), 10, 11.

24. "O vozrastnoi structure, urovne obrazovania, natsional'nom sostave, iazykakh i istochnikakh sredstv sushchestvovania naselenia Dnepropetrovskoi oblasti po dannym Vsessoiuznoi perepisis naselenia na 15 ianvaria 1970 goda," *Dneprovskaia Pravda,* June 26, 1971; Goskomstat USSR, Dnepropetrovskoe oblatnoe upravlenie statistiki, *Naselenie Dnepropetrovskoi oblasti po dannym Vsesoiuznoi perepisi naseleniia 1989 goda* (Dnepropetrovsk, 1991), 100, 102.

25. Goskomstat USSR, Dnepropetrovskoe oblatnoe upravlenie statistiki, *Naselenie Dnepropetrovskoi oblasti po dannym Vsesoiuznoi perepisi naseleniia 1989 goda,* 106,

108, 119, 122. According to contemporaries, the high salaries and better living conditions attracted representatives of various nationalities from different national republics who spoke also Russian rather than the Ukrainian language in Dniepropetrovsk. See my interviews with Evgen D. Prudchenko, Central Library of the Dniepropetrovsk Region, July 18, 2007; and with Galina V. Smolenskaia, Central Library of the Dniepropetrovsk Region, July 18, 2007. Natalia Vasilenko (b. 1959) also recalled how people from the Caucasus and the Russian Federation settled in the city of Dniepropetrovsk. See my interview with Natalia Vasilenko, Dniepropetrovsk, July 19, 2007. Vladimir Donets (b. 1953) recalled a similar development in another industrial city of the Dniepropetrovsk Region, Dnieprodzerzhinsk; see my interview with Vladimir Donets, Dniepropetrovsk, July 19, 2007.

26. Tsentral'noe Statisticheskoe Upravlenie Dnepropetrovskoi oblasti, *Dnepropetrovshchina v tsifrakh,* 55. Soviet statisticians singled out ten major marks of the region's increasing prosperity: number of workers (increased 3.5 times by 1984), retail trade per capita (6.9 times), city housing (5.4 times), number of students in secondary schools (1.3 times), number of students in vocational schools (6.5 times), number of students in colleges and universities (4.6 times), number of specialists with college decrees (14 times), number of children in kindergartens and elementary schools (8 times), number of physicians (5.3 times), and the number of beds in hospitals (20.8 times).

27. TsSU USSR, Statisticheskoe upravlenie Dnepropetrovskoi oblasti, *Molodiozh Dnepropetrovskoi oblasti: Statisticheskii sbornik,* ed. L. T. Glushkina and V. F. Iagniuk (Dnepropetrovsk, 1985), 1.

28. Ibid., 5.

Notes to Chapter 2

1. See the text of Lenin's essay "The Question of Nationalities or 'Autonomization,'" in *Lenin and the Making of the Soviet State: A Brief History with Documents,* ed. Jeffrey Brooks and Georgiy Chernyavskiy (Boston: Bedford / St. Martin's Press, 2007), 159–61. Also see Robert Service, *Lenin: A Biography* (Cambridge, Mass.: Harvard University Press, 2000), 455–58; Graham Smith, ed., *The Nationalities Question in the Soviet Union* (London: Longman, 1990), 2–7; Gerhard Simon, *Nationalism and Policy toward the Nationalities in the Soviet Union: From Totalitarian Dictatorship to Post-Stalinist Society,* trans. Karen Forster and Oswald Forster (Boulder, Colo.: Westview Press, 1991), 20–24; and Ben Fowkes, "The National Question in the Soviet Union under Leonid Brezhnev: Policy and Response," in *Brezhnev Reconsidered,* ed. Edwin Bacon and Mark Sandle (New York: Palgrave Macmillan, 2002), 72. On the results of de-Stalinization, see William Taubman, *Khrushchev: The Man and His Era* (New York: W. W. Norton, 2003), 270ff. On the effects of de-Stalinization on Ukraine, see Serhy Yekelchyk, *Ukraine: Birth of a Modern Nation* (New York: Oxford University Press, 2007), 154–63.

2. Derzhavnyi arkhiv Dnipropetrovs'koi oblasti (hereafter DADO), f. 9870, op. 1, d. 48, ll. 3–4.

3. Ibid.

4. During the post-Stalin era, similar problems existed in the Russian Federation as well. Some scholars called them a rise of "ethnonationalism." See Yitzhak M. Brudny,

Reinventing Russia: Russian Nationalism and the Soviet State, 1953–1991 (Cambridge, Mass.: Harvard University Press, 1998), 28ff.

5. What follows is based on documents from DADO, f. 9870, op. 1, d. 48, ll. 4–8.

6. The Historical-Philological Department later was divided in two different departments: History and Philology.

7. What follows is based on documents from DADO, f. 9870, op. 1, d. 48, l. 9–11.

8. A *kobza* is an old Ukrainian music string instrument similar to a mandolin.

9. This event is known in Ukrainian historiography as the Pereyaslav Rada of 1654.

10. Taras Shevchenko, "Velykyi liokh," in *Povne zibrannia tvoriv u dvanadtsiaty tomakh,* by Taras Shevchenko (Kyiv: "Naukova dumka," 1989), vol. 1, 221–33; also see his comments about the poem on 494–97.

11. On the Stalinist interpretation of these events, see Serhy Yekelchyk, *Stalin's Empire of Memory: Russian-Ukrainian Relations in the Soviet Historical Imagination* (Toronto: University of Toronto Press, 2004), 96–107.

12. DADO, f. 9870, op. 1, d. 48, l. 9.

13. Ibid., ll. 10–11.

14. See Shevchenko, *Povne zibrannia,* vol. 1, 494–97; and Dina Zisserman-Brodsky, *Constructing Ethnopolitics in the Soviet Union: Samizdat, Deprivation, and the Rise of Ethnic Nationalism* (New York: Palgrave, 2003), 26.

15. For official interpretations, see the documents of the Ukrainian Ministry of Culture devoted to preparation for the celebration of the 150th anniversary of Taras Shevchenko in Ukraine in 1964 in Tsenral'nyi Derzhavnyi Arkhiv Vyshchykh Organiv Vlady ta Upravlinnia Ukrainy, f. 5116, op. 4, d. 147, ll. 1–105.

16. On the movement of the clubs of creative youth in Kyiv and L'viv, see G. Kasianov, *Nezgodni: Ukrains'ka intelligentsia v rusi oporu 1960–80-kh rokiv* (Kyiv: Lybid, 1995), 18–21; and Borys Zakharov, *Narys istorii dysydents'kogo rukhu v Ukraini (1956–1987)* (Kharkiv: Folio, 2003), 81–86.

17. In April 1960, Natalia Televnaya, head of the literary workshop at the Palace of Students, was fired "for anti-Soviet remarks" in public. DADO, f. 9870, op. 1, d. 48, ll. 16–18. These young experimental poets, such as Oleksandr Zaivii and Yurii Zavgorodnii, read books by Ukrainian writers like Panteleimon Kulish and Volodymyr Vinnichenko.

18. As it turned out, during the years 1964–65, they actively corresponded (using various precautions) with poets who lived in Kyiv, such as E. Binushevsky, Yurii Zavgorodnii, L. Maksimets, and S. Plachinda, who "were notorious for their nationalistic aspirations." In September 1965, Yurii Zavgorodnii, a cousin of Vodolazhchenko, brought to Dniepropetrovsk a photocopy of a book "of nationalistic content" by Ivan Koshelivets, *A Modern Literature in the Ukrainian SSR,* which had been printed in the Federal Republic of Germany. Through Vodolazhchenko, copies of this book went to a student at DGU, I. Sokul'sky, and to G. Malovik, an editor in the agricultural department of the Dniepropetrovsk Television Studio. See DADO, f. 19, op. 50, d. 56, ll. 17–18; and Ivan Koshelivets, *Panorama nainovishoï literatury URSR: Poeziia, proza, krytyka* (New York: Proloh, 1963). On L'viv influences, see *U vyri shistdesiatnytskogo rukhu: Pogliad z vidstani chasu,* ed. Voldymyr Kvitnevyi (Lviv: Kameniar, 2003), 45, 52, 53; and Kasianov, *Nezgodni,* 119.

19. DADO, f. 19, op. 50, d. 56, ll. 17–19; the citation is on l. 19. By the end of November 1965, Vodolazhchenko left the editor's position at the radio station in the Magdalinovka District of Dniepropetrovsk Region. As a junior undergraduate student taking

evening classes at the Historical-Philological Department of DGU, he moved to the city of Dniepropetrovsk. The KGB informers wrote that he always criticized the old generation of Communists and once said that "the old generation of Soviet people was outdated; it does not know and does not understand a modern youth."

20. On September 16 and 26, 1965, two telegrams were sent from Dniepropetrovsk and Krivoi Rog to a secretary of the Communist Party of Ukraine in Kyiv with the demand to release Ivan Svitlichny, a poet who had been arrested by the KGB for nationalism. On Svitlichny, see Kasianov, *Nezgodni,* 121; Yurii Danyliuk and Oleg Bazhan, *Opozytsia v Ukraini (druga polovyna 50-kh–80-ti rr. XX st.)* (Kyiv: Ridnyi krai, 2000), 18, 19, 73, 74, 75; and Zakharov, *Narys istorii,* 36, 79–80, 82, 84–85, 87–88. The author of the first telegram was Vodolazhchenko, and the author of the second one was Sokul'sky. In November 1965, Vodolazhchenko, as a part-time correspondent of the weekly newspaper *Literary Ukraine,* visited a painting plant named Friendship in the village of Petrikovka. After this visit, he wrote an article about the unhealthy working conditions of the people who created a unique national Ukrainian paintings on wood. This article, "With a Fate of Step-Daughter," attracted the attention of the KGB as "nationalistic and anti-Soviet material." According to the KGB informers, Vodolazhchenko used Olga Piankovkaya, a typist from the district newspaper in Magdalinovka, to type and to disseminate documents of a "nationalistic character." Vodolazhchenko incorporated the published material on the Petrikovka painters into "his anti-Soviet pamphlets"; DADO, f. 19, op. 52, d. 72, l. 81. These documents included a book by I. Koshelivets and excerpts from an article by I. Mikhnovsky, "The Independent Ukraine."

21. DADO, f. 19, op. 50, d. 56, l. 20.

22. Ibid. On the similar events in Kyiv, see, in English, Kenneth C. Farmer, *Ukrainian Nationalism in the Post-Stalin Era: Myth, Symbols and Ideology in Soviet Nationalities Policy* (The Hague: Martinus Nijhoff,, 1980), 119–20.

23. DADO, f. 19, op. 50, d. 56, ll. 20–21.

24. Professor Pidgaetskii referred in his conversation to some of the participants in this group. See my interview with Vitalii Pidgaetskii, Department of History, Dniepropetrovsk University, February 10, 1996. Compare with my interview with Igor T., KGB officer, Dniepropetrovsk, May 15, 1991.

25. V. Zarichny, "Students'ka shchedrivka," *Prapor iunosti,* January 7, 1966. A group of the *koliadky* singers from Dniepropetrovsk also included a guest from Kyiv, the sculptor Oleksandr Nevecheria.

26. V.V. Ivanenko, ed., *Reabilitovani istorieiu,* vol. 2: *Svidchennia z mynuvshyny: Movoiu dokumentiv,* 281.

27. DADO, f. 19, op. 50, d. 56, ll. 22–24. Many of these young poets, participants in Gart, did not conceal the calls from KGB officials for interrogation or KGB official warnings, and even boasted to their friends about resisting KGB pressure and persecutions.

28. Two of the most active among these poets, a sophomore from the Historical-Philological Department of DGU, Mykhailo Romanushko (b. 1946), and a teacher of Ukrainian literature and language from High School No. 37 in Dniepropetrovsk, Gavrylo Prokopenko, had regular contacts with the "nationalistically disposed" O. Zavgorodnii, I. Sokul'sky, and O. Vodolazhchenko. Both Pomanushko and Prokopenko were loyal Soviet subjects; Romanushko was an active Komsomol member, and Prokopenko was a Communist, a hero of the Great Patriotic War. Both loved poetry and wrote good poems in Ukrainian as well. The KGB officials considered their poetry "na-

tionalistic," with "distortions of historic reality." In June 1966, Romanushko obtained from Vodolazhchenko a pamphlet by I. Dziuba titled *Internationalism, or Russification.* For the KGB, this was proof of his anti-Soviet activities. Romanushko read it attentively and then gave it to his friends. Six of them read it, and one of them denounced Romanushko to the KGB. Prokopenko kept in his office a prerevolutionary edition of *The History of Ukraine,* which "did not fit theoretical tenets of Soviet historical science, and which took non-Marxist approaches in interpretation of the certain historical stages of social development in Ukraine." It was also used by the KGB to incriminate him in "nationalistic activities"; DADO, f. 19, op. 50, d. 56, ll. 15–16. On the situation in other Ukrainian cities, see Zakharov, *Narys istorii,* 86. See also an old study: L. Alekseieva, *Istoria inakomyslia v SSSR: Noveishii period* (Moscow: Zatsepa, 2001), 16.

29. DADO, f. 19, op. 51, d. 74, l. 67.

30. The socialist countries of Poland and Czechoslovakia also supplied local intellectuals with "harmful" information. The poet Chkhan received newspaper clippings from his Czech friends about the student demonstrations in Poland and the events of the Prague Spring of 1968. Czech newspapers contradicted the official interpretations in the Soviet press. The active contacts between intellectuals in neighboring socialist countries, along with their listening to foreign radio, contributed to the Dniepropetrovsk intellectuals' critical attitude toward the ideological efforts of the local ideologists and KGB officials. On this, see DADO, f. 19, op. 51, d. 74, ll. 74–75.

31. DADO, f. 19, op. 52, d. 72, ll. 1–18.

32. DADO, f. 19, op. 52, d. 72, l. 2. On the NTS, see Arch Puddington, *Broadcasting Freedom: The Cold War Triumph of Radio Free Europe and Radio Liberty* (Lexington: University Press of Kentucky, 2000), 69, 102–3, 159, 162, 276–77, 296.

33. DADO, f. 19, op. 52, d. 72, l. 3.

34. G. S. Adorskii, an editor in the Dniepropetrovsk Television Department, idealized economic development in capitalist countries and "revisionist reforms" in socialist countries. His colleague from the same TV studio, K. S. Vakulenko, criticized the local Communist apparatchiks, who organized a persecution of the Ukrainian patriotic poets in the city. Ibid., ll. 4–5.

35. Ibid., ll. 4–5, 27.

36. This campaign followed the central directives from Moscow. Yuri Andropov, the head of the KGB, recommended in 1968 "to take measures to nip in the bud attempts to set up nationalist organizations" in Ukraine. See R. G. Pikhoya, *Sovetskii Soyuz: Istoria vlasti—1991* (Moscow: Rossiiskaya Akademiya, 1998), 294.

37. On March 26, 1968, the KGB reported to the regional Communist Party committee that a former active "Trotskyite" by the name of Sosnovich had published a series of articles in the regional Komsomol newspaper *Prapor iunosti.* Another writer for *Prapor iunosti,* a poet named Sirenko, who was expelled from the Communist party for his "anti-Soviet ideas" and who had an official interrogation by the KGB in October 1967, published his poem "Communist" in the main party daily periodical *Zoria* (A Dawn) on the very day of the fiftieth anniversary of October Revolution, November 7, 1967. DADO, f. 19, op. 52, d. 72, ll. 33–34.

38. DADO, f. 19, op. 52, d. 72, l. 34; on the rumors of the Krivoi Rog strikes, see l. 17. The police officers were afraid of a repetition of the workers' riots in the city that took place in June 1963. See Vladimir A. Kozlov, *Neizvestnyi SSSR: Protivostoianie naroda i vlasti 1953–1985 gg.* (Moscow: OLMA Press, 2006), 408–16.

39. DADO, f. 19, op. 52, d. 72, ll. 1–5.

40. On the KGB case of M. Mikhailov and N. Polesia, see DADO, f. 19, op. 52, d. 72, ll. 5–6; also see the similar case of Leonid S. Gavro, an engineer at the Dniepropetrovsk Institute of Metallurgy. Compare with a new approach toward the history of Soviet dissidents in recent anthropological studies, especially Sergei Oushakine, "The Terrifying Mimicry of Samizdat," *Public Culture* 13, no. 2 (2001): 191–214; and Alexei Yurchak, *Everything Was Forever, Until It Was No More: The Last Soviet Generation* (Princeton, N.J.: Princeton University Press, 2005), 102–8, 130–31, 143–45.

41. As Terry Martin noted: "Soviet policy did systematically promote the distinctive national identity and national self-consciousness of its non-Russian populations. It did this not only through the formation of national territories staffed by national elites using their own national languages, but also through the aggressive promotion of symbolic markers of national identity: national folklore, museums, dress, food, costumes, opera, poets, progressive historical events, and classic literary works. The long-term goal was that distinctive national identities would coexist peacefully with an emerging all-union socialist culture that would supersede the preexisting national cultures. National identity would be depoliticized through an ostentatious show of respect for the national identities of the non-Russians." See Terry Martin, *The Affirmative Action Empire: Nations and Nationalism in the Soviet Union, 1923–1939* (Ithaca, N.Y.: Cornell University Press, 2001), 13. See also Dina Zisserman-Brodsky, *Constructing Ethnopolitics in the Soviet Union: Samizdat, Deprivation, and the Rise of Ethnic Nationalism* (New York: Palgrave, 2003), 24–27.

42. This objective resulted in Khrushchev's and Brezhnev's national policy with "cultural-linguistic Russification and internal migration" that led to "the loss by ethnic groups of their cultural-linguistic identity." Zisserman-Brodsky, *Constructing Ethnopolitics,* 31, 32.

43. See the classical study of such a game as a form of performance in human presentation of self in: Erving Goffman, *The Presentation of Self in Everyday Life* (New York: Anchor Books, 1959).

44. DADO, f. 19, op. 52, d. 72, ll. 69–73.

45. This was a typical argument of many Ukrainian Soviet patriots who were accused in "bourgeois nationalism." Author's interview with Yurii Mytsyk, Dniepropetrovsk, January 15, 1992.

46. DADO, f. 19, op. 52, d. 72, l. 6.

47. Ibid., l. 103. See also about the theory of the merger of nations in Roman Solchanyk, "Politics and the National Question in the Post-Shelest Period," *Ukraine after Shelest,* ed. Bohdan Krawchenko (Edmonton: Canadian Institute of Ukrainian Studies, 1983), especially 1–3.

48. Brudny wrote: "A shared belief in socialism and a pride in the industrial, scientific, and cultural achievements of the Soviet state were supposed to give the members of different ethnic groups a sense of common civic identity. This idea was grounded in a theory of the dynamics of ethnic relations in the Soviet state. According to this theory, the federal structure of the Soviet Union was becoming increasingly obsolete because Soviet people of different nationalities developed similar fundamental concerns and common spiritual features in the process of building socialism. The theory postulated that the 'full-scale construction of communism constitutes a new stage in the development of national relations in the USSR in which the nations will draw still closer together, and their complete unity will be achieved.'" Brudny, *Reinventing Russia,* 43; he quoted from *KPSS v rezoliutsiyakh i resheniyakh siezdov, konferetsiy i plenumov Ts. K.* (Moscow: Politizdat, 1972), vol. 8, 282–83.

49. DADO, f. 19, op. 52, d. 72, ll. 103–4. According to Aleksandr Gusar, who knew a few members of this group, they were not the enemies of the Soviet political system. They wanted only to reform Soviet socialism "with respect of all nations and national cultures of the USSR." See my interview with Aleksandr Gusar, May 4, 1990. The police tried to find the connections between Kondratenko's group and the anti-Soviet demonstration in 1968 in Krivoi Rog, but they failed to do so.

50. DADO, f. 19, op. 52, d. 72, l. 7.

51. Ibid., l. 14.

52. On the KGB's persecution of Jewish nationalists in other regions of the USSR, see Robert O. Freedman, ed., *Soviet Jewry in the Decisive Decade, 1971–80* (Durham, N.C.: Duke University Press, 1984). See also a general survey of the Soviet policy toward Jews and Israel under Brezhnev: Alfred D. Low, *Soviet Jewry and Soviet Policy:* East European Monograph 281 (New York: Columbia University Press, 1990), 130–69.

53. "Banderovtsy" was derived from the name of Stepan Bandera, a leader of the Organization of Ukrainian Nationalists' radical branch. His name became a symbol of the Ukrainian national cause in the Western Ukraine starting at the end of the 1940s. On the connection between religion and nationalism in Soviet Ukraine, see Vasyl Markus, "Religion and Nationalism in Ukraine," in *Religion and Nationalism in Soviet and East European Politics,* ed. Pedro Ramet (Durham, N.C.: Duke Press Policy Studies, 1984), 59–80. See also Timothy Snyder, *The Reconstruction of Nations: Poland, Ukraine, Lithuania, Belarus, 1569–1999* (New Haven, Conn.: Yale University Press, 2003), 139–78; and Serhy Yekelchyk, *Ukraine: Birth of a Modern Nation* (New York: Oxford University Press, 2007), 125–28, 141–51.

54. DADO, f. 19, op. 52, d. 72, l. 9.

55. Ibid., ll. 8–9; the citation is on l. 8.

56. DADO, f. 19, op. 52, d. 72, l. 10.

57. See DADO, f. 19, op. 52, d. 72, l. 100. On the Ukrainian dissenters (including Dziuba), see, in English, Bohdan Nahaylo, "Ukrainian Dissent and Opposition after Shelest," in *Ukraine after Shelest,* ed. Bohdan Krawchenko (Edmonton: Canadian Institute of Ukrainian Studies, 1983), 30–54.

58. In 1967 in Kyiv, the local patriots organized a mass demonstration to celebrate this date. The KGB feared a repetition of this event in Dniepropetrovsk. See Kasianov, *Nezgodni,* 71–72; and Zakharov, *Narys istorii,* 93.

59. DADO, f. 19, op. 52, d. 72, ll. 100–102. In 1968, Zaremba approached the rector of DGU, Professor Mosakovsky, and asked him to write a positive review of Honchar's novel *The Cathedral.* Together with members of Sokul'sky's group, he criticized those authors who took part in the official campaign against Honchar's novel.

60. V.V. Ivanenko, ed., *Reabilitovani istorieiu,* vol. 2: *Svidchennia z mynuvshyny: Movoiu dokumentiv* (Dniepropetrovsk, 2000), 281.

61. DADO, f. 19, op. 52, d. 72, l. 11–12. By 1968, they had settled in Dniepropetrovsk. The Skoriks family got jobs at the publishing house of *Zoria,* the main daily periodical of the region. Uniat began his work as metal rigger at the local energy plant. Mikhailo Skorik, who was expelled in 1965, reentered the department of journalism at Kyiv State University later as an external student taking courses by correspondence. His wife, Tatiana Skorik (Chuprina), also had problems with the KGB. At Kyiv State University, her master's thesis, "M. O. Skrypnyk as a Publicist," was criticized by her colleagues for "Ukrainian nationalism." (Mykola Skrynyk was a famous Soviet Ukrainian Communist politician who committed suicide as a reaction to the oppression of

Ukrainians under Stalin.) That is why she had to change the topic of her thesis, which she defended in 1967. On Skrypnyk, see Martin, *Affirmative Action Empire,* 9, 23, 39, 45; and Andrew Wilson, *The Ukrainians: Unexpected Nation* (New Haven, Conn.: Yale University Press, 2002), 117.

62. V. D. Honchar and V. Ia. P'ianov, eds., *Vinok pam'iati Olesia Honchara: Spogady—Khronika* (Kyiv, 1997), 255. DADO, f. 19, op. 51, d. 74, ll. 78–79.

63. During the years 1962–63, when he was a student at L'viv State University, Ivan Sokul'sky had already participated in the similar club of creative youth in L'viv. See Ivan Sokul'sky, *Lysty na svitanku* (Dniepropetrovsk: Sich, 2002), vol. 2, 489.

64. DADO, f. 19, op. 52, d. 72, ll. 89–90. The same informer told the police that Uniat read anti-Soviet documents and urged others to discuss them during the same meeting on the bank of Dnieper.

65. Ibid., l.78.

66. Ibid., ll. 90–91, 99. Moreover, during May 1968, the KGB arranged at least twice the special (called "prophylactic" in the KGB report) interviews of Sokul'sky on the official premises of KGB on Korolenko Street in downtown Dniepropetrovsk.

67. Ibid., l. 99.

68. Ibid., l. 90. Compare with Pikhoya, *Sovetskii Soyuz,* 292 ff.

Notes to Chapter 3

1. Also see the brief mention of this story by Serhy Yekelchyk, *Ukraine: Birth of a Modern Nation* (New York: Oxford University Press, 2007), 164; and Leonid M. Mlechin, *Brezhnev* (Moscow: Molodaia gvardia, 2008), 388–89.

2. See the new, post-Soviet edition of the novel: Oles Honchar, *Sobor,* in *Vybrani tvory u 2-kh tomakh,* by Oles' Honchar (Dniepropetrovsk, 2001), vol. 2, 5–272.

3. On this church, see N. F. Karpenko, S. G. Koldunenko, and D. S. Shelest, "Novomoskovsk," in *Istoria gorodov i siol Ukrainskoi SSR v 26-ti tomakh: Dnepropetrovskaia oblast',* ed. I. V. Vasiliev et al. (Kyiv: Glavnaia redaktsia Ukrainskoi Sovestskoi Entsiklopedii, 1977), 470.

4. See the first scholarly analysis of the scandal around Honchar's novel in English: Kenneth C. Farmer, *Ukrainian Nationalism in the Post-Stalin Era: Myth, Symbols and Ideology in Soviet Nationalities Policy* (The Hague: Martinus Nijhoff, 1980), 106–9.

5. See Vitalii Koval, *"Sobor" i navkolo "Soboru"* (Kyiv, 1989); V. D. Honchar and V. Ia. P'ianov, eds., *Vinok pam'iati Olesia Honchara: Spogady—Khronika* (Kyiv, 1997); and P. T. Tron'ko, O. G. Bazhan, and Yu. Z. Danyliuk, eds., *Ternystym shliakhom do khramu: Oles' Honchar v suspil'no-politychnomu zhytti Ukrainy* (Kyiv, 1999). See also, in English, Bohdan Nahaylo, *The Ukrainian Resurgence* (Toronto, 1999), 36; and Farmer, *Ukrainian Nationalism,* 106–9.

6. On this, see "Lyst tvorchoi molodi Dnipropetrovs'ka," typed manuscript, Dniepropetrovsk, 1968. This document was circulating in handwritten (and later typed) form during the period 1968–69. Later on, it was published in Ukrainian emigrant periodicals in Germany and Canada. See *Suchacnist'* (Munich) 9, part 2 (February 1969): 78–85. Here, I use another edition of this document that is a verbatim reprint of the original version: "Lyst tvorchoi molodi Dnipropetrovs'kogo," in *Molod' Dnipropetrovs'ka v borot'bi proty rusyfikatsii: The Youth of Dnipropetrovsk in a Fight against Russifica-*

tion (Munich: Suchacnist', 1971), 9–19. See also the recent reprint editions of the document: *Ternystym shliakhom do khramu,* ed. Tron'ko, Bazhan, and Danyliuk, 169–80; and *Tysiacha rokiv Ukrains'koi suspil'no-politychnoi dumky. V 9-ty tomakh. Tom 8 (40-vi–80-ti roky XX ct.),* ed. Taras Hunchak (Kyiv, 2001), 230–37. An English translation appears in *The Ukrainian Review* 16, no. 3 (1969): 46–52.

7. Derzhavnyi arkhiv Dnipropetrovs'koi oblasti (hereafter DADO), f. 19, op. 52, d. 72, ll. 47–50. See also Farmer, *Ukrainian Nationalism,* 158–59.

8. DADO, f. 19, op. 52, d. 72, l. 49. See also a publication of this document in *Ternystym shliakhom do khramu,* ed. Tron'ko, Bazhan, and Danyliuk, 143–45. The KGB also spied on a Communist hero of the Great Patriotic War, and a teacher of Ukrainian, Gavrilo Prokopenko (b. 1922), who wrote the article "Air, Water and Bread of the People," defending the ideas in Honchar's novel against ideological accusations. On Prokopenko, see DADO, f. 19, op. 52, d. 72, l. 51. Another poet, Vladimir Sirenko, also supported Honchar and criticized the newspaper *Zoria* for participating in the anti-Honchar campaign. The KGB confiscated his short poem-epigram and insisted on firing him from his work. In his epigram, Sirenko called Honchar a great man and a daily periodical "shit." In the original Ukrainian, this was a very nasty and funny epigram: "Zoria' na sirykh shpal'takh z krykom / Na Honchara pleska bagnom. / Honchar zalyshyt'sia velykym, / "Zoria"—zalyshyt'sia govnom." See DADO, f. 19, op. 52, d. 72, l. 94; compare with the epigram's publication in *Ternystym shliakhom do khramu,* ed. Tron'ko, Bazhan, and Danyliuk, 145–47.

9. DADO, f. 19, op. 52, d. 72, l. 53. See also the memoirs of the famous Ukrainian political dissident Leonid Plyushch, with a contribution by Tatyana Plyushch, *History's Carnival: A Dissident's Autobiography,* ed. and trans. Marco Carynnyk (New York: Harcourt Brace Jovanovich, 1979), 174–75.

10. What follows here in the text is based on an archival document: DADO, f. 19, op. 52, d. 72, ll. 95–96; and the author's personal conversation with Yurii Mytsyk, April 10, 1990.

11. On the KGB's decision about this secret surveillance, see DADO, f. 19, op. 52, d. 72, ll. 95–96. Also see the published version of this document in *Ternystym shliakhom do khramu,* ed. Tron'ko, Bazhan, and Danyliuk, 148–49, 256. Only during perestroika did Mytsyk told us, his former students, about the details of this story. See also Yu. Mytsyk, "'Sobor' i navkolo 'Soboru,'" *Kur'er Kryvbasu,* 1998, no. 9, 102–9.

12. Among them were the writers N. Mikolaenko and M. Nechai and the literary critic I. Lutsenko. See DADO, f. 19, op. 52, d. 72, l. 55. Oles Honchar, who began his undergraduate studies in Kharkiv in 1935–38, eventually finished his studies and graduated from Dniepropetrovsk University after World War II.

13. DADO, f. 19, op. 52, d. 72, l. 58; see ll. 63–68 about the KGB's collection of biographical data and personal information on Honchar.

14. Tron'ko, Bazhan, and Danyliuk, *Ternystym shliakhom do khramu,* 156–63.

15. Ibid., 261. See the English translation of this letter in *The Ukrainian Review* 16, no. 3 (1969): 46–52. As a result of the international publicity about this case, the first scholarly analysis of these events appeared in English; see Farmer, *Ukrainian Nationalism,* 158–59. Compare with Ludmila Alexeyeva, *Soviet Dissent: Contemporary Movements for National, Religious, and Human Rights,* trans. Carol Pearce and John Glad (Middletown, Conn.: Wesleyan University Press, 1985), 40.

16. On the eve of his arrest, Sokul'sky worked as "a sailor-cashier on a board of a small tourist boat" because he was fired from his "normal job" for "Ukrainian national-

ism." Immediately after his arrest, he was accused not only of writing the letter but also of disseminating copies of the letters "in defense of Crimean Tartars" by the general-dissident P. Grigorenko, of the article "A Current State of the Soviet Economy" by the Soviet academician A. Aganbegian, and of a book by the Czechoslovak scholar Molnar, *Slovaks—Ukrainians,* all of which were considered "anti-Soviet propaganda" by the Dniepropetrovsk KGB. Moreover, the police discovered originals of Sokul'sky's poems "Freedom," "Nostalgia," and "Sviatoslav," whose ideas about the protection of Ukrainian culture the KGB officers also interpreted as "anti-Soviet, nationalistic material." Later on, the KGB removed its accusations about the dissemination of Aganbegian's article and Molnar's book. See DADO, f. 19, op. 54, d. 113, ll. 29–31; Tron'ko, Bazhan, and Danyliuk, *Ternystym shliakhom do khramu,* 260, 261; and Ivan Sokul'sky, *Lysty na svitanku* (Dniepropetrovsk: Sich, 2001–2), vol. 1, 22; vol. 2, 489, 491. See also G. Kasianov, *Nezgodni: Ukrains'ka intelligentsia v rusi oporu 1960–80-kh rokiv* (Kyiv: Lybid, 1995), 84–85; A. Rusnachenko, *Natsional'no-vyzvol'nyi rukh v Ukraini: seredyna 1950-kh—pochatok 1990-kh rokiv* (Kyiv: Vyd-vo im. Oleny Teligy, 1998), 173; and Borys Zakharov, *Narys istorii dysydents'kogo rukhu v Ukraini (1856–1987): Kharkivs'ka pravozakhysna grupa* (Kharkiv: Folio, 2003), 95.

17. "Lyst tvorchoi molodi," 9, 17.

18. Ibid., 12.

19. Ibid., 15, 15–16. They reminded their opponents of Lenin's advice on how to fight nationalism in the former Russian Empire. First of all, Communists had to resist "the great Russian chauvinism," and only afterward should they fight with the oppressed nation's nationalism, which was always a reaction to Russian chauvinism.

20. Ibid., 18–19.

21. See, especially, F. Tsukanov, "Maska i oblychia naklepnykiv," *Zoria,* February 7, 1970. The author even asked a question: "What is criminal in a concern for Ukrainian language?" See also L. Vyblaia, "Tak, tse—zrada," *Prapor iunosti,* February 7, 1970; and I. Shylo, "Otravlennye per'ia: Pravda o tak nazyvemom 'Pis'me tvorcheskoi molodiozhi,'" *Dneprovskaia Pravda,* February 8, 1970. Compare with a similar confusing situation in the Russian Federation at the same time: Solomon Volkov, *The Magical Chorus: A History of Russian Culture from Tolstoy to Solzhenitsyn,* trans. Antonina W. Bouis (New York: Alfred A. Knopf, 2008), 235.

22. On Savchenko, see Derzhavnyi arkhiv Sluzhby Bezpeky Ukrainy, Fond upravlinnia v Dnipropetrovs'kii oblasti, Sprava 24613, t. 7, ark. 300–317; and V. V. Ivanenko, ed., *Reabilitovani istorieiu,* vol. 1: *Vidrodzhena pam'iat'* (Dniepropetrovsk, 1999), 561–68. Savchenko became a famous Ukrainian writer. See also Savchenko' memoirs: *Reabilitovani istorieiu,* ed. V. V. Ivanenko, vol. 2: *Svidchennia z mynuvshyny: Movoiu dokumentiv* (Dniepropetrovsk, 2001), 278–81. On the cult of the historian Hrushervsky among Soviet Ukrainian intellectuals, see Serhii Plokhy, *Unmaking Imperial Russia: Mykhailo Hrushevsky and the Writing of Ukrainian History* (Toronto: University of Toronto Press, 2005). The police used the term "beat music" for rock and roll in the 1960s.

23. See the text of these resolutions in DADO, f. 19, op. 57, d. 25, ll. 9–11. See also V. V. Zhuravlev and Iu. Aksiutin, *Vlast' i oppozitsia: Rossiiiskii politicicheskii protsess XX stoletia* (Moscow: Rosspen, 1995), 235–72.

24. The Communist Party of the Soviet Union's resolution of April 23, 1973, was a revision of the "secret" resolution of 1971. See this text in *Reabilitovani istorieiu,* ed. Ivanenko, vol. 2: *Svidchennia z mynuvshyny: Movoiu dokumentiv,* 285–86.

25. See the documents of his criminal case of 1980 given by Sokul'sky, *Lysty na svitanku,* vol. 2, 392–493.

26. The quotation here is from Roman Solchanyk, "Politics and the National Question in the Post-Shelest Period," in *Ukraine after Shelest,* ed. Bohdan Krawchenko (Edmonton: Canadian Institute of Ukrainian Studies, 1983), 13; and *Literaturna Ukraina,* April 21, 1981.

27. G. Nikolenko and A. Pankratov, "Pis'mo, napisannoe zhelchiu: Istoria moral'nogo padenia odnogo neudavshegosia dissertanta (iz zala suda)," *Dneprovskaia Pravda,* April 2, 1974.

28. Author's interview with Igor T., KGB officer, Dniepropetrovsk, May 15, 1991. On the Shocking Blue song and Ukrainian identity among Dniepropetrovsk's young consumers of popular music, see chapter 5 in the present volume.

29. The most popular books were Semen Skliarenko, *Sviatoslav* (Kyiv: Radians'kyi pys'mennyk, 1961); Semen Skliarenko, *Volodymyr* (Kyiv: Radians'kyi pys'mennyk, 1963); and Ivan Bilyk, *Mech Areia* (Kyiv: Radians'kyi pys'mennyk, 1972). Bilyk thought that the Latin authors had misspelled this Slavic name "Hatylo" as "Attila." As a result, the real Ukrainian origin of the legendary prince was forgotten by contemporary historians, who misinterpreted the entire history of the collapse of the Roman Empire. According to Bilyk, these historians dismissed the historical role of the Ukrainians in the creation of Attila's tribal confederation. In 1980, another book caused a sensation among college students: Pavlo Zagrebel'nyi, *Roksolana* (Kyiv: Radians'kyi pys'mennyk, 1980).

30. This was mentioned by a KGB officer; see my interview with Igor T., May 15, 1991. Compare with my interviews with Yurii Mytsyk, Dniepropetrovsk, January 15, 1992; and with Vitalii Pidgaetskii, Department of History, Dniepropetrovsk University, February 10, 1996. See also Myroslav Shkandrij, "Literary Politics and Literary Debates in Ukraine 1971–81," in *Ukraine after Shelest,* ed. Krawchenko, 55–72. On the popularity of Bilyk's book, also see Oles Buzyna, *Tainaia istoria Ukrainy-Rusi: Vtoroe izdanie* (Kyiv: Dovira, 2007), 32–35.

31. The Helsinki Group, an influential nongovernmental organization, was founded in 1976 to monitor the Soviet Union's compliance with the recently signed Helsinki Final Act of 1975, which included clauses calling for the recognition of universal human rights.

32. P. T. Tron'ko, O. G. Bazhan, Yu. Z. Danyliuk, eds., *Ternystym shliakhom do khramu: Oles' Honchar v suspil'no-politychnomu zhytti Ukrainy* (Kyiv, 1999), 204; V. V. Ivanenko, ed., *Reabilitovani istorieiu,* vol. 3: *Mynule z girkym prysmakom: Represii v istorychnii retrospektyvi radians'kogo suspil'stva* (Dniepropetrovsk, 2002), 204–9. See also Zakharov, *Narys istorii,* 123, 124. During the 1980s, the KGB still persecuted people who had the old connections to Sokul'sky's group. See in L. Gamol'skii, "Iz-za ugla," *Dnepr vechernii,* March 30, 1984—about the ideological pressure on Oleksandr Kuz'menko, a former friend of Sokul'sky.

33. Volodymyr Makarenko now lives in Paris. Eventually, Feodosii Humeniuk came back to Ukraine. Now he lives in Kyiv. See John-Paul Himka, "Ukrainian Art in the Soviet Union: Makarenko and Humeniuk," *Journal of Ukrainian Graduate Studies* 2, no. 2 (Fall 1977): 89–90; Oleksa Vusyk, "Koly spadaie maska" "(Oberezhno! Ideologichna dyversia)," *Zoria,* November 26, 1982; V. Starienko, "Prychetnist' do dzherel: Koly zh ofitsiinyi Dnipropetrovsk vyznaie Feodosiia Humeniuka?" *Prapor iunosti,* January 14, 1989; O. Godenko, "Povernennia," *Zoria,* June 20, 1990; Yu. Pokal'chuk,

"'Kozak Makar,' paryzskyi ukrainets," *Kyiv,* 1994, no. 2; V. Vitenko, "Kozak Makar z Pushkarivky," *Prydniprovs'kyi komunar,* August 19, 1995; and Vitalii Starchenko, "Paryzh 'Kozaka Makara,'" *Golos vremeni,* January 15, 1998, no. 2 (18), 11.

34. See my interview with Igor T., May 15, 1991. Compare with my interviews with Vladimir Demchenko, a former public lecturer for Znanie (Society of Knowledge), Dniepropetrovsk, January 12, 1992; and with Pidgaetskii, February 10, 1996. On how Brezhnev supported Vatchenko, see Mlechin, *Brezhnev,* 389.

Notes to Chapter 4

1. Derzhavnyi arkhiv Dnipropetrovs'koi oblasti (hereafter DADO), f. 9870, op. 1, d. 48, l. 14. See also my interview with Oleksandr Ponezha, Dnipropetrovsk, July 22, 2008.

2. DADO, f. 9854, op. 1, d. 42, l. 60; f. 22, op. 15, d. 39, ll. 59–61, 120. During the 1960s, the term "beat music" (*beet muzyka*) was used in the USSR for Western rock music. Also see how the Dutch used the same words for rock music during the 1960s: Mel van Elteren, *Imagining America: Dutch Youth and Its Sense of Place* (Tilburg: Tilburg University Press, 1994), 118, 130–38.

3. DADO, f. 19, op. 52, d. 72, l. 25.

4. Ibid.

5. Ibid., ll. 25–26.

6. S. Budrevich, "O tekh, kto zasoriaet efir," *Dneprovskaia Pravda,* June 4, 1969.

7. DADO, f. 19, op. 60, d. 92, ll. 3, 4, 8–9, 14–15.

8. DADO, f. 19, op. 60, d. 85, ll. 7, 17. See the complaints of the party leaders in DADO, f. 22, op. 19, d. 2, ll. 142–43; and the author's interview with Igor T., KGB officer, Dniepropetrovsk, May 15, 1991. On Soviet illegal black marketers of Western goods, called *fartsovshchiks,* see A. Panov, *Fartsovshchiki* (London, 1971), 34; Alexei Yurchak, *Everything Was Forever, Until It Was No More: The Last Soviet Generation* (Princeton, N.J.: Princeton University Press, 2005), 138, 142, 201–2. On the anti-hippie campaigns in L'viv, see William Jay Risch, "Soviet 'Flower Children': Hippies and the Youth Counter-Culture in 1970s L'viv," *Journal of Contemporary History* 40, no. 3 (July 2005): 565–84.

9. For the obvious similarities with the German ideologists' reaction toward American rock and roll, see Uta G. Poiger, *Jazz, Rock, and Rebels: Cold War Politics and American Culture in a Divided Germany* (Berkeley: University of California Press, 2000), esp.184–97.

10. DADO, f. 22, op. 19, d. 2, ll. 142–43; author's interview with Igor T., May 15, 1991.

11. See S. Frederick Starr, *Red and Hot: The Fate of Jazz in the Soviet Union 1917–1980* (New York: Limelight Editions, 1985), 235–88. Compare with a recent book by Solomon Volkov, *The Magical Chorus: A History of Russian Culture from Tolstoy to Solzhenitsyn,* trans. Antonina W. Bouis (New York: Alfred A. Knopf, 2008), 175–78.

12. Author's interview with Vitalii Pidgaetskii, Department of History, Dniepropetrovsk University, February 10, 1996. Compare with Starr, *Red and Hot,* 243–44.

13. Author's interviews with Pidgaetskii, February 10, 1996; and with Vladimir Demchenko, a former public lecturer for Znanie (Society of Knowledge), Dniepropet-

trovsk, January 12, 1992. See also the KGB reports for 1968 in DADO, f. 19, op. 52, d. 72, ll. 22–25. Compare with the memoirs of a famous Soviet jazz musician, a founding father of the Soviet "fusion": Alexei Kozlov, *Dzhaz, rok i mednye truby* (Moscow: EKSMO, 2005), esp. 89–98. Also see his old book of memoirs: Alexei Kozlov, *Kozyol na sakse* (Moscow: Vagrius, 1998).

14. Yurii Lukanov, *Tretii president: Politychnyi portret Leonida Kuchmy* (Kyiv, 1996), 9–12.

15. For a good description of the priorities in the Soviet system of education in Ukraine, see Catherine Wanner, *Burden of Dreams: History and Identity in Post-Soviet Ukraine* (University Park: Pennsylvania State University Press, 1998), 88–90, 217–18.

16. Author's interview with Tamara Antonovna Kozintseva, Dniepropetrovsk, June 20, 2005.

17. Later, Kuchma explained to his friends that he chose Dniepropetrovsk because he had relatives there. V. P. Gorbulin et al., eds., *Zemni shliakhy i zoriani orbity: Shtrykhy do portreta Leonida Kuchmy* (Kyiv, 1998), 9, 62–63.

18. Compare with the similar stories of the Kuchma's contemporaries from another Soviet city: Donald J. Raleigh, trans. and ed., *Russia's Sputnik Generation: Soviet Baby Boomers Talk about Their Lives* (Bloomington: Indiana University Press, 2006).

19. Gorbulin et al., *Zemni shliakhy i zoriani orbity,* 3–43, 61–69.

20. Ibid., 12.

21. See the first satirical description of Moscow's stylish man in the humor magazine *Crocodile:* D. Belyaev, "Stilyaga," *Krokodil,* March 10, 1949, 10. This description was used by the Soviet ideologists for their anti-jazz campaigns. Compare with English translation of this material in *Mass Culture in Soviet Russia: Tales, Poems, Songs, Movies, Plays and Folklore, 1917–1953,* ed. James von Geldern and Richard Stites (Bloomington: Indiana University Press, 1995), 450–53.

22. See Alexei Kozlov's description of styliagi and how his father bought him his first tape recorder, Dnepr-3, in 1953. Kozlov, *Dzhaz,* 80–81, 89.

23. Artemy Troitsky, *Back in the USSR: The True Story of Rock in Russia* (London: Omnibus Press, 1987), 2–3. Compare with the portrayal of youth cultural consumption in West Germany and East Germany at the same time given by Uta G. Poiger, "Rock 'n' Roll, Female Sexuality, and the Cold War Battle over German Identities," *Journal of Modern History* 68 (September 1996): 577–616; and Poiger, *Jazz, Rock, and Rebels.*

24. On the fashion culture of the Teddy Boys, see Dick Hebdige, *Subculture: The Meaning of Style (New Accents)* (London: Routledge, 1981), 50 ff.

25. Alena V. Ledeneva, *Russia's Economy of Favours: Blat, Networking and Informal Exchange* (New York: Cambridge University Press, 1998), 1. See also an anthropologist's perspective: Yurchak, *Everything Was Forever,* 155.

26. See Gorbulin et al., *Zemni shliakhy i zoriani orbity,* 13. Also see the author's interviews with Aleksandr Gusar, Dniepropetrovsk, May 4, 1990; and with Vladimir Solodovnik, Dniepropetrovsk, June 21, 1991.

27. See Gorbulin et al., *Zemni shliakhy i zoriani orbity,* 11. Also see the author's interviews with Pidgaetskii, February 10, 1996; and with Evgen D. Prudchenko, Central Library of the Dniepropetrovsk Region, July 18, 2007.

28. Vladimir Zadontsev, "'Ves' etot dzhaz' v Dnepropetrovske," *Dnepr vechernii,* November 21, 2001; Aleksandr Kabakov, "Kak vsio nachinalos'," *Apel'sin,* 2002, no. 1, 10–11.

29. "U vecheri, v 'Chipolino,'" *Zoria,* January 29, 1965.

30. See Ivan Nasekan, "A treba sperechatycia!" *Molod' Ukrainy,* February 16, 1966; and G. Panfilova, "Mira vidpovidal'nosti," *Molod' Ukrainy,* December 13, 1967. Nasekan based his anti-jazz campaign on the old publications from the central Soviet periodicals against American jazz and its Soviet imitators by A. Mitrofanov, "Garmonia improviziruet," *Klub i khudozhestvennaia samodeiatel'nost',* 1964, no. 8, 24–26; and A. Mitrofanov, "Rabota ili iskussstvo," *Klub i khudozhestvennaia samodeiatel'nost',* 1964, no. 24, 14–16.

31. The Soviet generation of the 1960s called rock music, usually associated with the Beatles, "big beat" or just "beat music." Music bands that performed such music were called "beat bands." See the author's interview with Demchenko, January 12, 1992. Also see the author's interview with Prudchenko, July 18, 2007.

32. DADO, f. 19, op. 52, d. 72, l. 82.

33. Ibid., l. 83.

34. In 1968, the average monthly salary for a young worker was 90 rubles a month. A loaf of bread cost 20 kopeks, and 1 liter of milk cost 30 kopeks.

35. DADO, f. 19, op. 52, d. 72, l. 84.

36. Author's interviews with Solodovnik, June 21, 1991; with Demchenko, January 12, 1992; with Igor T., May 15, 1991; and with Pidgaetskii, February 10, 1996. See also the author's interview with Prudchenko, July 18, 2007.

37. Kozlov, *Dzhaz,* 101, 113. On the jazz clubs of Leningrad, see Yurchak, *Everything Was Forever,* 168, 170, 181.

38. See G. Vasil'ev, "Chy tak my mriialy 'Mriiu'?" *Prapor iunosti,* January 23, 1966; K. Oleksandrov, "Dzhaz: Tse seriozno," *Prapor iunosti,* April 9, 1968; O. Kabakov, "Tak, tse: Muzyka!" *Prapor iunosti,* May 1, 1968; and O. Kabakov, "Sviato veslykh rytmiv: Traditsiinyi dzhaz-festyval' 'Yunist'-70," *Prapor iunosti,* October 17, 1970.

39. See O. Marchenko, "Zvitue 'Yunist'-73," *Prapor iunosti,* April 19, 1973; and T. Karpushenko, "Do novykh zustrichei, 'Students'ka vesno'!" *Prapor iunosti,* April 19, 1973.

40. Troitsky, *Back in the USSR,* 7–8; Starr, *Red and Hot,* 241. On "jazz on bones" and "rock on bones" consumption by the youth of Leningrad, see Yurchak, *Everything Was Forever,* 181, 185.

41. See the calculation of participants in the music market in DADO, f. 19, op. 60, d. 85, ll. 7, 17; and in the author's interviews with Igor T., May 15, 1991, and with Pidgaetskii, February 10, 1996.

Notes to Chapter 5

1. See S. Frederick Starr, *Red and Hot: The Fate of Jazz in the Soviet Union 1917–1980* (New York: Limelight Editions, 1985); Artemy Troitsky, *Back in the USSR: The True Story of Rock in Russia* (London: Omnibus Press, 1987); Timothy W. Ryback, *Rock around the Bloc: A History of Rock Music in Eastern Europe and the Soviet Union* (New York: Oxford University Press, 1991); Richard Stites, *Russian Popular Culture: Entertainment and Society since 1900* (New York: Cambridge University Press, 1992); and Sabrina Petra Ramet, ed., *Rocking the State: Rock Music and Politics in Eastern Europe and Russia* (Boulder, Colo.: Westview Press, 1994). Two books are based on a material of the Leningrad rock club: Thomas Cushman, *Notes from Underground: Rock*

Music Counterculture in Russia (Albany: State University of New York Press, 1995); and Yngvar Bordewich Steinholt, *Rock in the Reservation: Songs from the Leningrad Rock Club, 1981–86* (New York: Mass Media Music Scholars' Press, 2004). See also a book based on Moscow and Leningrad sources: Michael Urban with Andrei Evdokimov, *Russia Gets the Blues: Music, Culture, and Community in Unsettled Times* (Ithaca, N.Y.: Cornell University Press, 2004). Good portrayals of how the Soviet consumption of jazz and rock music was related to the idealization of America and the West as a whole are given by Eric Shiraev and Vladislav Zubok, *Anti-Americanism in Russia: From Stalin to Putin* (New York: Palgrave, 2000), 19–21; and Yale Richmond, *Cultural Exchange and the Cold War: Raising the Iron Curtain* (University Park: Pennsylvania State University Press, 2003), 11–13, 205–9. On pop music consumption in Leningrad and Moscow, see Polly McMichael, "'After All, You're a Rock and Roll Star (At Least, That's What They Say)': *Roksi* and the Creation of the Soviet Rock Musician," *Slavonic and East European Review* 83, no. 4 (2005): 664–84; and Alexei Yurchak, *Everything Was Forever, Until It Was No More: The Last Soviet Generation* (Princeton, N.J.: Princeton University Press, 2005).

2. I quote a book of memoirs with a remarkable title: David Gurevich, *From Lenin to Lennon: A Memoir of Russia in the Sixties* (San Diego: Harcourt Brace Jovanovich, 1991), 128. Gurevich was born in the Ukrainian city of Kharkiv, graduated from the prestigious Soviet Institute of Foreign Languages in Moscow, and then emigrated to the United States in the 1970s. There he published his memoirs about the everyday life in the Soviet Union during the 1960s. On the veneration of the Beatles among Soviet youth, see Yury Pelyushonok, *Strings for a Beatle Bass: The Beatles Generation in the USSR* (Ottawa : PLY, 1999) and A. Bagirov, *"Bitlz": Liubov' moia* (Minsk: Parus, 1993). Even the older generation of those who grew up in the Russian provincial city of Saratov during the late 1950s and early 1960s were exposed to the influence of the Beatles. See a wonderful collection of the interviews in English: *Russia's Sputnik Generation: Soviet Baby Boomers Talk about Their Lives,* trans. and ed. Donald J. Raleigh (Bloomington: Indiana University Press, 2006), 38, 65, 68, 69, 139, 166, 237, 256.

3. Pavel Palazchenko, *My Years with Gorbachev and Shevardnadze: The Memoir of a Soviet Interpreter* (University Park: Pennsylvania State University Press, 1997), 3. Even the Russian president, Vladimir Putin, was influenced by the Beatles. His favorite Beatles song was "Yesterday." Adi Ignatius, "A Tsar Is Born," *Time,* December 31, 2007–January 7, 2008, 48. On the influence of the Beatles on youth in Moscow and Leningrad, see Andrei Makarevich, *"Sam ovtsa": Avtobiograficheskaia proza* (Moscow: Zakharov, 2002), 53, 90–91, 109–10, 116–18. See also Bagirov, *"Bitlz": Liubov' moia,* 3–4; Pelyushonok, *Strings for a Beatle Bass;* and Richmond, *Cultural Exchange and the Cold War,* 205–9. Compare with Walter LaFeber, *America, Russia, and the Cold War, 1945–2006, Tenth Edition* (Boston: McGraw-Hill, 2007), 337.

4. Author's interview with Vitalii Pidgaetskii, Department of History, Dnipropetrovsk University, February 10, 1996.

5. See Dmitrii Popov and Ilia Mil'shtein, *Oranzhevaia printsessa: Zagadka Yulii Timoshenko* (Moscow: Izdatel'stvo Ol'gi Morozovoi, 2006), 55.

6. Author's interview with Serhii Tihipko, a director of "Privatbank" in Dnipropetrovsk, October 12, 1993.

7. Author's interview with Eduard Svichar, Vatutino, Cherkassy Region, Ukraine, June 8, 2004.

8. V. P. Gorbulin et al., eds., *Zemni shliakhy i zoriani orbity: Shtrykhy do portreta*

Leonida Kuchmy (Kyiv, 1998), 14. Author's interview with Vladimir Demchenko, a former public lecturer for Znanie (Society of Knowledge), Dniepropetrovsk, January 12, 1992. See also the author's interviews with Evgen D. Prudchenko, Central Library of the Dniepropetrovsk Region, July 18, 2007; and with Galina V. Smolenskaia, Central Library of the Dniepropetrovsk Region, July 18, 2007.

9. Author's interviews with Vladimir Solodovnik, June 21, 1991; and with Demchenko, January 12, 1992. On similar developments among the youth in Moscow, see Makarevich, *"Sam ovtsa,"* 90–91, 109–10.

10. See the summer school diaries of Vladimir Solodovnik, February 12, 1966; and of Aleksandr Gusar, February 21, 1966. As far as I can recall, I had the similar impression after the listening to the tape of the Beatles album *Rubber Soul* in February 1966. In those days, I was a seven-year-old kid and lived in the small town Vatutino, in the Cherkassy Region of Ukraine. My elder brother, a college student, brought audiotapes with the Beatles' music from Moscow and invited his friends to listen to his tapes. I fell in love with the Beatles' music, and later I became a serious Beatles fan.

11. *Molod' Ukrainy,* May 28, 1964.

12. O. Levandovs'ka, "Do novykh zustrichei, Muslim!" *Zoria,* December 18, 1964; E. Torchyshnyk, "Pisni tvogo rovesnyka (Muslim Mafomaev u Dnipropetorvs'ku)," *Prapor iunosti,* December 16, 1964. On 'Beatlemania," see P. Kushch, "Modna khvoroba," *Prapor iunosti,* July 7, 1965. On the popularity of Robertino Loretti, see Yu. Oleksandrov, "Khlopchyk z ryms'koi okolytsi," *Prapor iunosti,* December 30, 1964. On Magomaev and Loretti, see, in English, Stites, *Russian Popular Culture,* 131, 132, 179.

13. Stites, *Russian Popular Culture,* 157. On the popularity of bard ("author's") poetry among the Soviet people of different ages and different social status, from young rockers to Communist Party apparatchiks, see Cushman, *Notes from Underground,* 53, 71, 72ff.; and Yurchak, *Everything Was Forever,* 123–24, 128, 129. On the tremendous popularity of Vladimir Vysotsky's songs among the Soviet population during the late 1960s and 1970s, see, in English, Gerald Stanton Smith, *Songs to Seven Strings: Russian Guitar Poetry and Soviet "Mass Song"* (Bloomington: Indiana University Press, 1984), especially the chapter on Vysotsky, 145–79; on Okudzhava, see 111–44; and on Aleksandr Galich, see 181–217. On Soviet *estrada,* see David MacFadyen, *Red Stars: Personality and the Soviet Popular Song, 1955–1991* (Montreal: McGill–Queen's University Press, 2001).

14. See my interviews with Vladimir Solodovnik, June 21, 1991; with Prudchenko, July 18, 2007; and with Smolenskaia, July 18, 2007. Natalia Vasilenko (b. 1959) also recalled the beginning of Beatlemania in the city of Dniepropetrovsk. See my interview with Natalia Vasilenko, Dniepropetrovsk, July 19, 2007. Vladimir Donets (b. 1953) recalled a similar development in another industrial city of the Dniepropetrovsk Region, Dnieprodzerzhinsk. See my interview with Vladimir Donets, Dniepropetrovsk, July 19, 2007.

15. In 1965 and 1966, three Beatles albums appeared on audiotapes in Dniepropetrovsk before the original vinyl records reached local consumers. They were *Help!, Rubber Soul,* and *Revolver.* The most popular songs for all dance parties at the local high schools and colleges were songs "Girl" and "Michelle" from the *Rubber Soul* album of 1965. This information came from my interview with Pidgaetskii, February 10, 1996. See also my interview with Solodovnik, June 21, 1991. On the Beatles' East German compilation, see Ryback, *Rock around the Bloc,* 91; and Olaf Leitner, "Rock Music in the GDR: An Epitaph," in *Rocking the State,* ed. Ramet, 29.

16. Author's interview with Mikhail Suvorov, Dniepropetrovsk, June 1, 1991.

17. Derzhavnyi arkhiv Dnipropetrovs'koi oblasti (hereafter DADO), f. 416, op. 2, d. 1565, ll. 306–7.

18. Author's interview with Suvorov, June 1, 1991. Also see the author's interviews with Vasilenko, July 19, 2007; with Prudchenko, July 18, 2007; and with Smolenskaia, July 18, 2007.

19. Author's interview with Svichar, June 8, 2004. See also a good article about the black market in Odessa: V. Tarnivs'kyi, "Tse tam, de tovkuchka," *Molod' Ukrainy,* May 16, 1967.

20. Author's interview with Pidgaetskii, February 10, 1996. On complaints about "beat music" influences on Ukrainian jazz in Kyiv, see Petro Masokha, "Estradni dysonansy," *Molod' Ukrainy,* February 28, 1965; and in Dniepropetrovsk, see Ivan Nasekan, "A treba sperechatysia," *Molod' Ukrainy,* Febraury 16, 1966.

21. Troitsky, *Back in the USSR;* Ryback, *Rock around the Bloc,* 106.

22. The local Komsomol periodicals covered a member of Dniepriane's career in detail. See K. Klimenko, "Charuiuchi melodii fol'kloru," *Prapor iunosti,* February 20, 1982; and Yu. Lystopad, "'Dniepriane' na beregakh Seny," *Prapor iunosti,* February 17, 1983.

23. DADO, f. 22, op. 28, d. 74, l. 7. Author's interview with Demchenko, January 12, 1992. On Soviet *estrada* mass songs, see Stites, *Russian Popular Culture,* 154–64. Also see the author's interviews with Tatiana Yeriomenko, a former singer with the band Dniepriane, Dniepropetrovsk, April 20, 1988; and with Yurii Kolomoets, a former musician of the band Dniepriane, March 12, 1991.

24. The Soviet places (or houses) of culture became the major centers of the socialist enlightenment during the Brezhnev era. As Ann White noted, during the late socialist period, "the core activities organized officially by houses of culture consisted of amateur theatricals, music-making and dance; non-school education in the form of courses and lectures; entertainments such as films, dances and performances by visiting professional and local amateur groups; and new socialist rites and festivals." See Ann White, *De-Stalinization and the House of Culture: Declining State Control over Leisure in the USSR, Poland and Hungary, 1953–89* (London: Routledge, 1990), 2.

25. For 1972, see DADO, f. 17, op. 7, d. 11. 31–33; for 1978, see DADO, f. 17, op. 10, d. 46, l. 9; and for 1979, see DADO, f. 1860, op. 1, d. 2425, l. 1-1ob. Soviet musicologists supported and promoted this style. See Yu. Ferkel'man, "VIA: Moda ili novyi zhanr?" *Klub i khudozhestvennaia samodeiatel'nost',* 1974, no. 10, 30–31.

26. Author's interviews with Andrei Vadimov, Dniepropetrovsk, July 20–21, 2003; and with Sergei Pulin, Dniepropetrovsk, April, 15, 1990.

27. Author's interview with Pidgaetskii, February 10, 1996. Because of the immense popularity of the tapes with Beatles recordings among Dniepropetrovsk youth, many high school students learned Beatles songs by heart. When Soviet TV used Beatles songs in broadcasts, local kids watched these TV shows and informed each other about this. Everybody remembers how in 1966 Soviet TV suddenly broadcast the Beatles song "Can't Buy Me Love" one Sunday on its show *International Panorama.* It was a sensation for all the young people of Dniepropetrovsk. After that evening, they watched this TV show every Sunday, expecting to hear another rock-and-roll song. On similar developments in other cities in the USSR, see Pelyushonok, *Strings for a Beatle Bass,* 3–4, and Bagirov, *"Bitlz,"* 3–4.

28. Author's interviews with Pidgaetskii, February 10, 1996; with Yeriomenko, April 20, 1988; and with Kolomoets, March 12, 1991.

29. Author's interviews with Pidgaetskii, February 10, 1996; and with Demchenko, January 12, 1992. On "Westernization," see T. Savytskyi, "Perevertni," *Zoria,* June 6,

1965. See also criticism of the "new music" in "Chaikovs'kyi i modni rytmy," *Prapor iunosti,* July 23, 1965.

30. DADO, f. 19, op. 52, d. 72, l. 26.

31. Ibid., ll. 25–26.

32. Author's interviews with Suvorov, June 1, 1991; with Vadimov, July 20–21, 2003; with Pulin, April, 15, 1990; with Yeriomenko, April 20, 1988; and with Yurii Kolomoets, March 12, 1991.

33. See my interviews with Svichar, July 28–29, 2007; with Suvorov, June 1, 1991; and with Vadimov, July 20–21, 2003. Compare with my interview with Vasilenko, July 19, 2007. When Beatles fans in Ukraine learned about the collaboration by Denny Laine, a guitarist from the British band the Moody Blues, and McCartney and his band Wings, everyone tried to get the tapes. Similarly, after a Soviet journalist wrote about the musicians featured in the Rolling Stones Rock and Roll Circus Show on December 11, 1968, those musicians, including Eric Clapton, Taj Mahal, and Jethro Tull, became the most popular names in the list of beat music for the Soviet kids.

34. See my interview with Suvorov, June 1, 1991. This was typical for both the Cherkassy and Dniepropetrovsk regions of Ukraine. See my interview with Svichar, July 28–29, 2007. Compare with my interview with Vasilenko, July 19, 2007.

35. The data on the sale of the records came from my interviews with Pidgaetskii, February 10, 1996; with Demchenko, January 12, 1992; with Suvorov, June 1, 1991; with Vadimov, July 20–21, 2003; with Svichar, June 8, 2004; with Yeriomenko, April 20, 1988; and with Kolomoets, March 12, 1991.

36. On the immense popularity of Creedence Clearwater Revival's music during dance parties all over the Soviet Union, see Pelyushonok, *Strings for a Beatle Bass,* 67. Also see the author's interviews with Yeriomenko, April 20, 1988; and with Kolomoets, March 12, 1991.

37. According to Eric Shiraev and Vladislav Zubok, Elvis Presley and Bob Dylan were the most popular American rock musicians among Soviet youth in the 1960s. In fact, a majority of Soviet consumers of rock music did not like Bob Dylan's music because they could not understand his lyrics. See Eric Shiraev and Vladislav Zubok, *Anti-Americanism in Russia: From Stalin to Putin* (New York: Palgrave, 2000), 20.

38. The quotation is from the summer school diary of Solodovnik, August 16, 1966. All my interviewees mentioned this; see, especially, my interviews with Pulin, April, 15, 1990, with Vladimir Sadovoi, Dniepropetrovsk, March 10, 1992; with Oleksandr Poniezha, Dniepropetrovsk, July 22, 2008; with Smolenskaia, July 18, 2007; with Solodovnik, June 21, 1991; with Suvorov, Dniepropetrovsk, June 1, 1991; and with Svichar, June 8, 2004, and July 28–29, 2007. Compare with my interviews with Pidgaetskii, February 10, 1996; and with Demchenko, January 12, 1992. Even Muscovites considered the Beatles more interesting than Elvis or Dylan. "Elvis was nice," they used to say, "But the Beatles had melodies. The Beatles were wonderful. The Beatles came knocking at our hearts." See Reggie Nadelson, *Comrade Rockstar: The Life and Mystery of Dean Reed, the All-American Boy Who Brought Rock 'n' Roll to the Soviet Union* (New York: Chatto & Windus, 1991), 81.

39. American consumers of pop music know the disco version of the song "Venus" by the band Bananarama. Author's interviews with Suvorov, June 1, 1991; with Vadimov, July 20–21, 2003; with Svichar, June 8, 2004; with Yeriomenko, April 20, 1988; and with Kolomoets, March 12, 1991.

40. Mel van Elteren, *Imagining America: Dutch Youth and Its Sense of Place* (Tilburg: Tilburg University Press, 1994), 138.

41. Even in 1974, the central Komsomol magazine published an article about Shocking Blue as a response to the immense popularity of the Dutch rock band among the Soviet youth. See M. Freed, "Tochnyi pritsel 'Shocking Blue,'" *Rovesnik,* 1974, no. 10, 24. See also a recent novel about the Soviet youth culture of the 1970s: Sergei Souloukh, *Shizgara* (Moscow: Vremia, 2005). This novel demonstrates the popularity of the song "Venus" among the Siberian youth of the 1970s. The very title of the novel is derived from "She's got it," a mispronounced refrain of this song. In Russian, this phrase was mispronounced as "Shizgara." On this, see Souloukh, *Shizgara,* 92–93.

42. Author's interview with Demchenko, January 12, 1992. For many Ukrainian rock musicians, Shocking Blue's music became what Thomas Cushman called "cultural fixation." See Cushman, *Notes from Underground,* 41–45.

43. "Dnipro vpadae v Chorne more, to turkam bude gore, koly kozaky pryplyvut' i turkiv vsikh ub'iut'. Kozaky, zaporiz'ki kozaky, . . ." in Ukrainian. The Ukrainian musicians transformed a refrain "She's got it Your baby, she's got it I'm your Venus I'm your fire At your desire" in a refrain about Cossacks. Author's interviews with Suvorov, June 1, 1991; with Vadimov, July 20–21, 2003; and with Svichar, June 8, 2004. Svichar still remembers all lyrics of this song in Ukrainian. See my recent interview with Svichar, July 28–29, 2007.

44. On Byelorussian rock musicians' linguistic choice, see Maria Paula Survilla, "'Ordinary Words': Sound, Symbolism, and Meaning in Belarusan-Language Rock Music," in *Global Pop, Local Language,* ed. Harris M. Berger and Michael Thomas Carroll (Jackson: University Press of Mississippi, 2003), 187–206. See also her old essay: Maria Paula Survilla, "Rock Music in Belarus," in *Rocking the State,* ed. Ramet, 219–41.

45. Ryback, *Rock around the Bloc,* 106; MacFadyen, *Red Stars,* 312. On the popularity of the song "Yellow River" among the Soviet audience, see Andrei Makarevich, *"Sam ovtsa,"* 130. Unfortunately, a good essay about rock music in Ukraine focuses mainly on the period after 1985 and misses the origin of the rock music culture in Ukraine; see Romana Bahry, "Rock Culture and Rock Music in Ukraine," in *Rocking the State,* ed. Ramet, 243–96.

46. See Semen Skliarenko, *Sviatoslav* (Kyiv, 1961); Semen Skliarenko, *Volodymyr* (Kyiv, 1963), Ivan Bilyk, *Mech Areia* (Kyiv, 1972); and Pavlo Zagrebel'nyi, *Roksolana* (Kyiv, 1980). See my interviews with Pidgaetskii, February 10, 1996; with Prudchenko, July 18, 2007; and with Smolenskaia, July 18, 2007. On the popularity of Bilyk's book, see Oles Buzyna, *Tainaia istoria Ukrainy-Rusi: Vtoroe izdanie* (Kyiv: Dovira, 2007), 32–35.

47. This was mentioned by Suvorov in my interview with him, June 1, 1991. Also see my interviews with Vadimov, July 20–21, 2003; and with Igor T., KGB officer, Dniepropetrovsk, May 15, 1991.

48. *Smerichka* means a small spruce in Ukrainian.

49. See Svitlana Frenets', "Chervona ruta (Rozpovid' pro zolotykh laureativ ogliadu khudozhnioi samodial'nosti)" *Ranok,* 1971, no. 3 (March), 17–18. On how the title of the *Smerichka* song was used during perestroika for a rock festival, "Chervona ruta," which contributed to the rise on national pride in the Ukraine during the 1990s, see Catherine Wanner, *Burden of Dreams: History and Identity in Post-Soviet Ukraine* (University Park: Pennsylvania State University Press, 1998), 121–34.

50. Author's interviews with Suvorov, June 1, 1991; with Vadimov, July 20–21, 2003; and with Svichar, June 8, 2004.

51. Author's interview with Pidgaetskii, February 10, 1996. See also a report of the music schools in the Dniepropetrovsk Region during the years 1974–75 in Tsenral'nyi

Derzhavnyi Arkhiv Vyshchykh Organiv Vlady ta Upravlinnia Ukrainy (herafter TsDAVOVU), f. 5116, op. 19, d. 308, ll. 1–128. Compare with the decisions of the officials in the Ukrainian Ministry of Culture in 1974 in TsDAVOVU, f. 5115, op. 19, d. 25, ll. 1–97, and d. 27, ll. 1–78.

52. These are "*firmennyi*" and "*classnyi*" in Ukrainian.

53. This quotation is from the summer school diary of Gusar, August 12, 1972, whose native language is Ukrainian.

54. Harris M. Berger, "Introduction: The Politics and Aesthetics of Language Choice and Dialect in Popular Music," in *Global Pop, Local Language,* ed. Berger and Carroll, xv.

55. Survilla, "'Ordinary Words,'" 204. On the indigenization of Western pop music in Russian youth culture, see Hilary Pilkington et. al., *Looking West? Cultural Globalization and Russian Youth Cultures* (University Park: Pennsylvania State University Press, 2002), 210. Compare with a good sociological analysis of Leningrad rock music taste culture and Russification of the Western rock music by Cushman, *Notes from Underground,* 36–39, 51–54. On nationalism in Russian rock music during perestroika, see Mark Yoffe, "Conceptual Carnival: National Elements in Russian Nationalist Rock Music," in *Rock 'n' Roll and Nationalism: A Multinational Perspective,* ed. Mark Yoffe and Andrea Collins (Newcastle: Cambridge Scholars Press, 2005), 96–119.

56. Simon Frith, "Music and Identity," in *Questions of Cultural Identity,* ed. S. Hall and P. du Gay (London: Sage, 1996), 121, 124.

57. Colin Campbell, *The Romantic Ethic and the Spirit of Modern Consumerism* (Oxford: Basil Blackwell, 1987), 89; Grant McCracken, *Culture and Consumption* (Bloomington: Indiana University Press, 1990), 104. On the imaginary West, see Yurchak, *Everything Was Forever,* 34, 35, 161–62, 164ff.

Notes to Chapter 6

1. According to Eduard Svichar, five of ten records in Kyiv's black market directly came from foreigners; author's interview with Eduard Svichar, Vatutino, Cherkassy Region, Ukraine, June 8, 2004. According to Mikhail Suvorov, in the Odessa black market, called the *tolkuchka,* five of ten records usually came from foreign tourists and five from Soviet sailors; author's interview with Mikhail Suvorov, June 1, 1991. On the *tolkuchka,* or Privoz, see a letter by Tatiana I. Karetnikova, March 25, 1978, in the Library of Congress, Rubinov Collection, box 15, folder 28C, letter 21418, p. 2. On the black market, called *tolchok,* in the city of Zaporizhie, a 1-hour drive from Dniepropetrovsk, see Library of Congress, Rubinov Collection, box 26, folder 60A, letter 39847, p. 1.

2. Derzhavnyi arkhiv Dnipropetrovs'koi oblasti (hereafter DADO), f. 22, op. 19, d. 2, ll. 142–43; author's interview with Igor T., KGB officer, Dniepropetrovsk, May 15, 1991.

3. See the memoirs of Andrei Makarevich, a representative of the Soviet generation of "the Beatles men" and a leader of the Soviet rock band Time Machine from Moscow: Andrei Makarevich, *"Sam ovtsa": Avtobiograficheskaia proza* (Moscow: Zakharov, 2002), 53–54 Also see A. Bagirov, *"Bitlz": Liubov' moia* (Minsk: Parus, 1993), 3, 157.

4. The Soviet compilations of Beatles songs included "Can't Buy Me Love" and "I Should Have Known Better" from the album *A Hard Day's Night;* "With a Little Help

from My Friends," "When I'm Sixty-Four," and "Lovely Rita" from the album *Sgt. Pep-per's Lonely Hearts Club Band;* "Eleanor Rigby," "Penny Lane," and "Lady Madonna," from various Beatles singles; "Come Together," "Something," "Maxwell's Silver Ham-mer," "Here Comes the Sun," "Octopus Garden," and "Because" from the album *Abbey Road;* and "Let It Be," "I, Me, Mine," and "Across the Universe" from the album *Let It Be.* For some reason, the three last tracks from *Abbey Road* ("Golden Slumbers," "Carry That Weight," and "The End") were released as one track on one of those *minions* un-der the title *Beatles Potpourri.* See the complete list of the Melodia discs with the Bea-tles recordings given by Bagirov, *"Bitlz,"* 157–58. Bagirov mistakenly wrote that VIA Golubye gitary (instead of Vesiolye rebiata) was the first Soviet rock band to cover the song "Ob-La-Di, Ob-La-Da." See Bagirov, *"Bitlz,"* 82.

5. Eventually, Melodia agreed to buy a license for a release of "Imagine" and "Band on the Run" in the Soviet Union in the mid-1970s. See Bagirov, *"Bitlz,"* 160–62.

6. On *Krugozor,* also see Alexei Kozlov, *Dzhaz, rok i mednye truby* (Moscow: EKSMO, 2005), 187–88; and Alexei Yurchak, *Everything Was Forever, Until It Was No More: The Last Soviet Generation* (Princeton, N.J.: Princeton University Press, 2005), 190. On the Soviet bands' covering of Beatles songs, see also Timothy W. Ryback, *Rock around the Bloc: A History of Rock Music in Eastern Europe and the Soviet Union* (New York: Oxford University Press, 1991), 106. See, e.g., a special appendix with a good ar-ticle about the British band Jethro Tull and a *minion* with this band's music given by A. Troitskii, "Folk-Rock," *Klub i khudozhestvennaia samodeiatel'nost',* 1978, no. 18. See also *Krugozor,* 1974, no. 4, with the songs "The Luck of the Irish" and "New York City" by John Lennon; *Krugozor,* 1974, no. 12, with the songs "My Sweet Lord," "Awaiting on You All," and "Bangla Desh" by George Harrison; and *Krugozor,* 1981, no. 3, with "(Just Like) Starting Over" and "Dear Yoko" by Lennon. More compilations were released on flex discs of *Klub i khudozhestvennaia samodeiatel'nost'.* See Mc-Cartney's songs "Man, Who Was Lonely" and "Give Ireland Back to the Irish" in *Klub i khudozhestvennaia samodeiatel'nost',* 1972, no. 10; "You Gave Me the Answer" and "Mrs. Vanderbilt" in *Klub i khudozhestvennaia samodeiatel'nost',* 1976, no. 12; "With a Little Luck" and "Mull of Kintyre" in *Klub i khudozhestvennaia samodeiatel'nost',* 1978, no. 10; and "Ebony and Ivory" and "Tug of War" in *Klub i khudozhestvennaia samodeiatel'nost',* 1984, no. 8. See also the Beatles songs in *Klub i khudozhestvennaia samodeiatel'nost',* 1980, no. 13; and Lennon's songs "Working Class Hero" and "Iso-lation" in *Klub i khudozhestvennaia samodeiatel'nost',* 1981, no. 13. See the complete Soviet discography of ex-Beatles songs given by Bagirov, *"Bitlz,"* 156–68, 160–62.

7. On the role of *Rovesnik,* the most influential magazine for Soviet rock music fans, see chapter 13 of this book.

8. Makarevich, *"Sam ovtsa,"* 163.

9. This was mentioned in my interviews with Suvorov, June 1, 1991; with Andrei Vadimov, Dniepropetrovsk, July 20–21, 2003; and with Igor T., May 15, 1991. Also see DADO, f. 19, op. 52, d. 72, ll. 25–28. On the radio stations Maiak and Yunost', see Alek-sandr Sherel', *Audiokul'tura XX veka: Istoria, esteticheskie zakonomernosti, osoben-nosti vliaiania na auditoriu—Ocherki.* (Moscow: Progress-Traditsia, 2004), 90–94. Also see the entries in the summer school diary of Aleksandr Gusar, May–August 1972, May–August 1973, and May–August 1974; and the summer school diary of Vladimir Solodovnik, June 12, 1970, July–August 1971, and July–August 1972.

10. Summer school diaries of Gusar, May–August 1972, May–August 1973, and May–August 1974; and of Solodovnik, June 12, 1970, July–August 1971, and July–

August 1972. See also the author's interviews with Svichar, June 8, 2004; with Igor T., May 15, 1991.

11. O. Iaseneva, "Krapka nad 'I'," *Prapor iunosti,* September 16, 1966. Compare with the situation in Moscow: S. Frederick Starr, *Red and Hot: The Fate of Jazz in the Soviet Union 1917–1980* (New York: Limelight Editions, 1985), 238; Artemy Troitsky, *Back in the USSR: The True Story of Rock in Russia* (London: Omnibus Press, 1987), 3; and Yurchak, *Everything Was Forever,* 193.

12. Inturist was the name of the All-Union Soviet administration for foreign tourism. As some historians argue, in 1964 the Soviet government stressed that the central for the profits of Inturist was "organization of trade in foreign currency" and the establishment of bars and cafés in the main Inturist hotels throughout the Soviet Union. See Shawn Salmon, "Marketing Socialism: Inturist in the Late 1950s and Early 1960s," in *Turism: The Russian and East European Tourist under Capitalism and Socialism,* ed. Anne E. Gorsuch and Diane P. Koenker (Ithaca, N.Y.: Cornell University Press, 2006), 193–94. See also an order by Vladimir Ankudinov, head of Inturist from 1947 to 1968, about the establishment of special bars for foreigners in "Prikaz po upravleniu po inostrannomu turizmu pri Sovete Ministrov SSSR no. 24," November 19, 1964, Gosudarstvennyi arkhiv Rossiiskoi Federatsii, f. 9612, op. 1, d. 598, l. 66.

13. See O. Iaseneva, "Krapka nad 'I'," *Prapor iunosti,* September 16, 1966; and O. Iaseneva, "Sud," *Prapor iunosti,* December 16, 1966. Compare with the author's interview with Vladimir Demchenko, a former public lecturer for Znanie (Society of Knowledge), Dniepropetrovsk, January 12, 1992.

14. What follows is based on O. Iaseneva, "Krapka nad 'I'," *Prapor iunosti,* September 16, 1966; O. Iaseneva, "Sud," *Prapor iunosti,* December 16, 1966, and on the author's interviews with Demchenko, January 12, 1992; and with Vitalii Pidgaetskii, Department of History, Dniepropetrovsk University, February 10, 1996.

15. Author's interview with Suvorov, June 1, 1991; DADO, f. 19, op. 60, d. 85, l. 7, 17; f. 19, op. 60, d. 92, l. 3, 4, 8–9, 14–15.

16. On how the local newspaper tried to blame Arnold in connection to the violent crimes committed by his customers, consumers of beat music, see Iaseneva, "Krapka nad 'I'"; and Iaseneva, "Sud." Also see the author's interview with Igor T., May 15, 1991.

17. See Iaseneva, "Krapka nad 'I.'" On the role of *fartsovshchiks* in the spread of rock music in the city, see the official Komsomol documents: DADO, f. 22, op. 19, d. 2, l. 143.

18. DADO, f. 19, op. 54, d. 113, ll. 9–10.

19. Author's interview with Igor T., May 15, 1991; DADO, f. 19, op. 54, d. 113, ll. 9–10. Compare with the hippie movement in L'viv as described by William Jay Risch, "Soviet 'Flower Children': Hippies and the Youth Counter-Culture in 1970s Lviv," *Journal of Contemporary History* 40, no. 3 (July 2005): 565–84.

20. DADO, f. 19, op. 54, d. 113, ll. 9–10; f. 22, op. 19, d. 2, l. 143.

21. Author's interviews with Svichar, June 8, 2004; and with Suvorov, June 1, 1991. See the letter about an infamous family of *fartsovshchiks,* the Fedins from Dniepropetrovsk, in Library of Congress, Rubinov Collection, box 24, folder 59B, letter 46674, pp. 1–2. On the similar developments in Leningrad, also see Yurchak, *Everything Was Forever,* 196–97, 200–202. And see the interesting information on the history of jeans consumption in "Eta staraia novaia moda," *Rovesnik,* January 1971, no. 1, 22.

22. DADO, f. 416, op. 2, d. 1565, ll. 306–7.

23. See Sapelkin's report in DADO, f. 19, op. 54, d. 113, ll. 11–12.

24. Author's interview with Demchenko, January 12, 1992. On Znanie, see Ellen Propper Mickiewicz, *Media and the Russian Public* (New York: Praeger, 1981), 125–27.

25. See Andrei Makarevich, *"Sam ovtsa"*, 126 ff.; and Yurchak, *Everything Was Forever,* 181–237. See also Thomas Cushman, *Notes from Underground: Rock Music Counterculture in Russia* (Albany: State University of New York Press, 1995).

Notes to Chapter 7

1. Summer school diary of Vladimir Solodovnik, June 6, 1964. Solodovnik referred to Mayne Reid, *Sochinenia v shesti tomakh,* ed. R. M. Samarin, vol. 1: *Belyi vozhd', Kvarteronka* (Moscow: Gosudarstvennoe izdatel'stvo detskoi literatury Ministerstva Prosveshchenia RSFSR, 1956).

2. Summer school diary of Andrei Vadimov, May 29, 1971.

3. Summer school diary of Aleksandr Gusar, May 30, 1973. As we see, all the authors mentioned the six-volume edition of Mayne Reid, which was the most popular book collection during the Brezhnev era. See Mayne Reid, *Sochinenia v shesti tomakh,* ed. R. M. Samarin (Moscow: Gosudarstvennoe izdatel'stvo detskoi literatury Ministerstva Prosveshchenia RSFSR, 1956–58): vol. 1: *Belyi vozhd', Kvarteronka;* vol. 2: *Otseola, vozhd' seminolov, Morskoi volchonok;* vol, 3: *Okhotniki za rasteniiami, Polzuny po skalam, Zateriannye v okeane;* vol. 4: *V debriakh Iuzhnoi Afriki, Uinye okhotniki, Okhotniki za zhirafami;* vol. 5: *Belaia perchatka, V debriakh Borneo, V poiskakh belogo bizona;* vol. 6: *Marony, Vsadnik bez golovy.*

4. For how Dmitry Medvedev, the future Russian president, loved to read books by Conan Doyle and Jules Verne during his childhood in Leningrad, see Nikolai Svanidze and Marina Svanidze, *Medvedev* (Saint Petersburg: Amfora, 2008), 300–301.

5. See my interviews with Yurii Mytsyk, Dniepropetrovsk, January 15, 1992; with Vitalii Pidgaetskii, Department of History, Dniepropetrovsk University, February 10, 1996; with Evgen D. Prudchenko, Central Library of the Dniepropetrovsk Region, July 18, 2007; and with Galina V. Smolenskaia, Central Library of the Dniepropetrovsk Region, July 18, 2007. Mytsyk referred to a Ukrainian translation, published in the series "A Library of Adventures and Science Fiction": Robert Stevenson, *Ostriv skarbiv* (Kyiv: Vydavnytstvo TSK lksmu Molod, 1957).

6. See the author's interviews with Natalia Vasilenko, Dniepropetrovsk, July 19, 2007; with Vladimir Donets, Dniepropetrovsk, July 19, 2007; and with Eduard Svichar, Vatutino, Cherkassy Region, July 28–29, 2007. I, myself, read Louis Boussenard's books only in Ukrainian translation in the 1970s.

7. See the summer school diaries of Vadimov, August 24, 1975; and of Gusar, January 5, 1976.

8. See the author's interviews with Pidgaetskii, February 10, 1996; and with Vladimir Demchenko, a former public lecturer for Znanie (Society of Knowledge), Dnipropetrovsk, January 12, 1992. See also the KGB reports for 1968 in Derzhavnyi arkhiv Dnipropetrovs'koi oblasti (hereafter DADO), f. 19, op. 52, d. 72, ll. 22–25.

9. DADO, f. 19, op. 60, d. 85, ll. 7, 17. See the complaints of the party leaders in DADO, f. 22, op. 19, d. 2, ll. 142–43. And see the author's interview with Igor T., KGB

officer, Dniepropetrovsk, May 15, 1991. On Fedin's family, see Library of Congress, Rubinov Collection, box 24, folder 59B, letter 46674; box 26, folder 60G, letter 43113.

10. Stephen Lovell, *The Russian Reading Revolution: Print Culture in the Soviet and Post-Soviet Eras* (New York: St. Martin's Press, 2000), 57–58.

11. M. D. Afanasiev, *Za knigoi: Mesto chtenia v zhizni sovetskogo rabochego* (Moscow: Kniga, 1987), 36 ff; O. Chubarian, ed., *Kniga i chtenie v zhizni nebol'shikh gorodov: Po materialam issledovania chtenia i chitatel'skikh interesov* (Moscow: Kniga, 1973), 133 ff., 199; O. I. Nikiforova, *Psikhologia vospriiatia khudozhestvennoi literatury* (Moscow: Kniga, 1972), 137; V. D. Stel'makh and N. K. Lobachev, eds., *Kniga i chtenie v zerkale sotsiologii* (Moscow: Knizhnaia palata, 1990), 134.

12. Lovell, *Russian Reading Revolution,* 55–56. "The book boom," Lovell wrote, "had provided welcome evidence of the rising cultural level of Soviet society, but it was also associated with a less desirable phenomenon: 'book hunger' (*knizhnyi golod*)."

13. Gregory Walker, "Readerships in the USSR: Some Evidence from Post-War Studies," *Oxford Slavonic Papers* 19 (1986): 167.

14. Maurice Friedberg, *A Decade of Euphoria: Western Literature in Post-Stalin Russia, 1954–64* (Bloomington: Indiana University Press, 1977), 57; and Lovell, *Russian Reading Revolution,* 65.

15. Lovell, *Russian Reading Revolution,* 70.

16. A. Volkov, *Volshebnik izumrudnogo goroda* (Moscow: Detskaia literatura, 1968); A. Volkov, *Urfin Dzhus i ego dereviannye soldaty* (Moscow: Detskaia literatura, 1968); A. Volkov, *Sem' podzemnykh korolei* (Moscow: Detskaia literatura, 1969); A. Volkov, *Ognennyi bog Marranov* (Moscow: Detskaia literatura, 1969).

17. Dnevnik knig (hereafter book diary) of Aleksandr Gusar, February 12–December 23, 1970; and book diary of Andrei Vadimov, January 15–December 30, 1970. See also the summer school diary of Solodovnik, May 10, 1969. See also my interviews with Prudchenko, July 18, 2007; and with Smolenskaia, July 18, 2007. Compare with my interviews with Vasilenko, July 19, 2007; and with Donets, July 19, 2007. See also my interview with Svichar, July 28–29, 2007.

18. Book diaries of Gusar, January 11–December 31, 1971; and of Vadimov, January 10–December 30, 1971.

19. Book diaries of Gusar, January 5–December 31, 1972; and of Vadimov, January 1–December 20, 1972.

20. Book diaries of Gusar, January 1–December 30, 1973; and of Vadimov, January 6–December 23, 1973.

21. Book diaries of Gusar, January 5, 1974–December 27, 1976; and of Vadimov, January 9, 1974–November 12, 1976.

22. Summer school diary of Gusar, June 21, 1975. On the popularity of Bilyk's book, see Oles Buzyna, *Tainaia istoria Ukrainy-Rusi: Vtoroe izdanie* (Kyiv: Dovira, 2007), 32–35.

23. Kenneth C. Farmer, *Ukrainian Nationalism in the Post-Stalin Era: Myth, Symbols and Ideology in Soviet Nationalities Policy* (The Hague: Martinus Nijhoff, 1980), 132.

24. Author's conversation with Yurii Mytsyk, Dniepropetrovsk, May 12, 1991. He expressed similar feelings.

25. See my interviews with Prudchenko, July 18, 2007; and with Smolenskaia, July 18, 2007. Compare with my interviews with Vasilenko, July 19, 2007; and with Donets, July 19, 2007. See also my interview with Svichar, July 28–29, 2007.

26. Summer school diary of Solodovnik, May 10, 1969.

27. See Dniepropetrovsk Central City Library, readers' records, 1970–75, especially the files of readers' records for 1974 and 1975. Compare with my interview with Pidgaetskii, February 10, 1996. See the interviews with Dniepropetrovsk readers who preferred Ukrainian historical novels, such as M. Starytskyi's novels about Bohdan Khmel'nytskyi in "Na svoi vkus," *Dnepr vechernii,* January 21, 1982.

28. Interview with Andrei Z., Dniepropetrovsk, June 12, 2005. These apartment buildings were called also *khrushchoba.* As William Taubman wrote: "Under Khrush-chev, the annual rate of housing construction nearly doubled. Between 1956 and 1965 about 108 million people moved into new apartments. In his haste to provide Soviet cit-izens with what had so long been denied them, Khrushchev encouraged rapid, assem-bly-line construction of standardized five-story apartment houses built out of fabricated materials. Many of the new complexes welcomed occupants before they were actually completed and were still unsafe. Millions were grateful, but it was not long before the buildings became known as *khrushchoba,* a word combining Khrushchev's name and *trushchoba,* the Russian word for "slum." In Khrushchev's eyes, the new houses were a stopgap quick fix, . . . to be replaced in twenty years or so by new and better build-ings." William Taubman, *Khrushchev: The Man and His Era* (New York: W. W. Norton, 2003), 382. Compare with Donald Filtzer, *Soviet Workers and De-Stalinization: The Consolidation of the Modern System of Soviet Production Relations, 1953–1964* (Cam-bridge: Cambridge University Press, 1992), 51–52; and Donald Filtzer, *The Khrushchev Era: De-Stalinization and the Limits of Reform in the USSR, 1953–1964* (London: Macmillan, 1993), 33–34.

29. Dmitrii Popov and Ilia Mil'shtein, *Oranzhevaia printsessa: Zagadka Yulii Timo-shenko* (Moscow: Izdatel'stvo Ol'gi Morozovoi, 2006), 53.

30. Author's interview with Andrei Z., June 12, 2005; Popov and Mil'shtein, *Oranzhevaia printsessa,* 53.

31. Popov and Mil'shtein, *Oranzhevaia printsessa,* 56.

32. Author's interview with Andrei Z., June 12, 2005.

33. Ibid. Also see the author's interviews with Vasilenko, July 19, 2007; with Ta-tiana Yeriomenko, a former singer with the band Dniepriane, Dniepropetrovsk, April 20, 1988; and with Smolenskaia, July 18, 2007.

34. Dniepropetrovsk Central City Library, readers' records, 1970–75, especially the entries for 1971 and 1975.

35. See the numerous studies of Soviet book reading and consumption discussed by G. N. Goreva, "Khudozhestvennaia literatura v chtenii molodykh rabochikh na rubezhe 60-kh–70-kh godov XX v.," in *Istoria russkogo chitatelia,* Vyp. 1, ed. I. Barenbaum (Leningrad: Leningradskii gosudarstvennyi institut kul'tury im. N. K. Krupskoi, 1973), 176–92, esp. 181–82; Chubarian, *Kniga i chtenie v zhizni nebol'shikh gorodov,* 133 ff., 199; and O. I. Nikiforova, *Psikhologia vospriiatia khudozhestvennoi literatury* (Moscow: Kniga, 1972), 137. See also a summary of the Soviet research in the studies of the Western scholars: Walker, "Readerships in the USSR," 170; and Friedberg, *Decade of Euphoria,* 58–81.

36. According to the statistics of all Ukrainian city libraries in 1977, the correspon-ding numbers were on average 91, 63, 23, 69, and 77 percent. See A. Reitblat and T. Frolova, eds., *Chitatel'skii spros v massovykh bibliotekakh v 1977 g. (Dinamika cht-enia i chitatel'skogo sprosa) Instruktivno-metodicheskie rekomendatsii* (Moscow, 1978), 52.

37. Dniepropetrovsk Central City Library, readers' records, 1980–84.

38. They would become popular again among the black marketers only during perestroika, when a resumed interest in Ukrainian history and culture stimulated reading in Ukrainian. Author's interview with Mikhail Suvorov, Dniepropetrovsk, January 10, 1993. Suvorov was an active participant in the black market for music and books during the period 1976–86. On the popularity of books in Russian among Ukrainian readers, see N. E. Dobrynina, "Mnogonatsional'naia otechestvennaia literatura i chitatel'skie orientatsii," in *Kniga i chtenie v zerkale sotsiologii,* ed. V. D. Stel'makh and N. K. Lobachev (Moscow: Knizhnaia palata, 1990), esp. 134, 135. On the role of the black market for books in the city of Dniepropetrovsk, see M. Stryl'chuk and O. Chaplygin, "Kolroleva Margo? Ogo-go!" *Prapor iunosti,* January 17, 1981. During the period 1979–83, one black marketer in books, Stepan Sizonenko, bought books that cost him 45,785 rubles. But he sold each book for 25 rubles. For one year only, he had a profit of 4,300 rubles. On him, see L. Gamol'skii, "Knizhnyi cherv'," *Dnepr vechernii,* December 10, 1983.

39. Author's interviews with Mytsyk, January 15, 1992; and with Pidgaetskii, February 10, 1996. Compare with the author's recent interviews with Oleksandr Poniezha, Dniepropetrovsk, July 22, 2008; and with Oleksandr Beznosov, Department of History, Dniepropetrovsk University, July 19, 2008.

40. See my interviews with Prudchenko, July 18, 2007; and with Smolenskaia, July 18, 2007. Compare with my interviews with Vasilenko, July 19, 2007; and with Donets, July 19, 2007. See also my interview with Svichar, July 28–29, 2007. See also my interviews with Poniezha, July 22, 2008; and with Beznosov, July 19, 2008.

41. Author's interview with Pidgaetskii, February 10, 1996.

42. See, especially, N. Dobrynina, *Cherty dukhovnoi obshchnosti: Russkaia khudozhestvennaia literature v chtenii mogonatsional'nogo sovetskogo chitatelia* (Moscow: Kniga, 1983), 70 ff. On the same, see the author's interviews with Poniezha, July 22, 2008; and with Beznosov, July 19, 2008.

43. See my interviews with Vasilenko, July 19, 2007; Donets, July 19, 2007; and Svichar, July 28–29, 2007.

Notes to Chapter 8

1. On the role of movies during the Brezhnev eras, see Ellen Propper Mickiewicz, *Media and the Russian Public* (New York: Praeger, 1981), 73–88. For a good survey of Soviet filmmaking during the Brezhnev era, see Dmitry Shlapentokh and Vladimir Shlapetokh, *Soviet Cinematography 1918–1991: Ideological Conflict and Social Reality* (New York: Aldine de Gruyter, 1993), 147–75. On film consumption in the USSR, see Anna Lawton, *Kinoglasnost: Soviet Cinema in Our Time* (New York: Cambridge University Press, 1992), 7–51; George Faraday, *Revolt of the Filmmakers: The Struggle for Artistic Autonomy and the Fall of the Soviet Film Industry* (University Park: Pennsylvania State University Press, 2000), 87–109; and Denise J. Youngblood, *Russian War Films: On the Cinema Front, 1914–2005* (Lawrence: University of Kansas Press, 2007). On the Soviet film audience during the Khrushchev era, see Josephine Woll, *Real Images: Soviet Cinema and the Thaw* (London and New York: I. B. Tauris and St. Martin's Press, 2000). On the popularity of Indian films among Soviet moviegoers, see Sudha

Rajagopalan, "Emblematic of the Thaw: Hindi Films in Soviet Cinemas," *South Asian Popular Culture* 4, no. 2 (October 2006): 83–100; and Sudha Rajagopalan, *Indian Films in Soviet Cinemas: The Culture of Movie-Going after Stalin* (Bloomington: Indiana University Press, 2009).

2. See my interview with Evgen D. Prudchenko, Central Library of Dniepropetrovsk Region, July 18, 2007. See also my interviews with Andrei Vadimov, Dniepropetrovsk, July 20–21, 2003; and with Eduard Svichar in Vatutino, Cherkassy Region, Ukraine, June 8, 2004. Natalia Vasilenko noted that movie theaters became especially popular for dating and sexual adventures. See my interviews with Natalia Vasilenko, Dniepropetrovsk, July 19, 2007; and with Tatiana Yeriomenko, April 20, 1988, Dniepropetrovsk.

3. Tsentral'noe Statisticheskoe Upravlenie Dnepropetrovskoi oblasti, *Dnepropetrovshchina v tsifrakh: K 40-letiu pobedy v Velikoi Otechestvennoi voine,* ed. L. G. Glushkina (Dniepropetrovsk, 1985), 77; TsSU USSR, Statisticheskoe upravlenie Dnepropetrovskoi oblasti, *Molodiozh Dnepropetrovskoi oblasti: Statisticheskii sbornik,* ed. L. T. Glushkina and V. F. Iagniuk (Dniepropetrovsk, 1985), 28.

4. *Sovetskii ekran,* 1971, no. 6, 2.

5. I. Levshina, "Ia smotriu vse kina": Razdumia nad anketami, kotorye prislali samye iunye zriteli," *Sovetskii ekran,* 1973, no. 14, 17.

6. See the summer school diary of Andrei Vadimov, June–August 1971; and the summer school diary of Aleksandr Gusar, May 30–June 7, and June 7–27, 1970.

7. A. G. Bolebrukh et al., eds., *Dnipropetrovs'k: Vikhy istorii* (Dniepropetrovsk, 2001), 229; TsSU USSR, Statisticheskoe upravlenie Dnepropetrovskoi oblasti, *Molodiozh Dnepropetrovskoi oblasti,* 25, 28. On the role of the Palaces of Culture during the Brezhnev years, see Anne White, *De-Stalinization and the House of Culture: Declining State Control over Leisure in the USSR, Poland and Hungary, 1953–89* (London: Routledge, 1990), 39–41.

8. *Sovetskii ekran,* 1971, no. 6, 2. Compare with the data from Mickiewicz, *Media and the Russian Public,* 76.

9. See such complaints in T. Savytskyi, "Perevertni," *Zoria,* June 6, 1965.

10. Vladimir Shlapentokh, *The Public and Private Life of the Soviet People: Changing Values in Post-Stalin Russia* (New York: Oxford University Press, 1989), 147.

11. *Novyny kinoekranu,* 1973, no. 12, 13. See also Vladimir Baskakov, "V ritme vremeni," *Iskusstvo kino,* 1980, no. 1, 26–58.

12. J. Hoberman, *The Dream Life: Movies, Media, and the Mythology of the Sixties* (New York: New Press, 2003), 31–32, 33, 34–50; Stanley Corkin, *Cowboys as Cold Warriors: The Western and U.S. History* (Philadelphia: Temple University Press, 2004), 174, 179–80, 181–84, 186, 189, 190.

13. See the complaints about this movie in *Izvestiia,* June 9, 1962, and *Pravda,* November 24, 1963. See also Maurice Friedberg, *A Decade of Euphoria: Western Literature in Post-Stalin Russia, 1954–64* (Bloomington: Indiana University Press, 1977), 288, 320–21, 331, and Mickiewicz, *Media and the Russian Public,* 78. For information about the American films on the Soviet screen from 1957 to 1980, see Val S. Golovskoy with John Rimberg, *Behind the Soviet Screen: The Motion-Picture Industry in the USSR 1972–1982,* trans. Steven Hill (Ann Arbor: Ardis, 1986), 132–37, esp. 133. Golovskoy mistakenly dated the Soviet release of *Stagecoach* as early as the end of the 1930s. (This film was released in the United States in 1939!) Compare this with a description of Western movies in the USSR, which came from the so-called trophy fund, by Solomon

Volkov, *The Magical Chorus: A History of Russian Culture from Tolstoy to Solzhenit-syn,* trans. Antonina W. Bouis (New York: Alfred A. Knopf, 2008), 175–76.

14. See *Dneprovskaia pravda,* June 20, 1966, and July 19, 1966.

15. "Z poshty 'Zori': Proty zakhidnykh fil'miv shcho nabuly populiarnosti u Dnipropetrovs'ku," *Zoria,* August 12, 1966. During the 1960s and 1970s, Ukrainian film magazines always criticized the mass popularity of the western among the Soviet youth. See such a typical criticism in the article "Kovboi bez legendy," *Novyny kinoekranu,* 1971, no. 2, 15.

16. Summer school diary of Vladimir Solodovnik, July 19, 1966.

17. Summer school diary of Solodovnik, May 30–August 28, 1966.

18. Author's interviews with Vitalii Pidgaetskii, Department of History, Dniepropetrovsk University, February 10, 1996; and with Vladimir Demchenko, a former public lecturer for Znanie (Society of Knowledge), Dnipropetrovsk, January 12, 1992.

19. Author's interview with Serhiy Tihipko, a director of "Privatbank" in Dniepropetrovsk, October 12, 1993.

20. Corkin, *Cowboys as Cold Warriors,* 22–28, 38–41. On John Ford, see Lindsay Anderson, *About John Ford* (New York: McGraw-Hill, 1983).

21. Vladimir Dmitriev, "Prostye istiny Dzhona Forda," *Sovetskii ekran,* 1975, no. 7, 5. See also an announcement about a release of this film in *Sovetskii ekran,* 1975, no. 6, 17.

22. Dmitriev, "Prostye istiny Dzhona Forda."

23. See *Zoria,* August 12, 1966.

24. G. Makarov, "Portret iastreba," *Sovetskii ekran,* 1970, no. 21, 16–17. Also see an essay about the actor John Wayne as a political reactionary and anticommunist enemy of the Soviet Union in the popular youth magazine *Rovesnik,* 1972, no. 7, 16–17.

25. Author's interview with Igor T., KGB officer, Dniepropetrovsk, May 15, 1991. See also *Zoria,* Februaury 7, 1975, and *Dneprovskaia Pravda,* February 14, 1975.

26. Many young moviegoers were disappointed with *My Darling Clementine,* this black-and-white classic American western. As one high school student wrote in his diary, referring to the article in the March issue of the Soviet film magazine, "What did *Sovetskii ekran* discover good and progressive in this boring American film? It is too slow without any action. *Zoloto Makenny* is much better, and it is a real great American western." The citation is from the summer school diary of Vadimov, March 30, 1975.

27. V. Dmitriev, "Vtrecha s vesternom," *Sovetskii ekran,* 1974, no. 18, 5–6.

28. Ibid. Dmitrii Medvedev, a future Russian president, also loved Western movies. See in Nikolai and Marina Svanidze, *Medvedev* (Saint Petersburg: Amfora, 2008), 304–5.

29. Vsevolod Revich, "Dva litsa parodii," *Sovetskii ekran,* 1967, no. 15, 14–15; V. Kisun'ko, "Vestern: Pominki ili?" ("Synovia Bol'shoi Medveditsy"), *Sovetskii ekran,* 1967, no. 5, 12.

30. Peter Hames, a British film critic, wrote about Lemonade Joe: "Apart from demanding lemonade ('Kolaloka'), he reveals himself to be a superb marksman, dispensing with a fly and [a bad guy] trouser belt with consummate ease. Joe is nothing if not simpleminded, but is still able to foil a bank raid with his casual under the arm shooting." See Peter Hames, *The Czechoslovak New Wave* (Berkeley: University of California Pres, 1985), 290 n. 45; and Peter Hames, *Way Out West: Oldrich Lipsky's Lemonade Joe* (Chicago: Facets Cine-Notes, 2006), 4, 5. Also see his comments on the *Lemonade Joe* DVD.

31. As these critics noted, the director Lipsky showed "an uncanny ability to toss every conceivable type of sight gag into his film and always get a laugh: undercranked action, a gunfight with the shots scratched onto the emulsion (they meet in midair and are deflected by each other), horses that gallop down 90-degree grades, and matte shots of a sphinx and the Taj Mahal superimposed in the background of a mountainous landscape (across which [a main character] rides, singing as he goes)." James Michael Martin, "Lemonade Joe," *Film Quarterly* 20, no. 2 (Winter 1964): 62–63.

32. For a positive review of the Czech comedies *Esli by tysiacha klarnetov, Limonadnyi Dzho,* and *Prizrak zamka Morrisvil,* see Vsevolod Revich, "Dva litsa parodii," *Sovetskii ekran,* 1967, no. 15, 14–15; and Vsevolod Revich, "Valdemar Matushka," *Sovetskii ekran,* no. 24, 14.

33. Summer school diary of Solodovnik, July 19, 1966; *Dneprovskaia Pravda,* June 9, 1966; author's interview with Pidgaetskii, February 10, 1996.

34. Author's interview with Pidgaetskii, February 10, 1996.

35. *Dneprovskaia Pravda,* January 17, 1967. See also a recent article in a popular Russian magazine: Vladimir Tikhomirov, "Nastoiashchii Chingachguk," *Ogonek,* March 6–12, 2006, no. 10, 62.

36. Summer school diary of Gusar, June 22 and June 24, 1970.

37. Gerd Gemunden, "Between Karl May and Karl Marx: The DEFA Indianerfilme (1965–1983)," *New German Critique,* no. 82, issue on East German film, Winter 2001, 25–38; the citation is on 26.

38. Gemunden, "Between Karl May and Karl Marx," 26.

39. Ibid., 27. "Like many Hollywood westerns," Gerd Gemundhen noted, "*Indianerfilme* are far more revealing about the political agenda of their makers than about the objects which they pretend to portray. Not surprisingly, in the DEFA films the various responses of the Indian tribes to the ever-advancing western frontier of the United States look like blueprints for a better socialist Germany." Gemunden gives an example of the ending in *The Sons of Great Mother Bear* when an Indian chief (Gojko Mitic) leads his people to a better and safer location by announcing: "Farming, raising domesticated buffaloes, being blacksmiths and making plows—that's our new path," "a message that had to resonate in the workers' and farmers' state." "Similarly," he continues, "Chief Osceola's most important victory is not won on the battlefield but at the bargaining table, as he secures fair wages for all plantation workers." In both *Chingachgook* and *Osceola,* Mitic "succeeds in ending warfare among rival tribes by persuading them to unite against a common enemy, following the motto "Indians of all lands, unite!"—which sounds like the old Marxist slogan "Working men of all countries, unite!" Compare with Karl Marx and Friedrich Engels, *The Communist Manifesto,* ed. David McLellan (New York: Oxford University Press, 1998), 39.

40. See Gojko Mitic's interview in a Ukrainian film magazine: Leonid Pavliuchyk, "Dubler ne potriben: Na zapytannia nashogo korespondenta vidpovidae yugoslavs'kyi actor Goiko Mitych," *Novyny kinoekranu,* 1978, no. 11, 14. Gojko Mitic explained that "The Sons of Great Bear" was a kind of "an anti-western"—in contrast to Hollywood westerns, the DEFA films showed Indians as main heroes. As Gemunden noted, "Born in Yugoslavia to a father who fought Hitler's army as a partisan, Mitic had moved to East Berlin in the mid-1960s after having already acted in some English and Italian productions and some of Reinle's Karl May films [the West German westerns]. Mitic was thus a highly visible exception to the westward flow of East German actors and film professionals." See in Gemunden, "Between Karl May and Karl Marx," 34. East German di-

rectors such as Konrad Petzold highly praised Gojko Mitic as a professional and ideological role model for the socialist countries: "It is not as if Gojko had no other choice that to portray Indians here in the East. He had, and as far as I know he continues to have, offers from the capitalist countries. It is a sign of his straightforwardness and honesty that he chooses to exclusively work here. He is really serious about this work, and it is importance to him to participate in the new discoveries and the new developments of this genre (Indian film), according to our Marxist view of history." Ehrentraud Novotny, *Gojko Mitic* (Berlin: Henschel, 1976), 27. See also a recent article in a popular Russian magazine: Vladimir Tikhomirov, "Nastoiashchii Chingachguk," *Ogonek,* March 6–12, 2006, no. 10, 62.

41. Kisun'ko, "Vestern," 12.

42. Gemunden, "Between Karl May and Karl Marx," 26, 32. See also Horst Peter Koll, "Der traumende Deutsche: Die *Winnetou*-Filmtrilogie," in *Idole des deutschen Films: Eine Galerie von Schusselfiguren,* ed. Thomas Koebner (Munich: Text & Kritik, 1997), 384–97. On the German westerns in modern German popular culture, see Lutz P. Koepnick, "Unsettling America: German Westerns and Modernity," *Modernism/ Modernity* 2, no. 3 (1995): 1–22. See also Christopher Frayling, *Spaghetti Westerns: Cowboys and Europeans from Carl May to Sergio Leone* (London: Routledge & Kegan Paul, 1981), 103–17; and Howard Hughes, *Once upon a Time in the Italian West: The Filmgoers' Guide to Spaghetti Westerns* (London: I. B. Tauris, 2004), xii–xvi.

43. L. Anninskii, "Vernaia ruka i Bol'shoi zmei," *Sovetskii ekran,* 1968, no. 22, 16–17. See also a recent study of the DEFA and West German films about Indians by Andrei Sharyi, *Znak W: Vozhd' krasnokozhikh v knigakh i na ekrane* (Moscow: Novoe literaturnoe obozrenie, 2007).

44. An overwhelming majority of the readers voted for this film in 1970. See *Sovetskii ekran,* 1970, no. 10, 2.

45. See the summer school diary of Gusar, June 29 and 30, 1970. The entries for both days had sentences: "We played Indians." Notice that a few days before Gusar and his friends had watched the DEFA Indian films.

46. Author's interview with Igor T., May 15, 1991.

47. On the cartoon films of the director V. Dakhno, see Olena Kryzhanivs'ka, "Kozaky na ekrani," *Novyny kinoekranu,* 1970, no. 12, 8–9. See also an announcement about the release of *Chiortova diuzhina* by the Odessa film studio in *Sovetskii ekran,* 1972, no. 10, 20, and in *Dneprovskaia Pravda,* February 7, 1973.

48. Manfred Bekman, "Goiko Mitych," *Novyny kinoekranu,* 1971, no. 11, 15; Ol'ga Bilan, "Din Rid: 'Til'ky v borot'bi znakhodzhu shchastia'," *Novyny kinoekranu,* 1979, no. 4, 12; "Spivai, kovboe, spivai!" *Novyny kinoekranu,* 1982, no. 6, 15; and Diter Vol'f, "DEFA: Fil'my i problemy," *Novyny kinoekranu,* no.10, 14–15. Compare with my interviews with Mikhail Suvorov, June 1, 1991; and with Natalia Vasilenko, Dniepropetrovsk, July 19, 2007.

49. *Sovetskii ekran,* 1967, no. 10, 8–9.

50. See the summer school diary of Gusar, June 18 and 19, 1970. On the first day, he saw the American adventure comedy film *Vozdushnye prikliuchenia,* the next day he saw *Beloe solntse pustyni,* and a few days later he saw "a DEFA Indian films' marathon," which consisted of three Gojko Mitic movies.

51. See the announcements about these films in the local press: *Dneprovskaia Pravda,* January 17, 1967, July 17, August 6, 1968, and December 4 and 14, 1969.

52. See *Dneprovskaia Pravda,* May 29, 1970, and July 15, 1973.

53. See how the Soviet film critics praised a progressive Italian cinema: V. Bozhovich, "Vittorio de Sika," *Sovetskii ekran,* 1967, no. 3, 16–17; V. Bozhovich, "Kuda vedet doroga?" (a review of the Fellini's film "La Strada," which was shown in USSR under the title "Oni brodili po dorogam"), *Sovetskii ekran,* no. 8, 14–15; and another article on the same pages, "V masterskoi Fellini." See also numerous articles in *Iskusstvo kino,* e.g., in G. Bogemskii, "Rabochii klass vykhodit na ekran," *Iskusstvo kino,* 1974, no. 11, 140–68; and G. Bogemskii, "Boevye rubezhi italianskogo kino," *Iskusstvo kino,* 1975, no. 6, 137–53. See also the article by the Ukrainian film critic Oksana Vyshyns'ka, "Prokliati liudstvom: Antyfashysts'kyi fil'm Lukino Viskonti" *Novyny kinoekranu,* 1971, no. 5, 15.

54. V. Mikhalkovich, "Rekviem po vesternu," *Sovetskii ekran,* 1969, no. 21, 18. On the Americanization of Italian cinema, especially the critical remarks about the films by Sergio Leone, see G. Bogemskii, "Sdelano v Itallii," *Sovetskii ekran,* 1971, no. 6, 13–14.

55. On spaghetti westerns, see Christopher Frayling, "Spaghetti Westerns," *Film Quarterly* 34, no. 4 (Summer 1981): 37–38; Marcia Landy, "'Which Way Is America?' Americanism and the Italian Western," *Boundary 2* 23, no. 1 (Spring 1999): 35–59; and Hughes, *Once upon a Time.*

56. On this film and the actor who played the main character, see Paul Smith, *Clint Eastwood: A Cultural Production* (Minneapolis: University of Minnesota Press, 1993), 19–26.

57. Summer school diary of Gusar, June 29, 1971, 36–37. On the Film Festival in Moscow and showing spaghetti westerns, see V. Mikhalkovich, "Rekviem po vesternu," *Sovetskii ekran,* 1969, no. 21, 18.

58. This film was released later in the United States as *A Bullet for the General.* See the announcements about this film in *Dneprovskaia Pravda,* December 4 and December 17, 1968.

59. Viktor Orlov, "Edinstvennyi vystrel," *Sovetskii ekran,* 1968, no. 17, 17. See also Hughes, *Once upon a Time,* 95–96.

60. Howard Hughes, one of the specialists in spaghetti westerns, gives a detailed description of this film in his book. Following a train robbery, Bill Tate joins Chuncho's "bandits" as they steal arms and ammunition for the Mexican rebel General Elias. Returning to the Elias's headquarters, Chuncho's gang participates in a rebellion by the people from the town of San Miguel. Instead of protecting rebellious town from the regular army, Chuncho removes his gang from the town. Only his brother Santo stays in the town to help the poorly armed rebellious peasants. Meanwhile, the regular army attacks Chuncho's gang, and only Tate and Chuncho survive this attack. Eventually they reached General Elias's hideout alive, but Tate catches malaria. "During Tate's convalescence," Hughes continues, "Chuncho finds a mysterious golden bullet in Tate's valise. At Elias's camp, Chuncho is sentenced to death for leaving San Miguel, where poor Mexican peasants were punished by the regular army. A brother of Chuncho, Santo, wants to carry out the sentence, but during the execution Tate shoots both Elias and Santo. As it turned out, Tate was a hired government assassin; for his contract to kill rebellious General Elias, he earns 100,000 pesos. Tate offers Chuncho half his fee, as a token of his gratitude to Chuncho for leading him to Elias. But in the last Mexican railway station on their way to the U.S. border, Chuncho at last sees his country as something worth fighting for. As Tate is boarding a train back to the United States, Cuncho guns him down and gives the money to a Mexican shoeshine boy, yelling 'Don't buy bread with that money hombre,

buy dynamite.'" Hughes, *Once upon a Time,* 95. Compare with this film description in Frayling, *Spaghetti Westerns,* 233, 235.

61. Summer school diary of Solodovnik, December 6, 1968.

62. Author's interviews with Tatiana Yeriomenko, Dniepropetrovsk, April 20, 1988; and with Natalia Vasilenko, Dniepropetrovsk, July 19, 2007.

63. Author's interview with Andrei Z., Dniepropetrovsk, June 12, 2005.

64. See, e.g., *Dneprovskaia Pravda,* June 22 and July 18, 1974.

65. On this, see V. Dmitriev, "Vtrecha s vesternom," *Sovetskii ekran,* 1974, no. 18, 5–6.

66. Brian Garfield, *Western Films: A Complete Guide* (New York: Rawson Associates, 1982), 224.

67. On the immense popularity of Gregory Peck among the Soviet audience, see *Sovetskii ekran* 1967, no. 10, 1–2.

68. Author's interviews with Pidgaetskii, February 10, 1996; and with Demchenko, January 12, 1992.

69. Summer school diary of Vadimov, August 25, 1974.

70. See the summer school diary of Gusar, August 12, 1974.

71. Author's interview with Suvorov, June 1, 1991. Askold B., who was eleven years old in 1974, expressed a similar enthusiasm about the film. See the author's interview with Askold B., a son of the head of the tourist department in the Dniepropetrovsk Trade Unions branch, Dniepropetrovsk University, April 15, 1993.

72. See the author's interviews with Natalia Vasilenko, Dniepropetrovsk, July 19, 2007; and with Tatiana Yeriomenko, Dniepropetrovsk, April 20, 1988.

73. In 2000, Alexander Suraev, a Russian reviewer of the *Mackenna's Gold* DVD who was from Moscow, shared his impressions of childhood for the Amazon.com Web site. "The only westerns we were allowed to see (in the Soviet Union)," he wrote, "were produced by East German studio DEFA with only one star—the Yugoslav hunk Goiko Mititch [*sic!*]. And mostly only one plot—the greedy prospectors come to take the Indian land and the feathered patriots put on the warpaint, flex their muscles—they all were very athletic, unlike the whites who were depicted as the degenerates in every sense—and gallop to sweep the terrain clean of that capitalist scum. But we were grateful even for that substitute, tired of seeing the other Red against White flicks—the films about the Russian Civil War heroes killing the White Guards by hundreds for the sake of Mother Russia's communist future. And then *Zoloto Makkeni* was imported. Why? The message was clear—'Look at these gold-crazed American bastards! Preachers, journalists, merchants, banditos, soldiers, adventurers—all of them are ready to sell their Momma's for a speck of golden dust! And this time they testify themselves, not our East German friends.' But who cared about all that? The authentic American western! With the real Indians instead of East German Olympic Team painted in gouache! The film's mildly idiotic background commentaries did not make us flinch—they fit into the didactic tradition we were used to. And the opening song! It was translated in Russian and sung in the film by the Russia's much-adored sweet-voiced drunk Valeri Obodzinskij. In the restaurants, at a campfires, in a streets the young males were singing—Vnov, vnov zoloto manit nas!—The gold lures us again and again!—I was 8 or 9 years old at that time. [I've] seen the film weekly. The boys in the playground asked in a whisper: 'Do they show something there? You know. . . .—' And I told them: 'Oh yeah! The Indian girl. . . .—They really do! Wow!' Well, speaking about childhood traumas. . . . Once I

took my mother along and seeing the bathing scene she suspected what was coming and obscured my view with her hand. . . . But seriously, the remastering crew did a superb job. The sights, the sounds—perfect! These were the times they were still happy to shoot in mostly natural—maybe slightly enhanced—colors, without these annoying tints and shades of today, when they seem to dip the freshly shot rolls of films in a can of blue paint [*sic*]." See Alexander Suraev's review in English at http://www.amazon.com/ MacKennas-Gold-Gregory-Peck/dp/B00004TJJU/ref.

74. Author's interviews with Suvorov, June 1, 1991; and with Andrei Z., Dniepropetrovsk, June 12, 2005.

75. The data about the films in Dniepropetrovsk movie theaters can be found on the last page of the local newspapers, *Dneprovskaia Pravda, Zoria,* and *Dnepr vechernii,* for 1974 to 1979. Ten years after the release of the Czech film, in June 1974, a high school student from the Dniepropetrovsk Region still enjoyed the humor of this parody of American westerns. But a few months later, he was able to appreciate the authenticity of a real American western as well. Being himself a fan of the DEFA Indian films for years, he finally noted in his diary entry for August 15, 1974, that the greatest "cowboy films ever made on this planet were not the stupid Gojko Mitic movies, but *Lemonade Joe* and *Mackenna's Gold.*" See the summer school diary of Gusar, June 26 and August 12, 1974. The Ukrainian filmmakers produced their own Ukrainian western *Lobo* to satisfy a growing demand among the Ukrainian filmgoers. See Mykahilo Vasyl'ev, "Vestern proty vesternu," *Novyny kinoekranu,* 1978, no. 9, 8–9.

76. On this film, see, in Soviet periodicals, Nina Zarkhi, "'O, schastlivchik!'—fil'm Lindseia Andersona," *Iskusstvo kino,* 1976, no. 4, 150–57; and Aleksandr Doroshevich, "Nesentimental'noe puteshestvie," *Sovetskii ekran,* 1976, no. 3 (March), 4–5.

77. Author's interview with Igor T., May 15, 1991.

78. A. Zorkii, "I oglianulis' vo gneve," *Iskusstvo kino,* 1971, no. 12, 121–41; G. Kapralov, "Utverzhdenie istiny," *Iskusstvo kino,* 1972, no. 2, 141.

79. *Iskusstvo kino,* 1973, no. 11, 192.

80. See my interviews with Suvorov, June 1, 1991; and with Pidgaetskii, February 10, 1996.

81. See especially Zorkii, "I oglianulis' vo gneve," 121, 123–25.

82. One of these reviewers, Elena Beliakova, who wrote a Web site review of *The Sandpit Generals,* emphasized the significant role of this film in the cultural imagination of the Soviet youth. "Many years ago in 1974, when I was a schoolgirl," she noted, "I saw a movie, which impressed me greatly, turned my soul upside down and determined my future life. It was Hall Bartlett's movie *The Sandpit Generals.* Up to now I can't forget that impression. I was shocked and fascinated and felt indissoluble ties with its characters—those homeless teenagers who, in spite of appalling conditions didn't lose their human dignity. They fought for their life, their future, their love. And music, that fascinating music! It penetrated into the depth of the heart, and the heart itself began sounding in unison with this doleful and courageous melody. I think the movie is a real masterpiece of the world cinematography and it isn't my opinion only. It is one of the most beloved movies in Russia, and is still being demonstrated in the cinemas. It is the favorite movie of Vladimir Putin. One can hardly imagine what a success it was. In 1974 the movie was called the best film by the young people of the Soviet Union. *The Sandpit Generals* became a kind of a cult for the whole generation. Unfortunately the movie was completely unaccepted in the US, it simply wasn't demonstrated there. Perhaps Hall Bartlett died without knowing how dear his movie was to millions and mil-

lions of Soviet people." See http://movies2.nytimes.com/gst/movies/movie.html?v_
id=13108.

83. See *Dneprovskaia Pravda,* November 13 and 20, and December 15, 1973.

84. *Dneprovskaia Pravda,* June 22 and July 18, 1974.

85. Summer school diary of Vadimov, July 5, 1974; summer school diary of Gusar, June 28, 1974.

86. Summer school diary of Vadimov, August 16, 1974. Gusar wrote it down on pages of his summer school diary as well. See the summer school diary of Gusar, August 23, 1974. They referred to a short article about the film and a publication of sheet music and notes of the song "Moi veterok, moia liubov' i plot" [My little wind, my love and boat] in an August issue of *Rovesnik.* This information was included in the most popular part of the magazine: "Chto govoriat, chto pishut" [What do they tell and what do they write about?]. See "Khol Bartlet i ego 'Generaly,'" *Rovesnik,* 1974, no. 8 (August), 23.

87. Derzhavnyi arkhiv Dnipropetrovs'koi oblasti (hereafter DADO), f. 17, op. 7, d. 1, l. 41; op. 10, d. 1, ll. 35, 40, op. 8, d. 44, ll. 5, 11, 123, 125, 141, 161–70.

88. They referred to *capoeira* (a Brazilian form of martial arts), elements of which were portrayed in the film. The youth magazine had to publish a brief information about this form of martial arts in 1974. See "Vzmakhni nogoi," *Rovesnik,* 1974, no. 3, 22. Even in 1985, Dniepropetrovsk filmgoers still loved to watch *The Sandpit Generals* in local movie theaters. See *Dnepr vechernii,* 1985, March 25, 4.

89. Author's interview with Igor T., May 15, 1991.

90. M. Bleiman, "Kak Vazhno byt' neserieznym," *Sovetskii ekran,* 1967, no. 24 (December), 13; on 12, also see the brief information "Milen Demonzho" about a French actress who played the fiancée of the journalist Fandor in *Fantomas.* On the original *Fantomas* film of 1913–14, see Alan Williams, *Republic of Images: A History of French Filmmaking* (Cambridge, Mass.: Harvard University Press, 1992), 67, 68, 69. See also a recent study of the *Fantomas* films: Andrei Sharyi, *Znak F: Povelitel' uzhasa: Fantomas v knigakh i na ekrane* (Moscow: Novoe literaturnoe obozrenie, 2007).

91. *Dneprovskaia Pravda,* July 25–August 28, 1967.

92. See the summer school diary of Gusar, June 16, 1973.

93. For the original story of the films, see Pierre Souvestre and Marcel Allain, *Fantômas* (New York: Morrow, 1986). Compare with the Soviet critic's films description by Bleiman, "Kak Vazhno byt' neserieznym."

94. Dimitris Eleftheriotis, *Popular Cinemas of Europe: Studies of Texts, Contexts and Frameworks* (New York: Continuum, 2001), 84. On the Soviet treatment of the Bond movies, see S. Mozhgunian, "'Bondiana' kak fenomen 'massovoi kul'tury,'" *Iskusstvo kino,* 1972, no. 10, 146–60.

95. On this, see Richad Stites, *Russian Popular Culture: Entertainment and Society since 1900* (New York: Cambridge University Press, 1992), 43–44, 153–54, 180–81.

96. Summer school diary of Solodovnik, August 20, 1968; author's interview with Pidgaetskii, February 10, 1996.

97. Author's interviews with Igor T., May 15, 1991; and with Pidgaetskii, February 10, 1996.

98. Author's interview with Pidgaetskii, February 10, 1996.

99. DADO, f. 19, op. 53, d. 109, ll. 1–9; author's interview with Igor T., May 15, 1991.

100. On Kurosawa's original film of 1943–45 see Rostislav Yurenev, "Odinokii

vsadnik v tumane: Ob iskusstve Akiry Kurosavy, " *Iskusstvo kino,* 1977, no. 5, 136. On the actor who played the major character in the film *Genii dziu-do,* see A. Lipkov, "Sem' samuraev Tosiro Mifune," *Iskusstvo kino,* 1972, no. 10, 155–68.

101. Summer school diary of Gusar, June 28 and July 2, 1970.

102. DADO, f. 19, op. 53, d. 109, ll. 23–28; author's interview with Igor T., May 15, 1991. Also see the information in *Dneprovskaia Pravda,* January 17, 1967, and *Dneprovskaia Pravda,* June 28 and July 19, 1969.

103. "Okh, uzh eto karate . . . ," *Dneprovskaia pravda,* January 5, 1982, 4.

104. See, e.g., Lipkov, "Sem' samuraev Tosiro Mifune."

105. Summer school diary of Vadimov, January 10, 1973. He referred to the article by Lipkov, "Sem' samuraev Tosiro Mifune." *Iskusstvo kino* was a more serious and analytical periodical than *Sovietskii ekran.* But many young Soviet film enthusiasts read this analytical periodical as well.

106. For a Westerner's opinion, see Hughes, *Once upon a Time,* 105.

107. See the information in *Dneprovskaia Pravda,* October 5, 1969.

108. Summer school diary of Gusar, July 19, 1970.

109. For information on how conservative Ukrainian film critics interpreted Damiani's films, see "Rozpovidaie Damiano Damiani," *Novyny kinoekranu,* 1971, no. 12, 15.

110. As Hughes wrote, "The opening scenes see LiPuma, a mentally unstable crook (played by bug-eyed Adolfo Lastretti), released from a mental institution by Bonavia and allowed to murder Dubrozio, a wealthy mobster (with dealings in the construction industry). LiPuma arrives at the hood's offices disguised as a policeman and proceeds to spray the room with a submachine gun. Later LiPuma's girlfriend (Marilu Tolo) is murdered by Dubrozio's henchmen. They sift her body from her flat in a packing case, take her to a nearby building site and cast her in a concrete stanchion that becomes part of Dubrozio's latest building development." Hughes, *Once upon a Time,* 105.

111. See, e.g., the first essay (of four essays) about the Moscow Film Festival written by the most prominent figure in Soviet film criticism. The entire essay was devoted to "the progressive Italian cinema," and its most talented representative, Damiano Damiani, who created honest films about corruption and the Mafia in Italy. G. Kapralov, "Utverzhdenie istiny, razoblachenie mifov," *Iskusstvo kino,* 1971, no. 11, 2–18.

112. *Dneprovskaia Pravda,* September 30, 1972.

113. See the results of the readers' survey in *Sovetskii ekran,* 1973, no. 10, 12.

114. Summer school diary of Gusar, June 17, 1974. He wrote, "I with friends visited our summer movie theater tonight and saw the Italian feature film by director Damiano Damiani *Priznanie komissara politsii prokuroru respubliki.* This film tells a story about an unsuccessful struggle of a police Commissaire Bonavia with Mafia in Sicily." A similar entry appeared in the summer school diary of Vadimov, June 23, 1974.

115. *Dneprovskaia Pravda,* June 22, 1974.

116. See Ryazanov's complaints about a prohibition of his film *Garage* because of Ryazanov's critical portrayal of the Soviet reality. See "Stenographic Report of Director Eldar Ryazanov's Speech at the Plenary Session of the Union of Film Workers of the USSR (Moscow, December 2, 1980)," in *Behind the Soviet Screen,* by Golovskoy with Rimberg, 118.

117. See Georgii Bogems'kyi's article in a Ukrainian film magazine: Georgii Bogems'kyi, "Talant i prystrast'," *Novyny kinoekranu,* 1978, no. 6, 13. See also my interviews with Pidgaetskii, February 10, 1996; with Demchenko, January 12, 1992; and with Igor T., May 15, 1991.

118. Georgii Bogems'kyi, "Politychne kino Italii," *Novyny kinoekranu,* 1972, no. 5, 14–15. See the series of articles by Bogemskii: G. Bogemskii, "Dzhan Mariia Volonte," *Iskusstvo kino,* 1973, no. 6, 137–47; G. Bogemskii, "Zakon 'po-italianski,'" *Iskusstvo kino,* 1974, no. 4, 156–62; G. Bogemskii, "Rabochii klass vykhodit na ekran," *Iskusstvo kino,* 1974, no. 11, 140–68; G. Bogemskii, "Boevye rubezhi italianskogo kino," *Iskusstvo kino,* 1975, no. 6, 137–53, and no. 7, 164–74; G. Bogemskii, "Vspominaia Viskonti," *Iskusstvo kino,* 1978, no. 9, 173–86, and no. 10, 140–52; and G. Bogemskii, "Italianskii politicheskii fil'm: Poteri i obretenia," *Iskusstvo kino,* 1979, no. 9, 146–65.

119. See also a positive review of another Mafia's film of Damiani by Evgen Margolit, "Liudyna stomylas' boiatysia," *Novyny kinoekranu,* 1982, no. 1, 14.

120. G. Bogemskii, "Franko Nero: Ot "zvezdy" k bortsu," *Sovetskii ekran,* 1974, no. 2, 14–15; Valerii Baranovs'kyi, "Buty 'lidynoi chesti,' . . ." *Novyny kinoekranu,* 1978, no. 5, 12–13.

121. Soviet ideologists also promoted the Romanian gangster "westerns" about the struggle of the Bucharest police with criminals in postwar socialist Romania. These films, such as *Chistymi rukami (With Clean Hands)* and *Poslednii patron (The Last Bullet),* also became popular movies among the young filmgoers in 1974–76. See the critical review by V. Revich, "V plenu u zhanra," *Sovetskii ekran,* 1974, no. 23, 4. On the popularity of these films, see *Sovetskii ekran,* 1976, no. 10, 18–19; and *Dneprovskaia Pravda,* December 15, 1974, and May 11, 1975.

122. Author's interview with Pidgaetskii, February 10, 1996. Even in 1984, "mafia films" were still popular in Dniepropetrovsk. See *Dnepr vechernii,* December 8, 1984.

Notes to Chapter 9

1. See, especially, *Sovetskii ekran,* 1971, no. 6, 2. Compare with the data from Ellen Propper Mickiewicz, *Media and the Russian Public* (New York: Praeger, 1981), 76. The most popular of Gaidai's comedies included *Operation "Y" and Shurik's Other Adventures* (1965), *Caucasian Captive, or Shurik's New Adventures* (1968), *Diamond Arm* (1969), and *Ivan Vasilievich Changes Occupation* (1973).

2. See *Dneprovskaia Pravda,* January 1, January 12, and February 16, 1966.

3. *Sovetskii ekran,* 1967, no. 10, 1–2.

4. Summer school diary of Aleksandr Gusar, May 31, 1970.

5. Summer school diary of Vladimir Solodovnik, March 7, 1966.

6. Summer school diary of Andrei Vadimov, July 5, 1969.

7. Author's interview with Vitalii Pidgaetskii, Department of History, Dniepropetrovsk University, February 10, 1996.

8. *Dneprovskaia Pravda,* March 8 and December 22, 1966. This periodical noted this unhealthy enthusiasm (*azhiotazh*) about two films, *Mister Pitkin in the Rear of Enemy* and *Mister Pitkin in the Hospital.*

9. *Dneprovakaia Pravda,* July 25, 29, 30, and 31, and August 20 and 22, 1967.

10. L. Anninskii, "Smeisia pervym, Freddy!" *Sovetskii ekran,* 1969, no. 10, 17.

11. Ibid.

12. See about the All-Union release of this film in 1969 in *Sovetskii ekran,* 1969, no. 24, 19. *Dneprovskaia Pravda,* July 19, 1969, and June 30, 1970.

13. Summer school diary of Vadimov, July 1, 1970. Compare with the summer school diary of Gusar, June 30, 1970.

14. Summer school diary of Vadimov, July 1, 1970.

15. As the film reviewers noted, this movie was set in 1910, "when the (lovingly re-created) airplanes of the period were likelier to sputter and crash than they were to go in a straight line." "The international contest," wrote the reviewer, Robert Horton, "requires an international cast, including Stuart Whitman as a cowboy American interested in the ladylove (Sarah Miles) of an English ace (James Fox). Alberto Sordi and Gert Frobe represent the Italian and German nations; Terry-Thomas plans frightful sabotage for race day. From the jaunty opening song and the great opening-credits drawings by Gerald Searle onward, the movie has a pleasingly breezy tone that sits well with the meticulous flying sequences. This is a delightful example of a certain kind of internationally flavored film of the period, somewhat similar to *The Great Race,* released the same year (1965)." See http://www.amazon.com/Those-Magnificent-Their-Flying-Machines/dp/B00014NEX0/ref.

16. *Dneprovskaia Pravda,* November 19 and December 18, 1968, and May 13, 1969. See also about the All-Union release of the film in *Sovetskii ekran,* 1969, no. 8, 20–21.

17. See information about the release of this film in the Soviet Union in *Sovetskii ekran,* 1976, no. 12, 9. On its release in Dniepropetrovsk, see *Dneprovskaia Pravda,* June 25, and October 3, 1976. As one of the American film reviewers, Richard Horton, noted, in 1965, "director Blake Edwards, fresh from the success of the first two Pink Panther movies, indulged his love of classic slapstick comedy with this long free-for-all, which throws in everything but Laurel and Hardy's kitchen sink. The film reunites *Some Like It Hot* stars Tony Curtis and Jack Lemmon, ably aided by a spunky Natalie Wood. The subject is a New-York-to-Paris auto race in the early years of the twentieth century, pitting the Great Leslie (Curtis), a goody-goody dressed all in white—even his teeth sparkle—against the malevolent Professor Fate (Lemmon), whose coal-black heart is reflected in his handlebar mustache. He looks like a bill collector from a silent-movie melodrama. Lemmon does double duty, also playing the pampered, drunken king of a small European country, whose laugh sounds like the wail of a cat in heat. The film may be too long for its own good, and you really have to love Jack Lemmon to put up with his over-the-top performance, but it's side-splitting in spots. It's one of those movies, if seen in childhood, that stays in your mind for years afterward. Some of the bigger routines, such as a pie fight of epic proportions, don't work as well as the simple chemistry between the perpetually exasperated Professor Fate and his much-abused assistant, Max (a terrific Peter Falk)." See http://www.amazon.com/Great-Race-Sub-Jack-Lemmon/dp/B000063K2R/ref.

18. Val S. Golovskoy with John Rimberg, *Behind the Soviet Screen: The Motion-Picture Industry in the USSR 1972–1982,* trans. Steven Hill (Ann Arbor: Ardis, 1986), 135.

19. Author's interviews with Pidgaetskii, February 10, 1996; and with Vladimir Demchenko, a former lecturer for Znanie (Society of Knowledge), Dnipropetrovsk, January 12, 1992.

20. See, e.g., *Dneprovskaia Pravda,* August 25, 1975; and *Zoria,* August 27, 1975.

21. The citations here are from the summer school diary of Gusar, June 18, 1970, and July 5, 1971.

22. See especially my interview with Andrei Z., Dniepropetrovsk, June 12, 2005.

23. Summer school diary of Solodovnik, May 14, 1969.

24. In 1975 another old American comedy, *How to Steal a Million,* directed by William Wyler and featuring Audrey Hepburn and Peter O'Toole, was released in the Soviet Union, ten years after its original release in the United States. But it was never a box office success in Dniepropetrovsk. See *Dneprovskaia Pravda,* February 14, 1975. Also see the review by Ian Berznitskii, "Poltora chasa udovol'stvia," *Sovetskii ekran,* 1975, no. 11, 4–5.

25. Summer school diary of Gusar, July 5, 1971, and May 31, 1973. Author's interview with Pidgaetskii, February 10, 1996.

26. M. Bleiman, "Kak Vazhno byt' neserieznym," *Sovetskii ekran,* 1967, no. 24, 13.

27. According to the American film critics, "Funès trained in music hall and appeared in small parts in over seventy films before his first leading roles. These came with *Ni vu, ni connu / Incognito* (1958), *Pouic-Pouic* (1963) and especially *Le gendarme de Saint-Tropez* (1964) and its sequels, which made him the French king of comedy. Throughout the 1960s and 1970s, in contrast to Alain Delon's and Jean-Paul Belmondo's flatteringly virile heroes, de Funès, with his slight physique and ultra-mobile face, portrayed Frenchmen as irascible and bumbling petit-bourgeois. He was often paired with contrasting stars like Yves Montand and Bourvil, with the latter in *Le Corniaud / The Sucker* (1965) and *La grand vadrouille / Don't Look Now—We're Being Shot At* (1966), two of the biggest French box offices hits. His hallmark was barely contained rage— against authority, domineering wives, foreigners (his films were regrettably often sexist and racist). But overblown and incompetent as his characters were (the gendarme was the archetype), they still triumphed, and that is one secret of his immense popularity. The other was the great comic talent, unfortunately not always matched by his films." Ginette Vincendeau, *The Companion to French Cinema* (London: Cassell for British Film Institute, 1996), 79. See also *Novyny kinoekranu,* 1979, no. 6, cover p. 3.

28. As one film critic noted, "From his first lead in *La ferme du pendu* (1945), a peasant melodrama, he drew on his origins as a farmer's son to develop his early persona of the 'village idiot.' He emerged as a star in Claude Autant-lara's *La traversée de Paris / A Pig across Paris* (1956), for which he won a prize at Venice Film Festival. From then on, he broadened his comic peasant to embody the 'average Frenchman' duped by more aggressive middle-class partners. For French audiences his enduring appeal was comic, the not-so-simple peasant and epitome of the man in the street, vindicated through stardom" Vincendeau, *Companion to French Cinema,* 39–40.

29. At the beginning of his career, Oury went to the Paris Conservatory of Dramatic Art and acted in numerous Swiss films. Yet apart from a handful of appearances—among them in Jacques Becker's *Antoine et Antoinette* (1947) and in *Le dos au mur* (known in America as *Back to the Wall,* 1958)—Oury made his mark in French cinema as a director. See the review by James Travers at http://filmsdefrance.com/FDF_goury.html. Travers wrote: "Oury's real name was Max Gérard Tannenbaum. He was born in Paris, on 29th April 1919, the son of the Jewish violinist Serge Tannenbaum and art critic Marcelle Oury. He studied drama under René Simon and then at the Conservatoire national d'art. In 1939, he entered the Comédie-Française, where he had a role in "Britannicus." In 1940, he evaded the Nazis with his wife, the actress Jacqueline Roman, by moving to the Free Zone in France, then Monaco, before settling in Switzerland, where he worked as an actor for the Compagnie de Genève. He adopted his mother's maiden name to be his professional name—Gérard Oury. Oury's first film job as an actor was a small part in Raymond Lebousier's 1942 comedy *Les petits riens,* which starred Raimu and

Fernandel, two of the top performers of the day. The film was made in France at the time of the Nazi occupation, but in the Free Zone. After the war, Oury returned to France and continued his career as an actor, appearing in minor roles in films such as Jacques Becker's 1947 drama *Antoine et Antoinette.* In the 1950s, he played a number of notable supporting roles in films made in both France and England—*Le passe-muraille* (1951), *The Heart of the Matter* (1953), *Father Brown* (1954), *Les héros sont fatigués* (1955). André Cayatte's 1958 film *Le miroir à deux faces* marked a key point in Oury's professional and personal life. As well as appearing in the film (in one of his most memorable roles), Oury also contributed to the script, and began a relationship with its star, the woman who would remain his companion for life (although they never married)— Michèle Morgan. Encouraged by the success of the film, Oury decided to embark on a career as a writer-director, beginning with *La main chaude* (1960). His first three films, thrillers in the classic French polar mould, were not particularly noteworthy and are now pretty much forgotten. It was Gérard Oury's fourth film—*Le Corniaud* (1964)—which was to establish him not just as a director, but as the most successful mainstream film-maker in France of his day. The film, a riotous comedy starring the two most popular comic actors of the time, Bourvil and Louis de Funès, had an audience of just under 12 million in France alone, yet its success was overtaken by Oury's next film. *La grande vadrouille* (1966)—a big-budget wartime comedy which reunited Bourvil and Louis de Funès—sold over 17 million seats in France, a record that stood until the blockbuster *Titanic* was released in 1998. For the next decade, the arrival of a new Gérard Oury comedy would be a national event, eagerly awaited by the public, who were seldom short-changed."

30. The Russian title *Razinia* is similar to the English translation *The Sucker.* See information about the release of this film in Dniepropetrovsk in *Dneprovskaia Pravda,* December 18, 1968.

31. Summer school diary of Solodovnik, June 1, 1969.

32. *Dneprovskaia Pravda,* June 19, 1971.

33. In the United States, it was released under the title *Don't Look Now—We're Being Shot At.*

34. As one American film critic, Miles Bethany, wrote: "Louis De Funès, Terry-Thomas, Bourvil—if these names don't mean anything to you, your credentials as a cosmopolitan might be extremely suspect. Three of the biggest figures in the history of European filmed comedy signed on to Gérard Oury's *La Grande Vadrouille* (*The Big Stroll*), and the resulting alchemy brought forth box office gold: $17.2 million in ticket sales, a French national record which stood for 30 years until *Titanic,* the very symbol of the ugly American film industry if there ever was one, knocked it from its perch. Terry-Thomas sparkles as an English pilot lost in occupied France during the Second World War; Bourvil and Louis De Funès play Parisians who somewhat involuntarily aid the ubiquitous Resistance by smuggling a British major across German lines. De Funès, best known for his portrayal of the wacky French police officer in the highly popular series of *Gendarme* films, is a manic, elastic comic genius, a proto-Rowan Atkinson with a rubbery face and a knack for physical humor. Here, his portrayal of conductor Stanislas LeFort remains alert, witty and moving—even when he's spazzing out. The antic script, cowritten by the intelligent and able Danièle Thompson (*Cousin, Cousine*), plays more like *Hogan's Heroes* than any war movie really ought to—the stodgy, autocratic Germans are perpetually undermined by those scruffy, resourceful French scalawags—

but humor is Vadrouille's, and Oury's, justification, and almost all of the jokes work. It would be another few years before French cinema could muster up the courage to treat the Vichy period, and France's wartime complicity, with anything like genuine honesty." See http://www.amazon.com/gp/product/B00004VY6P/ref=imdbap_t_3/102-8620400-4872168.

35. Dimitris Eleftheriotis, *Popular Cinemas of Europe: Studies of Texts, Contexts, and Frame Works* (New York: Continuum, 2001), 81.

36. M. Dolinskii and S. Chertok, "Piero iz derevni Burvil," *Sovetskii ekran,* 1967, no. 17, 15.

37. I. Lishchinskii, "Posledniaia progulka Burvilia," *Sovetskii ekran,* 1971, no. 10, 16–17. See also Vincendeau, *Companion to French Cinema,* 39–40. After Bourvil's death in 1970, a series of films with Loius de Funès were released in the Soviet Union. The Soviet film critics praised them as the "humane comedies without violence and pornography." See the good essay about Louis de Funès by I. Lishchinskii, "Put' nakhodok, put' poter'," *Sovetskii ekran,* 1972, no. 1, 18–19. See also the announcements about a release of the comedies featuring Louis de Funès such as *Malen'kii kupal'shchik, Zamorozhennyi,* and *Chelovek-orkestr* in *Sovetskii ekran,* 1971, no. 24, 19, and 1973, no. 2, 21; and *Iskusstvo kino,* 1971, no. 6, 199.

38. See *Dneprovskaia Pravda,* February 19 and April 30, 1972.

39. Summer school diary of Gusar, May 31, June 17, June 27, and June 29, 1973. The citation is from the entry on June 30, 1973.

40. See about this film in a review by KGF Vissers on the IMDB Web site: "Louis-Philippe Fourchaume, another typical lead-role for French comedy superstar Louis de Funès, is the dictatorial CEO of a French company which designs and produces sail yachts, and fires in yet another tantrum his designer André Castagnier, not realizing that man is his only chance to land a vital contract with the Italian magnate Marcello Cacciaperotti. So he has to find him at his extremely rural birthplace in 'la France pro-fonde,' which proves a torturous odyssey for the spoiled rich man; when he does get there his torment is far from over: the country bumpkin refuses to resume his slavish position now the shoe is on the other foot, so Fourchaume is dragged along in the boor-ish family life, and at times unable to control his temper, which may cost him more credit then he painstakingly builds up." See http://www.imdb.com/title/tt0062120/plotsummary.

41. Author's interview with Pidgaetskii, February 10, 1996.

42. See especially the film *Le grand blond avec une chaussure noire* (*The Tall Blond Man with One Black Shoe*) (1972), about a hapless orchestra player who became an un-witting pawn of rival factions within the French secret service after he was chosen as a decoy by being identified as a super secret agent. As a Soviet film reviewer explained a plot of the film: "Two factions of the French Secret Service involve a seemingly normal orchestra player, Francois Perrin, into their battle as one side uses him as a decoy. Soon, agents are all over the place, and one of them, Christine, is sent to seduce François. Meanwhile, François has his own problems, tangled up in an affair with his best friend's wife." See T. Khlopliankina, "Prilkiuchenia skripacha," *Sovetskii ekran,* 1975, no. 1, 9. Another socially crtical film with Pierre Richard was *Le jouet* (*The Toy*) (1976). In this film, François, a journalist, during his touring a big store for an article, was chosen by the son of the owner, Rambal-Cochet, as his new toy. All afraid of the despotic indus-trial also the newspaper's owner, François was forced to agree in this masquerade. Be-

coming the friend of the child, he induced him who wants to make a newspaper, to publicly unveil the real tyrannical way of life of his father. See also B. Pakhomov, "Pier Rishar," *Novyny kinoekranu,* 1979, no. 9, 12.

43. See how popular French comedies were in 1974–75. *Malen'kii kupal'shchik* and *Razinia* were still a box office hits for two years. See, especially, *Dnepropvskaia Pravda,* December 15, 1974, 4, and January 17, 1975, 4. On the popularity of Pierre Richard's films, also see *Dneprovskaia Pravda,* June 25, 1976.

44. Author's interview with Pidgaetskii, February 10, 1996.

45. Author's interview with Yurii Mytsyk, Dniepropetrovsk, January 15, 1992.

46. Author's interview with Pidgaetskii, February 10, 1996.

47. On Gérard Philipe, see Vincendeau, *Companion to French Cinema,* 113–14.

48. See a recent review of this film: "Fanfan, a lazy young man from Paris, escapes from a forced marriage to the daughter of farmer and joins the army after Adeline promised him a glorious career in the French Army. After signing the contract, he finds out that Adeline is the daughter of his sergeant. In spite of this, he tries to make the "promised faith" in him true, but he is caught when he tries to introduce himself to Louis XV's daughter Henriette, who he shall marry due to his promised faith. He is sentenced to death, but Adeline convinces Louis XV that he shall be free. But Louis XV hasn't done this for free. So he tries to kidnap Adeline. Fanfan chases the kidnappers, but he has no success in this, but he captures the military enemy's supreme command. For this he receives the thanks of Louis XV. He promotes him and he's allowed to marry one of his daughters, Adeline, who has been adopted by Louis XV." This review, by Stephan Eichenberg, is at http://www.imdb.com/title/tt0044602/plotsummary.

49. *Dneprovskaia Pravda,* March 25, 1970; and *Zoria,* March 30, 1970.

50. See the summer school diary of Gusar, June 21, 1970, and May 31, 1972. Compare with the summer school diaries of Solodovnik, March 25, 1970; and of Vadimov, June 25, 1973. On the official fascination with Gérard Philipe in the Soviet film magazines, see I. Rubanova, "Vernost' prizvaniu," *Sovetskii ekran,* 1969, no. 9, 18–19; Galyna Mykhailenko, "Mytets'—gromadianyn (Do 50-richchia z dnia narodzhennia Zherara Filipa)," *Novyny kinoekranu,* 1973, no. 1, 14–15.

51. On *Black Tulip,* see L. Anninskii, "Pochernevshii tul'pan," *Sovetskii ekran,* 1970, no. 14, 15. According to one review of this film, "Alain Delon stars as twin brothers in Christian-Jaque's film based on a novel by Alexandre Dumas. Set in 18th-century France during rumblings of revolution, Guillaume De Saint-Preux is the legendary Black Tulip, battling for the people against the monarchy. In reality, he is not much more than a self-serving thief who steals from the rich in the name of the people, but keeps it for himself rather than giving to those in need. After his face is scarred to mark him as a bandit, he enlists the aid of his identical twin, Julien, to carry on his work. Unfortunately for him, Julien is a revolutionary at heart and the ensuing events are nowhere close to Guillaume's expectations."

52. Vincendeau, *Companion to French Cinema,* 101.

53. On Henri Decoin, see Vincendeau, *Companion to French Cinema,* 62–63; and on Alain Delon, see in ibid., 65. See also the numerous positive esays by Soviet film critics about Jean Marais and Alain Delon as well: M. Bleiman, "Kak Vazhno byt' neserieznym," *Sovetskii ekran,* 1967, no. 24, 13; Natalia Pankratova, "Skazki i real'nost' Zhana Mare," *Sovetskii ekran,* 1977, no. 23, 19; I. Lishchinskii, "Alen Delon," *Sovetskii ekran,* 1967, no. 7, 14–15; and Inna Solovieva and Vera Shitova, "Alen Delon bez

svoei teni," *Sovetskii ekran,* 1976, no. 3, 18–19. On Alain Delon, also see Viktor Diomin, "Portret mytsia iz shpagoiu," *Novyny kinoekranu,* 1977, no. 9, 15.

54. Tatiana Bachelis, "Voprositel'nyi znak," *Sovetskii ekran,* 1967, no. 11, 14–15; "Milen Demonzho," *Sovetskii ekran,* 1967, no. 24, 12. On the popularity of French films among Ukrainian filmgoers, see "Milen Demonzho," *Novyny kinoekranu,* 1972, no. 2, 14–15.

55. See documents of the executive committee of Dniepropetrovsk city Soviet in Derzhavnyi arkhiv Dnipropetrovs'koi oblasti (hereafter DADO), f. 416, op. 2, d. 1565, ll. 28–32, and f. 6327, op. 1, d. 840, ll. 7–29.

56. DADO, f. 416, op. 2, d. 1565, ll. 28–32, and f. 6327, op. 1, d. 840, ll. 7–29. On the popularity of Alain Delon's characters, such as the legendary Zorro, also see Andrei Sharyi, *Znak Z: Zorro v knigakh i na ekrane* (Moscow: Novoe literatirnoe obozrenie, 2008).

57. Summer school diary of Solodovnik, June 22, 1966.

58. The first time this film was shown in Moscow was during the International Film Festival in the summer of 1967. On the foreign films at the Moscow Film Festival of 1967, see Yu. Khaniutin, "Lenty spokoinye i bespokoinye," *Sovetskii ekran,* 1967, no. 19, 12–14. See also *Sovetskii ekran,* 1968, no. 24, 21.

59. On the release of the first film, see *Sovetskii ekran,* 1969, no. 24, 19. On its release in Dniperopetrovsk, see *Dneprovskaia Pravda,* October 10, 1968, and November 22, 1969.

60. *Dneprovskaia Pravda,* May 31, 1973.

61. Dmitrii Popov and Ilia Mil'shtein, *Oranzhevaia printsessa: Zagadka Yulii Timoshenko* (Moscow: Izdatel'stvo Ol'gi Morozovoi, 2006), 70. On Yulia Tymoshenko, see my interview with Andrei Z., June 12, 2005. See also my interviews with Natalia Vasilenko, Dniepropetrovsk, July 19, 2007; and with Vladimir Donets, Dniepropetrovsk, July 19, 2007. Compare with my interviews with Evgen D. Prudchenko, Central Library of the Dniepropetrovsk Region, July 18, 2007; and with Galina V. Smolenskaia, Central Library of the Dniepropetrovsk Region, July 18, 2007.

62. A majority of the interviewees mentioned this. See especially my interviews with Vasilenko, Donets, Prudchenko, and Smolenskaia. On *Zakhar Berkut,* see *Novyny kinoekranu,* 1971, no. 2, 8–9; and G. Êapralov, "O doblesti narodnoi," *Sovetskii ekran,* 1972, no. 11, 4. On *Yaroslav Mudryi,* see *Novyny kinoekranu,* 1982, no. 1, 8–9; and Vitalii Korotych, "Uroky na vsi chasy: Notataky pislia pem'ery," *Novyny kinoekranu,* 1982, no. 5, 5. See also the summer school diary of Gusar, June 12, 1972.

63. *Sovetskii ekran,* 1972, no. 10, 20. On this film in Dniepropetrovsk, see *Dneprovskaia Pravda,* February 7, 1973.

64. See the summer school diary of Vadimov, May 12, 1973. See also my interviews with Pidgaetskii, February 10, 1996; and with Askold B., a son of a head of tourist department in Dniepropetrovsk Trade Unions branch, Dniepropetrovsk University, April 15, 1993. See also DADO, f. 416, op. 2, d. 1565, ll. 22–26.

65. Author's interview with Igor T., KGB officer, Dniepropetrovsk, May 15, 1991. See how Vatchenko repeated the same theme of ideological education of the youth at the regional Komsomol meeting in 1972 in DADO, f. 22, op. 19, d. 2, ll. 135–45.

66. *Dneprovskaia Pravda,* February 7 and March 8, 1967.

67. For the details about this film, see James Howard, *Stanley Kubrick Companion* (London: B. T. Batsford, 1999), 63–72.

68. As J. Hoberman noted, "Even in America, the Spartacus scenario—preproletarian uprising against the mightiest ruling class on earth—was imagined largely by onetime Communists. Adapted by blacklisted Dalton Trumbo, a member of the so-called Hollywood Ten, from a book that helped to win the Stalin Peace Prize for its then-Communist author, Howard Fast, *Spartacus* marked a comeback for the Hollywood Left. [This film] was a story of universal liberation that ultimately reflected on social injustice within America—the legacy of slavery—and, implicitly, on America's potential to right that injustice elsewhere in the world." J. Hoberman, *The Dream Life: Movies, Media, and the Mythology of the Sixties* (New York: New Press, 2003), 3–4, 5. On the Cold War and the film, see p. 13. Stanley Konkin also emphasized the left-liberal "overtones" of the film: Kirk Douglas "was also an avowed liberal who had been instrumental in getting Dalton Trumbo off the blacklist by helping him find work as a screenwriter for two much-honored films of 1960, *Exodus* and *Spartacus*." See also Stanley Corkin, *Cowboys as Cold Warriors: The Western and U.S. History* (Philadelphia: Temple University Press, 2004), 213. According to Hoberman, *Spartacus* "was a movie awash with free-floating progressive tropes. As the Howard Fast novel gave American Communism a religious credo and a human face, Dalton Trumbo's adaptation provided a retrospective anthology of Popular Front attitudes. The slaves demand a New Deal. Their army is a WPA mural brought to life—all manner and color of kids and dogs, feisty grandmothers and sinewy laborers as virtuous as they humble." Hoberman, *Dream Life,* 26. And he continued: "It is tempting to read *Spartacus* as an allegory of Hollywood "swimming pool" Stalinism. The revolution is led by entertainers—the gladiators Spartacus and Crixus (John Ireland), and the poet Antoninus (Tony Curtis). There is even an injunction against informing: the defeated slaves refuse to denounce Spartacus." See this citation on p. 27.

69. Hoberman, *Dream Life,* 27. On the reception of the film in the United States, see Howard, *Stanley Kubrick Companion,* 69–70.

70. Yu. Khaniutin, "Dva poedinka Spartaka," *Sovetskii ekran* 1967, no. 7, 16–17; the citation is on 17. See also the Ukrainian magazine *Novyny kinoekranu,* 1970, no. 2, 16. For a good essay about the American actor Kirk Douglas as a fighter with capitalist society, see E. Lyndina, "Zrelost' talanta i kanony Gollivuda," *Sovetskii ekran,* 1971, no. 9, 16–17.

71. See the summer school diaries of Solodovnik, July 3, 1970; of Gusar, July 13, 1970; of Andrei Vadimov, July 14, 1970; and of Mikhail Suvorov, July 15, 1970. They were watching the film in Dniepropetrovsk and the towns of the region such as Sinel'nikovo and Pavlograd.

72. See, especially, *Dneprovskaia Pravda,* September 23, 1970, and May 18, 1972.

73. See the review of this film: "The Persian king of kings Xerxes has devoted his reign to realizing the ambition of his father, stopped by Greeks, to extend his Achaemenid slave empire to and beyond Greece, and marches in 480 BC with an unprecedentedly vast army. When a captured Spartan explorer shows unconditional courage even on the chopping block, he is spared and sent to the assembled Greek states at Corinth to report the Persian might. There the Athenian leader Themistocles manages to turn the defeatist tide by formally placing the Athenian fleet under the supreme command of Sparta, whose king Leonidas promises to defend Greece regardless who follows—but back in Sparta, the ruling council hesitates to commit the whole army until the Persians approach the Corinthian Isthmus, and even after an encouraging Delphi oracle—lose a king or all Sparta—is forbidden to lead it before the end of a religious

festival, so he takes off first, keeping his promise, with only his 300-men-strong body-guard. Realizing there is no time to wait for sufficient reinforcements, but abandoning the northern access to Greece proper may allow the Persians to swarm the country before it can make a proper stand, he decides to take a heroic suicidal stand: fight impossible odds till the last man at the narrow pass of Thermopylai to minimize the numeric disadvantage, in the hope this will buy enough time. They prove that Spartans deserve the reputation of the fiercest and best-disciplined fighters, ingeniously creating the element of surprise and driving the overconfident aggressor to growing despair by inflicting humiliating losses at every failing attack wave, even by the imperial body guard of 10,000 'immortals.' Just when Xerxes plans to return, faking a divine message, the traitor Ephialtes arrives." K. G. F. Vissers at http://www.imdb.com/title/tt0055719/plotsummary.

74. Author's interview with Askold B., April 15, 1993. The most popular was an old Italian novel about Spartacus. See Raffaele Giovagnoli, *Spartak* (Kiev: Dzherelo, 1966).

75. See the summer school diary of Gusar, September 23, 1970.

76. *Dneprovskaia Pravda,* May 28, 1972, and June 5, 1972; and *Zoria,* May 29, 1972.

77. D. Ch., "Romeo i Dzhulieta," *Sovetskii ekran,* 1969, no. 3, 16. A recent Western reviewer, Tom Keogh, described this film as follows: "Franco Zeffirelli's 1968 adaptation of Shakespeare's *Romeo and Juliet* was unique in its day for casting kids in the play's pivotal roles of, well, kids. Seventeen-year-old Leonard Whiting and 15-year-old Olivia Hussey play the titular pair, the Bard's star-crossed lovers who defy a running feud between their families in order to be together in love. Typically played on stage and in previous film productions by adult actors, the innocent look and rawness of Whiting and Hussey resonated at the time with a burgeoning youth movement from San Francisco to Prague. The tragic romance at the center of the story also clicked with anti-authority sentiments, but even without that, Zeffirelli scores points by validating the ideals and passions of strong-willed adolescents. Less successful are scenes requiring the actors to have a fuller grasp of the text, though the best thing going remains the unambiguous duel between Romeo and Tybalt (Michael York). Lavishly photographed by Pasquale de Santis on location in Italy, this *Romeo and Juliet* brought a different tone and dimension to a story that had become tiresome in reverential presentations." See http://www.amazon.com/Romeo-Juliet-Leonard-Whiting/dp/0792165055/ref.

78. Valerii Geideko, "Shakespeare po-italianski," *Sovetskii ekran,* 1972, no. 13, 15. See "Olivia Khassi: Leonard Uaiting," *Novyny kinoekranu,* 1972, no. 9, 16.

79. Summer school diary of Vadimov, July 21, 1972. And he added: "I need to watch this film again. I especially like the song from this film."

80. See my interview with Andrei Z., June 12, 2005. See also my interviews with Vasilenko, July 19, 2007; with Tatiana Yeriomenko, a former singer with the band Dniepriane, Dniepropetrovsk, April 20, 1988; and with Smolenskaia, July 18, 2007.

81. See the results of the readers' survey in *Sovetskii ekran,* 1973, no. 10, 12. Compare with reaction of the young filmgoers: I. Levshina, "Ia smotriu vse kina": Razdumia nad anketami, kotorye prislali samye iunye zriteli," *Sovetskii ekran,* 1973, no. 14, 17.

82. See "Nastupit vremia," *Rovesnik,* January 1974, no. 1, 23. It is noteworthy that the Soviet journalist who wrote this essay mentioned the role of Nino Rotta in composing music for the American film *The Godfather,* which was forbidden to be shown in the Soviet Union.

83. Author's interviews with Serhiy Tihipko, a director of "Privatbank" in Dniepro-

petrovsk, October 12, 1993; with Demchenko, January 12, 1992; and with Igor T., May 15, 1991.

84. Summer school diary of Gusar, October 14, 1972. He referred to *Ukroshchenie ognia,* the Soviet film about the origins of the Soviet space program and rocket-building industry. The paradox of the situation is that the film was showed in the empty movie theaters. Nevertheless, *Sovetskii ekran* considered *Ukroshchenie ognia* as one of the best Soviet feature films of 1972. See *Sovetskii ekran,* 1973, no. 10, 12.

85. These films were *Daki* (*Dacians*) and *Kolonna* (*Column*). They successfully competed with the French and American historical films for popularity among Dniepropetrovsk filmgoers during the 1970s. See *Dneprovskaia Pravda,* August 30 and September 8, 1970.

86. Author's interview with Igor T., May 15, 1991. The film was shown in July 1969 in the major movie theaters of Dniepropetrovsk. See *Dneprovskaia Pravda,* July 11, 1969. See a Soviet review of this film: "'Bikini' i dinozavry," *Sovetskii ekran,* 1969, no. 9, 17. See also a recent film review: "In this vivid view of prehistoric life, a man from the mean-spirited Rock People (John Richardson) is banished from his home. He soon finds himself among the kind, gentle Shell People and falls in love with one of their loving tribeswomen (Raquel Welch). The twosome decide to face the world together, cut off from all tribal support, alone in a deadly world of hideous beast and earth-shattering volcanic eruptions. The film's pioneering special effects have made it a true science-fiction classic."

87. Calculations were made on the basis of information from the film ads on the last page of the local newspapers *Dneprovskaia Pravda* and *Zoria* for the 1960s and 1970s. Besides of the Western movies, the melodramatic films from India and Arab countries were also very popular among the middle aged filmgoers.

88. Mickiewicz, *Media and the Russian Public,* 18–40, 73, 74. See also the recent article about the beginnings of Soviet television broadcasting and its impact on the cultural consumption in the 1950s and 1960s: Kristin Roth-Ey, "Finding a Home for Television in the USSR, 1950–1970," *Slavic Review* 66, no. 2 (Summer 2007): 278–306. For the details of television's development in the USSR, see Kristin Roth-Ey, "Mass Media and the Remaking of Soviet Culture, 1950s–1960s" (PhD diss., Princeton University, 2003). On television in Soviet Ukraine at the end of the 1960s and 1970s, see Ivan Mashchenko, *Telebachennia Ukrainy* (Kyiv, 2004), 52–54, 91ff.; and the documents in Tsentral'nyi derzhavnyi arkhiv vyshchykh organiv vlady ta upravlinnia Ukrainy, f. 4915, op. 1, d. 3438, ll. 4–9. The Dniepropetrovsk premier of *Spartacus* took place in the newly opened Panorama movie theater.

89. Mickiewicz, *Media and the Russian Public,* 73, 74. These films were *Ad'iutant ego prevoskhoditel'stva* (*An Adjutant of His Excellency*) and *Semnadtsat' mgnovenii vesny* (*Seventeen Moments of the Spring*). They attracted an attention of the millions of the Soviet TV viewers all over the Soviet Union. On the immense popularity of these TV series, see *Sovetskii ekran,* 1973, no. 10, 12, and no. 24, 4–5.

90. Author's interview with Askold B., April 15, 1993. The most popular TV series for children was a Polish film about the adventures of the Polish tank crew during World War II, *Chetyre tankista i sobaka* (*Four Members of Tank Crew and a Dog*). See *Novyny kinoekranu,* 1970, no. 2, 14. See the article about the BBC's adaptation of *David Copperfield,* which was shown on Soviet TV: Aleksandr Anikst, "Bez vdokhnovenia," *Sovetskii ekran,* 1975, no. 24, 4. See also a negative review of the British TV film *The Moonstone* based on Wilkie Collins's detective novel, which was shown on Soviet TV as

well: Aleksandr Anikst, "Kamen' okazalsia ne dragotsennym," *Sovetskii ekran,* 1975, no. 20, 4.

91. On the similar processes among Siberian youth who idealized images from *Le Magnifique (Velikoplepnyi),* a French movie (a spy film parody) starring Jean-Paul Belmondo, see Andrei Makine, *Once upon the River Love,* trans. from the French by Geoffrey Strachan (New York: Arcade, 1998; orig. pub. 1994), 77–89.

92. *Dneprovskaia Pravda,* August 27, 1969, and February 19, 1972.

93. Author's interview with Igor T., May 15, 1991.

94. See the summer school diary of Vadimov, August 25, 1970. For a positive review of the film, see A. Vasiliev, "Na kvartire mistera Bakstera," *Sovetskii ekran,* no. 13, 17. Having been originally released in the United States in 1960, this film appeared in Soviet movie theaters in July 1970.

95. Author's interviews with Askold B., April 15, 1993; and with Vasilenko, July 19, 2007.

96. Author's interview with Pidgaetskii, February 10, 1996.

97. As Gusar noted in his diary after watching an American film, the police drama *New Centurions,* "It is good to live in the West when you have money and power, but it is very dangerous to live there if you are just ordinary poor man. I would rather stay in my own country." Summer school diary of Gusar, July 5, 1975. *New Centurions,* originally released in the United States in 1972, became a very popular film in 1974–75 in the Soviet Union. See *Sovetskii ekran,* 1975, no. 10, 6. Even in the early 1980s, Dniepropetrovsk ideologists complained about the immense popularity of Western movies, especially French and American ones, which had replaced "good Soviet films" on the silver screen of movie theaters. See especially E. Iakovlev, "Navazhdenie (kinoobozrenie)," *Dneprovskaia Pravda,* February 4, 1982.

Notes to Chapter 10

1. Many of the people I interviewed characterized this social group as "the upper middle class" of Soviet society. See my interviews with Mikhail Suvorov, Dniepropetrovsk, June 1, 1991; and with Eduard Svichar, Vatutino, Cherkassy Region, Ukraine, June 8, 2004, and July 28–29, 2007.

2. Dnipropetrovs'koi oblasti (hereafter DADO), f. 19, op. 60, d. 85, l. 7, 17. Also see the author's interviews with Andrei Vadimov, Dniepropetrovsk, July 20–21, 2003; and with Sergei Pulin, April, 15, 1990. It was an article about London hippies, with some history of the American hippie movement. See Yu. Ustimenko, "Liudi s tsvetami i bez tsvetov," *Rovesnik,* December 1967, no. 12, 10–11. On the different influences on Moscow hippies, see Andrei Makarevich, *"Sam ovtsa": Avtobiograficheskaia proza* (Moscow: Zakharov, 2002), 121–24.

3. Author's interview with Suvorov, June 1, 1991. Compare with a very idealistic description of hippies in L'viv: William Jay Risch, "Soviet 'Flower Children': Hippies and the Youth Counter-Culture in 1970s Lviv," *Journal of Contemporary History* 40, no. 3 (July 2005): 565–84. Many of the people who were interviewed by Risch represented the small number those in the local elite of the city of L'viv. Some of them assumed the hippie role later as a common fashion during the 1970s. I used information from other sources, including Eduard Svichar. See my interview with Svichar, June 8,

2004. Many friends of mine called themselves "hippies" because it was very "cool" to do this in the 1970s. But their style of life was very different from the Western type of hippie. Sometimes Western scholars, like Risch, took the words of their post-Soviet interviewees at face value and mistakenly interpreted a common youth fashion for a real mass movement among Soviet youth.

4. Author's interview with Vladimir Sadovoi, Dniepropetrovsk, March 10, 1992. See also Alexei Kozlov, *Dzhaz, rok i mednye truby* (Moscow: eksmo, 2005), 257–60; Risch, "Soviet 'Flower Children'"; and Alexei Yurchak, *Everything Was Forever, Until It Was No More: The Last Soviet Generation* (Princeton, N.J.: Princeton University Press, 2005), 138, 142, 201–2. See also my interviews with Oleksandr Beznosov, Department of History, Dniepropetrovsk University, July 19, 2008; and with Oleksandr Poniezha, Dniepropetrovsk, July 22, 2008.

5. During the Brezhnev era, the Soviet government introduced the vocational school form of education for those children who did not fit the intellectual requirements of the Soviet high school level because they had bad grades in middle school. Therefore, Soviet PTUs provided cadres from the Soviet working class and peasantry for factories and collective farms.

6. Author's interviews with Suvorov, June 1, 1991; with Aleksandr Gusar, May 4, 1990; and with Vladimir Solodovnik, Dniepropetrovsk, June 21, 1991.

7. All two hundred of my interviewees used the word "democratization." See especially my interviews with Solodovnik, June 21, 1991; and with Svichar, June 8, 2004. Compare with my interview with Sadovoi, March 10, 1992.

8. See my interview with Svichar, June 8, 2004.

9. Dmitrii Popov and Ilia Mil'shtein, *Oranzhevaia printsessa: Zagadka Yulii Timoshenko* (Moscow: Izdatel'stvo Ol'gi Morozovoi, 2006), 55. See also my interview with Andrei Z., Dniepropetrovsk, June 12, 2005. Compare with the summer school diaries of Vladimir Solodovnik, May 22, 1971, June, 10, 1972, and July 15, 1973; and of Aleksandr Gusar, June 2, 1972, and August 14, 1973. In September 1970, at the beginning of the academic year, new foreign students began their studies at the Krivoi Rog colleges. Some of these students brought the Deep Purple record with them to their dorms. Local Soviet students then recorded this album on tapes. In this way, music reached the student dormitories in the "closed" city of Dniepropetrovsk by October 1970. After this time, student parties held dances for only Deep Purple's music. In 1972 and 1973, the most popular among all college students in Dniepropetrovsk were three Deep Purple albums, which were released after *Deep Purple in Rock: Fireball,* 1971; *Machine Head,* 1972; and *Who Do We Think We Are,* in 1973.

10. On this, see Leonid Parfenov, "Dvukhetazhnoe soznanie," *Ogonek,* March 10–16, 2008, no. 11, 20; compare with *Ogonek,* March 10–16, 2008, no. 11, 17. On his love for Deep Purple, see Nikolai Svanidze and Marina Svanidze, *Medvedev* (Saint Petersburg: Amfora, 2008), 126–27, 128–31.

11. Kozlov, *Dzhaz,* 261.

12. Author's interviews with Suvorov, June 1, 1991; with Gusar, May 4, 1990; and with Solodovnik, June 21, 1991. See also the author's interview with Sadovoi, March 10, 1992

13. On Uriah Heep's and Deep Purple's popularity among Siberian youth in the 1970s, see Sergei Soloukh, *Shizgara* (Moscow: Vremia, 2005), 481, 482 ff.

14. Author's interview with Svichar, July 28–29, 2007. Soviet Deep Purple fans were interested in all music related to their idols. During the 1970s and 1980s they in-

cluded in their collections any records released by the legendary musicians, including Deep Purple guitarist Ritchie Blackmore's new project, Rainbow, and its vocalist David Coverdale's new band Whitesnake.

15. Author's interview with Natalia Vasilenko, Dniepropetrovsk, July 19, 2007. See also similar observations in my interviews with Tatiana Yeriomenko, a former singer with the band Dniepriane, Dniepropetrovsk, April 20, 1988; and with Yurii Kolomoets, a former musician with the band Dniepriane, Dniepropetrovsk, March 12, 1991.

16. The most popular Western musicians who represented the beginning of the glam-rock movement in Soviet Ukraine included (besides Slade and T. Rex) British bands such as Sweet, Gary Glitter (with his legendary long anthem "Rock and Roll"), Geordie, and the old hard-rock boogie band Status Quo. On Leningrad, see Thomas Cushman, *Notes from Underground: Rock Music Counterculture in Russia* (Albany: State University of New York Press, 1995), 42, 44, 47. On Moscow, see Makarevich, *"Sam ovtsa,"* 126 ff.; and Kozlov, *Dzhaz,* 261 ff. On L'viv, Odessa, and Kyiv, see the author's interview with Svichar, June 8, 2004. Also see the summer school diaries of Solodovnik, May 22, 1971, June, 10, 1972, and July 15, 1973; and of Gusar, June 2, 1972, and August 14, 1973.

17. Author's interview with Solodovnik, June 21, 1991.

18. Author's interview with Svichar, June 8, 2004. Compare with the author's recent interviews with Beznosov, July 19, 2008; and with Poniezha, July 22, 2008.

19. Will Straw, "Characterizing Rock Music Culture: The Case of Heavy Metal," in *The Cultural Studies Reader,* ed. Simon During (London: Routledge, 1993), 368–81; the quotations here are on 375, 377–78, 380. This is a reprint of Straw's essay in *On Record: Rock, Pop, and the Written Word,* ed. Simon Frith and Andrew Goodwin (New York: Pantheon Books, 1990), 97–110. Straw also noted here: "While the terms 'rock' and 'rock and roll' recur within song lyrics and album titles, this is always in reference to the present of the performance and the energies to be unleashed now, rather than to history or to myth. Any 'rebel' or non-conformist imagery in heavy metal may be seen as a function of its masculine, 'hard' stances, rather than as a conscious participation in rock's growing self-reflexivity. . . . If, within a typology of male identity patterns, heavy metal listeners are usually in a relationship of polar opposition to 'nerds,' it is primarily because the former do not regard certain forms of knowledge (particularly those derived from print media) as significant components of masculinity—if the 'nerd' is distinguished by his inability to translate knowledge into socially acceptable forms of competence, heavy metal peer groups value competence demonstrable in social situations exclusively. . . . Heavy metal . . . provides one of the purest examples of involvement in rock music as an activity subordinate to, rather than determinant of, peer group formation."

20. On ethnodemographic developments in the big industrial cities of Ukraine, also see Bohdan Krawchenko, *Social Change and National Consciousness in Twentieth Century Ukraine* (London: Macmillan, 1985), 171–258; and Wsevolod Isajiw, "Urban Migration and Social Change in Contemporary Soviet Ukraine," *Canadian Slavonic Papers,* March 1980, 56–66.

21. On the typical situation in PTU dormitories, see M. Karpov, "Vechir u gurto-zhytku," *Prapor iunosti,* August 24, 1982.

22. See my interviews with Yurii Mytsyk, Dniepropetrovsk University, January 15, 1992; and with Vitalii Pidgaetskii, Department of History, Dniepropetrovsk University, February 10, 1996. See also numerous complaints about a loss of Ukrainian identity on the dance floor in DADO, f. 17, op. 8, d. 44, ll. 1–3, 175–76; f. 416, op. 2, d. 1353, ll. 23–26, 40-49; d. 1991, ll. 4–7, 14–23. Some experts connected a loss of identity to the

rise of crime among the local youth. See DADO, f. 416, op. 2, d. 1694, ll. 6–14; f. 18, op. 60, d. 28, ll. 74–76, 79.

23. DADO, f. 19, op. 53, d. 109, ll. 28–31, 38, 39, 40, 41, 46. See also the statistics for 1980–84 in DADO, f. p-18, op. 60, d. 28, l. 79. Compare with the post-Soviet identification of Russian youth discussed by Hilary Pilkington et. al., *Looking West? Cultural Globalization and Russian Youth Cultures* (University Park: Pennsylvania State University Press, 2002), 180.

24. Author's interview with Mytsyk, January 15, 1992. On homogenization as a part of the Soviet cultural project, see Stephen Lovell, *The Russian Reading Revolution: Print Culture in the Soviet and Post-Soviet Eras* (New York: St. Martin's Press, 2000), 22–23. Compare with the roots of this project in the Stalin era: Jeffrey Brooks, *Thank You, Comrade Stalin! Soviet Public Culture from Revolution to Cold War* (Princeton, N.J.: Princeton University Press, 2000). On the effect of the Soviet urban culture of the big industrial cities on the new workers, migrants from the villages and small towns, see M. D. Afanasiev, *Za knigoi: Mesto chtenia v zhizni sovetskogo rabochego* (Moscow: Kniga, 1987), esp. 36–43.

25. As Hilary Pilkington noted, Soviet ideologists were against mass consumption of Western pop music. They claimed that Western pop music was "primarily designed to help destroy rationality as well as the ability to appreciate 'real' culture, by inculcating blind consumerism, and it encouraged social passivity through a process of gradual stupefaction (*effekt ogluplenia*)." Western rock music, especially, was "condemned for its anti-Soviet nature; it was declared to constitute psychological warfare against the Soviet Union that had been targeted specifically at youth since they were a psychologically and emotionally susceptible section of the population." Hilary Pilkington, "'The Future Is Ours': Youth Culture in Russia, 1953 to the Present," in *Russian Cultural Studies: An Introduction,* ed. Catriona Kelly and David Shepherd (New York: Oxford University Press, 1998), 374.

26. Author's interviews with Suvorov, June 1, 1991; with Gusar, May 4, 1990; and with Solodovnik, June 21, 1991. See also the author's interview with Sadovoi, March 10, 1992.

27. These ballads represented a wide variety of songs—from "Soldier of Fortune" by Deep Purple and "July Morning" by Uriah Heep to "Black Magic Woman" by Santana and "Hotel California" by the Eagles. The favorite heroes of beat music of the 1960s, such as the ex-Beatle Paul McCartney with his new band Wings and the old Rolling Stones, became popular again on Dniepropetrovsk's dance floors in the middle of the 1970s. All the dance parties at all the Dniepropetrovsk colleges from 1975 to 1978 included obligatory hits from old rock stars, such as "Mrs. Vanderbilt" and "Let Me Roll It" by Paul McCartney and "Wild Horses" and "Angie" by the Rolling Stones. See my interviews with Suvorov, June 1, 1991; with Gusar, May 4, 1990; and with Solodovnik, June 21, 1991. See also my interview with Sadovoi, March 10, 1992.

28. On Soviet entertainment, including dancing, parks of culture and relaxation, and so on, during Stalinist times, see Sheila Fitzpatrick, *Everyday Stalinism: Ordinary Life in Extraordinary Times. Soviet Russia in the 1930s* (New York: Oxford University Press, 1999), 53, 90, 93, 94, 103. According to the Soviet system of cultural enlightenment, the special locations for socialist artistic activities were palaces of culture and parks of culture and relaxation, where the Soviet people could relax and spend their free time.

29. These associations were called "circles" (*kruzhki* or *sektsii* in Russian). For a good description of the system of Soviet palaces of culture, see Anne White, *De-Stalin-*

ization and the House of Culture: Declining State Control over Leisure in the USSR, Poland and Hungary, 1953–89 (London: Routledge, 1990).

30. See the official commentary about this in the Communist Party files in Derzhavnyi arkhiv Dnipropetrovs'koi oblasti (hereafter DADO), f. 22, op. 19, d. 2, ll. 142, 143; and f. 22, op. 22, d. 4, l. 110.

31. The number of high school students in the region of Dniepropetrovsk who regularly visited the local dance grounds increased from 42,200 during the 1960–61 academic year to 125,900 in 1970–71 and to 108,800 in 1983–84. The number of vocational school students, who were regular visitors to dance parties, grew from 13,800 in 1960 to 29,500 in 1970 to 49,600 in 1984. The number of technical school students increased from 20,200 in 1960–61 to 54,400 in 1970–71 and to 56,700 in 1983–84. The number of college students on the dance floor also grew from 21,700 in 1960–61 to 36,800 in 1970–71 and to 52,200 in 1983–84. TsSU USSR, Statistiche-skoe upravlenie Dnepropetrovskoi oblasti, *Molodiozh Dnepropetrovskoi oblasti: Statisticheskii sbornik,* ed. L. T. Glushkina and V. F. Iagniuk (Dniepropetrovsk, 1985), 8, 10, 12. For slightly different numbers, see Tsentral'noe Statisticheskoe Upravlenie Dnepropetrovskoi oblasti, *Dnepropetrovshchina v tsifrakh: K 40-letiu pobedy v Velikoi Otechestvennoi voine,* ed. L. G. Glushkina (Dniepropetrovsk, 1985), 75.

32. TsSU USSR, Statisticheskoe upravlenie Dnepropetrovskoi oblasti, *Molodiozh Dnepropetrovskoi oblasti,* 23; TsSU USSR, Statisticheskoe upravlenie Dnepropetrovskoi oblasti, *Dnepropetrovskaia oblast' za tri goda deviatoi piatiletki (1971–1973 gody): Kratkii staisticheskii sbornik* (Dniepropetrovsk, 1974), 64; Ispolkom Dnepropetrovskogo oblastnogo Soveta narodnykh deputatov, *Sotsial'no-ekonomiceskoe razvitie Dnepropetrovshchiny za 1986–1990 gg. Statisticheskii sbornik* (Dniepropetrovsk, 1991), 17–18.

33. DADO, f. 1860, op. 1, d. 2615, ll. 1–1ob.; d. 2938, ll. 1–1ob.; d. 3145, ll. 1–1ob.; f. 17, op. 10, d. 46, l. 9. As a Komsomol apparatchik noted, "On these fourteen dance grounds, there were professional vocal instrumental ensembles which are officially registered and their repertoire followed the officially approved program."

34. DADO, 7, op. 11, d. 1, l. 30.

35. TsSU USSR, Statisticheskoe upravlenie Dnepropetrovskoi oblasti, *Molodiozh Dnepropetrovskoi oblasti,* 14.

36. DADO, f. 22, op. 19, d. 2, ll. 142–43.

37. See DADO, f. 17, op. 7, d. 1, l. 76. Author's interviews with Suvorov, June 1, 1991; and with Vadimov, July 20–21, 2003.

38. DADO, f. 17, op. 8, d. 44, ll. 1–3.

39. Ibid., ll. 175–76; author's interview with Vadimov, July 20–21, 2003.

40. Author's interview with Vadimov, July 20–21, 2003. Also see the author's interviews with Suvorov, June 1, 1991; and with Svichar, July 28–29, 2007.

41. See the letter about an infamous family of *fartsovshchiks,* the Fedins from Dniepropetrovsk, in the Library of Congress, Rubinov Collection, box 24, folder 59B, letter 46674, ll. 1–2.

Notes to Chapter 11

1. Derzhavnyi arkhiv Dnipropetrovs'koi oblasti (hereafter DADO), f. 19, op. 52, d. 72, ll. 2–3, 16.

2. DADO, f. 19, op. 52, d. 72, ll. 1–18.

3. DADO, f. 22, op. 24, d. 141, l. 11; f. 1860, op. 1, d. 1248, l. 57; d. 1532, l. 68; d. 2278, l. 122.

4. DADO, f. 19, op. 52, d. 72, ll. 1–18.

5. Despite a few general works about the persecution of religion in the Soviet Union, there have been no recent historical studies of popular religiosity and cultural consumption in the closed Soviet cities such as Dniepropetrovsk. I refer to the standard works by Dimitry Pospielovsky, *The Russian Church under the Soviet Regime, 1917–1982* (Crestwood, N.Y.: St. Vladimir's Seminary Press, 1984), vol. 2; and Dimitry Pospielovsky, *A History of Soviet Atheism in Theory and Practice, and the Believer:* Vol. 1: *A History of Marxist-Leninist Atheism and Soviet Antireligious Policies;* Vol. 2: *Soviet Antireligious Campaigns and Persecutions;* Vol. 3: *Soviet Studies on the Church and the Believer's Response to Atheism* (New York: St. Martin's Press, 1987–88). Also see Walter Sawatsky, *Soviet Evangelicals since World War II* (Scottdale, Pa., 1981); Vasyl Markus, "Religion and Nationalism in Ukraine," in *Religion and Nationalism in Soviet and East European Politics,* ed. Pedro Ramet (Durham, N.C.: Duke Press Policy Studies, 1984), 59–81; and Sergei N. Savinskii, *Istoria evangel'skikh khristian-baptistov Ukrainy, Rossii, Belorussii Chast' II (1917–1967)* (Saint Petersburg, 2001). See also the beginning of Zoe Knox, *Russian Society and the Orthodox Church: Religion in Russia after Communism* (London: RoutledgeCurzon, 2004); and Catherine Wanner, *Communities of the Converted: Ukrainians and Global Evangelism* (Ithaca, N.Y.: Cornell University Press, 2007).

6. For the opinions of those who lived through persecutions during Stalin's and Khrushchev's times, see Savinskii, *Istoria evangel'skikh khristian-baptistov Ukrainy, Rossii, Belorussii Chast' II,* 193–209. On Khrushchev's assault on religion, see V. A. Alekseev, *Illiuzii i dogmy* (Moscow, 1991), 364–65, 368–75; and William Taubman, *Khrushchev: The Man and His Era* (New York, 2003), 512ff. On the results of the antireligious campaigns during late socialism, see Vasyl Markus, "Religion and Nationalism in Ukraine," in *Religion and Nationalism,* ed. Ramet, 59–81; and Yitzhak M. Brudny, *Reinventing Russia: Russian Nationalism and the Soviet State, 1953–1991* (Cambridge, Mass.: Harvard University Press, 1998), 28–39.

7. See *Ogonek,* April 17–23, 2006, no. 16, 63; Pospielovsky, *The Russian Church,* 327ff.; Pospielovsky, *Soviet Antireligious Campaigns and Persecutions,* 98ff.

8. See the KGB report about this in DADO, f. 19, op. 52, d. 72, ll. 1–18.

9. By the end of 1962, 35 priests were preaching in 31 Orthodox churches of the region, with 82 monks and thousands of active parishioners. At the same time, the police registered 38 communities with almost five thousand evangelical Christian Baptists, 105 Adventists, 88 Old Believers, and 64 Catholics in the region. In 1962, unregistered denominations, illegal according to the Soviet laws, included 77 the Jehovah Witnesses, 1,197 Pentecostals, 30 Seventh-Day Adventists, 80 members of the Orthodox monarchist underground movement, 80 Baptists, and 37 "Ioannite sectarians." DADO, f. 9870, op. 1, d. 48, ll. 19–20.

10. DADO, f. 6465, op. 2, d. 2, l. 15.

11. DADO, f. 22, op. 19, d. 2, l. 143. During 1962, 15,890 children were baptized in 39 Orthodox churches of the region; during 1966, 17,022 infants were baptized in 26 churches according to Orthodox tradition. Even in 1971, every third newborn baby in the region was baptized according to Christian rituals (in the Orthodox and non-Orthodox Christian churches).

12. DADO, f. 9870, op. 1, d. 48, ll. 26–27.

13. Ibid., ll. 26–28.

14. See the KGB report of July 22, 1967 in DADO, f. 19, op. 51, d. 74, ll. 65–66; see also f. 6465, op. 2, op. 2, ll. 16–18.

15. DADO, f. 9870, op. 1, d. 48, ll. 24, 28. From 1963 to 1967, almost 40 percent of former Orthodox Christians joined various evangelical groups in the region. A majority of them were younger than forty years old.

16. See, in detail, about the Initiative group, the split of 1961, and the formation of STs EKhB in 1965: Savinskii, *Istoria evangel'skikh khristian-baptistov Ukrainy, Rossii, Belorussii Chast' II,* 208–35. See also Sawatsky, *Soviet Evangelicals,* 157–99. The KGB also discovered a growing efficiency of the evangelical Christian propaganda in the region. In 1966, each congregation of Baptists in the region held approximately three meetings for worship per week; and by 1966, they had five to six meetings per week. During 1963, 120 preachers delivered their sermons for 40 Baptist congregations of the region. Three years later, despite the forcible closings of meeting houses, there were 300 preachers for 35 Baptist congregations. In 1963, the Baptists preached for approximately 1 hour during each meeting for worship, which made 3 hours per week, and approximately 15 hours per month. In 1966, the sermons usually lasted 2 to 3 hours or 15 hours per week and 60 hours per month. At the beginning of the antireligious campaign, only a few Evangelical Christian Baptist congregations had music orchestra. By 1966, every congregation had a music orchestra with a guitar band as the most popular form of such an orchestra, which performed during each meeting for worship. See in DADO, f. 19, op. 51, d. 74, ll. 6–7. Compare with material about Kharkiv evangelicals during the 1960s in Wanner, *Communities of the Converted,* 63–89.

17. See KGB reports about this in DADO, f. 19, op. 52, d. 72, ll. 17–18.

18. DADO, f. 9870, op. 1, d. 48, ll. 21–22. In 1961 alone, Pentecostals involved in their activities more than 20 local students, the best pupils of regional middle and high schools. These students became Pentecostal activists in 1962. Later, they took an active part in various public ceremonies such as funerals, weddings, etc., playing musical instruments and singing religious songs at the meetings for worship. In 1962, during the funeral of a member of local Pentecostal church in the town of Piatikhatki, 200 "sectarians" arrived. Many of them were the secondary school students ("*deti shkol'nogo vozrasta*") who played a prominent part in this ceremony.

19. DADO, f. 9870, op. 1, d. 48, l. 22.

20. Ibid., l. 28; see my interview with Eduard Svichar, Vatutino, Cherkassy Region, June 20, 2002. During 1964–67, more than half the new tape recorders in the region were bought by the members of various religious communities. The KGB data were based on department stores' statistics; DADO, f. 19, op. 52, d. 72, ll. 15–18. See also my interview with Igor T., KGB officer, Dniepropetrovsk, May 15, 1991.

21. DADO, f. 9870, op. 1, d. 48, l. 23.

22. Authors interview with Igor T., May 15, 1991.

23. DADO, f. 19, op. 48, d. 146, ll. 44–45.

24. DADO, f. 9870, op. 1, d. 48, l. 23.

25. See the most detailed KGB report in DADO, f. 19, op. 52, d. 72, ll. 1–18.

26. DADO, f. 19, op. 48, d. 146, l. 202.

27. Ibid., ll. 203–4.

28. DADO, f. 6465, op. 2, d. 2, l. 6. In April 1966, Baptist dissenters organized a meeting for more than 100 young activists in the city of Krivoi Rog. Representatives of different regions of Ukraine came to Krivoi Rog for this meeting of *initsiativniki.* The

police arrested all participants of this meeting. As it turned out, young Baptists from regions of Dniepropetrovsk, Kirovograd, and Cherkassy were the most active and enthusiastic representatives of this radical branch of the Ukrainian evangelicals. By the end of 1966, among 959 participants of all illegal religious meetings of Baptist dissenters, Pentecostals, and Adventists, 327 were people younger than thirty years old. See in DADO, f. 19, op. 50, d. 56, ll. 6–14; and f. 19, op. 51, d. 74, ll. 4–5.

29. DADO, f. 6465, op. 2, d. 2, ll. 174–75. Many young people joined Christian communities, and some of them later became successful college students. Even Oleksii Vatchenko, the first secretary of the regional committee of the Communist Party of the Soviet Union, noted that members of different religious denominations entered various colleges in the city of Dniepropetrovsk, such as the metallurgical and medical institutes, and became good students there. Despite the prevalent official atheist education, Communist ideologists still worried about religious influences, especially among the young intellectuals of the region. The most dynamic and expanding groups among religious young people were radical evangelicals. See DADO, f. 22, op. 15, d. 252, l. 62.

30. DADO, f. 6465, op. 2, d. 4, l. 4.

31. Ibid., ll. 33–34.

32. DADO, f. 6465, op. 2, d. 15, ll. 42, 72, 75, 98–99. Many of these young people were attracted to these meetings because of the new and interesting musical and theatrical forms. At the beginning, some of them became participants in the musical bands or choirs of local religious congregations without any serious involvement in other religious activities. Later, they became more interested in religious issues. Soviet officials noted this tendency and commented on the gradual evolution of interest among the young participants in the Baptist meetings from mere musical and theatrical forms to the religious substance behind these forms. More and more students of local schools became active participants in and organizers of mass religious celebrations in the Baptist communities, which were called "Days of Harvest." The police discovered in 1977 that almost one thousand young people (seventeen to twenty years old) who were not members of the Baptist congregation participated in these "Days of Harvest" of the Baptist churches in the region of Dniepropetrovsk.

33. DADO, f. 19, op. 52, d. 72, ll. 13–14.

34. DADO, f. 6465, op. 2, d. 2, ll. 19–20.

35. DADO, f. 19, op. 52, d. 72, l. 14.

36. DADO, f. 6465, op. 2, d. 4, l. 190; d. 18, l. 132. The Orthodox Church had twenty-five religious buildings for twenty-five Orthodox communities with 44 priests and 160–70 staff members during the 1970s. See DADO, f. 6464, op. 2, d. 3, l. 20 (figures for 1972), l. 49 (figures for 1973); f. 6465, op. 2, d. 6, l. 32 (figures for 1974), l. 88 (figures for 1975); and f. 6465, op. 2, d. 9, l. 49 (figures for 1976).

37. DADO, f. 19, op. 52, d. 72, ll. 29–32.

38. DADO, f. 6465, op. 2, d. 2, ll. 119–22, 240; f. 6465, op. 2, d. 4, ll. 14–18.

39. DADO, f. 6465, op. 2, d. 4, ll. 14–18. As a result of this KGB campaign against Bishop Antonii, the number of religious rituals decreased in the region after 1970. During that year, 30 percent of all newborn babies were baptized, and 42 percent of all those who died were buried according to Orthodox Christian rituals. In 1978, only 16 percent of infant babies were baptized and 32 percent of all dead were buried according to Orthodox rituals. Still, Communists and Komsomol members continued to baptize their children according to Orthodox ritual. In select localities, the number of funerals and

weddings performed according to Orthodox rituals continued to increase, even after bishop Antonii's removal. See DADO, f. 6465, op. 2, d. 18, l. 132. In 1976, 4 Communists and 108 Komsomol members baptized their children in the Orthodox Church. The number of funerals conducted according to Orthodox ritual increased to 200 during one year, 1976. See ibid., d. 15, l. 42.

40. DADO, f. 6465, op. 2, d. 15, l. 12.

41. DADO, f. 6465, op. 2, d. 4, ll. 225–26.

42. DADO, f. 6465, op. 2, d. 4, l. 239, 242–45; author's interview with Mikhail Suvorov, June 1, 1991.

43. DADO, f. 6465, op. 2, d. 23, ll. 175, 176.

44. See my interview with Vitalii Pidgaetskii, Department of History, Dniepropetrovsk University, February 10, 1996.

45. See my interview with Vladimir Demchenko, a former public lecturer for Znanie (Society of Knowledge), Dnipropetrovsk, January 12, 1992. See also my interviews with Evgen D. Prudchenko, Central Library of the Dniepropetrovsk Region, July 18, 2007; and with Galina V. Smolenskaia, Central Library of the Dniepropetrovsk Region, July 18, 2007.

46. See my interviews with Vladimir Solodovnik, Dniepropetrovsk, June 21, 1991; Demchenko, January 12, 1992; and Pidgaetskii, February 10, 1996; as well as my more recent interview with Eduard Svichar, Vatutino, Cherkassy Region, July 28–29, 2007, and the annual librarian reports for 1968–73 at the Central Library of the Dniepropetrovsk Region.

47. DADO, f. 19, op. 60, d. 85, ll. 7, 17. Some police officers reported that the hippies had publicly displayed various religious symbols, such as Christian crosses and icons, as well as "portraits of Krishna and Buddha."

48. Summer school diary of Solodovnik, June 12, 1971.

49. See my interviews with Anatolii T., a member of the Dnepropetrovsk Hare Krishna Community, Dniepropetrovsk, July 20, 2005; and with Solodovnik, April 3, 1990.

50. See how Soviet ideologists idealized folk rock and country music as "people's music" vs. "capitalist rock music." See, especially, "Narodnye intonatsii i sovremennye estrady," *Klub i khudozhestvennaia samodeiatel'nost'*, 1978, no. 15, 33; and Yu. Melov, "'Kantri': Liudi, legendy i biznes," *Yunost'*, 1979, no. 10, 88–93.

51. On the obligatory "folklorism" of official Soviet "mass culture," see Richard Stites, *Russian Popular Culture: Entertainment and Society since 1900* (New York: Cambridge University Press, 1992), 78–79ff. The band Dniepriane, from Dniepropetrovsk University, was the best-known folk-rock band to perform Ukrainian Cossack religious songs. See K. Klimenko, "Charuiuchi melodii fol'kloru," *Prapor iunosti,* February 20, 1982; Iu. Lystopad, "'Dniepriane' na beregakh Seny," *Prapor iunosti,* February 17, 1983; author's interview with Tatiana Yeriomenko, a former singer with Dniepriane, April 20, 1988; and author's interview with Iurii Kolomoets, a former musician with Dniepriane, March 12, 1991. On Dniepriane's trip to England, October 2–11, 1981, see DADO, f. 22, op. 30 (1981), d. 85, ll. 57–62.

52. Summer school diaries of Solodovnik, May 22, 1971, June 10, 1972, and July 15, 1973; and of Gusar, June 2, 1972, and August 14, 1973.

53. Timothy W. Ryback, *Rock around the Bloc: A History of Rock Music in Eastern Europe and the Soviet Union* (New York: Oxford University Press, 1991), 149. For how

Alexei Kozlov and his bad Arsenal were influenced by the music of *Jesus Christ Superstar,* see Alexei Kozlov, *Dzhaz, rok i mednye truby* (Moscow: EKSMO, 2005), 264–66; and author's interview with Solodovnik, June 21, 1991. On the real cult of Weber's opera among the Soviet youth in Siberia during the 1970s, see Sergei Soloukh, *Shizgara* (Moscow: Vremia, 2005), 450, 452.

54. See my interview with Suvorov, June 1, 1991. My mother, who was a librarian in the town of Vatutino in the Cherkassy Region of Ukraine, had the same complaints about this "Jesus" hysteria in 1974, when the opera *Jesus Christ Superstar* became suddenly popular among local kids. Other people mentioned this "Jesus" hysteria as well. See my interview with Svichar, June 20, 2002.

55. See the Russian editions of the works of the Polish author Zenon Kosidowski, *Bibleiskie skazania* (Moscow, 1966); and Zenon Kosidowski, *Skazania evangelistov* (Moscow, 1977). Also see the Russian translation of the work of the French author Leo Taxil, *Zabavnoe evangelie, ili Zhizn' Iisusa* (Moscow, 1963).

56. See my interviews with Svichar, June 20, 2002; and with Suvorov, June 1, 1991. My mother also confirmed the fact of this growing interest in Christianity among the young reading audience. See also the summer school diaries of Solodovnik, May 22, 1971, June, 10, 1972, and July 15, 1973; and of Gusar, June 2, 1972, and August 14, 1973. And see the "Yearly Reports" of the Dniepropetrovsk Central City Library, 1972–77. On how the Soviet atheistic magazine reacted to "Jesusmania," see T. Golenpol'skii, "Iisus Khristos: Superzvezda," *Nauka i religia,* 1973, no. 9, 87–90.

57. The leaders of the local tourist groups that traveled abroad complained about the new obsession with the metal crosses among young tourists. See DADO, f. 22, op. 24, d. 141, l. 11; f. 1860, op. 1, d. 1533, ll. 7, 8–9 (for 1972); f. 1860, op. 1, d. 1993, ll. 59, 70, 90–91, 119 (for 1976).

58. Summer school diary of Gusar, April 29, 1973.

59. The police recorded 11,400 young people who visited the church in 1972. The following year, only 8,500 people could get in the church through the police lines. See my interview with Suvorov, June 1, 1991. Compare with the official description in DADO, f. 6465, op. 2, d. 4, l. 23. See also my interviews with Igor T., May 15, 1991; with Yurii Mytsyk, Dniepropetrovsk, January 15, 1992; with Pidgaetskii, February 10, 1996; with Prudchenko, July 18, 2007; and with Smolenskaia, July 18, 2007.

60. Author's interviews with Sergei Pulin, April, 15, 1990; with Suvorov, June 1, 1991; and with Eduard Svichar, Vatutino, Cherkasy Region, Ukraine, June 8, 2004.

61. DADO, f. 6465, op. 2, d. 37, ll. 235–36. On Likhachev's archeological career, see V. Cherednichenko, "Zagadky syvykh kurganiv: Iz shchodennyka uchasnyka arkheologichnoi ekspedytsii," *Prapor iunosti,* September 11, 1981.

62. Author's interview with Aleksandr Gusar, May 4, 1990. See also author's interviews with Igor T., May 15, 1991; with Mytsyk, January 15, 1992; and with Pidgaetskii, February 10, 1996.

63. Author's interview with Solodovnik, June 21, 1991. Compare with the similar developments in the Cherkasy Region of Ukraine in the author's interview with Svichar, June 8, 2004.

64. Compare Alexei Kozlov, *Dzhaz, rok i mednye truby* (Moscow: EKSMO, 2005), 278–80, with the author's interview with Svichar, June 20, 2002.

65. See my interviews with Svichar, July 28–29, 2007; and with Suvorov, June 1, 1991.

66. DADO, f. 6465, op. 2, d. 15, l. 11. The tradition of *subbotniki* came from the old revolutionary ideas during the first years of the Soviet power, when Lenin and other Bolsheviks emphasized voluntary work by Communists as a main element of the new "Communist approach to work" in the socialist society. Given the fact that these "holidays of Communist work" were often organized on Saturdays, during weekends, people called them *subbotniki* (*subota* is Saturday in Russian). Traditionally, Communist ideologists devoted the most popular mass spring *subbotnik* to the anniversary of Vladimir Lenin on his birthday, April 22. In reality, they tried to organize these celebrations of Communist work on the eve of main religious holidays such as Easter. Thus, in 1977 the Dniepropetrovsk party leaders organized a *subbotnik* on Saturday, April 9, which was actually Easter Eve. On March 22, 1977, the Soviet administration of the region offered local ideologists a special program of activities for local youth. The goal of these activities was to prevent young people from visiting religious ceremonies at various churches. This program included antireligious lectures, dance parties, concerts, movies, and sports events. According to this anti-Easter program, the local administration had to ban baking and selling paschal bread and rolls with symbols of Easter and to forbid the use of personal and public automobiles for religious services. But the most important alternative to religious holidays, according to local ideologists, was *subbotniki*—"holidays of communist work." On *subbotniki,* see Alexei Yurchak, *Everything Was Forever, Until It Was No More: The Last Soviet Generation* (Princeton, N.J.: Princeton University Press, 2005), 94, 155.

67. DADO, f. 6465, op. 2, d. 15, l. 11. In the city of Dniepropetrovsk, more than eighty thousand people took part in a *subbotnik* organized for Easter Eve 1977, cleaning city streets, fixing furniture and sports equipment for schools, improving parks, planting more than 10,500 trees in the city, and so on. A week later, during the All-Union *subbotnik* of April 16, 1977, more than 2.2 million people participated in various forms of voluntary work in the region.

68. See my interviews with Suvorov, June 1, 1991; with Gusar, May 4, 1990; and with Igor T., May 15, 1991.

69. DADO, f. 6465, op. 2, d. 15, l. 20; author's interviews with Vadim Ryzhkov, May 18, 1995; with Solodovnik, June 21, 1991; with Pulin, April, 15, 1990; with Suvorov, June 1, 1991; and with Svichar, June 20, 2002. Komsomol activists played popular music through amplifiers outdoors to create a holiday atmosphere and boost the enthusiasm of the youth. As many participants recalled, sometimes these activists played not only songs of Soviet pop stars, such as Alla Pugacheva or Sophia Rotaru, but also popular melodies of Anglo-American rock bands. In downtown Dniepropetrovsk, the most popular music of the *subbotnik* of 1977 were Paul McCartney songs from his band Wings' album *Band on the Run,* some hits of the American band Creedence Clearwater Revival, and songs of the British bands Queen and Slade. Some old Communists criticized young rock music enthusiasts for playing "foreign tunes during a holiday of the Communist labor." As it turned out, the Komsomol ideologists had borrowed music tapes from the people in charge of the disco called Club Melodia. See DADO, f. 6465, op. 2, d. 15, l. 19.

70. DADO, f. 6465, op. 2, d. 38, ll. 356–63; author's interview with Suvorov, June 1, 1991.

71. DADO, f. 1860, op. 1 pr., d. 3157, l. 128. Compare with a description of international tourism during the Khrushchev era by Anne E. Gorsuch, "Time Travelers: So-

viet Tourists to Eastern Europe," in *Turizm: The Russian and East European Tourist under Capitalism and Socialism,* ed. Anne S. Gorsuch and Diane P. Koenker (Ithaca, N.Y.: Cornell University Press, 2006), 205–26.

72. See these reports in DADO, f. 22, op. 24, d. 141, l. 11; and f. 1860, op. 1, d. 1248, l. 57; d. 1532, l. 68; and d. 2278, l. 122. On the "criminal activities" of Z. Krupakova, a group leader during a Mediterranean cruise of 1978, see DADO, f. 1860, op. 1, d. 2278, l. 215; and author's interviews with Igor T., May 15, 1991; and with Askold B., the son of the former head of a tourism department of the Dniepropetrovsk Trade Union branch, Dniepropetrovsk University, April 15, 1993.

73. DADO, 6465, op. 2, d. 20, ll. 92–93.

74. DADO, f. 6465, op. 2, d. 40, ll. 4–5.

75. DADO, f. 5465, op. 2, d. 16, ll. 55–59, 62–65. In 1977, a group of people from Dniepropetrovsk sent a large donation to Pochaev Monastery and ignored the Soviet Peace Fund and any other Soviet funds that used to accept voluntary donations from the Soviet state.

76. The Russian Orthodox Church controlled 25 religious buildings, where 43 priests performed religious rituals, which included 26 weddings and 11,573 burial services in 1984. These priests conducted 5,611 baptismal ceremonies. It is noteworthy that there were 12 students and 93 adults among the newly baptized adults. Despite an increase of Jewish emigration to Israel and the United States from the region during the 1970s, Dniepropetrovsk's synagogue still functioned on a regular basis, with at least 200 staff members in 1984. Evangelical Christian Baptists registered 32 congregations with 88 ministers and 5,374 members in the region. Pentecostals had 2 registered congregations with 6 ministers and 242 registered members and 755 nonregistered members who rejected state interference. The Seventh-Day Adventists had 4 registered congregations with 6 ministers and 299 registered members. The Council of Churches of Evangelical Christian Baptists (*initsiativniki*) had 4 unregistered congregations with 5 ministers and 301 members. The Adventists-Reformists had 3 unregistered congregations with 6 ministers and 125 members. The Jehovah's Witnesses had 2 unregistered congregations with 6 ministers and 136 members. DADO, f. 6465, op. 2, d. 42, l. 52. If we add to these numbers the 100,000 regular visitors to the Orthodox Church and the 500 activists of Judaism, we have approximately 107,732 people whom the Communist ideologists considered religious. In 1984, the population of the region was 3,771,200. So according to our calculations of the official numbers, so-called religious people made up only 3 percent of the entire population, and at least 2 percent of these religious people lived in Dniepropetrovsk itself. See Statisticheskoe upravlenie Dnepropetrovskoi oblasti, *Dnepropetrovshchina v tsifrakh: K 40-letiu pobedy v Velikoi Otechestvennoi voine,* ed. L. T. Glushkina (Dniepropetrovsk, 1985), 10.

77. DADO, f. 6465, op. 2, d. 42, l. 33.

78. Author's interview with Igor T., May 15, 1991.

79. Author's interviews with Svichar, July 28–29, 2007; and with Suvorov, June 1, 1991.

80. Andy Bennett, *Popular Music and Youth Culture: Music, Identity and Place* (New York: St. Martin's Press, 2000), 198.

81. See my interviews with Natalia Vasilenko, Dniepropetrovsk, July 19, 2007; with Tamara M. Kozintseva, Dniepropetrovsk, June 20, 2005, with Vladimir G. Donets, Dniepropetrovsk, July 19, 2007; and with Oleksandr Poniezha, Dniepropetrovsk, July 22, 2008.

Notes to Chapter 12

1. Artemy Troitsky, *Back in the USSR: The True Story of Rock in Russia* (London: Omnibus Press, 1987), 25.

2. Timothy W. Ryback, *Rock around the Bloc: A History of Rock Music in Eastern Europe and the Soviet Union* (New York: Oxford University Press, 1991), 107–8. See also the author's interview with Vladimir Demchenko, a former public lecturer for Znanie (Society of Knowledge), Dniepropetrovsk, January 12, 1992.

3. Derzhavnyi arkhiv Dnipropetrovs'koi oblasti (hereafter DADO), f. 22, op. 19, d. 73, ll. 13–14.

4. As Ryback noted, "The disco evenings opened with an informational segment, which included discussions about individual rock bands supplemented with transparencies, musical examples, and appropriate ideological commentaries. At one discotheque, the Riga Pantomime Theater entertained the audience by dancing to the music of the British group Renaissance. With the pedagogical requirements fulfilled, the disco evenings gave way to uninterrupted dancing. At the end of the weeklong conference, the participants concluded that *diskoteki* could provide an effective means of entertaining young people while indoctrinating them with proper political and ideological guidance." Ryback, *Rock around the Bloc,* 159–60.

5. According to Ryback, "In the summer of 1978, Moscow contracted a British company to provide sound systems and music tracks for four hundred discos across the Soviet Union." Ibid., 160. See also Richard Stites, *Russian Popular Culture: Entertainment and Society since 1900* (New York: Cambridge University Press, 1992), 160.

6. The information about Kyiv and Odessa came from my interview with Eduard Svichar, Vatutino, Cherkassy Region, Ukraine, June 8, 2004. The information about L'viv came from my interview with Vitalii Pidgaetskii, Department of History, Dniepropetrovsk University, February 10, 1996. See also my interviews with Mikhail Suvorov, June 1, 1991; and with Vladimir Sadovoi, March 10, 1992. On the situation in the early 1980s, see Anne White, *De-Stalinization and the House of Culture: Declining State Control over Leisure in the USSR, Poland and Hungary, 1953–89* (London: Routledge, 1990), 76.

7. DADO, f. 17, op. 7, d. 1, l. 76.

8. Author's interview with Pidgaetskii, February 10, 1996. Also see the author's interview with Suvorov, June 1, 1991.

9. Yu. Milinteiko, "Pervye shagi diskoteki," *Prapor iunosti,* February 26, 1977; author's interview with Pidgaetskii, February 10, 1996.

10. Yu. Milinteiko, "Pervye shagi diskoteki," *Prapor iunosti,* February 26, 1977. For more information about Tukhmanov's album, see chapter 13 in the present volume.

11. See the author's interview with Igor T., KGB officer, Dniepropetrovsk, May 15, 1991. He always praised the ideological reliability of the Yuzhmash ideologists' entertainment efforts.

12. V. Ivashura and I. Manevich, "Rizhane dariat prazdnik," *Dnepr vechernii,* March 23, 1977.

13. M. Zobenko, ". . . I muzyka, povna vidkryttiv," *Prapor iunosti,* March 22, 1977.

14. On the transformation of this bar into the most popular disco club of 1982, see *Prapor iunosti,* January 9, 1982. Valerii Miakotenko, a disc jockey of the central city discotheque, rented the Red Coral in 1981–82, and organized very popular, but very ex-

pensive, dance parties there. Also see my interviews with Suvorov, June 1, 1991; with Aleksandr Gusar, May 4, 1990; with Vladimir Solodovnik, June 21, 1991; and with Sadovoi, March 10, 1992.

15. See the author's interview with Andrei Z., Dnipropetrovsk, June 12, 2005.

16. Author's interviews with Pidgaetskii, February 10, 1996; with Demchenko, January 12, 1992; with Suvorov, June 1, 1991; and with Andrei Vadimov, Dniepropetrovsk, July 20–21, 2003.

17. The Komsomol leaders declared these goals in public; see V. Ivashura, "Diskoteka stanovitsia populiarnoi," *Dnepr vechernii,* May 24, 1977. For the official report by Ivan Litvin, the first secretary of the city Komsomol committee, on December 17, 1977, see DADO, f. 17, op. 10, d. 1, ll. 32, 87, 98.

18. DADO, f. 17, op. 10, d. 1, ll. 97–98.

19. Ivashura, "Diskoteka stanovitsia populiarnoi."

20. DADO, f. 17, op. 10, d. 1, l. 98; Ivashura, "Diskoteka stanovitsia populiarnoi." See also O. Marchenko, "Tsia charivna dyskoteka," *Prapor iunosti,* May 21, 1977. Demchenko, who was present at the opening of this discotheque, also mentioned "a good cultural level" of this event; see my interview with Demchenko, January 12, 1992.

21. I. Chenous'ko, "Disko-klubu: Zelenuiu ulitsu," *Dnepr vechenii,* July 1, 1978.

22. Ibid.

23. M. Zobenko, "Supermodno: Tse ne modno," *Prapor iunosti,* October 20, 1979.

24. Chenous'ko, "Disko-klubu"; DADO, f. 22, op. 28, d. 1, ll. 41, 87.

25. DADO, f. 17, op. 11, d. 1, ll. 28–29; Chenous'ko, "Disko-klubu." Also see the author's interviews with Suvorov, June 1, 1991; and with Vadimov, July 20–21, 2003.

26. In 1982, this disco club rented the pavilion called Dnieper Dawn four days a week and a special dance hall in Chkalov Park two days a week. See B. Gran'ko, "Karbovanets' za tansi, try: Za kokteil', abo chomu vpav avtorytet 'Melodii,'" *Prapor iunosti,* June 24, 1982.

27. On the number of guests of the disco club in 1979, see I. Rodionov, "Vecher v diskoklube," *Dneprovskaia Pravda,* January 14, 1979. On guest numbers and admission fees and alcohol beverages in 1982 and 1983, see Gran'ko, "Karbovanets' za tansi, try"; and *Prapor iunosti,* January 15, 1983. On the profits of Melodia, see the author's interview with Suvorov, June 1, 1991. Also see the documents in DADO, f. 17, op. 11, d. 1, l. 28; f. 22, op. 36, d. 1, ll. 36, 37, 39, 40.

28. Rodionov, "Vecher v diskoklube."

29. Ibid.; DADO, f. 17, op. 11, d. 1, l. 29.

30. For a good description of this mechanism of sponsorship and management in Petrov's disco club, see L. Titarenko, "Tsikavi tsentry vidpochynku," *Zoria,* August 15, 1978; and my interview with Vadimov, July 20–21, 2003. See also the official documents in DADO, f. 22, op. 28, d. 1, l. 41. And see Alena V. Ledeneva, *Russia's Economy of Favours: Blat, Networking and Informal Exchange* (New York: Cambridge University Press, 1998), 1. Using the traditional structure of the original Yuzhmash discotheque of 1977, Petrov organized five groups of people who formed his club's council: (1) a technical department, (2) a music department, (3) a literary department, (4) an informational department, and (5) a department of translations. Sergei Varava, an engineer and enthusiast of rock music who used to play rock guitar himself, imitating Jimi Hendrix, became a disc jockey for Courier. Nine other enthusiasts were in charge of the five main departments of this disco club. They created special music programs, which won not only an official acknowledgement from the Dniepropetrovsk Komsomol

leaders but also the high prizes at the USSR competition of discotheques "Amber Spring-78" in Kaliningrad in 1978. Their programs included such themes as "How Beautiful Is the World," which covered music by a popular Soviet composer, David Tukhmanov; "Mysterious Cheslav Nieman," about a famous Polish rock musician; and "The Sound World of Aleksandr Gradskii," about a pioneer of Soviet rock music. See Titarenko, "Tsikavi tsentry vidpochynku."

31. V. Koroteieva, "Dyskoteka rozvazhae i vchyt': Nova forma dozvillia molodi," *Dzerzhynets'*, March 25, 1978; V. Koroteieva, "Rozbazhaiuchi, vchyty," *Dzerzhynets'*, September 22, 1978; O. Uzhvii, "Vechir u dyskotetsi," *Dzerzhynets'*, November 25, 1978.

32. A. Belkina, "Vechir u dyskotetsi," *Prapor iunosti*, December 11, 1979.

33. Author's interviews with Suvorov, June 1, 1991; and with Vadimov, July 20–21, 2003

34. A. Belich, "Diskoteka: ot fakta k priznaniu," *Komsomol'skoe znamia*, October 20, 1979; A. Belich, "Pervye: Vse—v Dnepropetrovske podvedeny itogi 1-go respublikanskogo smotra-konkursa diskotechnykh program," *Komsomol'skoe znamia*, October 24, 1979.

35. *Zdes' mozhno uznat' mnogo pouchitel'nogo: Iz opyta raboty Dnepropetrovskogo molodezhnogo diskokluba "Melodia"* (Dniepropetrovsk, 1979), 1–4.

36. DADO, f. 17, op. 11, d. 1, l. 28.

37. DADO, f. 22, op. 32, d. 1, l. 44. In the USSR, there were more than 50,000 officially registered disco clubs. See A. Gavrilenko and I. Galichenko, eds., *Sbornik rukovodiashchikh materialov i normativnykh dokumentov po kul'turno-prosvetitel'noi rabote* (Moscow: Ministerstvo kul'tury SSSR, 1983), 25; and G. Nikitiuk, "Razvlekaia, prosveshchat'," *Dnepr vechernii*, May 31, 1983.

38. Gavrilenko and Galichenko, *Sbornik rukovodiashchikh materialov*, 24–27, 133–35. As Anne White wrote, "There was a sustained attempt not only to render discos harmless but also to transform them into events of 'high ideological and artistic quality.' Soviet ideologists worried that it was youth music which was most often used by bourgeois propaganda for ideological sabotage on a variety of scales. This was the reason why the disco had to become a field of active ideological struggle, a channel for propaganda and counterpropaganda." White, *De-Stalinization*, 76, 77–79. At one disco that White visited in Voronezh in 1982, the participants protested by dancing between the projector and the slide screen during the "educational" sections of the evening. See also *Sovetskaia kul'tura*, December 1, 1984; and *Klub i khudozhestvennaia samodeiatel'nost'*, 1987, no. 14, 5.

39. See the definition of the "socialist discotheque" by Gavrilenko and Galichenko, *Sbornik rukovodiashchikh materialov*, 133.

40. The official resolutions of 1980 about the disco movement in the USSR complained about a widespread imitation of the worst patterns of capitalist mass culture by the Soviet disco clubs. See Gavrilenko and Galichenko, *Sbornik rukovodiashchikh materialov*, 26; and White, *De-Stalinization*, 76–77.

41. Gavrilenko and Galichenko, *Sbornik rukovodiashchikh materialov*, 26; White, *De-Stalinization*, 76–77.

42. Gavrilenko and Galichenko, *Sbornik rukovodiashchikh materialov*, 26; White, *De-Stalinization*, 77–78. White witnessed the discotheque movement in the central Russian provinces of the Soviet Union: "In the USSR, . . . there have been continued attempts to insert a socializing element or theme or merely provide an ideological label.

For example, dances are often preceded by a thematic evening with slides and speeches about, for example, heroic youth brigades; a fashion show may be punctuated with satirical sketches and interrogation by the compere of members of the audience ('what is your definition of beauty?', 'how would you describe contemporary woman?' and 'men, should women wear trousers?'); a lecture on religious burial rites may be titled 'Graves as a minor architectural form and atheist-patriotic education'; or a concert by a famous pop star may be 'in honor of the Great Patriotic War.'" See White, *De-Stalinization,* 78–79.

43. DADO, f. 22, op. 28, d. 1, l. 41.

44. DADO, f. 17, op. 12, d. 18, l. 15.

45. Meanwhile, since 1980, the USSR Ministry of Culture and All-Union Methodical Center of People's Creativity and cultural-educational work had published a series of special books about disco clubs, information about popular music, and music records. See the special series *Diskoteka: Muzykal'naia Estrada—Rekomendatel'nyi ukazatel' knig, statei, grampalstinok,* ed. N. V. Aksionova, (Moscow, 1980–85), 5 vols. See also *Diskoteka dlia shkol'nikov (Metodicheskie rekomendatsii),* ed. E. S. Tsodokov (Moscow: VNMTs NT and KPR, 1982). Compare with the Krasnoiarsk regional Komsomol publication: *Diskoteki, Muzykal'naia programma (Rekomendatel'nyi ukazatel' knig, statei, gramplastinok),* ed. A. Mertsalov, (Krasnoiarsk, 1985). And compare with the more conservative attitude toward disco clubs in Dniepropetrovsk: M. Dubilet, "'Za' i 'Protiv' 'Kolobka,'" *Dnepr vechernii,* April 10, 1981 (about children's disco club in downtown Dniepropetrovsk); M. Dubilet, "Gde uchastsia muzykanty?" *Dnepr vechernii,* June 2, 1981; V. Zan'kovskii, "'Gor'ko!' i nemnozhko grustno," *Dnepr vechernii,* December 17, 1981 (about commercialization of disco clubs and rock bands); and V. Machula, "Ne potakat', a vospityvat'," *Dnepr vechernii,* April 6, 1982 (about the city competition of disco clubs). The local Komsomol newspaper started a new series of publications with the title "The Secrets of Discotheques"; see Yu. Makova, "Daite veduchomu tochku opory," *Prapor iunosti,* January 20, 1981; and P. Lydovs'kyi, "Fantazuvaty rukhamy chy tovkatysia?: Dozvol'te zaprosyty do tantsiu," *Prapor iunosti,* April 2, 1981.

46. Gran'ko, "Karbovanets' za tansi, try"; F. Sukhonis, "Karbovanets' za tansi, try: Za kokteil'," *Prapor iunosti,* January 15, 1983.

47. Author's interviews with Suvorov, June 1, 1991; and with Vadimov, July 20–21, 2003. See also Ryback, *Rock around the Bloc,* 159. See also the author's interviews with Evgen D. Prudchenko, Central Library of the Dniepropetrovsk Region, July 18, 2007; with Galina V. Smolenskaia, Central Library of the Dniepropetrovsk Region, July 18, 2007; and with Natalia Vasilenko, Dniepropetrovsk, July 19, 2007.

48. On the national Ukrainian and Byelorussian theme in the city disco clubs in DADO, f. 17, op. 10, d. 1, ll. 87, 98; op. 11, d. 25, l. 88; op. 12, d. 18, l. 15; f. 22, op. 36, d. 1, ll. 36–37. See also the articles in local periodicals: Chenous'ko, "Disko-klubu"; L. Titarenko, "Tsikavi tsentry vidpochynku"; I. Rodionov, "Vecher v diskoklube"; and Belkina, "Vechir u dyskotetsi."

49. Author's interview with Igor T., May 15, 1991.

50. Ibid.; also see the author's interviews with Askold B., a son of a head of the tourist department in the Dniepropetrovsk Trade Unions branch, Dniepropetrovsk University, April 15, 1993; and with Serhiy Tihipko, a director of "Privatbank" in Dniepropetrovsk, October 12, 1993.

51. Author's interviews with Suvorov, June 1, 1991; and with Vadimov, July 20–21, 2003. Compare how Russian nationalism influenced the perception of Western rock mu-

sic in Soviet Russia during the same time: Yitzhak M. Brudny, *Reinventing Russia: Russian Nationalism and the Soviet State, 1953–1991* (Cambridge, Mass.: Harvard University Press, 1998), 148, 149.

52. Author's interviews with Suvorov, June 1, 1991; and with Vadimov, July 20–21, 2003. See also the author's interviews with Tatiana Yeriomenko, a former singer with the band Dniepriane, Dniepropetrovsk, April 20, 1988; and with Yurii Kolomoets, a former musician in the band Dniepriane, Dniepropetrovsk, March 12, 1991. Compare with the author's interview with Vasilenko, July 19, 2007. And see the author's interviews with Prudchenko, July 18, 2007; and with Smolenskaia, July 18, 2007.

Notes to Chapter 13

1. The band Teach In became popular among Melodia administrators because it won the Eurovision competition in 1975. Officially, Teach In's record was released under a license from CNR b. v. Grammofoonplaten Maatschappij (Leiden, the Netherlands). The Melodia record's number was GOST 5289-73 (C60-07403), and its price was 1.90 rubles. I still have this record in my music collection. The most popular Melodia compilations in the 1970s included "House of the Rising Sun," by the Animals; "Holiday," "I Can't See Nobody," and "To Love Somebody," by the Bee Gees; "Mary Long," and "Super Trouper," by Deep Purple; "Coz I Lov You," by Slade; "Funny Funny," by Sweet; and "Hot Love" and "Bang a Gong (Get It On)," by T. Rex. In the 1970s and early 1980s, Melodia also released popular hits by Elton John, Creedence Clearwater Revival, Pink Floyd, Jethro Tull, and other rock musicians from the West. Of course, the Beatles and Rolling Stones were represented by six *minions* ("small records," the Soviet version of single-song records), which were released by Melodia without any official license from Western recording companies. See my interviews with Eduard Svichar in Vatutino, Cherkassy Region, Ukraine, June 8, 2004; with Evgen D. Prudchenko, Central Library of the Dniepropetrovsk Region, July 18, 2007, and with Galina V. Smolenskaia, Central Library of the Dniepropetrovsk Region, July 18, 2007. Compare with my interviews with Natalia Vasilenko, Dniepropetrovsk, July 19, 2007; and with Vladimir Donets, Dniepropetrovsk, July 19, 2007.

2. A. Bagirov, *"Bitlz": Liubov' moia* (Minsk: Parus, 1993), 160–62. See my interview with Mikhail Suvorov, June 1, 1991; my interview with Aleksandr Gusar, May 4, 1990; and my interview with Vladimir Solodovnik, June 21, 1991. Also see my interview with Vladimir Sadovoi, March 10, 1992.

3. They were songs by the major stars of Western rock music, from Elton John and Pink Floyd to Jethro Tull. On these journals, see Timothy Ryback, *Rock around the Bloc: A History of Rock Music in Eastern Europe and the Soviet Union* (New York: Oxford University Press, 1991), 161; and Alexei Yurchak, *Everything Was Forever, Until It Was No More: The Last Soviet Generation* (Princeton, N.J.: Princeton University Press, 2005), 190, 217. *Krugozor* was very popular among Dniepropetrovsk consumers. In 1981 the local periodical devoted a big essay to this musical magazine, which began publication in 1963 with 100,000 copies and reached the height of its popularity in 1980 with 500,000 copies (including a popular journal for children, *Kolobok*). See S. Avdeenko, "Zvuchashchie gorizonty 'Krugozora,'" *Dnepr vechernii,* January 5, 1981, 4.

4. On détente, from the American point of view, see Walter LaFeber, *America, Russia, and the Cold War, 1945–2006* (New York: McGraw-Hill, 2007), esp. 282–98.

5. Young enthusiasts of rock music such as Solodovnik and Gusar requested a replay of Golubkina's show with a Moscow band covering McCartney's hit "Ms. Vanderbuilt" at least two times. See my interview with Gusar, May 4, 1990; and my interview with Solodovnik, June 21, 1991. See also my interviews with Prudchenko, July 18, 2007; with Smolenskaia, July 18, 2007; my interview with Vasilenko, July 19, 2007; and my interview with Donets, July 19, 2007.

6. Author's interview with Vladimir Demchenko, a former public lecturer for Znanie (Society of Knowledge), Dnipropetrovsk, January 12, 1992. See reports of trade union libraries in the region in Derzhavnyi arkhiv Dnipropetrovs'koi oblasti (hereafter DADO), f. 1860, op. 1, d. 2267, ll. 1–37, d. 2268, ll. 1–18 (for 1978), d. 2425, ll. 1–23, d. 2430, ll. 1–35 (for 1979), d. 2627, ll. 1–37 (for 1980), d. 2992, ll. 1–12 (for 1982), and 204 libraries for 1983 d. 3145, ll. 1–42. My mother, a librarian, who was in charge of reading room in a town of Vatutino, Chekassy Region, confirmed the same fact of immense popularity of *Rovesnik* during the 1970s.

7. On the role of *Rovesnik* in Soviet and post-Soviet Russian youth culture, see Hilary Pilkington, Elena Omel'chenko, et al., *Looking West? Cultural Globalization and Russian Youth Cultures* (University Park: Pennsylvania State University Press, 2002), 51.

8. Author's interviews with Suvorov, June 1, 1991; with Gusar, May 4, 1990; and with Solodovnik, June 21, 1991. See also the author's interview with Sadovoi, March 10, 1992. And see the Komsomol's publication in Dniepropetrovsk in 1979: *Zdes' mozhno uznat' mnogo pouchitel'nogo: Iz opyta raboty Dnepropetrovskogo molodezhnogo diskokluba "Melodia"* (Dniepropetrovsk, 1979), 1–4.

9. *Rovesnik,* February 1964, no. 2, 25. Apparently, this publication preceded a critical essay from *Krokodil* magazine in March 1964, which Timothy Ryback considers the first Soviet official publication about the Beatles. See Ryback, *Rock around the Bloc,* 62.

10. V. Orlov, "Sdelano na eksport," *Rovesnik,* July 1964, no. 7, 11.

11. This phrase was a title of the article: Leonid Mitrokhin, "Liudi, dostoinye pesni," *Rovesnik,* July 1964, no. 7, 14–15. *Rovesnik* published an article from French magazine about the "rockers" and "mods": *Rovesnik,* November 1964, no. 11, 14–15.

12. See Mark Traverse's song "Sixteen Tons" in *Rovesnik,* July 1965, no. 7, 25.

13. See an explanation by V. Zviagin in *Rovesnik,* September 1965, no. 9, 19, and an article about the Canadian singer Paul Anka: V. Voinov, "Ne prints iz skazki," *Rovesnik,* September 1965, no. 9, 8–9. See also the criticism of the Western pop idols such as Adriano Chelentano and Rita Pavone in Italy and the Beatles in England by D. Proshunina and V. Zviagin, "O buntariakh i sinei ptitse," *Rovesnik,* October 1965, no. 10, 16–17. At the same time the magazine published a serious and balanced article about the history of jazz music in 1966; see A. Volyntsev and V. Voinov, "Dzhaz," *Rovesnik,* May 1966, no. 5, 9, 16–17.

14. The journal reprinted an article from the French Communist newspaper about Bob Dylan, Joan Baez, and Barry McGuire: Klod Kro, "Slyshu, poiot Amerika," *Rovesnik,* July 1966, no. 7, 16–17, 19; and see Dylan's song "Blowing in the Wind" on p. 24 of the same issue.

15. See Oleg Feofanov, "Zhokei plastinok," *Rovesnik,* August 1967, no. 8, 16–17; Oleg Feofanov, "Gitary v ogne," *Rovesnik,* April 1968, no. 4, 15–18; and M. Kriger and

L. Pereverzev, "Dylan: Snova v puti," *Rovesnik,* September 1974, no. 9, 19–21. Despite the lack of interest in Dylan's music among a majority of Soviet rock music fans, *Rovesnik* kept publishing information about Dylan almost every year.

16. Mikhail Bruk, "Dean Reed," *Rovesnik,* February 1967, no. 2, 23–24.

17. On the Dean Reed phenomenon, see Ryback, *Rock around the Bloc,* 131–34; and Richard Stites, *Russian Popular Culture: Entertainment and Society since 1900* (New York: Cambridge University Press, 1992), 160, 176. See also Dmitrii Rozanov, "Krasnyi kovboi," *Rovesnik,* December 1971, no. 12, 15, 25; *Rovesnik,* May 1974, no. 5, the last page of a cover had sheet music and the lyrics of his song; and N. Rudnitskaia, "Dean Reed: Khudozhnik dolzhen riskovat'," *Rovesnik,* April 1978, no. 4, 23–25. Only the Beatles had more articles devoted to their work than Dean Reed in *Rovesnik.* See also a popular biography in English: Reggie Nadelson, *Comrade Rockstar: The Life and Mystery of Dean Reed, the All-American Boy Who Brought Rock 'n' Roll to the Soviet Union* (New York: Chatto & Windus, 1991).

18. A. Volyntsev, "Koroleva estrady," *Rovesnik,* September 1967, no. 9, 16–17.

19. Ibid., 17.

20. Compare with Ryback, *Rock around the Bloc,* 63. Ryback referred to a piece written by A. Martynova in 1968 as the first positive Soviet article about the Beatles. In fact, *Rovesnik* began this positive reevaluation of the Beatles' music for the Soviet youth's consumption. See also Martynova's article in *Sovetskaia kul'tura,* December 3, 1968.

21. M. Aleksandrova, "Zheltaia submarina," *Rovesnik,* July 1969, no. 7, 17.

22. See about popularity of this magazine among the Siberian rock music fans in the 1970s in Sergei Soloukh, *Shizgara* (Moscow: Vremia, 2005), 49.

23. During my student days in Dniepropetrovsk, I checked the annual reviews of the readers' records from the 1960s and 1970s through 1985 at the Regional State Library in Dniepropetrovsk and from 1966 to 1985 at the Vatutino City Library in the Zvenigorodka District of Cherkassy Region. Alexandr Gusar did the same for the Central City Library of Pavlograd, Dniepropetrovsk Region. His conclusions supports my findings as well. See also the comments about the popularity of the Komsomol publications, such as *Rovesnik,* among the young musicians and artists of the region of Dniepropetrovsk in DADO, f. 22, op. 22, d. 361, ll. 10–14. On the trade union libraries, also see DADO, f. 1860, op. 1, d. 2861, ll. 1–26; d. 2992, ll. 1–5. And see my interview with Gusar, May 4, 1990; and my recent interview with Eduard Svichar, Vatutino, Cherkassy Region, July 28–29, 2007.

24. Author's interviews with Suvorov, June 1, 1991; with Andrei Vadimov, Dniepropetrovsk, July 20–21, 2003; with Gusar, May 4, 1990; and with Solodovnik, June 21, 1991. See also the author's interview with Sadovoi, March 10, 1992.

25. *Rovesnik,* April 1968, no. 4, 25.

26. *Rovesnik,* December 1968, no. 12, 25. Author's interviews with Solodovnik, June 21, 1991; with Demchenko, January 12, 1992; and with Vitalii Pidgaetskii, Department of History, Dniepropetrovsk University, February 10, 1996. My mother, who was a librarian in charge of the reading room at Vatutino city library in Cherkassy region, recalled the same situation with issues of the magazine *Rovesnik.* See also my recent interview with Svichar, July 28–29, 2007.

27. *Rovesnik,* July 1969, no. 7, 25; February 1970, no. 2, 24; and March 1970, no. 3, 25. See the sheet music and lyrics in Russian for "Back in the USSR" in *Rovesnik,* August 1970, no. 8, 24. The English lyrics for "Give Peace a Chance" were short-

ened in the reprinting to remove "the awkward words" for the Soviet reader, such as "masturbation." See *Rovesnik,* November 1970, no. 11, 25

28. In July 2007, this author discovered that the pictures of the Beatles were cut out from the issues of the youth magazine in the Russian (Lenin) State Library in Moscow. In the collection of this library, see *Rovesnik,* 1973, no. 7, 21; and no. 10, 21–22.

29. A. Valentinov, "Dilaila: Poklonniki i khuliteli," *Rovesnik,* April 1969, no. 4, 14–15. See also *Rovesnik,* August 1970, no. 8, 19.

30. M. Belen'kii, "Kuda katiaitsia 'Rolling Stones'?" *Rovesnik,* September 1973, no. 9, 20–21.

31. This was an article about London hippies. See Yu. Ustimenko, "Liudi s tsvetami i bez tsvetov," *Rovesnik,* December 1967, no. 12, 10–11. See also a good article about the history of jeans consumption: "Eta staraia novaia moda," *Rovesnik,* January 1971, no. 1, 22.

32. On the story of hippies and rock music in Moscow, see S. Frederick Starr, *Red and Hot: The Fate of Jazz in the Soviet Union 1917–1980* (New York: Limelight Editions, 1985), 289–321; Artemy Troitsky, *Back in the USSR: The True Story of Rock in Russia* (London: Omnibus Press, 1987), 15–25; and Ryback, *Rock around the Bloc,* 112–14. See also Stites, *Russian Popular Culture,* 161. On the Ukrainian hippies from L'viv, see William Jay Risch, "Soviet 'Flower Children': Hippies and the Youth Counter-Culture in 1970s L'viv," *Journal of Contemporary History* 40, no. 3 (July 2005): 565–84. Andrei Makarevich and his friends in Moscow were influenced by an article in *Vokrug sveta;* see Andrei Makarevich, *"Sam ovtsa": Avtobiograficheskaia proza* (Moscow: Zakharov, 2002), 121–24.

33. People who lived in 1967 in Dniepropetrovsk confirmed this fact; see my interviews with Demchenko, January 12, 1992; and with Pidgaetskii, February 10, 1996.

34. L. Filippov, "Zolotaia likhoradka na Golgofe," *Rovesnik,* July 1972, no. 7, 20–21.

35. Author's interview with Solodovnik, June 21, 1991.

36. *Rovesnik,* August 1978, no. 8, 24. See also another article about the Who concert in Sweden in *Rovesnik,* November 1974, no. 11, 22; and March 1974, no. 3, 22.

37. M. Freed, "Kometa 'Kridens,'" *Rovesnik,* June 1974, no. 6, 24–25; M. Freed, "Tochnyi pritsel 'Shocking Blue,'" *Rovesnik,* October 1974, no. 10, 24. Also see the author's interview with Suvorov, June 1, 1991.

38. A. Troitskii, "Piaterka 'Tiomno-lilovykh,'" *Rovesnik,* March 1975, no. 3, 24–25.

39. See the two Pete Seeger songs in *Rovesnik,* August 1972, no. 8, 25; and see the reprints from Woody Guthrie's book, Woody Guthrie, "Zdorovo, Drug," *Rovesnik,* August 1973, no. 8, 19–21. On Joan Baez, see M. Kriger, "Iasnost' gornogo potoka," *Rovesnik,* April 1974, no. 4, 24–25. On Dylan, see M. Kriger and L. Pereverzev, "Dylan: Snova v puti," *Rovesnik,* September 1974, no. 9, 19–21. On Phil Ochs, see D. Berendt, "Ivot vam boli portret," *Rovesnik,* July 1977, no. 7, 14–16.

40. On this idealization of Afro-American blues in present-day post-Soviet Russia, also see Michael E. Urban and Andrei Evdokimov, *Russia Gets the Blues: Music, Culture, and Community in Unsettled Times* (Ithaca, N.Y.: Cornell University Press, 2004).

41. On Louis Armstrong, see L. Pereverzev, "Ia i dzhaz rodilis' vmeste," *Rovesnik,* March 1974, no. 3, 19–21. On Duke Ellington, see G. Donaldson, "Poslednee interv'iu Diuka Ellingtona," *Rovesnik,* December 1974, no. 12, 24–25. For the general contribution of African American musicians to modern popular music, see L. Pereverzev, "Tsveta chernoi muzyki," *Rovesnik,* February 1975, 18–21. On the origins of reggae music, see *Rovesnik,* July 1977, no. 7, 22; and 1982, no. 1, 28–30. On the concert tour of B. B. King

in Moscow in the spring of 1979, see N. Rudnitskaia and Yu. Filinov, "Vse khotiat znat', pochemu ia poiu bliuz," *Rovesnik,* August 1979, no. 8, 30–31. Also see a good article about American jazz by Leonid Pereverzev in *Rovesnik,* 1981, no. 4, 28–31; no. 8, 25–27; no. 12, 28–31; 1983, no. 1, 23–26; and no. 5, 27–28.

42. *Rovesnik,* January 1973, no. 1, 22.

43. "Beatles i bitlomania," *Rovesnik,* July 1973, no. 7, 18–21. See the new updated edition of this book: Hunter Davis, *The Beatles: Illustrated and Updated Edition* (New York: W. W. Norton, 2006).

44. See the interview with Petrov in *Rovesnik,* 1984, no. 9, 16–19. Hunter Davis's book was reprinted in Russian in *Rovesnik,* 1983, no. 8, 25–28; no. 9, 24–27, no. 10, 23–26, no. 11, 24–28; no. 12, 27–31; and 1984, no. 4, 15–17. See also the interview with Paul and Linda McCartney by Ch. Shaar Murrei, "Razgovor s 'bogami,'" *Rovesnik,* 1976, no. 8, 19–21. On Ringo Starr, see B. Yoffinden, "'Udarnaia' rabota skromnogo Ringo Starra," *Rovesnik,* 1977, no. 4, 22–23. On George Harrison, see L. Robinson, "Tridtsat' tri i odna tret'," *Rovesnik,* 1977, no. 5, 24–25, On John Lennon, see L. Robinson, "Delo," *Rovesnik,* 1977, no. 8, 20–21, 25. Also see the interview with George Harrison in *Rovesnik,* 1979, no. 10, 28–29. See also *Rovesnik,* 1982, no. 1, 27. For an essay about John Lennon and sheet music and the lyrics of John Lennon's "Woman Is the Nigger of the World," see *Rovesnik,* 1982, no. 8, 28–31; and also see *Rovesnik,* 1983, no. 4, 26, and other issues of this journal.

45. See, e.g., the article about Elton John in *Rovesnik,* 1975, no. 6, 25; and *Rovesnik,* 1979, no. 2, 30–31; about Jim Morrison and The Doors in *Rovesnik,* 1976, no. 4, 13–15; about Led Zeppelin in *Rovesnik,* 1976, no. 4, 24–25; about Uriah Heep in *Rovesnik,* 1976, no. 9, 23; about Emerson, Lake, and Palmer in *Rovesnik,* 1976, no. 10, 18–21; about Queen in *Rovesnik,* 1978, no. 1, 25; about Pink Floyd in *Rovesnik,* 1981, no. 11, 24–26; about punk rock and "new wave" in *Rovesnik,* 1978, no. 2, 19–21, and no. 6, 13–15. Also see other issues of this magazine.

46. The first information about ABBA appeared in *Rovesnik,* 1977, no. 1, 22. On the disco music of the Bee Gees, see Frenk Rouz, "Bratia po krovi," *Rovesnik,* 1979, no. 3, 26–27; and on disco clubs in socialist countries, see *Rovesnik,* 1979, no. 4, 25–27. See also L. Pereverzev, "Fenomen disko," *Rovesnik,* 1979, no. 11, 26–29; 1979, no. 12, 26–29; and 1980, no. 4, 29–31.

47. See, e.g., the summer school diary of Aleksandr Gusar, August 24, 1975.

48. See I. Porudominskaia, "'Pudis' poluchaet premiu" (about Puhdys), and A. Troitsky, "Spesha vniz" (about Slade) in *Rovesnik,* 1977, no. 9, 24–25.

49. Artemy Troitsky wrote three articles in this issue of *Rovesnik:* "Raduga Richi Blekmora" (about Rainbow), "'Nesushchie dozhd' o svoikh zadachakh konkretno" (about a band from East Germany), and "'Orly': Chisto kaliforniiskaia raznovidnost" (about the Eagles). And Ondzhei Konrad wrote "I snova 'M. Effekt'" (about a band from Czechoslovakia). See *Rovesnik,* 1979, no. 9, 28–31.

50. Given the average monthly salary of 100 rubles of a young Soviet specialist, such as a teacher or an engineer during the first years of their career, these products were very expensive.

51. Information about prices in Kyiv came from the author's interview with Svichar, June 8, 2004. The information about prices in Dniepropetrovsk is from the author's interviews with Suvorov, June 1, 1991; and with Sadovoi, March 10, 1992. The information about Supertramp appeared in *Rovesnik,* 1980, no. 1, 28.

52. See how Artemy Troitsky wrote about this album in 1987: "David Tukhmanov,

a professional composer already in his thirties who, unlike the other craftsmen of 'easy listening,' had an inkling of certain new trends and as a result recorded two 'concept' albums of quasi-rock titled 'The World Is So Beautiful' and 'The Waves of My Memory.' The formula for both was more or less the same: modern electric arrangements, guest 'underground' rock soloists (including Gradsky and Mekhrdada Badi, the Iranian vocalist from Arsenal), and the use of classical verses from the likes of Goethe and Baudelaire as lyrics. I can't say that Tukhmanov's songs were really strong, but compared to the unbelievably pathetic pop product options then available, his albums seemed like a real achievement and were bought up in record quantities by the music-starved youth." Troitsky, *Back in the USSR,* 36–37. Compare with Timothy Ryback's evaluation of this album in 1990: "'In the Waves of My Memory,' envisioned as a concept album, combined the lyrics of nineteenth- and twentieth-century poets with the sounds of Pink Floyd, Neimen, and the art-rock band Renaissance." Ryback, *Rock around the Bloc,* 158. In contrast to Ryback's opinion, the Ukrainian consumers of rock music never considered the Tukhmanov's album *How Beautiful Is This World* as the first Soviet rock album.

53. Besides British rock music hits, songs from Tukhmanov's album became popular for dance parties in the region of Dniepropetrovsk during 1976 and 1977. One particular song, with lyrics from medieval poetry about the adventures of an unfortunate student (*vagante*), survived musical fashions in the late 1970s and was included in the official programs of all student discotheques in the region by 1980. Author's interview with Gusar, May 4, 1990; see also the author's interviews with Solodovnik, June 21, 1991; with Sadovoi, March 10, 1992; and with Demchenko, January 12, 1992.

54. See how Soviet ideologists praised folk-rock music as "authentic music of the laboring masses." Komsomol journalists loved especially the Byelorussian folk-rock band Pesniary and its rock opera *Dolia* (The Fate). Mikhail Katiushenko, "Pesnia dlia nas," *Smena,* 1976, no. 24, 20–22. See also an article in the Ukrainian youth journal about Pesniary and praise for the Beatles' music as good Western music: Mykahilo Katiushenko and Pavlo Yakubovych, "Od 'Liavonov' do 'Pisniariv,'" *Ranok,* 1978, no. 4, 16–18. See an article about the Ukrainian disco clubs "Siogodni, zavtra, zavzhdy," *Ranok,* 1978, no. 6, 2–4. On Komsomol and rock music consumption, see Yurchak, *Everything Was Forever,* 207–37.

55. See the comments about this during the regional Komsomol conferences in Dniepropetrovsk, when the first secretaries of the Central Committee of the VLKSM from Moscow, B. Pastukhov (in 1980), and V. Mironenko (in 1984), warned about a danger of popularity of the Western mass culture among the Soviet youth. See, in detail, DADO, f. 22, op. 28, d. 1, l. 177; op. 36, d. 1, l. 36.

56. *Rovesnik,* November 1980, no. 11, 30–31.

57. Sharapov's letter was approved by the Komsomol ideologists and published under the title "People Think about Music" in "O muzyke . . . dumaiut," *Rovesnik,* November 1980, no. 11, 30–31; also see *Rovesnik,* June 1983, no. 6, and other issues for that year.

58. Author's interview with Gusar, May 4, 1990.

59. Author's interview with Suvorov, June 1, 1991.

60. See the positive Soviet reviews of this film in the main Soviet film magazines: Nina Zarkhi, "'O, schastlivchik!' Fil'm Lindseia Andersona," *Iskusstvo kino,* 1976, no. 4, 150–57; and Aleksandr Doroshevich, "Nesentimental'noe puteshestvie," *Sovetskii ekran,* March 1976, no. 3, 4–5.

61. Author's interviews with Igor T., KGB officer, Dniepropetrovsk, May 15, 1991;

and with Pidgaetskii, February 10, 1996. See also *Dneprovskaia Pravda,* August 19 and August 24, 1975.

62. Author's interviews with Solodovnik, June 21, 1991; with Suvorov, June 1, 1991; and with Gusar, May 4, 1990.

63. Author interview with Igor T., May 15, 1991.

64. Eduard Svichar recalls long lines of people waiting for beginning of *O Lucky Man!* shows in Kyiv, Cherkassy, and Odessa. Author's interview with Svichar, June 8, 2004.

65. Summer school diary of Andrei Vadimov, September 3, 1975. See also the similar reaction in the summer school diary of Gusar, August 24, 1975.

66. On Czech music parodies, see *Sovetskii ekran,* 1967, no. 24 (December), 14. On Polish music films, see *Sovetskii ekran,* 1970, no. 24, 19; and *Dneprovskaia Pravda,* December 1, 1970. On Soviet-Romanian films, see *Sovetskii ekran,* 1971, no. 6 (March), 20; and *Dneprovskaia Pravda,* April 17, 1971. On the Mikhalkov-Konchalovskii film, see *Iskusstvo kino,* 1974, no. 2, 32–40, no. 12, 29–38; *Sovetskii ekran,* 1975, no. 1, 10–13; and *Dneprovskaia Pravda,* December 15, 1974, 4; and January 10, 1975, 4.

67. Michael Makin of the University of Michigan, who visited the Russian city of Voronezh as a research scholar at the end of the 1970s, witnessed the mass enthusiasm of the local Soviet audience for the British film *O Lucky Man!* According to Makin, this enthusiasm was reminiscent of the beginning of Beatlemania on the British Isles in 1963–64. My conversation with Makin at the University of Michigan, Ann Arbor, June 1, 2007.

68. *Rovesnik,* February 1976, no. 2, 23, and July 1976, no. 7, 23. Author's interview with Suvorov, June 1, 1991. Yulia Grigian (Tymoshenko) classmates also wrote letters to the journal with the similar requests. See my interview with Andrei Z., Dnipropetrovsk, June 12, 2005.

69. Author's interviews with Sergei Pulin, April, 15, 1990; with Suvorov, June 1, 1991; with Gusar, May 4, 1990; and with Vadimov, July 20–21, 2003. See also the Komsomol recommendations of 1979 in *Zdes' mozhno uznat' mnogo pouchitel'nogo,* 1–4. As late as 1983, the local ideologists praised the serious rock music that was recommended by *Rovesnik:* V. Machula, "Shchedra muza: Muzyka," *Prapor iunosti,* December 15, 1983.

70. Author's interview with Serhiy Tihipko, a director of "Privatbank" in Dniepropetrovsk, October 12, 1993.

71. Author's interview with Suvorov, June 1, 1991. On Angela Davis, see Regina Nadelson, *Who Is Angela Davis? The Biography of a Revolutionary* (New York: Peter H. Wyden, 1972).

72. See the comments about this in my interview with Tihipko, October 12, 1993.

73. See my interview with Tihipko, October 12, 1993. *Rovesnik*'s publication of material about Manfred Mann was in response to a request from a Dniepropetrovsk student, Dmitrii Yarmosh. See *Rovesnik,* January 1984, no. 1, 26–27.

74. "The most popular Western bands," according to Yurchak, "played a version of art rock or hard rock; their music was neither 'light' nor 'melodious'; their compositions included multiple parts, with rich instrumental arrangements, complex, passionate, often operatic vocals, improvisational passages, changes in key, heavy guitar riffs, overdrive sounds and distortions, and an overall trancelike quality. Despite differences in styles, these different groups shared a musical aesthetic marked by a break with realism and the predictable, circular, and immutable aesthetic of light 'melodious' music. It was

precisely that break that made Western rock seem so perfectly appropriate for the work of constructing vibrant imaginary worlds." Yurchak, *Everything Was Forever,* 236.

75. Ibid. See the similar ideas in Dniepropetrovsk publications as well. A leader of the Dniepropetrovsk medical institute's disco club Galaktika shared the same ideas in 1982. See, especially, his article: M. Sukhomlin, "Teatr tinei grae . . . rock," *Prapor iunosti,* January 30, 1982. Compare with Machula, "Shchedra muza."

76. See also my interviews with Prudchenko, July 18, 2007; with Smolenskaia, July 18, 2007; with Vasilenko, July 19, 2007, and with Donets, July 19, 2007.

77. On the questionnaire, see DADO, f. 17, op. 11, d. 1, ll. 28–29; and the document of the Komsomol City Committee, *Zdes' mozhno uznat' mnogo pouchitel'nogo,* 1–4; author's interview with Suvorov, June 1, 1991. See also complaint about this music in the documents of the Dniepropetrovsk Regional Committee of Komsomol: DADO, f. 22, op. 28, d. 1, "Protokol XXIV Dniepropetrovskoi oblastnoi otchetno-vybornoi komsomol'skoi konferentsii," ll. 1–221, esp. ll. 26–27, 110, 201. On anti-Soviet music and the antisocial behavior of young people, see also, for 1980, DADO, f. 22, op. 28, d. 38, ll. 1–12; d. 74, ll. 1–21; For 1981, see DADO, f. 22, op. 30, d. 35, ll. 1–10; d. 63, ll. 1–46. As late as 1984, the Dniepropetrovsk audience had similar preferences. See L. Mishchenko, "I pochuty melodiu dushi," *Prapor iunosti,* August 16, 1984.

78. Author's interview with Suvorov, June 1, 1991. See also a similar situation in other regions of Ukraine, as related in the author's interview with Svichar, June 8, 2004. Also see the author's recent interview with Svichar, July 28–29, 2007; and the thoughts about this given by Machula, "Shchedra muza."

79. Author's interview with Suvorov, June 1, 1991. See also the author's recent interview with Svichar, July 28–29, 2007.

80. Author's interview's with Suvorov, June 1, 1991.

81. Ibid.

82. Author's interview with Eduard Svichar in Vatutino, Cherkassy Region, Ukraine, July 15, 2005. See also the author's recent interview with Svichar, July 28–29, 2007.

83. See my interviews with Svichar, June 8, 2004; with Sergei Pulin, April, 15, 1990; with Suvorov, June 1, 1991; with Gusar, May 4, 1990; with Vadimov, July 20–21, 2003; with Tihipko, October 12, 1993; with Solodovnik, June 21, 1991; with Demchenko, January 12, 1992; and with Pidgaetskii, February 10, 1996.

84. Author's interview with Igor T., May 15, 1991. On the domination of the Russian language in disco programs and rock concerts in Dniepropetrovsk, see V. Zan'kovskii, "'Gor'ko!' i nemnozhko grustno," *Dnepr vechernii,* December 17, 1981.

85. Author's interviews with Suvorov, June 1, 1991; and with Svichar, June 8, 2004. See also the author's recent interview with Svichar, July 28–29, 2007. On complaints that Western rock music ousted the Ukrainian language and brought Russified versions of rock songs in Dniepropetrovsk—a concert of the Moscow band Tsvety (Flowers) triggered these complaints—see I. Naidenko, "Iake nasinnia zronyly 'Kvity,'" *Prapor iunosti,* January 15, 1981. Compare with Yu. Makova, "Daite veduchemu tochku opory," *Prapor iunosti,* January 20, 1981.

86. From 1968 to 1975, the Moscow radio station Maiak (established in 1964) broadcast every Sunday a special music show by the journalist Viktor Tatarskii with the title *Zapishite na vashi magnitofony* (Please make your own tape-recording). Besides Tatarskii's radio shows, for many Ukrainian rock music fans, the most popular source of their music was "socialist" radio broadcast of Romania from Bucharest. This was mentioned by Mikhail Suvorov in the author's interviews with Suvorov, June 1, 1991;

and with Vadimov, July 20–21, 2003. Also see DADO, f. 19, op. 52, d. 72, ll. 25–28. Also see the author's interview with Igor T., May 15, 1991. On the radio stations Maiak and Yunost', see Aleksandr Sherel', *Audiokul'tura XX veka: Istoria, esteticheskie zakonomernosti, osobennosti vliaiania na auditoriu—Ocherki* (Moscow: Progress-Traditsia, 2004), 90–94. Also see the entries in the summer school diary of Gusar, May–August 1972, May–August 1973, and May–August 1974; and the summer school diary of Vladimir Solodovnik, June 12, 1970, July–August 1971, and July–August 1972.

87. Summer school diary of Gusar, June 1, 1974. Gusar mentioned an article by Mykola Solomatin, "Zhertvy chornoi magii," *Ranok,* 1974, January, no. 1, 18–19, and a book devoted to the history of Western pop music by the Moscow journalist Oleg Feofanov, *Tigr v gitare* (Moscow: Detskaia literatura, 1969). See also other articles in *Ranok:* Anatolii Povnytsia, "Tvoi dity, Brytanie," *Ranok,* 1970, no. 6, June, 17; 1971, no. 4, 8–9; and Valerii Voronin, "Amerykans'ki zustrichi," *Ranok,* 1975, no. 9, 17–18.

88. L. Vdovina, "Khto vidkrye molodi talanty?" *Prapor iunosti,* May 25, 1982. See also the official reports about the concerts organized by the trade unions and Komsomol in DADO, f. 22, op. 26 (1979), ll. 1–160; f. 1860, op. 1, d. 2427, ll. 1–26; and articles about the domination of the Russian language in pop culture: "Nebo muzyky," *Prapor iunosti,* June 1, 1982; June 3, 1982; and many other issues of this periodical for 1982.

89. V. Sotnikova, "Eti alye 'Maki,'" *Dnepr vechernii,* January 13, 1983; L. Tsaregorodtseva, "Na stsene: 'Vodograi,'" *Dnepr vechernii,* January 17, 1983.

90. I refer also to my conversation with Natalia Ambrosimova, a journalist from the Komsomol newspaper *Prapor iunosti,* Dniepropetrovsk, May 12, 1991. See also T. Vin'kova, "Profesionaly chy dyletanty," *Prapor iunosti,* June 13, 1983.

91. See the summer school diary of Gusar, May–August 1976; see especially the entry for August 29, 1976.

92. See Ralph S. Clem, "The Integration of Ukrainians into Modernized Society in the Ukrainian SSR," in *The Soviet West: Interpaly between Nationality and Social Organization,* ed. Ralph S. Clem (New York: Praeger, 1975), 60–70; L. I. Poliakova, "Zminy v etnonathional'nomu skladi naselennia pivdnia Ukrainy v 60–80-ti roky XX st.," in *Pivdenna Ukraina XX stolittia: Zapiski naukovo-doslidnoi laboratorii istorii Pivdennoi Ukrainy Zaporiz'kogo Derzhavnogo Universytetu,* ed. A. V. Boiko (Moscow: Zaporizhzhia, 1998), 227–37. See also a good analysis of these trends in English: Bohdan Krawchenko, "Ethno-Demographic Trends in Ukraine in the 1970s," in *Ukraine after Shelest,* ed. Bohdan Krawchenko (Edmonton: Canadian Institute of Ukrainian Studies, 1983), 101–19. See also Goskomstat USSR, Dnepropetrovskoe oblastnoe upravlenie statistiki, *Naselenie Dnepropetrovskoi oblasti po dannym Vsesoiuznoi perepisi naseleniia 1989 goda* (Dnepropetrovsk, 1991), 100, 102, 106, 116.

93. The quotations here are from the summer school diary of Vadimov, September 10, 1976, and the summer school diary of Gusar, October 21, 1976. See also the summer school diary of Solodovnik, June 12, 1972. Compare with the entries from the summer school diary of Mikhail Suvorov, February 12, 1977.

94. Stephen Lovell, *The Russian Reading Revolution: Print Culture in the Soviet and Post-Soviet Eras* (New York: St. Martin's Press, 2000), 22–23. On the homogenization of Soviet culture during Stalin's time, see Evgeny Dobrenko, *The Making of the State Reader: Social and Aesthetic Contexts of the Reception of Soviet Literature,* trans. Jesse M. Savage (Stanford, Calif.: Stanford University Press, 1997); and during the Brezhnev era, see Natalia E. Dobrynina, *Cherty dukhovnoi obshchnosti: Russkaia khudozhestvennaia literatura v chtenii mnogonathional'nogo sovetskogo chitatelia* (Moscow:

Kniga, 1983), esp. 51–69. On the concept of the "Soviet people," see Yitzhak M. Brudny, *Reinventing Russia: Russian Nationalism and the Soviet State, 1953–1991* (Cambridge, Mass.: Harvard University Press, 1998), 7, 43, 92. On the Soviet evaluation of the homogenization of the youth culture through cultural consumption, see Sergei I. Plaksii, *Tvoi molodoi sovremennik: Problemy sovershenstvovania obraza zhizni rabochei molodiozhi v zerkale sotsiologii* (Moscow: Molodaia gvardia, 1982), esp. 146–60. Compare with a sociological survey of the Ukrainian students in 1991: *Natsional'na samosvidomist' studets'koi molodi,* ed. N. I. Chernysh, I. V. Vasilieva, et al. (Toronto: Canadian Institute of Ukrainian Studies Press, 1993), esp. 29–76.

Notes to Chapter 14

1. Hilary Pilkington, *Russia's Youth and Its Culture: A Nation's Constructors and Constructed* (London: Routledge, 1994), 79.

2. See *Pravda,* July 15, 1983; *Ob ideologicheskoi rabote KPSS: Sbornik dokumentov* (Moscow: Izdatel'stvo politicheskoi literatury, 1983), 127. See the translation of this phrase in English by Paul Easton, "The Rock Music Community," in *Soviet Youth Culture,* ed. Jim Riordan (Bloomington: Indiana University Press, 1989), 56.

3. See, especially, his theoretical article: Yuri Andropov, "Uchenie Karla Marksa i nekotorye aspekty stoitel'stva sotsializma v SSSR," *Kommunist,* 1983, no. 3, 9, 23. See also his speech in *Pravda,* August 16, 1983.

4. The Illich Palace was known as a place where all the famous guest musicians from the capital cities performed. On a seminar for disco activists, see M. Sukhomlin, "Shkola zaproshue dysk-zhokeiv," *Prapor iunosti,* November 6, 1982. On ideological control, see Yu. Lystopad, "Ideologichna borot'ba i molod' (Notatky z oblasnoi naukovo-praktyuchnoi konferentsii)," *Prapor iunosti,* December 17, 1983.

5. See F. Sukhonis, "Pisniu druzhby zaspivuie molod'," *Prapor iunosti,* December 13, 1983.

6. On the anti–rock music campaign in 1983–84, see Artemy Troitsky, *Back in the USSR: The True Story of Rock in Russia* (London: Omnibus Press, 1987), 89–93 ff.; Timothy W. Ryback, *Rock around the Bloc: A History of Rock Music in Eastern Europe and the Soviet Union* (New York: Oxford University Press, 1991), 220–22; and Sabrina Petra Ramet, Sergei Zamascikov, and Robert Bird, "The Soviet Rock Scene," in *Rocking the State: Rock Music and Politics in Eastern Europe and Russia,* ed. Sabrina Petra Ramet (Boulder, Colo.: Westview Press, 1994), 190–91.

7. Ryback, *Rock around the Bloc,* 220; Easton, "Rock Music Community," 57.

8. *Komsomol'skaya pravda,* April 7, 1984. In another issue, this newspaper informed its readers that the spread of rock music in the Soviet Union was the result of "Operation Barbarossa Rock and Roll," a plan by the U.S. Central Intelligence Agency and NATO military intelligence to undermine the USSR. See *Komsomol'skaya pravda,* September 16, 1984. On the mass arrests of black marketers in the city of Dniepropetrovsk, see M. Skoryk, "Komersant (sudovyi narys)," *Prapor iunosti,* July 14, 1983; and in the region, see M. Larin, "Khytryi rynok," *Prapor iunosti,* August 4, 1983.

9. This list was published for the first time in *Komsomol'skaya pravda,* November 10, 1985. On first publications of the Soviet lists with "forbidden bands" in Englishm see Ryback, *Rock around the Bloc,* 221; and Ramet, Zamascikov, and Bird, "Soviet Rock

Scene," 191. Alexei Yurchak recently reprinted a similar list used by the Nikolaev regional Komsomol committee (in Ukraine) in January 1985. See Alexei Yurchak, *Everything Was Forever, Until It Was No More: The Last Soviet Generation* (Princeton, N.J.: Princeton University Press, 2005), 213–16.

10. Troitsky, *Back in the USSR,* 42–43. Troitsky explained that there were various reasons for rejecting punk in the Soviet Union in those days: "A psychological reason: having always been put down as a poor cousin of 'real' (high) culture, our rockers humbly strove for symbols of 'prestige,' meaning complex musical arrangements, technical virtuosity, poetic lyrics or even just chic costumery. The anarchic, consciously seedy pathos [of punk music] was alien to our musicians. . . . Another reason was that our listeners had an acute case of disco fixation. Teenagers who only recently had idolized Deep Purple, Slade and Sweet now couldn't live without Boney M and Donna Summer. [Another reason was] in the Russian understanding of music. We have no tradition of playing loud and fast and dirty. Maybe our love for melody and a 'clean' sound is embedded in the genes. How else can one explain the boundless love for a miserable group like Smokie or the enormous popularity of The Eagles in the late seventies . . . and the total disregard for The Sex Pistols, although everyone knew of their odious name." Troitsky referred to famous images of Sid Vicious (from the Sex Pistols) with swastika. On the Web, also see http://samaroundtheworld.blogspot.com/2006/08/sid-and-nancy.html; http://www.myspace.com/siddenyvicious; and http://www.geocities.com/punkscenes/ swazsid.nolanpurehell.jpg.

11. On the Clash, see *Rovesnik,* 1978, no. 6, 13–15; 1980, no. 10, 26; 1982, no. 4, 22–23. *Rovesnik* reprinted the sheet music and lyrics for two Clash songs, "The Guns of Brixton," in no. 4 for 1982; and "Know Your Rights," in no. 10 for 1983. On the album *The Wall* by Pink Floyd, see *Rovesnik,* 1981, no. 11, 24–26.

12. See the author's interviews with Igor T., KGB officer, Dniepropetrovsk, May 15, 1991; especially with Mikhail Suvorov, June 1, 1991, and with Andrei Vadimov, Dniepropetrovsk, July 20–21, 2003.

13. Author's interviews with Vladimir Demchenko, a former public lecturer for Znanie (Society of Knowledge), Dnipropetrovsk, January 12, 1992; and with Serhiy Tihipko, a director of "Privatbank" in Dniepropetrovsk, October 12, 1993. On the persecutions of punk musicians in socialist Hungary, see Anna Szemere, *Up from the Underground: The Culture of Rock Music in Postsocialist Hungary* (University Park: Pennsylvania State University Press, 2001).

14. Even during perestroika, local journalists and KGB officials still used these materials. They reprinted some British punks' declarations for the use of Komsomol ideologists. See L. Gamol'sky, N. Efremenko, and V. Inshakov, *Na barrikadakh sovesti: Ocherki, razmyshlenia, interviu* (Dniepropetrovsk, 1988), 139. Also see the author's interviews with Igor T., May 15, 1991; and with Suvorov, June 1, 1991. On the Hungarian situation, see Szemere, *Up from the Underground.*

15. M. Pozdniakov, "Piraty vid muzyky (v tumani antymystetstva)," *Prapor iunosti,* June 14, 1984. For Dniepropetrovsk, see the author's interviews with Suvorov, June 1, 1991; with Demchenko, January 12, 1992; and with Igor T., May 15, 1991. For Cherkassy and Kyiv, see the author's interview with Eduard Svichar, Vatutino, Cherkassy Region, Ukraine, June 8, 2004.

16. Author's interviews with of Igor T., May 15, 1991; and with Suvorov, June 1, 1991. On the similar situation in other regions of Ukraine, see the author's interview with Svichar, June 8, 2004.

17. See especially *Rovesnik,* 1981, no. 11, 24–26.

18. Author's interview with Igor T., May 15, 1991. Both Suvorov and Aleksandr Gusar mentioned that during an interrogation after confiscation of "The Final Cut" album, KGB officers gave them this explanation. See the author's interviews with Suvorov, June 1, 1991; and with Aleksandr Gusar, May 4, 1990. See also Yurchak, *Everything Was Forever,* 216–17. Yurchak obviously recalls his life in Leningrad during the same period.

19. On a public trial that took place on December 22, 1982, in Dniepropetrovsk, see the letter of a Communist Party of the Soviet Union veteran, Nadezhda Sarana, against local punks under the title "We Declare War on Everybody Who Interferes in Our Life and Work!" [*"Boi tem, kto meshaet nam stroit' i zhit'!"*], *Dnepr vechernii,* December 23, 1982; and A. Liamina and L. Gamol'skii, "Grazhdaninom byt' obiazan," *Dnepr vechernii,* December 23, 1982. Compare with the reaction of activists in "Iz vystuplenii uchastnikov sobrania," *Dnepr vechernii,* December 3, 1982. See also L. Vasil'eva, "Takim ne mesto sredi nas!" *Dnepr vechernii,* January 10, 1983. And see my interview with Suvorov, June 1, 1991.

20. "Spetsvypusk 'Politychnogo klubu Plu.',"*Prapor iunosti,* October 20, 1983.

21. Ibid.

22. A majority of the local youth periodicals demonstrated the obvious incompetence and ignorance of the Komsomol journalists about Western music. For typical essays about the ideological danger of foreign music for Soviet youth, see Yu. Lystopad, "Ideologichna borot'ba i molod' (Notatky z oblasnoi naukovo-praktychnoi konferentsii)," *Prapor iunosti,* December 17, 1983; S. Mykytov, "Khto zamovliaie rok-rytmy, abo pogliad na suchasnyi show business," *Prapor iunosti,* February 7, 9, and 11, 1984; M. Pozdniakov, "Piraty vid muzyky (v tumani antymystetstva)," *Prapor iunosti,* June 14, 1984; and O. Razumkov, "Prestyzhni detsybely," *Prapor iunosti,* November 27 and 29, 1984. Some of these publications were reprinted in a special collection of ideological material during perestroika; see the reprint of the old newspaper articles in a collection: L. Gamol'sky, N. Efremenko, and V. Inshakov, *Na barrikadakh sovesti: Ocherki, razmyshlenia, interviu* (Dniepropetrovsk, 1988), esp. 133–37.

23. Igor Tishchenko, "Poiot VIA 'Zemliane,'" *Dnepr vechernii,* January 21, 1984.

24. O. Rozumkov and M. Skoryk, "Komu zemliaky 'Zemliane'? (Rozdumy pislia kontsertu)," *Prapor iunosti,* March 15, 1984; M. Skoryk, "Komu zemliaky 'Zemliane' (Rozdumy nad poshtoiu), *Prapor iunosti,* April 17, 1984; *Prapor iunosti,* April 24, 1984.

25. Gamol'sky, Efremenko, and Inshakov, *Na barrikadakh sovesti,* 133.

26. Ibid., 134. Some university students suffered persecutions for posters of the British band Black Sabbath in 1984–85. See my interview with Oleksandr Beznosov, Department of History, Dnipropetrovsk University, July 19, 2008.

27. And the journalist continued: "Let's think again! There is no justification for collection of the Nazi regalia! Many people in the West understand this. And Leon Rappoport, an American professor from the University of Kansas, was absolutely right, when he sincerely declared: 'Collecting of Nazi relic is certainly one of the forms of fascist propaganda.'" Gamol'sky, Efremenko, and Inshakov, *Na barrikadakh sovesti,* 135–36. On Frolin's phrase, also see my interview with Suvorov, June 1, 1991.

28. Lystopad, "Ideologichna borot'ba i molod'." Oleksandr Beznosov, a professor of history at Dniepropetrovsk University, recalls how during the same period of time he (as an undergraduate history student in 1983) and his roommates were interrogated by the student dorm supervisors for the possession of records and posters of Black Sabbath,

Iron Maiden, and Kiss. Beznosov was almost expelled from the university. Only the interference of his academic mentor saved him. I refer to my conversation with Beznosov, Department of History, Dnipropetrovsk University, June 26, 2006.

29. G. Dubovyi, "Oberezhno! Zakhidna otruta!" *Prapor iunosti,* November 24, 1983; Mykytov, "Khto zamovliaie rok-rytmy"; Pozdniakov, "Piraty vid muzyky"; Razumkov, "Prestyzhni detsybely."

30. Gamol'sky, Efremenko, and Inshakov, *Na barrikadakh sovesti,* 137.

31. See my interviews with Oleksandr Poniezha, Dniepropetrovsk, July 22, 2008; and with Beznosov, July 19, 2008. On this film and similar cases during perestroika, see Richard Stites, *Russian Popular Culture: Entertainment and Society since 1900* (New York: Cambridge University Press, 1992), 152, 168, 170.

32. This was mentioned in the author's interview with Igor T., May 15, 1991.

33. See "Otchet Dnepropetrovskogo OK lksmu ot 23 dekabria 1983 g." in Tsentral'nyi Derzhavnyi Arkhiv Gromads'kykh Ob'ednan' Ukrainy, f. 7, op. 20, d. 3087, l. 43.

34. Author's interview with Igor T., May 15, 1991. On the arrests of black marketers, also see M. Skoryk, "Komersant (Sudovyi narys)," *Prapor iunosti,* July 14, 1983; and O. Ivangora, "'Dyskostoianka'. . . dlia khapug," *Prapor iunosti,* July 5, 1984. The students at Dniepropetrovsk University and Medical Institute were constantly harassed for their music preferences, especially the music of the group AC/DC. See my interviews with Beznosov, July 19, 2008; and with Poniezha, July 22, 2008.

35. See my interviews with Evgen D. Prudchenko, Central Library of the Dniepropetrovsk Region, July 18, 2007; with Galina V. Smolenskaia, Central Library of the Dniepropetrovsk Region, July 18, 2007; and with Natalia Vasilenko, Dniepropetrovsk, July 19, 2007.

36. Here I am quoting my interviews with Suvorov, June 1, 1991; and with Svichar, June 8, 2004. See also my interview with Gusar, May 4, 1990.

Notes to Chapter 15

1. On the role of tourism in Soviet society, see G. P. Dolzhenko, *Istoria turizma v dorevoliutsionnoi Rossii i SSSR* (Rostov, 1988), 150ff. See also Denis J. B. Shaw, "The Soviet Union," in *Tourism and Economic Development in Eastern Europe and the Soviet Union,* ed. Derek R. Hall (London: Belhaven Press, 1999), 137–40. On tourism and Soviet trade unions, see Blair Ruble, *Soviet Trade Unions: Their Development in the 1970s* (Cambridge: Cambridge University Press, 1981). Also see the papers in a recent collection about tourism in socialist countries, especially Karl D. Qualls, "'Where Each Stone Is History': Travel Guides in Sevastopol after World War II," in *Turizm: The Russian and East European Tourist under Capitalism and Socialism,* ed. Anne S. Gorsuch and Diane P. Koenker (Ithaca, N.Y.: Cornell University Press, 2006), 163–85; Shawn Salmon, "Marketing Socialism: Inturist in the Late 1950s and Early 1960s," ibid., 186–204; Anne E. Gorsuch, "Time Travelers: Soviet Tourists to Eastern Europe," ibid., 205–26; Wendy Bracewell, "Adventures in the Marketplace: Yugoslav Travel Writing and Tourism in the 1950s–1960s," ibid., 248–65; Scott Moranda, "East German Nature Tourism, 1945–1961: In Search of a Common Destination," ibid., 266–80; and Christian Noack, "Coping with the Tourist: Planned and 'Wild' Mass Tourism on the Soviet Black Sea Coast," ibid., 281–304.

2. Dolzhenko, *Istoria turizma,* 150. See also Shaw, "Soviet Union," 137–40. On tourism and Soviet trade unions, see Ruble, *Soviet Trade Unions.* According to the official data, for only the first six months of 1972, 79,601 Soviet tourists traveled in socialist countries, and 15,156 Soviet citizens visited capitalist and developing countries through the trade union travel agency. All together, from January to June 1972, 94,757 Soviet tourists visited thirty-nine foreign countries. During the same period, 6,119 foreign tourists visited the Soviet Union. Among them, 1,943 tourists from capitalist countries and 398 from socialist countries traveled on the equal exchange basis (*na bezvaliutnoi osnove*), i.e., without paying for travel plans in hard currency. In addition, 728 tourists came from West Germany, Italy, Austria, Belgium, and Finland, with a payment in foreign currency (equivalent to 27,800 so-called *invaliutnykh* rubles). Between 1,600 and 1,800 foreign tourists traveled daily in the Soviet Union in 1972. Soviet trade unions gave Inturist 770 rooms in hotels and tourist bases, and 2,500 rooms in camping zones for the reception of the foreign tourists. During the second half of 1972, the Central Council of the All-Union trade unions planned to send more than 165,000 Soviet tourists abroad and receive more than 9,000 foreign tourists in the Soviet Union. Moreover, the main emphasis was on profits. In 1973, Soviet trade union travel agency planned to increase a number of foreign tourists with payment in hard currency from 3,000 to 10,000. See Gosudarstvennyi arkhiv Rossiiskoi federatsii (hereafter GARF), f. 5451, op. 68, d. 483, l. 48.

3. See the KGB report on the situation in the region, which was submitted to the Communist Party regional committee on July 4, 1968: Derzhavnyi arkhiv Dnipropetrovs'koi oblasti (hereafter DADO), f. 19, op. 52, d. 72, ll. 1–4.

4. For the Soviet classification of tourism and recreation, see Shaw, "Soviet Union," 120–36.

5. In 1940, the region had only 2 sanatoria with 70 beds. By 1984, there were 33 sanatoria, pensions, and tourist hotels with 7,407 beds. Overall, in the USSR, the number of these facilities increased from 469 in 1940 to 2,566 in 1988. The region of Dniepropetrovsk had 39,600 summer camps for children with special children's tourist facilities in 1950, with more than 142,600 camps with tourist facilities for children in 1984. See Tsentral'noe Statisticheskoe Upravlenie Dnepropetrovskoi oblasti, *Dnepropetrovshchina v tsifrakh: K 40-letiu pobedy v Velikoi Otechestvennoi voine,* ed. L. G. Glushkina (Dniepropetrovsk, 1985), 69, 68; and Shaw, "Soviet Union," 122. In 1973, the Komsomol tourist organization Sputnik in the Dniepropetrovsk Region used three facilities to accommodate more than 6,000 young tourists, mainly secondary school students, from 160 cities in the Soviet Union. In 1980, this organization used six tourist facilities, including a fashionable hotel, the Dniepropetrovsk, to accommodate more than 36,000 Soviet tourists, and one modern hotel, the Kiev in Krivoi Rog, to accommodate 100 foreign tourists. See i DADO, f. 22, op. 19, d. 156 (1973–74), ll. 1, 2, 14; f. 22, op. 26, d. 102 (1979–80), ll. 1, 2, 4, 5.

6. On the origin of all these forms of tourism in Stalin's times, see Anne E. Gorsuch, "'There's No Place Like Home': Soviet Tourism in Late Socialism," *Slavic Review* 62, no. 4 (Winter 2003): 760–85; the citation here is on 769–70. On international tourism in the Khrushchev era, also see Gorsuch, "Time Travelers."

7. DADO, f. 1860, op. 1d, d. 7, l. 1.

8. DADO, f. 1860, op. 1d., d. 62, l. 28. In 1970, all the regional trade unions organized travel abroad for 2,027 people. This number included 1,930 tourists who bought their travel plans through Intourist, 82 workers who were sent by the trade unions, which

covered all their travel expenses, and 15 people who were taking medical care in health centers abroad. See DADO, f. 1860, op. 1, d. 1249, ll. 45, 46.

9. In 1972, the trade unions sent 3,192 local tourists to various locations in different countries. DADO, f. 1860, op. 1, d. 1533, l. 5.

10. DADO, f. 22, op. 22, d. 62, ll. 1–11. On the history of Sputnik's activities (1972–83) in Dniepropetrovsk, see an article on the regional leader of this organization: M. Blokha, "Klyche dalechyn' vitchyzny (Do 25-richchia BMMT 'Sputnyk')," *Prapor iunosti,* June 7, 1983. Also see the annual reports of the Ukrainian Republican office of Sputnik in the documents of the Ukrainian Komsomol in Tsentral'nyi Derzhavnyi Arkhiv Gromads'kykh Ob'ednan' Ukrainy (hereafter TsDAGOU), f. 7, op. 20, d. 1495, ll. 1–47 (for 1975); d. 1689 , ll. 1–43 (for 1976); d. 1732, ll. 1–32 (for 1977); d. 2041, ll. 1–43 (for 1978).

11. The citation here is in DADO, f. 22, op. 19, d. 156, l. 7.

12. Author's conversations with Karlo A. Markov, Dniepropetrovsk University, April 12, 1992; and with Natalia V. Bocharova, Dniepropetrovsk University, March 15, 1993. DADO, f. 22, op. 24, d. 67, ll. 10, 13, 16.

13. In 1974, Sputnik received 131 foreign tourists into the region and sent 13,031 people as domestic tourists and 488 as international tourists. At the same time, 4,167 local tourists went abroad through the trade unions traveling agency. In addition to these numbers, the Komsomol tourist organization usually sent approximately 300 young tourists to the international youth camps each year. See DADO, f. 22, op. 22, d. 4, l. 110. TsSU SSSR, Statisticheskoe upravlenie Dnepropetrovskoi oblasti, *Dnepropetrovskaia oblast' za tri goda deviatoi piatiletki (1971–1973 gody): Kratkii statisticheskii sbornik* (Dnepropetrovsk, 1974), 6.

14. In 1975, Sputnik sent 700 local tourists to foreign countries and 17,300 to domestic destinations. In 1976, it sent 828 as international tourists and 16,111 as domestic tourists. In 1976, the Ukrainian Sputnik organized travels and excursions for more than 1 million Soviet and foreign tourists; more than 20,000 Komsomol members from Ukraine traveled abroad. More than 10,000 Ukrainian young people relaxed in the international youth camps. More than 100,000 foreign young people visited Ukraine as tourists from 70 countries all over the world. See an article by an official of the Kyiv administration of Sputnik: Oleksandr Iemchenko, "Marshruty druzhby," *Ranok,* 1977, no. 2, 15–17. Compare with the numbers for Dniepropetrovsk in DADO, f. 22, op. 24, d. 67, l. 16. See also Gennadii Naumenko, "Orbity druzhby 'Suputnyka,'" *Ranok,* 1978, no. 3, 19.

15. DADO, f. 22, op. 24, d. 67, l. 16.

16. See the documents for the Dniepropetrovsk branch of Sputnik and the reports of leaders of tourist groups in DADO, f. 22, op. 22, d. 62, ll. 1–64; f. 22, op. 24, d. 141, ll. 1–42; f. 22, op. 30, d. 85, ll. 1–84. For figures on the population of the Dniepropetrovsk Region see, in official statistics, Tsentral'noe Statisticheskoe Upravlenie Dnepropetrovskoi oblasti, *Dnepropetrovshchina v tsifrakh,* 10. For the numbers of tourists see Sputnik's reports: DADO, f. 22, op. 19, d. 156 (1973–74), ll. 1, 2, 14; f. 22, op. 26, d. 102 (1979–80), ll. 1, 2, 4, 5; f. 22, op. 22, d. 61 (1974), l. 8; op. 22, d. 403 (1975), l. 4ob.; op. 23, d. 86 (1976), l. 4; op. 24, d. 67 (1977), l. 10; op. 30, d. 83 (1981), l. 3; op. 32, d. 71 (1982), l. 11; op. 34, d. 73 (1983), l. 14; op. 36, d. 73 (1984), l. 14. A number of the trade unions' tourists came from DADO, f. 1860, op. 1, d. 1991 (1976), l. 5; d. 2441 (1979), l. 3; d. 2836 (1981), ll. 1–206; d. 2837 (1981), ll. 1–201. In 1990, the zenith of perestroika, the number of trips abroad reached a peak for the entire history of the re-

gion. During this year, 2,130 people visited capitalist and developing countries on business trips or as guest scholars and scientists; 5,123 and 23,000 local inhabitants went, respectively, to capitalist and socialist counties as tourists. In general, 30,253 tourists from the region of Dniepropetrovsk went abroad that year. Even then, they still represented less than 1 percent of the entire regional population (0.77 percent of 3,905,200 people). Yet, with the addition of the number of emigrants who left the region for Israel and the United States (7,368 people), the overall number of those who traveled abroad was still very small, less than 1 percent (0.96 percent). See Ispolkom Dniepropetrovskogo oblsatnogo Soveta narodnykh deputatov, *Sotsial'no-ekonomicheskoe razvitie Dniepropetrovshchiny za 1986–1990 gg. Statisticheskii sbornik* (Dniepropetrovsk, 1991), 3, 78.

17. See, especially, John Urry, *The Tourist Gaze: Leisure and Travel in Contemporary Societies* (London: Sage, 2002). The citation here is from John Urry, "The 'Consumption' of Tourism," in *The Consumption Reader,* ed. David B. Clarke, Marcus A. Doel, and Kate M. L. Housiaux (London: Routledge, 2003), 117–21. See also John Urry, "Consuming Places: Cites and Cultural Tourism," in *Consuming Cities,* ed. Steven Miles and Malcolm Miles (London: Palgrave Macmillan, 2004), 66–85.

18. Even those Soviet apparatchiks who used to live in the West still had these ambiguous feelings about foreign countries. For an interesting analysis of a Stalinist apparatchik's feelings about his trips to Europe, see Michael David-Fox, "Stalinist Westernizer? Aleksandr Arosev's Literary and Political Depictions of Europe," *Slavic Review,* 62, no. 4 (Winter 2003): 733–59.

19. I refer to the Soviet movie *The Diamond Arm* (director: Leonid Gaidai; Mosfilm, 1969).

20. See complaints about these preferences in official reports: DADO, f. 1860, op. 1, d. 1532, ll. 11–112 (for 1972). See also DADO, f. 22, op. 22, d. 62, ll. 1–64; f. 22, op. 24, d. 141, ll. 1–42; f. 22, op. 30, d. 85, ll. 1–84.

21. See my interview with Serhiy Tihipko, a director of "Privatbank" in Dniepropetrovsk, October 12, 1993; my conversation with Karlo A. Markov, Dniepropetrovsk University, April 12, 1992; and my conversation with Natalia V. Bocharova, Dniepropetrovsk University, March 15, 1993.

22. On the criminal activities of Z. Krupakova, a group leader during a Mediterranean cruise in 1978, see DADO, f. 1860, op. 1, d. 2278, l. 215. Also see the author's interviews with Igor T., KGB officer, Dniepropetrovsk, May 15, 1991; and with Askold B., a son of a head of the tourist department in the Dniepropetrovsk Trade Unions branch, Dniepropetrovsk University, April 15, 1993. And see the author's conversations with Markov, April 12, 1992; and with Bocharova, March 15, 1993.

23. DADO, f. 1860, op. 1, d. 1532, ll. 111–12.

24. See my interview with Tihipko, October 12, 1993; my conversation with Markov, April 12, 1992; and my conversation with Bocharova, March 15, 1993.

25. See both documents: DADO, f. 22, op. 22, d. 62, ll. 1–64; f. 22, op. 24, d. 141, ll. 1–42; f. 22, op. 30, d. 85, ll. 1–84; and the personal opinions of the travelers: the author's interview with Askold B., April 15, 1993, and his conversations with Markov, April 12, 1992; and with Bocharova, March 15, 1993.

26. The citation here is from DADO, f. 1860, op. 1, d. 1022, l. 114. See also DADO, f. 22, op. 19, d. 73, l. 15 (for 1972) and f. 22, op. 24, d. 141, l. 21 (for 1978). And see a typical report about attempts of the Soviet tourists to bring illegally extra Soviet currency in DADO, f. 22, op. 22, d. 62, l. 40, or an exchange of Soviet goods into money

in DADO, f. 1860, op. 1d., d. 62, l. 31 (for 1966), and f. 22, op. 32, d. 73, ll. 85–86 (for 1982).

27. DADO, 1860, op. 1, d. 2278, l. 95.

28. See, especially, DADO, f. 1860, op. 1, d. 1533, ll. 7, 8–9, d. 2637, ll. 26, 27–27ob., and also f. 22, op. 22, d. 62, ll. 1–64; f. 22, op. 24, d. 141, ll. 1–42; f. 22, op. 30, d. 85, ll. 1–84. And see the author's interview with Askold B., April 15, 1993; his conversation with Markov, April 12, 1992; and his conversation with Bocharova, March 15, 1993. Finally, see Alexei Kozlov, *Dzhaz, rok i mednye truby* (Moscow: EKSMO, 2005), 181–83, 191.

29. See the most typical cases in DADO, f. 1860, op. 1, d. 1533, ll. 7, 8–9; d. 1532, ll. 10, 22–47, 51, 55, 65, 68, 78, 94–95,109, 111–12, 146, 147, 167; f. 1860, op. 1, d. 2278, ll. 12, 30–32, 59, 62, 97, 172, 184. See also the documents about *fartsovka* among tourists in TsDAGOU, f. 7, op. 20, d. 1689, ll. 7, 10ob., 11 (for 1976).

30. Author's conversations with Markov, April 12, 1992; and with Bocharova, March 15, 1993. See also David L. Edgell, *International Tourism Policy* (New York: Van Nostrand Reinhold, 1990), 40.

31. Author's conversations with Markov, April 12, 1992; and with Bocharova, March 15, 1993. See also Edgell, *International Tourism Policy,* 43.

32. See my interviews with Igor T., May 15, 1991; and with Askold B., April 15, 1993. See also Edgell, *International Tourism Policy,* 41.

33. See my interview with Tihipko, October 12, 1993; my conversation with Markov, April 12, 1992; and my conversation with Bocharova, March 15, 1993.

34. Alena Ledeneva gave many examples of these tokens of loyalty in her description of *blat* as "the Soviet system of personal favors." See Alena V. Ledeneva, *Russia's Economy of Favours: Balt, Networking, and Informal Exchange* (New York: Cambridge University Press, 1998), 3, 63, 67, 151, 196.

35. Tsentral'noe Statisticheskoe Upravlenie Dnepropetrovskoi oblasti, *Dnepropetrovshchina v tsifrakh,* 78.

36. These books were so popular that even Soviet military officers who were stationed in the socialist countries used to bring them—together with pieces of furniture, jewelry, etc.—to their Soviet homes. See my interviews with Vladimir Donets, Dniepropetrovsk, July 19, 2007; with Tihipko, October 12, 1993; and with Natalia Vasilenko, Dniepropetrovsk, July 19, 2007. Also see my conversations with Markov, April 12, 1992; and with Bocharova, March 15, 1993.

37. For a typical case of exchange of a pack of the Soviet cigarettes into a music records, see DADO, f. 22, op. 32, d. 73, l. 85 (for 1982).

38. DADO, f. 22, op. 22, d. 62, ll. 1–64; f. 22, op. 24, d. 141, ll. 1–42; f. 22, op. 30, d. 85, ll. 1–84. For an account of new Western music equipment among Ukrainian musicians, see Kozlov, *Dzhaz,* 364, 365.

39. For a discussion of how they provided information about foreign disco clubs and dancing parties in their reports as early as 1972, see DADO, f. 22, op. 19, d. 73, ll. 13–14.

40. Author's interviews with Tihipko, October 12, 1993; and with Igor T., May 15, 1991. See also the memoirs of the famous Soviet jazz musician Alexei Kozlov, *Dzhaz,* 181, 182–83, 194, 230. After 1980, Soviet customs rejected only items that were bought in Poland and did not permit them to be brought into Ukraine. For the Soviet customs officers, Polish music markets were ideologically wrong because of the anti-Soviet Solidarity movement. Compare with my interview with Askold B., April 15, 1993.

41. DADO, f. 19, op. 60, d. 85, ll. 7, 14–17. Author's interviews with Mikhail Su-

vorov, June 1, 1991; with Aleksandr Gusar, May 4, 1990; with Vladimir Solodovnik, June 21, 1991; and with Igor T., May 15, 1991.

42. Summer school diary of Aleksandr Gusar, August 24, 1975. Gusar referred to the Dniepropetrovsk tourist groups (altogether 700 people) that traveled abroad through Sputnik in 1975. See a Sputnik report for 1975: DADO, f. 22, op. 22, d. 403, ll. 1–4ob. Gusar mentioned a Dutch rock band, Shocking Blue, and an Andrew Lloyd Weber opera. Gusar's notion of the authentic West is very close to what Hilary Pilkington discovered in her analysis of the Russian provincial cities. See Hilary Pilkington, Elena Omel'chenko, et al., *Looking West? Cultural Globalization and Russian Youth Cultures* (University Park: Pennsylvania State University Press, 2002), 181.

43. Yu. Milinteiko, "Pervye shagi diskoteki," *Dnepr vechernii,* February 26, 1977; B. Ivashura and I. Manevich, "Rizhane dariat prazdnik," *Dnepr vechernii,* March 23, 1977.

44. From February to July 1972, in the location of the traditional city music market, the police organized 100 raids, arrested 200 such dealers, and confiscated hundreds of music records and tapes. See DADO, f. 19, op. 60, d. 85, ll. 7, 17.

45. See Yu. Nepomniashcha, "Rok, folk, dysko . . . i drevo nazhyvy," *Prapor iunosti,* January 5, 1982. The author of this article obviously censured these connections with black market. But a majority of the readers supported Miakoteko's position and attitudes toward the black market as an important source of the fresh music information. They did not see any alternative to the black market, which was a stable source of music products. See the discussion about this in "Povertaiuchys' do nadrukovannogo: 'Rok, folk . . . i dysko,'" *Prapor iunosti,* March 4, 1982. On the range of prices for music recordings in other towns of the Dniepropetrovsk Region, see M. Larin, "Khytryi rynok," *Prapor iunosti,* August 4, 1983. On the higher prices on black market in downtown Dniepropetrovsk in February 1983, see G. Nikitiuk, "Na kriuchke u superzvezdy," *Dnepr vechernii,* February 7, 1983. According to this information, audiotapes with Western music cost 5 rubles, Pink Floyd's album *The Wall* cost 95 rubles, and Donna Summer records cost 50 rubles. The most popular object was an album form the German band Kraftwerk. The typical black marketer was a college student age sixteen to twenty-three years. Officially, Komsomol and trade union apparatchiks worked together with the "discotheque activists" from the early stages of the discotheque movement in 1976. Moreover, the rapid spread of this movement made this region exemplary for many Soviet ideologists, who used the success of the Dniepropetrovsk central discotheque as proof of the ideological efficiency of propaganda about the new forms of socialist leisure for Soviet youth. The region of Dniepropetrovsk was praised by the republican Komsomol ideologists in Kyiv for "the efficient organization of disco club movement." Despite the Communist ideologists' criticism that discotheques spread bourgeois mass culture among the local youth, the Komsomol leaders maintained their collaboration with the activists of the discotheque movement. The Komsomol activists emphasized professionalism and a variety of forms of entertainment in the regional disco clubs. High professionalism depended on fresh music information that came from the black market. See T. Vin'kova, "Profesionaly chy dyletanty," *Prapor iunosti,* June 30, 1983; and V. Machula, "Shchedra muza: Muzyka," *Prapor iunosti,* December 15, 1983.

46. See the Sputnik reports for 1979 in DADO, f. 22, op. 26, d. 102, l. 17, item 43; and for 1980 in DADO, f. 22, op. 28, d. 94, l. 11. On the financial scandal in December 1981, see DADO, f. 1860, op. 1, d. 2835, ll. 1–4. On how the leadership of Sputnik tried to justify Komsomol tourist business in the Dniepropetrovsk Region, see M. Blokha,

"Orbity 'Sputnyka,'" *Prapor iunosti,* September 25, 1982. On the financial scandals, which involved disco clubs, cafés, and travel agencies in 1982, see V. Machula, "Iz bara ta kafe pishov, u 'Kolobok' pryishov," *Prapor iunosti,* July 15, 1982. On the financial crimes of 1983 and 1984, which involved the local rock musicians and restaurant administration (e.g., the band Kruiz from Staraia bashnia and a band Ogni from Maiak), see R. Gordon, "'Chaiovi' za . . . pisniu, abo shche raz pro okremi negarazdy v roboti doomadu," *Prapor iunosti,* June 28, 1984. See also M. Skoryk, "Restoranyi marafon zdiiusniuiut' dekotri libyteli vypyty v robochyi chas," *Prapor iunosti,* February 13, 1983.

47. See Tetiana Honchatova, "Serhiy Tihipko on Sharp Turns," *The Ukrainian,* 2001, no. 2, 60–65; Ukrains'kyi Nezalezhnyi Tsentr Politychnykh Doslidzhen', *"Dnipropetrovs'ka sim'ia": Informatsia stanom na 25 lystopada 1996 roku,* ed. V. Pikhovshek a.o. (Kyiv, 1996), 246–24; and the author's interview with Tihipko, October 12, 1993.

48. Starting in 1986, he was in charge of the regional Komsomol department of propaganda; author's interview with Tihipko, October 12, 1993. On the similar situation for the Leningrad Komsomol apparatchiks, see Alexei Yurchak, *Everything Was Forever, Until It Was No More: The Last Soviet Generation* (Princeton, N.J.: Princeton University Press, 2005), 209–12.

49. As an American historian of rock music in the Soviet bloc wrote, in "the Soviet Union seven thousand discotheques also felt repercussions of the 1984 crackdown. By 1982, about 90 percent of the music played in Soviet discotheques was of Western origin, primarily hits by the Bee Gees, Donna Summer, and other disco music groups. The 1984 crackdown banned the playing of all Western groups, including officially promoted bands like ABBA and Boney M. Disc jockeys caught spinning Western albums received fines. Some discotheques, deemed to be of a 'low artistic' level, were simply closed down. Many establishments, anxious to appease officials, introduced political and cultural instruction." Timothy W. Ryback, *Rock around the Bloc: A History of Rock Music in Eastern Europe and the Soviet Union* (New York: Oxford University Press, 1991), 221. See also the excellent analysis of Soviet scholars' and executives' reactions to the new ideological campaigns of 1984–85: Hilary Pilkington, *Russia's Youth and Its Culture: A Nation's Constructors and Constructed* (London: Routledge, 1994), 80–85.

50. "Zdobuttia i vtraty," *Prapor iunosti,* March 24, 1984; L. Mishchenko, "I pochuty melodiu dushi," *Prapor iunosti,* August 16, 1984.

51. A famous discotheque at the cultural center of Dniepropetrovsk University was transformed into a music lecture club named Dialogue: Music in Ideological Struggle. Instead of dancing, students now listened to boring lectures about modern music and important issues of international politics. The local ideologists preferred this kind of cultural consumption to the spontaneous dance parties of bourgeois music, which were difficult to control. At Dniepropetrovsk University, I became the new head of the music club Dialogue in September 1986, when I started my teaching career there. See my interviews with Tihipko, October 12, 1993; and with Mikhail Suvorov, June 1, 1991.

52. The police complained that the major records of these young businessmen represented the "hostile anti-Soviet bands such as Kiss, AC/DC and Black Sabbath." See O. Ivangora, "'Dyskostoianka' . . . dlia khapug," *Prapor iunosti,* July 5, 1984; Yu. Lystopad, "Ideologichna borot'ba i molod' (Notatky z oblasnoi naukovo-praktyuchnoi konferentsii)," *Prapor iunosti,* December 17, 1983; and M. Larin, "Khytryi rynok," *Prapor iunosti,* August 4, 1983.

53. I. Rodionov, "Vecher v diskoklube," *Dneprovskaia Pravda,* January 14, 1979. On guest numbers and admission fees and alcohol beverages in 1982 and 1983, see B.

Gran'ko, "Karbovanets' za tansi, try—za kokteil', abo chomu vpav avtorytet 'Melodii,'" *Prapor iunosti,* June 24, 1982, and January 15, 1983. On the profits of Melodia, see my interview with Suvorov, June 1, 1991. See also the documents in DADO, f. 17, op. 11, d. 1, l. 28; f. 22, op. 36, d. 1, ll. 36, 37, 39, 40.

54. DADO, f. 22, op. 19, d. 2, 143, f. 19, op. 60, d. 85, ll. 9–11. See also my interview with Tihipko, October 12, 1993.

55. Author's interviews with Suvorov, June 1, 1991; and with Vladimir Sadovoi, March 10, 1992. See also the author's interviews with Gusar, May 4, 1990; with Solodovnik, June 21, 1991; with Igor T., May 15, 1991; and with Askold B., April 15, 1993.

56. On this, see the author's interviews with Gusar, May 4, 1990; and with Suvorov, June 1, 1991. Also see DADO, f. 22, op. 36, d. 73, ll. 13–15; and the author's interview with Igor T., May 15, 1991.

57. Video salons were rooms equipped with videocassette recorders and television sets that allowed people to watch Western video films. On the police's persecution of illegal "video salons" in private homes, see L. Gamol'sky, N. Efremenko, and V. Inshakov, *Na barrikadakh sovesti: Ocherki, razmyshlenia, interviu* (Dniepropetrovsk, 1988), 146–47.

58. A restaurant waiter, Boris Shafrai, brought to Dniepropetrovsk a Japanese videocassette recorder made by JVC, which he had bought for 8,500 rubles in Moscow. He sold videocassettes to his customers, who had bought Western music recordings for 150 rubles each. See L. Gamol'sky, "Zhazhdal Boria naslazhdenii," *Dnepr vechernii,* September 29, 1983.

59. The most famous criminal case of illegal showings of "forbidden Western videos" involved Konstantin Prokop, a famous leader of a disco club at the Illich Palace of Culture, and Valentin Shashkov, a disc jockey for another prestigious discotheque. See Igor Puppo, "U zamorskikh 'muz' na posylkakh," *Dnepr vechenii,* October 15, 1985.

60. See my interviews with Vitalii Pidgaetskii, Department of History, Dniepropetrovsk University, February 10, 1996; with Evgen D. Prudchenko, Central Library of the Dniepropetrovsk Region, Dniepropetrovsk, July 18, 2007; and with Sergei Pulin, Dniepropetrovsk, April, 15, 1990.

61. See my interview with Pidgaetskii, February 10, 1996.

62. See my interview with Eduard Svichar, Vatutino, Cherkassy Region, July 28–29, 2007.

63. Author's interview with Igor T., May 15, 1991.

64. Author's interview with Suvorov, Dniepropetrovsk, June 1, 1991.

65. See my interview with Igor T., May 15, 1991. See also my interviews with Prudchenko, July 18, 2007; with Galina V. Smolenskaia, Central Library of the Dniepropetrovsk Region, July 18, 2007; and with Vasilenko, July 19, 2007. Vladimir Donets (born in 1953) recalled a similar development in another industrial city of the Dniepropetrovsk Region, Dnieprodzerzhinsk; see my interview with Donets, July 19, 2007.

66. This information is from my interviews with Suvorov, June 1, 1991; with Sadovoi, March 10, 1992; with Gusar, May 4, 1990; with Solodovnik, June 21, 1991; with Igor T., May 15, 1991; and with Askold B., April 15, 1993.

67. This system of personal favors was called *blat* in Russian. See Ledeneva, *Russia's Economy of Favours.*

68. Dmitrii Popov and Ilia Mil'shtein, *Oranzhevaia printsessa: Zagadka Yulii Timo-*

shenko (Moscow: Izdatel'stvo Ol'gi Morozovoi, 2006), 55. See also Dmytro Pona-marchuk, "Prosto Yulia," *Izvestia,* September 20, 2007.

69. Popov and Mil'shtein, *Oranzhevaia printsessa,* 64–67. Some disco movement activists recalled the Tymoshenko family dancing. See my interview with Suvorov, June 1, 1991.

70. See the updated biographies of Tymoshenko given by Popov and Mil'shtein, *Oranzhevaia printsessa,* 52–89; and Ponamarchuk, "Prosto Yulia."

71. Author's interview with Tihipko, October 12, 1993.

72. Author's interview with Askold B., April 15, 1993.

73. Author's interview with Suvorov, June 1, 1991.

74. Author's interviews with Sadovoi, March 10, 1992; with Solodovnik, June 21, 1991; with Igor T., May 15, 1991; and with Askold B., April 15, 1993.

Notes to the Conclusion

1. Author's interview with Vitalii Pidgaetskii, Department of History, Dniepro-petrovsk University, February 10, 1996.

2. Many contemporaries also noted the role of L'viv and Moscow in the consumption of Western cultural products in the closed city, and in shaping the local identity of Dniepropetrovsk. See my interviews with Mikhail Suvorov, Dniepropetrovsk, June 1, 1991; with Natalia Vasilenko, Dniepropetrovsk, July 19, 2007; and with Oleksandr Poniezha, Dniepropetrovsk, July 22, 2008.

3. Andy Bennett, *Popular Music and Youth Culture: Music, Identity and Place* (New York: St. Martin's Press, 2000), 198.

4. *Dneprovskaia Pravda,* June 26, 1971.

5. In the city of Dniepropetrovsk 33.2 percent of ethnic Ukrainians reported that their native language was Russian, and only 0.9 percent of ethnic Russians claimed that their native language was Ukrainian. Goskomstat USSR, Dniepropetrovskoe oblatnoe upravlenie statistiki, *Naselenie Dnepropetrovskoi oblasti po dannym Vsesoiuznoi perepisi naseleniia 1989 goda* (Dnepropetrovsk, 1991), 100, 102, 106, 116, 117.

6. Soviet Ukrainian officials followed the Ukrainian patriots' efforts to preserve cities of the "Cossack glory" in the Dnipro Region. See a collection of documents about this: *Zbereshemo tuiu slavu: Gromadskyi rukh za uvichnennia istorii ukrains'kogo kozastva v drugii polovyni 50-kh-80-kh rr. XX st.,* ed. Iu. Danyliuk (Kyiv: Ridny krai, 1997).

7. I quote my former colleague, Vitalii Pidgaetskii, from my interview with him, February 10, 1996.

8. I refer to James C. Scott, *Weapons of the Weak: Everyday Forms of Peasant Resistance* (New Haven, Conn.: Yale University Press, 1985); and James C. Scott, *Domination and the Arts of Resistance: Hidden Transcripts* (New Haven, Conn.: Yale University Press, 1990).

9. Michel de Certeau, *The Practice of Everyday Life,* trans. Steven Rendall (Berkeley: University of California Press, 1989; orig. pub. 1984), 31.

10. E.g., consider the cynical and practical interests of different Dniepropetrovsk leaders like Leonid Kuchma, Pavlo Lazarenko, and Yulia Tymoshenko. Kuchma's career is a pure product of the Brezhnev era. In 1980, Kuchma was elected the first secre-

tary of Yuzhmash's Communist Party committee. In 1982, he took a position as the deputy head of Yuzhmash's secret design office; and in 1986, during perestroika, he became the successor of Makarov as the new director of Yuzhmash. Pavlo Lazarenko's career started during Chernenko's rule. Lazorenko, the first prime minister during the presidency of Kuchma, graduated from Dniepropetrovsk Agricultural Institute in 1978. Starting his career as a village driver, he became the head of agricultural administration in the rural district of Tsarichanka in 1984. During perestroika, he became the secretary of the regional committee of the Communist Party and was responsible for the agriculture and food industry in the region of Dniepropetrovsk. From 1992 to 1994, he was the head of the Dniepropetrovsk regional administration. During this time, he built relations with Kuchma, who later brought him to Kyiv as his first prime minister in 1994. In a contrast to Kuchma and Lazorenko, Tymoshenko's career is a typical product of the perestroika years. Through the Communist Party and Yuzhmash connections of her father-in-law, she became involved in the organization of a music video rental chain, the first business operations of the local Komsomol elite, and during perestroika she laid a foundation for her own lucrative enterprise. In the 1990s, the same connections raised her into the circle of the Dniepropetrovsk oligarchs and influential politicians such as Kuchma and Lazarenko. See "Ukrains'kyi Nezalezhnyi Tsentr Politychnykh Doslidzhen,'" in *"Dnipropetrovs'ka sim'ia": Informatsia stanom na 25 lystopada 1996 roku,* ed. V. Pikhovshek et al. (Kyiv, 1996), 84–85. The best portrayal of this post-Soviet cynicism is in the novel by Gary Shteyngart, *Absurdistan* (New York: Random House, 2006).

Selected Bibliography

The Most Important Interviews

Interview with Oleksandr Beznosov, Department of History, Dniepropetrovsk University, July 19, 2008.

Interview with Vladimir Demchenko, a former public lecturer for Znanie (Society of Knowledge), Dniepropetrovsk, January 12, 1992.

Interview with Vladimir G. Donets, Dniepropetrovsk, July 19, 2007.

Interview with Aleksandr Gusar, Dniepropetrovsk, May 4, 1990.

Interview with Yurii Kolomoets, a former musician with the band Dniepriane, Dniepropetrovsk, March 12, 1991.

Interview with Tamara Antonovna Kozintseva, Dniepropetrovsk, June 20, 2005.

Interview with Professor Yurii Mytsyk, Dniepropetrovsk University, January 15, 1992.

Interview with Vitalii Pidgaetskii at the Department of History, Dniepropetrovsk University, February 10, 1996.

Interview with Oleksandr Poniezha, Dniepropetrovsk, July 22, 2008.

Interview with Evgen D. Prudchenko, the Central Library of Dniepropetrovsk Region, Dniepropetrovsk, July 18, 2007.

Interview with Sergei Pulin, Dniepropetrovsk, April, 15, 1990.

Interview with Vladimir Sadovoi, Dniepropetrovsk, March 10, 1992.

Interview with Galina V. Smolenskaia, Central Library of the Dniepropetrovsk Region, Dniepropetrovsk, July 18, 2007.

Interview with Vladimir Solodovnik, Dniepropetrovsk, June 21, 1991.

Interview with Mikhail Suvorov, Dniepropetrovsk, June 1, 1991.

Interview with Eduard Svichar, Vatutino, Cherkassy Region, Ukraine, June 8, 2004.

Interview with Eduard Svichar, Vatutino, Cherkassy Region, July 28–29, 2007.

Interview with Anatolii T., a member of the Dniepropetrovsk Hare Krishna Community, Dniepropetrovsk, July 20, 2005.

Interview with Igor T., a retired KGB officer, Dniepropetrovsk, May 15, 1991.

Interview with Serhiy Tihipko, a director of Privatbank, Dniepropetrovsk, October 12, 1993.

Interview with Andrei Vadimov, Dniepropetrovsk, July 20–21, 2003.

415

Selected Bibliography

Interview with Natalia Vasilenko, Dniepropetrovsk, July 19, 2007.
Interview with Tatiana Yeriomenko, a former singer with the band Dniepriane, Dniepropetrovsk, April 20, 1988.
Interview with Andrei Z., classmate of Yulia Grigian (Telegina; now Tymoshenko), Dniepropetrovsk, June 12, 2005.

Personal Documents

Book diary of Aleksandr Gusar, Pavlograd, Dniepropetrovsk Region, 1970–76.
Book diary of Andrei Vadimov, Dniepropetrovsk, 1969–75.
Summer school diary of Aleksandr Gusar, Pavlograd, Dniepropetrovsk Region, 1970–76.
Summer school diary of Vladimir Solodovnik, Sinel'nikovo, Dniepropetrovsk Region, 1966–72.
Summer school diary of Mikhail Suvorov, Dniepropetrovsk, 1972–77.
Summer school diary of Andrei Vadimov, Dniepropetrovsk, 1969–75.

Archival Sources

Derzhavnyi arkhiv Dnipropetrovs'koi oblasti, Dniepropetrovsk:
  Fond 17, Dnepropetrovskii Gorkom LKSMU (Komsomola Ukrainy).
  Fond 18, Dnepropetrovskii Gorkom KPU (Kommunisticheskoi partii Ukrainy).
  Fond 19, Dnepropetrovskii Obkom KPU (Kommunisticheskoi partii Ukrainy).
  Fond 22, Dnepropetrovskii Obkom LKSMU (Komsomola Ukrainy).
  Fond 416, Ispolnitel'nyi komitet Dnepropetrovskogo gorodskogo Soveta deputatov trudiashchiksia.
  Fond 1860, Dnepropetrovskii Oblastnoi Sovet Professional'nykh soiuzov.
  Fond 3383, Ispolnitel'nyi komitet Dnepropetrovskogo oblastnogo Soveta deputatov trudiashchikhsia.
  Fond 6463, Sovet po delam religioznykh kul'tov pri Sovete Ministrov SSSR, Upolnomochennyi i Soveta po Dnepropetrovskoi oblasti, g. Dniepropetrovsk.
  Fond 6464, Sovet po delam Russkoi pravoslavnoi tserkvi pri Sovete Ministrov SSSR, Upolnomochennyi Soveta po Dnepropetrovskoi oblasti.
  Fond 6465, Sovet po delam religii pri Sovete Ministrov SSSR, Upolnomochennyi po voprosam religioznykh kul'tov po Dnepropetrovskoi oblasti, g. Dniepropetrovsk.
  Fond 9854, Dnepropetrovskii promyshlennyi Obkom LKSMU (Komsomola Ukrainy).
  Fond 9870, Dnepropetrovskii Obkom KPU (Kommunisticheskoi partii Ukrainy), Otdel: Osobyi sector. Sektor: Sekretnaiu chast'.

Tsentral'nyi derzhavnyi arkhiv vyshchykh organiv vlady ta upravlinnia, Kyiv:
  Fond 4648, Upolnomochennyi Soveta po delam religioznykh kul'tov pri Sovete Ministrov SSSR po Ukrainskoi SSR.
  Fond 5116, Ministerstvo kul'tury URSR.

Tsentral'nyi Derzhavnyi Arkhiv Gromads'kykh Ob'ednan' Ukrainy, Kyiv:
Fond 7, Tsentral'nyi Komitet LKSMU.
Viddil kul'tury.
Viddil Propagandy i agitatsii.

Gosudarstvennyi arkhiv Rossiiskoi Federatsii, Moscow:
Fond 5451, VTsSPS, Obshchii otdel, Osobyi sector.
Fond 6991, Sovet po delam religii pri Sovete Ministrov SSSR, Dokumenty upolnomochennykh Soveta po oblastiam Ukrainy (1966–82 gody).
Fond 9520, Sovet po turizmu VTsSPS, Otdel po mezhdunarodnomu turizmu.
Fond 9612, Glavnoe upravlenie po inostrannomu turizmu pri Sovete Ministrov SSSR, Otdel reklamy i pechati.

Rubinov Collection (Papers of a Former Editor of *Literaturnaia gazeta,* 1964–84), Library of Congress, Washington.

Contemporary Newspapers and Journals, 1964–84

Dneprovskaia Pravda	*Novyny kinoekranu*
Dnepr vechernii	*Perets*
Iskusstvo kino	*Prapor iunosti*
Izvestia	*Pravda*
Klub i khudozhestvennaia samodeiatel'nost'	*Ranok*
Komsomol'skaia Pravda	*Rovesnik*
Krokodil	*Smena*
Krugozor	*Sovetskii ekran*
Molod' Ukrainy	*Vokrug sveta*
Nauka i religia	*Zoria*

Printed Sources

Brezhnev, Leonid I. *Report to the 24th Congress of the CPSU 1971.* Moscow: Progress, 1971.
———. *Report to the 25th Congress of the CPSU 1976.* Moscow: Progress, 1976.
Chitatel'skii spros v massovykh bibliotekakh v 1977 g. (Dinamika chtenia I chitatel'skogo sprosa) Instruktivno-metodicheskie rekomendatsii, ed. A. Reitblat and T. Frolova. Moscow, 1978.
Gorbulin, V. P., et al., eds. *Zemni shliakhy i zoriani orbity: Shtrykhy do portreta Leonida Kuchmy.* Kyiv, 1998.
Goskomstat USSR, Dnepropetrovskoe oblatnoe upravlenie statistiki. *Naselenie Dnepropetrovskoi oblasti po dannym Vsesoiuznoi perepisi naseleniia 1989 goda.* Dniepropetrovsk, 1991.
Gurevich, David. *From Lenin to Lennon: A Memoir of Russia in the Sixties.* San Diego: Harcourt Brace Jovanovich, 1991.

Honchar, V. D., and V. Ia. P'ianov, eds. *Vinok pam'iati Olesia Honchara: Spogady—Khronika.* Kyiv, 1997.

Hunchak, Taras, ed. *Tysiacha rokiv Ukrains'koi suspil'no-politychnoi dumky: V 9-ty tomakh—Tom 8 (40-vi–80-ti roky XX ct.).* Kyiv, 2001.

Ispolkom Dnepropetrovskogo oblastnogo Soveta narodnykh deputatov. *Sotsial'no-ekonomiceskoe razvitie Dnepropetrovshchiny za 1986–1990 gg. Statisticheskii sbornik* Dniepropetrovsk, 1991.

Ivanenko, V. V., ed. *Reabilitovani istorieiu.* Vol. 1: *Vidrodzhena pam'iat';* vol. 2: *Svidchennia z mynuvshyny: Movoiu dokumentiv;* vol. 3: *Mynule z girkym prysmakom: Represii v istorychnii retrospektyvi radians'kogo suspil'stva.* Dniepropetrovsk, 1999–2002.

Kozlov, Alexei. *Dzhaz, rok i mednye truby.* Moscow: EKSMO, 2005.

———. *Kozyol na sakes.* Moscow: Vagrius, 1998.

Kuznetskii, M. I., and I. V. Stazheva, eds. *Baikonur: Cudo XX veka—Vospominania vevteranov Baikonura ob akademike Mikhaile Kuz'miche Yangele.* Moscow, 1995.

Makarevich, Andrei. *"Sam ovtsa": Avtobiograficheskaia proza.* Moscow: Zakharov, 2002.

Ministerstvo kul'tury SSSR, Upravlenie kul'turno-prosvetitel'skikh uchrezhdenii. *Sbornik rukovodiashchikh materialov i normativnykh dokumentov po kul'turno-prosvetitel'skoi rabote,* ed. A. Ya. Gavrilenko and I. M. Galichenko. Moscow, 1983.

Molod' Dnipropetrovs'ka v borot'bi proty rusyfikatsii [The Youth of Dnipropetrovsk in a Fight against Russification]. Munich: Suchacnist', 1971.

"O vozrastnoi structure, urovne obrazovania, natsional'nom sostave, iazykakh i istochnikakh sredstv sushchestvovania naselenia Dnepropetrovskoi oblasti po dannym Vsessoiuznoi perepisis naselenia na 15 ianvaria 1970 goda." *Dneprovskaia Pravda,* June 26, 1971.

Palazchenko, Pavel. *My Years with Gorbachev and Shevardnadze: The Memoir of a Soviet Interpreter.* University Park: Pennsylvania State University Press, 1997.

Pelyushonok, Yury. *Strings for a Beatle Bass: The Beatles Generation in the USSR.* Ottawa : PLY, 1999.

Plyushch, Leonid, with a contribution by Tatyana Plyushch. *History's Carnival: A Dissident's Autobiography,* ed. and trans. Marco Carynnyk. New York: Harcourt Brace Jovanovich, 1979.

Raleigh, Donald J., trans. and ed. *Russia's Sputnik Generation: Soviet Baby Boomers Talk about Their Lives.* Bloomington: Indiana University Press, 2006.

Sokul'sky, Ivan. *Lysty na svitanku.* 2 vols. Dniepropetrovsk: Sich, 2001–2.

Tron'ko, P. T., O. G. Bazhan, and Yu. Z. Danyliuk, eds. *Ternystym shliakhom do khramu: Oles' Honchar v suspil'no-politychnomu zhytti Ukrainy.* Kyiv, 1999.

Tsentral'noe Statisticheskoe Upravlenie Dnepropetrovskoi oblasti. *Dnepropetrovshchina v tsifrakh: K 40-letiu pobedy v Velikoi Otechestvennoi voine,* ed. L. G. Glushkina. Dniepropetrovsk, 1985.

TsSU USSR, Statisticheskoe upravlenie Dnepropetrovskoi oblasti. *Dnepropetrovskaia oblast' za tri goda deviatoi piatiletki (1971–1973 gody): Kratkii staisticheskii sbornik.* Dniepropetrovsk, 1974.

———. *Molodiozh Dnepropetrovskoi oblasti: Statisticheskii sbornik,* ed. L. T. Glushkina and V. F. Iagniuk. Dniepropetrovsk, 1985.

Vishniak, A. I., and N. N. Churilov, eds. *Sotsial'nyi oblik molodiozhi (na materialakh Ukrainskoi SSR).* Kiev: Naukova dumka, 1990.

VTsSPS, Tsentral'nyi Sovet po turizmu i eskursiiam. *Sbornik ofitsial'nykh materialov.* Moscow, 1982.

Zdes' mozhno uznat' mnogo pouchitel'nogo: Iz opyta raboty Dnepropetrovskogo molodiozhnogo diskokluba "Melodia." Dniepropetrovsk, 1979.

Secondary Sources

Afanasiev, M. D. *Za knigoi: Mesto chtenia v zhizni sovetskogo rabochego.* Moscow: Kniga, 1987.

Bacon, Edwin, and Mark Sandle, eds. *Brezhnev Reconsidered.* New York: Palgrave Macmillan, 2002.

Bagirov, A. *"Bitlz": Liubov' moia.* Minsk: Parus, 1993.

Barker, Adele Marie, ed. *Consuming Russia: Popular Culture, Sex, and Society since Gorbachev.* Durham, N.C.: Duke University Press, 1999.

Berkhoff, Karel C. *Harvest of Despair: Life and Death in Ukraine under Nazi Rule.* Cambridge, Mass.: Belknap Press, 2004.

Bolebrukh A. G., a.o., ed. *Dnipropetrovs'k: vikhy istorii.* Dniepropetrovsk: Grani, 2001.

Boym, Svetlana. *Common Places: Mythologies of Everyday Life in Russia.* Cambridge, Mass.: Harvard University Press, 1994.

Brooks, Jeffrey. *Thank You, Comrade Stalin! Soviet Public Culture from Revolution to Cold War.* Princeton, N.J.: Princeton University Press, 2000.

Brudny, Yitzhak M. *Reinventing Russia: Russian Nationalism and the Soviet State, 1953–1991.* Cambridge, Mass.: Harvard University Press, 1998.

Certeau, Michel de. *The Practice of Everyday Life,* trans. Steven Rendall. Berkeley: University of California Press, 1989. Orig. pub. 1984.

Chernysh, N. I., I. V. Vasilieva, et al., eds. *Natsional'na samosvidomist' studets'koi molodi (Sotsiologichnyi analiz).* Toronto: Canadian Institute of Ukrainian Studies Press, 1993.

Cushman, Thomas. *Notes from Underground: Rock Music Counterculture in Russia.* Albany: State University of New York Press, 1995.

Danyliuk, Yurii, and Oleg Bazhan. *Opozytsia v Ukraini (druga polovyna 50-kh–80-ti rr. XX st.).* Kyiv: Ridnyi krai, 2000.

Dnepropetrovskii raketno-kosmicheskii tsentr: Kratkii ocherk stanovlenia i razvitia—DAZ-YuMZ-KBYu—Khronika dat i sobytii. Dniepropetrovsk, 1994.

Dobrynina, N. *Cherty dukhovnoi obshchnosti: Russkaia khudozhestvennaia literatura v chtenii mogonatsional'nogo sovetskogo chitatelia.* Moscow: Kniga, 1983.

Dyczok, Marta. *Ukraine: Movement without Change, Change without Movement.* London: Routledge, 2000

English, Robert D. *Russia and the Idea of the West: Gorbachev, Intellectuals, and the End of the Cold War.* New York: Columbia University Press, 2000.

Farmer, Kenneth C. *Ukrainian Nationalism in the Post-Stalin Era: Myth, Symbols and Ideology in Soviet Nationalities Policy.* The Hague: Martinus Nijhoff, 1980.

Fitzpatrick, Sheila. *Everyday Stalinism: Ordinary Life in Extraordinary Times—Soviet Russia in the 1930s.* New York: Oxford University Press, 1999.

Foucault, Michel. *Aesthetics, Method, and Epistemology,* ed. James Faubion. New York: New Press, 1998.

Friedberg, Maurice. *A Decade of Euphoria: Western Literature in Post-Stalin Russia, 1954–64.* Bloomington: Indiana University Press, 1977.

Frith, Simon, and Andrew Goodwin, eds. *On Record: Rock, Pop, and the Written Word.* New York: Pantheon Books, 1990.

Gorsuch, Anne E. "'There's No Place Like Home': Soviet Tourism in Late Socialism." *Slavic Review* 62, no. 4 (Winter 2003): 760–85.

Gorsuch, Anne E., and Diane P. Koenker, eds. *Turizm: The Russian and East European Tourist under Capitalism and Socialism.* Ithaca, N.Y.: Cornell University Press, 2006.

Gudkov, L. D. "Pererozhdeniia 'Sovetskogo cheloveka' (Ob odnom issledovatel'skom proekte Levada-Tsentra)." In *Odissei: Chelovek v istorii—2007—Istoria kak igra metaphor.* Moscow: Nauka, 2007.

Highmore, Ben. *Everyday Life and Cultural Theory: An Introduction.* London: Routledge, 2002.

Kasianov, G. *Nezgodni: Ukrains'ka intelligentsia v rusi oporu 1960–80-kh rokiv.* Kyiv: Lybid, 1995.

Kelly, C., and D. Shepherd, eds. *Constructing Russian Culture in the Age of Revolution: 1881–1940.* New York: Oxford University Press, 1998.

Knox, Zoe. *Russian Society and the Orthodox Church: Religion in Russia after Communism.* London: RoutledgeCurzon, 2004.

Koval, Vitalii. *"Sobor" i navkolo "Soboru."* Kyiv, 1989.

Krawchenko, Bohdan. *Social Change and National Consciousness in Twentieth-Century Ukraine.* London: Macmillan, 1985.

———, ed. *Ukraine after Shelest.* Edmonton: Canadian Institute of Ukrainian Studies, 1983.

Kuromiya, Hiroaki. *Freedom and Terror in the Donbas.* New York: Cambridge University Press, 2003.

Kuzio, Taras. *Ukraine: State and Nation Building.* London: Routledge, 1998.

LaFeber, Walter. *America, Russia, and the Cold War, 1945–2006, Tenth Edition.* Boston: McGraw-Hill, 2007.

Lazebnik, Valentina I. *Oziorka nasha: Istoricheskii ocherk o Dnepropetrovskom Tsentral'nom rynke,* ed. G. A. Efimenko. Dniepropetrovsk, 2001.

Ledeneva, Alena V. *Russia's Economy of Favours: Balt, Networking, and Informal Exchange.* New York: Cambridge University Press, 1998.

Lefebvre, Henry. *The Production of Space,* trans. Donald Nicholson-Smith. Oxford: Blackwell, 1991.

Liber, George O. *Alexander Dovzhenko: A Life in Soviet Film.* London: British Film Institute, 2002.

———. *Soviet Nationality Policy, Urban Growth and Identity Change in the Ukrainian SSR 1923–1934.* New York: Cambridge University Press, 1992.

Lovell, Stephen. *The Russian Reading Revolution: Print Culture in the Soviet and Post-Soviet Eras.* New York: St. Martin's Press, 2000.

Lukanov, Yurii. *Tretii President: Politychnyi portret Leonida Kuchmy.* Kyiv, 1996.

MacFadyen, David. *Red Stars: Personality and the Soviet Popular Song, 1955–1991.* Montreal: McGill–Queen's University Press, 2001.

Makine, Andrei. *Once upon the River Love,* trans. from the French by Geoffrey Strachan. New York: Arcade, 1998. Orig. pub. 1994.

Markus, Vasyl. "Religion and Nationalism in Ukraine." In *Religion and Nationalism in*

Soviet and East European Politics, ed. Pedro Ramet. Durham, N.C.: Duke University Press, 1984.

Martin, Terry. *The Affirmative Action Empire: Nations and Nationalism in the Soviet Union, 1923–1939.* Ithaca, N.Y.: Cornell University Press, 2001.

McMichael, Polly. "'After All, You're a Rock and Roll Star (At Least, That's What They Say)': *Roksi* and the Creation of the Soviet Rock Musician." *Slavonic and East European Review* 83, no. 4 (2005): 664–84.

Mickiewicz, Ellen Propper. *Media and the Russian Public.* New York: Praeger, 1981.

Millar, J. R. "The Little Deal: Brezhnev's Contribution to Acquisitive Socialism." *Slavic Review* 44, no. 4 (Winter 1985): 694–706.

Mlechin, Leonid M. *Brezhnev.* Moscow, 2007.

Nadelson, Reggie. *Comrade Rockstar: The Life and Mystery of Dean Reed, the All-American Boy Who Brought Rock 'n' Roll to the Soviet Union.* New York: Chatto & Windus, 1991.

Nahaylo, Bohdan. *The Ukrainian Resurgence.* Toronto: University of Toronto Press, 1999.

Nikiforova, O. I. *Psikhologia vospriiatia khudozhestvennoi literatury.* Moscow: Kniga, 1972.

Omel'chenko, Elena. *Molodiozh: Otkrytyi vopros.* Ulianovsk: Simbirskaia Kniga, 2004.

Osokina, Elena. *Za fasadom "stalinskogo izobilia": Raspredelenie I rynok v snabzhenii naselenia v gody industrializatsii, 1927–1941.* Moscow, 1998.

Oushakine, Sergei. "The Terrifying Mimicry of Samizdat." *Public Culture* 13, no. 2 (2001): 191–214.

Parfionov, Leonid, *Namedni, 1961–70. Nasha Era.* Moscow: Kolibri, 2009.

Pilkington, Hilary. "'The Future Is Ours': Youth Culture in Russia, 1953 to the Present." In *Russian Cultural Studies: An Introduction,* ed. Catriona Kelly and David Shepherd. New York: Oxford University Press, 1998.

———. *Russia's Youth and Its Culture: A Nation's Constructors and Constructed.* London: Routledge, 1994.

Pilkington, Hilary, Elena Omel'chenko, et al. *Looking West? Cultural Globalization and Russian Youth Cultures.* University Park: Pennsylvania State University Press, 2002.

Pikhovshek, Vyacheslav, et al., eds. *Dnipropetrovsk vs. Security Service.* Kyiv, 1996.

Poiger, Uta G. *Jazz, Rock, and Rebels: Cold War Politics and American Culture in a Divided Germany.* Berkeley: University of California Press, 2000.

Poliakova, L. I. "Zminy v etnonathional'nomu skladi naselennia pivdnia Ukrainy v 60–80-ti roky XX st." In *Pivdenna Ukraina XX stolittia: Zapiski naukovo-doslidnoi laboratorii istorii Pivdennoi Ukrainy Zaporiz'kogo Derzhavnogo Universytetu,* ed. A. V. Boiko. Moscow: Zaporizhzhia, 1998.

Popov, Dmitrii, and Ilia Mil'shtein. *Oranzhevaia printsessa: Zagadka Yulii Timoshenko.* Moscow: Izdatel'stvo Ol'gi Morozovoi, 2006.

Pospielovsky, Dimitry. *A History of Soviet Atheism in Theory and Practice, and the Believer.* Vol. 1: *A History of Marxist-Leninist Atheism and Soviet Antireligious Policies;* vol. 2: *Soviet Antireligious Campaigns and Persecutions;* vol. 3: *Soviet Studies on the Church and the Believer's Response to Atheism.* New York: St. Martin's Press, 1987–88.

———. *The Russian Church under the Soviet Regime, 1917–1982.* 2 vols. Crestwood, N.Y.: St. Vladimir's Seminary Press, 1984.

Puddington, Arch. *Broadcasting Freedom: The Cold War Triumph of Radio Free Europe and Radio Liberty.* Lexington: University Press of Kentucky, 2000.

Rajagopalan, Sudha. *Indian Films in Soviet Cinemas: The Culture of Movie-going after Stalin.* Bloomington: Indiana University Press, 2009.

Ramet, Sabrina Petra, ed. *Rocking the State: Rock Music and Politics in Eastern Europe and Russia.* Boulder, Colo.: Westview Press, 1994.

Richmond, Yale. *Cultural Exchange and the Cold War: Raising the Iron Curtain.* University Park: Pennsylvania State University Press, 2003.

Riordan, Jim, ed. *Soviet Youth Culture.* Bloomington: Indiana University Press, 1989.

Risch, William Jay. "Soviet 'Flower Children': Hippies and the Youth Counter-Culture in 1970s Lviv." *Journal of Contemporary History* 40, no. 3 (July 2005): 565–84.

Ruble, Blair. *Creating Diversity Capital: Transnational Migrants in Montreal, Washington, and Kyiv.* Baltimore and Washington: Johns Hopkins University Press and Woodrow Wilson Center Press, 2005.

———. *Soviet Trade Unions: Their Development in the 1970s.* Cambridge: Cambridge University Press, 1981.

Rusnachenko, A. *Natsional'no-vyzvol'nyi rukh v Ukraini: Seredyna 1950-kh–pochatok 1990-kh rokiv.* Kyiv: Vyd-vo im Oleny Teligy, 1998.

Ryback, Timothy W. *Rock around the Bloc: A History of Rock Music in Eastern Europe and the Soviet Union.* New York: Oxford University Press, 1991.

Sabic, Claudia, and Kerstin Zimmer. "Ukraine: The Genesis of a Captured State." In *The Making of Regions in Post-Socialist Europe: The Impact of Culture, Economic Structure and Institutions—Case Studies from Poland, Hungary, Romania and Ukraine,* ed. Melanie Tatur. Wiesbaden, 2004.

Sarup, Madan. *Identity, Culture and the Postmodern World.* Edinburgh: Edinburgh University Press, 1996.

Savinskii, Sergei N. *Istoria evangel'skikh khristian-baptistov Ukrainy, Rossii, Belorussii Chast' II (1917–1967).* Saint Petersburg: Biblia dlia vsekh, 2001.

Sawatsky, Walter. *Soviet Evangelicals since World War II.* Scottdale, Pa.: Herald Press, 1981.

Sherel', Aleksandr. *Audiokul'tura XX veka: Istoria, esteticheskie zakonomernosti, osobennosti vliaiania na auditoriu—Ocherki.* Moscow: Progress-Traditsia, 2004.

Shiraev, Eric, and Vladislav Zubok. *Anti-Americanism in Russia: From Stalin to Putin.* New York: Palgrave, 2000.

Shlapentokh, Dmitry, and Vladimir Shlapetokh. *Soviet Cinematography 1918–1991: Ideological Conflict and Social Reality.* New York: Aldine de Gruyter, 1993.

Shlapentokh, Vladimir. *A Normal Totalitarian Society: How the Soviet Union Functioned and How It Collapsed.* Armonk, N.Y.: M. E. Sharpe, 2001.

———. *The Public and Private Life of the Soviet People: Changing Values in Post-Stalin Russia.* New York: Oxford University Press, 1989.

———. *Soviet Intellectuals and Political Power: The Post-Stalin Era.* Princeton, N.J.: Princeton University Press, 1990.

Siddiqi, Asif A. *Sputnik and the Soviet Space Challenge.* Gainesville: University Press of Florida, 2003.

Sklovs'kyi, Ihor. *Robitnycha molod' v etnosotsial'nykh zryshenniakh Ukrains'kogo suspil'stva: 70-ti–pochatok 90-kh rokiv XX stolittia.* Kirovograd, 2001.

Smith, Gerald Stanton. *Songs to Seven Strings: Russian Guitar Poetry and Soviet "Mass Song."* Bloomington: Indiana University Press, 1984.

Soloukh, Sergei. *Shizgara.* Moscow: Vremia, 2005.

Starr, S. Frederick. *Red and Hot: The Fate of Jazz in the Soviet Union 1917–1980.* New York: Limelight Editions, 1985.

Steinholt, Yngvar Bordewich. *Rock in the Reservation: Songs from the Leningrad Rock Club, 1981–86.* New York: Mass Media Music Scholars' Press, 2004.

Stel'makh, V. D., and N. K. Lobachev, eds. *Kniga i chtenie v zerkale sotsiologii.* Moscow: Knizhnaia Palata, 1990.

Stites, Richard. *Russian Popular Culture: Entertainment and Society since 1900.* New York: Cambridge University Press, 1992.

Storey, John. *Cultural Consumption and Everyday Life.* London: Arnold, 1999.

Survilla, Maria Paula. "'Ordinary Words': Sound, Symbolism, and Meaning in Belarusan-Language Rock Music." In *Global Pop, Local Language,* ed. Harris M. Berger and Michael Thomas Carroll, Jackson: University Press of Mississippi, 2003.

Svanidze, Nikolai, and Marina Svanidze. *Medvedev.* Saint Petersburg: Amfora, 2008.

Taubman, William. *Khrushchev: The Man and His Era.* New York: W. W. Norton, 2003.

Troitsky, Artemy. *Back in the USSR: The True Story of Rock in Russia.* London: Omnibus Press, 1987.

Tumarkin, Nina. *Lenin Lives!: The Lenin Cult in Soviet Russia.* Cambridge, Mass.: Harvard University Press, 1997.

———. *The Living & the Dead: The Rise and Fall of the Cult of World War II in Russia.* New York: Basic Books, 1994.

"Ukrains'kyi Nezalezhnyi Tsentr Politychnykh Doslidzhen'." *"Dnipropetrovs'ka sim'ia": Informatsia stanom na 25 lystopada 1996 roku,* ed. V. Pikhovshek et al. Kyiv, 1996.

Urban, Michael, with Andrei Evdokimov. *Russia Gets the Blues: Music, Culture, and Community in Unsettled Times.* Ithaca, N.Y.: Cornell University Press, 2004.

U vyri shistdesiatnytskogo rukhu: Pogliad z vidstani chasu, ed. Voldymyr Kvitnevyi. Lviv: Kameniar, 2003.

van Elteren, Mel. *Imagining America: Dutch Youth and Its Sense of Place.* Tilburg: Tilburg University Press, 1994.

Vasiliev, I. V., et al., eds. *Istoria gorodov i siol Ukrainskoi SSR v 26-ti tomakh: Dnepropetrovskaia oblast'.* Kyiv: Glavnaia redaktsia Ukrainskoi Sovestskoi Entsiklopedii, 1977.

Verdery, Katherine. *National Ideology under Socialism: Identity and Cultural Politics in Ceaușescu's Romania.* Berkeley: University of California Press, 1991.

———. *What Was Socialism, and What Comes Next?* Princeton, N.J.: Princeton University Press, 1996.

Wanner, Catherine. *Burden of Dreams: History and Identity in Post-Soviet Ukraine.* University Park: Pennsylvania State University Press, 1998.

———. *Communities of the Converted: Ukrainians and Global Evangelism.* Ithaca, N.Y.: Cornell University Press, 2007.

White, Anne. *De-Stalinization and the House of Culture: Declining State Control over Leisure in the USSR, Poland and Hungary, 1953–89.* London: Routledge, 1990.

Wilson, Andrew. *The Ukrainians: Unexpected Nation.* New Haven, Conn.: Yale University Press, 2002.

Yekelchyk, Serhy. *Stalin's Empire of Memory: Russian-Ukrainian Relations in the Soviet Historical Imagination.* Toronto: University of Toronto Press, 2004.

————. *Ukraine: Birth of a Modern Nation.* New York: Oxford University Press, 2007.

Yoffe, Mark. "Conceptual Carnival: National Elements in Russian Nationalist Rock Music." In *Rock 'n' Roll and Nationalism: A Multinational Perspective,* ed. Mark Yoffe and Andrea Collins. Newcastle: Cambridge Scholars Press, 2005.

Youngblood, Denise J. *Russian War Films: On the Cinema Front, 1914–2005.* Lawrence: University of Kansas Press, 2007.

Yurchak, Alexei. "The Cynical Reason of Late Socialism: Power, Pretense and the *Anekdot.*" *Public Culture* 9, no. 2 (1997): 161–62.

————. *Everything Was Forever, Until It Was No More: The Last Soviet Generation.* Princeton, N.J.: Princeton University Press, 2005.

Zakharov, Borys. *Narys istorii dysydents'kogo rukhu v Ukraini (1956–1987): Kharkivs'ka pravozakhysna grupa.* Kharkiv: Folio, 2003.

Zhuk, Sergei Ivanovich. "Building the Ukrainian Identity through Cultural Consumption in the 'Closed' City of Soviet Ukraine: Dnipropetrovs'k KGB Files and 'Transgressions' of Everyday Life during Late Socialism, 1959–1985." In *Nationalisms Today,* ed. Tomasz Kamusella and Krzysztof Jaskulowski. Oxford: Peter Lang, 2009.

————. "The Modernity of a 'Backward Sect': Evangelicals in Dniepropetrovsk under Khrushchev and Brezhnev." *East-West Church & Ministry Report* 15, no. 4 (Fall 2007): 3–5; 16, no. 1 (Winter 2008): 3–5.

————. "Popular Culture, Identity, and Soviet Youth in Dniepropetrovsk, 1959–84." In *The Carl Beck Papers in Russian and East European Studies, No. 1906.* Pittsburgh: University of Pittsburgh Press, 2008.

————. "Religion, 'Westernization,' and Youth in the 'Closed City' of Soviet Ukraine, 1964–84." *Russian Review* 67, no. 4 (October 2008): 661–79.

Zisserman-Brodsky, Dina. *Constructing Ethnopolitics in the Soviet Union: Samizdat, Deprivation, and the Rise of Ethnic Nationalism.* New York: Palgrave, 2003.

Zubkova, Elena. *Russia after the War: Hopes, Illusions, and Disappointments, 1945–1957,* trans. and ed. Hugh Ragdale. Armonk, N.Y.: M. E. Sharpe, 1998.

Zubok, Vladislav M. *A Failed Empire: The Soviet Union in the Cold War from Stalin to Gorbachev.* Chapel Hill: University of North Carolina Press, 2007.

———— *Zhivago's Children: The Last Russian Intelligentsia.* Cambridge, Mass.: Belknap Press of Harvard University Press, 2009.

Index

ABBA, 173; and disco clubs, 230, 235; and ideology of pop music consumption, 240, 248, 250, 258

AC/DC, 175, 176, 310; and antifascist hysteria, 266, 268, 270–75; and ideology of pop music consumption, 257, 258, 260; and tourism and cultural consumption, 293, 294, 295

The Adventures of Angelique, 157, 158, 160, 161

Akhmatova, Anna, 249

Amado, Jorge, and *Captains of the Sand,* 139

Amel'chenko, Aleksandr, 272–73

American films, 8; and ancient history, 161, 163, 164; and westerns, 138, 139, 153

Amiga (East German state-owned music record label), 83–84

Andropov, Yuri, 17, 24, 52; and antifascist hysteria, 265, 266, 267. *See also* antipunk campaigns

The Animals: and "House of the Rising Sun," 89–90, 96, 139, 174, 235; *Rovesnik* and film *O Lucky Man!,* 245, 252, 258. See also *O Lucky Man!;* Price, Alan

Anka, Paul, 250

Annychka, 167

antifascist hysteria, 265–79

antipunk campaigns, 265–79; and human rights, 269–79. *See also* Andropov, Yuri

antireligious campaigns, 188–90. *See also* Khrushchev, Nikita

anti-Semitism, 14, 46, 197

Antonii (bishop of Dniepropetrovsk Diocese of Orthodox Church; Onufrii I. Vikarik), 197–98

Antonov, Yurii, 258, 260

The Apartment: and Billy Wilder, Jack Lemmon, and Shirley MacLaine, 168

Aquarium, 266

Armstrong, Louis, 247

Baadi, Mekhrdad, 249

Baccarat, 240, 250

Bacon, Edwin, 11

Badfinger, 88, 235

Baez, Joan, 243, 247, 256

Balashov, Aleksandr, and Trade Corporation, 301, 312

ballistic missiles, 20–23, 142. *See also* Yuzhmash

Baltic Soviet Republics ("the Soviet West"), 216, 291, 300, 316; and disco clubs, 220, 221, 225

Bandera, Stepan, 276

Banderovtsy (Banderites), 47, 276. *See also* Ukrainian Insurgent Army

425

Yangel, Mikhail, 19–20, 71. *See also* Yuzhmash
Yaroslav Mudryi, 161
Yeltsin, Boris, 14
Yes, 81, 179, 232, 258, 259
Young, Paul, 250
Youngblood, Denise J., 11
youth culture, 4, 7–9, 17; and its commercialization, 104–5; and disco, 237, 241, 262, 264, 271, 276; and ideology, 303–17; and role of jazz and beat music, 65–94, 103, 104, 176, 205
Yugoslavia: as a model in socialist consumption, 208, 216, 246; and tourism, 285, 286, 287, 290, 316
Yunost' (restaurant, formerly club Chipollino), 74
Yunost' (Soviet youth literary magazine), 97, 241
Yurchak, Alexei, 6, 12–14, 257, 258
Yuzhmash (rocket factory known as Dniepropetrovsk Automobile Factory before 1951 and Southern Machine-Building Factory since 1966), 5, 18–28; and beat music, 81, 86–87, 98, 118, 182; and disco, 221–28, 230–31, 234; and jazz, 69, 71, 73, 75, 76; and practices of cultural consumption, 299, 300, 313

Zagrebel'nyi, Pavlo, 91
Zakhar Berkut, 161
Zaporizhie, 95, 260–61
Zaremba, Volodymyr, 49–52, 57–60
Za rubezhom, 244
Zavgorodnii, Oleksandr, 35–36, 37–40, 48–52
Zavgorodnii, S., 56
Zemliane and Igor Romanov, 273–74
Zhurnal mod, 244
Ziama (a barber), 73
Zionism, 26, 197. *See also* Jewish nationalism
Znanie (Society of Knowledge), 104, 215, 269, 272, 296
Zolotaia pulia (Quien Sabe?), 135, 136
Zonal'naia Komsomol'skaia shkola, 261
Zvenkovskaya, M., 34
Zykina, Liudmila, 90
ZZ Top, 174